Land Transport in Europe

To Béla Gunda
– in friendship

Folkelivs studier

Studies of Folklife

4

Land Transport in Europe

EDITED BY

A. FENTON, J. PODOLÁK
AND
H. RASMUSSEN

NATIONALMUSEET
1973

Edited by Alexander Fenton, Ján Podolák and Holger Rasmussen
Cover by Erik Hjørne
Printed by Andelsbogtrykkeriet i Odense
Copyright © The National Museum of Denmark, Copenhagen 1973
ISBN 87 480 5901 3

Cover picture: Milk-maids from Haraldsund, Faroe Islands,
carrying pails for milking in the outfields. Photo by Johs. Klein 1898.

Contents

List of Contributors

V. V. Antropova, Institut für Ethnographie, Moskva.
John R. Baldwin, National Museum of Antiquities of Scotland, Edinburgh.
Ludvík Baran, University of Arts, Famu, Prague.
Kerstin G:son Berg, Nordiska Museet, Stockholm.
Jorge Diaz, Centro de Estudos de Etnologia, Lisbon.
Alexander Fenton, National Museum of Antiquities of Scotland, Edinburgh.
Karel Fojtík, Institut für Etnographie, Brno.
Hans Griessmair, Haus der Kultur »Walther von der Vogelweide«, Bozen.
I. S. Gurwitsch, Institut für Ethnographie, Moskva.
Helmut Hagar, Institut för folklivsforskning, Stockholm.
Karl Haiding, Landschaftsmuseum Schloss Trautenfels, Steiermark.
J. Geraint Jenkins, Welsh Folk Museum, St. Fagans, Cardiff.
Bogumil Jewsiewicki, Université de Lodz.
B. Kopczyńska-Jaworska, Ethnographical Department, University of Lodz.
Vasil Marinov, Institut für Ethnographie, Sofia.
Attila Paládi-Kovács, Ethnographical Research Group of the Hungarian Academy of Sciences, Budapest.
Mykola P. Prychodko, Institut Mistectvoznavsta, folkloru ta etnografii, Akademii Nauk, Kyjev.
Holger Rasmussen, National Museum, 3rd Department, Copenhagen.
Ants Viires, Institute of History, Tallinn.
Kustaa Vilkuna, Finlands Akademi, Helsinki.
Ørnulv Vorren, Tromsø Museum, Tromsø.
Robert Wildhaber, SAVK, Basel.

Preface

Like many other good ideas, the idea of a volume on the subject of Land Transport in Europe was born whilst the three editors were sitting around a table in a small Slovakian hotel, discussing the why and wherefore of ethnological problems over a glass of wine.

Land transport is one of the fundamental subjects of ethnology. The equipment, terminology, and techniques of carrying and of being carried, especially in areas where pre-industrialised conditions have existed until relatively recent times, can provide material of much comparative value in international studies. In the glow of Karpatenské Zlato, the three of us agreed to see what could be done to stimulate and co-ordinate fresh thinking on land transport.

But if we needed further stimulation, it was already present in the person of Professor Béla Gunda, head of the Ethnological Institute of the Lajos Kossuth University of Sciences in Debrecen. Béla Gunda was participating with us in the Seminarium Ethnologicum which one of the present editors, Professor Ján Podolák, had organised. Himself a specialist in questions of land transport, especially in the Carpathian Mountain region, he had been teaching us a great deal through discussion and by the practical application of his field research methods.

The idea and the man coincided. The occasion also appeared when it was remembered that Béla Gunda had his sixtieth birthday on Christmas Day, 1971. It was decided there and then that we should send a preliminary circular to people whom we knew to be working on aspects of land transport, to see if sufficient material could be assembled in the time available to make a worthwhile volume. It was not to be a Festschrift in the usual sense, with a heterogeneous collection of articles, but a solid contribution to a substantial theme, dedicated to Béla Gunda in friendship and as a token of respect for his work.

The response to the circular was so good that the Editors were unwillingly obliged to set a firm time limit on the date for accepting contributions, otherwise a book of unmanageable size and expense would have resulted. As it is, the territory covered is wide: North Asia, Austria, the Baltic countries, Bulgaria, Czechoslovakia, the Faroe Islands, Hungary, Lappland, Norway,

Poland, Portugal, Russia, Scotland, Sweden, Switzerland, Wales. The time-scale is also broad, ranging from prehistoric Scandinavian ski-finds through medieval Polish wheeled vehicles to a variety of obsolescent or recently obsolete transport methods. The emphasis, however, lies mainly on the nineteenth and twentieth centuries.

In the main we have succeeded in assembling data according to the outline suggested in our Preliminary Circular, which asked for material relating to:

1. Transport by human beings, on the head, back, or shoulders, in association with baskets, boxes, or bundles; or using the hands to carry hand-barrows, or push wheel-barrows, or pull load-bearing poles or sledges.

2. Transport on the backs of horses and other animals, with the relevant types of harness and containers.

3. Transport in carts (2-wheeled), wagons (4-wheeled), and sledges, with the relevant methods of harnessing and yoking.

The material presented by the different authors is not only of value in itself for advancing our knowledge of these themes, but is also of general significance for the methodology of ethnological studies, with special stress on the necessity for integrating a number of approaches: through prehistoric finds, historical documents, linguistic investigation of the terminology, and above all, field observation and enquiry.

The necessary knowledge for such wide integration is not lightly acquired, for it involves deep penetration into a number of related fields. The study of ethnology at a fully scientific level is no easy option. It involves total dedication and constant striving not only to acquire fresh knowledge but to learn to exploit more fully every aspect of experience already gained. It is because Professor Béla Gunda is a man of this calibre that so many of his friends and fellow-workers from so many countries, have willingly spared the time to contribute to this volume on Land Transport in Europe.

The Editors and authors are proud to dedicate this volume to Béla Gunda.

Full details of "Béla Gunda—His Life and Work" can be found in English in the introduction to "Studia ethnographica et folkloristica in honorem Béla Gunda" edited by Dr. Zoltán Ujváry, but it is appropriate to give a brief synopsis here.

Béla Gunda was born on 25 December 1911 and was brought up in areas of farms and big estates in Hungary. At the university he studied geography and geology on the one hand, and Hungarian literature, Slavic and eastern philology, and archaeology on the other. Under the influence of Hungarian ethnographers he turned from his intention of being a geologist and took his doctor's degree in economic geography, economic history, and ethnography.

A Swedish state scholarship took him to Stockholm in 1938–9 where he learned from Sigurd Erixon the method of Swedish ethnology, and got to know the work of the Nordiska Museum and the Statens Etnografiska Museum, experience he was able to put to good use later in the Ethnographic Museum in Budapest.

He combined museum work with university teaching and became professor in 1943.

Throughout his working life he has been active in editing and writing books and articles, not only in Hungarian but in several other languages. At whatever university he has been (on one occasion, for example, for a year at the University of California as holder of a Ford Scholarship) he has made good use not only of his teaching abilities but also of his genius for field research.

The depth of knowledge he brings to bear on the science of ethnology, added to the international breadth of his experience, has been of immense value in the organisation of ethnological studies in Hungary and has not only helped to push Hungary to the forefront in the subject, but has been a source of inspiration for workers in other countries as well.

Ethnology is not a subject that can be fettered in time or place. Its main function is the investigation and analysis of cultural and ethnic movement, interaction and change. It has to be studied not as a dead subject, not with a butterfly-net that seeks to capture stray specimens of the past surviving into the present, but as a dynamic process constantly being worked upon by innumerable factors at all levels of existence.

This approach is one of the corner-stones of Béla Gunda's work and teaching. It is also a corner-stone of ethnology as a whole, and it was a matter of great regret to the Editors that they could not ask Béla Gunda for a contribution to this volume to exemplify his ethnological techniques.

The contributions published here include much primary material from Europe and Asia. It is still only the tip of the iceberg, for land transport is a vast subject, and it is the Editors' hope that this volume will stimulate much more future activity within this field. In the course of preparing this volume, contacts were made with many scholars who had material to offer, but who were prevented by the time factor from contributing. We wish to thank them for the interest they showed, and look forward to seeing their works in print in the near future, in journals and books. We also wish to thank the many people who helped us with advice in private discussion and in other ways, and in particular Professor Gösta Berg, author of the fundamental work, "Sledges and Wheeled Vehicles" (1935), Dr. Eszter Kisbán, Budapest, and Mrs. Elisabeth Henningsen, Helsingør.

Alexander Fenton
National Museum of Antiquities of Scotland

Ján Podolák
Institute of Ethnology, Comenius University, Bratislava

Holger Rasmussen
National Museum of Denmark

Dog-Driving in North Asia

By V. V. ANTROPOVA

Dog-driving is widespread on the vast territory of North Asia from Ural to the Pacific coast including the Amur basin and the island of Sakhalin. Outside Asia it is known in North America and Greenland. There are two distinct ways of using dogs: first, in the dog-team, and second, in assistance to a man pulling the *narta*.[1] Dog-driving suggests the breeding of special draught-dogs, used solely for transporting people and freight, as well as the existence of special *nartas*, harness and certain methods of dog-driving. It is characteristic of the sedentary and semi-sedentary population of North Asia, for fishermen and seahunters who until recently had dog-driving as the only means of conveyance.

Utilization of dogs as subsidiary power was limited to the only breed, the Eskimo dog, that was harnessed together with a man in a hand-pulled *narta*. This way of transportation was employed mostly by foot-hunters who were short of reindeer.

Dog-driving in North Asia has been given a rather complete analysis in ethnographical literature. There are detailed descriptions of *nartas*, harness, methods of driving, and there have appeared a good many hypotheses concerning the origin, development and role of dog-driving in the culture of northern and other peoples (e.g. Levin 1946). On the basis of these studies several authors have made attempts to work out classifications of dog-driving, e.g. to mark its specific types (Bogoras 1904.1; Jochelson 1908.2; Montandon 1934; Levin and Potapow 1961).

The main elements of dog-driving are the *nartas*, the harness and the mode of arranging the dog-team. In North Asia we know three types of *nartas:* marked by straight, arched, or slanting stanchions. When defining the type of harness the distinguishing feature taken as a criterion is the mode of placing the straps on a dog. Depending on what part of the dog's body the straps are placed we distinguish the following types of harness: neck, chest, loin and shoulder harness. The mode of arranging dogs in the team may be either lengthwise or abreast.

The combination of all these elements is not casual. As a rule a certain type of *narta* corresponds to a specific type of harness as well as to a certain mode of arranging dogs. Considering these elements in a complex we can distinguish within the chronological bounds of the 18th–20th centuries six types of dog-driving:

East Siberian type. This type is characterized by the straight-stanchion *narta* (with one horizontal arch in the front part); lengthwise arrangement of the dog-team (in pairs along a trace-strap); harness of chest type. An additional sign of this type is the way in which a man sat sideways on the right side of the *narta* and drove the dog-team by means of an *ostol* (massive iron tipped stick).

Amuro-Sakhalin type. A straight-stanchion *narta* with two horizontal arches (front and rear); lengthwise arrangement of dog-team, alternating on each side of the trace-strap in herring-bone fashion; neck-harness; sitting astride of the *narta*, driving by means of two *ostols*.

Chukotsk type. Main features: low *narta* with 7–8 arched stanchions, no *narta*'s body; a fan-like arrangement of dog-team with the dogs abreast, each one fastened to a common ring set in the *narta*; shoulder-type harness; sitting astride the *narta*, driving by means of a whip.

Kamchatka type. High *narta* with two arched stanchions and a peculiar boat-like body. The original type of harness is unknown. In the 18th–19th centuries dogs were arranged lengthwise but probably other types of arrangement had also existed. A driver sat sideways on the *narta* and drove the dog-team by means of an *ostol* and a rein (Levin and Potapow 1961.62).[2]

North-western type. *Narta* with angled stanchions; dogs fastened abreast to the *narta* through pulleys; chest, or sometimes loin harness (the latter looping the loins of the dog); driving by the *khorei* (a pole for driving reindeer) and a rein; a man sat sideways on the left side of the *narta* (Khomich 1966).[3]

West-Siberian type. More evidence is needed, for the information available is very scarce. Neither the design of the *narta* (probably the straight-stanchion type) nor the mode of arranging the dog-team are identified.

The six types of dog-driving mentioned above are widespread in definite areas.[4] The Chukotsk type existed among the peoples of Chukotka Peninsula, e.g. among coastal Chukchee and Eskimo of Asia till the second half of the 19th century. Later on the old type was employed only in dog-racing. Very interesting in this type of dog-driving is the *narta*. Its design is identical with that of the reindeer *narta* which still exists among the Chukchee and the Koryak. On the grounds of this similarity some authors considered the arched-stanchion *narta* to be the prototype of the reindeer *narta*. New information has shaken this opinion. Archaeological excavations conducted in the 1940s–

1960s did not provide any objects relating to dog-driving. The earliest finds date to the late Punuk-complex, dated by S. I. Rudenko to the beginning of the 17th century (Rudenko 1947.96,109). These data make us look with caution not only at the identification of the prototype of the reindeer *narta* but also at the problem of the age of dog-driving in North-eastern Asia.

The Kamchatka type was known to the Itelmen and probably to the Koryak. In written sources this type can be traced from the 18th century to the second half of the 19th century. In spite of detailed descriptions of the Itelmen dog-driving given in 18th–19th centuries and museum collections relating to the same period (Antropova 1949), many problems in this topic remain unsolved. Apparently as early as the 18th century the dog-driving of the Itelmen had undergone strong influence from Russian folk culture. For instance, the lengthwise arrangement of the dog-team has obvious traces of borrowings from the elements of the Russian arrangement of horses two by two in line ahead, the use of iron chains for fastening together leather parts, etc. Some remnants of evidence suggest that before the advent of the Russians the Itelmen employed the fan-shaped arrangement for the dog-team and another type of harness which differed from that used at the end of the 18th–beginning af the 19th century (Levin and Potapow 1961.58). Knowledge of the original forms of Itelmen dog-driving would probably help to solve the problem of the relationship between Chukotsk and Kamchatka types.

The third almost completely forgotten type of dog-driving is the Amuro-Sakhalin one. It has been spread among the Nivkhi, Nanaj, Oroks, Ainu, and partially among the Negidal and Udege. Its disappearance dates to the beginning of the 20th century. At present this type is very rare. The Nivkhi still employ the old dog-team but only in racing (Taksami 1967.190).

So, beginning from the middle of the 19th century, three types of dog-driving in Eastern Siberia have gradually disappeared and have been supplanted by a new East-Siberian type. At the beginning of the 20th century besides the above-mentioned ethnic groups which used Chukotsk, Kamchatka and Amuro-Sakhalin types of dog-driving, the East-Siberian dog-team was employed by the old Russian inhabitants of eastern Siberia, by the sedentary Even of the Okhotsk area, and partially by the Yakut and Yukaghir. Undoubtedly this type of dog-driving is originally connected with Russians (Levin 1946.98–99). Probably some version of the native dog- or hand-pulled *narta* served as a prototype for the East-Siberian *narta,* and the native harness was replaced by the chest harness in imitation of horse harness. The same is true for the pair-file dog-team.

The problem of the origin of dog-driving in Western Siberia is open to discussion. Information on this subject is scarce and rather discrepant. By the end of the 19th–beginning of the 20th century there was no single type of the *narta* in this region and methods of arranging dog-teams were numerous. Thus the Khanty and Mansi used to harness dogs to the hand-pulled or reindeer *narta* employing both a lengthwise and cross arrangement of dogs in the team. Harness was more uniform. The peoples of Western Siberia employed loin harness unknown in other regions of North Asia, though chest and neck harness was also rather common.

The lack of clear forms in the dog-driving of this region led W. G. Bogoras to think that it was of very late origin and appeared as an imitation of reindeer sledge driving (Bogoras 1927.44). This thesis is refuted by a good deal of evidence. Historical sources of the 15th–18th centuries prove the existence of dog-driving in these regions. There are even pictures of dog-teams (Levin 1946.100–101), and linguistic evidence exists that proves the ancient origin of dog-driving (Chernetsov 1937.350). We must also keep in mind that the earliest remnants of dog-driving were found in Western Siberia in the Ust-Poluj culture, dated by the majority of scholars (V. N. Chernetsov, V. I. Moshinskaya, L. R. Kyzlasov) to the end of the last millennium B.C. V. I. Moshinskaya dates the Ust-Poluj finds to the 5th–3rd centuries B.C. (Moshinskaya 1965.8)[5]. Specific type of harness (loin harness) also proves the existence of a distinct type of dog-driving. Ethnically the West-Siberian type apparently relates to the Khanty and Mansi.

Bogoras's point of view that dog-driving came into being in imitation of reindeer sledge-driving can be applied only to modern Nenetz dog-driving. The Nenetz really developed dog-driving of a new type which has all the characteristic features of reindeer-driving, they employ a *narta* very similar to the reindeer one and fasten dogs through pulleys. L. V. Khomich's essays contain drawings which show that dog and reindeer harness also look very much alike (Khomich 1966.93,98). Identity with the elements of reindeer-driving is further supplemented by the same way of sitting upon the *narta* (on the left side) and by using the *khorei* and rein in driving.

So with good reason we may speak about the existence of two kinds of dog-driving in Western Siberia: first, the early kind which preceded reindeer-driving and was typical for the Ugric peoples (West-Siberian type); and, second, the late type (north-western) which came into being in imitation of reindeer-driving and was not genetically connected with the first type. The north-western type is common only among certain groups of the Nenetz (those of Novaya Zemlya, Kanin, Vaigatch island) who for one reason or another had lost their reindeer and took up hunting for subsistence.

The second method of dog-driving—that of employing a dog in a hand-pulled *narta* to supplement a man—is widespread in North Asia. This way of employing dogs was common among the Khanty, Mansi, Ket, Selcup, some groups of the Evenk (for instance the Sym, Nepa, Tokma, Amur Evenks), Yukaghir, Oroks, Udege and among some other peoples during migrations or on hunting trips. Besides that dogs in a hand-pulled *narta* were employed for transporting firewood, water and other household loads.

Forms of hand-pulled *nartas* used both with and without a dog are very numerous, but so far they have not been described adequately in the scientific literature, so it is difficult to classify them as yet.

We can distinguish non-stanchion and stanchion hand-pulled *nartas*. The first type includes various *volokushas* and hand-sleds. The *volokusha* is known to the Evenks. Thus the Evenks of the Nepa and Tokma used for transportation a wide board with the front edge turned upwards (Vasilevich 1949.96–97), the Sym Evenks employed a trough-like *narta* (consisting of a wide board on runners with both edges turned upwards and side-boards which form the side-walls) with two trace-straps, one for a man and another for a dog (Vasilevich 1949.95–96).

Sleds consist usually of two runners joined by several cross-pieces. They were widespread among the coastal Chukchee and Eskimo. These *nartas* were generally employed without dogs.

Apparently there were also other types of non-stanchion hand-pulled *nartas* but information on them is very scarce.

Among the stanchion hand-pulled *nartas* that employed by the Ket, Selcup, Khanty and Mansi is worth notice (Alekseenko 1961). It is a *narta* of straight-stanchion type but the stanchions are usually inclined slightly backwards. At the front this *narta* has a horizontal arch, and there is also a deep single body at full length. This *narta* was a hand-pulled one but the harnessing of one or two dogs together with a man was rather common. The Mansi sometimes used this *narta* as a driving one in which case they employed a lengthwise team when in *taiga*, or a fan-shaped team, when in an open space.

Rather interesting for the genetical aspect is the hunting *narta* of straight-stanchion type which is widespread in Western Siberia and in the forest regions of South Siberia. In design it is identical to the East-Siberian dog-pulled *narta*. We have good grounds for considering the hand-pulled *narta* to be the prototype of the dog-pulled one, but in that case it is difficult to explain why the former is never employed with a dog.

The hunting *narta* of the Amur peoples has no essential distinctions from the driving *narta* of Amuro-Sakhalin type. A man pulling the *narta* is always assisted by a dog.

In comparing the designs of hand-pulled and driving *nartas,* it is impossible to avoid noting the similarity between Eskimo hand-pulled sleds and the dog-pulled *narta* existing among the Eskimo of Greenland and Canada. The main constructional features of both *nartas* are identical and include two runners which support thin cross-piece planking. An interesting analogy can also be observed in the harness of this dog-driving type. The picture drawn by the Eskimo Unuk and published by S. A. Arutyunov and D. A. Sergeyev depicts the hunter's equipment including the strap which is used by the hunter to drag the killed animal (Arutyunov and Sergeyev 1969.145). This strap exactly reproduces the dog's harness of shoulder type consisting of two loop straps joined by the cross-belts at the back and on the chest. Though refraining from drawing conclusions, we suppose that this similarity it not a mere coincidence.

1. All kinds of dog-, reindeer-, and hand-pulled vehicles are called *nartas.* This term is generally accepted in ethnographical literature.
2. In the article "Dog-driving" Chukotsk and Kamchatka types were considered as mere versions of one general type, but taking into account the substantial difference between the Chukotsk and the Kamchatka *nartas,* as well as the different ways of sitting and driving, it seems more probable that these versions are two independent types.
3. This type of dog-driving has been described in detail by L. V. Khomich whose material may add a lot to the analysis of dog-driving in Western Siberia as given in the Ethnographical Atlas of Siberia.
4. Outside Asia in Greenland and Canada there exists one more type of dog-driving which is characterized by a non-stanchion *narta,* shoulder harness and a cross arrangement of dog-team.
5. M. P. Gryaznov dates the Ust-Poluj culture by 7th–8th centuries A.D. but even in this case dog-driving in West Siberia must be of early origin.

Bibliography

Alekseenko, E. A.: The Ket Means of Conveyance, in Papers of the Institute of Ethnography 1961. (N.S.) LXIV.

Е. А. Алексеенко. Средства передвижения кетов. Труды Института этнографии, нов. сер. Т. LXIV М.–Л. 1961.

Antropova, V. V.: Old Kamchadal Sledge, in Collected Papers of the Museum of Anthropology and Ethnography, 1949. X.

В. В. Антропова. Старинные камчадальские сани. Сборник музея антропологии и этнографии, т. X, М.–Л., 1949.

Arutyunov, S. A. and Sergeyev, D. A.: Ancient Cultures of the Asian Eskimo (Uelen tomb). Moscow 1969.

С. А. Арутюнов, Д. А. Сергеев. Древние культуры азиатских эскимосов (Уэленский могильник), М. 1969.

Bogoras, W.: The Chukchee. Memoir of the American Museum of Natural History 1904. VII.

Bogoras, W. G.: Ancient Migrations of Peoples in Northern Eurasia and America, in Collected Papers of the Museum of Anthropology and Ethnography, Leningrad, 1927. VI.

В. Г. Богораз. Древние переселения народов в северной Евразии и Америке. Сборник музея антропологии и этнографии, т. VI. Л., 1927.

Chernetsov, V. N.: Terms for Means of Conveyance in the Mansi Language. Papers in Memoriam Bogoras (1865–1936). Moscow-Leningrad 1937.

В. Н. Чернецов. Термины средств передвижения в мансийском языке. Сб. статей "Памяти В. Г. Богораза (1865–1936)". М.–Л., 1937.

Jochelson, W. I.: The Koryak, in Memoir of the American Museum of Natural History, 1908. VI.

Khomich, L. W.: The Nenetz. Ethnographical Essays. Moscow-Leningrad 1966.

Л. В. Хомич. Ненцы. Историко-этнографические очерки. М.–Л., 1966.

Levin, M. G.: On the Origin and Types of Dog-driving, in Sovietskaya Ethnographiya 1946. No. 4.

М. Г. Левин. "О происхождении и типах упряжного собаководства" ("Советская Этнография", 1946 № 4).

Levin, M. G. and Potapow, L. P.: Historical-Ethnographical Atlas of Siberia, 1961.

Potapow, L. P.: Историко-этнографический атлас Сибири. М.–Л., 1961.

Montandon, G.: L'ologénèse culturelle. Paris 1934.

Moshinskaya, V. I.: Archaeological Relics of North-western Siberia. Moscow 1965.

В. И. Мошинская. Археологические памятники Северо-Западной Сибири. М. 1965.

Rudenko, S. I.: The Ancient Culture of the Bering Sea and the Eskimo Problem, Moscow-Leningrad 1947.

С. И. Руденко. Древняя культура Берингова моря и эскимосская проблема. М.–Л. 1947.

Taksami, Ch. M.: The Nivkhi (Modern Economy, Culture and Family Life). Leningrad, 1967.

Ч. М. Таксами. Нивхи (Современное хозяйство, культура и быт). Л., 1967.

Vasilevich, G. M.: The Trough-shaped Narta of the Sym Evenks, in Collected Papers of the Museum of Anthropology and Ethnography, Leningrad, 1949. X.

Г. М. Василевич. Корытообразная нарта сымских эвенков. Сборник Музея Антропологии и Этнографии, т. X, Л., 1949.

Land Transport in Gásadalur and Mykines, Faroe Islands

By JOHN R. BALDWIN

The Faroe Islands lie between Norway (c. 575 km) and Iceland (c. 430 km), with the Shetland Islands at the northern tip of Scotland and about half-way to Norway as their nearest neighbours (c. 300 km). They lie between latitudes 61° 20′ and 62° 24′ N and longitudes 6° 15′ and 7° 41′ W but, because of the Gulf Stream, have a north Atlantic rather than Arctic climate and vegetation, in spite of being considerably further north than the south of Greenland (Mitens 1966.7–9).

The most westerly of the island group are Vágar and Mykines, visited in July-August 1970. (Fig. 1). Fourteen days of field-work were spent in Gásadalur and Mykines and the present material represents part of that accumulated during the visit. Oral information was gathered by the writer directly from a number of unfailingly helpful local sources; material from direct observation—sketches, measurements, notes on construction and use—was assembled both by the writer and by members of the Brathay Exploration Group's Faroes Expedition under his guidance.

PHYSICAL BACKGROUND

a. Gásadalur

The village, nucleated save for one dwelling, is situated on the north western peninsula of the island of Vágur, above the sea-cliff, at between 80 m and 90 m. The 18 *merkur bøur* (the original infield area, measured in marks), together with later added infield *(tillegg* and *trøð)* rises from c. 50 m to c. 150 m in c. 0.65 km, whilst the steeply U-shaped, *hamar*-sided valley behind (studded with bands of basalt cliffs) is some 2.6 km long by 2.6 km across the ridges. The encircling watershed is mainly over 500 m, rising to 722 m in the Arnafjall.

All this terrain has to be covered to a greater or lesser extent during the annual round of work and is served by a minimal network of tracks. The only stretch of earthen road (c. 0.5 km) fit to take a cart or mini-tractor, spans the

20

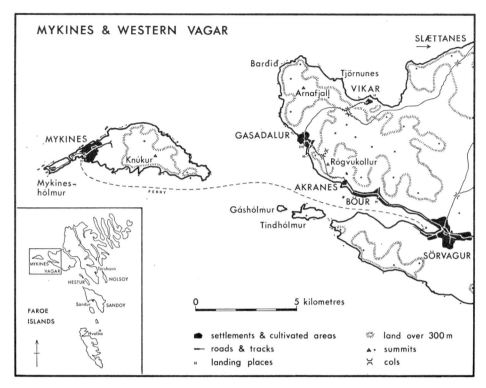

Fig. 1. Compiled with permission (A. 494/71) of the Geodetic Institute, Copenhagen.

bøur from the main hill-dyke gate to the village, with a feeder (c. 0.3 km) out to the newer landing place. Otherwise, apart from the path to Sörvágur, there is just one man-made track leading up the valley. One branch goes over to the Reipsá river and the former small *trøð* settlement of Slættanes, abandoned in 1965 (Coull 1967.165). The other goes over to Víkar—once merely *trøð* land for Gásadalur, then settled because of the difficulties of all-weather access and increasing population, and finally abandoned, apparently about the turn of the century, on account of its isolation and lack of facilities. The inhabitants of Gásadalur, within one of whose three *hagar* (hill and moorland common grazings) Víkar lies, and some from Bøur, still use it for grazing and fowling. Transport over this difficult track is, therefore, still necessary.

Land access to the whole area from Sörvágur is by a narrow, twisting, unmetalled road along the northern shore of the Sörvágsfjörður, past the small village of Bøur, as far as Akranes. Only the drystone pillars of a footbridge over the Skarðsá river remain, while beyond, a track—intermittently

Fig. 2. Land access to Gásadalur is just to the left of the highest cliffs, over the ridge: small boats tied up at the nearest rocks. Electricity poles, also providing street lighting, skirt much of the earthen track across the *bøur*.

distinct—zigzags up and around the partly eroded southern shoulder of the Rógvukollur, before reaching its maximum on a col at c. 435 m—a rise of c. 350 m in a direct line of c. 1.4 km. The descent to Gásadalur is far more precipitous down steep, loose and water-worn scree and then steep grassy slopes—a drop of c. 320 m in just over 0.5 km, and a total descent of c. 380 m to the village bridge in just under 1 km. (Fig. 2).

So rough and steep, in fact, is this track, that cattle are taken by a different, more stable and grassy route over the Neytaskarð, slightly to the north-east. Similarly, at the head of the valley, near the point where the Víkar and Slættanes tracks diverge, cattle and horses are kept a little to the south of the normal path, nearer to the stream.

Access to Gásadalur by sea is also possible. Until c. 1940 the landing place was merely some flattish rocks at the foot of the cliffs between Langanes and the Foss. People climbed the cliff and goods were hauled up and down. The new harbour at Reyðastiggjatangi, even though subject to rock-falls, gives a far better service with its space for lashing down boats on the lower rocks (in the summer, at least), its steps hewn out of the 60 m cliff face and its aerial cable-way for cargo. Unfortunately, it has only a very narrow entrance and is otherwise encircled by mainly submerged rocks. It cannot, therefore, be used by boats much bigger than an *áttamannafar* (an eight-man boat, c. 7.5 m long, but nowadays fitted with an engine), and even then only when the weather favours a more or less westerly approach. There is no ferry service for cargo or passengers. The villagers' own boats must be used.

Consequently, access and transport by sea are but marginally better now than before the 1939–45 War and the land route, for all its roughness, must be considered the only reliable way.

b. Mykines

Mykines, an island some 4.5 km off the west of Vágar, across the Mykines-fjörður, has better communications with Sörvágur than Gásadalur even though further away and accessible only by sea. Whilst its harbour can also be impossible to use, especially in winter, it is able to take somewhat bigger boats and receives a regular twice weekly ferry service. There is a good track, slip and cargo hoist to its boat sheds and stores some 40 m above the sea and a more sophisticated slip and stairway has been installed recently to augment the earlier structures.

This apart, however, the island is largely as rough and steep as the Gása-dalur region. It is some 8.4 km long by 2.5 km wide overall, and everywhere surrounded by sea-cliffs which at one point rise to 460 m in 300 m. A water-shed culminating in the Knúkur (560 m) separates the three precipitous easterly valleys, used for livestock grazing and fowling, from the main part of the island. This has to be crossed when use of the emergency landing-places, accessible only by a greater or lesser rock-climb, is necessary in stormy weather. Similarly a ravine, narrow and sea-filled but bridged, separates the Mykineshólmur, where at one time there was a separate settlement, with its own school, to serve the lighthouse. The light is now automatic and the last keeper left in August 1970, but in recent years he had been living in the main settlement and owned a house in Sörvágur. The compact village area of Mykines proper is situated at between 40 m and 60 m, by the side of the main stream and sewer and c. 0.3 km from the harbour. Its 40 *merkur bøur* rises from c. 25 m to 165 m in just under 0.9 km in one direction, and to 128 m in c. 0.5 km in another.

Fig. 3. A wooden skate with separate, shaped foot-piece. The sledge-like runner is metal-bound and punctured strips of tin give extra grip. The tie-cords pass through grooves on the upper edge of the runner. Gásadalur.

The *bøur* is crossed by an earthen track c. 0.7 km long, from the harbour head, through the village and out to the former peat-cuttings on the Heimangjógv. Like the Gásadalur infield road, this will take carts or tractors; and it has the added advantage of extending onto the *hagi*, allowing in particular the easier transport of peat (Williamson 1948.64). Otherwise, apart from a steep, sometimes stony sometimes slimy path through the nearest puffinries, Dalið and Lambi, to the *hólmur* and the lighthouse, there are no formal tracks. Some fowling is still done and a good many sheep kept in the more remote parts of the island. Thus various methods have to be employed here, as in Gásadalur, to transport produce back to the settlement over steep and rough terrain.

LAND TRANSPORT

The aim is to consider forms of transport still extant in both communities and to record not only some now largely defunct although still recalled by the

Fig. 4. A wheeled muck-barrow. Mykines.

local inhabitants, but also some of the more recent innovations and changes that have occurred, and the reasons for these.

The materials for which transport was normally required were: – manure, potatoes, turnips, rhubarb, hay, grain, peat, milk, wool, stone, fowls, fish and fishing equipment and various miscellaneous loads. To a greater or lesser extent, and with the exception of barley which has disappeared entirely in the settlements, all have still to be carried today, together with a range of more modern imported goods.

The methods employed can be classified under three main groupings, incorporating:

1. Man power
2. Horse power
3. Mechanical power.

It should not be forgotten, however, that land transport and sea transport may complement each other in matters other than basic access, where the geographical environment encourages it. This is particularly relevant to aspects of Gásadalur life (see 1 b i, ii, iii).

Fig. 5. A wheel-barrow, used primarily for carrying peat. Gásadalur.

1. Man Power

Transport by man power alone is still of considerable importance in the more isolated Faroese settlements. The two principal methods of carrying materials are:

    a. on a quite separate load-bearing frame

    b. directly on the person, with or without aids.

a. Separate Load-Bearing Frames

The methods observed involved frames that made contact with the ground by means of a wheel or runners. Methods incorporating team transport, where such a frame is not in contact with the ground (as with a hand-barrow), were not noted.

There is evidence on Mykines for the possible use of a small, simple, hand-drawn sledge (a flat, wooden platform on two metal-shod wooden runners) to move peat out on the moor; and thick-runnered skates (Fig. 3) are still to be found in Gásadalur, along with the iron-spiked wooden staff (*fjallstavur* or *píkstavur*) for man's own use. Nothing else was apparent, however, to suggest runnered transport.

Wheeled transport in any form is a fairly modern phenomenon, dependent

26

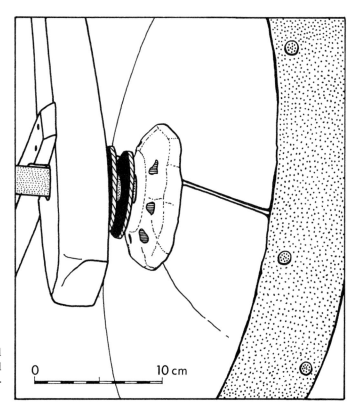

Fig. 6. Axle detail and the solid wooden wheel of a Gásadalur wheel-barrow.

0   10 cm

to a large extent upon local topographical factors (cf. Williamson 1948.59; see also 2 b). Hand carts, for instance, were introduced to Hestur c. 1920 for the transportation of hay (Nyman 1958.102) – although no example was noted in the settlements visited. Within the immediate neighbourhood of the buildings, however, there is more scope for the small, wheeled container, as against the larger cart.

i. The Wheelbarrow

The wheelbarrow, either pushed or pulled, is used for all manner of small jobs. In Gásadalur, for instance, it brings in peat from the moor to the stores below the houses; in Mykines it is used for shifting dung out from the byre or for collecting goods from the boat. It also takes rubbish to the stream below the village.

A fairly conventional example on Mykines (Fig. 4) has a locally-made body and a rubber-tyred wheel. The container sits firmly on the top of two shafts

27

Fig. 7. The bogey for transporting boats from harbour-head to village. Mykines.

running the whole length of the barrow and protruding at either end. At the rear they form two handles and narrow at the front to provide pivot supports for the fixed-axle wheel slung between them. Two wooden legs are jointed into the rear corners of the container. Fundamentally it is merely a wheeled hand-barrow, identical in principle to that of e.g. Foula in Shetland.

A mid-twentieth century Gásadalur barrow *(trillibøra)*, however, shows a distinctly different mode of construction (Fig. 5), which can scarcely be put down nowadays to lack of suitable wood. It is essentially a box, rather than a hand-barrow, to which a pair of handles and a wheel have been added. The legs penetrate upwards through the rear corners.

The wheel axle is supported by two perpendicular boards nailed to and partly set under the front of the box. These are strengthened by thin struts below, whose front ends are nailed to them and whose rear ends are set about the barrow legs. The perpendicular boards also serve to keep the overhanging box clear of the wheel. Clearly, the effect of these various bearers is to create a cradle to fulfil a function carried out far more simply and efficiently by the two through shafts of the conventional design.

The solid wooden wheel is also of considerable interest. It has a diameter of 35.5 cm and a rim width of 6.5 cm. The axle and wheel turn as one unit with the former passing through one of the two semi-circular wooden blocks,

Fig. 8. Transporting wool with the aid of a *fetil*. The cap gives extra protection. Víkar.

presumably dowelled together, which form the wheel. There is a pair of very roughly shaped wooden hub discs or bosses, nailed in position on one side by six and on the other by seven nails set in recessed holes, and at each side two hide washers have been placed round the axle (Fig. 6). These all combine to strengthen the structure, minimize wear and to promote smoother running. Around the wheel a thin rim of iron has been nailed and this, apart from the axle and some thin reinforcement strips at the corners of the box and across the handles, is the only piece of metal used.

The barrow wheel appears to be inscribed I J J J and 1951 I F, although the latter reading in particular is doubtful. The Js presumably indicate the maker's name. J J would identify with the particular *kongsbóndi* (a farmer holding his land from the Crown) to whom the barrow belongs, whilst J J J corresponds to the names of one of his sons. The figures doubtless indicate the year of construction.

Overall dimensions of the barrow are 162.75 cm × 58 cm. The box is 76.25

Fig. 9. Carrying wool to the boat – over the head, and over the shoulder. Tjørnunes, near Víkar.

cm × 53.5 cm × 18.5 cm internal depth, the horizontal struts 75 cm long, the perpendicular boards 53 cm high and the leg length below the box 25.5 cm.

ii. The Bogey

On Mykines, boats are sometimes stored for the winter outside the houses in the village itself and a bogey is now used to transport them along the track from the top of the harbour slip-ways to the settlement (Fig. 7). It is pulled by two teams of men, their numbers varying according to availability and the size of the boat.

The equipment is modern, comprising a maroon-painted wooden frame, 258 cm × 175 cm overall, formed of two parallel shafts linked by three shorter parallel bars. The foremost cross-bar, which takes the strain, is reinforced on either side by a nut and bolt through a square iron plate. On top of this framework, as well as a further cross-bar, two lengthways shafts (346 cm × 11 cm × 5 cm) have been added later. Towards the rear end of each of these, a small triangular frame (67 cm high × 67 cm base length) rises up as extra support.

Between the two main shafts sit two wooden rollers (16 cm diameter) en-

Fig. 10. Carrying wool with the aid of a walking-stick. Tjørnunes, near Víkar.

circled at their ends by iron bands and, a little further in, by narrow, hard rubber rings (2 cm deep). These latter form the only contact with level ground. The iron axles, fixed to the rollers, revolve in iron loops, parts of short metal bars attached to the underside of the two shafts.

Round the front cross-bar is spliced a loop of 3 cm diameter rope, further secured to either side of the centre by nails. Into a small loop lashed out of the doubled apex, two lengths of thinner rope (each c. 682 cm long × 1 cm diameter) have been spliced. It is on these longer ropes that the men haul. Apart from the upper frame, the bogey appears to be the work of a professional joiner.

b. Body Loads

Sometimes articles are carried just in the hands or arms, but heavy loads, especially over difficult terrain, are normally strapped to the human frame. Three methods were noted involving:

   i. the rope
  ii. the sack or bag
 iii. the wooden container.

i. The Rope

Use of the rope in transporting hay is well documented (cf. Landt 1810. 298–9; Williamson 1948.202–4; Nyman 1958.102–6). According to Nyman, a large hay-cock or *sáta* would be split into three *byrður* (bales), each weighing c. 120 lbs and tied round with a rope *(hoyberareip)*, some 15 yards (c. 13.7 m) long. This used formerly to be of horsehair.

In Gásadalur and Mykines, as elsewhere, it is used in conjunction with the *held*. Nyman mentions a goathorn *held*, but normally it appears to have been made from ram's horn. After boiling (Niclasen 1968.97), it is drawn out a little and shaped, and a hole made near one end. The other end is passed through the hole to make a ring, and when cool it is entirely immoveable.

The doubled rope on which the hay has been laid is passed over and across the load in such a way as to quarter it. The circular *held* is used to change the direction of the rope and also, finally, as a tie ring. To raise the *byrða*, the bearer lies on top and then gradually bends forward first to his knees and then to his feet, whilst a second man helps to lift and keep a balance (Williamson 1948.202–3). Since the cross-rope is also used as a *fetil* or carrying band, care must be taken to keep the *held* to one side, out of the way. That the weight of hay and the pressure of the rope is normally very great can sometimes be seen from friction grooves worn into the horn.

Ropes are also in common use for raising and lowering man and sheep, and sometimes birds, on the cliffs. It is essential, for instance, when transporting sheep in the spring to otherwise inaccessible islets *(hólmar)* or grassy bands sandwiched between the basalt cliffs *(hamrar)*. On one particular sea cliff, close by Barðið, near the extreme north-western tip of Vágar, the Gásadalur men hoist up four sheep (thirty years ago it was only one) on a rope from the boat below. In the autumn, they again climb up and lower the sheep back into the boat.

Although this particular cliff is climbed without a rope, they and the men on Mykines sometimes use one when out fowling, as an aid both to access and to security, depending on the location and objective.

Once taken and killed, the birds are often carried on ropes, either back to the settlement (cf. Landt 1810.339–42; Williamson 1948.152–3), or from house to harbour if destined for export – a means of disposal currently favoured on Mykines.

In Gásadalur, a bunch of three puffins is made by tying the necks together. It is called a *kneppa*. The same term was also used elsewhere in the Faroes to describe a pair of large birds held together by the beaks (Svabo 1781–2.39).

A bunch of five puffins, their necks tied together in a loop on a rope—

heads above and bodies below—is known as a *lundavørða* (cf. also Svabo 1781–2.34). Six such bundles would be normal in Gásadalur for one rope, as it is said that too many, causing the rope to extend too far down the back, would upset a man's balance when climbing back to the village. The two ends of the rope are tied to a woollen *fetil* which crosses, as is usual, a little above the forehead. Some men, however, claim that they have carried as many as 25 bunches or 125 puffins at a time on their backs by this method—i.e. about half as many as a horse would carry (see 2a ii & iii). And indeed, on Mykines, where the same method and terminology (*lundavørða*) is employed, it would seem normal for some 20 bunches or 100 puffins to be attached to one rope— if, that is, such a number be caught. These figures represent well nigh the maximum a man can carry.

A waist line is also used on Mykines. In the spring, when puffins are taken from the burrow with a *lundakrókur*, a short wooden stick with an iron hook at one end (Williamson 1948.152–3), and not caught from the air with a *fleygistong* (a triangular net attached to a long pole), some 30–40 may be tucked under this rope by their necks. To prevent the weighty load from slipping down, a separate length of rope can be attached to the centre of the waist belt, and passed over both a man's shoulders, thus forming a kind of harness. Williamson records the term *beltisgyrði* for Mykines. Svabo has *bæltislunder* for Hvalba, where 60 puffins might be carried by this method (Svabo 1781–2.40), but this refers rather to the number of birds making up the fowler's personal reward than to the belt itself—a sense that *beltisgyrði* can also have (Poulsen).

ii. The Sack or Bag

More recently there has been a tendency in Gásadalur to transport birds in sacks rather than on ropes. Once the sack has been filled, a rope is tied to one of the bottom corners and a second round each of the two top corners which are then drawn and bound together. This gives two primary attachment points and a roughly triangular shaped sack. The *fetil* is tied to the rope ends. As with the older, rope-only method, 30 or so birds would be thus carried, depending upon size. Puffins *(lundar)* and fulmars *(havhestar)* are the usual victims; shags *(skarvar)* are also sometimes still taken.

Bags of one sort or another are used in various other ways. A broad, white sack is taken by the Gásadalur postman when he goes to Sörvágur for letters and packets. When empty it is hung loosely over the shoulder and the *fetil* held in front by the hand(s); when full, the *fetil* lies above the forehead.

Fig. 11. Empty sacks are carried with the *fetil* crossing the chest. The man is sharpening a lug-marking knife. Víkar.

For transport of wool, hessian sacks between c. 1 m and 1.5 m deep are normal and may be borne in several ways. A sack may be carried with the aid of a *fetil,* in which case the woollen band is tied to two short lengths of rope attached in turn to an old sack or piece of cloth passed round the full bag about two-fifths the way up. The man must crouch down to pull the band over his head and, when lifted, perhaps a quarter of the load extends above the head (Fig. 8). Otherwise, the sack may be gripped at the top by the hands and held either above the head like a sack of coal, or over the shoulder (Fig. 9). Sometimes the curved handle of a walking stick is hooked under the top edge of the sack (Fig. 10). These last methods in particular—all in use in Gása-dalur—are very elementary.

Sheep shears, syringes, hack-saws, doses, empty sacks and suchlike are rolled into a small bundle or put into a single sack tied up in the same way as the sack for puffins, and slung over the back with the *fetil* diagonally crossing the chest (Fig. 11). Food and provisions for a day's work away from home may also be carried like this or kept in a small rucksack or haversack. It

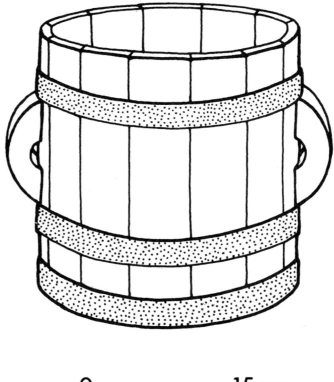

Fig. 12. A *dylla*, used by
the women for carrying
milk back to the settlement.
Gásadalur.

0   15 cm

should be noted that after shearings across at Tjörnunes and Víkar, wool,
dogs and shearers are brought back by boat if weather conditions allow. This
saves a steep, tiring return trek over the main ridge.

A slightly different 'bag' remembered by some people in Gásadalur was
made from a scraped and treated sheepskin and also carried by a rope
passing crossways over the chest. Seemingly it had several names—e.g.
taska, skjátta, hít—and was used for carrying milk or bread. It may have
been similar to the sealskin 'wallets', closely resembling Icelandic examples, which were slung over the shoulders by means of a woollen rope tied
round the tail and neck (Annandale 1903.256). It may also resemble the
pridla, a completely clean lambskin, gathered up and tied at the outer end
with a cord and used for carrying birds' eggs, especially in rain when they
would otherwise become wet and slippery (Svabo 1781–2.30).

iii. The Wooden Container

The Dylla

Although Williamson quotes the term *dylla* as referring to a wooden yoke for carrying two milk pails (Williamson 1948.173), field evidence seems to refer it more generally to the cylindrical wooden pail used by the women to bring the milk back from the outfield pastures. One in Gásadalur (Fig. 12) 23.5 cm high × 24.5 cm overall diameter, is made of 12 × 1 cm thick wooden staves and bound round by three iron bands (2.5 cm wide × 0.2 cm thick). Such bands were formerly made of wood. There are two solid wooden handles placed opposite each other, 6.5 cm down from the top of the staves. Each has a small semi-circular hole taken centrally out of its inner edge and through this passes the rope which goes round the woman's arms and chest a little below arm-pit level (Landt 1810.310; Rasmussen 1957.71, fig. 2; Rasmussen 1968.35, fig. 8 A). A processed piece of sheepskin, secured on the outside by a woollen cord, is placed over the top of the pail as a lid to prevent spilling.

The Leypur

The chief container, however, is the *leypur*—basically an upright rectangular wooden box with four corner posts *(stulur)*, slatted sides *(riim)* and a slatted base *(niit)* (Svabo 1781–2.138). Examples for use with a horse (see 2 a ii) have a base that can be opened to release the load, but these may equally well be borne on the human back, in which case a separate *fetil* is added, quite independent of the harsher rope which hooks round the pack-saddle horn.

Gásadalur has three versions of the standard back *leypur*. The *roka-leypur* (a) is the largest and the only one to have five slats per side. It is used for carrying hay. A medium sized one, for peat and puffins, is called

	Overall Height	Overall Widths — Top	Corner Posts	Slat Height from Corner Post	
				Bottom	Top
a...........	70.5 cm	51.0 cm × 48.0 cm	3.5 cm × 3.5 cm	3.5 cm	9.0 cm
b...........	61.5 cm	43.0 cm × 40.0 cm	3.25 cm × 3.0 cm	3.5 cm	2.25 cm
c...........	48.5 cm	37.0 cm × 31.0 cm	3.0 cm × 3.0 cm	5.0 cm	5.0 cm
Svabo ⎫ Landt ⎭	61.0 cm [1 ell]	40.6– 40.6– 44.1 cm × 44.1 cm [16″–17″ square]			

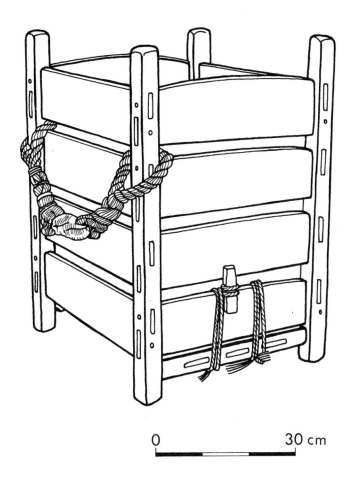

Fig. 13. A medium-sized *leypur* used with a pack-pony to transport mainly potatoes and puffins. Gásadalur.

0   30 cm

	Number and Depth of Slats	
	Side	Base
a...........	5 (8.0–9.0 cm)	5 (6.0–11.0 cm)
b...........	4 (10.0–11.0 cm)	3 (8.0–11.0 cm)
c...........	4 (8.0 cm)	3 (5.0–11.5 cm)
Svabo ⎱	4 (7.6–10.1 cm)	
Landt ⎰	[4 (3″–4″)]	

the *tunnuleypur* (b) and has four slats. So also does the *fjórðingsleypur* (c), the smallest type and used currently for puffins and potatoes. Some of the *leypar* are absolutely straight-sided, others expand a little towards the top. The latter are said to be more recent. They are locally made and should last for over 30 years.

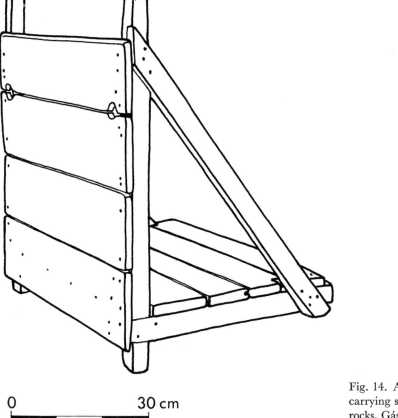

0   **30 cm**

Fig. 14. A *grótleypur* for carrying stones and rocks. Gásadalur.

All the *leypar* observed have the gaps between the side slats between 2 cm and 4 cm deep and the slats themselves are 0.25 cm to 0.5 cm thick, mortised into the corner posts with staggered tenons, in such a way as to form regular rows all round (Fig. 13). The tenons of the top and bottom slats are secured with dowels, to help keep the framework rigid. In earlier drawings the slats themselves are shown staggered to avoid the overlapping of joints, and consequently the gaps between appear wider than is currently so, and wider indeed than the measurements of Svabo and Landt, for a *rossleypur*, would suggest (Svabo 1781–2.138–40; Landt 1810.278–9).

In the base, the centre slat of three (b & c) is the narrowest, the others being of equal width. The five base slats of (a) are of varying widths. (b) would seem to have been reconstructed at some stage, since circular blind holes for a pivoting base strut appear near the top of two corner posts (see 2 a ii). This

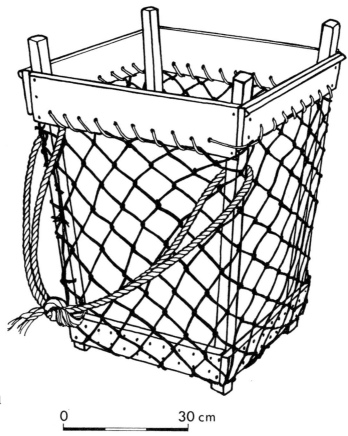

Fig. 15. A *línuleypur* covered with nylon fishing net, to hold and carry a fisherman's long-lines. Mykines.

0   30 cm

would probably also explain the surprisingly short distance between the top slats and the tops of the corner posts.

A knitted woollen carrying band is tied to two short lengths of rope attached to two of the corner posts just below the top slats. That for (a) is 62 cm long by 14 cm wide.

The *leypur* is also used for carting e.g. dung to the fields or fish up from the harbour, and at least one inhabitant of Mykines takes a regular evening walk down the village street, to the stream, with a *leypur* full of domestic waste.

Apart from the standard *leypar*, there are two rather specialised types still in use. The *grótleypur* or *steinleypur* is a wooden chair-like construction used for carrying large stones from a quarry or beach to a building site (cf. Williamson 1948.58). A Gásadalur example (Fig. 14), unlike that shown by Jirlow (1937.140) or the one seen at Sandur, Sandoy in 1930 (photograph

39

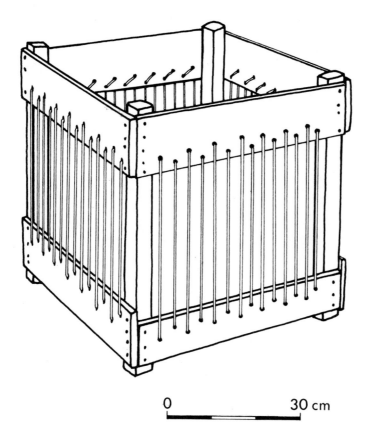

Fig. 16. An older form of *línuleypur* with straight sides and an infill of vertical cording. Mykines.

0   30 cm

R.3:14 in the Göteborgs Historiska Museum), has a back of four slats, not gapped but solid (overall height 56 cm by 50.75 cm wide), nailed to a pair of parallel struts (64.75 cm high). The base, attached at right angles to the back, is similarly formed (48.25 cm long by 54.5 cm wide). Two diagonal side struts, each 63.5 cm long and running from base to back, add strength and support to the load. The *grótleypur* is carried by rope and *fetil*, just like the ordinary *leypur*. Holes, one on each side, have been made where the top two slats of the back meet, for the short ropes to pass through.

The second particular type is the *línuleypur*. It is the normal rectangular shape but has only two rows of side slats which are, moreover, nailed rather than jointed on to the corner posts. The intervening space is filled on the outside by a pattern of thin rope or netting which continues round the base. Vertical cording through staggered holes, 0.3 cm in diameter, is the older form and found on the quite upright models; square or diamond meshed nylon is a recent modification, found especially on those which expand somewhat towards the top. One of each type was noted on Mykines. The *línuleypur* is used for carrying a fisherman's long-lines, coiled inside with the hooks set side by side over the top row of slats. This occasionally incorporates an extra outside lip to keep the hooks from slipping off. (Fig. 15 = (a): Fig. 16 = (c)).

	Overall Height	Overall Widths — Top	Corner Posts	Slat Height from Corner Post	
				Bottom	Top
a..........	25.0 cm	54.5 cm × 48.0 cm	3.5 cm × 2.7 cm	4.0 cm	3.0 cm
b..........	65.0 cm	48.0 cm × 47.5 cm	3.0 cm × 3.0 cm	6.0 cm	4.5 cm
c..........	50.0 cm	53.0 cm × 52.0 cm	3.0 cm × 3.0 cm	1.5 cm	1.5 cm

	Depth of Slats	Sides	No. of Hooks
a....	7.5–11.0 cm	Diamond Mesh	106
b....	6.5–7.0 cm	Square Mesh	40
c....	9.5–11.5 cm	Vertical Cord	87

It is unlikely that this form of *leypur* is ever carried very far on land, other than from the harbour to the boat sheds and stores and perhaps to the village. Even then it could be taken in the hands. However, (a) was fitted with a doubled rope (105 cm long), attached to two adjacent corner posts, under the upper slats, in such a way that it could either have been carried with a head-band or have been hooked over the horn of a pack saddle.

Its existence underlines the adaptation of a form of land transport to a marine environment, most prominent presumably in the nineteenth century when traditional methods were still everywhere strong and fishing grew in importance. The lesser number of slats would doubtless reflect the general scarcity of wood and the need, therefore, to cast around for suitable alternatives. Line or mesh is quite adequate where the contents are unlikely to spill out easily.

That no *línuleypar* were noted in Gásadalur serves as a further reminder that this community, because of environmental difficulties, never betook itself to fishing to the same degree as other Faroese settlements.

2. Horse Power

The pony has long been used as a servant in the islands. The strong and sturdy Faroese type, between twelve and thirteen hands, is usually roan-coloured, but

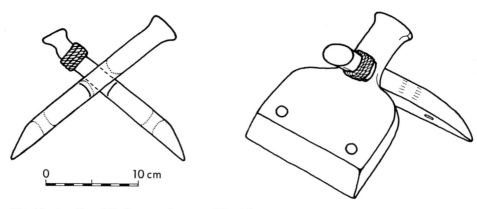

Fig. 17. A split-saddle for a pack-pony. Gásadalur.

sometimes almost black (Landt 1810.314; Williamson 1948.59; Cardél 1968. 45). The original breed is now virtually extinct and new strains have been produced by crossing with the Norwegian Westlander and Icelandic types. The former cross, in particular, is considered good for draught: the latter for riding (Cardél 1968.45). Not everyone could ever hope to keep such a horse, however, and several families would share in the upkeep and use of a single animal. In recent times there were about eight on Mykines although numbers have dropped. In Gásadalur there are only two.

a. Pack

In the past, the horse was considered primarily as a pack animal. Indeed, though sometimes used for riding, it is said never to have been used for draught in earlier times (Landt 1810.209; Rasmussen 1957.71). A similar situation used also to exist in Shetland.

i. Pack Harness

The necessary equipment has been comprehensively described by several writers (Svabo 1781–2.138–41; Landt 1810.277–8; Williamson 1948.59). Information from Gásadalur and Mykines largely confirms these earlier reports. No reference to a sod or skin was noted: otherwise a mat of wool, straw or hay underlies the wooden split-saddle which is secured to the beast by two ropes, one of which passes round the breast, the other under the tail. The creels or baskets are hung by a short rope from the saddle and are sometimes secured by a further rope round the horse's fore or hind quarters.

42

Terminology, too, is virtually identical:

Svabo (1781–2. 138–40)	Landt (1810. 277–8)	Williamson (1948. 59)	Gásadalur (1970)	Mykines (1970)	
à raja	a raia				carrying by pack-pony
tujggind	tuyggind	rossatýggj	rosstýggj	týggini	pack harness and creels
metta			ull metta		wool mat
			strá metta	strá metta	straw mat
klibbari	klibbari	klibbari	klibbari	klibbari	split-saddle
rossa-lejpur	loiper/				
-lejpar	leipar	rossaleypar	leypar	leypar	creels, baskets
léàrabaand			sperruband		thigh rope to creels
héàla tøgvi					matted wool twisted round tail-girth

A Gásadalur split saddle (Fig. 17) is noteworthy, not only on account of the extreme roughness of its construction but also on account of its size. The side boards measure 19 cm × 11 cm × c. 2 cm thick and the overall height of the bigger piece, from the tip of the horn to the base of the board, a mere 22 cm. Each lower outer edge, below the two holes (1.5 cm diameter and 12 cm apart) for the breast and tail girths, has a 25°–30° bevel over 3.5 cm—doubtless to permit the load to lie more easily against the side. Each of the two sections is carved from a single piece of wood and one horn (4 cm wide) passes through a hole in the other (6 cm wide), the two being secured, not by a pin as e.g. in the Northern Isles of Scotland, but by a piece of woollen cord wound round the upper part of the thinner shaft. This prevents any slip-back.

Another feature is the slight but distinct knob at the end of each horn. That on the thinner one has a somewhat angled head. They are not marked enough to allow the load to be hung from the nearest rather than from the opposite horn and it is improbable that they are trace survivals of the hook found, for example, on some one- and two-horned Norwegian and Scottish pack-saddles. Certainly, there appears to be no tradition of such hooks in the Faroe Islands.

However, it may be permissible to speculate that they are now-meaningless stylisations stemming from the insert-and-turn method of securing one piece to the other, as illustrated in earlier works (Svabo 1781–2, fig. 8; Landt 1810, fig. 2; see also Fenton p. 128). Alternatively, or maybe as an indirect adaptation of this, they may have a specific functional use—to prevent the rope carrying-band from jumping off the horn as the pony jogs up and down steep slopes. This would be particularly relevant in the case of such a small saddle—not just because it is shorter than most but because it must, therefore, sit at a wider angle on the horse's back and thus lower the angle of the horns relative to the ground.

As well as being attached to the horn by a carrying band, the *leypar* are further secured by a loop of rope attached between the two lowest slats of the nearest corner-post and passing above the forelegs. Like the breast and tail girths, the purpose of this *sperruband* is to prevent the equipment from shifting unduly on hillsides. An attachment forward would help when ascending, replaced presumably by one round the rear quarters for the descent. Such a girth was also noted by Svabo who indicates that a woollen rope or *léàra-baand* passed round the thighs and was fixed to the after-most corner-post on the nearest side (Svabo 1781–2.138; cf. also Landt 1810.279–80).

ii. The Horse Leypur

The *rossleypur* is very much the same as the ordinary *leypur*, and it can equally well be carried by a man (see 1 b iii). Its primary difference is in the base which, instead of being fixed, may be opened by releasing a small wooden peg anchored between the two lower slats on a side adjacent to that bearing the carrying band. A thin cord from the middle of the peg is tied round the central base slat. These latter, normally three in number, are mortised into two supporting cross-struts, one of which swivels in small blind holes cut into the lower part of two of the corner posts (Svabo 1781–2, fig. 7; Landt 1810, fig. 1). In this way, the *leypar* do not have to be removed for emptying. However, in order not to unbalance the horse, care must be taken to allow the load to fall in roughly equal quantities from each side.

This opening device appears to have become less common than formerly by the beginning of the present century (Annandale 1903.257–8), although several examples were noted in 1970, particularly in Gásadalur. Most, however, also incorporate one or two lengths of rope which pass round the base strut, through the gaps between the base slats and up round the lowest side slat, and this may indicate that the base is now primarily thought of as fixed (Fig. 13). Previously one or other method might have been employed, but not both apparently (Svabo 1781–2.140).

The horse-*leypur*—by Svabo's figures, almost identical in size with the

Fig. 18. A single-horse box-cart. Gásadalur.

tunnuleypur—is used in Gásadalur mainly for carrying potatoes *(eplir)* from the *bøur,* and puffins *(lundar)*—especially when the latter are taken on the cliffs near the former *trøð* settlement of Víkar on the far side of the main ridge. In July 1970, it took two journeys to bring back some 400 puffins along a track where a loaded pony sometimes has difficulty in passing between rocks and boulders. In Mykines, too, a load is reckoned at 100–150 puffins per *leypur.*

Dung used also to be carried in this manner (although Williamson's *tøðleypur* was solid, with no gaps between the slats—Williamson 1948.58). Svabo (again, apparently, followed by Landt) remarks that a two-basket load was called a *kliiv* and adds that such *leypar* were somewhat smaller (or filled less) than those used for peat. He estimated that c. 3300–3500 cubic inches of peat were contained in one *leypur* 16–17″ square by 24″ high (see 1 b iii), a figure that would roughly tally with the Mykines estimate of 50–70 dried peats per side. Peat-cutting is virtually obsolete on Mykines nowadays, and this figure, in fact, refers to the number until recently carried on a pack-horse in each of two sacks. However, it used also to be carried in the *rossleypur* —as well as by cart or on the back.

iii. The Sack or Bag

Like peats in Mykines, grain in Gásadalur was carried in bags in the days when barley was still grown. These *tunnusekkur*, thought to have been made from coconut flax or coir and, apparently, containing about 200 lb., would be hooked over the horns of the pack-saddle.

At present on Mykines, a long sack passing right over the horse's back and down either flank can be used for transporting puffins without a pack-saddle. It is slung over a hay, wool or straw mat and secured by breast and tail girths, *reip*, tied to the sides of the sack. This sack, known as a *lunda-posi*, has two slits on the upper side through which the puffins are slipped: it is said that 200–250 can be carried on each side.

Hay was not carried on horse-back, however, as far as could be ascertained: nor should it be thought that this was necessarily the major way of transporting any specific commodity. Certainly on Mykines, whilst the horse took dung to the fields and brought back peat from the moor, yet it was more usual sometimes to cart peats back, or for a man to carry them on his back. Equally, though the horse would bring sea-birds from the more remote parts of the island, a man would carry those from closer by. Similar distinctions are found in Gásadalur practice.

b. Draught

i. The Cart

Where conditions allow, the pony is harnessed to a cart and used in the same way as the tractor, which is only marginally the more recent of the two techniques. The hand-cart reached Hestur about 1920 (see 1 a) but even in the late 1950s it was still considered strange enough to merit special mention (Nyman 1958.102) and Williamson, speaking of the early 1940s, clearly emphasises the "very recent introduction" of the wheeled cart—both the two-wheeled single-horse box-cart, found then in great numbers around Sandur in Sandoy, and a longer, narrower and somewhat deeper four-wheeled waggon of Danish origin (Williamson 1948.59). The cart bodies were seemingly of local construction although, because there were no wheelwrights in the Faroes, wheels were imported from Norway. Gásadalur boasts two horses and carts at present (Forster & Smith 1969.38) and the cart specification relates closely to that given by Williamson. It is a rectangular wooden container, little larger than the *trillibøra* box (see 1 a i), and secured to a pair of wooden shafts. The only concession to the 1970s is a pair of new inflatable rubber tyred wheels attached to an iron axle (Fig. 18).

46

On Mykines, a small wooden cart wheel—certainly not the work of a professional wheelwright and probably of local construction—was noted in an uninhabited house (Fig. 19). Overall diameter is 82 cm, hub diameter 15 cm and axle hole diameter 3 cm. Eight rectangular wooden spokes (27 cm × 2 cm × 4 cm) slot into the hub (12 cm deep) and divide the eight quite separate segments of an inner rim. The wooden outer rim, approximately twice the thickness of the inner one and with its eight felloes splice-jointed over each other, is encircled by a 3 cm wide iron strip, apparently attached cold. This and a band around the hub, are the only pieces of metal used.

ii. Harness

A set of cart harness examined in Gásadalur had been imported directly from Norway. It consists of bridle, bit and rein, collar and wooden hames, harness and saddle. The two-piece iron bit has a rope rein attached by a snap-link to one of its rings. Two leather-covered, swivelling, wooden pads support a strongly arched brass-covered, iron saddle bar complete with shackles and rings. The equipment is known locally as *selatoy*—from the Danish *seletøj*.

3. Mechanical Power

This category comprises machinery powered by electricity or fuel oil. Mykines now has its own electricity generator, and pylons stretch high over the mountains from the Böur road-end into Gásadalur. Electricity has arrived only during the last few years and provides light, heat and power, replacing oil-based fuels in some spheres. Both sources of energy are included here only in so far as they have taken over from man and horse in the realm of transport.

a. The Tractor

Where the two-wheeled box-cart came into use in the two settlements earlier this century, there is now a tendency to harness it to a mini-tractor, mainly on the short stretches of earthen road running through the *bøur*. Goods from the harbour or large loads of e.g. hay from quite near to the track, can thus be carted mechanically. The single Gásadalur machine, which is for the benefit of all, is driven by the youngest working member of the community, who has just left the village school. The cart it draws is virtually identical to the rubber-tyred, single-horse example already noted (see 2 b i), except for its central traction bar.

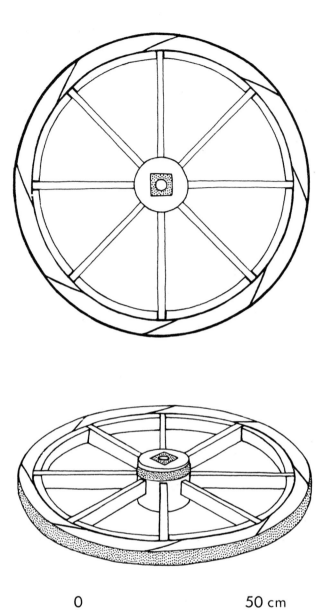

0   50 cm

Fig. 19. A small wooden cart-wheel. Mykines.

b. The Cable-way

Mechanically-powered cable-ways are found in both Gásadalur and Mykines for shifting up or down anything and everything, including boats, between harbour and cliff-top. In Mykines, a new winch and power house, to accompany the recently-built concrete slipway, has only to be fitted out: meantime,

48

a system of ground-level, steel cables zig-zagging round pulley-wheels down the old slip with its fixed wooden rollers, serves to haul up the boats—right up to the village road-end, if need be. There is also a somewhat elementary overhead cable hoist for materials.

The need for a sound cable-way is even more necessary in Gásadalur. The winch-house here is set back a little from the cliff to allow for loading and unloading immediately over the earthen track. The steel cradle, with wood-planked base, incorporates two cantilevered arms attached to pulley-wheels running along a steel cable (Fig. 20). Once over the cliff-top the angle increases sharply and the cable swoops down in one stretch to its terminal point on the flattish rocks beside the landing place. Not only do objects have to be securely lashed on, but the villagers make it a rule that no-one be caught on the cliff steps when the cradle is overhead. When boats are carried, depending on overall size, some two-thirds or more of their length and about half their width may overhang the cradle.

Examples of aerial ropeways, doubtless somewhat less sophisticated and perhaps more like the old Mykines hoist, were noted in the early 1940s on Nólsoy and Hestur for moving peat (Williamson 1948.65), so this method of transport is not an entirely recent innovation. However the use of power-assisted transport is limited in those more remote communities still isolated from an expanding system of communications.

PROGRESS AND CHANGE

The subject of transport, in the various aspects discussed, highlights the endemic nature of change due to innovation and obsolescence in the Gása-dalur and Mykines communities. Skins are no longer in use except as a cover for the *dylla,* and sacks have largely replaced rope-tied bundles; the former vertical cording is disappearing as nylon-netting now covers the *línuleypur;* horse-hair has given way first to hemp and now to nylon for ropes; the man-powered barrow and the horse- or engine-powered cart are replacing the *ley-pur* for back burdens. The pack-horse is being ousted by the draught-horse, and the construction of roads together with the introduction of mechanization and electricity is doing away with both man and beast as the primary sources of transport.

Other developments have hastened change—the demise of barley as a crop, the disuse of peat as a fuel, the importation of food and bulky goods beyond the capacity of traditional transport methods.

Fig. 20. The steel cradle transports goods to and from the landing-place. Mini-tractor and converted box-cart are parked at the head of the cliff where electric lighting enables work to continue during the night, if necessary. Gásadalur.

Rates of change vary, here as elsewhere, but Gásadalur, because of its physical remoteness and severity, has maintained a greater dependence upon mainly subsistence agriculture than probably any other settlement in the Islands. Elsewhere, the second half of the nineteenth century saw a great increase in fishing, closely associated with population growth (Hansen 1965.25), the arrival of the potato, and the changeover from a subsistence to an exchange economy (Coull 1967.162). Since the Second World War, in particular, the fishing has outstripped agriculture (John 1968.8). Farming in the Faroes is still of importance—especially for milk, lamb, mutton and potatoes—but an increasingly large proportion of these products is now imported (Kallsberg 1970.313) and the old, purely agricultural settlements have gradually declined (Hansen 1965.25) as primarily full-time fishermen have moved nearer to the main ports (Kallsberg 1970.319–20).

By its survival so long under peculiarly difficult conditions Gásadalur is an anomaly in present-day terms, although its population too is now dropping rapidly. It is one of the few places where peat is still cut regularly—although the recent introduction of electricity will doubtless soon bring about a rapid decrease in this activity. Furthermore, since they cannot fish regularly direct from the settlement, the inhabitants still set much store by fowling and cultivation. Indeed, one man in 1970 had recently acquired from the government —as an extension to his arable—an extra 1100 sq. m. approximately, of *trøð* land, from the *hagi* immediately adjacent to the western dyke.

Because of such factors, the system of land transport in Gásadalur remains more traditional in character than in many other Faroese settlements, with apparently an almost total reliance on the human back and the pack horse until the mid 1960s.

On Mykines, however, a cash economy has a far stronger hold. The returns from the long-term distant-water fisheries and from the quite heavy annual crop of tourists enable the inhabitants to buy in an increasingly large proportion of their needs. Fuel is supplied by the generator rather than the peat bank and fowling is no longer essential although it still continues to some extent. Puffins are sometimes sent away to friends, relatives or for sale, by the same boat that brings in the regular supplies of potatoes and other necessities. In 1970, it was expected that only about one-quarter of the hay would be cut and therefore requiring transport since, apart from the still constant sheep, the number of cows (14), calves (6) and bullocks (3) had dropped considerably. Informants recalled figures of 40, 12 and 8 as obtaining quite recently, although 20 bullocks were recorded as recently as the early 1940s, grazing on the Mykineshólmur (Williamson 1948.176)—precisely the same number as laid down in law last century (Winther 1870.152 ff.) and noted in the eighteenth century (Svabo 1781–2.373).

Within the context of transport, moreover, a marked difference in social organisation is evident between the two communities. The mini-tractor in Gásadalur is driven by the youngest working male as a service to the whole community, and at the harbour everyone present will lend a hand with loading and unloading, regardless of ownership. On Mykines, however, a man will normally deal only with what belongs to him. Materials destined for another will be left on the rocks by the landing-stage even though other islanders may return empty-handed to the village after the arrival of a boat. It is hard to say whether this is due to relatively recent changes in social and economic conditions or to the somewhat looser groupings of a larger community where universal co-operation for survival is less pressing.

What is clear is that at present, in Gásadalur, the recently-acquired mechanical power is still being used primarily to move traditional materials. On Mykines, however, a whole new range of goods has arrived, reflecting changes in general outlook and aspirations which will sooner or later also materially alter the character of Gásadalur. Indeed this settlement can now boast of one mechanical hand-mower for hay, although Mykines, which for long had just one, has had four for the past six years.

In terms of transport, a tractor-drawn cart can save on the overall number of journeys and the time taken for each, as well as on manpower—particularly important factors when there is a declining population or change of emphasis in the economy. Consequently, the more new tracks created in the infield as at Böur and Sörvágur, the greater the accessibility and saving— also, the greater the amount of time for fishing, the acquisition of money, the purchase first of necessities and then of luxuries, and the concomitant lessening of local subsistence activities.

Soon the old ways of transport will be relegated to a secondary position, for use only in emergencies or for some minor purpose. Even the carrying of e.g. birds and wool down from the more remote parts of the hill grazings is threatened, since these activities depend to a large extent on the survival of the old economy. Moreover the *hagar* themselves, on the main islands, are slowly becoming more accessible as roads are driven across them to link otherwise isolated settlements.

The projected tunnel development from Akranes to Gásadalur will, like the roads elsewhere, have far-reaching effects on the character of the settlement. Not only will the old access routes be rendered quite obsolete, but it will also allow free passage to consumer imports and the hot-dog stands of Sörvágur. The movement will be one-way in terms of merchandise, since the settlement has virtually nothing to export. The aim of such a tunnel is to stem depopulation by removing the element of isolation and hardship, but people in Sörvágur are quick to point out that the new road to Böur has done little to remedy the problem there. As in rural Britain, improved transport and communications seem only to hasten emigration when the surrounding environment is not only naturally hostile, but fundamentally imcompatible with the consumer-based cash economy and way-of-life which floods in along the new 'life-line'. The physically deprived region may become a leisure time environment but does not remain a primary working one.

Note

Photographs	All photographs by John R. Baldwin, July-August, 1970.
Figure 1	Based on the 1:100,000 and 1:20,000 Færoe maps of the Geodætisk Institut, Copenhagen.
Figures 6, 13, 14, 15, 16	Based on photographs.
Figures 12, 17, 19	Based on field-drawings.
Figures 13, 15, 16	Back and bottom have been omitted from the drawings.

Acknowledgements

Thanks are due to many individuals in the Faroes who made my visit and research both re-
markably pleasant and rewarding – to H. O. Danielsen, Sverri Dahl and Oddur Arge for
offering their time and knowledge and for arranging access to the archives and collections of
the Matrikulstovan, Fornminnissavn and Landsbókasavn during my very brief stay in Tórshavn; also to many farmers, fishermen and local officials on Vágur and Mykines for their co-
operation, patience and hospitality – in particular, Peter Weihe and family, Sörvágur;
Hjalgrim Petersen, and the households of Jóannis Joensen, John Joensen and Hanni Mikkelsen,
Gásadalur; Mrs. Benadikt Davidsen and the schoolmaster, Mykines.

Credit is also due to members of the Brathay Exploration Group's Faroes Expedition, 1970,
who assembled an impressive collection of field sketches, measurements and notes relating to
many of the specific objects and techniques observed. Drawings are by Miss H. Jackson.

Finally, I should like to thank Professor Chr. Matras, Jóhan Hendrik W. Poulsen, Holger
Rasmussen and Alexander Fenton for later guidance on certain linguistic matters: any remaining errors are mine alone.

Glossary of Faroese Words

a. Plural forms are indicated in parenthesis if they have been included in the text.

b. G = Gásadalur (1970) S = Svabo (1781–82) W = Williamson (1948)
   M = Mykines (1970) L = Landt (1810) N = Nyman (1958)
   H = Hammershaimb (1891) CM = Matras (1971)
   P = Poulsen (1971)

c. The orthography of earlier written sources has been retained.

áttamannafar	boat, previously rowed by eight men, but now almost universally fitted with an engine (G/M)
bæltis-lunder	puffins carried in a waist-band – the fowler's personal reward (S/P): cf. *beltislundi (-lundar)* (P)
beltisgyrði	(a) waist band used in carrying puffins (W) (b) puffins carried in the waist-band (P)
byrða (byrður)	bale of hay, carried by a man on his back (N/W)
bøur	enclosed and cultivated infield area around the settlement (G/M)
dylla	(a) wooden milk pail, normally carried strapped to a woman's back (G/M) (b) yoke to carry milk pails (W) [considered incorrect by Poulsen]
epli (eplir)	potato (G/M)

53

fetil	knitted or woven woollen carrying band, worn just above the forehead when carrying loads on the back (G/M)
fjallstavur	wooden staff with a two- or four- barbed iron ferrule at the end, used as an aid in hill-climbing or in icy conditions (G): = *píkstavur*
fjórðingsleypur	smallest form of *leypur* in Gásadalur – for potatoes and puffins (G)
fjørður	fiord, firth (G/M)
fleygistong	long pole with triangular-shaped net, used in fowling (G/M)
grótleypur	wooden frame for carrying stones on the back (G): = *steinleypur*
hagi (hagar)	uncultivated common land divided between settlements and with specific rights allocated to individual landholders for e.g. grazing, fowling (G/M)
hamar (hamrar)	bands of rock, alternating with steep grassy slopes on precipitious cliffs – coastal and inland (G)
havhestur (havhestar)	fulmar (G/M)
héàlatøgvi	matted wool twisted round girths on a pack-pony (S): cf. *hali* + *togvi* – tail + felt/matted wool (H); *halatógvi* (CM/P)
held	ring, generally of ram's horn, used as an eye when baling hay with a rope (G/M)
hít	skin bag – to carry milk and bread and slung across the back (G): = *taska, skjátta*
hólmur (hólmar)	holm, islet (M)
hoyberareip	rope used in baling and carrying hay: formerly of horsehair (N)
klibbari	wooden split-saddle forming part of a pack-horse harness (G/M): cf. *klyvberi* (H)
kliiv	a horse-load, split equally between two *leypar* (S): cf. *klyv* (H)
kneppa	(a) bunch of two or three puffins, tied together in a loop on a rope to transport them back to the settlement (G) (b) two guillemots tied together by their bills (P)
kongsbóndi	farmer holding land from the crown which must be passed on, un-divided, to the heir (G/M)
léàrabaand	woollen band passing from the rear-most posts of the *leypar* and round a pack-pony's thighs (S): cf. *læra* + *band* – thigh + band (H): = *sperruband*. Usually used in the plural – *lærabond* (P)
leypur (leypar)	rectangular wooden container, with slatted base and sides, which may be carried singly on a man's back supported by a carrying band or *fetil* from the head, or in pairs slung over the horns of a pony's pack saddle (G/M)
línuleypur	rectangular wooden container for carrying long-lines used in fishing (M)
lundakrókur	short wooden stick with an iron hook at the end, used to pull puffins out of their burrows (W)
lundaposi	sack stretching right over the back of a horse and used for carrying puffins (M)
lundavørða	bunch of five puffins, tied together in a loop on a rope to transport them back to the settlement (G/M)
lundi (lundar)	puffin (G/M)
metta	mat of wool, straw or hay underlying a pack-saddle on a pony's back (M)
mørk (merkur)	a variable unit of land measurement (G/M)
niit	(a) base of three wooden slats in a *leypur* (S): cf. *nit* (CM/P) (b) two pieces of wood on which the base slats rest (P)

óðalsbóndi	freeholder whose land is shared out among many heirs, thus leading to fragmentation of holdings (G/M)
píkstavur	= *fjallstavur* (G/M)
pridla	lambskin bag, cleaned and with the hairy side outermost, used for carrying birds' eggs in wet weather (S): cf. *prilla* (CM/P)
(à) raja	carrying of loads on a pack-pony (S): cf. *reiða* – borne on horseback (H/CM/P)
reip	rope (M)
riim	wooden slats forming the sides of a *leypur* – generally four per side, but sometimes five (S): cf. *rim* (*rimar*) – small, thin board (H/CM/P)
rokaleypur	(a) largest of the *leypar* used in Gásadalur for carrying hay. Has five slats per side instead of the usual four (G) (b) any *leypur*, the contents of which form a top or *roki* (P)
ross	horse (G)
rossleypur	rectangular wooden container carried in pairs on horseback by means of a pack-saddle (W)
rosstýggi(r)	see *týggini*, *týggj* (G)
sáta (sátur)	large, conical hay-cock (G/M)
selatoy	harness used for a draught horse (G/P). Dan. *seletøj*
skarvur (skarvar)	scarf, shag (G/M)
skjátta	skin bag carried on the back by a band passing across the chest – for milk or bread (G): = *taska*, *hít*: cf. also *matskjátta* – leather bag (H)
sperruband	rope that passes from the corner posts of the *rossleypar* and round the front or rear quarters of a horse, to help support the *leypar* and to prevent them moving backwards or forwards on steep slopes (G): = *léàrabaand*
steinleypur	= *grótleypur* (G)
strámetta	straw mat underlying a pony's pack-saddle (G/M)
stulur	wooden corner-post of a *leypur* (S): cf. *stuðul/stuðlur* (*stuðlar*) – post (H/CM/P)
taska	skin bag carried on the back by a band across the chest – for milk or bread: = *skjátta*, *hít* (G)
tillegg	land enclosed at a later date than the original *bøur*, but generally earlier than *trøð* (G/M/P). Dan. *tillæg*
torv	turf, peat (G/M)
trillibøra	wheelbarrow, used for carrying peat and other loads within the settlement (G/CM/P). From Dan. *trillebør*
trøð	infield created at a later date than the original *bøur*. All newly-enclosed land has latterly been called *trøð* (G/M)
tunnuleypur	medium-sized *leypur* used in Gásadalur for carrying peat and puffins (G)
tunnusekkur	sack hooked over the pack-saddle, for carrying grain on a pony's back (G/CM/P)
týggi týggj } (týggi[r])	see *týggini* (CM/P)
týggini	pack-pony harness and equipment (M/CM): cf. *tujggind* (S), *tuyggind* (L), *týggi* (W), *týggj* (*týggi[r]*) (CM/P)
tøðleypur	rectangular container with solid wooden sides for carrying dung (W)
ullmetta ullarmetta }	woollen mat underlying a pony's pack-saddle (G/CM/P)

Bibliography and References

Anderson, A.: Agriculture in Faroe, in *Zetland County Council, Report on the Visit to Faroe, May–June 1962.*

Annandale, N.: The Survival of Primitive Implements, Materials and Methods in the Faroes and South Iceland, in *The Journal of the Anthropological Institute of Great Britain and Ireland*, 1903, XXXIII.

Cardél, J. ed.: The Faroese Pony, in *Welcome to the Faroes*, 1968.

Copland, P. J. M. & Walker, H. C.: Demography of the Faroe Islands, with special reference to Vaagö – an unpublished student project report, Durham University Dept. of Geography Expedition to the Faroe Islands, 1968.

Coull, J.: A Comparison of Demographic Trends in the Faroe and Shetland Islands, in *Transactions and Papers of the Institute of British Geographers*, 1967, XLI.

Djurhuus, N.: J. Chr. Svabo, Indberetninger fra en Reise i Færøe 1781 og 1782, 1959.

Edge, G.: Geographical Research in the Faroe Islands, 1966, in *Brathay Exploration Group, Annual Report and Account of Expeditions in 1966.*

Edmonston, T.: An Etymological Glossary of the Shetland and Orkney Dialect, 1866, with additional ms. notes by Barclay, T. (Library of National Museum of Antiquities of Scotland).

Forster, J. & Smith, F.: Agriculture on the Island of Vágur, Faroe Islands, in *Journal of the Durham University Geographical Society*, 1969, XI.

Hammershaimb, V. U.: Færøsk Anthologi, (1891) 1947, Vol. II.

Hansen, N. E.: The Faroe Islands, in Rying, B., ed., *The Farthest Shore*, 1965.

Helmsdal, M.: Road Construction on the Faroes, in Nyborg, A., ed., *Welcome to the Faroes*, 1969.

Jacobsen, J.: The Dialect and Place Names of Shetland, 1897.

– An Etymological Dictionary of the Norn Language in Shetland, 1928.

– The Place Names of Shetland, 1936.

Jirlow, R.: Das Tragen mit dem Stirnband, in *Acta Ethnologica*, 1937, II.

John, B. S. et al.: Village Studies from the Faroe Islands – a project report of the Durham University Dept. of Geography Expedition to the Faroe Islands, 1968.

Kallsberg, E.: The Faeroes Today, in Williamson, K., *The Atlantic Islands*, (1948) 1970.

Landt, G.: A Description of the Feroe Islands, 1810.

Lockwood, W. B.: The Language and Culture of the Faroe Islands, in *Saga-Book of the Viking Society*, 1946–53, XIII.

– An Introduction to Modern Faroese, 1955.

Mitens, E.: The Country and the People ⎤
– Economic Life ⎦ in Hiort, E., ed. *Facts about the Faroe Islands*, n. d. [1966]

Niclasen, B.: Some Remarks on the Present-Day Use of the "held", in *The Fifth Viking Congress, Tórshavn, July 1965*, 1968.

Nyman, A.: Hay Harvesting Methods in the Faeroe Islands, in *Folk-Liv*, 1958, XXI–XXII.

Ølgaard, A. ed.: Færinger – Frænder, 1968.

Orme, J. R. & Sterry, D. R.: The Impact of Recent Changes in the Transport Structure of Vágur, in *Journal of the Durham University Geographical Society*, 1969, XI.

Petersen, K. H.: Borger i Danmark, 1969.

Rasmussen, H.: Der pfluglose Feldbau auf der Färöer, in *Agrarethnographie*, 1957, XIII.

– Føroysk Fólkamenning, 1968.

Small, A.: The Distribution of Settlement in Shetland and Faroe in Viking Times, in *Saga-Book of the Viking Society*, 1967–8, XVII.

Svabo, J. Chr.: see Djurhuus, N.

Williamson, K.: The Atlantic Islands, 1948 & 1970.

Winther, M. A. et al.: Taxations Protokol: Vaagø Præstegjæld, 1870.

Transport in Czechoslovakia as an Ethnographical and Social Phenomenon

By LUDVÍK BARAN

The traditional methods of transport in Bohemia, Moravia, Silesia and Slovakia stem from certain economic and production conditions, from technical and technological possibilities, and from the nature of the terrain. From the ethnographical point of view, the territory of Czechoslovakia is very rich in forms of transport. Besides the ancient methods, there is a whole sequence of types representing: 1. back transport, 2. wheel or runner transport, drawn by man or animal power, natural force or special mechanisms.

We can further characterize transport according to the distance carried: 1. local short distance transport, 2. long distance transport of extended duration.

Carrying in the hands or arms, on the back or head, is common in all the ethnographically interesting areas of Czechoslovakia, for the transport of both individual loads and economic products and goods. Over shorter distances, burdens are carried in the hands or arms. Over longer distances, heavier burdens of 40–50 kg, are hung on the shoulders and supported only by the back, or, exceptionally, carried on the head.

Carrying Sheets

Carrying of little children. In western Slovakia, around Žilina, in the vicinity of Beskid, in Orava, in northern Spiš, in central Slovakia (the region of higher Hron, of Zvolen), and in eastern Slovakia, there has survived a method of carrying little children of 3–4 years old in sheets (often embroidered), slung over the shoulders, so that the child is on the left side of the chest. The left hand holds the child, the right hand is free to carry other things or to feed, treat and soothe the child. Such a burden is characteristically borne by women. Men do not carry children, for it would be beneath their dignity. Little Slovakian children were not only carried by their mothers, but also by 10–11 year old girls. These little nurses did not transport the children for considerable distances. Women with loads carried their child to the field, often more than 5 km up the hill. For such distances they used to put the

Fig. 1. Transport of child in carrying sheet, Závadka nad Hronom, di. Brezno. The right shoulder and hand of the mother is free. Ph.: Staňková 1960.

children into the *loktushe* (*loket* = elbow), a band of linen, fastened with a knot on the chest, that held the child astride the mother's back. Women of Tzigane (gipsy) minorities carried their children during the whole day time. At the field, the women made the sheet into a cradle by suspending it from a tripod of branches cut on the spot.

In the western parts of Bohemia and Moravia this sort of transport and carrying was unknown in the 18th and 19th centuries.

The sheets for child transport were of white, sometimes embroidered linen, measuring 70–80 cm × 250 cm. In similar sheets were also transported bread, cheese, meal, shopping. In coarse sheets of hemp or flax fibre, of mop or tow scrap, were transported such products as grass, hay, straw, flax, hemp, poppy-heads and wood, as well as manure for the fields. Transport in *loktushe* and in sheets is still very much alive in the Orlice Mountains, in the Bohemian-Moravian highlands, in Beskid, in western Slovakia as far as the Little Carpathian Mountains, and in the whole eastern mountainous part of Slovakia.

Fig. 2. The weight of the child or of the errands rests on the left shoulder, the right hand is free. Shopping bags changed the traditional sort of transport, overburdened the hands, restricted movements. Ph.: Staňková 1960.

The technique is very simple: into a sheet 150 cm square, in the corners of which are sewn 4 solid bands, the load of grass, hay, etc. is put. The bundle must be tied up tightly: The woman lies down on her back, passes her shoulders under two of the four bands, and, whilst still sitting, raises the complete load of 35–40 kg. Then, she transports it down or even uphill, two or more kilometres in a 1–1½ hour period. Women from the Carpathian Mountains and also from Central Slovakia and the Lower-Tatra region suffer, as a result, from varicose veins, and, when older, from respiration troubles. At hay-making and harvest time, the women are enormously overburdened, often transporting loads throughout the day for long distances, according to the position of the fields.

In Wallachia (Morava) and in Beskid, these sheets are called *trávnice* (*trava* = grass).

Only in one single locality, Huty under Tatra, the sheet for hay is carried on the head.

Fig. 3. A little carrying sheet loaded with straw, Central Slovakia. Ph.: Staňková 1960.

The inhabitants of the region of Jablunkov carried hay and grass in sheets from steep hills in a rather strange way. They slid it on the grassy meadows, moist with the evening dew. They had to wear their special home-made, heelless sandals, called *krpce*.

Baskets and carrying hampers

For *load carrying and transport* baskets, hand-baskets, and hampers were and still are in use. Wicker-work baskets of different sizes of birch, willow or hazel rods are still used, in different ways, for carrying grass, hay, straw, potatoes, fruit and vegetables, for the farm and household.

In every farm in south-west Bohemia, Moravia and Slovakia, we find many basket types, and in winter we meet, in nearly every cottage, a man who makes such baskets and hampers. For longer distances, quadrangular wicker- and hazel-rod-hampers are still in use in Bohemia and Moravia. They are about

Fig. 4. Transport of cabbage in sacks which are put into a carrying sheet. Liptovská Teplička. Ph.: Staňková 1960.

1 m high, conical, the upper part being ca. 70 cm square. Flat hampers were known in the vinicultural areas of central Bohemia, southern Moravia and southern Slovakia. Loads carried in hampers were transported for long distances, but, very often, the hampers were also used for local carriage.

For burdens of grain, maize, flour etc. for household and farm use, there were also containers of straw. This gave rise to a vast home-production of baskets, straw "wallets", and hampers, through which craft the relatively poor mountain areas became famous: Šumava (Böhmerwald), the Bohemian-Moravian highlands, the slopes of Krkonoše (Riesengebirge), Wallachia (in Moravia), western, central and eastern Slovakia, and the lowlands of central Bohemia and of southern and central Moravia.

These products were sold on a large scale at the country and village fairs. Such fairs were and still are places where transport methods and equipment

Fig. 5. Hamper of hazel-rods is carried for sale by the maker. Kašperské hory, Šumava, south-western Bohemia. Ph.: Staňková 1967.

can be studied. Baskets and hampers loaded with cheese, eggs, flour, spices and herbs are arranged in different ways for safe transport and for display to the customers. Wickerwork bodies for medium sized carts or sledges for transporting cabbage, vegetables and fruit, used to be made in an interweaving technique.

Ropes and Bands

Far simpler devices are home plaited bands and ropes. Faggots, sheaves of corn, flax or hemp are bound with them in Wallachia, in central and northern Slovakia, in the mountainous parts of Bohemia and the Bohemian-Moravian highlands. A bundle is ingeniously fastened on the back, so that, at the moment of unloading, a single tug at the knot frees the whole load. Householders, and farmers carrying grain, maize, or flour, used straw containers.

Fig. 6. A big basket of rods for grass. Liptovská Teplička. Ph.: Staňková 1960.

Loads bound with bands or rope are never firmly attached to the human body; but are balanced so as to be controlled by one hand only, leaving the other free.

Hampers

Besides the sheets and simple ropes, hampers fastened on the back also served for transport. This was so especially in Krkonoše (Riesengebirge) and on its slopes, and in the Bohemian-Moravian highlands. In the surroundings of Žďár in Moravia, the hampers were carried even in relatively level terrain and for shorter distances, especially by women. The hampers of Krkonoše are typical mountaineer's devices. In construction, they are very like the Alpine "Traggerät". A ladder-frame construction, ca. 1 m high, lies flat against the back. The burden of up to 40 kg is loaded onto two short cross-bars usually

63

provided with ropes. From the frame sometimes protrudes a little wooden platform for containers of different kinds. This platform is usually attached by a rope. Such frames appear in paintings, pictures, and illustrations, in an unchanged form from the 18th century. They are used for the household transport of grass, straw, hay, wood, branches, and also for the transport of goods in pieces, e.g. bread, cans, meat, a cask of beer, cabbage etc. In weaving areas, in the region under Krkonoše, in the Bohemian-Moravian highlands, in Wallachia, in Horňácko in Moravia etc. such frames were used to transport rolls of linen to the factor, and knapsacks to transport materials for the loom. The hampers served as a means of transport for home-craftsmen. They were equivalent to a small case and pedlars' frames. Glaziers, tinkers, linen-drapers etc. transported materials for their customers in similar containers. We can find similarly shaped hampers still in full function at the shopkeepers' market places nowadays.

Another type has, instead of rungs, a plank platform, and an additional little platform that protrudes over the head. This type of frame is still in use in certain parts of Krkonoše. On this superior type of frame enormous loads of hay are transported, under which we can scarcely see the stooping figure of the mountaineer. In this case the carriers are men, rarely women. The pile of hay is firmly attached with a rope wedged in a wooden clamp on the chest. On top of the head is put a round cloth head-pad. The burden is very often transported for rather long distances, up to 2 km, downhill. These frames are practical for carrying back-burdens downhill in terrain that is unsuitable for wheels or runners. The bearer sometimes takes a rest at a convenient place, generally a knoll, against which the burden may be leaned, to give him some relief. The man usually remains standing. At his destination, he gets rid of the load by tugging the rope suddenly. The sling of the clamp loosens and the whole pack of grass or hay falls into a yard or into a little barn.

Hampers are not used for local transport on farms. This device for the transport of grass or hay was more frequent in Krkonoše, among the Germans, than among the Czechs who preferred to use runners or skids.

Runner-devices and Skids

A simple skid-device is a solid, longish branch, on which the load is slung to be dragged down. This relatively rare ancient mode of transport is still in use nowadays in Bohemian countries and in Slovakia. It serves for short and long distances, notably on steep, grassy hollows. This type of transport is advantageous in dew, but the presence of dew is not a pre-condition, the use of skids

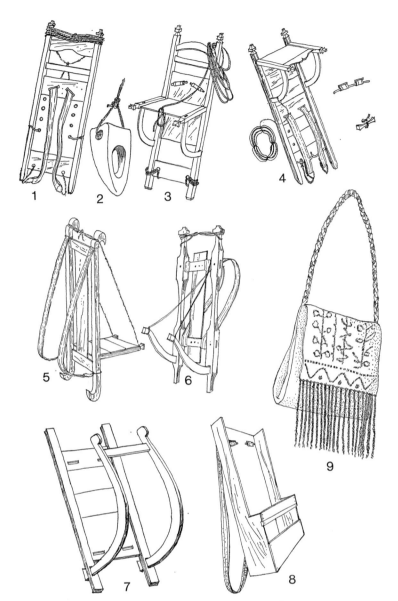

Fig. 7. (1) *Žebříkové ploché krůsně* (flat ladder hampers), Velkà Úpa, Krkonoše (Riesengebirge), 80–100 cm h., 45–50 cm l., straps 70 cm, rope to attach the burden 2–3 $\frac{1}{2}$ m is drawn through the holes in the middle plank. These hampers transported loads in pieces (salt, casks, chopped wood, branches). It is possible to elongate the hampers vertically with laths. Material: ash. – (2) *Žabka* (nut); auxiliary device to turn the rope tight. – (3) *Lavičkové krůsně* (platform hampers), Špindlerův Mlýn, Krkonoše, 85 cm h., 42 cm l., low part of the platform 55 cm h., rope 2$\frac{1}{2}$ m. For food, sacks, casks, receptacles, cans, wood, compost. Material: ash. Load, ca. 50 kg. – (4) *Pultové krůsně* (hamper with platform), Špindlerův Mlýn, Jelení boudy, Krkonoše (all in the Riesengebirge), 100 cm h., 57 cm l., besides a ring for head, bottomed with horsehair. For hay or corn, ca. 9 bundles arranged 5 behind, 4 over the head, attached with a rope. Detail of the straps being attached and securing the end of the rope. Material: ash. Load 70 kg. – (5) "Krosna" (hamper) for a roll of linen and of a warp, Frenštát under Radhošť, Beskid, 75–80 cm h., 40 cm l. Material: ash or beech. – (6) Hamper for grass, hay, with fixed turned up supports, Fryšava, dep. Žďár, the Bohemian-Moravian highlands, 80 cm h., 38 cm l. Material: beech; load up to 35 kg. – (7) Hamper for hay, bundles of corn, grass, with movable supports, Vysoké nad Jizerou, Krkonoše. In similar use in Vimperk in Šumava and in central Bohemia – Jílové near Praha (for compost), 80–85 cm h., 40 cm l. Material: ash. – (8) Small hamper used by glaziers, tinkers, home craftsmen, Turzovka near Žilina, 70 cm h., 40–45 cm l. Material: pine, fir, larch wood. For glass, tools, utensils, plate metal, wires. – (9) Wallet, bag, *cedidlo, cedilo* (strainer, filter), Čierný Balogh. A woollen sack for wood-cutters, shepherds, for food, small things of personal use; dimens. 55–60/60–70 cm.

Fig. 8. Sledging of the compost by *stragle*, Vyšná Boca, Slovakia. Photo: Staňková 1960.

being possible at any time of day. We can see branches used as skids in Krkonoše, in Jeseniky, in Beskid, in Little and Big Tatra, in Low Tatra. The present author saw this sort of transport used for the last time, in 1962 in Donovaly and in 1969 in Krkonoše.

Wherever this form of transport is in frequent or even occasional use, the hand-pulled skid devices were specially made, light constructions, which could be carried without difficulty up the hills.

The simplest form of travois consists of two parallel bars 2–2¹/₂ m long, set about 70 cm apart, and connected by two rungs or one crossbar. Sometimes the back part of the travois is a little broadened. The cross-bars are of ash. At the end where they are held with the hands, they are stripped of the bark, smoothed, and rounded, with terminal knobs or notches to which a stitched hempen band is attached. This band is slung over the shoulder and across the chest so that the body would absorb some of the strain and the weight would not lie on the hands alone. The hands then direct and lighten this travois. Such a device is typical for Beskid, the region of Jablunkov and

Fig. 9. Transport of an empty
sledge up the hill. Vyšná Boca.
Photo: Staňková 1960.

Teshin, and western Slovakia, for transporting branches, dry wood, grass, hay, compost.

Travois for heavier loads, drawn by manpower are sometimes attached to a short summer sledge or to a chassis of two little wheels on one pole. In the latter case, the travois is made a little longer, broadening out in a fanshape behind, with a rung fixed in front and provided with a hole by which it is attached to the handle of the sledge or the axle of a small light carriage. Sometimes these travois are provided with short rods notched for ropes or small chains.

All these combined hand-drawn devices can be found on steep, grassy slopes, in mountain areas which have a regular economic system and especially where the fields lie above the cottages, for example in the surroundings of Jablonec (on Jizera under Krkonoše, in the Jizera and Orlice Mountains, in Spišska Magura). In Oravskà Magura an interesting type of device not unlike the sledge is in use. It is called *vlatchuvky,* or *vlatchushky,* from the verb *vláčeti, vléci,* to trail, drag. It is a strong branch split into two halves, now in use for the transport of harrows and cultivating tools to the field and back, in spring and in autumn. Formerly it must have had a far wider application.

The travois can easily be transformed into a vehicle. Its back part is taken by a person who helps to transport the load on flat terrain. In this form it can well serve a modest farmer's needs.

From these facts it is evident that hand-travois or skids can be: 1. natural, e.g. cut branches, tree-bark, a piece of wood or leather, and 2. artificially made or arranged—according to local traditions and conditions—either hand-drawn or attached to sledges, small carriages and carts. These latter are, in fact, the simplest types of communication with a stabilized construction. The weight of the burden reposes on this construction and the whole transport-device is in contact with earth, ice, snow or water. The means of communication, then, include travois or skids, sledges, carts, boats etc. whilst sheets, baskets, frames, ropes, household carrying-frames, saddles, knapsacks, wallets, snow-shoes, and skis are subsidiary devices which facilitate the transporting and unloading of burdens in an organized way. The weight of the burden is still carried by the man. No real advantage is taken of slipways, friction, and other mechanical aids, nor is application made of the relevant physical laws.

Sledges

The sledge is a perfect and constructionally advanced sliding-device. The whole surface of the runners lies in the same plane, their path being the point at which braking is applied. The sledge is generally driven and manipulated with a fixed draught-pole, leaning against the upright front-part of one runner and attached to the first cross-bar. The hand sledge of Krkonoše (Riesengebirge) and of Šumava (Böhmerwald) has no pole and is manipulated by high upright front-parts. The driving of the sledge on grass or snow-covered soil requires considerable dexterity, a ready capacity for anticipation and prompt reaction.

For driving hand and horse sledges in hilly terrain, a complete system of braking has been developed. The simplest brake is a bar lying against the handle which digs into the soil or snow. From this bar has been developed, in Šumava and Krkonoše, since the 19th century, heavier brakes, provided with a metal point and connected directly with the runner. A good brake is a small block, lying crossways under both runners and attached to the poles. For the tranport of wood by hand sledge, logs called *berany, byky* (= rams,

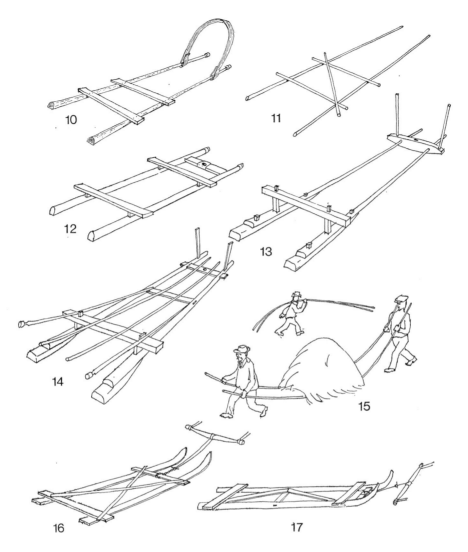

Fig. 10. (10) Gliding-device for grass, hay, corn, branches, Pražmo, Silesia of Tesin, $2\frac{1}{2}$–3 m l
Material: pine; load 30–50 kg. – (11) A light sled, Karlovice, Wallachia, Beskid, $2\frac{1}{2}$ ml., 80–90
cm br., for hay, bunches, branches. – (12) Skid for elongating the platform of the sledge, *berany*,
attached to the back crossbar, 3 m l., 90–100 cm br., Chlístov, distr. Klatovy, southern Bohemia. – (13) *Vleki*, sliding-device for elongating a short sledge, *gnotky*, or for attachment behind
a cart on steep slopes, 4–6 m l., up to 120 cm large behind, Jezersko, distr. Spišská Belá,
northern Slovakia. – (14) *Vlačuhy*, from Ždiar under Tatra, northern Slovakia, Tatra, Magura,
attached to short sledges or a cart. – (15) Aluminium, turned up bars, for the transport of hay,
Pec, Krkonoše, 7 m l. – (16) Sled made of old skis for the transport of hay, of different loads
in winter, Pec under Snežka, Krkonoše, 2 m l. – (17) *Vleky*, a low sledge from Krkonoše, 4 m l.,
for sacks of hay, wood etc.

piledrivers) are attached by chains, and slow down the speed in a controllable measure. On icy terrains, there are suspended from the poles of the sledge, under the runner, short chains—one, two, even four, to achieve really effective braking.

In Bohemian countries and in Slovakia the sledge as a universal means of popular transport has a very long tradition. Lubor Niederle and other investigators consider that the Slavs, who colonized our countries in the 5th and 6th centuries, transported their goods and chattels from the East on sledges drawn by draught animals. Undoubtedly, they also had carts, as proved by archeological discoveries. The essential ways of transport in our countries have a tradition over a thousand years old. The forms of transport were modified through time. Geographical and climatic conditions, and the manner of cultivating and exploiting the fields, meadows and woods, led to the preservation of certain archaic forms of popular transport, as in other countries with comparable conditions.

For Bohemia, Moravia and Slovakia, there is a characteristically rich variety of forms, some of which have survived till now, as the only possible ones in a limited number of localities, not as an index of outdated forms of work but as an ingenious and well-tried practice.

A special type of sledge is a hand summer sledge of light construction, from 150 cm to 200 cm long, provided with high or low uprights, with or without a draught pole. This type of sledge is easily transportable on the back. In Krkonoše it was called *rohatchky* (from *roh*, corner), in the region of Mount Jeshted in northern Bohemia, *samotížky* ("selfweight", by its own weight), and, similarly in the Orlice Mountains and in the Bohemian-Moravian highlands. In the Beskid of Wallachia and Teshin this type is known under the name *kozy* (goats), *smytchky* (slidings). The bigger summer sledge was called *grunarky* in Slovakia, and in Oravská Magura *krivule* (from *krivy*, crooked), etc. The summer sledge of ash, beech or hornbeam is never metal shod and is made of wood without a single nail. It has, only exceptionally, a vertically movable draught-pole. This sledge transports grass, hay, corn, branches, firewood, sometimes a sack of grain to a water-mill, or flax or hemp to the stampmill etc. The sledge was mostly driven by men from 14–65 years old. I have never seen women transporting loads in sledges. They carried and still carry them on their backs.

The sledge moves easily on short mountain grass, especially in dew, but not after rain, when the runners catch in the soil. When transporting branches from the wood, where the slope is not sufficient, the sledge sinks in the leaves, and is difficult to pull. Small straight hornbeam branches, of about finger

70

Fig. 11. Two sledges, one with the body, the other without staves, a cart with side boards loaded with compost, racks before the house. Ždiar under Tatra, Slovakia. Photo: Paul 1949.

thickness, are therefore laid at 1–2 m intervals, creating a path along which to draw the loaded sledge out of the wood. They do not remove the small branches after work, and the traces may stay for a long time there. The mountaineers may either slide their loads directly on the slip-way, or they may zig-zag down grassy slopes, taking advantage of knolls and mounds to turn and to brake. On flat terrain or a mild declivity, they draw the sledge with a rope or with a band passed always over the chest. A bigger summer sledge, adjusted for a team of draught animals, was in use in central Slovakia and in Beskid. Nowadays this sort of transport can be seen only rarely. For big burdens four-wheeled waggons are used. In eastern Slovakia and in southern Zemplin, in swampy and marshy regions, a hand summer sledge with enlarged runners is also in use. In the whole Carpathian arc, in accordance with the nature of the terrain, the summer sledge is commonly enlarged and elongated with laths to extend the freight-platform. Behind the loads are attached, if necessary, logs called *barance* (rams, piledrivers), for braking on an abrupt slope; on a milder slope the logs are detached and are left behind.

For the exploiting of timber and for its transport to roads that are practicable for carts and lorries, there is in use, in Wallachia, in Spishská Magura and in the Low Tatra, a short solid metal-shod summer sledge with a movable draught-pole for horses or oxen to be put in the collar or the yoke. In this way are transported long trunks and metre lengths of fire-wood, *shtipy, shaity* (from *štípat,* to chop).

The use of the winter hand sledge, naturally, is more universal. We find it everywhere in Bohemian countries and in Slovakia, in the same functions as a hundred years ago. The slippery envelope of snow and ice that covers the mountain country from November or December till April, can be crossed only on sledges. The manipulation of the Bohemian *rohatchky* (corners) and *shmejtchky* (sliders) in winter is very much as in summer. The man stands braced between the high uprights of the sledge and controls its speed. On a mild descent he pulls the sledge by the uprights with both hands. In Moravia and Slovakia, the sledges are not provided with such high uprights, but are manipulated by a fixed or movable draught-pole.

The transport of timber on the forest paths is carried out in winter in two ways; 1) by a team of horses, without a sledge, or 2) by a short sledge *klotchary,* to the back of which the trunks are attached and slide by their own weight, at the same time braking the load, as in summer, or on a hand sledge, *shnepky,* with one cross-handle.

Throughout the Carpathian arc, there is a system of using two sledges attached one behind the other for the transport of long beams on flat terrain. The rear sledge, having no draught-pole, is called the "back sledge", *shnepy,* the "small sledge", the small *gnotky.* Such a load, perhaps 12 m long, is very heavy and requires considerable dexterity and promptness in guiding the horses, and in correctly applying the brakes. Both the fore- and the back-sledges for this kind of transport are perfectly solid and well shod with metal.

In Bohemian countries, in Šumava, in the Orlice Mountains, in Horňácko, in Jeseniky, these two sorts of sledges are also used. They are called "the half-sledge", *pulky* (halves), *polouky.* In the North of Bohemia the winter sledge is used for transporting the compost in the fields. A hand sledge with a body is used for the lower lying fields, with a team of horses or other draught animals for going up the hill. The winter sledge has specially arranged staves and bigger side boards. As soon as the snow has disappeared in spring, the compost is transported on steep Carpathian slopes on sledges, hand barrows, or, on the Moravian-Slovak border, still in canvas sheets and hampers. The deep snow would wash away the compost from the small fields during the thaw.

Fig. 12. A summer *smyk* for the transport of hay from Liptovská Teplička, Central Slovakia. It is hung on natural hooks of wood. The enlarging of the platform is done with natural coarsely hewn bars. Photo: Staňková 1960.

In Krkonoše, in the Orlice Mountains, and in the Beskid of Teshin, there is in use a well-known and well-tried technique of transporting compost by means of a winch. On the descent the rope is stretched over the pulleys, and a small draught rope is attached, which is connected to a small cart with one or two wheels. The transport of compost in high-lying fields is facilitated, nowadays, by human force or by electric motor. The investigation of this technique showed its great popularity in Jesenik, in Beskid and in the Little Carpathian Mountains. The rope is usually 200–300 m long. In a single day it is possible to haul up to 50 sledges each containing 2 q. The hay and corn harvests are brought down on the same principle.

The summer and winter sledge, especially when drawn by a team of animals, is everywhere combined with a man-made section attached to the sledge to enlarge the freight-platform. This auxiliary advice is referred to as *vlaky, vloky, zvlaky, shnepy, shlepy, smyky* (trailers, draggers, gliders, sliders).

In Spishska Magura the fore-sledge is changed, in summer, for a two-

73

wheeled cart, and the auxiliary sled effectively counterpoises the declivity of the slope by its length of 6 m.

The range of means of transport on mountain farms is extremely wide. Against the outer and inner walls of the barns, there are suspended various types of summer and winter sledges, and in yards before cottages, near little gardens, are sledges and sledging equipment leaning against each other. The men always knew how to make the sledges themselves as home-craftsmen, but an anxiety to have such essential devices kept the cartwrights busy. They made them to order and still do so today. The big bulky sledge was also made by the carpenter and metal-shod by the smith. In order to spare the runners, the sledge was often provided with additional flat pieces of wood fixed underneath, which, when worn out, could be changed like used tyres.

Besides the sledge as a household-device for the transport of tools, farm produce and wood on the slopes and especially on the lowlands, there were also in use light coach-sledges, for personal transport, with one or two draught-poles and covered bodies. The horse harness was varied, decorated with small and bigger bells. This sort of transport is quite obsolete today.

Very important and still found is a light personal sledge used by workers going regularly from their mountain cottages into the manufacturing enterprises in the Beskid valleys. This type is only convenient for beaten tracks, whilst on the snow-covered plains of Krkonoše, of Šumava and Slovakia, adults and children (going to school) transport themselves on skis.

The children's sledges, and sledges made for children's pleasure, were always constructed for one person only in popular culture, while, later, industrial production began to offer longer ones.

To complete my enumeration, I shall mention the types of quasi-boat-sledges used since the 19th century in mountainous areas by the mountain rescue service or by guides for transporting wounded, sick and dead persons, and also for the urgent transport of goods and food to mountain chalets and hostels. This sledge has a fixed draught-pole and is propelled by a man going ahead on skis, while it has on the side at the rear one or two fixed bars by the aid of which other skiers guide the sledge when descending. The sledge, made of wood, plastic, or metal is still in use today, notably in deep, untrodden snow away from the normal mountain ways.

Carts and Waggons

The most common current means of transport in agriculture and forestry are waggons, but even waggons, as traditional kinds of popular transport, have recently been made obsolete by mechanized modern forms of transport.

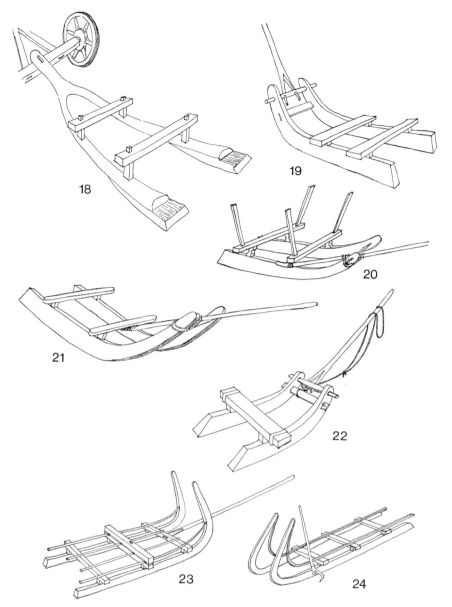

Fig. 13. (18) *Vlacúvky, vlacúsky*, Dlhá, Podbiel, northern Orava, Slovakia, for ploughing equipment, attached to the ploughing wheels, 250 cm l., 100 cm large behind. Material: ash. – (19) *Krivule*, Zuberec, Northern Orava, Slovakia, hand-drawn solid sledge for compost, grass, hay, 130 cm l., 80–90 cm br. Material: beech; load 2–3 q., used summer and winter. – (20) *Samotížky*, a foot-propelled summer sledge, Fryšava, distr. Ždiar, Bohemian-Moravian highlands, for hay, compost, wood; load 2 q., 160 cm l., 85 cm br. Material: beech, not metal-shod. – (21) *Kozy*, summer foot-propelled sledge, Horní, Bečva, distr. Valašské Meziříčí, Beskid, for branches, wood, brushwood; 150 cm l., 80 cm br. Material: ash; load 2–4 q.; not metal-shod. – (22) *Kločary*, a foot summer sledge for transport of long pieces of wood, Staré Hamry, distr. Frýdek, Beskid; 150 cm l., 80 cm br.; load up to 8 q.; metal-shod runners. – (23) *Rohačky*, a foot-propelled winter sledge, with or without metal, Stràžné, Krkonoše, distr. Vrchlabí. With the draught-pole usable even by a team of horses. The harness traces for lighter freight attached to the lower part of the sled uprights. 180–200 cm l., 80 cm br. Material:ash, beech or maple. – (24) *Šmejček*, foot-propelled winter sledge, Záblatí, distr. Prachatice, southern Bohemia, 180–200 cm l., 80–90 cm br., for wood, sacks, other burdens. Material: beech; runners metal-shod; hand-control stick brake.

Among the oldest types are reckoned carts and small carts with two wheels, still used for local transport in southern Wallachia and central Slovakia. This is, in fact, half a four-wheeled waggon, essentially lighter and more convenient for mountainous terrains with steep fields.

Such carts transported compost, hay, corn, potatoes, ploughing equipment etc. They do not have a historical or typological continuity with the ancient two-wheeled Roman chariots, as is the case e.g. in the Rhineland. Our half-carts have the normal wheel dimensions, a fixed draught-pole and usually wooden friction brakes applied to the tires of the metal-shod wheels.

The waggons vary in length from 3,5–6 m and the wheel-base varies from 1,20–1,80 m, depending on the terrain and on the weight of the freight, usually 10–100 q. That is why we still find various types of waggons serving on different occasions for long and short draughts. At the end of the 19th century the trade of carter disappeared. The carters who saw to the long distance transport in our territory, were equipped with big solid covered waggons drawn by two or three pairs of horses. For them had been established the system of carters' inns with stalls for horses, with farriers and wheel-wrights. Nowadays, the carters' trade is completely replaced by international autocar- and railway transport.

For local transport the farmers use various types of waggons with cart bodies, ribbed frames, plain waggons or waggons with poles only. The freight is traditional: compost, hay, corn, stone, brick, chopped wood, short and long logs, planks, branches, sacks of grain, potatoes, meal, vegetables, fruit, etc. Every sort of freight has its special device, construction and kind of transport.

Very interesting are the light two wheeled carts with flat bodies on which are transported loads that are too heavy or awkward for transport in canvas sheets, hampers or carriers' frames. We quite often meet this sort of transport in the northern part of the Orava region, in southern Wallachia, in southern Slovakia, in Moravia and even in Bohemia, wherever the terrain is mostly level. The light cart is a typical means of transport by the craftsmen of the towns: decorators, housepainters, joiners, upholsterers, locksmiths, coopers, etc. These carts are always constructed in a frame with two shafts.

We can find, as a speciality, carts with one draught-pole only, and some-times with solid home-made wheels of strong laths. The spoked wheel has been current in our countries since the Middle Ages. A solid or primitively made wheel is really an absolutely atypical and for our popular culture rare exception.

Very popular, mainly in Bohemian countries, is a small light waggon of four wheels with body or ribbed frame which is an exact miniature of the big

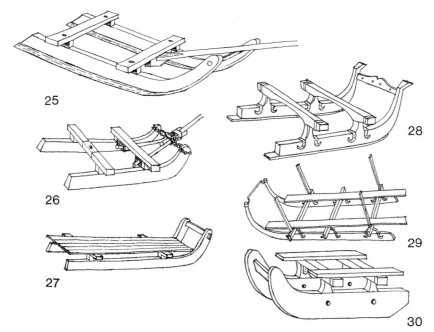

Fig. 14. (25) "Big horse sledge", Skřiváň, distr. Rokycany, western Bohemia, 260–320 cm l., 90–100 cm br., metal-shod, for different heavy loads, 30–50 q. Material: oak. – (26) *Berany*, a short winter sledge for a team of horses, Chlístov, distr. Klatovy, south-western Bohemia, 150–180 cm l., behind are attached sleds up to 3 m l., notably for wood freights. – (27) "Pious sledge", summer and winter sledge for a team of draught animals, Liptovská Lužné, distr. Ružomberok, Central Slovakia, 4 m l., 90 cm br., for corn, hay, wood in winter; load 40–50 q. – (28) "Horse sledge" for transport of wood in winter, Železná Ruda Šumava, 180 cm l., 90 cm br., metal-shod; load, 20 q. – (29) *Šmejček*, a foot-propelled sledge for the transport of wood in winter, Lenora, distr. Vimperk, Šumava, 2½ m l., metal-shod, with a carriage body; equally serviceable for the transport of compost. – (30) *Koňské těžké saně*, Cikhàj, distr. Ždár in Moravia, Bohemian-Moravian highlands, winter sledge for wood, metal-shod, 2½–3 m l. Braking chains go through holes in the runners. Load up to 60 q.

waggons. It is used for the transport of small loads, up to 2 q of potatoes, grass, a sack of salt, of meal, of cement, a number of bricks or stones, etc., and for local transport, in farmsteads from time to time, for moving heavier loads.

Yokes, tub-bars, wallets, sacks, wheel-barrows

Typical for certain regions, especially mountain areas of dispersed settlement where there is no water in the house, are the carrying yokes. They are shaped bars about 150 cm long notched at the ends. To the notches are attached thongs or strings or natural wooden hooks, onto each of which is hung a bucket

Fig. 15. A cart loaded with compost, drawn by a team of yoked oxen, Nedašova Lhota, distr Brumow, Wallachia. Photo: Baran 1948.

or tub of water. The balanced yoke is put on the neck and shoulders. Water is transported from the wells in this way, summer and winter.

The simplest auxiliary device is a stick put over the shoulder. On it is hung a sack, a leather knapsack, a bundle or any heavy thing. The weight is carried by the body, not by the hand; the hand balances, with the stick, only the weight of the load.

For local transport buckets and pails were typical in the past. The wooden buckets are carried, e.g. in mountain dwellings, with one hand holding a round stick, which is inserted into the holes in the two upright ears of the bucket. If a wooden withy is intertwined through the handles, it must be removed. For cattle feeding and local transport, there were, in all Bohemian and Slovak countries, wooden buckets and tubs of typically flat form.

Wood-cutters, shepherds, workers in wood, used and still use satchels slung over the shoulder, in which they carry food, tools, and items of dress to their work. With much variety are ornamented the woollen wallets of men from central Slovakia. Equally interesting are the leather wallets of shepherds, watchmen, and certain craftsmen such as gelders of male-animals.

Fig. 16. A cart with ribbed sides, Dlha, northern Orava, Slovakia. Photo: Baran 1948.

Easily storable carrying devices, coverings in fact, are sacks, which are carried when full for short or long distances on the back or on the shoulder, with a cover or rope tied round the middle. Heavy sacks are put on a barrow, by which it is possible to transport loads over great distances. This form of transport is widely dispersed and well known all over Europe.

Snowshoes, mud-boards, skis on leaf-covered surfaces

The use of snowshoes for personal transport on unbeaten snow is of very ancient origin and enormously widely dispersed. In Bohemian countries, they are known as *kropie, krpie, karpie, snieznice,* in Slovakia, *krnie, karpce, lazidla.* They are used by hunters, foresters, workers in woods, for work or for pulling the sledge up hilly places. In Šumava, we can find old types of snowshoes made of convergent or slightly upturned parallel boards. The same can be found in Krkonoše, in Beskid, in High and Low Tatra and in the whole arc of the Slovak Carpathian Mountains.

79

Fig. 17. A double team of oxen drags an empty cart up the hill. A wide track evident behind, the same before. Rusava, distr. Vsetín, Wallachia. Photo: Baran 1948.

The Finns call the snowshoes *karpponen* or *snokenka,* which signifies a device for walking on mud. Till about 1934 the smugglers on the Germano-Czech frontier in Šumava, used interesting snowshoes for muddy terrains, *bahnice* (from *bahno,* mud, marsh), in German known as Sumpfschuhe. They were very like skis, turned up at both ends. The wood-cutters fixed them with screws on their wooden shoes, which were padded with felt to complete the set of snowshoe equipment.

A special device for walking on leaves was a type of large ski, used up to 1930–32, in deep beech woods around Banska Bystrica in Slovakia and in the Transcarpathian Ukraine. The wood-cutters and workers in forestry used these 140 cm long skis in summer to traverse drifts of leaves, or to descend slopes covered with leaves or short mountain grass. These skis only appeared after World War II, and were used merely in extraordinary conditions, in the big Carpathian woods.

Fig. 18. A wheel of the cart in a wooden runner brake, Rusava, distr. Vsetín, Wallachia. Photo: Baran 1948.

Boats, rafts, water-gliders

In Bohemian countries, water-transport was developed for the conveyance of freight and for fishing. Boats of planks are known and illustrated from the beginning of the 14th century. They are not very much different from the boats used in other countries. Less widespread are the boats which were cut out of one single piece of wood. This type of boat disappeared in Bohemia about the 1850s. In the region of the river Labe (Elbe) were excavated in some places *dubovky* (from *dub* = oak), i.e. boats of one piece of oak. Their period of life was, in regard to the material, rather long, often even a hundred years. The excavated boats date from the 18th century.

In Kysuca, near Zilina, was recorded the last fishers' monoxyle, nearly 8 m long and 50 cm high which had been used for fishing, not long ago, in fresh river water. Owing to tourism, monoxyles have been preserved till the present day on Dunajec, the Slovako-Polish frontier. These are not so long (5–5$^1/_2$ m), but are constructed in the same way as in ancient times. On the Slovak

Fig. 19. Harness of oxen yoked in a medium cart with body, loaded with compost. Švermovo, distr. Brezno. Photo: Staňková 1960.

river side, about 30 examples are stored up, on the Polish side about 50. They are usually joined together in units of 4 or 5 to make small rafts, by the aid of which tourists are taken for a short trip on the white rapids of Dunajec. The boats are made of one piece of pine or of a poplar trunk. The boat is manipulated with a punt-pole. The composite raft is able to carry up to 6 q. The Polish farmers transport, from time to time, by means of rafts made of boats, grass or hay from the fields lying upstream from their farms.

The last rafts floated on Vltava (Moldau) in Bohemia, on Orava and Vah in Slovakia in the 1950s, before the deep-water constructions, dams, had been finished, which changed the current of the rivers into cascades of big or small lakes. The raftmen's trade was an old traditional trade. It effectively used the force of water currents for floating 8–12 m long logs. The rafts were joined into a number of clusters with ingeniously plaited withy ropes. The first and the last cluster was provided with a huge oar, necessary for directing the raft on the water current. The run through the dams was most dramatic. The raftsmen had their shore inns, where they could spend a night, and during the rafting time they were supplied with provisions from accompanying boats.

Fig. 20. The commonest type of wheelbarrow, Svratka, distr. Hlinsko, Bohemian-Moravian highlands. Photo: Staňková 1959.

A special culture of songs, recitals and rituals developed in the environment of these people.

A remarkable sort of water transport for wood chopped in metre lengths was used since the 18th century, in Šumava, in Jesenik, in Beskid, and in the Carpathian Mountains of Slovakia. In higher lying areas were created water reservoirs, from which were dug and regulated the channels of brooks and mountain rivers. In Šumava the Schwarzenberg exemplified a perfectly regulated channel, which brought the water from one river-basin to the other (Vltava-Dunaj). In east Slovakia and in the Transcarpathian Ukraine the flow is regulated by wooden-panels and an intertwining technique. At an exactly determined moment, the water reservoirs were opened and the high water carried the wood, which had been thrown into the bed of the stream, down the valley, to be stock-piled or to come to the plains, where lignite was burnt into charcoal. We can still find the water reservoirs and regulated water channels, but the fire-wood is transported, nowadays, in other ways.

My last remark concerns the water propelled devices, which are constructed, in summer, in the Carpathian Mountains of Slovakia and in Jesenik in Moravia. This device is, essentially, a 2–3 km long water channel. It is constructed of long beams, firmly put together, and lined with planks. The existence of these water channels is general on abrupt slopes which end on a plain with a stock of wood. There are brought small mountain brooks into the water channel so that the water might go through. The long beams are thrown from the top of the slope into the water channel, and slide on their own down the valley. This transport by water propulsion, which requires very solid preparations, is rather dangerous, but very quick. It is very useful in places where there is a great exploitation of wood.

Transport in Czechoslovakia as a social phenomenon

A number of different types of transport devices and methods have been preserved till the present day. This is partly due to tradition and an uninterrupted continuity of use from the Middle Ages, partly because of natural conditions of terrain and climate, and partly because of the way of farming and cultivating fields, woods and meadows. On some estates and farmsteads certain practices and proceedings in timber exploitation were stabilized in the 19th century and these ways of working survived till the 1950s, principally in relation to the artificial sliding-devices, sledges and carts.

The socialization of agriculture after 1948, the ending of the cooperative system and the development of agriculture in big complex units led to mechanization, which displaced a whole series of traditional forms of agricultural transport and put it on a small-farmer basis. Transport in the lowlands and in the hills soon changed its fashion. Tractors, bogies, containers, traction engines, funiculars, and a permanent network of roads, fields- and woods communications changed the transport system. By the regulation of rivers and brooks, by the construction of dams, by the transforming of ponds and basins, even conditions in water-transport were changed after some years.

With these changes, since the 1850s, even certain popular handicrafts disappeared and traditional professions degenerated. Traditional artisans' trades disappeared: carpenters, axemakers, peddlers, stall-keepers, guides and carriers.

Equally the countryside changed. By the construction of new roads and express highways, traditional roadside inns were displaced, by the construction of dams and barrages, old craftmen's inns disappeared, craftmen's wharves and docks changed, mountain dams, 150 years old, dried up; colliers' points, where the coal had been burnt, became overgrown with grass. Archaic districts with

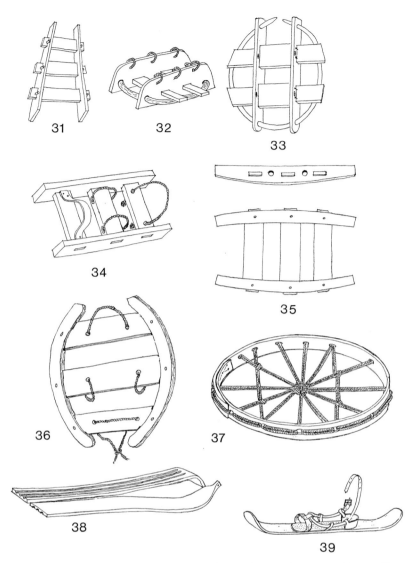

Fig. 21. (31) Snowshoes, formed of rod rings intertwined with rope; 32 cm diam., used currently in Krkonoše, end of 19th century for tourism, Erlebachovy boudy near Špindlerův Mlýn, 1958. – (32) *Karpie*, Lysà Hora, Beskid, conical snowshoes, 35 cm l., 19 cm wide at the back, 14 cm wide at the front. Material: hornbeam. 1948. – (33) Mountain *karple* from the northern Slovak Carpathian Mountains, region of Tatra, 38 cm l., 33 cm wide. Material: small beech boards, pine withy. 1935. – (34) *Krpě* from Beskid, Horní Bečva and Karlovice. Material: ash; 33 cm l., 31 cm wide. 1951. – (35) Snowshoes of parallel boards, Vrchlabí, Krkonoše, 32 cm l., 18 cm wide. Material: maple. 1960. – (36) *Kropě*, snowshoes, Vrchlabí, Krkonoše, a little upturned, 34½ cm l., 18 cm wide. Material: oak. 1952. – (37) Snowshoes, roughly turned up, Horská Kvilda, Šumava, 35 cm l., 28 cm wide. Material: maple. 1946. – (38) Skis for leaf-covered terrain. Material: ash. Báňská Bystrica, Central Slovakia, made in Jilemnice in Bohemia in 1952. 140 cm l., 11–13 cm wide, with three grooves. – (39) Snowshoes for muddy terrains, Horská Kvilda, Šumava. 1934. 60–80 cm l., 15–18 cm wide, without grooves. The wood-cutters fixed them with nails directly onto the wooden-shoes.

slip-ways and steep icy twisting slopes, where the logs and fire-wood had been brought down, changed their nature. Even the old field roads, sometimes narrow and compressed with hollow ways and bordered with small chapels, disappeared or had their arches improved. Wide dusty ways going directly up the hills, in spring and in autumn full of mud, were replaced by narrower roadways on a stone base. Some of the former transport equipment, therefore, became obsolete, and lay for some time out of action behind small barns or in front of houses, before being burned out of the way.

Krkonoše, Šumava and the Slovak Mountains have been slowly losing, since the 1850s, their complex of traditional transport. They became places of recreation, and the exploitation of timber, grass, and hay was modified according to the new economic and social conditions. But we have numerous records of popular fashions of transport as well, gathered in the 1950s, because in some mountainous parts of our territory it was not possible, due to difficult terrain, from the economical point of view and in such a short time, fully to realize mechanization. Secondly this phenomenon of retardation is due to the influence of the two disastrous wars, which hindered the general introduction of modern transport in agriculture and forestry, and for short and long distance travelling.

Changes in the farming of the highland and mountain areas, which had a dispersed form of settlement, leading from small-scale farming to cattle-breeding, the movement of the population to the cities, changes in professions due to the influence of factories and industrial enterprises produced shifts in the structure of the professions. Industrialization, mechanization, socialization deeply affected the old structure of life. The transformation is still going on.

The snowshoes, once absolutely indispensable for mountaineers, workers in woods, and hunters, were replaced by skis. Belt-transporters with trailers replaced the travois and sledges, petrol- and oil motors replaced animal force, the dangerous downhill transport of trunks was mechanized by means of funiculars. Motorised cranes and pick-up transporters help to load heavy burdens.

Of course, man himself changed too. After World War II we could still meet on an asphalt road or concrete speed-way a team of yoked oxen with a cart full of hay, straw or compost. Today the traffic sign directs them on to the side roads. The carters were replaced by motorised or rail transport.

Petrol and electricity replaced animal- and human force. Summer and winter, red tractors and transporters can be seen around the cottages, and stables have been converted into garages. Traditional sorts of transport slowly but

Fig. 22. The binding of rafts on Dunajec, Červený Kláštor, Spiš, Northern Slovakia. Photo: Baran 1951.

surely became in summer and in winter as well, a romantic memory of our grandparents' days. Twenty years ago, a team of yoked oxen or cows was a rarity, nowadays a team of horses in yoke is already a rarity too.

Transport by human force in agriculture and forestry, especially in hills and mountains, did not change as rapidly as the transport of heavy burdens in the country. Once the farmers went to the fields in carts or sledges, nowadays they have a small lorry or, very often, a tractor with a platform. Once they went to the fields on foot, carrying rakes, scythes, hampers and baskets, nowadays both men and women go on bicycles, motor cycles, scooters or motorcars. In the mountains, they must still go to the fields on foot. There can be found a range of transport methods, unchanged for decades. The transport revolution became most marked in the local and individual forms of transport, notably for women, but new forms of transport took away from the women much of the natural elegance of movement and is also physically less good for them. Carrying-sheets fastened in a practical way over the left shoulder, hampers, peddlers' frames, yokes, carrying devices etc., constructed to suit the carrier's abilities, have gone. An adequate division of weights, adaptation to a natural movement, a convenient lowering of the burden according to a certain terrain and state of the road, all this cultivated and maintained a tradition of popular culture that is lost. Also lost are bundles and hand-baskets for fragile loads like eggs, cakes, pastry, and knapsacks and rucksacks of all forms are very rarely used. Buckets and containers did not, of course, change their forms much, but even they often do not preserve a form convenient for the hand, stature or manipulation of the load.

With new forms of transport, equally, the old arrangements became obsolete. Even the structure of the burdens and their contents changed. Today we travel with luggage, bags, boxes and sacks. Very often we do not know what to do with them, our hands are full; but our backs and shoulders are empty. The ancient wallets had a strap or a plaited rope to be hung over the shoulder, but the new bags have handles badly formed for the hand. Cases and boxes loaded with big, heavy and also fragile objects are difficult to handle. In cities there is a complete transport system, organizations of porters, purveyors and caterers. In the country, however, the transport problems for new types of loads are not yet resolved. Actually the finished articles are carried from one place to another, while once they originated in the place. Equally the frequency of the loads which are brought and carried away is greater. The coverings and loads adapted their forms more for storage needs than for the needs of transport and local transport. Occasional carrier bags of a short service life, intervened into the structure of town and country transport. The original and traditional culture of transport has broken down. Burdens transported without ingenuity and solidity took, in a measure, dignity away from the man. We met the most miserable forms of transport during the wars, when the man possessed only what he was able to carry himself. The popular forms of individual transport are very inspiring for us by their serviceable nature. They developed in a certain structure of life, a structure, which, in regard to place, time, rhythm and the whole style, is different from the present life culture, form and needs of man. I consider then that the great majority of traditional forms of popular transport, whether in farming or in individual transport form a closed, dying chapter which, as a phenomenon, characterized and accompanied the individual. Transport as an ethnographical phenomenon is much less expressive in cultures and ethnic spheres which are differentiated one from the other. The Bohemian countries have, in comparison to Slovakia, a whole series of differentiations relating to aspects of popular culture. The differentiations in transport that we meet are not too much expressive in form, in comparison with other countries. The survivals of old forms are, however, best observed in the Carpathian arc, in mountain areas, while the lowlands and plateaus advanced to the modern system of transport.

Literature

1. Niederle, Lubor. *Život starých Slovanu* [The Life of the Ancient Slavs] Vol. I, 269–272; vol. III: 2, 347–440.
2. Zelenin, Dmitrij. *Russische Volkskunde*. 1927, 134.
3. Moszyňski, Kazimierz. *Kultura ludowa Słowian*. 1929, 629.
4. Voràček, Josef – Baran, Ludvík. Transport by Sliding-devices, in *Český lid* [Bohemian People] 1948, 74.
5. Baran, Ludvík. Čundrování s dřevem, in *Český lid* 1947, y.v. 20, 74.
6. Baran, Ludvík. Report on research of NSC, in *Český lid* 1953, y.v. 40, 239.
7. Baran, Ludvík. Krkonošské krůsně [Hampers of Riesengebirge], in *Český lid* 1954, y. v. 41, 84.
8. Baran, Ludvík. Smyky a saně v zemích českých a na Slovensku [Sliding-devices in Bohemian countries and sledges in Slovakia], in *Ceskoslovenskà etnografie* 1957, y.v. V, 333.
9. Baran, Ludvík. Krpě – valašské sněžnice, [Krpě – The Snowshoes of Wallachia] in *Český lid* 1951, y.v. 6, 114.
10. Baran, Ludvík. Sněžnice na bahna – šumavské bahnice [Snowshoes for muddy terrain], in *Český lid* 1970, 35.
11. Baran, Ludvík. Monoxyly na Dunajci [Monoxyles on the river Dunajec], in *Nàrodopisný věstník československý* 1951, y.v. 32.
12. Bednàrik, Rudolf. *Slovenska vlastivěda* [The Slovak Civics]. 1943, vol. II, 188.
13. Novotný, Bohumil. *Nejstarší plavidla na českých vodàch, NVČ* [The oldest crafts on Bohemian waters, National Czechoslovak Bulletin], 1951, y.v. 32.

Some Sledges with Handles and their Relations to the Kick-sleigh

By KERSTIN G:SON BERG

In the course of the preparations for a uniform nomenclature for the collections of the Nordiska Museet in Stockholm, the category *meddon*, i.e. vehicles on runners, has been accorded special attention. The largest group of runner-vehicles are the sledges, and among them the kick-sleigh is one of the later types. The older types had already had their evolution scientifically demonstrated, when Göran Rosander in collaboration with the Cultural History research department (KU) of the Nordiska Museet in 1966 issued a special questionnaire (number Sp. 188) on *Sparkstöttingar* (Kick-sleighs). Rosander published the results of his investigations in a paper "Sparkstöttingar" in 1969, giving an account of the history and development of the kick-sleigh from the 1870's to the present day. The answers to Sp. 188, however, contained several references to certain sledges bearing a definite resemblance to the kick-sleigh in construction and use, without having all the characteristics of the fully developed *sparkstötting*. From a terminological point of view it appeared necessary to investigate these kick-, drag- and steering-sledges and their relations to, on the one hand, the common sledge-types and, on the other hand, the different types of the kick-sleigh.

The construction of the sledge and the kick-sleigh

According to the definition in the nomenclature list of runner-vehicles the sledge is a vehicle consisting of two or more runners and posts, fastened to the runners. The posts, called *fjätar*, sing. *fjäte*, are connected by a cross-bar, *bank*. On the bars there frequently is a platform, *flak*, but sometimes there are only two rails along the sides. Usually the posts are low and end at the cross-bar, but they can also be high, reaching over the loading plane. The tall uprights are called *ståndare*. Sometimes, loose stakes, *stakar*, sing. *stake*, have been inserted at the sledge-sides instead of uprights to keep the load from falling off.[1]

The kick-sleigh is treated as a sledge with uprights. There are both kick-sleighs with two runners (in exceptional cases the runners are divided) and

90

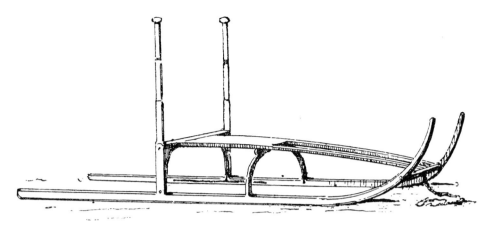

Fig. 1. "Sparkstötting", kick-sledge. From V. Balck, Vinteridrott, 1889.

kick-sleighs with one runner, the single-runner kick-sleigh. The runners are
very long and the fore-part or brim, *brätte,* is turned up. The kick-sleigh with
two runners has two uprights. The cross-bar is tenoned into the uprights,
and at the front the runner-brims are connected by a cross-rail, a so-called
noströ (nose-rail). Running between cross-bar and nose-rail there are two long
braces, *strävor* (fig. 1). There are some examples of braces from the cross-bar
to the front end of the runners, a construction giving a primitive, archaic
impression. The seat, if there is one, is fastened to the cross-bar. The uprights
are usually placed so that at least one-fourth of the runners projects behind
their point of attachment. Between the uprights there is a handle-bar, on all
kick-sleighs of later times fastened at the top of the uprights. This basic construction can be supplemented by quite a number of different additions, which
have been described by Rosander.

The kick-sleighs have often been used in winter-fishing or for transport on
ice. There is, however, another category of runner vehicles, that are expressly
built for such purposes (fig. 2). These are the *kälklädarna* (sledge-convey-
ances). They have heavy frames with two or more pairs of posts and cross-
bars, and a whole sledge-basket or box. They can be equipped with handles,
but in that case these are attached to the sledge-body, not to the runners as on
the kick-sleigh.

Sledges resembling kick-sleighs

Several answers to the questionnaire speak of sledges that were in use before
the kick-sleigh, or of so-called *sparkkälkar* (kick-sledges), which look like

91

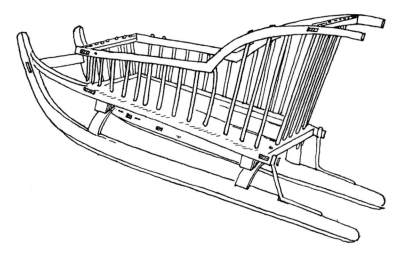

Fig. 2. *Kälksläde* "Torsöskrinna", sledge conveyance from Västergötland.
NM 184 809. Drawing after photo (Maria Berkoff-Urbonas).

sledges, except for two (additional) uprights at the rear end of the platform.
Instances of such *sparkkälkar*, to borrow a name from Gothenburg, are to be
found in the provinces Västergötland, Bohuslän, Dalsland, Västmanland and
Uppland. There are also instances from Åland. There are further kick-sledges
in the northern provinces of Medelpad, Ångermanland, Jämtland, Lappland,
Västerbotten and Norrbotten. The examples from Jämtland are illustrated by
photographs of sledges, sent to the exhibition of kick-sleighs in Östersund in
1968. The kick-sledges seem to have been especially frequent in coastal
regions and on the shores of large lakes.

Two uprights have been used in several different types of sledges, when it
was considered more practical to push the sledge forwards instead of hauling
it behind. Well known over great parts of Sweden is the long sledge with four
uprights. The rear uprights are usually taller than those at the front of the
platform. As regards the construction, the uprights can be connected with the
cross-bar in three different ways. The cross-bar may be tenoned into the
uprights, or there are two holes pierced in the bar and the uprights emerge
through the holes (fig. 3). In modern times, a childrens' sledge called "stak-
kälke" (stake-sledge) has the cross-bar and the uprights screwed together. The
nomenclature list suggests the name *ståndarkälke* (uprights-sledge) for the
sledge with tenoned cross-bar (fig. 4), and the name *flakkälke med ståndare*
(platform-sledge with uprights) for the sledge with pierced bar.

Furthermore, there are sledges with only the two uprights at the end of the
platform. They may be constructed in the same manner as the above-men-

Tenoned cross-bar   Pierced cross-bar

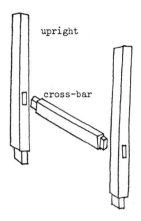
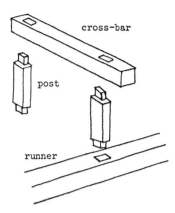

Fig. 3. Tenoned cross-bar and pierced cross-bar. Drawing (Maria Berkoff-Urbonas).

tioned, but there is also a more primitive form. The side-rails are here made from pieces of wood with natural bends, so that the stakes are all in a piece with the side-rails, as can be seen on the sledge from Dalsland (fig. 5). A handle-bar, now lost, has been tenoned into the stakes of this so-called *rot-kälke* (root-sledge). Sledges with detachable stakes, more or less securely stuck down in the platform or in the cross-bars, might resemble sledges with uprights, but the construction was too weak to allow the stakes to be used as handles.

Sledges with four or two uprights have been used for transporting firewood and water, and for other small loads, e.g. goods from the rural general shops, and besides that, for pleasure sledging. Two uprights to take hold of was, however, so practical, that they were also introduced on sledges of quite different types, e.g. the sledge with bow-shaped posts and cross-bars, which we have been wont to see as a sledge mainly for sledging. Uprights and handle-bar have even been added to the East European sledge with the high curved runner-brims, the *snabelbrättade kälken* (proboscis sledge), which is found in Sweden in the extreme north in Norrbotten and Lappland (fig. 6). The proboscis sledge is generally long and heavy, and the informant from Pajala gives it the name of "dragkälke" (drag sledge). It has a hauling-rope at the front and a handle-bar at the rear (KU 543).

As soon as the sledge had been furnished with two uprights, with or without a cross-rail to be used as a handle-bar in pushing and sliding, it had already approached the kick-sleigh both in appearance and in use. It only remained for the runners to be extended behind the uprights for the emergence of a

93

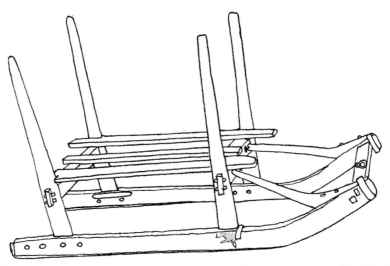

Fig. 4. *Ståndarkälke* "dragkälke", uprights sledge from Östergötland. NM 187 763. Drawing after photo (Maria Berkoff-Urbonas).

type of sledge, which in nearly all aspects corresponded to those kick-sleighs that have supports under the front part of the seat. It is a matter of taste if the "sparkstötting" without a handle-bar, that Balck shows, is to be called a kick-sleigh or a kick-sledge (see fig. 1). Closer inspection shows that it has curved posts and a cross-bar at the front of the platform and a hauling-rope fastened to the nose-rail. On page 6 in Rosander's paper there is a picture of real kick-sleighs with nothing but supports of wire under the braces or the seat.

Kick-sledges seem to have existed in many different forms, some of them fairly heavy, in different parts of the country. From Bohuslän and Gothenburg they are mentioned by several informants (KU 462, KU 640, KU 893, KU 541, KU 717). In Gothenburg they were used for sports sledging (fig. 7), but in the countryside there existed bigger specimens meant for carrying firewood, school-children, fishing-tackle etc., as well as smaller specimens for the children's sledging. The informants from Gothenburg call it "sparkkälke" (kick-sledge) and "drög" (sled) and remark, that it could be steered in the sledging-run by a long pole, trailing behind. More than one person could find a seat on a "drög".

An informant from Fagersta, Västmanland, Anton Lindström, has much to tell about the kick-sledge. It had the runners extended backwards and four uprights, and it might be equipped with a box instead of a platform: "The kick-sledge was undoubtedly the best transport vehicle in the winter to carry

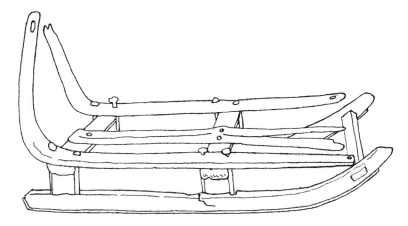

Fig. 5. *Rotkälke*, root-sledge from Dalsland. NM 180 707. Drawing after photo (Maria Berkoff-Urbonas).

goods from the shops, situated as a rule about 2–3 km from the works (4–5 miles from the Fagersta iron works).—A good thing to be able to bring the children along on the trip, there was room for two. In my childhood 1890–1900 there were kick-sledges in every home. The most suitable wedding-present it was too. Most of them were home-made, to be sure. Per Pettersson (Carpenter-Pelle)'s workshop made kick-sledges to order and the axe-smith Aug. Olsson in Björbo (six miles from Fagersta) mounted them with iron and painted them. The price of such an iron-lined and painted kick-sledge was 8 crowns in the year 1898. My father paid that and it was considered rather dear. Those who were good wood-workers made their own according to their own ideas and the pattern began to alter slowly. There emerged turned uprights with overlying handle-bar, the runners grew longer at the rear and at the same time more flexible." (KU 519).

The "sparkkälke" (kick-sledge) from Vittinge parish in Uppland was a children's sledge with two uprights for handles and a small seat, and it was used for sledging and on the way to school. It was in existence before the kick-sleigh (KU 599). Likewise the "styrkälken" (steering-sledge) in Dalsland, that was used as a drag vehicle and children's sledge and had a straight, vertical handle and short rear runners. The rough draft by the informant shows that the rear runners indeed were shorter than those of the kick-sleigh, but still long enough as to offer a foothold. The informant thinks that it was generally used from the 1850's onwards (KU 610).

The answers to the questionnaire do not show if these sledges were made with pierced or tenoned cross-bars. Both constructions are possible. In the

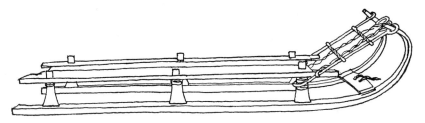

Fig. 6. *Snabelbrättad kälke* "långsläde", East European or proboscis sledge from Norrbotten. NM 76 739. Drawing after photo (Maria Berkoff-Urbonas).

collections of the Nordiska Museet there are several examples of sledges with tenoned cross-bar from the northern part of Götaland and all the way to the north, and with pierced cross-bar from Västmanland and further north. The descriptions of the kick-sledges from Norrland are on the whole the more detailed, and the sledges seem there to have been constructed with tenoned cross-bar, i.e. the same construction as in the modern steel kick-sleighs.

From Borgsjö in Jämtland we have a description of a "knoppkälke" (knob-sledge), simply the common 'uprights'-sledge with four uprights, of which the two rear ones are taller. The rear uprights were placed in such a way that the runner-ends "were just right to stand on going downhill, where the sledge ran by itself because of the law of gravity. These rear uprights were often connected at the top by a cross-rail, in the form of a handle, or, if you prefer that expression, handle-bar." At the nose-rail there was a piece of rein so that another person might help with the hauling. "The knob-sledge was, without doubt, the predecessor to that which later on would receive the name sparken (the kick), sparkkälken (the kick-sledge) or sparkstöttingen (the kick-sleigh)." (KU 467). The informant adds that the knob-sledges were in use until about 1910.

In Ångermanland, Långsele, there has existed a very peculiar short-sledge that could carry a tub of water. The vehicle consisted of two long runners, two heavy uprights with a low-lying cross-bar, and a cross-pole that was set in grooves in the tops of the uprights. On the cross-pole the tub was suspended. The sledge was called "vattendrög" (water-sled) (KU 941).

The kick-sledges from Jämtland, that were exhibited in Östersund in 1968, represent two types. One, undoubtedly the more ancient, gives a decidedly home-made impression, and moreover, it seems to have been put together from what in the case of bicycles is called "assembled parts" (fig. 8). Runners and nose-rail belong to a timber-sledge, seat and fore-posts to some sort of sports or children's sledge, while the uprights and the handle-bar in fact are turned on the lathe in the same way as on those of a kick-sleigh. The more

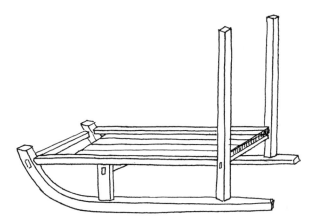

Fig. 7. *Sparkkälke*, kick-sledge from Gothenburg. After rough drawing by the informant, KU 462.

recent kick-sledge on the other hand is a well-made creation, which differs from the turned wooden kick-sleighs only in having turned baluster-shaped posts under the front of the platform, which is built like a box with rail-and-post sides (fig. 9). We meet the same sort of body in small hand drawn waggons, and it has certainly carried the same load: a baby has been placed in the box or basket. To make the kick-sleigh serve as perambulator has been fairly common, and the problem of joining the body and the seat has been solved in many different ways. Sometimes the body, as in this instance, has been built as one with the frame, at other times it has been detachable. I remember from the days of the Second World War, when it was still possible to slide on a kick-sleigh over the Swedish roads, a particularly practical kind of board or plywood box, half-covered and adapted to the curve of the kick-sleigh. In this box the baby lay well wrapped up in a fur-lined driving sack. The box was fastened to the kick-sleigh with leather straps. Also from Uppsala, about 1910, there is an example of a sledge with a fixed rail-and-post body and uprights with handle-bar, but the rear ends of the runners are so short, that it can not have been propelled by kicking (fig. 10).

The answers from Tärna in Lappland (KU 2330), Umeå in Västerbotten (KU 603) and Överluleå in Norrbotten (KU 1747) all give about the same picture of the development. There has existed a long sledge with uprights at the rear, sometimes with a handle-bar, used for hauling water, wood, hay and similar loads. The rear ends of the runners were so long that they could be used as a foothold. The informants look upon it as a fore-runner to or as contemporaneous with the early forms of the kick-sleigh. The oldest informant in Överluleå was born in 1863 and according to his statement "sparken" (the kick, a fairly common abbreviation of *sparkstötting*) was a vehicle used

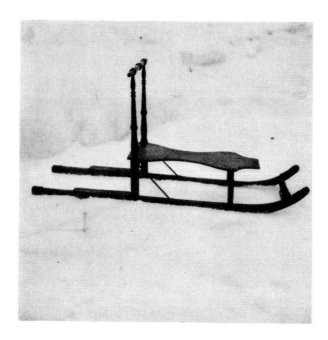

Fig. 8. "Sparkstötting", kick-sledge from Jämtland. Photo in Jämtlands läns museum, Östersund.

for sledging, while "kälken" (the sledge) or "vattenkälken" (the water-sledge) was the name of the sledge for hauling. In Tärna too the hauling sledge was named "tjalk" (a dialectal form of *kälke*), but in Umeå it was called "drög" (sled).

However, in Tärna there were, besides the sledge, so-called "sparkstöttin-gar" for children, built after approximately the same model. The rough drawing by the informant actually shows a sledge with uprights at the rear and posts at the fore end of the short platform, as well as low runner-brims. The lack of braces between cross-bar and nose-rail is worth noticing and underlines the close relationship to the sledge with four uprights.

In spite of the fact that the appearance and the use of several of the above-mentioned steering- and kick-sledges have presented a close resemblance to those of the kick-sleigh, the informants have not chosen to regard them as real kick-sleighs, except when used by children. The kick-sleigh, therefore, was seen in the first place as a vehicle for the transport of persons, and the carrying capacity was a matter of secondary importance. The kick-sleigh is often compared with the bicycle, cf. the nickname "lapp-cykel" (lapp-bike), but the victorious progress of the kick-sleigh over northern Sweden lies some twenty or thirty years before that of the bicycle, and unlike the bicycle, the kick-sleigh was cheap and accessible to everybody. Perhaps it should be pointed out that kick-sleighs in children's sizes have also been manufactured.

Fig. 9. "Sparkstötting", kick-sledge from Jämtland. Photo in Jämtlands läns museum, Östersund.

When kick-sleighs grew more common, they took over some of the functions previously filled by different types of sledges, both in carrying, sledging and winter fishing on ice.

The single-runner sleigh

The single-runner sleigh seems to have a course of development different from that of the two-runner kick-sleigh, although some of its forms presumably derive from the kick-sleigh with two runners.

The single-runner sleigh has been found in types with and without a seat, but the ranges of use of the two types are clearly defined. The single-runner sleigh *without seat* was exclusively a sports sleigh for downhill racing. The sleigh *with seat* has been used in the same way as the kick-sleigh with two runners, i.e. for the transport of persons and for carrying small loads, especially liquids. The single-runner kick-sleigh was considered faster and handier than the common kick-sleigh (fig. 11).

Many informants answer in the negative to the question of the existence of the single-runner sleigh in their neighbourhood, and its diffusion also seems to have been sporadic. It probably came into existence spontaneously several times, sometimes with the two-runner kick-sleigh as the model, and perhaps in

Fig. 10. *Flakkälke*, platform sledge with handle. Uppsala, about 1910. KU 3099.

a few instances as an improvement of the ancient push-runner. Rosander mentions an instance of the latter from Medelpad and there is one from Västergötland (KU 503).

If one may judge from the few statements, the single-runner sleigh without seat, used for downhill racing, has had a more continuous distribution in those regions, where *kässjan* ("karsar", "kajsa"), a short ski with handle also was in use for downhill racing or sledging (fig. 12). An informant from Mockfjärd parish in Dalarna, in fact, calls the single-runner sleigh "kajsa": "Single-runner vehicles there were on the other hand, which were called 'kajsa', made like a heavy ski, rather thick in the middle where the upright went down, but for the rest the nose (brim) was thin and turned up like a ski. The handle-bar was about 3 dm—1 foot long." (KU 2602). They had apparently changed the low bow-shaped handle of the *kässja* for an upright with a handle-bar. The *kässjorna* are known from Dalarna and Hälsingland.[2]

It is always best to be circumspect in default of sufficient information. Perhaps the *kässja* has been known in Härjedalen and Jämtland too and served as a prototype for the single-runner sleigh there. But the idea can also have been transmitted through some other vehicles. There are records of other ski-like runners, that a person was able to propel by kicking. One example is the *skridstång* (slide-pole), the long runner of the seal-hunter, on which he kicks himself forward, when he is still out of sight of the quarry.

100

Fig. 11. *Enmedsspark*, single-runner kick-sleigh made at the Bosjö joinery shop, Värmland, in the 1890's. Nordiska Museet, Bildarkivet.

Another example is the "enskidan" (single-ski), that is mentioned from the parish of Boda in Dalarna. It was used in the same manner as the *kässja*, but there was nothing but a leather strap to take hold of, threaded through a hole in the ski-tip. The single-ski had a strap over the toes, as had certain *kässjor*.

Names for the kick-sleigh

Rosander has mentioned, among dialect terms for the kick-sleigh: "stål-" (steel) or "trähäst" (wooden horse), "sparkare" (kicker), "stött" (short one), "sprätt" (scratcher), "rännstötting" (racing sleigh) and "kurir" (courier). The word "rännulv" (racing wolf), which Balck has given, has been applied e.g. to the single-runner kick-sleigh in Säfsnäs in Dalarna (Geete, b.c.), and to the common kick-sleigh in northernmost Uppland and in Östergötland, where the name "rännåk" (racing vehicle) also occurred. The informants who write of "rännulv" all point out that nowadays the name has disappeared.

Different compound words with *spark* (kick) have been reported from different places. From Dalsland there come "längspärk" (long-kick) and "mespärk" (runner-kick). The word "isspark" (ice-kick) is recorded from Skel-

101

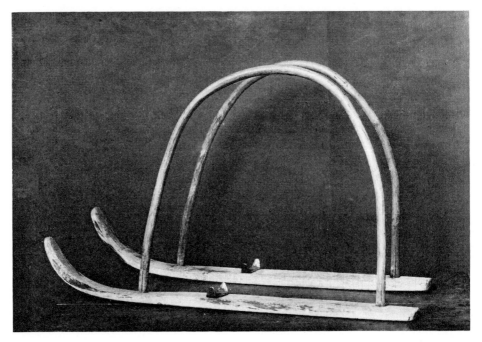

Fig. 12. *Kässjor*, a pair of short skis with handles from Dalarna. NM 96 082. Phot. Nordiska Museet.

lefteå in the 1910's and has been used in the suburbs of Stockholm too at the same time, in both instances denoting the new type of kick-sleigh with steel runners. In the trade directory "Svenska Varor" (Swedish Goods) from 1916 it is called "järnsparkstötting" (iron kick-sleigh). "Sparkkälke" (kick-sledge) the vehicle was named "gammalt i världen" (in olden days) in Ovansjö parish in Gästrikland. Besides,"sparkkälke " has been, as indicated above, one of the names of the sledge with two uprights and extended runner ends in western Sweden. In the Swedish dialects in Finland, "sparkkälke" is also known as a name for the kick-sleigh.

The word "sprätt" (scratcher) is not known from Dalarna alone, but has been recorded from Småland too, and in Ydre in Östergötland they said "sprättkälke" (scratch-sledge) as well as "stötting" (short sledge).

Skidkälke (ski-sledge) is, according to ethnological terminology and in most dialects, the name of a special sledge: a long, low, slender sledge with the runners and the side-rails parallel and connected with each other at the fore end. This name however, an informant in the parish of Länna to the north of Stockholm has applied to a kick-sleigh with the runners replaced by skis, yet with a handle-bar as for the common kick-sleigh. According to the

102

answers to the questionnaire a horse or a dog might be harnessed in front of the kick-sleigh. It happened occasionally, but there are also several instances of a conveyance formed like a kick-sleigh in the fore part, while the rear ends of the runners are shortened and a board or platform is nailed on to give the driver a foot-hold. Such a type of conveyance or sledge was called "skidsläde" (ski-conveyance) in the Kulling district in Västergötland (KU 696). This type of sledge has had relations among the winter vehicles of the Swedish army.

Kick-sledges and kick-sleighs

The above-mentioned "drög" (sled) from Umeå has its nearest counterpart in a sledge from Steneby in Dalsland, which the informant describes as follows: "The kick-sleigh was supposed to come from Värmland. But I wonder if it is so. Did it not naturally evolve from a sledge, that hereabouts went under the name of 'styrkälke' (steering-sledge) and at least from 1850 on was common both as a cart-sledge and as a running-sledge for children and looked like this: that is, a sledge with straight vertical uprights and handle-bar and short rear runners." (KU 610). The rough outline drawn by the informant shows a sledge, where the rear runners are long enough to give a foothold, and there is a strong resemblance to the older wooden kick-sleighs, which did not possess rear runners either of that conspicuous length which the steel kick-sleighs afterwards have been equipped with.

This "styrkälke" (steering sledge) and the informant's speculations about it, introduces the problem of the origin of the kick-sleigh. As appears from the previous account, there have existed a number of different types of sledges in the provinces all the way from northern Götaland to the far North, that have been the forerunners of the kick-sleigh both in construction and in appearance. To the examples already cited may be added an uprights-sledge from Östergötland in the collections of the Nordiska Museet, with rear runners long enough to give a foothold (see fig. 4).

Concerning the origin of the kick-sleigh, the investigators have on the whole based their opinions on what Balck wrote in his "Idrottsbok" (Book of Sports) of 1888 and in "Vinteridrott" (Winter Sports) of 1889. To be sure, Balck is a contemporary source, but he had probably no reason to do any profound research, and the information available today gives a different picture from the one he drew. Balck thought that the kick-sleigh, from its place of origin in the Norrbotten-Västerbotten area, would not have had time to advance further south than to Nordmaling, while Rosander (p. 2) has been able to show that kick-sleigh running already in 1888 had reached the capital "in earnest", and evidently it was coming into vogue at about the same time in Uppsala and Södertälje.

That Nordmaling should have been the south boundary also appears unlikely when compared with Balck's statement as to the invention in 1887 of the handlebar, in the Sundsvall region. Nordmaling is situated in the south of Västerbotten, more than 200 km north of Sundsvall. The statement rather indicates that the kick-sleigh already had some diffusion in Sundsvall and its surroundings. The handle-bar or cross-rail is, as Rosander points out, of an origin much more ancient. In addition to the parallels brought forward by this author, attention should be paid to the sleds with high runners and two uprights with a handle-bar, so common in the Dutch winter landscapes with motifs from the icebound canals. Drag vehicles with handles are especially suited for use on ice; it is characteristic that in Sweden so many sledges with handles are to be found in the coastal districts both on the West and the East coast. The *sparkstötting* has another advantage besides, that W. R. Mead and H. Smeds have described in their work "Winter in Finland", p. 108: "The *sparkstötting* is a practical method of transport which distributes the weight of the user over a relatively large surface area, making it especially suitable for employment in the archipelagoes." Sledge and toboggan with handle-bar have been reported from the Uppland coast, but I have not included them in the survey, as there is no indication of their being propelled by kicking.[3]

Runners with the rear ends extended have their main counterparts among the conveyances. A foothold on the runner-ends has been the rule on all small and light conveyances of the old type in central Sweden and southern Norrland, cf. Berg, "Sledges", fig. 30. Such conveyances had handles at the upper angles at the rear of the body. On the runner ends the driver accordingly stood, cf. Berg, fig. 29. The *trollhoppa* (troll-jumping sledge), a horse-drawn sledge on high posts, where the travellers sat astride the narrow platform, might also have the runner ends extended.

The two uprights of the real kick-sleigh are connected by a tenoned cross-bar, likewise on the rear short-sledge, "bakstötting", that Rosander illustrates. The accompanying text may give the impression that the timber-sledge in Sweden was generally constructed in that way. This, however, was not the case. Usually the timber-sledge had the pierced bar, making the sledge more stable and more suited to heavy loads. Jerker Öström, author of "Studier över meddonsterminologien i Övre Norrland" (Studies in the terminology of runner vehicles in Upper Norrland) only briefly mentions a type of short-sledge having posts raised above the cross-bar and doing service as sledge stakes.[4] As far north as middle Västerbotten the pierced cross-bar was dominant,

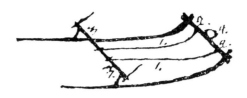

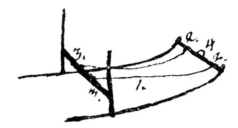

Fig. 13. *Enbankskälke* "stötting", short-sledge (above) and *ståndarstötting* "stötting", boys' sleigh (below). From P. Stenberg, Ordbok över Umemålet 1804, 1966.

even in its most primitive form with one naturally grown post on the cross-bar. North from here began the domain of the bound cross-bar (the soft cross-bar), which belongs to the East-European (proboscis) sledge.

The insignificant rôle played by the short-sledge with tenoned cross-bar in lumbering according to Öström, is explained if we retrace our steps to bygone epochs. Linnaeus illustrated in 1732 a short-sledge from Kalix, that had been linked with a similar one to a double-sledge. Linnaeus' short-sledge has a pierced cross-bar and is meant for timber and wood transport. A similar short-sledge, intended for the same use, is found in a dictionary of the Umeå dialect, completed in 1804 by Per Stenberg.[5] The only difference consists in the fastening of the braces which in the Umeå sledge are nailed to the nose-rail instead of to the runner brims. The Stenberg drawing does not show how the posts and the cross-bar were put together, but the detachable sledge-stakes are quite clearly depicted. In addition to this short-sledge Stenberg has drawn and described: "The sleighs, that the boys use for sledging downhill", and the rough drawing shows a sleigh with tall posts (fig. 13). The similarity to the kick-sleigh from Holmön in Västerbotten, illustrated by Rosander, is really striking. The single new feature of the kick-sleigh is the handle-bar on the uprights. The absence of a seat on the older kick-sleighs is also explained by the supposition that they were meant only for the children's sledging and as sports articles.

The hypothesis may be made, that some time during the first part of the 19th century the boys' running sleigh was taken over by the grown-ups and

105

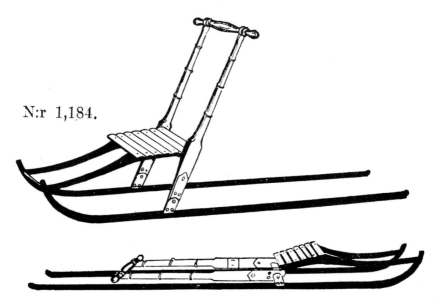

N:r 1,177.

N:r 1,184.

Fig. 14. *Hopfällbar sparkstötting*, folding kick-sleigh of Finnish design and make. From a catalogue from Scoutmagasinet, Stockholm, 1916.

turned into a kick-sleigh. Afterwards it spread, as we know, all over the country. However, the older types of kick-sleighs are so numerous and so different in shape, that obviously it cannot have been *the sleigh as an object* that was diffused in the first place, but *the idea of kicking oneself forwards* on a pair of long runners with uprights. If there was a seat, extra posts or supports and other details in the construction were of no great consequence. The construction of the Umeå boys' sleigh of 1804 did not in fact gain supremacy until the kick-sleigh with steel runners had been generally accepted. Especially the factory-made kick-sleighs of the 1890's offered such a variety and imagination in the design, that they appear far removed from the prototype, as e.g. the kick-sleigh from Kärfsta on p. 7 by Rosander. The joinery shop at Bosjö in the neighbourhood of Filipstad in Värmland made models of, if possible, still more original constructions, among others folding single-runner kick-sleighs (see fig. 11).

Folding or collapsible two-runner kick-sleighs also existed, but they might be rather treacherous and collapse when least desired (fig. 14). The Swedish author Erik Asklund related such a deplorable accident in 1962 in an ode to the kick-sleigh "Ode till sparkstöttingen": "There are (or were) collapsible kick-sleighs too, but they were a nuisance, for once upon a time when I was the unfortunate owner of one of that kind and kicked (yes, that is the correct expression!) my first flame on the ice on Årstaviken, the catches came unfastened and we came tumbling down to the rejoicing of the rest of our form. Nevermore did she look at me."[6]

Balck was chiefly interested in sports, and consequently the kick-sleigh without seat and its diffusion as a sports vehicle stood in the focus of his interest. But the idea of kicking as a means of forward locomotion reached farther, by reason of its satisfying a need. During the second half of the 19th century there was a growing population of landless people, for whom it was a necessity to get along swiftly to certain centres, to their places of work, to the country shops and to the elementary schools. Country shops were not established earlier than 1846, and factories with many workmen only after 1850. The state elementary school was introduced four years before the country shops. The school-children were in great need of something to shorten their long way to school during the dark winter half-year in the sparsely populated regions of Upper Sweden. And for other groups of people of slender means and long ways to walk the kick-sleigh was an excellent solution, as it carried both the person and the load. Erik Asklund calls it "the means of transporting the country postman and the midwife on slippery roads."

Notes

1. The terminology here used is that of G. Berg in "Sledges and Wheeled Vehicles", where *sled* means a platform on two runners, *sledge* the built-up sledge with pairs of posts and cross-bar, and *conveyance* a horse-drawn sledge for travelling. The author has made some additions and alterations, e.g. *sleigh* for G. Berg's short-sledge. W. R. Mead and H. Smeds in "Winter in Finland" write chair-sled for *kick-sleigh*. In this instance, as the seat does not seem to belong to the original construction, I have adopted a more literal translation of the Swedish *sparkstötting*.
2. The *kässja* is usually treated as one of a pair, but it could be used singly, cf. E. Geete, Kässjor, in the yearbook "På skidor" 1947. Instances from Hälsingland had not yet been brought forward when Geete wrote his paper.
3. The toboggan with two uprights and a handle-bar was called "issloda" in the neighbourhood of Östhammar, according to Norrtelje Tidning 22.1.1968. An informant from Nacka south of Stockholm gives the name "sloda" for the sledge with four uprights (KU 440). "Sloda" is an unusual dialect word, in other regions meaning slide-car.
4. In stencil. The Institution of Nordic Languages, University of Uppsala.
5. Ordbok över Umemålet. Publications of the Landsmåls- och Folkminnesarkivet, Uppsala 1966.
6. Svenska Dagbladet 8.IV.1962.

Sources and Literature

Collections, registers etc. in the Nordiska Museet.

The archive of the Institution of Cultural History at the Åbo Academy, Finland.

Professor Gösta Berg's collections concerning the kick-sleigh.

Letter from Landsantikvarie Göran Rosander 10.X.1969.

I am greatly indebted to Professor Gösta Berg and Landsantikvarie Göran Rosander for their most generous help.

Balck, V., Illustrerad idrottsbok, 1888.

Balck, V., Illustreradt bibliotek för idrott. 9. Vinteridrott, 1889.

Berg, G., Sledges and Wheeled Vehicles, 1935.

Geete, E., Kässjor. In "På Skidor", 1947.

Linné, C. von, Iter lapponicum. Second ed., 1913.

Luther, C. I., Geschichte des Schnee- und Eissports. In Bogeng, Der Sport, 1926.

Nilsson (Eskeröd), A., Samfärdsel och fordon. In Gruddbo på Sollerön, 1938.

Nordisk Familjebok, Second ed., art. Släddon.

Norrländska Socialdemokraten, 8.XII.1969.

Norrtelje Tidning, 22.I.1968.

Rosander, G., Sparkstöttingar, 1969, also in Fornvårdaren, X: 4, 1970, with references.

Stenberg, P., Ordbok över Umemålet. Skrifter utg. genom Landsmåls- och Folkminnesarkivet i Uppsala, 1966.

Svenska Dagbladet, 8.IV.1962.

Öström, J., Studier över meddonsterminologien i Övre Norrland. In stencil, Institutionen för Nordiska Språk, Uppsala Universitet.

Drawings by Maria Berkoff-Urbonas. Photographs by Nordiska Museet.

Margit Stoye has shown great kindness and patience in revising the English translation of this paper.

Wie Frauen in Portugal Lasten tragen

Von JORGE DIAS

Eine der elementarsten Notwendigkeiten des Menschen ist der Transport von Gegenständen verschiedener Natur und Grösse von einem Ort zum anderen.

Unter dieser, allen Völkern gemeinsamen Notwendigkeit steht in erster Linie das Tragen der Kinder, welches – zu einem gewissen Grad – sogar in Gesellschaften mit hohem, technischen Niveau fortbesteht.

In Völkergruppen mit niederem technischen Niveau ist, ausser dem Kindertragen, das Herbeischaffen der primären Grundlagen zur Erhaltung des Lebens – Wasser und Brennmaterial – der beinah allen Völkern der Erde gemeinsame Hauptgegenstand des Transports.

Nachdem einmal die verschiedenen Methoden des Lastentragens in jedem der Völker festgelegt waren, haben sie sich natürlich, im Lauf der Zeit, dem Transport vieler anderer Gegenstände angepasst, welche je nach neu entstandenen Bedürfnissen einer fortschreitenden Evolution des ökonomischen Lebens dieser Völker auftauchten. Schliesslich machte die grosse technische Entwicklung gewisse Formen körperlicher Anstrengung überflüssig, da sie durch mehr praktische, und den verschiedenen Zwecken besser angepasste Mechanismen ersetzt wurden.

Je nach der, aus diversen Umständen (physischer, historischer, ökologischer und kultureller Natur) sich bildenden Tradition ergeben sich Unterschiede in den Methoden, mit welchen Frauen die Lasten befördern, und mit welchen Männer sich dieser Aufgabe unterziehen; was nicht ausschliesst, dass einige Arten beiden Geschlechtern gemeinsam sind.

Wir wollen hier nur die den Frauen gemässen Gebräuche des Tragens in Portugal behandeln.

Vor allem ist den Frauen die Aufgabe des Kindertragens bestimmt. Im ländlichen Portugal existieren noch heute verschiedene Arten davon.

Ausser dem in Europa sehr verbreiteten Brauch das Kind in den Armen liegend oder auf dem Arm der Mutter sitzend zu transportieren, gibt es Frauen, welche es auf ihrer Hüfte reitend mit sich nehmen (Abb. 1). Dies geschieht, ausser unter Portugiesen, besonders unter Zigeunern und ausserdem meist mit Kindern, welche schon laufen können, jedoch nicht dem eiligen

Abb. 1. Transport eines Kindes auf der Hüfte reitend. (Cântanhede)

Tempo der Mütter und den weiten zu durchlaufenden Entfernungen stand-
halten können. Leroi-Gourhan erwähnt noch die Tatsache, dass diese Technik
den Ländern warmen Klimas, in denen das Kind nicht zu sehr in Kleider
eingewickelt ist, eigen sei.[1]

In den Küstengebieten Nord-Portugals tragen die Frauen zum Teil ihre
kleinen Kinder, in einem länglichen Korb *(canastra)* liegend, auf dem Kopf.

In anderen, deutlich umgrenzten Gebieten werden Arten des Kindertragens
vorgezogen, die den Müttern die Arme für die Arbeit, sei es auf dem Felde
oder im Haus, freilassen. Bei beiden Prozessen, die wir kennen, benützt man
ein grosses Wolltuch, in welchem das Kind entweder auf dem Rücken oder, im
zweiten Fall, vor der Brust der Mutter hängend, festgebunden wird.

Der ersten Art begegnen wir in der Gegend um Miranda do Douro, wo sie
unter der Bezeichnung *chinchim* bekannt ist. Das Tuch umfasst das Kind auf
dem Rücken der Mutter, die beiden Enden werden über ihre Schultern nach
vorne gezogen, über der Brust gekreuzt und wieder nach hinten geführt und
unterhalb des Kindes geknotet (Abb. 2). Wir können diese Art als eine
europäische Variante der in weiten Gebieten der Welt, hauptsächlich in

Abb. 2. Transport
eines Kindes auf dem
Rücken.
(Miranda do Douro)

Afrika, China und Japan verbreiteten Form betrachten. Man weiss, dass sie auch in Ägypten, um 2.000 v. Ch. gebräuchlich war[2]. Die Frauen von Miranda transportieren ihre Kinder, selbst wenn sie zu Pferde reiten, auf diese Weise und haben somit die Hände frei für gleich welche Art von Tätigkeit. Leite de Vasconcellos bezog sich darauf im 19. Jahrhundert[3]. Wir selber konnten sie noch vor wenigen Jahren beobachten und es ist sehr wahrscheinlich, dass sie in diesen Gebieten auch heute noch genau so beibehalten wird.

Die andere Technik dieser Art ist sehr viel seltener und existiert in der Gegend von Castro Laboreiro[4]. Die Kinder werden in die Mitte eines Woll-tuchs, das der Länge nach gedoppelt wurde, eingewickelt, das eine freie Ende des Tuches über die linke Schulter, das andere unter der rechten Achsel der

Abb. 3. Transport
eines Kindes im
»fateiro«. (Castro
Laboreiro)

Frau durchgezogen und beide Enden hinter dem Rücken zusammengebunden. Das Kind hängt somit vor der Brust, oder besser, vor dem Oberkörper der Mutter, was ihr ebenfalls die Hände frei zum Arbeiten lässt (Abb. 3). Wenn sie das Kind stillen will, braucht sie es nicht einmal auszuwickeln, die Position erlaubt auch das. Dieses Tragsystem, dort unter dem Namen „*fateiro*" bekannt[5], muss in früheren Zeiten eine viel grössere Verbreitung gehabt haben, denn man kennt es z. B. in Rumänien, wo Florescu es sogar auf einer Metope an einem römischen Denkmal, dem Tropaeum Traiani (aus dem Anfang des 2. Jhdts.) abgebildet fand.[6] Florescu hat 1956 dasselbe Tragsystem in Viseul de Sus (Oberwischau) beobachtet und gibt sogar die Masse des Tuches an: 4,00 m lang und 40 cm breit. Er versichert, seines Wissens nach existiere

Abb. 4. Der Tragring
unter dem Korb ist
sichtbar.
(Ponto do Lima)

dieses System bei keinem anderen Volke[7]. Jedoch, wenn auch heutigentags sehr selten, braucht es dies nicht vor einigen Jahrhunderten gewesen zu sein. Nach einem Bild von Lukas van Leyden zu schliessen, muss es diese Art des Kindertransportes auch in den Niederlanden im 16. Jahrhundert gegeben haben[8]. Der Mangel an Dokumentation ist kein Beweis für die Nichtexistenz in verschiedenen Gebieten Europas in früheren Epochen.

Das Tragen schon grösserer Kinder wird häufig der Frau abgenommen und geht dann auf ältere Brüder oder den Vater über, welche das Kind auf die Schultern setzen, mit den Beinen nach vorn, und es an den Füssen festhalten, während das Kind sich mit den Händen an der Stirn des Trägers sichert.

Abb. 5. Den Wasserkrug auf dem Kopf transportierend. (Mira)

Im übrigen findet der Transport grösserer und kleinerer Lasten bei den Frauen hauptsächlich auf dem Kopfe statt.

Zur besseren Verteilung des Gewichts auf eine grössere und ebenere Oberfläche, wie auch um den Kopf vor schmerzendem Kontakt mit der oft unebenen Last zu schützen, benützen sie ein Tragpolster, „rodilha" oder „sogra" (Schwiegermutter) genannt, eine Art von Strohring mit Stoff bezogen, den sie lose auf den Kopf legen. (Abb. 4). Sehr oft wird solch ein Ring einfach improvisiert, indem man ein Tuch, häufig die eigene Schürze, zu einem Ring zusammendreht. Dieses System der Tragstütze ist nicht nur in Portugal und Westeuropa verbreitet, auch in Afrika drehen die Frauen Buschgrasringe zum Transport der Wasserkrüge[9] und identische Prozesse kennt man in Melanesien, in gewissen Gebieten Japans, in Indonesien und in Zentralamerika[10].

Sehr typisch für den Küstenstreifen Nord-Portugals, zwischen den Flüssen Minho und Mondego, wo der Transport der Lasten auf dem Kopf bis vor wenigen Jahren allgemein war, sind die eigenen, schönen Trachtenhüte der Frauen, welche dort – obwohl in verschiedenen Formen – alle mit einer Art von eingenähter „Schwiegermutter" im Innern des Hutkopfes (oder über

114

Abb. 6. Auf dem Weg zur Kirchweih mit der *merenda*. (Caminha)

diesem) versehen sind und auf diese Weise das Tragen der grossen Körbe mit landwirtschaftlichen Produkten zu den Märkten, oder mit Essen *(merenda)* für Kirchweihbesuche oder sonstige Feste, erleichtert wird ohne dass der Tragring zu sehen ist.

Die Fischverkäuferinnen trugen vor dem letzten Krieg und zum Teil noch heute, selbst in den Städten, einen Ring, entweder auf dem von einem Tuch bedeckten Kopf oder über dem Hutkopf, zur sicheren Stütze ihres breitausladenden Fischkorbes.

Die in Portugal verbreitetste Traglast der Frauen war und ist noch der

Abb. 7. Frau mit einem
Mehlsack aus einem
Tierbalg.
(Vilarinho da Furna)

Krug, mit dem sie das Wasser vom Brunnen ins Haus befördern (Abb. 5).
Dies geschieht in den meisten Fällen auf dem Kopf, kommt jedoch in einigen
Gegenden, wie z. B. in der Provinz Entre-Minho-e-Douro und benachbarten
Gebieten[11], auch auf der Schulter vor. Nur im Süden des Landes transpor-
tiert man die Wasserkrüge auf Eseln oder in kleinen Handkarren, die mit
einem Gitter zum Hineinstellen der Krüge versehen sind.

Die Fähigkeit der Frauen, das Gleichgewicht schwerer oder grosser Lasten
(Körbe, Säcke, Fässer etc.) auf dem Kopf zu wahren, ist bewundernswert,
aber noch erstaunlicher die Geschicklichkeit mit welcher sie leichte oder zer-
brechliche Gefässe mit kleiner Basis balancieren (Abb. 6–9).

Abb. 8. Eine Tonne auf dem Kopf transportierend. (Coimbra-Souzelas)

Abb. 9. Töpferinnen transportieren ihre Ware zum Markt. (Ponte da Barca)

Abb. 10. Pappschachteltransport. (S. João da Madeira)

Das Tragen gewisser leichter Lasten kann in Portugal von Frauen jedoch auch auf andere Weise als auf dem Kopf ausgeführt werden. Dazu dienen Körbe oder Taschen verschiedener Formen mit Henkeln, die mit der Hand gefasst oder am Arm hängend ihren Dienst erfüllen.

Auch benützen die Frauen in gewissen Gegenden (z. B. Tras-os-Montes oder Algarve), ebenso wie die Männer, wenn sie zum Markt gehen, den *alforje,* einen Sack, der auch über den Esel gelegt werden kann. Er besteht aus einem etwa 45 cm breiten und 2,30 m langen Streifen festen Wollstoffes, an dem die beiden Enden um ungefähr 45 cm aufgeschlagen und an den Längsseiten zugenäht werden, sodass zwei sich gegenüberliegende Säcke entstehen, welche mit Gegenständen gefüllt werden können. Der *alforje* wird über der Schulter getragen.

Die nördliche Küstenzone des Landes, die wir schon öfter erwähnt haben, war die am frühesten von der Auswanderung betroffene Gegend. Die Frau musste dort deshalb notgedrungen ebenso die landwirtschaftliche Tätigkeit übernehmen, wie bei allen, ihr zustehenden[12] und nicht zustehenden Arbeiten

118

Abb. 11. Transport von Kiefernnadeln als Brennmaterial. (Anadia)

Abb. 12. Die Tradition des Lastentragens auf dem Kopf wird auch auf dem Rad beibehalten. (S. Tirso)

einspringen. Daraus ergab sich eine weitgehende Anpassung der verschiedensten Transportsysteme – sogar solcher aus der Kleinindustrie wie z. B. Töpferei, Möbelschreinerei und Pappschachtelanfertigung – an die der Frau eigene, typische Art des Lastentragens auf dem Kopf (Abb. 10–12).

Mit den Anfängen der Industrialisierung, die verhältnismässig spät stattfand, kam nach und nach auch für die Frauen in gewissen Gegenden die Benützung des Fahrrades auf, was manche körperliche Anstrengung erleichterte. Trotzdem wird manchmal die Tradition des auf-dem-Kopfe-tragens mit dem Fahren kombiniert, was nur dank der enormen und von Jugend auf geübten Fähigkeit zum Gleichgewichthalten in dieser Generation noch möglich ist und beinahe etwa an Zirkuskünste erinnert.

Obwohl heute die Hilfe des mechanischen Transports den menschlichen zum grossen Teil entbehrlich macht, sehen wir in Portugal in vielen Gegenden immer noch Frauen, die ihren Wasserkrug von Brunnen heimtragen oder die zum Teil festlich bereiteten Körbe zum Markt oder zu den Kirchweihfesten an weit entfernte Orte auf dem Kopf transportieren.

Anmerkungen

1. André Leroi-Gourhan, L'Homme et la Matière, Paris 1943, p. 123.
2. André Leroi-Gourhan, op. loc. cit.
3. J. Leite de Vasconcellos, Um costume transmontano, in Revista do Minho, I, Barcelos 1886, p. 77.
4. Sie ist heute nur in den Dörfern, welche zu Castro Laboreiro, Melgaço, gehören, bekannt.
5. Das Lexikon der portugiesischen Sprache von Cândido de Figueiredo registriert die Wörter *fateira* und *fateiro* als in der Provinz Tras-os-Montes gebrauchte und bezieht sich auf einen Artikel von Rocha Peixoto in Revista Portugália, vol. II, Seite 375. Dort ist Seite 374, unten, der »fateiro de burel« von Castro Laboreiro erwähnt, den Rocha Peixoto im Vergleich zu einem, in der Gegend von Miranda bestehenden, ähnlichen Brauch zitiert. Seine Bemerkung beweist uns, dass auch in Miranda die Körper der kleinen Kinder von der Mitte bis nach unten eingewickelt wurden, wie in Castro Laboreiro im »fateiro«.
6. Florea Bobu Florescu, Das Siegesdenkmal von Adamklissi, Tropaeum Traiani, Bukarest 1965.
7. Florea Bobu Florescu, op. cit., p. 632. Siehe Abb. 232 und 316 a, b, c, und d.
8. Das Bild Lukas van Leyden's (1489?–1533) im Rijks Museum in Amsterdam stellt eine Frau dar, welche ein Kind über der Schulter festgebunden trägt, ähnlich wie beim »fateiro«.
9. Jorge Dias e Margot Dias, Os Macondes de Moçambique, vol. II, Cultura Material, Lisboa 1964, Abb. 159.
10. André Leroi-Gourhan, op. cit., p. 119.
11. Jorge Dias, Vilarinho da Furna, Porto 1948, Abb. Tafel VIII, unten.
12. Zum Beispiel: die Textil-, Spitzen- und Stickerei-Industrie in Guimarães, Fafe, Vizela und Viana do Castelo war zum grossen Teil eine weibliche Tätigkeit. Auch darf man nicht die Beteiligung der Frauen an der Herstellung des Filigran-Goldschmucks in Gondomar und Póvoa de Varzim, wie diejenige an den Tonfiguren in Barcelos, vergessen.

Transport with Pack-Horse and Slide-Car in Scotland

By ALEXANDER FENTON

In Scotland, as in most other parts of Britain, roads and communications are now so well developed and organized that the question of transport in track-less conditions has become almost a matter for historical study. Nevertheless in the hilly or boggy areas of north and west Scotland, in parts of the islands, and to some extent in the Scottish Borders (as in Northern England), wherever roads are few or makeshift, the older forms of transport survive. Peat to fuel the fire may be carried on horseback from the bogs, and on the big estates during the shooting season, game-birds that fall victim to the sportmen's guns may be carried in wickerwork creels slung on either side of a saddle. Deer may also be dragged on sledges or slide-cars to the shooting-lodges (Fig. 1). On the shores, too, where stake-net fishing for salmon is carried on, the fish are sometimes carried to the solid land in wicker creels on horseback (Fig. 2). When deer-fences are to be built, the long wooden posts can be carried into the hills and moors at the horse's sides, lying over a hooked iron bar bolted across the crub of the saddle (Fig. 3), with their front ends attached to the collar.

Such survivals are due to special conditions of terrain, and especially to the practical difficulties of making roads, or the lack of need for them, in certain areas. They are survivals that reflect what was everywhere commonplace (along with transport on the human back) before the road-system began to be expanded in the eighteenth century. Nevertheless there are areas outside the main trade and communication routes, such as some of the islands of the north and west, where roads have only appeared within the last generation. The gradual disappearance of trackless forms of transport has to be viewed on a different historical perspective in different parts of the country.

Disappearance and survival must also be considered in relation to the skills of craftsmen and the products of wheelwrights and cartwrights. A local joiner in a rural community could make cart bodies at any time, but the production of spoked, iron-shod wheels was a more difficult task calling for collaboration with a local blacksmith, and in the early days of the spread of carts with spoked wheels to the farms of Scotland, wheels were often got from elsewhere.

Fig. 1. "Deerstalking on Jura", in Argyll, painted by Gourlay Steell (1819–1894) ? ante 1875. Left to right: Neil Clark, estate worker, Angus McKay, gamekeeper, Richard Campbell, the laird, and Angus McKay junr. The pony is pulling a slide-car. By courtesy of the Art Gallery and Museum, Kelvingrove, Glasgow.

For example, in the early nineteenth century, Thurso and Wick shopkeepers imported second-hand carriage-wheels from the Edinburgh market for sale to small tenants, at 15/- to £ 2.2 per pair. The tenant then bought birch-wood for an axle and shafts, and fir for a box, and a local cart-wright would finish the cart at his house (Henderson 1812.64–5). Amongst the imports to the Orkney islands during the period 1801–6 there are listed only 13 complete carts, but 287 pairs of cartwheels (Shirreff 1814. Appx. 46–53). Spoked wheels were expensive, however, and their initial spread was chiefly on the bigger farms. The smaller farms retained the older, cheaper forms of transport for a much longer period, and the question of social differentiation, therefore, constitutes a third element (alongside terrain and the availability of crafts-men) in the retention pattern of transport on horseback, sledges, slipes, slide-cars, and also of a form of cart consisting essentially of a slide-car with wheels added, an intermediate stage between slide-car and cart that was formerly common in Ireland as well as in parts of Scotland. The latter provides an example of an evolutionary sequence that has given rise to a good deal of

122

Fig. 2. A pack horse with wickerwork baskets for carrying salmon from the stake-nets on the coast at St. Cyrus, Kincardineshire. Photo: A. Macwhirter, 1957.

discussion from the nineteenth century onwards (Haddon 1898.163 ff; Fox 1931. V. 185; et al.).

Transport on Horseback. The carriage of goods on the backs of horses or ponies by means of a pack-saddle is or was common in a great many parts of the world. There is everywhere a basic similarity in the essential elements of the harness, but there are regional variations in the form of the saddle, its presence or absence, the nature of the material from which its retaining ropes are made, the type of creel or pannier, which could be changed to suit the load carried, and the kind of animal in use as a beast of burden.

In Scotland, the horse or pony or garron appears to have been the only animal much used as a pack-animal, though the ass was also used to a limited extent, as in Ireland (Mahaffy 1916–17. XXXIII. 530–538). An ass with a lady riding sidesaddle on its back appears, for example, in the foreground of an etching of a Tower at Glasgow, dating from before 1774 (Clerk 1825. Pl. 17).

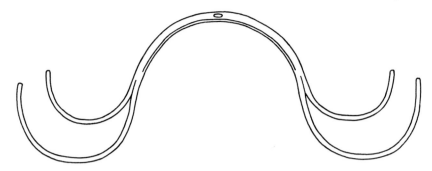

Fig. 3. An iron bar bolted across the crub of a cart-saddle, used in transporting wooden posts for fences in Ross. After a sketch by W. Munro. Width approximately 3 ft. 10 in. (117 cm). Not to scale.

The equipment for a pack-horse comprised a pad or cover, often consisting of a cloth next to the animal to absorb sweat and a mat of grass or straw on top; a wooden pack-saddle held in position by ropes passing under the horse's tail or attached to a wooden crupper under the horse's tail, by a rope under the belly and, more rarely, by a third rope round the breast; a pair of creels made of wood, wickerwork, or straw, slung on to the saddle either directly or through the medium of open-work nets of bent-grass or straw; or a pair of wooden "currachs", resembling the seat and back of a chair, also slung from the saddle.

The Back Cover. The cover on the horse's back was a standard feature. It could take the form of a lambskin or sheepskin with the wool still on, as in the Faroe Islands (Landt 1810.278), but was more often a cloth with an overlying mat of straw, grass, or rushes. Sometimes the cloth or sacking was sown on the matting to make a one-piece cover. In the Northern Isles, the covers were usually made of bunches of straw about 2.5 cm in diameter, drawn out straight and bound together with twine or thin ropes twisted by hand from bent grass or dried rushes. In the Western Isles the process and materials were similar. According to one description, a wooden bar was slung at a suitable height, and a warp of seventeen double-ply strands attached. The lower ends were fixed to a wooden bar on the floor, held down by weights. The single-ply weft was then woven in by hand, the work proceeding from bottom to top, each upright having part of the weft passing in front of and behind it. A South Uist maker added an extra centre-piece, tied on to the main cover, to give additional protection at the point where the saddle rested. There was a split running in about 30 cm at the middle of each of the sides, resulting in flaps that allowed the cover to lie more comfortably on the horse's back (Kissling 1960.34–35),

Fig. 4. A bent grass horse-cover being made in South Uist. The extra part added on top makes a pad for the saddle to rest on. The method of making split ends can be seen. Photo: Dr W.Kissling, 1953. By courtesy of Dr Kissling, and The School of Scottish Studies, University of Edinbugh.

but this feature is unknown in the Northern Isles (Fig. 4). When the wooden bars were withdrawn, the open loops were bound with rope to strengthen the ends.

There was not a great deal of variation in size. An Orkney cover was 90 cm square (Johnston 1908.246) and another in Sutherland was 90 cm long by 76 cm wide by 2 cm thick (Henderson 1812.60). Examples from Shetland in the National Museum of Antiquities of Scotland measure 84 × 50 cm and 80 × 51 cm. In places like Barra in the Hebrides where bent grass was more plentiful the whole pad could be made of this material (Grant 1961.202; Highland Folk Museum, Cat. No. 216), but otherwise the softer and less long-lasting straw served the purpose, for example in Moray where the pad was described as "a straw mattress covering the back and both sides of the horse" (Leslie 1811.

125

122), or else rushes might be used, as in Banffshire (Spence 1889.62) and Aberdeenshire (Jamieson 1825 s.v. Fosset).

Sometimes a grassy sod served as a pad (Carr 1809.471), a custom also known in South West Norway (Steinsnes 1961.44–52; Stigum 1963.579), the Faroe Islands, and Iceland (Annandale 1905.181). In Iceland, indeed, sods were in common use for this purpose. Across the horse's back was first laid a tough, rectangular grassy sod, *reiðingstorfa*, over which two others were laid as saddle pads, *reiðingsdýna*, one at each side, and another couple of thin sods, *framanundirlag*, were pushed in between these and the underlay towards the front. The cover could also be made of the interwoven roots of grass-wrack, *Zostera marina*, and the side pieces sewn into sacking or skin (Eldjárn 1963.580).

A cover of this nature meant that there was no need for the saddle itself to be padded, though the combination of pads and saddle involved only a short further step.

This simple piece of equipment was known by a variety of terms in the Lowland Scots dialects: *brot, brotach, brottie* (Bnff., Abd., Ags., Per.); *flackie, flaikie* (Shet., Ork.); *fle(a)t, flettie, fleatag* (Ork., Cai., Sth.); *forsel* (Ork.); *fosset* (N.E. Scot.); *leaves* (N.E. Scot.); *sheemach* (N.E. Scot.). In Gaelic the following terms were used: *minicreag, minguidh, peanan, plàta(ch), plàt-eich, sumag*. *Cadda* or *caddow* occurs in the dialects of Ulster. Such a wide range of names points clearly to the basic and widespread nature of the piece of equipment to which it is applied, and suggests some of the possible lines of cultural influence in the past. For instance, the Ulster name, known in both Old Scots and Early Middle English of the sixteenth century in the sense of 'a rough woollen covering or rug', has undergone a dialectal restriction in sense. The Insular and North Scots terms *flackie, fle(a)t,* derive from Norse words, and the *brot* forms of Lowland Scots, as well as *sheemach*, must be due to Gaelic influence. There are, therefore, indications of coming and going across the North Channel of the Irish Sea, between Highland and Lowland Scotland, and between Scandinavia and the North of Scotland, though in the latter case the original Scandinavian words have had a local development in sense.

The Pack Saddle. In Scotland there were two main forms, to which the names *crook-saddle* and *split-saddle* may be given. The crook-saddle was made in one fixed piece, but the split-saddle was in two separable halves, one half fitting into the other. Both types have two flat boards whose inner sides lie against the cover or pad on the horse's back. The horns or bows are attached to the

126

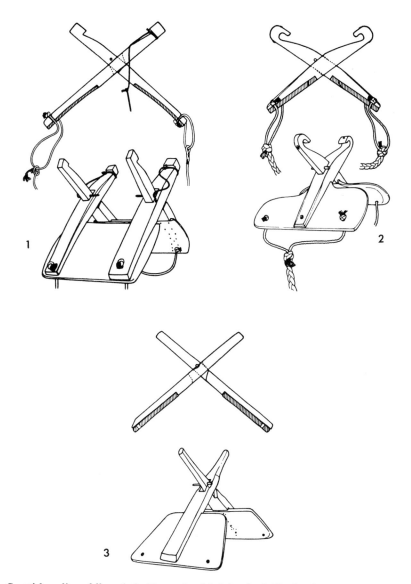

Fig. 5. Scottish split-saddles: 1–2. From the Mainland of Shetland; 3. From Papa Stour, Shetland. In the National Museum of Antiquities of Scotland.

outer sides of these boards. The feature that indexes typological variation is the manner in which the saddle boards are linked.

Both the split- and the crook-saddle may have one or two pairs of horns or bows. As far as the split-saddle is concerned, the one-horned form is commonest in Shetland. One horn is thicker than the other, and contains an opening through which the smaller one passes. Once in position, a wooden peg

127

or nail is put through a hole in the smaller horn, forming a check against the upper side of the thicker horn, to hold the two halves in position (Fig. 5). The ends of the horns are usually shaped by deep notching to form a pair of hooks to which the burden ropes are attached (Fig. 5,2), but in the island of Papa Stour and the neighbouring part of the mainland of Shetland (parish of Walls) the horns are straight, without hooked ends (Fig. 5,3). In this case the burden ropes are fixed by being taken from one side right over the top of the saddle to rest in the angle formed by the horn of one side, and the flat side piece of the other. A Shetland split-saddle with hooked horns, preserved in the Göteborgs Historiska Museum, was illustrated in the journal *Rig* (Jirlow 1931.93).

The single horned variety was used in Orkney too (Firth 1920. Pl. 5 facing page 106), and was recorded there *c.* 1770 (Aberdeen 1770 MS) but double-horned saddles were also found there, as well as to a lesser extent in the south Mainland of Shetland (Fig. 5,1). Their construction is exactly parallel to that of the single-horned split-saddles.

It is possible that the double-horned saddle is more recent than the single-horned, for the latter has a longer recorded history in the northern islands. Svabo illustrated one that he saw in 1781–2 in the Faroe Islands, where it was called a *klibbari* or *kløftsaddel* (Djurhuus 1959.138). *Kløfft sadeler* were also referred to there by Tarnovius in 1667, as part of the harness used in transporting peat (Hamre 1950.53). The same word, *klyfsaþul*, is recorded as early as 1345 in Sweden (Jansson 1963.580–1). According to a later description, the Faroese saddle consisted of "two strong pieces of wood, in form not unlike a pair of cards; but the shaft of the one has a hole, into which the shaft of the other is fitted, by which means they adhere together" (Landt 1810.278). Landt's illustration is similar to that of Svabo (Fig. 6,1). A saddle of this form is preserved in the Tórshavn Museum (Williamson 1948.59).

There is a Faroese variant with a single horn at one side, and a double horn at the other linked by a cross-wire at the top (Fig. 6,2). The single horn was passed sideways through the slot in the double horn, then turned through a right angle to make a firm joint (Jirlow 1931.93; Erixon 1938.138).

Like the Papa Stour saddles, none of the Faroese ones have hooks on the horns. This is also true of the Lappish pack-saddles, which consist of two curved boards like half barrel-staves, one of which passes through a key-hole slot at the top of the other (Jirlow 1931.90; Wiklund 1938. Pl. 64a, facing 385). Unlike the saddles of Iceland, the Faroes, Shetland and Orkney, these have no side-boards, which are thought to be a loan from the riding-saddle (Stigum 1963.579). Possibly the Lappish saddle has evolved from the use of

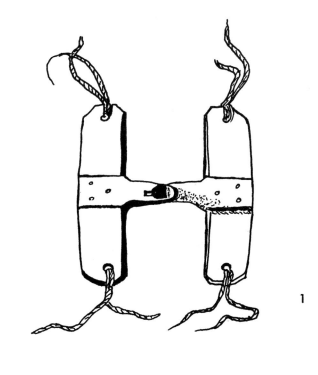

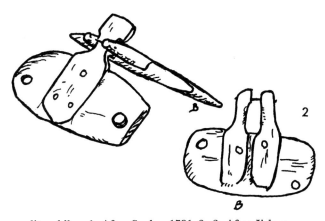

Fig. 6. Faroese split-saddles: 1. After Svabo, 1781–2; 2. After Jirlow.

suitable branches, since "provisorische Saumsattel werden aus kreisformig gebogenen, ineinander gekoppelten Baumästen verfertigt" (Wiklund 1938. 398).

The Lappish name, *svakah, spakka,* may be cognate with Old Norse *svigi,* a thin, curved piece of wood, a switch, and the object to which it refers may therefore also be a borrowing. According to oral tradition the "Lappish" type was formerly known in South-West Norway, under the name *kløvtre* (Steinsnes 1961.54–5; Stigum 1963.579). It is conceivable that it spread from Norway north into Lapland, and west to Shetland, Orkney, the Faroes, and Iceland, leaving the interlocking single-horned form as a legacy of somewhat older vintage than the double-horned variety.

A related question is the date at which saddle-boards began to be used on pack-saddles, but to this there is no easy answer and the antiquity of combined pack- and riding-saddles would first have to be established. Bronze mountings from finds of the early Migration Period in South Sweden, dated to the second half of the 5th century A.D., include long, narrow pieces that must have been attached to side-boards at the bottom and then run up the sides of the wooden bows or cantles of riding-saddles. Some rings were also found, and were probably attached to the saddles so that bags and burdens could be slung onto them (Norberg 1929.101 ff; Norberg 1931.106–109). Perhaps it was to such a ring or strap on a saddle-bow that Earl Sigurd tied the head of the Scottish earl Melbrigda tonn, after slaying him in a fight by the River Oykell in Sutherland, about the year 892 (Taylor 1938.139).

Though the riding-saddle could clearly be used in this way for carrying light loads, there is no definite evidence (apart from its existence in the 5th century) to suggest when its form began to influence the form of the pack-saddle by the addition of side-boards to the latter if, in fact, this suggestion is valid. It may nevertheless be suggested that this stage had been reached before the Vikings started raiding and settling west-over-sea.

The known distribution of the split-saddle in Britain is chiefly confined to Shetland and Orkney, and possibly Caithness. The only other area where there is evidence for it is Clare Island in Ireland (Evans 1961.170), and it may, therefore, be suspected that it could formerly have been found in the intervening areas, but there are no survivals or descriptions to support this possibility.

Just as split-saddles may have one or two pairs of horns, so also may crook-saddles have single or double bows or crooks, in Gaelic called *cairb* (Dwelly). Deep notches were cut in the tops of the bows leaving two hooks in which the burden ropes could lie. According to a description from Sutherland:

"The horse being equipped with a – – – – clubbar on his back, – – – made of crooked wood, like a saddle, to fit the horse's back above the straw mat, and secured by a rush or hair rope under the horse's belly. This clubber – – – has a deep notch in the top of it to receive the fettles or bands of two of the – – baskets" (for manure) (Henderson 1812.60).

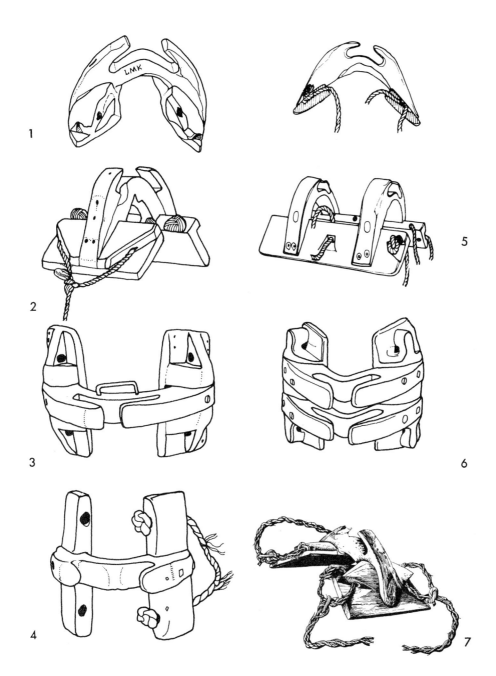

Fig. 7. Scottish crook-saddles: 1. From Skye. In The Skye Cottage Museum; 2. From Penine-rine, South Uist; 3. From South Uist; 4. From Highland Scotland, locality unknown; 5. From Islay; 6. From Highland Scotland, locality unknown; 7. From Rannoch, Perthshire. 2, 3, 4 and 6, in the Highland Folk Museum, Kingussie; 5, in the National Museum of Antiquities of Scotland.

Crook-saddles seem to have been the rule in the Western Islands, the Highlands, and, at an earlier period, in Lowland Scotland as well. The name *crook-saddle* goes back to the sixteenth century in North-East Scotland, though the saddle itself must certainly be much older, and in its origins and development should be considered jointly with the saddle over which the support for the shafts of a cart or slide-car was laid. Cart-saddles, "kar-sadillis", are recorded from 1496 in Scotland (DOST s.v. *Car-sadil*). In Highland Perthshire, a "hooked car-saddle" was referred to for carrying creels (Robertson 1799.92–3), but otherwise this term was applied to a 'small saddle put on the back of a carriage horse, for supporting the trams or shafts of the carriage' (Jamieson 1825 s.v.).

The majority of crook-saddles have single bows, but one example from Islay (Fig. 7,5) in the National Museum of Antiquities and another from Rannoch, Perthshire (Fig. 7,6), in the Highland Folk Museum, have each double bows. A painting done about 1875 or before, of a small horse yoked in a slide-car in the island of Jura, shows the same feature (Fig. 1). This double-bow form matches the pack-saddle used, for example, in steep country in Norway (Reinton 1969.39, 41) (Fig. 9).

A form of the crook-saddle, called a *crutch* or *straddle,* occurs in Donegal, Northern Ireland, in which there is an upright peg at each of the points where the bow is attached to the side-boards. Alternatively, the pegs may be fitted nearer the top of the curve of the bow (Fig. 8) (Evans 1958.106). These pegs take the place of the hooks on Scottish examples, and are also found on the bows of crook-saddles in Iceland, where they are called *klakkar* (Jirlow 1931. 94; Heiberg 1932.123; Steinsnes 1961.45–46).

The terminology of the saddle is more limited than that of the pad below it. The split-saddle is called the *clibber* or *clubber* in Shetland, Orkney, and Caithness, corresponding to the Faroese *klibbari,* Old Norse *klyf-beri, klybberi,* Norwegian *klyvbere* and dialectal *klyvbar, klyvber, klubbar* (Hellemo 1957. 47, 123; Reinton 1969.38). Its earliest recorded occurrence in Scotland appears to be in an Orkney inventory of 1734 where reference is made to "Eighteen pair sufficient Creills, Eighteen Clibers" (Hibbert 1923. I. 65), showing that for each split-saddle a pair of creels or baskets was required.

The first element of the name, Old Norse *klyf,* has the meaning of a 'pack or trunk on a pack-horse' and *klyfja* is 'to load a pack-horse' (Cleasby and Vigfusson 1874. s.v.). This is the same as the word *klyfja,* 'to split, cleave', presumably because the load on horseback has to be split into two equally balanced portions.

The crook-saddle has a little more terminological variety. The name *crook-*

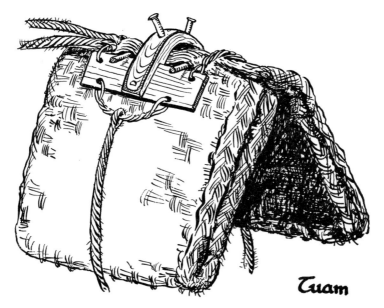

Tuam

Straw pads & straddle for Creels

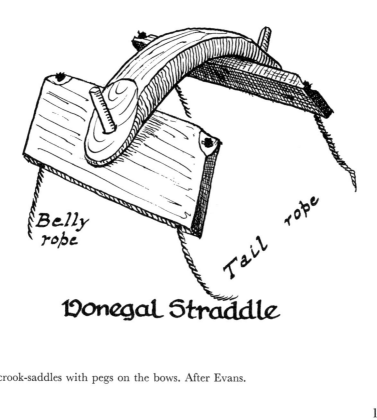

Belly rope

Tail rope

Donegal Straddle

Fig. 8. Irish crook-saddles with pegs on the bows. After Evans.

133

saddle itself was first recorded in an Action of Spuilzie in Aberdeenshire in 1557, when there were listed "four cruik saddellis" costing 2/- each (Littlejohn 1904. I. 155), and the name was later fairly widespread in north and north-east Scotland. In August, 1736, on the estate of Monymusk in Aberdeenshire, four crook-saddles cost 20d. (Hamilton 1946.26). In nineteenth century Banffshire one writer saw a crook-saddle—by implication no longer used—owned by a Mr. Findlater of Balvenie (Grant 1901–2.10). Another Banffshire source described the pack-saddle as resembling the skeleton of a common cart saddle, but the part arching across the back was deeper, and carved into two rough hooks on which the creels were hung (Spence 1889.62). There were crook-saddles in Ross in 1732 (MacGill 1911. II. 130), and in north Scotland in the 1790s they cost 6d. each (Grant 1961.100). The term was also used by the minister of Stornoway, Lewis in the late eighteenth century (Mackenzie 1795.248).

A name descriptive of function was *laid-saddle*, i.e. a saddle for carrying loads, known from the early eighteenth century in the proverbial expression, "Cadgers has ay mind of load Sadles" (Kelly 1720.77). It was also used in the dialect speech of Yorkshire, in the North of England. There is one reference from Sutherland to *straddle* (Jamieson 1825. s.v.), a term otherwise rare in Scotland, but commonly used in Northern Ireland. The usual name throughout the Gaelic speaking area is *s(t)rathair*.

Harness Ropes. The ropes that held the pack-saddle in position were made of a variety of materials—straw, rushes, horse hair, twisted birch or willow twigs, the fibrous roots of the sea-reed, *Arundo arenaria* (Neill 1806.17), and in more recent times not only coir yarn but also twisted silk stockings have been noted. Sealskin strips were seen at Boreray in North Uist (Beveridge 1911.326).

The rope round the horse's tail is called a *tailgirth* in the Northern Isles, with the term *croopan* occurring once in Orkney (Jamieson 1887. s.v.), and in Gaelic, *an eiseach* (Macinnes 1893–4.216), *eisleach* (Dwelly), *eibhsichean, eillsichean, eillisean* or *eiseachan* (Campbell 1958. s.v.). The ends could be tied to loops on the saddle, or could be taken round the front of the saddle over the top of the horns, in which case its length could readily be adjusted by tying a knot. In the Northern Isles, as in the Faroe Islands, there is no indication that a wooden crupper was used, and the *tailgirth* was padded where it passed under the horse's tail. Elsewhere, however, including Ireland, a wooden crupper about 90 cm long was a normal element in the harnessing of a pack

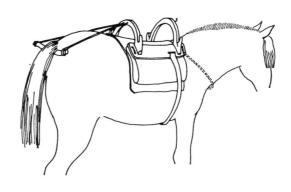

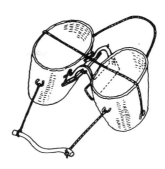

Fig. 9. A Norwegian crook-
saddle. After Reinton, 1969.

AFTER L. REINTON

horse, called in Gaelic *bod-chrann, botrachan* (Campbell 1958. s.v.), or *beart-
dheiridh-dialta* (Dwelly).

Split- and crook-saddles have two holes in each of the flat panels, usually
one in each of the lower corners. Alternatively the side boards were made
rather thick, with a raised outer piece through which vertical holes were
pierced in the same plane as the board (Figs. 7, 1, 2, 3, 6). Through these a
loop of rope was knotted, to the middle of which the belly-band was attached.
These loops were called *gointicks* in the Northern Isles, a word deriving from
Old Norse *gagn-tak,* a saddle-strap, and the belly-band was the *wime-girt*
(*wime* = stomach). Only one instance is known of a crook-saddle with a
central hole in the side boards to which the belly-band was directly attached
(Fig. 7,4). A belly-band of twisted willow or birch was known in Gaelic as
gad-tarraich (Macinnes) or *teannach*. Though *gad* has the sense of a withy,

135

the term nevertheless remained in use when leather replaced wood (Campbell 1895. V. 25).

To keep the load from slipping backwards a breast-band could be used. This appears to have been a relatively rare feature in the Northern Isles, though used in the Faroe Islands (Djurhuus 1959.138). In the Gaelic speaking areas, however, it was known as *uchdach* (Dwelly), or *gad-uchdaich*, "a twisted rope of twigs going round breast of horse, and attached to the two front ends of flat boards. The use of this is to keep the saddle from slipping when going up a hill" (Macinnes 1893–4.216).

The Bridle. A pack-horse wore a bridle which, according to a description of *c.* 1860, "has no bit, but two plates of wood or iron are placed at right angles to the horse's mouth, and are joined above and below by a rope, which is made of horse-hair, leather, or twisted bent. The horse's nose goes into it" (Campbell 1890. I. 62–63). The cheek-pieces, linked above the nose and behind the jaw, had each a central opening at right angles to the terminal openings, through which passed the cord that went over the animal's head, behind its ears. A bridle of this form, which could be used on tethered cows, as well as horses, was widely known in the Scots dialects as the *branks* from the sixteenth century onwards. The word was defined in the early nineteenth century as "a sort of bridle, often used by country people in riding. Instead of leather, it has on each side a piece of wood joined to a halter, to which a bit is sometimes added; but more frequently a kind of wooden noose resembling a muzzle" (Jamieson 1808. s.v.). A bit would not be necessary for a pack-horse, which was invariably led by a short length of rope, but would be desirable if the horse was ridden. A late nineteenth century writer noted that bits were occasionally made of wood (Campbell 1890. I. xix).

It was not always necessary, either, to have wooden cheek-pieces, and sometimes a simple rope halter was used. In the Northern Isles this was called the *grimek*, a word of Norse origin cognate with Norwegian *grime*, Faroese *gríma*, both meaning a halter.

The Gaelic name for the bridle was *srian*, the bit, *mìreanach*, or, in Lochaber, *cabastair* (per J. McInnes), and the chinstrap *smeachan* (Dwelly).

Creels. The final element in the harness of a pack-horse was the pair of creels or other containers for carrying loads. They took a variety of forms, and often differed from those carried on the human back only in being used in pairs. They varied in relation to the type of load carried. In the Northern Isles, for example, where the container was called the *kishie* or *caisie*, the normal size

136

Fig. 10. Andrew Hughson and William Hendry Jamieson loading a pony with a pair of equally filled *horse-kishies* in Fetlar, Shetland. Copied from a local photograph.

for pack-ponies, the *horse-kishie,* was smaller than that carried on the human back (Fig. 10), but differed in no other respect. It was usually made of bunches of straw bound together by hand-twisted cords of bent grass or rushes. Another more open type used on horse back, called a *reppa-* or *rivva-kishie* in Shetland, was in effect a net-work bag made of docken stalks and bent grass or rush ropes, or latterly coir yarn could be used for the verticals. *Kishies* were usually placed in a net of bent-grass attached to the saddle by the loops of rope at its ends (Fenton and Laurenson 1964.10–16).

The *horse-kishie* and *rivva-kishie* were suitable for carrying loads such as peat, but if grain had to be taken to the mill a special type of carrier was used, known as a *half-led,* "a bag made of straw ropes and floss [rush] bands, with loops at the mouth through which a floss-band was threaded to draw the mouth together" (Johnston 1907–8. I. 246). Unlike the *kishie,* it was longer than it was deep, and is said to have been like the carrier used by a joiner for his tools, or like the upside down shell of a crab. It was 90 to 120 cm long by 45 cm deep and could carry about a sack of oats (Omond *c.* 1912.20), roughly three bushels. The *half-led* was not slung directly on to the saddle, but was carried in a *maisie* or open net, that gave it extra support (Firth

1920.36). A loop on the side of the *half-led* by which it could be lifted was known in Orkney as a *sideack* (Marwick 1929. s.v.). Amongst the implements of husbandry noted in the parish of Assynt in Sutherland in the late eighteenth century were *"cabbies, crook-saddles* and *creels"* (Mackenzie 1795.187). The word *cabbie* is otherwise recorded in only one source, as 'a sort of box, made of laths, which claps close to a horse's side, narrow at the top, so as to prevent the grain in it from being spilled. One is used on each side of the horse in place of a pannier" (Jamieson 1808. s.v.). This is like a wooden version of the grain containers, but is not otherwise recorded.

Although in the Northern Isles, creels were normally made of straw, bent grass, rushes, and docken stalks, in other parts of Scotland they appear to have been almost exclusively of wickerwork for most purposes except the carrying of grain, when a more closely knit material was desirable. In North Uist, for example, special bags were made of bent-grass for this purpose, of which one in the National Museum of Antiquities, is 66 cm deep by 61 cm wide, with nine lugs each 10 cm wide along the top for suspension. Similarly, in early nineteenth century Caithness, small tenants used straw *cassies* instead of sacks for corn. They were made of oat-straw bunches bound by small ropes of rushes, in the same way as a mat. They were oblong in shape, 90 cm long at the bottom, by 76 cm long at the top, by 50 cm deep, and could hold half a boll (3 bushels) of oats or bere. Each had a handle or *fettle* at each side and end, and had two straw ropes to tie the mouth when full. Such containers were made by the tenant and his male servants, if any, during the winter evenings, the material costing about 2d. They would last for about two years. The horse carried two *cassies* of grain, one slung at each side, making a total load of one boll (6 bushels). The *cassies* were balanced equally, and held in position by a rope of straw or rushes across the horse's back, and turned up around each *cassie*. When both ends were fixed tight, the part of the ropes that passed over the split-saddle were put in the notch on top. During transport, the loaded horses were each tied by the halter to the tail of the one in front, up to 6 or 7 in a row. When unloaded, the halter of the first horse was tied to the tail of the last horse, so that they could not run away (Henderson 1812.70), a practice also recorded in Shetland, Orkney, and Aberdeenshire. A string of horses was known as a *cring* in the Northern Isles (Edmondston 1866. s.v.).

For the carriage of peat as fuel for the fires, or of sea-weed as manure for the fields, wickerwork creels were usual, however. There were two forms, a round one largely confined to peat carrying, and a D-shaped one with a flat side next to the horse and a rounded outer-side. The latter was used for both peats and manure, and had the special name of *cliabh spidrich*, the general

138

Fig. 11. Horses with open, D-shaped creels in Islay, Argyll. From a local postcard photograph.

name for creel being *cliabh*. The bottoms of such creels were made to open on hinges of twisted withy and were held close by a movable loop (Macinnes 1893–4.216).

There were also panniers of wood, like one seen in North Uist in the early twentieth century, "with a somewhat complicated attachment by which the bottom could be released at will" (Beveridge 1911.326). At Annochie in Aberdeenshire, in the late eighteenth-early nineteenth century, limestone was carried four or five miles to Brucklay and Whitehill in creels whose bottoms opened like dung-creels (Milne 1891.162). For carrying dung from the byre to the fields, creels were also very commonly used. For this purpose in the parish of Birse, Aberdeenshire, for example, they had "creels made of hazel, birch, or willow wands, with the bottoms hinged on one side and a *sneck* or catch on the other, which being taken off, the bottom fell down and emptied the creels. It is said that a pair of small-sized horses carried as much manure in one day, when the fields were near at hand, as a pair of carts would do at the present time with the same number of hands" (Dinnie 1865.20).

In Moray too, before the days of dung carts, manure was carried in semi-circular baskets on each side of a horse, slung from hooks on the saddle, below which was a straw mattress covering the back and both sides of the

139

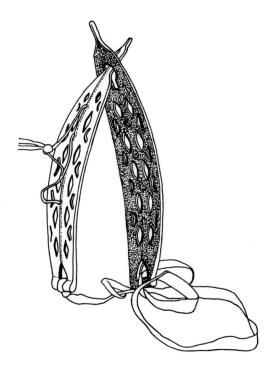

Fig. 12. A Lappish split-saddle. After Wiklund, 1938.

horse. "The bottom of the basket was connected by a hinge to the flat side, and fastened by a latch to the other, by the turning of which the bottom falling out, discharged the load, equal to about the twelfth part of the load of a single horse cart" (Leslie 1811.122–3).

The dung-creel with a bottom that could be opened seems to have been practically universal in Scotland as well as in other areas like the Faroe Islands (Djurhuus 1959.140, and Tab X, Fig. 7), Iceland and Norway (Steinsnes 1961.67–9). However, no evidence has come to hand from the Northern Isles for creels or baskets that opened in this way and, in fact, it would be difficult to make a straw container with a bottom that could be opened unless a rigid framework was included in its structure. These differences reflect the inter-relationship of form and of material drawn from local resources, leading to regional variation not always entirely due to aspects of function or techniques of use.

The D-shaped creels for carrying sea-weed could be fairly open in construction, like the one from Islay, Argyll, illustrated in Fig. 11, which parallels to some extent an Irish example from County Down (Evans 1961.169) (Fig. 13). Peat creels were of a closer construction, but nevertheless they still, as a rule, had a row of eyes round the middle, known in Gaelic as *briagan a'*

140

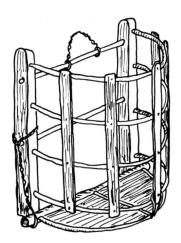

Fig. 13. An open, wooden sea-weed creel from County Down, Ireland. After Evans, 1951.

chleibh, taobhaisdean (Dwelly), *taghaisdean* (Campbell 1958. s.v.). The other parts of the creel were called *iris* or *iris mhuineil* for the bearing band, made of a rope of grass, *dula na h-iris* for the loop of the bearing band, *staingean* for the upright ribs of the frame and *mas* for the bottom (Dwelly). At the top of the creel the ribs stuck out a little way and these protrusions had the name of *fiaclan a' cleibh* (the teeth of the creel) (Campbell 1958. s.v.). They resulted from the manner in which creels were made by sticking the ribs into the ground to outline the shape and size required, and weaving the heather stalks or wickerwork of the body around them. When the body had been completed, the creel was lifted, so pulling the ribs out of the ground, and then the ends were trimmed off with a knife, leaving equal lengths all round (Kissling 1961.40). The three openings at each of the four corners of the bottom of a creel are called *car(r)-oiseanain* (Campbell 1958. s.v.).

Other terms applied to creels were *happrick* and *hot(t)*. *Happrick* is applied in Shetland to a creel used as a rule for carrying manure, recorded from the late nineteenth century (SND s.v.). *Hot(t)* belongs to South West Scotland and Northern England (Cowper 1898. IV. 20), and also refers to a basket or pannier for carrying manure, in this case with a hinged bottom to allow the contents to be easily emptied (SND s.v.). Though recorded in Scotland only from the early nineteenth century (Jamieson 1808. s.v.), it derives from Northern Middle English *hott*, a pannier (1300), from Old French *hotte*, idem, cognate with German *Hotte*, a creel, and therefore has a long ancestry.

Panniers. Creels were not the only fittings for carrying loads, and indeed they were of relatively little use when it came to carrying hay, straw, corn, ferns, or the like. In this case a more open and solider type of framework was

141

Fig. 14. A V-shaped wooden creel from Ireland, for carrying firewood. After Evans, 1951.

required, variously known as a *crubban* or *currach*. One Caithness writer made the distinction clear in speaking of the woods in the Berriedale area, where the trees were cut down for making, inter alia, "*crubbans,* for carrying corn or peats on horses' backs, and *criells,* or baskets, for carrying the manure to the land on horseback. The tenantry of these straths, having generally a mechanical turn, made these implements of husbandry and carried them for sale to the county fairs" (Henderson 1812.153).

The use of the word *crub(b)an* is confined to Caithness, where it was first recorded at the end of the eighteenth century, when the minister of Wick parish wrote that "the tenants carry home their peats, and some lead their corn, in what they call *crubans*" (Sutherland 1795.23). It may be a derivative of the Gaelic *crùbag,* 'wooden frame placed on a horse's back for the purpose of carrying anything bulky, as hay, corn, etc.' (Dwelly), a word that got itself into the speech of Sutherland and Perthshire almost unchanged in the form *crooback* (Jamieson 1825. s.v.). It is of interest to note that the word *crub* is used for a similar piece of equipment in South West England, at the diametrically opposite end of Britain. Here, there were two types of carrier, a "long crook" and a "short crook". The long crook consisted of two poles bent in a semicircle of 46 cm diameter, with one end much longer than the other. A pair was kept 60 cm apart, and parallel, by five or more wooden rungs. This frame was slung on the pack-saddle, pannier-wise, so that the long ends were upright, at least 90 cm above the horse's back. Since they were over 150 cm apart, a very large quantity of hay, straw, or corn could be loaded. The short crook was of similar construction, but smaller, with a greater number of rungs, and was intended for compact, heavy loads like logs, stones, etc. (E.D.D. 1898. s.v. *Crub, Crook*). It was this short crook to which the name

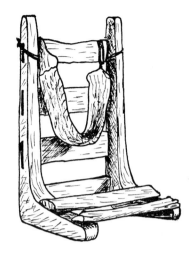

Fig. 15. A Faroese *grotleypur*, for transport on the human back. After Jirlow, 1937.

crub was given, and which must have resembled, for example, the V-shaped carrier (though more right-angled in form) used in Ireland for carrying firewood (Evans 1951.110) (Fig. 14), the Faroese *grotleypur,* for carrying stones (Fig. 15) (Jirlow 1937.137), and the *"Curracks,* pair of, in wood. Stamped "I.P." Used as panniers for carrying fuel etc. H.470 (cm), B.480 (cm). Aberdeenshire—Wilson Collection. Purchased 1910" (Reid 1912.49) (Fig. 16), in the Anthropological Museum in the University of Aberdeen.

It should be noted, however, that the *grotleypur* illustrated is for carrying on the human back, with a band round the forehead. It is also of interest that the V-shaped Irish creel for wood is reminiscent of the V-shaped individual wooden hooks (Fig. 17) used in pairs on crook-saddles in the Sogn district of Norway, as well as in parts of France, for a similar purpose (Heiberg 1932. 118–22).

A number of eighteenth century descriptions also point to the L-shape for a currach. In Moray, "the corn was carried from the field in a lighter conveyance of two sides only, hung similarly on the saddle; its outer side only rising to the same height, made an acute angle with that which rested on the side of the horse; the sheaves piled high over the saddle were kept together by a rope from the two extremities. Grain, meal, and lime were carried in sacks tied upon the back of the horse, 4 or 6 bushels making the load" (Leslie 1811.122–3).

In the late eighteenth century, a Banffshire writer made the comment that about 1750 creels or *currocks,* "a semicircular basket made of twigs", served for carrying dung and peats on horseback, adding that grain, meal, lime etc. were carried in sacks on the backs of horses (Donaldson 1794.19–20). It is possible, from his description, that he is confusing creels and currachs, as

143

Fig. 16. A pair of wooden panniers from Aberdeenshire. By courtesy of The Anthropological Museum, University of Aberdeen.

often happens in the dictionary definitions of "currach". That creels and currachs were different things, intended in the main for different types of loads, is clearly borne out by several of the sources, as when a later Banffshire writer, making an alternative, said that currachs or wicker creels were hung from the crook-saddle, and that currachs were used for carrying dung, loading corn, etc. (Grant 1901–2.10–11).

There is a clear distinction here, as also further south in Angus where in the 1790s, currachs for corn and creels for peat, at 1/- a pair, were still in use in the higher parts of the county. The currachs were described as frames of sticks, and the creels as panniers (Roger 1794.16.26). In Argyll, "peats and dung used to be carried on sledges, or on creels on the backs of horses; and the corn and hay was conveyed in small frames in the same manner. This is still the case in some parts where steep grounds and bad roads admit of no better conveyance" (Smith 1798.60–1). In the Perthshire Highlands, "the people performed some distant carriages of bulky commodities with handles, fixed on each side of the horse, by means of a hooked car-saddle, still remembered by the name of currans. Less bulky commodities were carried in hampers or baskets, made of young hazle, with a square mouth, and fixed on the horse's back with the same car-saddle" (Robertson 1799.92–3). In Skye, too, it was observed that sheaves were often carried home on a kind of open pannier, or "frame of sticks" on the horse's back (Johnson 1775.181),

144

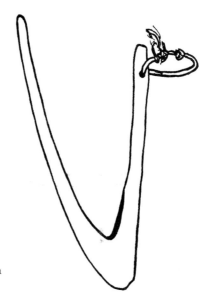

Fig. 17. A wooden hook, one of a pair attached to a crook saddle for the transport of firewood in the Sogn district of Norway. After Heiberg, 1932.

and in Galloway sheaves were carried on horseback in a so-called "basket-machine", with people at each side keeping the load in position with forks. This was still occasionally seen in the 1790s (Webster 1794.12). It is likely that the seventeenth century horse heavily laden with two bundles of hay, in the foreground of a view of the town of Brechin in Angus, is harnessed with a pack-saddle and pair of currachs (Slezer 1693. Pl. 53), though these cannot, of course, be seen under the load.

The term *currach,* or some variant spelling, was one of the most commonly used names for a carrier for bulky loads on horseback. It was chiefly found in Banffshire and Aberdeenshire, and stretched south into Kincardineshire and Angus. A late eighteenth century Lanarkshire writer referred to the curroch, but was imitating Highland speech at the time (MacGregor 1883. I. 272). It first appears in the variant form *currell* in 1620 when Alex. McWilliam Moir was given permission, as part of his lease of the half town and lands of Corthullie, to cut wood "for plewis, kartis, sledis, currellis, harrowis, barrowis and sicklyk" (Fraser 1883. III. 319), and forty years later the wife of the minister of Kennethmont got herself into trouble for borrowing a "pair of currecks" to help in leading home corn on a Sunday (Bell 1897.38). The first form is a Lowland Scots spelling of Gaelic *curral,* itself a variant of *curran,* with the same meaning. In 1736, two pairs of currachs cost 17d., and a pair of "Corn Curracks" 10d. on the Monymusk estate in Aberdeenshire, where on 19 October 1749, two men with two horses and currachs were paid 6/- for "drawing in the green corn to yard" (Hamilton 1946.26, 109). The difference in price between ordinary currachs and those for corn suggests some difference in form as well.

The widespread nature of transport on horseback, especially till about the end of the eighteenth century, is further indicated by the number of terms that remain to be considered.

The *packet*, or *packart*, a term confined to North-East Scotland, appears to have been a light kind of support for loads. In the Monymusk Papers, the cost of a pair of currachs at 6/- Scots contrasts, in 1738, with the cost of a pair of packets at 2/- Scots (Hamilton 1945.12). In the same source, "Muck Creels" and "Peat Creels" were 9/- each. The packet was therefore smaller than the currach and the two may have borne the same relationship to each other as the long crook and short crook of South West England. A Banffshire comment, that "for more extended travel were packets made of wooden rungs with a bend for holding the *birn* (load)" (Grant 1901–2.10–11), seems to confirm that the form was similar. A late Morayshire source that glosses the term "packart" as "a saddle made of birch wands fitted on the back of a pony on each side of which peats could be built up and carried" (SND s.v.), appears to confuse or conflate the pack-saddle and the carrier, but *may* be accurate, for such two-in-one pieces of equipment do exist, for example in Spain (Erixon 1938.138, Pl. 17b).

The term *houghams* is known in Old Scots from 1617, when "5 creillis . . . a pair of hochemis" are referred to in the Master of Works Accounts. The Edinburgh Testaments of 1625 mention "ane pair of Hochames and an cair sedill", and again in 1652, "two load saidells and ane pair of hochomes". In the Acts of 1649, there were "work horsis with their sleds, creills, hochimes, and such like" (DOST s.v. *Hochems*). The word is applied to a bent piece of wood slung over the back of a horse to support panniers or creels (Jamieson 1825. s.v.). The reference in *Hope's Practicks* to "a Crook-saddle, with a Pair of Creels and Gohams" (Spotiswood 1734.542) appears to incorporate a misprint for this word, though nevertheless confirming that the device was used in conjunction with a creel.

It was not always necessary to use a pack-saddle with creels or currachs to move loads on horseback. It was noted in the parish of Birse, Aberdeenshire, for example, that "when bags of corn, meal, or other grain had to be removed from one place to another, they were laid across the horse's back equally balanced on each side, and fastened with a rope round the belly of the horse" (Dinnie 1865.20). Attention should also be paid to a curious form of hay- or straw-rope "pack saddle" of which examples are known in County Louth, Ireland. It is described as "a pad, shaped like a long U, the sides of which extend along the horse's flanks parallel to the spine while the closed end rests just behind the withers. Three cross-ties prevent the sides from spreading apart and at the end of each side is a large eye or opening to which a crupper-rope, passing under the tail, is attached. The pad, excluding the crupper-rope, is 94 cm long. It is round in section, thickest at the closed end where it is 14 cm in diameter, and tapers gradually to the open end, where it is about 8 cm in diameter. ... When in use the saddle was held in place by a rope belly-band. The reason for the extra thickness at the closed end of the pad was to form a high roll on the horse's withers to obviate the danger of the sack slipping forward on to the neck when the animal was coming down a steep slope" (Lucas 1961.13–14).

This cross between a pack-saddle and a pad was used in carrying sacks of peat. It is likely that the carrying of loads without a pack-saddle was of frequent occurrence, provided some form of protective mat or cover was used when necessary, and even in recent times, for example at Wensleydale, in the North of England, pairs of milk cans could be seen on donkey back, in special holders of the "currach" type, linked across the donkey's back by leather straps over a pad of sacking (Hartley and Ingilby 1968. Pl. 99).

Slide-Cars, Kellach Sledges and Kellach Carts

The Slide-Car. Vehicles of the travois or slide-car type, in which loads are carried between a pair of poles whose lower ends trail on the ground behind the draught animal, are old in time, and wide in distribution. Amongst the oldest types may be that drawn between a pair of oxen, with the front ends of the poles attached to the centre of the ox-yoke, and therefore involving a yoke of sufficient length to give room for the travois, though space could be saved by arranging the poles in triangular fashion, with the apex at the yoke. Rock engravings of Early Bronze Age character from Val Fontanalba, Liguria, provide prehistoric evidence for the "yoke travois" (Jochstangenschleife) (Kothe 1953.83). Apart from this, however, the evidence is for slide-cars with poles whose front ends act as a pair of shafts between which the single draught animal, usually an equid, could walk.

For the simple pole travois, there is almost invariably a tendency towards a triangular or splayed-out form. The triangularity is carried to an extreme amongst the North American Indians, where the poles may come up alongside the horse's riding saddle, to which they are attached, and then cross each other above the horse's neck, in front of the saddle bow (Townshend 1913. 955). The triangular shape may be important from the evolutionary point of view, since the frame of the base of some early carts, like those from the third millenium B.C. burials of Transcaucasia, has a similar shape (Piggott 1968. 289 ff.). The Transcaucasian carts are the earliest known examples of the type and no unambiguous archaeological evidence of equivalent or earlier date has so far been found for the slide-car.

Possibly the earliest European find of a pair of travois poles was in the moor at Uchte in Lower Saxony. To them had been tied a bundle of clothes which, along with a fibula, are said to belong to the period 300–150 B.C. The poles were much worn at their thicker lower ends, and the upper ends contained openings with traces of thongs. The poles have not survived, and their length is not known (Dieck 1959.37–40). There is no information about the nature of the draught, and the straps may even have gone over the shoulders of the dead man who was found nearby. Another pair of poles was found in the moor at Alte Redoute in the Grafschaft Bentheim in 1866, with two bars attached as runners for a container (Dieck 1959.40–1). Presumably this was like the type, recorded, for example, in Italy, that has been described as a "double travois" (Doppelstangenschleife) (Kothe 1953.76.). This find has also disappeared.

Attention should also be paid to a shaped deer-horn in the museum at Geestemünde with two horizontal holes, one in the foot and one in the shank, as well as to another from a pile-dwelling at Zedmar, East Prussia, dated to the Early Bronze Age. The latter has a simple hole at the junction of foot and shank (Fig. 18) (Dieck 1959.42–3), and has been variously interpreted as a sole plough, "Sohlenpflug" (Gaerte 1929.24), and a foot operated cultivating implement, "ein furchenstockartiges Gerät" (Kothe 1953.88). Dieck may well be correct in interpreting these as the lower ends of travois poles, but the Uchte find so far appears to provide the earliest undoubted evidence. The almost world-wide distribution of the travois may be a further pointer to its antiquity, however (Berg 1935.132–136), and its survival till the present day in many areas, including parts of Scotland, northern England, Ireland and Wales is an indication of its continuing usefulness.

The earliest visual evidence from Scotland is in a seventeenth century source, where two types of slide-car are shown (Fig. 19). Both have a pair of shafts supported by a strap from a broad back band or light saddle and probably also attached to the collars of the horses, and each has an upright ribbed framework. In one example, the ends of the shafts run on the ground, in the normal fashion, but in the other, there is a substructure that raises the body almost to the horizontal. There is no sign of struts in the illustration, though they would appear to be necessary if the substructure were to have a

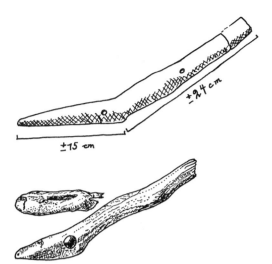

Fig. 18. Deer-horns from Geestemünde Museum (top) and from a pile-dwelling at Zedmar, East Prussia (bottom), the latter of Early Bronze Age date. Possibly used as skids on the ends of travois poles.

reasonable degree of stability. Each horse is being led, and one also has a rider, seated sideways. These slide-cars were in use in the Arbroath area of Angus, and the Dunblane area of Perthshire (Slezer 1693. Plates 27, 40).

The next illustration (Fig. 20), dating from *c.* 1734, shows a shaggy pony with a light saddle and collar, led by a cloaked and hooded figure, dragging a slide-car whose poles are joined by a pair of semi-circular hoops, with a lighter infilling of ropes or withies on them and on the base to retain a load.

These drawings are put into context and the details amplified by later references in the topographical and agricultural literature. In the island of Skye, the redoubtable Samuel Johnson saw one on which sheaves were being dragged by a horse. He said it had a frame of timber, with the two points behind pressing on the ground (Johnson 1775.181). His comrade James Boswell gave a fuller description: "They have also a few sledges, or *cars* as they are called in Ayrshire, clumsily made and rarely used. They are made of two crooked trees. Two ends drag on the ground; two lean on a horse, one on each side . . . and for a good way there are cross-bars between them and a back of sticks" (Pottle and Bennett 1963.198). Boswell also made a rough sketch, which has not been published.

There is a comparable description from the Central Highlands, by an agricultural writer conscious of evolutionary problems, for he commented that "from this simplest of implements, the present rude cart of the Highlands may still be traced (especially in the north of Scotland) through the several intervening stages; and, in the present one-horse cart of the Lowlands, it may be said to have reached its ultimate improvement". He applied the term "slipe"

149

a)

b)

Fig. 19. Slide-cars, (a) at Dunblane, Perthshire; (b) at Arbroath, Angus. After Slezer, 1963

150

to it, and noted that, when yoked, the front ends of the shafts were fastened to the harness on the collar (Marshall 1794.34–5). In Perthshire, "near carriages, particularly the ingathering of their hay and corns, were executed with a sledge, which consisted of two shafts reaching from the collar on the horse's neck to the ground, with cross-bars near the horse's hind-feet, for a bottom, and at least seven erect bars behind, for keeping on the load. This sledge succeeded the hurdle [i.e. a form of currach for transport on horse-back] and evidently required some road, whereas the hurdle could be used wherever it was possible for a horse to walk..." (Robertson 1799.92–3). In Arran, Bute, the story was the same, the "cars" having a "back of sticks" for bringing home peat and grain (Headrick 1807.317; Aiton 1816.166). A sketch was made of such a travois with an ill-balanced looking load of corn at Glen-croe, Argyll (Fig. 21), and several others loaded with peats were seen around Loch Tarf, Inverness-shire, though not confined to that area (Garnett 1811. I. 318–20). In the hilly Grampian districts of Angus, "sledges, like carts, but lacking wheels" were still also in use for carrying peat and corn on steep ground (Headrick 1813.511).

One of the most detailed nineteenth century descriptions comes from Wester Ross:

"There being no need of wheels in a roadless country in my young days, we had only sledges in place of wheeled carts, all made by our grieve. He took two birch trees of the most suitable bends and of them made the two shafts, with iron-work to suit the harness for collar straps. The ends of the shafts were sliced away with an adze at the proper angle to slide easily and smooth-ly on the ground. Two planks, one behind the horse and the other about half-way up the shaft ends, were securely nailed to the shafts, and were bored with holes to receive four-foot-long hazel rungs to form the front and back of the cart and to keep in the goods, a similar plank on the top of the rungs making the front and rear of the cart surprisingly stable and upright. The floor was made of planks, and these sledge carts did all that was needed for moving peats, and nearly every kind of crop. Movable boxes planted on the sledge floor between the front and back served to carry up fish from the shore and lime and manure, and it was long ere my father Sir Hector paid a penny a year to a cartwright. The sledges could slide where wheeled carts could not venture, and carried corn and hay, etc., famously." (Mackenzie 1924.31–2).

In some sources, "sledge" is the name applied to a travois, for example, in Dumbartonshire where "sledges, owing to the badness of roads, are still used in many places of the country" (Ure 1794.43), and in Stirlingshire, especially

Fig. 20. (1) a slide-car;
(2) a rung cart;
(3) a kellach cart.
After Burt, *c.* 1734.

the western part, single-horse sledges, generally made by the farmer himself, were in use for carrying hay and sheaves (Belsches 1796.41; Graham 1812.117).

In the mid-nineteenth century, a visitor to a glen on the mainland of Scotland opposite Skye saw a number of vehicles: a "plain sledge for hay, called in Gaelic, carn slaoid. The shafts continued along, with cross-pieces only to form, as it were, the body of the cart. Next came the sledge, with wattling at the bottom, and twisted sticks, arched in front and behind . . . (Fig. 22).

The basket-sledge for manure was next shown to us; this is called in Gae-

Fig. 21. A slide-car with a load of sheaves at Glencroe, Argyll. After Garnett, 1800.

lic, "lopan-an-slaoid". This is, of course, a much stronger vehicle, and well adapted for carting manure; it is worked with thick split sticks, as in a creel (Fig. 26). Each of these classes of vehicles is drawn by native ponies, stout, strong, and shaggy little animals and gifted with great powers of endurance" (? Pritchett 1867.479–80).

The downcurved ends of the wattled sledge (Fig. 22) form one piece with the side poles, but are nevertheless reminiscent of the Irish slide-cars in which hardwood shoes are attached to the ends of the poles by means of a wooden peg and an iron ring (Haddon 1898. Pl. III; Evans 1951.119; Evans 1958.108). They could lie full length, or might be slanted to lie in the same plane as the shafts (Haddon 1898.165) (Fig. 24). Although such replaceable shoes are a logical and economic way of minimizing wear they are nevertheless unknown in Scotland. They may be paralleled by the deer-horn artefacts discussed earlier (Fig. 18).

About the same time, in 1863–1864, Sir Arthur Mitchell saw two travois in Strathglass, Kintail (Fig. 23), one with semi-circular infilled hoops at the front and back, the other with side-hoops, an open front, and a back made of cross spars. At the front end of each shaft of the latter were two upright wooden pins for attaching the back and collar withies. He published diagrams of them

153

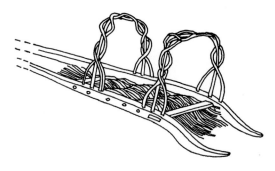

Fig. 22. A slide-car with a wattle bottom, from the Scottish Mainland opposite Skye. After Pritchett, 1867.

a few years later, along with an inaccurate copy of Burt's slide-car, which has been turned in the opposite direction, and a heavy horse substituted for the pony. Mitchell refused to accept Burt's comment that such vehicles provided evidence for the backward and degraded state of the north Highland population in the early eighteenth century. Rather, he wrote:

"When I saw what these carts were employed in doing, namely transporting peats, fern, and hay from high grounds down very steep hills entirely without roads, I saw that the contrivance was admirably adapted for its purpose, and that wheeled carts would have been useless for that work. But I saw more than this: I saw that these carts were used in doing the exact analogue of what is done every day in the advanced south . . . When boulders, for instance, are removed on sledges from the fields in which they have been turned up; when trees are transported on sledges from the high grounds on which they have been cut when a heavily laden lorry puts on the drag as it comes down hill: what is it that we see, but carts without wheels—carts without wheels preferred to carts with wheels, whenever the circumstances in which they are to be used makes the want of the wheels an advantage? It is not always an evidence of capacity or skill to use elaborate or fine machinery. A rough, rude tool may for certain purposes be the most efficient, and may show wisdom both in its contriver and employer. It would certainly show a want of wisdom in the Kintail Highlanders, if they used wheeled carts to do the work they require of their wheel-less carts. Indeed, they could not so use these, except by putting the drag on hard and fast—being first at the trouble of getting wheels, and then at the trouble of preventing them turning" (Mitchell 1880. 96–8).

It is clear, therefore, that until well into the nineteenth century, the travois consisting of two side shafts, a number of cross-bars, and a set of upright rungs, used for carrying the hay and grain harvest and for peat, was fairly common around the fringes of the Highlands. It has survived till the present

154

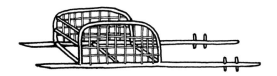

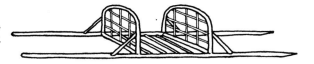

day in Argyll and in particular the island of Jura as a means of transporting
deer from the hills when they have been shot. A model of a "Jura car" in the
National Museum of Antiquities of Scotland (where there is also a full scale
example) was made by a joiner as a pattern some time in the nineteenth
century, and on it he has marked in ink the sizes of the various members
(Fig. 25). A lively scene of the Victorian sporting era, painted by Gourley
Steell (now in the Art Gallery and Museum, Kelvingrove, Glasgow), shows a
horse with a slide-car at the scene of slaughter, and a stag waiting to be
loaded, whilst the laird holds a telescope he has borrowed from one of his
stalkers to see if he can spot more game. In this case the horse has a crook-
saddle with a double-bow between which lies a withy rope to support the
shafts, and a straw collar with a pair of wooden hames to which the front ends
of the shafts are attached by further withies. The bridle is of rope, with a
pair of wooden cheek-pieces, and there is no bit (Fig. 1).

The Kellach Sledge. For the carriage of dung to the fields, the slide-car was
adapted by the addition to it of a wickerwork creel. On more level ground,
a simple, low sledge with two shallow runners was used for the same purpose.
The slide-car with a creel fitted to it is known especially in north-east and
north Scotland as a *kellach* sledge, a name derived from Gaelic *ceallach*,
"peat-cart, creel placed on a sledge to carry peats, manure, etc." (Dwelly). No
descriptions previous to the eighteenth century have been noted, and most
references lie broadly within the period 1750–1850. Presumably it replaced
manure creels on horseback. In Nairn the kellach sledge was said to consist of
a "conical basket framed on twigs", supported between the shafts and two

155

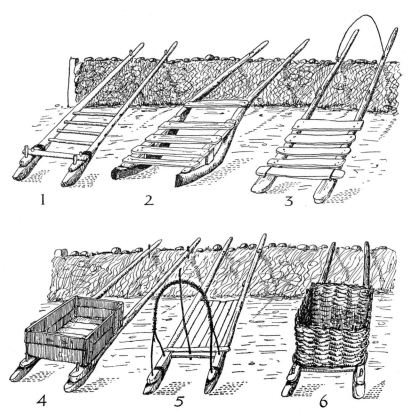

Fig. 24. Irish slide-cars. 1. Glens of Antrim; 2. South Fermanagh; 3. West Cavan; 4. Box slide-car; 5. Corn slide-car; 6. Peat slide-car. Four have shoes or skids on the ends of the runners. After Evans, 1951.

linking cross bars of the travois (Donaldson 1794.15). In the parish of Kiltarlity, Inverness, *keallachs* carried on sledges were still used in the higher parts of the parish (Fraser 1794.519). In Perthshire, where the name kellach is not recorded, the equipment itself was nevertheless known since a description of the travois for hay and grain is followed by a comment that "upon this sledge or car the farmers in the Highlands carried out the dung in large baskets, diverging towards the mouth in the shape of an equilateral triangle, one side of the basket lying on the bottom or floor of the sledge; . . . On these sledges they carried home their peats in other baskets of a square form and of such capacity as to hold a horse's load; but where the road was so steep that the car could not be used, they adopted small baskets of the same form, fixed on the horse's sides to the hooked car-saddle. In many parts of the Highlands, these sledges are still employed for carrying grain and hay, as well as peats; especially where the roads are so rugged and uneven as to render the use of

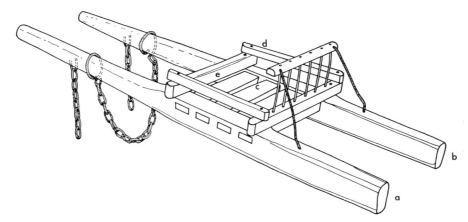

Fig. 25. A model slide-car from Jura, Argyll, used as a joiner's pattern. The ink markings on the members are:

(a) top of shaft at rear "Height of back 14 inches"; left side af shaft "Between Shafts at Point 2 Feet 6 Inches. Thickness 4 × 3 Inches. Over at Aft End 4 Feet 2 Inches".

(b) top of shaft at rear "4 Feet to Cross Bar; in middle, "2 Feet 2 Inches"; at front "7 Feet from Cross Bar". Side of shaft "Not to be made of Heavy Wood"; below frame, "Bolt Nut"; at front, "Chain 21 Inches".

(c) centre cross piece "Slots $3\frac{1}{2}$ × $\frac{1}{4}$ Inches".

(d) top of side piece "2 × $1\frac{1}{2}$ Inches"; side of side piece, "Bolt Nut".

(e) front of front piece "$2\frac{1}{2}$ × $1\frac{3}{4}$".

carts impracticable" (Robertson 1799.92–3). This is an interesting description, clearly exemplifying adaptation of equipment in relation to terrain, the nature of the loads, and the presence or absence of roads, which seem to have been desirable even for the wheelless travois. In Arran, Bute, creels were also fastened to the "cars" for carrying out dung, but the upright back of sticks was put on for loads of peat or corn (Headrick 1807.317).

By the end of the eighteenth century the pattern had become one of survival and even reminiscence in many areas, but remained one of necessity in others. This can be seen clearly from the references in the *Statistical Account of Scotland,* especially when these are set alongside the information from other sources given above. Thus in Kiltarlity parish, Inverness, there must have been a question of necessity in relation to terrain in the existence of 361 sledges (alongside 40 "coups or small waggons", and 376 carts) (Fraser 1794.519), and in Kilmallie, Argyll, where sledges were used for hay and corn and there were only 24 carts in the parish (Fraser 1793.446). Survival areas were Kilfinan, Argyll, where the peat, corn, and manure cars and sledges had been largely replaced by 58 carts (McFarlane 1795.239), Cawdor, Nairn, where the tenants stuck to their old style equipment (Grant 1792.

157

356), and the moorland districts of Killearn, Stirling (Ure 1795.115). In Torthorwald, Dumfries, the "trail cars" used about 1750 had become a matter of reminiscence (McMillan 1791.4), and the same could no doubt be said for most of Lowland Scotland.

Similar equipment was found in Northern Ireland, for example in the Antrim Glens and the Sperrins, where a comparable form of travois had a *kish* (cf. the *kishie* or *caisie* of the Northern Isles of Scotland) made of osiers of ash or of willow tied on to it (Thompson 1955.34). Slide-cars with square or rectangular baskets for peats have also been noted there (Evans 1951.120) (Fig. 24, 6).

Kellach Carts. It appears from the Perthshire reference of 1799 that some kind of a road was preferred for the travois. This factor may have had some influence in encouraging the addition of a pair of small wooden wheels to the ends of the travois poles. Wheels would cause less damage to the roads, at the same time permitting the carriage of slightly heavier burdens. The term *kellach* or *kellachie cart* is applied to this vehicle in the areas where the *kellach sledge* was used. It was recorded in Ross as early as 1713 (MacGill 1909. I. 132), and illustrated shortly after by Captain Burt, who showed, besides an ordinary slide-car, two types of wheeled vehicle, one with a body whose sides were composed of upright rungs linked by cross-bars at the top, the other with the *kellach* or creel slung between its poles, behind the horse (Fig. 20, 2, 3). The shafts of the latter are supported by a rope across a wooden saddle on a back-pad, and are also attached to a collar round the horse's neck. Such vehicles were used not only in the country, but in the town as well about 1734. Burt complained that in Inverness they filled up the streets so much that it was sometimes impossible to pass them on horseback, and difficult on foot. His attitude was clear:

"It is really provoking to see the Idleness and Inhumanity of some of the Leaders of this Sort of Carts; for as they are something higher than the Horse's Tail, in the Motion, they keep rubbing against it, till the Hair is worn off and the Dock quite raw, without any Care taken to prevent it, or ease the Hurt when discovered."

Women sometimes led the carts, usually walking barefoot, and wearing a blanket or plaid that could go over their heads in bad weather. "At other Times they wear a Piece of Linnen upon their Heads, made up like a Napkin Cap in an Inn, only not tied at-top, but hanging down behind."

The harness ropes were usually of twisted withies, but sometimes of horse-

158

hair rope, and the collar and crupper of straw bands. A "Parcel of old Rags" went under the cart saddle to save the horse's back. The horses were unshod.

Some of the carts were so light that "when the Carter has had Occasion to turn about one Sort of these Carts in a narrow Place, I have seen him take up the Cart, Wheels and all, and walk round with it, while the poor little Horse has been strugling to keep himself from being thrown" (Burt 1759. I. 86–9).

Further details come from descriptions at the end of the century. In Ross and Cromarty, a great many kellach carts were in use. In Kiltearn parish, on such solid-wheeled carts, manure was carried in "a coarse, strong basket, formed like a sugar loaf . . . of a conical form" (Robertson 1791.277). In Dingwall parish they were described in the same way. The minister there thought that "in hilly and uneven places, their lightness may be a reason for using them; but in places differently situated, blind attachment to inveterate customs can only account for the use of them" (Rose 1792.11). The situation was changing, however, for in places like Kirkmichael parish, small box-carts with spoke-wheels were replacing kellach carts (Arthur 1795.90), and in Rosemarkie farmers were beginning to use "coups" drawn by pairs of oxen (Wood 1794.336).

From Cromarty comes a very detailed description:

"The *kellach* has an axle fixed to the wheels, which are solid, 18″–24″ diam. The great ends of the shafts are joined by 2 cross-bars behind, the bars themselves crossed obliquely, and by others similar a short space forward. The extremity is thus placed on the axle by 2 slender wooden bows within which the axle turns. For turf, corn, or hay, 2–3 boards are laid across the shafts, and a railing or rungs erected on it, secured round by pieces of wood at the top into which the upper ends of the rungs enter. The cross-bars receive a conical wickered basket, carrying *c.* 140–160 lbs., which can be lifted off and on at will. It is in general use in the Northern Highlands, especially in the low parts or coast sides. The wheels wear to all sorts of shapes" (Sinclair 1795.23).

In Moray, the kellach carts were "for the most part made by the farmer himself; but when sold in the market, cost altogether about four shillings and six pence" (Donaldson 1794.22). The same was true of Nairn (Donaldson 1794.15) where the "kellocks", made of broom or juniper twigs, interwoven like basketry, were used by the poorer tenants for carrying compost manure (Paterson 1797.623). In Dyke and Moy, box-carts were beginning to replace kellachs (Dunbar 1798.203).

In the nineteenth century the kellach cart was still often seen in Moray. It could carry about a quarter of an ordinary cart load (Leslie 1811.123). Another writer assessed its capacity at a third of a cart load (Rhind 1839.13). It had disappeared by the end of that century, but was still remembered. It was said that there was a science in emptying it. A stick could be pulled out to make the creel lean over to one side on the frame, when it could easily be pushed over (Mason 1889.10). Another writer reminisced that the kellachs held a good lot of manure. The last one he saw was made into a chimney for a house at West Kellas, Delnies (Wilken 1887.26).

The Rung Cart. Alongside the kellach cart was the form whose body was constructed of upright rungs, as illustrated by Captain Burt (Fig. 20, 2). The Cromarty description quoted above (Sinclair 1795.23) implies that one could readily be converted into the other. The rung cart was for peat, grain, etc., rather than for manure, and great numbers were in use. There were, for example, 2,410 in Dingwall (Rose 1792.10), about 300 in Kiltearn (Robertson 1791.277), and 376 in Kiltarlity (Fraser 1794.519).

A term, "Morra cairt" (Moray cart) was used jocularly in Banffshire for a cart whose bottom was formed of rungs with spaces between, laid so that the flat side was downwards on the axle and the rounded side uppermost. The sides were formed by vertical rungs. The story is told that a nonagenarian in Cullen, on the Banffshire coast, remembered a certain George Kennedy, a strong man who did not shout Wo! to his horse, but simply put his legs firmly on the ground through the bottom of his "Morra' cairt" to make it stop (Scottish Notes & Queries 1900. II. 2nd Ser. 95). It also appears to have been rung carts, "made of bars and timber rods both in the sides and bottom", that were used to transport limestone for the building of Fort George, around 1747. Chips and small bits of stone could fall out through the openings (Leslie 1811. 263–4). Apart from this, however, the main periods of activity for rung carts appear to have been during the peat and harvest leading seasons.

Clog Wheels. The nature of the wheels of the kellach and rung carts, and the manner of their attachment to the axle, are of considerable interest. The wheels, called "tumbler wheels" (Sinclair 1795.101) or more often "clog wheels" (Wilken 1887.26), in the North of England as well as in Scotland, were generally of three pieces of wood dowelled together to form a solid disc, attached to the axle so that the axle turned together with them.

Solid, one-piece disc wheels go back in time to the fourth millenium B.C. in the Ancient Near East (van der Waals 1964.10; Piggott 1968.274), and three-piece wheels dating to the third millenium B.C. have been found on vehicles from Transcaucasia (Piggott 1968.278).

160

Fig. 26. A "loban" with spoked
wheels, seen on the Scottish Mainland opposite Skye. After Pritchett,
1867.

In Britain, there is one single-piece disc wheel of the Celtic Iron Age from
the Glastonbury Lake Village, in the south of England (Bulleid and Gray
1911. Fig. 84) and one three-part wheel from a bog at Blair Drummond, in
Perthshire, Scotland. The latter was found in 1830 with part of another that
has not survived. In 1850 it was presented to the National Museum of Antiquities of Scotland, where it was correctly registered as a wheel, though an
illustration of it in a book that appeared in the same year described it as a
"wooden shield" (Drummond 1850. V. 217–8). A prehistoric date has been
suggested for it, since its general form (Fig. 28), with a pair of lunate openings
by the nave, matches wheels of early date from, for example, Dystrup in Denmark and Buchau in South-West Germany (Piggott 1949.238–41).

It is a matter of interest to note that the early vehicles could sometimes be
more sophisticated than those of later times, for the Dystrup wheels had
tubular hubs within the pierced centres, and revolved round the axle (Berg
1935.102–3), whereas the wheels and axles of kellach, rung and tumbler
carts turned together.

Without radio-carbon dating, it is difficult to be certain of the age of the
Blair Drummond wheel, since it is strictly comparable with the wheels of
kellach carts of eighteenth century and later date, both in form and in size,
and the lunate openings can be paralleled on recent disc wheels from several
areas, including the Iberian peninsula and Bulgaria (Berg 1935.114 ff.). Its
diameter of 61 cm falls well within the range of recorded sizes for kellach
cart wheels.

In 1727, "calachie cairts" with small, solid wheels were used in Ross (Mac
Gill 1909. I. 133), and in the town of Inverness about 1734, Captain Burt saw
carts with three-part, solid wooden wheels, which, "when new, are about a
foot and half (46 cm) high, but are soon worn very small; they are made
of three pieces of plank, pinned together at the edges like the head of a butter

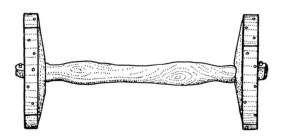

Fig. 27. A pair of clog wheels with a fixed axle from Westmorland. After Cowper, 1898.

firkin, and the axle-tree goes round with the wheel; which having some part of the circumference with the grain, and other parts not, it wears unequally, and in a little time is rather angular than round, which causes a disagreeable noise as it moves upon the stones" (Burt 1815.73–4).

A writer on the agriculture of Nairn commented that "the carts are framed on a form still further from perfection: the wheels, about two feet (61 cm) diameter, are composed only of three pieces of plank two or three inches thick, having square holes in the centre to receive the axle, which must therefore turn round with the wheels, moving in wooden bows fixed under the body of the cart. The shafts are formed of the larger, and the body of the carriage of bars or slender batons of the smaller branches of the alder tree" (Donaldson 1794.15).

In Kiltearn, Ross, rung carts had "instead of wheels, small solid circles of wood, between 20 and 24 inches (50–60 cm) diameter, called tumbling wheels" (Robertson 1791.277).

Some years later a traveller in the same county described the cars as "made of two pieces of straight wood fastened parallel by three or four spars, one of which projects from the parallels at a right angle, and answers for the axle of the cart, the wheels being a circular piece of wood, about the size of the broad rimmed bonnets, made at Kilmarnock" (Thom 1811. I. No. 4. 283–4).

As a rule the wheels were of birch or alder, and usually unshod, but pieces of iron were sometimes nailed over the felloe joints in lieu of tires. It was said that two horses might be used in tandem to pull such carts (Mason 1889. 11), implying that the drag and friction of the wheels and axle that turned with them was considerable. One writer said the axle was of birch (Wilken 1887.26).

Similar wheels and axles were known outside these areas, for example in Ayrshire where dung was said to have been dragged to the fields in the 1750s on "cars or sledges, or on what were called tumbler wheels, which turned with the axle tree" (Fullarton 1793.9).

In Northern England, the first clog wheels appeared at Borrowdale, in

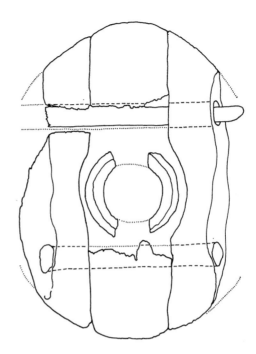

Fig. 28. A tripartite wooden wheel with lunate openings, from Blair Drummond Moss, Perthshire. After Piggott, 1949.

Westmoreland, after about 1770 (Fig. 27). A pair from Troutbeck were about 55 cm in diameter and 95 cm apart, with three iron *strakes* nailed on in lieu of an iron ring. The wheels and the axle turned together. It was said that a wide sweep was necessary to turn a corner, and the drivers carried a grease horn to lubricate the axle. The first improvement was said to be by making one wheel only revolve on the axle, the other still remaining fixed (Cowper 1898. IV. 21–2).

Similar fixed clog wheels and axles were seen between Kendal and Bowness in 1698 (Morris 1947.194), and at Penrith in 1760. The latter had a close resemblance to the Blair Drummond Moss wheel, "a small segment of a circle being cutt out of the two side pieces and a little from the middle piece" (Kemp 1887.36). A pair of lunate openings is a standard feature of recorded clog wheels from the North of England and the expansion in size of this opening, accompanied by the insertion of one, two, or four cross-spars as it grew bigger, is presumably to be interpreted as due to the influence of the spoked wheel. An illustration of 1814 (Fig. 29,1) shows a rung-sided peat cart whose tripartite wheels have simple lunate openings (Walker 1814. Plate 27) but more developed forms actually occurred at an earlier date, for in 1800 a wheel was illustrated which had an hour-glass shaped centre piece, two felloe segments, and two "spokes" (Fig. 29, 2). According to the latter source:

163

"The wheels are sometimes solid block wheels, but these being found heavy, and apt to carry dirt, they are sometimes lightened, by being constructed upon a very simple plan, of five pieces of wood only . . .

These wheels are generally fixed to the axletree, which, instead of being fixed, as usual, to the bottom of the cart, and having the wheels turning upon it, is detached from the cart, and fixed to the wheels, with which it turns, being kept in its place by two iron pins on each side of the cart" (Tuke 1800. 78–9).

The type of solid wheel to which he refers is represented by the Westmorland example referred to above (Fig. 27).

The Science Museum in London preserves a wheel (Fig. 29, 3) like the one in Tuke's sketch, differing only in having two pairs of spokes. The Bowes Museum, County Durham, has a pair of wheels and an axle (Fig. 29,4), probably of nineteenth century date, in which the wheels have each an hour glass centre, four felloes, and four pairs of spokes, having advanced to a stage where the term "clog" wheel is almost a misnomer (Atkinson and Ward 1964. 33–34, 40). They are 98 cm in diameter, and therefore larger than clog wheels proper. Such a typological range, involving solid wheels, wheels with lunate openings, and wheels with cross-bar "spokes", is paralleled in, for example, the Iberian peninsula (Haddon 1898.187).

The most recent survivals of composite solid wheels have been noted in Ireland, Wales and Orkney.

In Ireland block-wheels were common and their long survival has led to some degree of modernisation, for they are fitted with iron rings and revolve on, but not with, their axles. They have been frequently illustrated and discussed in the literature (Edgeworth 1813.57 ff.; Haddon 1898. Pl. IV, Figs. 25 and 33; Lane 1935.141; Herring 1944.44–5; Thompson 1955. Pl. VI et al.). Similar wheels were fitted to the Welsh "truckle car" (Fox 1931. 188–90).

In the small islands of Hoy, Graemsay and Flotta in Orkney they remained in use till the 1940s on low, four-wheeled vehicles known locally as "sleds", "coaches", "lorries" or "hurlies" (Fenton 1961.55; Simpson 1963.160 ff.). They were cut from old ships' hatches and measured about 61 cm in diameter. Like the Irish tripartite wheels, they had iron rings and revolved on their axles.

One example from Hoy had individual iron pegs serving as axles for each of the four wheels, and the pegs revolved in apertures in the framework of the vehicle (Simpson 1963.164–5).

Wheeled sledges with a pair of short runners at the back and disc wheels

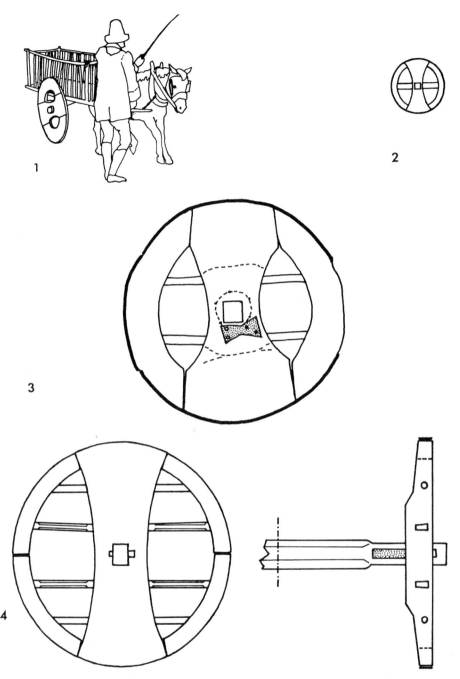

Fig. 29. Clog wheels from Northern England: 1. On a rung cart for peat, with plain lunate openings. After Walker, 1814; 2. With lunate openings and a pair of "spokes". After Tuke, 1800; 3. As 2, with two pairs of "spokes". In the Science Museum, London; 4. As 2 and 3, with four pairs of "spokes". In the Bowes Museum, Castle Barnard.

165

at the front were also in such recent use at Orphir in Orkney that they were drawn by tractors. An example of such a wheeled sledge is preserved in the National Museum of Antiquities of Scotland.

Solid wheels can also be found on peat-barrows, for example on the type used in the peat bog at Netherley, Kincardineshire. These are unshod, so that the wheels would not cut too deeply into the relatively soft ground, nor stick and slip as easily as when furnished with an iron rim.

The arrangement by which the axle and wheels turned as one was not, of course, confined to kellach and rung carts in Scotland. The *tumbrils* referred to in Angus in the early nineteenth century, had "wheels or rollers of solid wood", about 90 cm in diameter, with large wooden axles that turned with the wheels. The writer said he had seen similar ones in Northern England, and that they usually travelled in a string, like the pack horses, with the head of each horse tied to the tumbril in front (Headrick 1813.512). Further south in East-Central Scotland, it was said that *coups*, 'panniers fixed upon a sledge' had vanished everywhere in the area, surviving longest amongst the moorland people who used them for carrying dung, and that they had been replaced by *tumblers*, "a trifling species of carts which have for ages been used about Alloa for transporting coals to the shore." Their wheels were described as of "one solid piece of wood" (Ramsay 1888. II. 199–200). Another form of kellach cart was known in Gaelic as a *lòban* and in one or two Lowland dialects as a *loban*. According to Dwelly's *Illustrated Gaelic-English Dictionary*, "when peats are to be carted, the ordinary sides and ends of the cart in many districts are laid aside, and lighter ones *(lòban)* of spars or rods provided for the purpose. These had been evidently preceded by sides and ends of wicker or wattle-work".

It is possible that the kellach cart seen opposite Skye in 1867 (Fig. 26) is a *loban*. It shows the use of spoked wheels as well as solid wheels on such vehicles. There are metal hooks and fittings on the shaft that may suggest chains for attachment to the saddle and collar (? Pritchett 1867.480), in the manner of ordinary cart-harness.

Conclusion

This review of the evidence relating to aspects of pre-industrialised forms of transport in Scotland and neighbouring areas, is selective rather than comprehensive, and even within the range of subject matter dealt with, the whole of the field has not been fully covered. A number of pieces of horsedrawn equipment remain to be examined. Sledges and slipes with parallel and

166

Fig. 30. A romanticised late 19th century drawing of a rung cart with clog wheels, pulled by a horse with a wooden crook saddle and wooden hames over a collar of straw.

V-shaped runners, for transporting farm-dung, stones and other heavy loads, grass and hay were not uncommon, and examples of hermaphrodite construction with both wheels and runners are known. At the other end of the scale come the craftsman made farm carts of various shapes and sizes, with fittings of different kinds to accommodate different loads, and spoked wheels. These were being made and distributed in the late eighteenth century from several centres and their diffusion at one social level, and their subsequent local movement down the social scale is a study of some interest that should be set alongside pack-horse and slide-car transport in order to get a more rounded picture.

Transport by human beings on the back, or by means of poles and hand-barrows, of square or round wooden frames or yokes (as in water-carrying), of wheel barrows for everyday use and for special purposes like moving peat out of bogs, also requires close examination and can serve as an index to regional change and development.

So far, within Britain, it is the Irish evidence on these topics that has been most consistently published, and the complementary material from other areas, England as well as Scotland, awaits proper analysis.

167

Nevertheless, within the limited range of this present study, a number of significant factors appear. The forms of pack-saddles, creels, and panniers, of slide-cars and their wheeled equivalents, and the associated terminology, put the Scottish material firmly in a North European setting, and have a bearing on possible evolutionary processes that were already beginning to take place in the very distant past. The material has both local value, as an index to socio-economic development in relation to terrain and tradition, and general comparative and interpretative value. It throws into clear relief the fact that evolution and change are processes that rarely take place and are done with once and for all, but are subject to continual repetition, and even occasional retrogression, as the human situation and environment dictate.

Acknowledgments. Thanks are due to the many people who have helped, directly or indirectly, with this article.

Photographs have been supplied by Professor R. D. Lockhart, Hon. Curator of the Anthropological Museum, Aberdeen; by Dr. Werner Kissling; and by the School of Scottish Studies of the University of Edinburgh. Diagrams of comparative Irish material were provided by Professor E. Estyn Evans. Copies of articles otherwise unobtainable have been supplied by Dr. A. T. Lucas, Director of the National Museum of Ireland, and Dr. H. Rasmussen, Director of the Danish Folk Museum. The Gaelic terms have been checked by Mr. John McInnes, of the School of Scottish Studies. Diagrams are by Helen Jackson.

My greatest debt is due to the two great compendiums of all aspects of Scottish culture, The Scottish National Dictionary and The Dictionary of the Older Scottish Tongue, not only for etymologies, but for the range of sources pin-pointed under each entry.

Bibliography

Aberdeen, W. A Chart of the Orkney Islands. MS, *c.* 1770.
Aiton, W. *General View of the Agriculture of the County of Bute.* 1816.
Annandale, N. *The Faroes and Iceland.* 1905.
Arthur, R. Parish of Kirkmichael and Cullicudden, in *The Statistical Account of Scotland.* 1795. XIV.
Atkinson, F. and Ward, A. A Pair of "Clog" Wheels from Northern England, in *Transactions of the Yorkshire Dialect Society* 1964. XI. Pt. LXIV.
Bell, T. ed. *Records of the Meeting of the Exercise of Alford* (New Spalding Club) 1897.
Belsches, R. *General View af the Agriculture af the County of Stirling.* 1796.
Berg, G. *Sledges and Wheeled Vehicles.* Nordiska Museets Handlingar: 4. 1935.

Beveridge, E. *North Uist*. 1911.

Bulleid, A. and Gray, H. St. G. *The Glastonbury Lake Village*. 1911.

Burt, E. *Letters from a Gentleman in the North of Scotland*. 2 vol. 1759.

Campbell, J. F. *Popular Tales of the West Highlands*. 1890.

Campbell, J. L. ed. *Rev. Fr. A. McDonald. Gaelic Words ... from South Uist and Eriskay* (1859–1905). 1958.

Carr, Sir John. *Caledonian Sketches*. 1809.

Clark, J. G. D. *Prehistoric Europe. The Economic Basis*. 1952.

Cleasby, R. and Vigfusson, G. *An Icelandic-English Dictionary*. 1874.

Clerk, J. *Etchings, Chiefly of Views in Scotland MDCCLXXIII–MDCCLXXIX*. 1825.

Cowper, H. S. Some Old-fashioned Contrivances in Lakeland, in *The Reliquary* 1898. IV.

Craigie, W. A. and Aitken, A. J. *A Dictionary of the Older Scottish Tongue*. 1937.

Dieck, A. Eine Stangenschleife der Ripdorfstufe im Kreise Nienburg/Weser, in *Nachrichten aus Niedersachsens Urgeschichte* No. 28 (1959).

Dinnie, R. *An Account of the Parish of Birse*. 1865.

Djurhuus, N. ed. *J. Chr. Svabo, Indberetninger fra en Reise i Færøe 1781 og 1782*. 1959.

Donaldson, J. *General View af the Agriculture of the County of Banff*. 1794.

– *General View of the Agriculture of the County of Elgin or Moray*. 1794.

– *General View af the Agriculture af the County af Nairn*. 1794.

DOST. See Craigie, W. A. and Aitken, A. J.

Drummond, J. Notes on Ancient Shields and Highland Targes, in *Archaeologia Scotica* 1850. V.

Dunbar, J. Parish of Dyke in *The Statistical Account of Scotland*. 1798. XX.

Dwelly, E. *The Illustrated Gaelic-English Dictionary*. 1930.

E.D.D. See Wright, J.

Edgeworth, R. L. *Essay on the Construction of Roads and Carriages*. 1813.

Edmondston, T. *An Etymological Glossary of the Shetland and Orkney Dialect*. 1866.

Eldjárn, K. in *Kulturhistorisk Leksikon* 1963 VIII. s.v. *Kløv*.

Erixon, S. West European Connections and Culture Relations, in *Folk-Liv* 1938.

Evans, E. E. Some Archaic Forms of Agricultural Transport in Ulster, in W. F. Grimes, ed., *Aspects of Archaeology in Britain and Beyond*. 1951.

– *Irish Heritage*. 1958.

– *Irish Folk Ways*. 1961.

Fenton, A. Scottish Farm Carts, in *Scotland's Magazine* July 1961.

Fenton, A. and Laurenson, J. J. Peat in Fetlar, in *Folk Life* 1964. II.

Firth, J. *Reminiscences of an Orkney Parish*. 1920.

Fox, C. Sledges, Carts and Waggons, in *Antiquity* 1931. V.

Fraser, A. Parish of Kilmallie, in *The Statistical Account of Scotland*. 1793, VIII.

Fraser, J. Parish of Kiltarlity, in *The Statistical Account of Scotland*. 1794. XIII.

Fraser, W. *The Chiefs of Grant*. 1883. 3 V.

Fullarton, W. *General View of the Agriculture of the County of Ayr*. 1793.

Gaerte, W. *Urgeschichte Ostpreussens*. 1929.

Garnett, T. *Observations on a Tour through the Highlands*. 1800.

Graham, P. *General View of the Agriculture of Stirlingshire*. 1812.

Grant, A. Parish of Calder, in *The Statistical Account of Scotland*. 1792. IV.

Grant, J. Agriculture 150 Years Ago, in *Transactions of the Banff Field Club*. 1901–2.

Grant, I. F. *Highland Folk Ways*. 1961.

Grant, W. and Murison, D. *The Scottish National Dictionary*. 1929–.

Haddon, A. C. *The Study of Man*. 1898.

Hamilton, H. *Selections from the Monymusk Papers* (1713–1755). Scottish History Society. 1945.

– *Life and Labour on an Aberdeenshire Estate 1735–1750*. Third Spalding Club. 1946.

Hamre, H. Ferøers Beskrifvelser, av Thomas Tarnovius in *Færoensia* 1950. II.

Hartley, M. and Ingilby, J. *Life and Tradition in the Yorkshire Dales*. 1968.

Headrick, J. *View of the Minerology, Agriculture, . . . of the Island of Arran*. 1807.

– *General View of the Agriculture of the County of Angus*. 1813.

Heiberg, G. F. Kløvsal og Klyfberi in *Maal og Minne* 1932.

Hellemo, L. *Frå det gamle arbeidslivet* (Skrifter fraa Norsk Maalførearkiv, XII). 1957.

Henderson, J. *General View of the Agriculture of the County of Caithness*. 1812.

– *General View of the Agriculture of the County of Sutherland*. 1812.

Herring, I. The Scottish Cart in Ireland and its Contemporaries, *circa* 1800, in *Ulster Journal of Archaeology* 1944. VII.

Hibbert, Mr. A 1734 Orkney Inventory in *Proceedings of the Orkney Antiquarian Society* 1923. I.

Jamieson, J. *An Etymological Dictionary of the Scottish Language*. 1808, 1825, 1879–87.

Jansson, S. O. in *Kulturhistorisk Leksikon* 1963. VII. s.v. *Kløv*.

Jirlow, R. En lapsk Klövsadel och dess Ursprung, in *Rig* 1931.

– Das Tragen mit dem Stirnband, in *Acta Ethnologica* 1937. II.

Johnson, S. *A Journey to the Western Islands of Scotland*. 1775.

Johnston, W. A. Orkney Jottings, in *Orkney and Shetland Miscellany* 1907–8. I.

Kelly, J. *A Complete Collection of Scottish Proverbs*. 1721.

Kemp, D. W. ed. *Tours in Scotland 1747, 1750, 1760 by Richard Pococke* (Scottish History Society) 1887.

Kissling, W. Rope Harness and Horse-Covers, in *Scotland's Magazine* Dec. 1960.

– Country Creels and Baskets, in *Scotland's Magazine* April 1961.

Kothe, H. Verbreitung und Alter der Stangenschleife, in *Ethnographisch-Archäologische Forschungen* 1953. I.

Landt, G. *A Description of the Feroe Islands*. 1810.

Lane, R. H. Waggons and their Ancestors in *Antiquity* IX. 1935.

Leslie, W. *General View of the Agriculture of Nairn and Moray*. 1811.

Littlejohn, D. ed. *Records of the Sheriff Court of Aberdeenshire* (New Spalding Club) 1904. 3 V.

Lucas, A. T. A Hay-rope Pack-Saddle from County Louth in *Journal of the County Louth Archaeological Society* 1961. XV. No. 1.

McFarlane, A. Parish of Kilfinan, in *The Statistical Account of Scotland* 1795. XIV.

MacGill, W. *Old Ross-shire and Scotland*. 1909. 2 V.

MacGregor, G. *The Collected Writings of Dougal Graham*. 1883. 2 V.

Macinnes, D. Notes on Gaelic Technical Terms, in *Transactions of the Gaelic Society of Inverness* 1893–4. XIX.

Mackenzie, C. Parish of Stornoway in *The Statistical Account of Scotland* 1795. XIX.

Mackenzie, O. H. *A Hundred Years in the Highlands*. 1924.

Mackenzie, W. Parish of Assint, in *The Statistical Account of Scotland* 1795. XVI.

Mahaffy, Prof. J. P. On the Introduction of the Ass as a Beast of Burden into Ireland, in *Proceedings of the Royal Irish Academy* 1916–17. XXXIII.

McMillan, J. Parish of Torthorwald in *The Statistical Account of Scotland*. 1792. II.

Marshall, W. *General View of the Agriculture of the Central Highlands of Scotland*. 1794.

Marwick, H. *The Orkney Norn*. 1929.

Mason, T. L. *Rafford in the Past*. 1889.

Milne, J. The Making of a Buchan Farm in *Transactions of the Buchan Field Club* I. 1891.

Mitchell, A. *The Past in the Present*. 1880.

Morris, C. *The Journeys of Celia Fiennes*. 1947.

Neill, P. *A Tour through some of the Islands of Orkney and Shetland*. 1806.

Norberg, R. Om Forhistoriska Sadlar i Sverige, in *Rig* 1929. Bd. 12.

– Moor- und Depotfunde aus dem 5. Jahrhundert nach Chr. in Schonen, in *Acta Archaeologica* 1931. II.

Omond, J. *Orkney 80 Years Ago. c.* 1912.

Paterson, J. Parish of Auldearn in *The Statistical Account of Scotland*. 1797. XIX.

Piggott, S. A Tripartite Disc Wheel from Blair Drummond, Perthshire, in *Proceedings of the Society of Antiquaries of Scotland* 1956–7. XC.

– The Earliest Wheeled Vehicles and the Caucasian Evidence, in *Proceedings of the Prehistoric Society* 1968. XXXIV.

Pottle, F. A. and Bennet, C. H. *Boswell's Journal of a Tour to the Hebrides with Samuel Johnson*, LL.D. 1773. 1963.

Pritchett, R. T.? Up a Highland Glen, in *Once a Week* 19 Oct. 1867. IV (N.S.).

Ramsay, J. *Scotland and Scotsmen in the Eighteenth Century*. 2 V. 1888.

Reid, R. W. *Illustrated Catalogue of the Anthropological Museum, Marischal College, University of Aberdeen*. 1912.

Reinton, L. *Til Seters*. 1969.

Rhind, W. *Sketches of Moray*. 1839.

Robertson, H. Parish of Kiltearn, in *The Statistical Account of Scotland*. 1791. I.

Robertson, J. *General View of the Agriculture in the County of Perth*. 1799.

Roger, Mr. *General View of the Agriculture of Angus or Forfar*. 1794.

Rose, D. Parish of Dingwall, in *The Statistical Account of Scotland*. 1792. III.

Shirreff, J. *General View of the Agriculture of the Orkney Islands*. 1814.

Simpson, E. J. Farm Carts and Waggons of the Orkney Islands, in *Scottish Studies* 1963. VII.

Sinclair, J. *General View of the Agriculture of the Northern Counties of Scotland*. 1795.

Slezer, J. *Theatrum Scotiae*. 1693.

Smith, J. *General View of the Agriculture in the County of Argyle*. 1798.

SND. See Grant, W. and Murison, D.

Spence, M. A Small Farm 100 Years Ago, in *Transactions of the Banffshire Field Club*. 1889.

Spotiswood, J. *Practical Observations upon Divers Titles of the Law of Scotland commonly called Hope's Minor Practicks*. 1734.

Steinsnes, S. Klyvje- og ridesalar i Karmsund, in *Årbok for Karmsund* 1961.

Stigum, H. in *Kulturhistorisk Leksikon* 1963. VIII. s.v. *Kløv*.

Sutherland, W. Parish of Wick, in *The Statistical Account of Scotland* 1794. X.

Taylor, A. B. *The Orkneyinga Saga*. 1938.

Thom, Mr. Journal of a Tour in the North of Scotland, in *The New Agricultural and Commercial Magazine* I. No. 4. April 1811.

Thompson, G. B. Some Primitive Forms of Land Transport used in Northern Ireland, in *Ulster Folklife* 1955. I.

– *Primitive Land Transport of Ulster*. 1968.

Townshend, R. B. Indian Customs in North America, in *Customs of the World* 1913. Part XXV, Chapter XLI.

Tuke, J. *General View of the Agriculture of the North Riding of Yorkshire*. 1800.

Ure, D. *General View of the Agriculture in the County of Dumbarton*. 1794.

– Parish of Killearn, in *The Statistical Account of Scotland*. 1795. XVI.

Waals, J. D. van der. *Prehistoric Disc Wheels in the Netherlands*. 1964.

Walker, G. *Costumes of Yorkshire*. 1814.

Webster, J. *General View of the Agriculture in the County of Galloway*. 1794.

Wiklund, K. B. Die Renntierzucht, in *Folk-Liv* 1938.

Wilken, A. G. *Peter Laing, an Elgin Centenarian*. 1887.

Williamson, K. *The Atlantic Islands*. 1948.

Wright, J. *The English Dialect Dictionary*. 1898–1905.

Wood, A. Parish of Rosemarkie, in *The Statistical Account of Scotland* 1794. XI.

Die Bedeutung des Transport- und Verkehrswesens in Böhmen und Mähren im 16. und 17. Jahrhundert für die Gestaltung der Volksüberlieferung

Von KAREL FOJTÍK

In der Regel konzentriert das volkskundliche Studium des traditionellen Transport- und Verkehrswesens die Aufmerksamkeit der Forscher vor allem auf die möglichst vielseitige und gründliche Erfassung und Schilderung verschiedener bei der Beförderung von Lasten und Personen verwendeter Mittel und Geräte, auf ihre genaue Beschreibung und Klassifizierung nach den Gesichtspunkten ihrer Konstruktion, ihrer Handhabung und Anwendung, auf die Feststellung und Erläuterung aller Besonderheiten, durch welche sich diese traditionellen Mittel und Geräte in einzelnen Gebieten voneinander unterscheiden, sowie auch auf die Festsetzung der charakteristischen Merkmale, welche die "Volkstümlichkeit" einzelner Mittel und Geräte bestimmen sollen.[1] Weniger Aufmerksamkeit widmen diese Untersuchungen der Erforschung des Verkehrsnetzes: meistens begnügen sie sich mit einer Aufzählung der wichtigsten, vorhandenen Straßen und Wege, welche die untersuchte Ortschaft, das untersuchte Gebiet mit ihrer Umgebung verbinden, auf die Festsetzung der Grenzen, in welchen die Einwohner der untersuchten Ortschaft gewöhnlich verkehren, bzw. der Gelegenheiten, bei welchen sie sich in benachbarte Städte, Städtchen und Dörfer begeben. Wichtige und komplizierte Probleme bleiben dabei fast unberührt, wie z. B. das Problem der Möglichkeit einer Ausnutzung der Straßen- oder Wegeverbindungen durch einzelne Stadt- oder Dorfbewohner, des Charakters und der Intensität der Kontakte, welche auf diese Weise zwischen ihnen und den Bewohnern anderer Ortschaften zustandekommen und gepflegt werden, und der Einwirkung dieser Kontakte auf die Gestaltung einzelner Bereiche lokaler Kulturüberlieferung.

In den nachfolgenden Erwägungen wollen wir versuchen auf Grund tschechischer Urkunden und Zeugnisse aus dem 16. und 17. Jahrhundert ein unseres Erachtens wichtiges Problem, nämlich das der Beschaffenheit und Intensität des Verkehrs auf den vorhandenen Straßen und Wegen, der Möglichkeit und des Grades ihrer Benützung durch verschiedene Schichten der Stadt-, bzw. Dorfbewohner zu prüfen, sowie auch die Auswirkung dieser Momente auf die historische Gestaltung verschiedener Bereiche lokaler Kulturüberlieferung anzudeuten.[2]

172

Zu den wichtigsten Problemen zählt man in dieser Hinsicht das Problem der Bedeutung des vorhandenen Verkehrsnetzes für das Leben einzelner Gruppen der Stadt- und Dorfbewohner. Eine bloße Übersicht diesbezüglicher Urkunden und Zeugnisse aus dem 16. und 17. Jahrhundert und ihre Auswertung zeigt, daß die volkskundliche Forschung zur Lösung dieses Problems mehr Ausgangsinformationen braucht, als eine bloße, wenn auch vollständige Aufzählung der zur gegebenen Zeit vorhandenen Straßen und Wege, ihres Verlaufes und objektiven Zustandes: ihre kulturell gestaltende Wirkung beeinflußten einerseits verschiedene, die freie Wahl der Straße beschränkende Einrichtungen, z. B. zahlreiche an einzelne Städte und Städtchen erteilte Privilegien, welche die Handelsleute zwangen, mit ihrer Ware vorgeschriebene Routen zu benutzen und in genau festgesetzten Städten und Städtchen Halt zu machen, andererseits wurde ihre kulturell gestaltende Wirkung durch verschiedene Umstände, welche die Reisebereitschaft des einfachen Bürgers oder Bauern beträchtlich herabsetzten, gehemmt.

Eine große Bedeutung hatte in dieser Hinsicht ein fast allgemein schlechter Zustand der Straßen im ganzen Lande, darunter auch derer, welche die wichtigsten Zentren der weltlichen und kirchlichen Verwaltung, des inländischen und ausländischen Handels verbanden. Häufig war der Zustand einzelner Straßen so jämmerlich, daß der König gezwungen war, an verschiedene Städte und Städtchen Zoll- und Mautrecht zu vergeben mit der Verpflichtung, aus ihrem Ertrage die Wege in der unmittelbaren Umgebung der Stadt befahrbar zu erhalten. Eine noch größere Bedeutung hatten jedoch die Gefahren, welchen der Reisende unterwegs ausgesetzt wurde. Er war in einer steten Lebensgefahr seitens durchziehender oder herumstreichender Soldaten, der nicht ganzjährig gedungenen oder nach ihrer Dienstzeit „beurlaubten" und zeitweilig auf freiem Fuße stehenden Knechte,[3] der wandernden Angehörigen mancher verrufener oder entehrter Berufe, z. B. der Teichgräber oder Schafhirten. Noch mehr zu befürchten hatte er die richtigen Berufsräuber, welche in geschlossenen und gut organisierten Banden[4] selbst die Straßen in der unmittelbaren Nähe der größten Städte unsicher machten,[5] sowie auch die adeligen und nicht-adeligen "Anmelder",[6] d.h. Leute, welche noch im 16. Jahrhundert der oder jener Stadt, der oder jener Obrigkeit, ja nicht selten auch dem König „anmeldeten", eine Warnung schickten, daß sie das Unrecht, welches sie oder jemand von ihren Verwandten vor dem Stadtgericht oder durch die Obrigkeit erlitten hätten, an den Bürgern der Stadt und an den Untertanen der Obrigkeit, an ihren Personen und ihrer Habe rächen wollten, sie überall verfolgen und in Gefangenschaft nehmen würden.[7]

Neben den objektiv bestehenden Behinderungen, welche die Benützung der

Straßen und Wege erheblich erschwerten – dem schlechten Zustand der meisten Straßen und Wege, den Gefahren, welchen man unterwegs und in den einsamen Gasthäusern preisgegeben war, gab es zahlreiche und in der kulturellen Überlieferung fest verankerte subjektive Vorstellungen, welche als ebenso wirksame subjektive Behinderungen funktionierten und die Benützung bestimmter Straßen und Wege, namentlich zu bestimmten Tages- oder Jahreszeiten, dermaßen erschwerten, daß diese von einem großen Teil der Stadt- und Dorfbevölkerung gemieden wurden.

Es gab viele und mannigfaltige überlieferte Vorstellungen, deren Einwirkung auf die Gemüter so tief war, daß sie eine Straße oder einen Weg durch einen psychologischen Riegel absperren konnten. Es waren vorerst zahlreiche, dem Menschen feindlich gesinnte dämonische Wesen, deren Walten der abergläubische Dorf- und Stadtmensch namentlich in den Wäldern und an den Gewässern vermutete: so der heimtückische Wassermann, besonders gefährlich dadurch, daß er sich in verschiedene Gestalten verwandeln konnte und dem Menschen nicht nur an den Flüssen und Bächen, sondern auch im freien Felde nachstellte; das schadenfrohe Hemänchen, welches zur Nachtzeit in den Wäldern seinen Unfug trieb und – ebenso wie andere Aufhocker – den Wanderer aufschrecken, ihm jedoch auch schweren Schaden zufügen konnte; garstige, wilde Weiber, welche den Müttern ihre Kinder wechselten, und wunderschöne Feen, welche auf den Roden ihre Reigen tanzten und den Wanderer – besonders einen Jüngling – zu Tode tanzten: unberechenbare Irrlichter und Feuermänner, welche bald den Wanderer irreführten, bald ihm den richtigen Weg zeigten und beleuchteten usw. Zu ihnen gesellten sich verschiedene böse Geister, unerlöste Seelen der Selbstmörder, welche sich an jenem Platze aufhalten mußten, an welchem der Unglückliche sich das Leben genommen hatte, und die Seelen der Ermordeten, welche an der Stelle, wo der Mord geschah, ihrer Rache oder Erlösung harren; die Seelen der Hexenweiber, welche die gesegnete Erde des Friedhofes nicht aufnehmen wollte und welche nach dem Tode als Gespenster namentlich an den Kreuzwegen und Dreiwegen, wo man sie zu begraben pflegte, ihre Frevel weitertrieben, weiter die Seelen der Missetäter, welche in ihrem Leben die geheiligten Grenzsteine versetzten, usw. Der Glaube an alle diese Wesen, welcher sich in Hunderten von Sagen und Erzählungen manifestiert, war in verschiedenen Gebieten noch am Anfang des 20. Jahrhunderts in der Überlieferung so tief eingewurzelt, daß es mehreren Märchen- und Sagensammlern möglich war, unter der Bevölkerung Leute zu finden, welche beteuerten, solche Begegnungen selbst erlebt oder Erscheinungen gesehen zu haben.[8]

Die Eingliederung solcher Vermutungen in die Gesamtheit des traditionellen Systems weltdeutender Vorstellungen steigerte noch ihre einschränkende Wirkungskraft. Ihre Glaubwürdigkeit unterstützte z. B. die allgemein verbreitete feste Überzeugung von der Existenz der Wiedergänger, von der besonderen magischen Bedeutung, welche die Kreuz- und Dreiwege haben – vermöge dieser besonderen Kräfte konnten auf sie verschiedene Unheil bringende Geister gebannt werden, selbst der Teufel in seiner leiblichen Gestalt konnte hier beschwört und bezwungen werden, von der außerordentlichen Zauberkraft mancher Worte und Formeln, sowie auch andrerseits die in der volkstümlichen Überlieferung noch im 19. Jahrhundert nicht weniger verbreitete Überzeugung, daß es nicht allen Menschen gegeben ist, die Geister mit eigenen Augen zu sehen, ihre Anwesenheit zu vernehmen, sie in der Gestalt einer Katze, eines Hundes, einer Kuh oder eines Pferdes zu identifizieren, daß diese wunderliche Gabe nur die unter besonderen Umständen, z. B. an besonderen Tagen, geborene Kinder besitzen. Diese Überzeugung von der Unvernehmbarkeit der Geister durch gewöhnliche Leute verringerte im voraus die Möglichkeit, den Sachverhalt der Erzählungen über Begegnungen mit Geistern und anderen spuckhaften Gestalten auf seine Richtigkeit zu prüfen, stärkte die Glaubwürdigkeit dieser Erzählungen und Vorstellungen und den Glauben, daß es in der Umgebung Plätze gibt, an welchen es nicht geheuer ist, an welchen dem Menschen und seiner Seele immer Gefahr droht, welche daher besser zu meiden sind. Noch im 19. Jahrhundert gab es in der nächsten Umgebung zahlreicher Ortschaften viele solche sagenumwobene Plätze, welche der abergläubische Dorfbewohner zu betreten nicht wagte. Die feste Verbindung der Sagen und Memorate mit einzelnen Wegen und Straßen verursachte, daß manche Straßen und Wege namentlich für den einsam Wandernden so gut wie gesperrt waren.[9]

Die Existenz der objektiven Gefahren und Behinderungen einerseits und der vielen subjektiven Vorstellungen andererseits – gemeinsam mit der persönlichen rechtlichen Stellung namentlich der untertanen Bauernbevölkerung der Städtchen und Dörfer – bedeutete keineswegs, daß es überhaupt keine regelmäßige Verbindung zwischen einzelnen Ortschaften gegeben hat. Die Bevölkerung der Städtchen und noch mehr die der Dörfer war in mehr als einer Hinsicht auf solche wechselseitige, relativ häufige, regelmäßige und verläßliche Verbindung angewiesen, so z. B. bei der Wahl des Ehepartners – es war sehr schwierig, einen passenden Ehepartner unter den Kindern der wenigen in der Ortschaft angesessenen Familien zu finden,[10] zumal diese Familien durch zahlreiche Blut- und Wahlverwandtschaftsbeziehungen miteinander verbunden waren, wodurch die ohnehin beschränkte Auswahlmöglichkeit noch weiter eingeengt wurde.[11] Ihre Existenz bestimmte jedoch maßgebend das Gepräge dieser wechselseitigen Verbindungen und den Charakter ihrer Auswirkung auf die Gestaltung allgemeiner Umstände, unter welchen der Kulturkontakt und -austausch vor sich ging. Die Person des Vermittlers hatte für das Sich-Geltend-Machen der vermittelten Kulturmodelle eine besonders große Bedeutung.

Wenig einflußreich waren in dieser Hinsicht Personen, welche in eine andere Ortschaft einheirateten: ihre persönliche und gesellschaftliche Stellung gestattete ihnen nicht, einzelne Kulturelemente ihrer einheimischen Kulturüberlieferung zu behalten oder zu verbreiten, die Altgesessenen zwangen ihren neuen Nachbarn sich den ortsüblichen Kulturformen und -normen anzupassen; zum Konformismus mit der Umgebung wurde er übrigens von klein aufgezogen, und zu ihrer Wahrung verpflichtete er sich schon bei seiner Aufnahme in die Dorfgemeinschaft, und von dem erreichten Anpassungsgrad hing weitgehend auch sein persönliches Prestige ab. Den Kulturaustausch und -ausgleich zwischen verschiedenen ortsgebundenen Kulturüberlieferungen konnten diese einzeln eingewanderten, angesessenen Bauern nur wenig beeinflußen, und zwar auch in jenen Kulturbereichen, in welchen die traditionelle Volkskultur verschiedenen Mitgliedern der Dorf- und Stadtgemeinschaft bereitwillig wesentliche Konzessionen gewährte.[12] Ebensowenig einflußreich waren in dieser Hinsicht zahlreiche Bekanntschaften und Freundschaften, welche die Bewohner einzelner benachbarter Ortschaften bei verschiedenen Gelegenheiten schließen und erhalten konnten. Einflußreicher waren solche Ankömmlinge, wenn sie mit ihrer ganzen Familie in ein fremdes Dorf übersiedelten, wenn sie ihre relative wirtschaftliche Unabhängigkeit zu behaupten vermochten, durch eine besondere Begabung auffielen, sich auf eine Gruppe Freunde und ähnlich Gesinnte stützen konnten: sie konnten oft die mitgebrachten Kulturformen im Leben ihrer Familie, ihres Kameradschaftskreises aufrechterhalten. Die Verbindungen, welche auf diese Weise vermittelnd wirkten, wurden durch Personen zustande gebracht, welche die Altgesessenen meistens als ebenbürtig ansahen: die Tatsache, daß sie auf die kulturelle Überlieferung des Dorfes oder der Stadt nur wenig Einfluß ausüben konnten, ist darauf zurückzuführen, daß sie einerseits meistens aus den in der näheren Umgebung liegenden Ortschaften stammten, welche nur wenige und nicht auffallende Differenzen in der kulturellen Überlieferung aufzuweisen hatten, und andererseits, daß sie sich bereitwillig ihrer neuen Umgebung anpaßten. Der Zwang zum Konformismus, welchen die Dorf- oder Stadtgemeinschaft ausübte, verursachte, daß auch Besuche, zu welchen Verwandte und Bekannte von verschiedenen Ortschaften mehrmals im Jahr zusammenkamen, keine Gefährdung der Einheitlichkeit der örtlichen Kulturüberlieferung bringen konnten.

176

Mit den entfernten Gebieten außerhalb der Grenzen der feudalen Domäne und mit den großen Stadtzentren hatte die Bevölkerung der Dörfer und Städtchen meistens nur gelegentliche und einseitige Verbindung. Bedeutungsvolle Aufgaben bei der Vermittlung der Nachrichten über das Leben und die Geschehnisse in der großen Stadt und auf anderen Domänen hatten verschiedene wandernde Leute, welche ab und zu das Dorf oder das Städtchen besuchten. Die wichtigste Rolle unter ihnen erfüllten die wandernden Gesellen verschiedener Handwerke, sowohl jene, welche in dem Städtchen bei einem Zunftmeister Arbeit fanden, als auch jene, welche als freie, unzünftige Handwerker, Störer, allein oder mit der Familie von Dorf zu Dorf zogen und in den Bauernhäusern für den Bauern das Störschuster- oder Störschneiderhandwerk machten. Beide erfüllten wichtige kulturgestaltende Aufgaben: die Gesellen, welche bei dem Zunftmeister Arbeit und Unterkunft hatten, vermittelten dem Meister und anderen Handwerkern in dem Städtchen Neuigkeiten über den Zustand des Handwerkes in anderen, entfernten Städten, berichteten über die in der großen Stadt herrschende Mode, über Sitten und Bräuche des Handwerkslebens in fremden Ländern. Nicht weniger wichtige Aufgaben erfüllte auch der Störhandwerker, welcher auf dem Dorfe arbeitete, manchmal wochenlang bei einem Bauern lebte und arbeitete. In seinem Felleisen brachte er häufig verschiedenes Zubehör – eine sonst auf dem Dorfe unerreichbare Ware, silberne und goldene Häckchen, Spangen, Bänder, importierte Stoffe – mit welchen er die Kleider und Schuhe des Bauern verzierte; den Familienmitgliedern und ihren Besuchern erzählte er – mit dem Leben der Handwerksgesellen in der großen Stadt, mit ihren Bruderschaften und mit dem für diese Bruderschaften wichtigen Brauchtum vertraut – über das Leben der jungen Handwerker, über ihre Organisation und über die für das ehrenvolle Benehmen notwendigen Sitten und Bräuche, über ihre Vergnügungen. Manches in dem Gemeinschaftsleben der Dorfjugend in dem 19. Jahrhundert scheint durch diese Berichte der Störhandwerker angeregt zu werden.

Neben den zünftigen Handwerksgesellen und zunftlosen Störhandwerkern gab es auch manche andere fahrende Leute, die bei der kulturellen Vermittlung namentlich auf dem Dorfe eine nicht geringe Aufgabe erfüllten. Es waren vor allem Hirten, welche unter der Dorfbevölkerung oft jahrelang und in guten Beziehungen lebten, ohne jedoch mit ihr zusammenzuschmelzen und die Verbindung zu Hirten in der weiten Umgebung und das ausgeprägte Bewußtsein der Gruppenzusammengehörigkeit zu verlieren;[13] herumziehende Schüler und Schulmeister, welche von Ort zu Ort zogen und durch Gesang und Geigenspiel ihren Unterhalt erwarben; vazierende Jäger-, Müller- und

Malzerburschen, wegen ihrer angeblichen Hexenkünste von der Bevölkerung gefürchtet, deswegen immer bewirtet und willkommengeheissen – erwiesen sich als dankbar vor allem durch Erzählen; herumstreichende Bettler, denen auch wichtige Vermittlungsdienste von Ort zu Ort anvertraut werden konnten, da sie ihre Route durch die Ortschaften genau einhielten, usw.

Die Einwirkung der auf ihre Vermittlung zurückgreifenden Kulturelemente auf die Gestaltung des Kulturlebens der lokalen oder professionellen Gruppe konnte sich im 16. und 17. Jahrhundert nur in einem Teil der Kulturüberlieferung durchsetzen, und zwar mit verschiedener Stärke. Dabei kamen der soziale Status des Vermittlers einerseits und die Relevanz des überlieferten Kulturgutes für die Erhaltung der Stabilität der inneren Bindungen und Beziehungen in der Gruppengemeinschaft andererseits zur Geltung; am stärksten differenzierend beeinflußten sie jene additiven Bereiche der Kulturüberlieferung, welche der persönlichen Repräsentation dienen konnten, z. B. die Kleidung, weniger jene, welche in dieser Hinsicht irrelevant blieben, z. B. den Liederschatz oder das Erzählgut, den Unterhaltungstanz und die Unterhaltungsmusik, noch weniger verschiedene wirtschaftliche und weltdeutende Vorstellungen, während substitutive Bereiche der Kulturüberlieferung, z. B. Normen und Formen sozialen Verhaltens, so gut wie unberührt blieben.

1. Als »volkskundliche« werden angesehen z.B. »alle Sachen, die wir ohne Sonderberuf, nach Stoff, Form und Gebrauch schaffen, nachschaffen und anwenden können« (vgl. W. Mitzka, Volkskundliche Verkehrsmittel zu Wasser und zu Lande. In: W. Pessler (Red.), Handbuch der deutschen Volkskunde, Bd. III, Potsdam: Athenaion, s. a. (1938), S. 1).

2. Das historische, geographische und volkskundliche Schrifttum über die geschichtliche Entwicklung des Verkehrsnetzes in Böhmen, Mähren und Schlesien im 16. und 17. Jahrhundert ist nicht besonders zahlreich. Eine Zusammenfassung der Erkenntnisse über die Geschichte der Straßen in Böhmen bringt Fr. Roubík, Silnice v Čechách a jejich vývoj (Die Straßen in Böhmen und ihre Entwicklung), Praha 1938 (mit einer Landkarte und einer tabellarischen Übersicht der wichtigsten Straßenverbindungen); über die historische Entwicklung der Straßen in Mähren informiert Chr. d'Elvert, Geschichte der Verkehrsanstalten in Mähren und Schlesien (= Schriften der historisch-statistischen Sektion der k.k. mährisch-schlesischen Gesellschaft des Ackerbaues der Natur- und Landeskunde, Bd. VIII), Brünn: Nitsch 1858.

3. Diese Knechte wurden namentlich um St. Martini gefährlich: zu dieser Zeit verließen gedungene Knechte den Dienst bei den Bauern, versammelten sich für eine kurze Zeit vorwiegend in den größeren Städten und zogen dann in Scharen von Ort zu Ort, bettelnd und stehlend. Ihre Truppen waren so zahlreich und gut organisiert, daß sie auch manche befestigte Siedlung eines Adeligen plünderten. Man nannte sie "Martinkové", da sie meistens um den Tag St. Martini auftauchten.

4. Die Frau des Hauptmanns einer Räuberbande befehligte die Frauen in der Bande, organisierte auch ihre Aussendung auf Kundschaft. Die Mitglieder der Bande, welche einen verhältnismäßig genau festgesetzten Wirkungskreis gewöhnlich hatten, verständigten sich bereits im 16. Jahrhundert in einer Geheimsprache, einem Rotwelsch, z.B. den Hut nannten sie »Deckel«, den Ortsrichter »Hirt«, den Schergen »Springer«, die Goldmünze »Fuchs«, die Silbermünze »Staub«, usw.

5. Besonders gefährlich war es in der nächsten Umgebung von Prag, vor allem in den Weinbergen, in welchen sich die Räuber in den Preßhäusern aufhielten und bei den Winzern oft einen Unterhalt hatten. Von Zeit zu Zeit veranstalteten die Bürger gegen die Räuber Großfahndungen, an welchen die Bewohner mehrerer Städte teilnehmen mußten, und welche auch koordiniert durchgeführt wurden: so z.B. im Jahre 1524 die Bewohner der Städte Louny, Slaný und Žatec, im Jahre 1588 die Bewohner der Stadt Rakovník. Manche Städte errichteten für diesen Dienst gemeinsame Truppen gemieteter Soldaten, so z.B. die Bürger der Prager Altstadt, Neustadt und Kleinstadt am Anfang des 17. Jahrhunderts (vgl. Stadtarchiv Prag, Nr. 326, Fol. 116).

6. Der berühmteste unter den Anmeldern im 16. Jahrhundert war ein Adeliger Jiří Kopidlanský, welcher den Prager Bürgern die Rache anmeldete, da sie seinen Bruder ohne Gericht enthaupten ließen. Selbst der König vermochte nicht, die Prager vor ihm zu schützen (vgl. Mikuláš Dačický z Heslova, Prostopravda. Paměti (Schlichte Wahrheit. Erinnerungen), Praha: SNKLHU 1955, S. 166–167).

7. Der erwähnte Jiří Kopidlanský z.B. kam im Jahre 1508 »an jenem Donnerstag vor dem Tage der hl. Ludmila abends zum Schweinstor (in Prag) selbstdreizehnter (d.h. mit zwölf Begleitern) und behieb 6 Männer, Bürger und Instleute, als sie von den Weinbergen nach Hause gingen. In demselben Jahre am Montag vor dem Tage des hl. Wenzels brannte Kopidlanský die Vorstadt in Limburk nieder: er belog die Nachtwächter, Herr Hořický käme angeritten, und sie ließen ihn bereitwillig ein, und er schlug die Torwächter nieder und steckte die Vorstadt in Brand und lief davon. Am nächsten Tag brannte er Auwal nieder, wo unsere Prager Fußsoldaten in der Kneipe lagen« (vgl. Staré letopisy české (Alte Annalen von Böhmen), Praha: SNKLHU 1959, S. 332).

8. Vgl. z.B. in dem Riesengebirge J. Š. Kubín, Lidové povídky z českého Podkrkonoší. Úkrají východní (Volkserzählungen aus dem tschechischen Vorgebirge des Riesengebirges. Östlicher Teil). Praha: Akademie věd a umění 1926, Nr. 10, 11, 12, 30, 31, 39, 44, 48, 50, 51, 52, 53, 64, 70, 71, 72, 103, 148, 149, 150, 151, 197, 198, 199, 221, 222, 225; auf der Böhmisch-mährischen Hochebene Ig. Hošek, Nářečí českomoravské, díl II., část 2: Ukázky podřečí polnického (Bömisch-mährische Mundart, Teil II, Abt. 2: Proben der Polnitzer Untermundart [nebo des Polnitzer Idioms]). Praha: Akademie věd a umění 1905; vgl. auch Karel Fojtík, K otázce podmínek vývoje lidové kultury v 16. a 17. století (Zum Problem der Gestaltungsbedingungen der Volkskultur im 16. und 17. Jahrhundert). In: Český lid 53, 1966, S. 296 ff.

9. Vgl. dazu auch W.-E. Peuckert, Sagen. Geburt und Antwort der mythischen Welt (= Europäische Sagen, hg. von Will-Erich Peuckert: Sagen: Einführungsband). Berlin: Schmidt Verlag 1965, bes. S. 26 ff.

10. In den meisten Gebieten von Böhmen, Mähren und Schlesien hatten um 1600 kleine Siedlungen, in welchen weniger als 25 angesessene Familien wohnten, das Übergewicht. Nur in wenigen Gebieten, z.B. in Süd-Ostmähren, waren große Ortschaften zahlreicher (vgl. auch O. Placht, Lidnatost a společenská skladba českého státu v 16.–18. století (Die Bevölkerungsdichte und Gesellschaftsstruktur des böhmischen Staates im 16.–18. Jahrhundert). Praha: Akademie Verlag 1957, bes. S. 30–70; Fr. Matějek, Feudální velkostatek a poddaný na Moravě s přihlédnutím k přilehlému území Slezska a Polska (Das feudale Großgrundbesitz und der Untertan in Mähren mit Berücksichtigung des anliegenden Gebietes Schlesiens und Polens). Praha: Akademie Verlag 1959, bes. S. 234 ff.

11. Vgl. dazu Karel Fojtík, Svatba na střední a západní Moravě v 16. a 17. století (Das Hochzeitsfest in Mittel- und Westmähren im 16. und 17. Jahrhundert). In: Český lid 52, 1965, bes. S. 335 f.

12. Ihre eigene Tradition zwang sie z.B. sich der ortsüblichen Kleidung anzupassen und nicht einerseits die etwas andere Tracht ihrer Heimat zu tragen, andererseits sich nach der letzten städtischen Mode zu kleiden: nach der allerletzten Mode kleideten sich meistens nur die Scharfrichter und andere entehrte Leute.

13. Dieses Bewußtsein der Gruppenzusammengehörigkeit beruhte einerseits auf ihrem besonderen sozialen Status – ihr Beruf schloß sie als entehrte Leute aus der Gemeinschaft anderer Dorfbewohner aus, obwohl sie sich persönlicher Unabhängigkeit und Bewegungsfreiheit erfreuten, andererseits auf ausserordentlich festen, wechselseitigen Bindungen, welche sie zu anderen Hirten unterhielten und welche bei verschiedenen Gelegenheiten zutage kamen: z.B. anläßlich einer Hochzeit in der Familie eines Hirten versammelten sich alle Hirten aus weiter Umgebung, sie stellten alle Hochzeitsfunktionäre. Da sie jedoch oft ohne einen regelmässigen, wechselseitigen Verkehr waren und einander persönlich nicht kannten, somit manche Merkmale einer sozialen Gruppe nicht erfüllten, nenne ich ihre Gruppe eine Quasi-Gruppe. Vgl. dazu Karel Fojtík, Professional Groups in the Development of Folk Culture in Middle Europe. In: Man and Culture II (= Opera ethnologica 3), Praha: ČSAV 1968, S. 53–61.

Vom Holzziehen in Südtirol

Von Dr. HANS GRIESSMAIR

Im Gebirge eignet sich der Winter für den Landtransport besser als jede andere Jahreszeit. Gute Schneewege erlauben den Einsatz von Schlitten und damit eine Schonung der Zugtiere. Alles was der Bauer aus entlegeneren Grundstücken zu holen hatte, Bergheu, Streu oder Holz, wurde im Winter zum Hof gebracht.

Das Heimholen des Heues von den Bergwiesen wurde weit eifriger beobachtet und beschrieben[1] als etwa das Holzziehen; wohl nicht zuletzt deswegen, weil letzteres nicht so gefahrvoll war und auch der bäuerlichen Arbeit ferner steht. Denn soweit es sich nicht um Brennholz oder sonst kleinere Mengen handelte, besorgte es weder der Bauer selbst noch seine Dienstboten, sondern eigene Holzknechte. Diese hatten den Sommer über und bis in den Spätherbst hinein die Bäume gefällt und zu lieferbaren, meistens vier Meter langen Stämmen (Museln) zersägt, sie auch beim ersten Schnee über steile Rinnen und Riesen in gefährlicher Arbeit an die Waldwege herangetrieben. Hier blieben die Baumstämme liegen, bis die Schneeverhältnisse den Transport ins Tal möglich machten, wo dann bessere Wege den Einsatz von Pferdeschlitten gestatteten. In früheren Zeiten, ehe es Auto und Eisenbahn gab, wurden die Stämme in den Talbächen getriftet, wenn die Schneeschmelze genügend Wasser brachte.

Die mittlere Arbeitsstufe, der Transport des Holzes von den Hochwäldern herab zu breiteren Wegen und Straßen, soll hier in aller Kürze beschrieben werden. Inzwischen haben Seilbahnen und Forststraßen, die auf alle Höhen führen, den älteren Arbeitsmethoden ein Ende bereitet. Ohne ihr nachzutrauern, wird diese schwere Arbeit in ihrer letzten Blütezeit geschildert. Sie war durch die Wirtschaftslage nach dem Zweiten Weltkrieg, in der Zeit zwischen 1946 und 1955 gegeben. Ich habe genügend gewesene Holzknechte in meiner Bekanntschaft und Verwandtschaft, die von ihrer Arbeit erzählen können; allein das verwendete Arbeitsgerät verschwindet mit unglaublicher Schnelligkeit. In der genannten Zeit wurde im waldreichen westlichen Pustertal sehr viel Holz geschlagen; das brachte vielen Holzknechten Arbeit und Verdienst.

Fig. 1. Schlitten aus dem mittleren Pustertal (1971). Aufnahme H. Griessmair.

Auch die Betrachtung des hierfür verwendeten Holzschlittens[2] ergibt, daß diese Arbeit im mittleren Pustertal ausgiebiger betrieben wurde als in anderen Teilen des Landes. Das Gerät ist einfacher, zugleich auch zweckmäßiger; zwei leichtgebogene Kufen von 130 cm Länge; die Höhe der Hörner beträgt ungefähr 80 cm, die der Ladefläche 35 cm, deren Breite 80 bis 90 cm. (Zur Form des Gerätes siehe Abbildung 1.)

Gelegentlich ist auch eine drehbare Ladebank ("Reihbankl") angebracht; diese vergrößert nicht nur das Gewicht des Schlittens, das ohnehin schon an die 30 kg beträgt, sondern auch die Gefahr, in jähen Wegbiegungen die ganze Fuhre umzuwerfen. Der Schlitten mit "Reihbankl" fand dort Verwendung, wo wegen zu flachen Geländes manchmal auch ein Pferd vorgespannt werden mußte, obwohl der Halbschlitten sonst nur für menschliche Zugkraft gedacht war.

Eine eigene Form hat der Halbschlitten oder Hornschlitten im Ahrntal (siehe Abbildung 2). Auffallend ist hier: das "Reihbankl", das mit starken Eisenspitzen versehen ist, um den Baumstämmen das Rutschen zu verwehren,

182

Fig. 2. Schlitten aus dem
Ahrntal (1971).
Aufnahme H. Griessmair.

die Eisenschienen auf den Kufen, während sonst der Halbschlitten überall
unbeschlagen, "barfuß" ist, wie der mundartliche Ausdruck lautet. Noch
eigenartiger sind die zwei Kratzer, eine äußerst wirksame Bremsvorrichtung,
die sich in den Boden senkten, wenn der Fahrer die etwa 80 cm langen
Hebel anhob.[3] Alle diese Zutaten machen den Schlitten schwer, es dürften
gut vierzig kg sein; er wird auch nicht von Holzzieher selbst in den Wald
getragen, sondern von einem Pferd gezogen; bei der Talfahrt ist jedoch in
der Regel kein Pferd vorgespannt.

Wieder andere Formen hat der Halbschlitten im oberen Eisacktal und in
den westlichen Teilen Südtirols. Im oberen Eisacktal hat der Halbschlitten
bei sonst gleicher Form zwei Jöcher; ebenso im Vinschgau,[4] im Vorderpasseier
und im Ultental. Der Halbschlitten im Burggrafenamt und im äußeren Pas-

seiertal hat keine Hörner; zum Lenken dient ein Leitholz, das an der rechten Kufe befestigt ist; zum Ziehen ist ein eigenes Zugseil vorgesehen (siehe Abbildung 3).

Statt einer, sind beim Ultner Schlitten zwei Leitstangen, "Hörner" genannt, angebracht (siehe Abbildung 4); das zweite Jöchl, das beim Transport von Langholz ziemlich überflüssig ist und wohl nur zum Sitzen gut sein mag, macht diese Art von Schlitten schwerer als jene im Pustertal.

Mit wenigen Ausnahmen wurden die Halbschlitten aus Birken hergestellt. Im Hochpustertal wurden in früheren Zeiten Buchen aus Kärnten bestellt; Buchenholz wurde jedoch nur für die Kufen verwendet. Im Vinschgau nahm man Lärchenholz, wenn möglich mit gewachsener Krümmung.

Der Arbeitsvorgang selbst war überall ungefähr gleich, ebenso die übrige Ausrüstung der Holzknechte. Dazu gehörte das Bindzeug, ein gezopfter Lederstrick mit Bindekloben ("Spol") und eine lange Kette; zwanzig bis dreißig Eisenklammern, die je nach Bedarf in die Stämme eingeschlagen wurden, um die Ladung zusammenzuhalten; der "Zappin" als Gerät zum Heben und Ziehen. Besonders wichtig waren die zwei starken, zehn-bis zwölfgliedrigen Sperrketten. Alles zusammen ergab ein Gewicht von nahezu 50 kg, das der Holzknecht auf seinem Rücken den Berg hinaufzutragen hatte.

Konkret an einem viel benützten Holzweg betrachtet, sah die Arbeit so aus: Schon zwischen zwei und drei Uhr nachts brachen die Holzzieher von den Dörfern Kiens oder Mühlen (siehe Kartenskizze)[5] auf; mit der erwähnten Last auf dem Rücken benötigten sie für den Aufstieg in die Wälder am Georgenberg mindestens zwei Stunden, es war ein Höhenunterschied von ungefähr tausend Metern zu überwinden. Bei größeren Holzmengen waren nicht nur viele Holzzieher, sondern auch eigene Auflader und ein Wegmacher angestellt. Jeder "Holzer" trachtete, möglichst früh oben zu sein, um nicht zu lange warten zu müssen; auch der Ehrgeiz und die Aussicht auf einen früheren Feierabend spielten dabei eine Rolle.

Der Zieher beaufsichtigte das Beladen des Schlittens, er allein konnte abschätzen, was er seinen Kräften und seinem Gefährt zutrauen durfte. Das Binden besorgte dann jeder selbst, davon konnte Leben und Tod abhängen; gut gebunden ist halb gefahren, sagt das Sprichwort. Da es sich um Akkordarbeit handelte, wollte jeder so viel als möglich aufladen, im Durchschnitt einen Kubikmeter Holz, drei bis fünf Museln.

Die Abfahrt dauerte meistens nicht mehr als zwanzig Minuten. Der Fahrer hängte sich in den Schlitten (siehe Abbildung 5) und mit vorgestreckten Beinen rudernd und mit dem Körper gegen die Schlittenhörner drückend lenkte er die Fuhre auf abschüssigen Wegen talwärts. Wurde die Fahrt gar zu

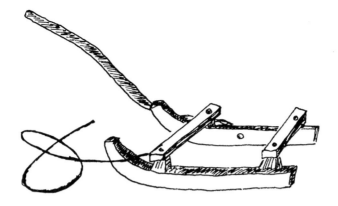

Fig. 3. Halbschlitten mit Leitholz. Zeichnung Verfasser, nach Entwürfen von M. Ladurner-Parthanes.

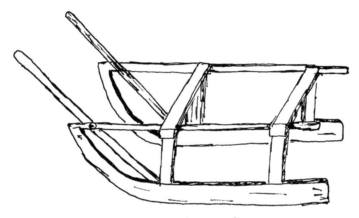

Fig. 4. Ultner Schlitten mit zwei Leitstangen. Zeichnung Verfasser.

schnell, warf er mit raschem Griff eine der Sperrketten unter die (dem Hang zugekehrte) Kufe, was sichere Wirkung tat. War die Bremswirkung nicht mehr nötig, wurde der Schlitten angehalten und die Kette mit dem Fuß unter der leicht angehobenen Kufe hervorgeholt. Zwischendurch durfte der Fahrer auch gemächlich die Füße auf die Kufen setzen, sich an die Museln lehnen und dem Gefährt seinen Lauf lassen, oder aber er mußte mit aller Kraft am Schlitten ziehen.

An gefährlichen Stellen wurden Baumstämme an den Wegrand gelegt; die Fahrbahn glich einer schmalen Rinne, aber einem Sturz in den Abgrund war dadurch vorgebeugt. Vereiste Steilstücke entschärfte der Wegmacher durch

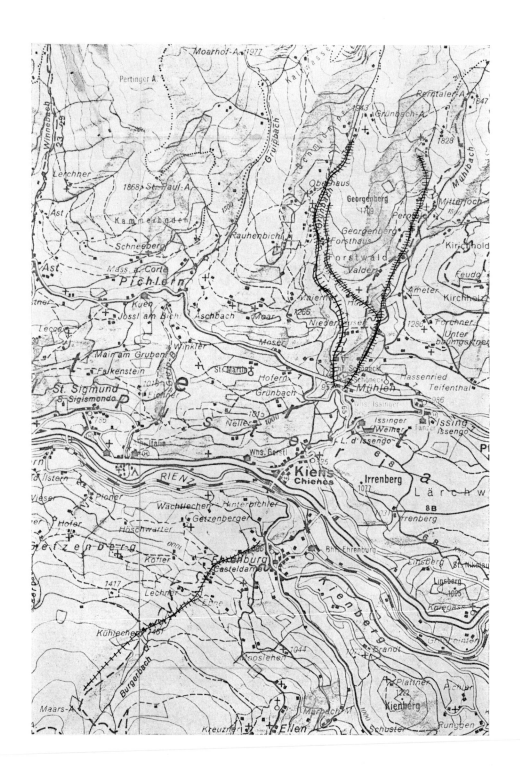

186

Fig. 5. Abfahrt mit beladenem Schlitten. Zeichnung Verfasser.

Einwerfen von Erde oder Sägemehl. Unglücksfälle waren unter zünftigen Holzziehern selten, dafür gingen immer zahlreiche Schlitten in Brüche.

In der Regel war nach zwei Fahrten das Tagwerk der Holzknechte getan. Schon gegen Mittag wurde es still auf den Wegen und Ladeplätzen. Wer nicht in Machkammer oder Werkstätte etwas an seinem Werkzeug auszubessern hatte oder unbedingt ins Gasthaus wollte, lag am warmen Ofen und holte die versäumte Nachtruhe nach. In den Stuben roch es nach feuchtem Loden und Lederzeug.

Die Holzzieher waren fast ausschließlich Selbstverpfleger; auf sie wartete kein fettes Mahl nach vollbrachter Arbeit wie bei den Bauernknechten, wenn diese vom Heuziehen heimkamen. Dafür war ihre Arbeit weitaus einträglicher; zur genannten Zeit wurde für die Fuhre ungefähr 800 Lire bezahlt; ein Holzknecht verdiente in einer Woche mehr als ein bäuerlicher Dienstbote im ganzen Monat; von einer Versicherung war freilich keine Rede. Das Holzknechtleben konnte auch sehr aufwendig sein; ein Schlitten beispielsweise kostete damals zwischen 3000 und 4000 Lire, der Wagner arbeitete daran tüchtig einen ganzen Tag.

Die Waldarbeit hat sich in kurzer Zeit grundlegend geändert. Die alten Holzwege und Ladeplätze sind nun von Jungwald überwachsen, über das morgenfrühe Treiben legt sich das Vergessen. Es geht rascher als man meint. Hier sollte nicht rückschauend harte Arbeit verklärt, sondern eine Form des Landtransports, wenngleich nur an einem winzigen Punkt der europäischen Landkarte, vorgestellt werden.

Literaturverzeichnis

1. Hermann Holzmann: Heuziehen in Tirol. In: Tiroler Heimat 20 (1956), S. 63–85; ders.: Der Bergbauer im Winter. In: Südtirol in Wort und Bild 5 (1961), S. 32–33 mit 4 Abbildungen, davon 2 zum Holzziehen im oberen Eisacktal.
   Vgl. auch: Maria Kundegraber: Vom Heutragen und Heuziehen in der Gottschee. In: Jahrbuch für ostdeutsche Volkskunde Bd. 11, Marburg/Lahn 1968, S. 62–85, mit 2 Karten und 17 Abbildungen; Franz J. Gstrein: Die Bauernarbeit im Ötztal einst und jetzt. Innsbruck 1932; Erika Hubatschek: Bauernwerk in den Bergen. Innsbruck 1961.
2. Vgl. dazu auch: Karl Haiding: Fahrzeuge des steirischen Ennsbereiches und des Ausseer Landes. In: Zeitschrift des Histor. Vereins f. Steiermark 60 (1969), S. 173–198, 61 (1970), S. 127–149; Erika Hubatschek: Zur bäuerlichen Arbeits- und Gerätekunde des inneren Stubaitales. In: Volk und Heimat, Graz 1949, S. 99–112; Viktor Herbert Pöttler: Ziehpflug, Rechenbock und Spangoaß aus Alpach. Ein Beitrag zur Arbeits- und Gerätevolkskunde Tirols. In: Tiroler Heimat, N.F. 18 (1954), S. 107–116; Hanns Koren: Altertümliche Schlitten in Steiermark. In: Zs. d. Histor. Ver. f. Steiermark 39 (1948), S. 126–136; Paul Scheuermeier: Bauernwerk in Italien, der italienischen und rätoromanischen Schweiz. Bd. I, Erlenbach-Zürich 1943, Bd. II, Bern 1956.
3. Siehe auch die Abbildung bei E. Hubatschek, Bauernwerk in den Bergen, S. 134.
4. Ich nenne besonders die Gewährsleute: Matthias Ladurner-Parthanes, Meran; Ferdinand v. Marsoner, Ulten; Josef Pardeller, Stilfs im Vinschgau; Luis Oberkalmsteiner, Sarnthein.
5. Ausschnitt aus: Kompass Wanderkarte 56, Maßstab 1:50000.

Sommerliches Nomadenzelt der allaichowschen Ewenen und Rentierschlitten-Schleppvorrichtung

Von I. S. GURWITSCH

Als wir 1951 in der Grossen Westtundra (der Nishni-Kolyma Rayon) arbeiteten, konnten wir mehrmalig die Erzählungen der Ewenen und Jukagiren hören, dass sie in der Vergangenheit, in den sommerlichen Nomadenlagern, nicht das kegelförmig-zylindrische Zelt, das Tschuora-dü, aufgeschlagen hatten, sondern eine leichtere Behausung von anderer Bauart, das sogenannte Boi. Wir hatten damals keine Gelegenheit, diese Behausung zu sehen. Laut der Erzählungen unserer nishni-kolymsker Informanten war sie vor etwa 20–30 Jahren aus dem Gebrauch gekommen. Aber im Sommer 1959 konnten wir in dem benachbarten Allaichower Rayon, in den Nomadenlagern der Jäger-Fischer am Ufer des Flusses Indigirka, fünf Kilometer von der Siedlung Oiotunga entfernt, drei Bois sehen (Abb. 1). Unsere Expeditionsroute verlief dann über den Kolyma-Kanal des Flusses Indigirka. Die Rentierzuchtbrigaden des Kolchoses "W. I. Lenin", die sich neben diesem Kanal aufhielten, benutzten auch die Nomadenzelte vom Typ Boi. Die Bauart dieser Behausung unterschied sich tatsächlich stark von der eines gewöhnlichen ewenischen Nomadenzeltes, das in der Literatur beschrieben ist.[1] Das Zelt Boi war nicht kreisrund, sondern ellipsenförmig im Grundriss. Seine Höhe ist kleiner als die des Tschuora-dü. Das Boi hat nicht einen, sondern zwei Eingänge. Das Gerüst des Boi besteht aus kurzen Stangen, den Tschuoren. Bekanntlich bilden sie die senkrechten Wände auch des gewöhnlichen, ewenischen, winterlichen Nomadenzeltes.

Die Bois, die wir sahen, hatten folgende Ausmasse im Grundriss: Längsdurchmesser – von 550 bis 670 cm, Querdurchmesser – von 480 bis 550 cm, Höhe – von 200 bis 415 cm (Abb. 2).

Das Boi wird folgenderweise aufgeschlagen: nach der imaginären Linie des Längsdurchmessers werden zwei hohe Stangen (Iruka) hineingesteckt. Die Entfernung zwischen ihnen beträgt 150–170 cm. In diesem Zwischenraum wird die Feuerstelle errichtet. Die Stangen werden im Winkel zueinander hineingesteckt, aber sie berühren sich nicht, sondern werden in der Höhe von 200–215 cm über der Erdoberfläche durch eine Querstange miteinander verbunden. Dann werden entlang der Kreislinie des Boi die Böcke

Abb. 1a, b. Sommerliche Nomadenzelten.

(von 110 bis 140 cm) aus kurzen Stangen (Tschuoras) aufgestellt. Die Tschuoras bindet man zu drei Stück zusammen: zwei Stangen werden in die Erde hineingesteckt und die dritte auf das nächste Paar Tschuoras aufgelegt und mit Riemen an der Verbindungsstelle befestigt. So werden auf den beiden Seiten der Herdstütze zwei stabile Halbringe errichtet, die aus den Böcken und den umbindenden Querstangen bestehen. Das Zentrum jedes Halbringes wird mit der Stützstange des Herdes verbunden. Diese Stützstange heisst (genauso wie die senkrechten Stangen) Iruka. Sie wird mit einem Ende an die Querumbindung und mit dem anderen – an die obere Verbindungsstange der Stütze festgemacht. Dadurch erlangt die Konstruktion des Gerüstes die nötige Festigkeit.

Als Dachdecke des Nomadenzeltes dienen zwei Bahnen aus gut zubereiteten Rentierhäuten. Diese Bahnen heissen auch Bois. Jede von ihnen wird so zugeschnitten, dass sie die Hälfte der Oberfläche des Zeltes umfasst. Der untere Rand der Bahn wird mit einem Saum aus dem enthaarten Rentierfell, dem Rowduga, oder einem festen Stoff besetzt und an diesen Saum werden in gleicher Entfernung von 10–15 cm Schlaufen angenäht. Die seitlichen Ränder jeder Bahn werden mit Riemenbändern versehen. Der obere Rand, der die Rauchöffnung umfasst, wird gewöhnlich mit einer Franse aus Rowduga besetzt. An den oberen Ecken der Bahnen werden lange Riemenbänder angenäht. Jede Hälfte der Zeltdecke wird mit Hilfe dieser Bänder an den senkrechten Stangen festgemacht, und zwar an den Stellen deren Verbindung mit

190

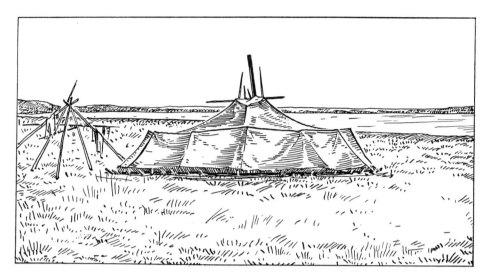

b.

der Querstange; und den unteren Rand dehnt man über das Gerüst aus. Die Schlaufen werden dabei straff gespannt mit Hilfe von Pflöcken, die in die Erde hineingesteckt werden. Die beiden Hälften der Zeltdecke werden seitlich durch die Bänder miteinander verbunden. Auf diese Weise überzieht die Decke dicht das Gerüst des Nomadenzeltes. Am Tage ist es im Zelt hell, da das Licht durch die breite Rauchöffnung durchdringt und der Sonnenschein durch die dünnen Rentierhäute durchleuchtet. Neben den Wänden werden Rentierfelle ausgebreitet – sie dienen als Liegestätten.

Zwischen den senkrechten Stangen wurde früher die Feuerstätte untergebracht. Jetzt setzen die Rentierzüchter an dieser Stelle einen eisernen Ofen mit hohem Schornstein. Über der Feuerstelle bzw. dem Ofen wird gewöhnlich an die senkrechten Stangen eine Querstange gebunden, an der eiserne Haken für Kessel und Teekessel hängen.

Das Gerüst des Sommerzeltes wird auf einer besonderen bügeleisenförmigen Rentierschlitten-Schleppvorrichtung befördert, in die ein Rentier eingespannt wird (Abb. 3).

Der Rentierschlitten stellt einen ausgehöhlten, kurzen, tiefen Trog dar, der vorne zugespitzt ist und keine Rückwand hat. Die von uns gesehenen Rentierschlitten hatten folgende Ausmasse: Länge 45–50 cm, Breite 28–33 cm, Höhe 18–20 cm, Stärke der Wände und des Bodens – 3–4 cm.

Im Rentierschlitten werden die Spitzen der Stangen festgemacht. Dafür gibt es an den Wänden vier-fünf Öffnungen, durch die die Riemen gezogen

Abb. 2a, b. Die konstruktiven Besonderheiten des Nomadenzeltes.

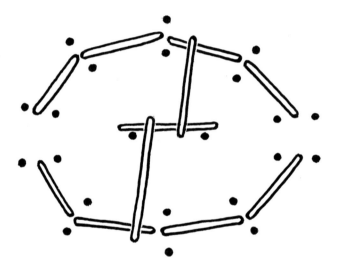

b.

werden. Die Öffnungen in dem massiven Vorderteil dienen zur Festigung des Tragriemens. Die Rentierschlitten-Schleppvorrichtung wird nur zur Beförderung des Gerüstes des Nomadenzeltes benutzt. Die Decken vom Zelt und alle ihre Sachen befördern die Ewenen als Traglast.

Es drängt sich die Frage auf, wie das beschriebene Nomadenzelt und der besondere Rentierschlitten zu betrachten sind: Ob die Sommerbehausung der allaichowschen Ewenen und Jukagiren, das Boi, eine besondere Art des Noma-

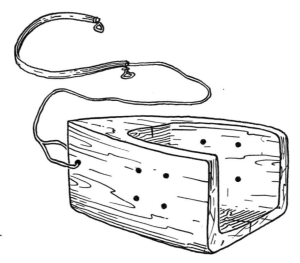

Abb. 3. Rentierschlitten-Schleppvorrichtung.

denzeltes oder eine Abart des kegelförmig-zylindrischen Zeltes Tschuora-dü
ist? Ob die Rentierschlitten-Schleppvorrichtung eine örtliche Erfindung oder
von aussen her hineingebracht ist?

Die Terminologie und die konstruktiven Besonderheiten des Nomadenzeltes Boi zeugen, unserer Meinung nach, davon, dass dieses Zelt eine örtliche,
erleichterte Sommervariante des ewenischen Nomadenzeltes ist. Es ist jedoch
möglich, dass diese Behausung irgendeine Abart des alten jukagirischen Nomadenzeltes ist, weil im XVII. Jahrhundert, zur Zeit, wo die Russen an den
Unterlauf des Flusses Indigirka gelangten, dieses Gebiet von den Jukagiren
bewohnt war.

Es ist schwer zu sagen, wie die Rentierschlitten-Schleppvorrichtung in diesem Gebiet erschienen ist. Unsere Informanten, die Greise, wiesen darauf hin,
dass solch ein Rentierschlitten von ihren Vorfahren benutzt worden war. Vielleicht erschien diese Vorrichtung für die Beförderung der Zeltstangen als
Ergebnis der Nutzbarmachung der ausgehöhlten Boote oder der alten ausgehöhlten Tröge, aus denen die Hunde in den Wirtschaften der russischen
Alteingesessenen des Indigirka-Gebiets gefüttert wurden. Zuerst hielten wir
die Rentierschlitten-Schleppvorrichtung für solch einen Trog ohne eine Wand.
Die konstruktiven Besonderheiten der allaichowischen Rentierschlitten-
Schleppvorrichtung weisen nichts Gemeinsames mit dem bekannten saami-
schen (lappländischen) Schlitten, dem Keresha auf, obwohl der Lastkeresha der
finnischen und norwegischen Saamen auch ohne Rückwand benutzt wurde und
seine Seitenwände durchgehende Öffnungen zum Durchstecken der Riemen
hatten.[2] Aber der Keresha stellte bekanntlich einen einküfigen Rentierschlitten

dar, während die allaichowsche Rentierschlitten-Schleppvorrichtung ausgehöhlt war.

Die speziellen zwei- und einstrebigen Rentierschlitten mit halbrunden Stre-
ben wurden für die Beförderung von Stangen der Tschuktschenbehausung,
der sogenannten Jaranga, benutzt. Auf diesen Rentierschlitten wurden nur
die oberen Enden der Stangen festgemacht, damit die unteren frei auf dem
Schnee geschleift werden konnten. Die Nenzen und Nganassanen beförderten
die Stangen vom Nomadenzelt auf dem zweistrebigen Rentierschlitten ohne
Belag.[3] Die Nachbarn der indigirischen Ewenen und Jukagiren, die nishne-
lensker und oleneksker Jakuten, sowie die Dolganen banden beim sommerlichen Nomadisieren in der Tundra die oberen Enden der Zeltstangen an den
Lastsessel des Rentiers, das die Karawane abschloss, und die unteren Enden
der Stangen wurden auf der Erde frei geschleift.

Also haben die Tundra-Gebiete des Nordens Eurasiens nichts aufzuweisen,
was der allaichowschen Rentierschlitten-Schleppvorrichtung ähnlich ist.

1. W. I. Jochelson. Nomadenstämme zwischen den Flüssen Indigirka und Kolyma, ihre
   ethnische Zusammensetzung, Dialekt, Lebensweise, eheliche und andere Gebräuche und
   Wechselwirkung von verschiedenen veränderlichen Elementen, »Das lebendige Alte«.
   Folgen 1–2. SPb. 1900; W. Jochelson. The Jukaghir and the Jukaghirized Tungus. The
   Jesup North Pacific Expedition. Memoir of the Amer. Mus. of Nat. His., vol. IX. Leiden-
   New York, 1926; G. M. Wassilewitsch. Ewenkisch-russisches Wörterbuch. M., 1958, S. 526.
2. T. Vuorela. The Finno-Ugric Peoples. Hague, 1964, p. 74; T. I. Itkonen. Suomen Lappa-
   laiset vuoten, 1945, Helsinki, 1948, vol. 1, p. 399, das Staatliche Museum für Ethnographie
   der UdSSR (Leningrad), Sammlung Nr. 1424, Ausstellungsgegenstand Nr. 2 – der saamische
   Lastkeresha.
3. J. A. Popow. Die Nganassanen. M.–L., 1948, s. 64–65.

Die Zugvorrichtungen bei dem zweispännigen Ackerwagen für Pferde in Skandinavien und Finnland

Von HELMUT HAGAR

Der vierräderige Ackerwagen ist in ganz Dänemark, in Schweden aber nur bis zu den mittleren Teilen des Landes verbreitet. Die approximative Grenze, welche das alte südliche Wagengebiet von dem exklusiven nordschwedischen Karrengebiet abtrennt, ist auf der Karte, Abb. 3:9 verzeichnet.[1] Die Verbreitung des Ackerwagens nördlich der angezeigten Grenzlinie ist im allgemeinen eine späte Diffusion.[2] – In Finnland ist Åland ein altes Wagengebiet. Aus dem südwestlichen Festlande sind nach einer älteren Kartierung Bruchstücke eines früheren Verbreitungsgebietes vom Ochsenwagen bekannt.[3] Eine spätere Aufnahme der Überlieferung erweist, dass der Ackerwagen (auch für Pferde) im Eigentlichen Finnland und den anschliessenden Teilen von Süd-Satakunta und Südwest-Häme verbreitet gewesen ist und noch heute vorkommt.[4] Obschon man hier teils nur eine Punktverbreitung vorfindet, die sich auf die grösseren Bauernhöfe und Gutshöfe bezieht, teils auch mit einer späten Diffusion zu rechnen hat, dürfte der Ackerwagen in diesen Teilen Finnlands doch alten Ursprungs sein.[5] Sonst wird das Land ebenso wie Nordschweden von dem zweiräderigen Karren beherrscht.[6] – Dasselbe gilt für Norwegen. Der zweiräderige Karren ist allgemein.[7] Nur der Südosten zeigt eine zerstreute Verbreitung des Ackerwagens, der auch hier verhältnismässig jungen Datums ist.[8] – Innerhalb dieses abgegrenzten Gebietes sollen nun die Zugvorrichtungen des zweispännigen Pferdewagens erörtert werden.

I

Das Material liegt kartographisch aufgenommen vor, Abb. 3.[9] Die Verbreitungskarte umfasst nur Dänemark und Schweden.

Die Karte zeigt, dass die wohlbekannte allgemeineuropäische Zugvorrichtung mit Mitteldeichsel, Waage und Strängen auch im Norden vorhanden ist, Abb. 3:7, vgl. Abb. 2:G.[10] Die lange Deichsel ist bei diesem Anspann nicht zum Ziehen, sondern nur zum Lenken und Bremsen des Wagens da. Sie wird von einer Koppel verschiedener Konstruktion getragen, welche ihr Vorderende mit dem Geschirr der Zugtiere verbindet. Diese Deichsel wird im folgenden

Koppeldeichsel und die ganze Zugvorrichtung *Waaganspann mit Koppeldeichsel* genannt.

Wir werden auf diesen Anspann noch später zurückkommen. Er ist ausser in den kartierten Gebieten auch in Finnland anzutreffen. Aber schon ein flüchtiger Blick auf die Verbreitungskarte zeigt, dass der Waaganspann mit Koppeldeichsel einheitlich nur in Dänemark vorkommt. In Schweden ist das Bild gemischt, es erscheinen auch Zugvorrichtungen, die ganz anders konstruiert sind. Gemeinsam für die letztgenannten ist, dass sie keine Koppeldeichsel besitzen. Nur zwei von ihnen sind mit der Waage, bzw. nur mit dem Waagbalken oder langem Zugholz ausgerüstet. Stränge sind überhaupt nicht vorhanden. Diese Zugvorrichtungen setzen sich aus verschiedenen Kombinationen von hölzernen Zugstangen oder auch Zugstangen und einer Deichsel ohne Koppel zusammen.

Das in Schweden übliche Pferdegeschirr, welchem die im folgenden behandelten Zugvorrichtungen angepasst sind, wird durch Abb. 1 veranschaulicht. Den Mittelpunkt des Geschirres bilden zwei grosse Eisenringe, die je einem Vorderbug des Zugtieres anliegen und alles wesentliche Riemenzeug des Geschirres aufnehmen. Die Zugkraft des Pferdes wird mittels besonderer, an den Ringen eingehängter Verbindungsglieder abgenommen. Diese werden durch die entsprechenden, an den Vorderenden der Zugstangen eingemeisselten Öffnungen hindurchgezogen und mit Hilfe von Schirrnägeln zurückgehalten. Das Geschirr ist auch in Norwegen und Westfinnland verbreitet und in Skandinavien schon in der Wikingerzeit nachweisbar.[11]

Unter den besonderen Zugvorrichtungen, die auf der Karte verzeichnet sind, scheiden wir zuerst eine Gruppe aus, für welche der Zug von den Enden der Vorderachse des Wagens aus charakteristisch ist. Es liegen vier Varianten vor, Abb. 2, A–D. Bei sämtlichen werden die beiden äusseren Zugstangen entweder durch einen ringförmigen Eisenbeschlag, oder, in gewissen Fällen, auch nur durch ein am Hinterende der Stange befindliches Loch an den Achsenenden ausserhalb der Radnaben befestigt, wo sie durch einen Querzapfen zurückgehalten werden. Die vier Varianten unterscheiden sich voneinander durch die Konstruktion der Mittelstangen, d.h. derjenigen Zugstangen, die auf der Innerseite der Pferde anzuschirren sind.

Bei der Variante A sind zwei separate Mittelstangen vorhanden, die zwischen Deichselarmen an der Mitte der Achse eingesetzt und durch einen Querzapfen befestigt werden. Es gibt auch Beispiele mit drei parallelen Deichselarmen, wodurch für je eine Zugstange ein besonderes Fach gebildet wird.[12] Zuoberst sind die Mittelstangen gewöhnlich durch ein kurzes Kettengelenk miteinander verbunden. Die Anordnungen zur Befestigung der äusseren Zug-

Abb. 1. Pferdegeschirr. Sveg, Härjedalen, Schweden. Nach Photo des Verf.

stangen werden im Detail von Abb. 4 und 5 beleuchtet. Das Loch am Hinterende der Stange ist nur aus Skåne (und überhaupt nur bei der Variante A)
bezeugt. Anstatt des hülsenförmigen Beschlages, der in ein rundes, verdünntes
Endstück ausläuft, kommt auch ein flacher Eisenring mit geradem Heft vor
(vgl. Abb. 7 und 8:a). Die Variante ist auf einem weiten Gebiet in Schweden
verbreitet, Abb. 3:1. Man könnte vielleicht behaupten, dass die Belege sich
vorzugsweise an der westlichen und nördlichen Peripherie des alten Wagengebietes anhäufen. Auf Öland und in Blekinge im Südosten existieren sie
nicht. Aus Småland sind nur zwei verstreute Belege bekannt. Ausserhalb
Schwedens kenne ich einen Beleg aus dem südöstlichen Häme in Finnland.[13]
In Norwegen kommt die Variante nicht vor, wie auch die übrigen Varianten
dieser Gruppe durch das rezente Material daselbst nicht bezeugt sind.

Bei der Variante B liegen die Mittelstangen nicht dicht aneinander, sondern
in einem gewissen Abstand von einander. An der Vorderachse befinden sich
zwei keilförmige Deichselarme, an welche die Hinterenden der Zugstangen,

197

die bei dieser Konstruktion gegabelt sind, durch einen gemeinsamen Bolzen befestigt werden. Auch hier kann sich zwischen den Vorderenden der Stangen ein Kettengelenk befinden, Abb. 6. Dies ist doch nicht immer der Fall. Es liegen Berichte vor, dass die äusseren Stangen der Zugvorrichtung beseitigt und die Mittelstangen umgewendet werden konnten, wodurch die nach aussen gerichtete Biegung derselben nach innen zu liegen kam und der Wagen als Einspänner angeschirrt wurde.[14] Soweit bekannt, sind die äusseren Zugstangen an den Achsenenden durch einen Eisenring befestigt gewesen, welcher an einer Öse am Hinterende der Stange eingehängt war.[15] Die Variante liegt nur aus einem begrenzten Gebiet in Västergötland in Schweden vor, Abb. 3:2, sonst ist sie durch das rezente Material nicht bezeugt.

Bei der Variante C besteht der Mittelteil der Zugvorrichtung aus einer langen, zwischen den Deichselarmen des Wagens eingefügten Stange, welcher eine kürzere Stange angegliedert ist. Die beiden Zugstangen werden zuoberst durch ein Kettengelenk zusammengehalten. An den Hinterenden der äusseren Zugstangen befinden sich die üblichen flachen Eisenringe, Abb. 7. Die Zusatzstange in der Mitte kann von verschiedener Länge sein. Es gibt Beispiele, wo sie viel kürzer als auf Abb. 7 erscheint,[16] aber auch Fälle, wo sie ganz an der Basis der längeren Stange ansetzt.[17] Es ist offenbar, dass die Konstruktion typologisch der Variante A nahesteht, und entwicklungsgeschichtlich von ihr hergeleitet werden könnte. Sie ist beinahe über das ganze alte Wagengebiet in Schweden verbreitet, wobei doch zu merken ist, dass sie sich im Gegensatz zur Variante A in der südöstlich-nordwestlichen Richtung orientiert, und damit auch eine zentralere Lage als diese einnimmt. Die Verbreitungsdifferenzen sind doch bei dem vorliegenden dünnen Belegmaterial eher als Tendenz wahrzunehmen. Der isolierte Beleg aus West-Värmland, weit von der alten Wagengrenze entfernt, ist nur als eine zufällige Ausnahme zu bewerten. Aus Finnland sind zwei Belege dieser Variante bekannt, von denen der eine aus Åland,[18] der andere aus dem südöstlichen Häme stammt.[19]

Die Variante D schliesslich weicht von den übrigen Varianten dieser Gruppe am meisten ab. Der Mittelteil der Vorrichtung besteht hier aus einer kräftigen Deichsel, welcher an den beiden Seiten eine Zugstange angehängt ist. Die Zugstangen sind mit der Deichsel durch Eisengelenke verschiedener Konstruktion verbunden. Ein paar Beispiele dafür bringt ausser der schematisierten Darstellung Abb. 8. Auch die Länge der Deichsel ist verschieden. Es kommen Deichseln vor, die entweder zu einem ganz kurzen Stumpf am Vordergestell des Wagens reduziert sind, oder auch genau bis zu den Vorderenden der äusseren Zugstangen reichen. In dem letztgenannten Falle sind die angegliederten Zugstangen nur ganz kurz.[20] Die Funktionsweise der Zug-

198

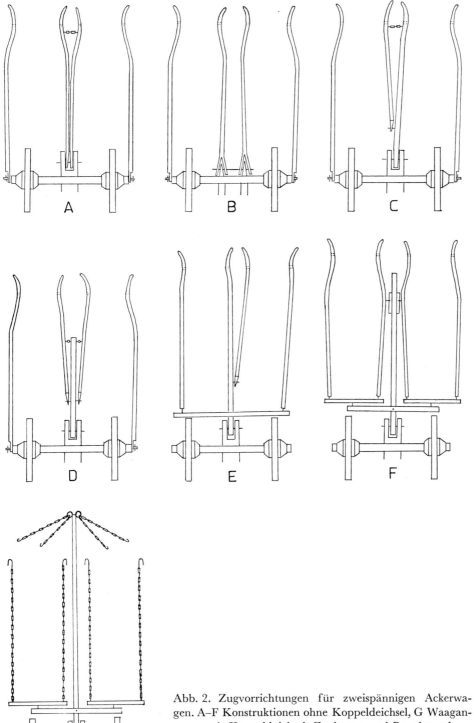

Abb. 2. Zugvorrichtungen für zweispännigen Ackerwagen. A–F Konstruktionen ohne Koppeldeichsel, G Waaganspann mit Koppeldeichsel, Zugketten und Brustkoppel.

199

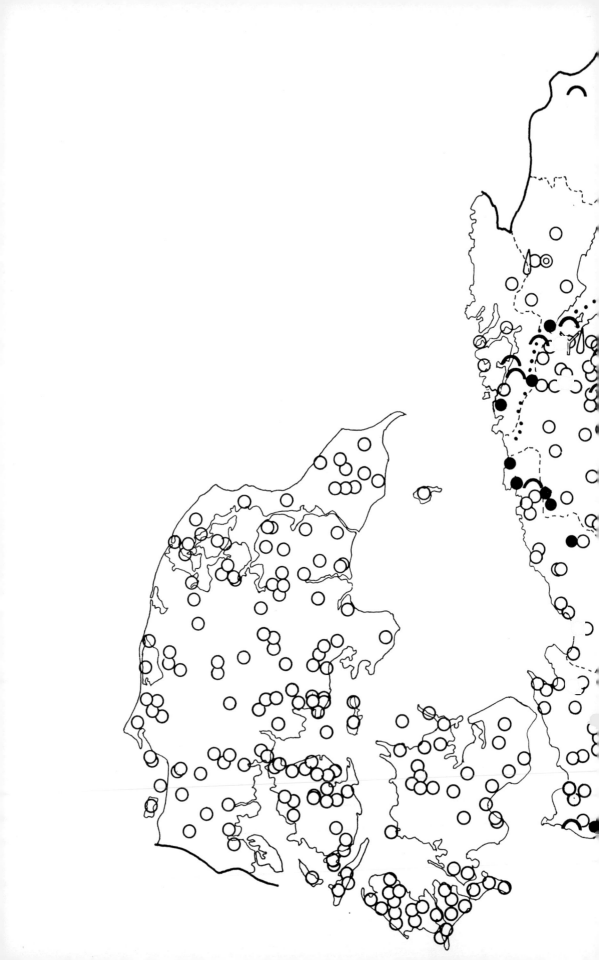

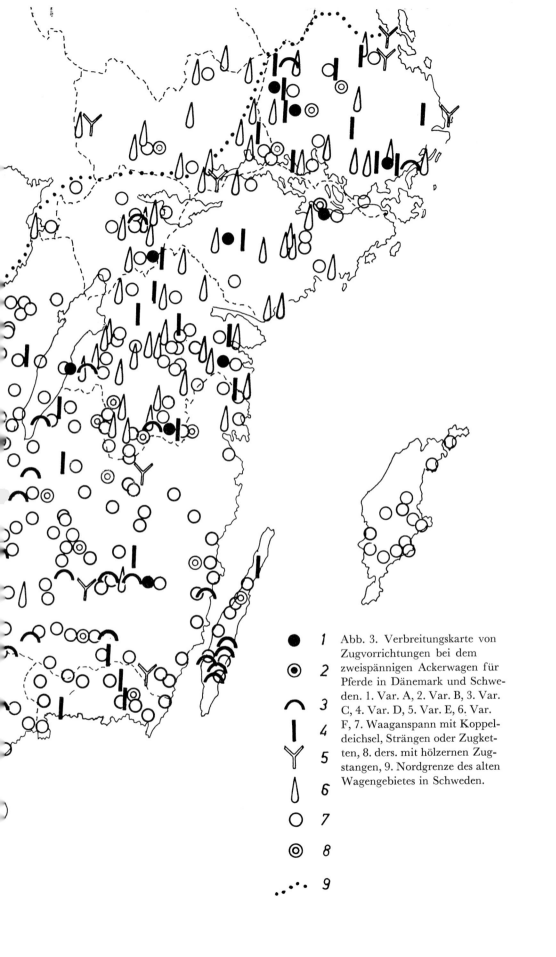

Abb. 3. Verbreitungskarte von Zugvorrichtungen bei dem zweispännigen Ackerwagen für Pferde in Dänemark und Schweden. 1. Var. A, 2. Var. B, 3. Var. C, 4. Var. D, 5. Var. E, 6. Var. F, 7. Waaganspann mit Koppeldeichsel, Strängen oder Zugketten, 8. ders. mit hölzernen Zugstangen, 9. Nordgrenze des alten Wagengebietes in Schweden.

vorrichtung bleibt doch immer dieselbe. Ein Teil der Zugkraft wird bilateral auf die Deichsel überführt. Die Deichsel selbst steht in keinem unmittelbaren Kontakt mit dem Geschirr, sondern wird von den beiden inneren Zugstangen getragen. Die Variante ist nur aus Schweden bekannt und weist hier eine weite Verbreitung in den meisten Teilen des alten Wagengebietes ausser dem äussersten Westen auf, Abb. 3:4.

Ausser der Gruppe A-D kommen noch zwei Konstruktionen ohne Koppeldeichsel vor. Keine der beiden besitzt Radnabenzug. Sie werden als E und F bezeichnet, Abb. 2.

Von ihnen besitzt die Variante E ein langes Zugholz, an dessen Enden die äusseren Zugstangen eingehakt sind. Die mittleren Zugstangen sind von derselben Konstruktion wie bei Varianten C und D. Die Zugvorrichtung wird entweder zwischen Deichselarmen am Vorgestell des Wagens befestigt, Abb. 9, oder auch an die Vorderachse eingehakt, Abb. 10 und 11. Die Variante ist ungeachtet der angedeuteten konstruktiven Verschiedenheiten durch ein gemeinsames Zeichen auf der Karte verzeichnet, Abb. 3:5. Es sind nur verstreute Belege aus Småland, Södermanland, Uppland, Västmanland und Västergötland bekannt.[21] In Finnland liegen zwei Belege von den Ålands-Inseln vor, vgl. Abb. 9.[22] Die Variante hat auch in Norwegen eine Tradition. Sie knüpft aber hier hauptsächlich an die Kutsche an, weil der Ackerwagen überwiegend einspännig gezogen wird.[23] Doch liegen einzelne Berichte über ihre Anwendung bei Lastwagen vor.[24] Die Konstruktion der Mittelstangen ist in Norwegen immer derjenigen der Variante C gleich.

Die Variante F schliesslich ist auf einer regelrechten Waage aufgebaut, Abb. 2 und 12. Es sind die Ortscheite und der Waagbalken da, doch keine Stränge, sondern vier Zugstangen, welche an den Ortscheiten angehängt sind. Auch die Funktion der Deichsel ist derjenigen des Waaganspannes gleich. Sie wird aber von keiner geschirrverbundenen Koppel getragen, sondern durch eine bilaterale Verbindung mit den inneren Zugstangen in ihrer Lage festgehalten. Zwei verschiedene Verbindungsmechanismen werden von Abb. 12 dargestellt. Noch mehrere sind vorhanden, von welchen einige schon bei den vorher behandelten Varianten vorgefunden wurden (vgl. Abb. 8 und 11). Es ist augenscheinlich, dass die Variante F Bestandteile sowohl von Varianten D-E, als auch vom Waaganspann aufnimmt, aber doch eine eigene Zugvorrichtung darstellt. Ihr Verbreitungsgebiet in Schweden ist scharf abgegrenzt, Abb. 3:6. Es umfasst den nördlichen Teil des Wagengebietes bis Småland und Mittel-Västergötland, und überschreitet überall die alte Nordgrenze dieses Gebietes. Der Schwerpunkt der Verbreitung liegt im Nordosten. In Finnland

202

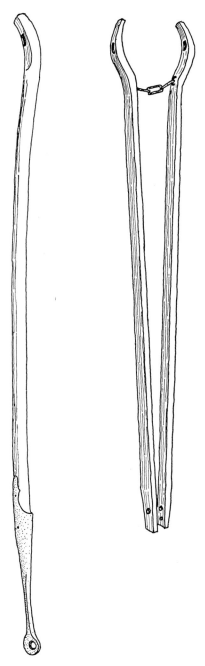

Abb. 4. Zugvorrichtung für zweispännigen Ackerwagen, Var. A. Mittelstangen und eine der beiden äusseren Zugstangen. Heimatsmuseum in Älghult, Småland, Schweden. Gez. v. Verf.

ist die Variante durch einen Einzelbeleg aus der Landschaft Eigentliches Finnland bezeugt.[25]

Was über die beschriebenen Konstruktionen hinaus vorkommt, ist nur eine Ausnahme. Aus Västergötland in Schweden wird berichtet, dass der Zug auch aus vier Einzelstangen bestehen konnte, welche, jede für sich, an das Untergestell des Wagens eingehakt wurden,[26] und aus Skåne liegt eine Skizze vor, laut welcher der Paarzug aus zwei Gabeldeichseln gebildet ist. Die Gabeldeichseln sind an einem langen Querbalken am Vordergestell des Wagens festgesetzt. – Es soll nun versucht werden, die im Norden auftretenden Zugvorrichtungen kulturhistorisch zu erfassen.

II

Der Waaganspann mit Koppeldeichsel ist in weiten Gebieten des europäischen Kontinentes allgemein. Sein Verbreitungsgebiet erstreckt sich von England über Mitteleuropa, die Alpenländer, Nordbalkan und Polen bis zum Dniepr in der südwestlichen Ukraine.[28] Im Nordwesten läuft die Ostgrenze des Verbreitungsgebietes durch Mittellitauen,[29] Westlettland,[30] berührt die kleine Schwedeninsel Runö im Rigischen Meerbusen[31] und durchkreuzt zuletzt die Insel Ösel an der Westküste Estlands.[32] Innerhalb des abgerissenen Gebietes wird, bzw. wurde, der Waaganspann mit Koppeldeichsel sowohl beim Acker- und Lastwagen als auch bei der Kutsche gebraucht. Was die kontinentale Sonderverbreitung des Anspannes nur in der letztgenannten Funktion betrifft, wird hier nicht berücksichtigt.

Es dürfte genügend bekannt sein, dass dieser Anspann mittelalterlichen Ursprunges ist. Aus verschiedenen Teilen seines kontinentalen Verbreitungsgebietes liegt altes graphisches Beweismaterial dafür in der einschlägigen Literatur vor. R. Freudenberg hat durch zeitgenössische Miniaturen die Waageinrichtung bzw. das Zugholz am Wagen bis zum ersten Drittel des 14. Jahrhunderts zurückgeführt.[33] Der älteste mir bekannte Beweis liegt durch die sogen. „korssunschen" Bronzetüren in Gross-Nowgorod vor. Bei der Himmelfahrt des Elias, die auf einer Einzelplatte der Türen dargestellt wird, ist der Zweispännerwagen mit einem langen Zugholz, Strängen und Deichsel angeschirrt. Die Türen sind bekanntlich sächsische Arbeit aus der Mitte des 12. Jahrhunderts.[34] Die vorhandenen frühen Bilddokumente weisen untereinander gewisse Konstruktionsunterschiede auf, die namentlich für die Entwicklungsgeschichte der Waageinrichtung von Gewicht sind. Die Stränge und die Koppeldeichsel sind doch überall zu erkennen. Auf einer Darstellung um etwa 1460 ist auch eine Halskoppel klar ersichtlich.[35] Derselbe Bestandteil des

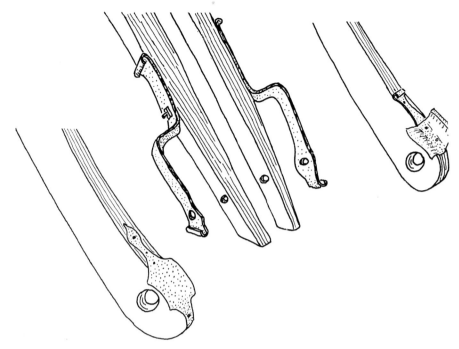

Abb. 5. Detail von Zugvorrichtung für zweispännigen Ackerwagen, Var. A. Gegend von Simrishamn, Skåne, Schweden. Österlens museum. Gez. v. Verf.

Anspannes geht aus einem Bilddokument des mittelalterlichen Englands hervor.[36]

Dem alten kontinentalen Verbreitungsgebiet schliesst sich Dänemark sowohl topographisch als auch chronologisch unmittelbar an. Ich weise hier auf die Darstellung eines bäuerlichen Leiterwagens auf der Landstrasse zwischen Kopenhagen und Roskilde aus dem 16. Jahrhundert hin,[37] sowie auf die Abbildung eines Last- oder Ackerwagens im Kataster Jacob Ulfeldts aus Holckenhavn um die Wende desselben Jahrhunderts.[38] Sprachlich ist *halskobbel* um 1576,[39] *vogn stert* 'temo' 1514,[40] *vognreb* 'rebskagle' (d.h. Wagenstrang) 1580,[41] und *hammelreb* 'skagle' (d.h. Strang am Zugholz) 1583[42] belegt. *Vognhammel* (d.h. Zugholz am Wagen) erst um 1626 sprachlich dokumentiert,[43] muss aber nach dem oben Erwähnten viel früher bekannt gewesen sein. In ein paar plattdeutsch verfassten Rechenschaften aus dem Jahre 1494 werden Wagendeichsel *(1 nige distelle to deme wagen)* und Zughölzer *(2 ortschede;* es gilt eine Wagenreise nach Berlin und Kalundborg) erwähnt.[44] Ein mittelalterliches Sprichwort: *stangh kenner hæst at draffwe*[45] deutet ohne Zweifel Waaganspann mit Koppeldeichsel an. Obwohl einige von den

205

hier vorgeführten Belegen sich auf Kutsch- oder Staatswagen beziehen mögen, kann nicht bezweifelt werden, dass der Waaganspann mit Koppeldeichsel und Strängen in Dänemark schon im Mittelalter die allgemeine Zugvorrichtung auch beim Ackerwagen war.

Ganz im Gegensatz zu Dänemark liegt das Aufkommen des Waaganspannes mit Koppeldeichsel beim Ackerwagen in Schweden noch fast überall in mündlicher Überlieferung. Eine Ausnahme bildet nur Gotland, das später besonders behandelt wird. Die Zeitgrenze variiert, übersteigt jedoch in keiner Landschaft die Mitte des vorigen Jahrhunderts. Die frühesten Angaben datieren um 1860 (Skåne, Halland, Flachlandsdistrikte Östergötlands),[46] die spätesten aus den 1890-er Jahren und sogar dem Anfang dieses Jahrhunderts (alle übrigen Landschaften, besonders Mittel- und West-Småland).[47] Diese späte Chronologie wird durch Auskunft über eine Funktionsverschiebung bei dem betreffenden Anspann ergänzt. Es wird mitgeteilt, dass derselbe früher nur bei den Kutschen des höheren Standes bezeichnend war, sich dann in derselben Funktion über grössere Höfe zu den gewöhnlichen Bauernhöfen verbreitete, und zuletzt auch Zugvorrichtung beim Ackerwagen wurde.[48] – Der Anspann mit Koppeldeichsel heisst auf schwedisch *stångsele*. Die Bezeichnung ist in den herrschaftlichen Nachlassverzeichnissen aus dem 18. Jahrhundert allgemein und wird dort immer nur mit der Kutsche oder Equipage verknüpft, fehlt aber vollständig in den bäuerlichen Inventarien jener Zeit.[49] In den letztgenannten taucht der Terminus sporadisch erst nach der Mitte des 19. Jahrhunderts auf. Es ist daraus zu schliessen, dass der Waaganspann mit Koppeldeichsel in Schweden vor etwa 1850 (in den meisten Distrikten noch viel später) ein Zeichen internationaler Standeskultur war und als Anspann bei dem herrschaftlichen Kutschwagen nur eine Punktverbreitung im Lande besass.

Es ist aus Raummangel nicht möglich, hier auf alle Einzelheiten des Waaganspannes einzugehen. Nur einiges, was die kontinental-dänische Konstruktion von der schwedisch-finnländischen unterscheidet, sei kurz erwähnt. – Anstatt der Stränge und Zugketten sind bei dem Koppeldeichselanspann in Schweden und Finnland auch hölzerne, an den Ortscheiten angehängte Stangen vorgekommen. Sie sind auf der Verbreitungskarte durch ein besonderes Zeichen angegeben, Abb. 3:8.[50] Von den zwei gewöhnlichen Koppelformen, namentlich Hals- und Brustkoppel, wird in Schweden und Finnland nur die letztgenannte gebraucht.[51] Bei der Brustkoppel fehlt der freistehende Lederriemen, der jedem Pferd über den Nacken gelegt wird und der am unteren Ende die Deichselkette trägt, sondern die Deichselkette wird hier direkt an Kummethölzer, oder, wenn Sielengeschirr gebraucht wird, am Brustblatt fest-

206

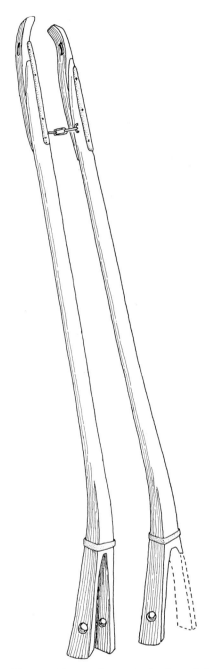

Abb. 6. Mittelstangen zur Zugvorrichtung des zweispännigen Ackerwagens, Var. B. Västergötland, Schweden. Västergötlands museum. Gez. v. Verf.

gemacht. Diese Koppelform ist entwicklungsgeschichtlich jünger als die Hals-koppel. In Dänemark wurde sie erst spät beim Ackerwagen in Gebrauch genommen.[52] Die Einrichtungen zur Befestigung der Koppelketten an die Deichsel bestehen in Schweden immer nur aus festen eisernen Ösen an der Deichselspitze, von welchen die 8-förmige Doppelöse die gewöhnlichste ist. Sie ist ursprünglich für die Kutschendeichsel bezeichnend gewesen. In Finn-land befindet sich am Deichselende oft ein kurzes Querholz, von welchem die Koppelketten oder Koppelriemen ausgehen. Das Detail rührt vom Anspann der modernen Erntemaschine her, wie von den verschiedenen Gewährsleuten ganz richtig angegeben wird.[53] Sowohl auf dem Kontinent als auch in Däne-mark hat die Koppelkette an ihrem freien Ende einen Ring, der über die Deichselspitze gestreift und von einem Zapfen oder Haken gehalten wird. Die letztgenannte Einrichtung ist in Schweden nur aus Gotland bezeugt, wo sie mit der Anwendung vom Halskoppeljoch, gewöhnlich bloss Halsjoch genannt, zusammenhängt. Man kann nicht umhin, diese wenig bekannte Form der Deichselkoppel hier etwas näher zu betrachten, weil sie bei der nordischen Chronologie des Koppeldeichselanspannes eine Rolle spielt.

Ein gotländisches Halskoppeljoch wird durch Abb. 13 veranschaulicht. Es besteht aus einem Querholz, das an Halsriemen den Pferden vor die Brust gehängt wird. Auf der Unterseite des Holzes befindet sich ein Ring, welcher über die Deichselspitze gestreift wird. Das Halskoppeljoch ist früher auf Got-land allgemein gewesen. Im Jahre 1741 wird es von Carl v. Linné als Deich-selkoppel beim Wagen beschrieben.[54] Das älteste mir bekannte Zeugnis davon ist in einem bäuerlichen Nachlassverzeichnis aus Süd-Gotland im Jahre 1680 enthalten: *Et p: Zeelar medh halßååk Betzel och tömmor Zwenglar . . .*[55] 'ein Paar Geschirre mit Halsjoch Zaum und Leinen Ortscheiten'. Ein anderes Inventar aus dem Jahre 1696 gibt die Wagenstränge an.[56] Damit ist der Waaganspann mit Koppeldeichsel für den gotländischen Ackerwagen aus dem 17. Jahrhundert direkt bewiesen.

Das Halskoppeljoch hat eine sporadische kontinentale Verbreitung und ist auch in Dänemark bekannt gewesen. In einer französischen Publikation wird es schon im Jahre 1756 als Bestandteil des Waaganspannes bei einem bestimmten Fisch- und Mehlhändlerkarren beschrieben und abgebildet.[57] Weitere Berichte über sein früheres Vorkommen sind aus dem Elsass,[58] Nau-ders am Finstermünzpass in Tirol,[59] Volhynien,[60] den Mittel-Karpaten,[61] Westfalen,[62] Holland,[63] Litauen,[64] der Insel Runö im Rigischen Meerbusen[65] und West-Ösel in Estland[66] bekannt. Wahrscheinlich ist das Halskoppeljoch mit der europäischen Kolonisation schon im 17. Jahrhundert nach Südafrika gelangt, wo es beim zweiräderigen Karren noch gegen Ende des vorigen Jahr-

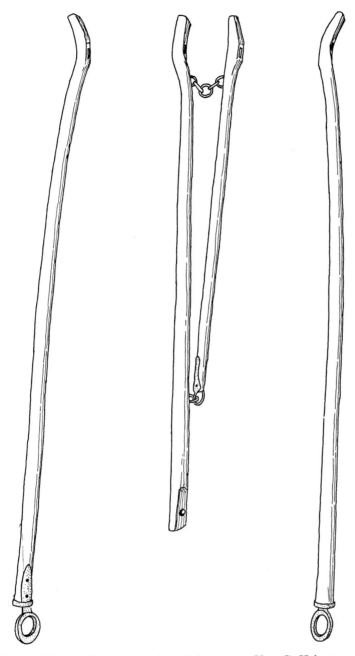

Abb. 7. Zugvorrichtung für zweispännigen Ackerwagen, Var. C. Heimatmuseum in Ölmstad, Småland, Schweden. Gez. v. Verf.

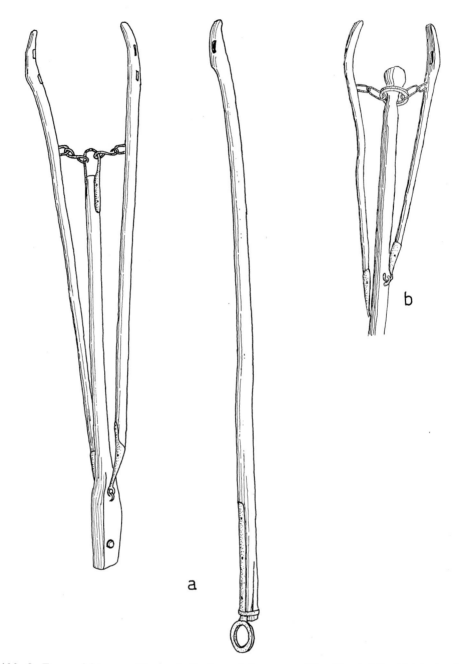

Abb. 8. Zugvorrichtungen für zweispännigen Ackerwagen, Var. D. a) Mitteldeichsel mit Zugstangen und eine der beiden äusseren Zugstangen. Sammlungen der Volkshochschule in Lunnevad, Östergötland, Schweden. b) Detail von Mitteldeichsel mit Zugstangen. Heimatmuseum in Sjösås, Småland, Schweden. Gez. v. Verf.

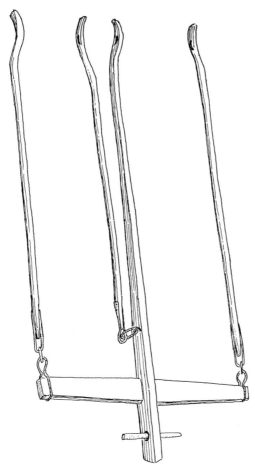

Abb. 9. Zugvorrichtung für zweispännigen Ackerwagen, Var. E. Föglö, Åland, Finnland. SLS 549: 12. Gez. nach Photo.

hunderts Anwendung fand.[67] An einigen Orten scheint es nur beim Pflügen im Gebrauch gewesen zu sein (Tirol, Volhynien, Litauen, Holland; in Groningen ist die Anwendung jedoch nicht auf diese Weise beschränkt), wobei das Holz den Pferden quer unter den Bauch gehängt wurde. Auch die früheste Nachricht vom Koppeljoch in Dänemark, die durch zwei, aus den 1750-er Jahren herrührenden Zeichnungen auf der Insel Bornholm vorliegt, stellt das Joch beim Pflügen dar. Das Gerät hing an Rückenriemen unter dem Bauche der Pferde um die lange Arldeichsel zu tragen, welche in einem Bügel auf der Oberseite des Querholzes ruhte.[68] Sonst sind mehrere Koppeljoche mit Halsriemen, aber auch hölzernen oder eisernen Halsbügeln, aus Jylland und

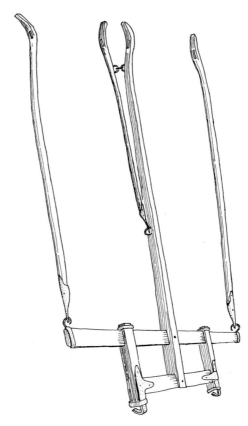

Abb. 10. Zugvorrichtung für zweispännigen Ackerwagen, Var. E. Rumskulla, Småland, Schweden. Tjustbygdens kulturhistoriska museum, Västervik. Gez. v. Verf.

Fyn in den dänischen Museen bewahrt.[69] Sie sind mit einem Ring wie auf Gotland ausgerüstet, nur ist der Halsriemen, bzw. der Halsbügel, immer an einer einzigen Öse an jedem Ende des Jochholzes festgemacht. Diese Halsjoche werden von den Museumskatalogen fast durchgehend als *studekobbel*, d.h. Ochsenkoppeln bezeichnet, und damit als Bestandteile der Ochsenanschirrung hingestellt. Es muss nun damit gerechnet werden, dass die Jochanspannung der Paarochsen wahrscheinlich auch in Dänemark, ebenso wie in Norddeutschland und Böhmen,[70] schon spätestens am Ausgang des Mittelalters durch die von der Pferdeanspannung übernommenen Ortscheite und Stränge ersetzt wurde und dass das Halskoppeljoch folglich zu den mittelalterlichen Bestandteilen der Pferdeanschirrung gezählt werden dürfte.[71] In derselben Richtung ist auch die rezente Verbreitung des Gerätes zu deuten. Die Zusammenstellung der zugänglichen Belege erweist, dass das Halskoppeljoch inner-

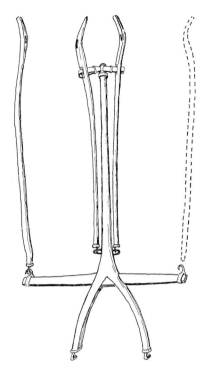

Abb. 11. Zugvorrichtung für zweispännigen Ackerwagen, Var. E. Herråkra, Småland, Schweden. Gez. v. Verf.

halb des Verbreitungsgebietes des Koppeldeichselanspannes eine Randerscheinung ist und damit vielleicht als die älteste Form der Koppeldeichsel überhaupt bewertet werden soll. Das gotländische Halskoppeljoch erhält dadurch einen Beweiswert, der den Schluss ermöglicht, dass die Insel als einziger Distrikt Schwedens sich schon im Mittelalter völlig dem kontinentalen Verbreitungsgebiet des Waaganspannes mit Koppeldeichsel anschliesst.

III

Es dürfte aus dieser Übersicht ohne weiteres hervorgehen, dass die Zugvorrichtungsvarianten A-F, welche oben beschrieben wurden, wenigstens beim Ackerwagen in Schweden älteren Ursprunges als der Waaganspann mit Koppeldeichsel sein müssen. Der Nachweis ist indes möglich, dass gewisse von ihnen bis auf das frühe Mittelalter zurückgehen.

Von den genannten Konstruktionen liegt nur die Entstehung der Variante F in der mündlichen Überlieferung. Laut einiger Berichte wurde sie erst in den 60-er Jahren des 19. Jahrhunderts in Gebrauch genommen.[72] Aus mehreren Teilen ihres Verbreitungsgebietes wird mitgeteilt, dass sie im Vergleich mit den Varianten A-E sekundär sei.[73] Sie ist als eine ganz moderne Kontaminationsform entstanden, hat in Uppland und Södermanland, teilweise auch in Östergötland die älteren Konstruktionen schon vor dem Auftreten des Koppeldeichselanspannes abgelöst und sich mancherorts bis zur jüngsten Zeit im Gebrauch erhalten. Die Konstruktion tritt auch als Fabrikware auf, wodurch die zerstreuten Belege ausserhalb ihres geschlossenen Verbreitungsgebietes zu erklären sind. – Die Entstehungszeit der Varianten A-E wird dagegen von der Überlieferung nicht erreicht. Diese Varianten werden von der mündlichen Tradition bloss als älter als der Waaganspann mit Koppeldeichsel und die Variante F bezeichnet. Nur in Mittel- und West-Småland, dem südlichen Västergötland und Närke scheint diesbezügliche Tradition ganz zu fehlen.[74] Dies dürfte daraus zu erklären sein, dass der für diese Gebiete speziell charakteristische, intensive Zugochsenhandel und die damit zusammenhängende expansive Ochsenzucht den Pferdebestand schon früh derart herabgesetzt hatten, dass in den meisten Bauernhöfen in den letzten Jahrzehnten des vorigen Jahrhunderts höchstens nur noch ein einziges Pferd gehalten wurde.[75] Das Pferd wurde dann nur vor den leichten Reisewagen gespannt, während der Ackerwagen von Ochsen mit einer Jochdeichsel gezogen wurde. Dass aber auch in diesen Gebieten, wie z. B. in Mittel- und West-Småland, die vom Koppeldeichselanspann abweichenden Zugvorrichtungen früher vorkamen, wird durch die in Museen aufbewahrten Gegenständen bewiesen. – Beweismaterial über die tiefere chronologische Kontinuität dieser Zugvorrichtungen liegt wie folgt vor.

Im Jahre 1827 wird ein Leiterwagen mit Variante A aus Südwest-Skåne abgebildet,[76] und mehrere, mit derselben Zugvorrichtung ausgerüstete Bauernwagen treten auf einer Lithographie vom Marktplatze der Stadt Lund um 1830 auf.[77] Aus Südost-Skåne wird um die Wende des 18. Jahrhunderts berichtet, dass daselbst nur Wagen mit hölzernen Zugstangen im Gebrauch waren. Es wird ausdrücklich betont, dass keine Stränge vorhanden waren, und damit höchst wahrscheinlich auf die Variante A abgezielt ist.[78] Der Radnabenzug bei dem zweispännigen Acker- oder Lastwagen geht weiter aus folgenden bildlichen Darstellungen hervor: um 1825 aus Österhaninge in Södermanland,[79] 1752 aus Kungsbacka in Nord-Halland,[80] 1707 aus Vimmerby im nordwestlichen Småland,[81] 1677 aus der Stadt Landskrona in Skåne[82] und um etwa 1450 durch ein Freskogemälde in der Kirche in Rinkaby in derselben Landschaft.[83] Zur Befestigung an die Wagenachse gibt es in Rinkaby und wahrscheinlich auch in Landskrona an dem hinteren Stangen-

214

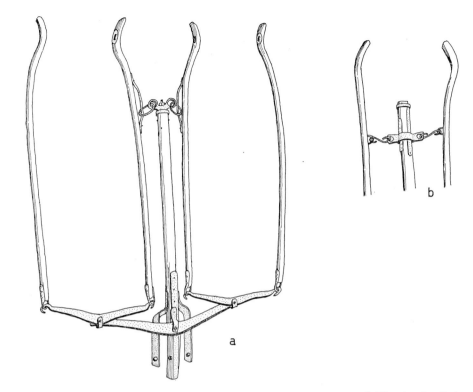

Abb. 12. Zugvorrichtungen für zweispännigen Ackerwagen, Var. F. a) Björnlunda, Södermanland, Schweden. b) Detail von Mitteldeichsel und inneren Zugstangen. Heimatmuseum in Ringarum, Östergötland, Schweden. Gez. v. Verf.

ende ein Loch. Über die Konstruktion der mittleren Zugstangen kann bei diesem Bildmaterial nicht näher entschieden werden.

In dem berühmten, ins frühe 9. Jahrhundert datierten Osebergsfund aus Vestfold in Südost-Norwegen ist ein reichlich ornamentierter vierräderiger Wagen enthalten, der Teile von seiner ursprünglichen Zugvorrichtung behalten hat. An der Vorderachse des Wagens befinden sich zwei dünne, mit Schnitzereien verzierte Deichselarme, an welchen je eine Zugstange mit gegabeltem Hinterende durch einen Querzapfen befestigt ist. Am Vorderende der Stangen ist eine rechteckige Öffnung eingemeisselt, und zuoberst werden die Stangen von einem kurzen Kettengelenk miteinander verbunden.[84] Diese Konstruktion ist mit den mittleren Zugstangen der Variante B aus Västergötland in Schweden vollständig identisch.

Die Entdeckung der Mittelstangen am Osebergswagen wird von den Wagenbildern vervollständigt, die auf den Wandbehängen aus demselben

Fund dargestellt sind. Es liegen sowohl Reise- als Lastwagen vor. Die Wagen sind zweispännig angeschirrt. Das Pferdegeschirr ist von derselben Beschaffenheit wie das oben abgebildete Geschirr aus Schweden, nur mit Ausnahme von Kummethölzern, die von einem Brustblatt ersetzt werden. Auf der Aussenseite der Pferde sieht man zwischen dem Sielenring und dem Ende der Vorderachse des Wagens einen Strich.[85] Ob dieser eine hölzerne Zugstange oder aber eine Zugleine oder Zugkette darstellt, kann nicht entschieden werden. Es steht aber ausser jedem Zweifel, dass hier ein Radnabenzug vorliegt, welcher von derselben Funktion wie bei dem vorgeführten rezenten Material ist.

Derselbe Zugvorrichtungskomplex wie in Oseberg kann auch aus dem wikingerzeitlichen Gotland bewiesen werden. Auf einem Bildstein, der aus der Kirche im Kirchsp. Alskog stammt und spätestens ins 9. Jahrhundert datiert wird, befindet sich ein zweispänniger Reisewagen, bei welchem sich eine äussere Zugstange bzw. gerade gespannte Zugleine oder Zugkette feststellen lässt, die an der Vorderachse ausserhalb des Rades befestigt sein dürfte.[86] Der Mittelteil der Zugvorrichtung gleicht der in den Stein eingehauenen Figur einer Deichsel mit gespaltenem Hinterende. Mit Rücksicht auf die Perspektive der Darstellung ist es kaum zu bezweifeln, dass hier zwei parallele Zugstangen derselben Art wie in Oseberg vorliegen.

Zur Beleuchtung der frühen Geschichte des Radnabenzuges in Skandinavien tragen noch gewisse Erdfunde aus Gotland und Skåne in Schweden sowie Fyn in Dänemark bei. Es handelt sich um eine Gruppe von flachen Eisenringen, die zuerst von Bertil Almgren als Beschläge zur Befestigung der Zugketten an den Enden der Vorderachse des Wagens interpretiert wurden.[87] Die Ringe aus Gotland sind in einem aus Schmiedezeug bestehenden, ins 11. Jahrhundert datierten Depotfund aus Mästermyr im Kirchsp. Silte enthalten.[88] Es sind zwei Paar Ringe vorhanden, von welchen je einer hier abgebildet wird, Abb. 14. Das eine Paar ist mit einfachen Ösen versehen, das andere mit geraden, spiralgewundenen Heften, welche ebenfalls in eine Öse auslaufen. Die Innenweite der Ringe misst ungefähr 5–6 cm, der äussere Diameter etwa 10–11 cm. Die Ringe sind an der Innerkante nicht voll 1 cm dick und verschmälern sich nach aussen.

Die Ringe aus den übrigen Fundorten unterscheiden sich von den gotländischen nur durch gewisse Einzelheiten. In Skåne sind zwei Paar Ringe gefunden worden, von welchen das eine aus dem Kirchsp. Lackalänga im Südwesten,[89] das andere aus Nosaby im Nordosten der Landschaft stammt.[90] Die Ringe aus Lackalänga rühren von einem Gräberfund aus dem 8. Jahrhundert her und sind mit geraden Heften versehen, deren Vorderenden

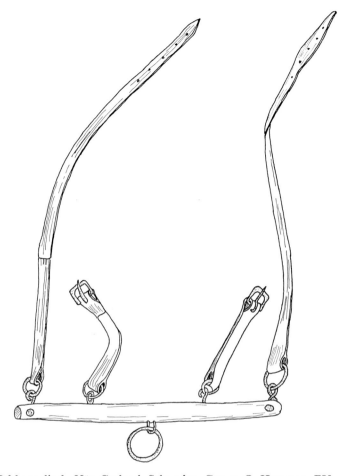

Abb. 13. Halskoppeljoch. Näs, Gotland, Schweden. Gez. v. O. Homman. EU.

hakenförmig umgebogen sind. Die Nosabyringe sind ebenso wie die gotländischen in einem Depotfund aus dem 11. Jahrhundert enthalten. An den Ösen der Ringe hängen Fragmente von Eisenketten.

Mit Eisenketten sind auch die dänischen Ringe aus den Kirchsp. Hillerslev und Søllested auf Fyn ausgerüstet. Die Ringe sind Gräberfunde aus dem frühen 10. Jahrhundert. Aus Hillerslev liegen drei Ringe mit einfachen Ösen vor. Die übrigen Beigaben bestehen hauptsächlich aus Geschirrteilen.[91] Aus Søllested gibt es zwei Ringe, welche mit einer Doppelöse zur Befestigung der Zugkette versehen sind. Die übrigen Beigaben bestehen unter anderem aus Geschirrteilen für ein Paar Pferde, unter welchen ein etwa 8 cm langer Eisen-

217

pflock mit bronzenem Tierkopf zu bemerken ist.[92] Der Vergleich mit dem rezenten Material aus Schweden und Norwegen ergibt, dass derselbe als ein Schirrnagel ausgedeutet werden muss.

Die besprochenen ringförmigen Beschläge mit daranhängenden Kettenfragmenten sind früher in Dänemark als Deichselkoppeln interpretiert worden.[93] Dieser Deutung können wir nicht länger beipflichten. In Hillerslev sind zwei pflockförmige Endstücke der Ketten vorhanden, die an dem Vorderende mit einem Querzapfen versehen sind, welche vermutlich zur Befestigung der Zugketten am Geschirr gedient haben. Der Schirrnagel aus Søllested setzt die Anwendung von hölzernen Mittelstangen etwa von der gleichen Konstruktion wie in Oseberg voraus. Andererseits ist es verfehlt, wenn B. Almgren den wikingerzeitlichen Radnabenzug mit den Verstärkungsleinen bei dem Einspännerwagen im Baltikum und in Osteuropa vergleicht, die sich zwischen den Vorderenden der Gabeldeichselstangen und Radachse ausserhalb der Radnaben befinden.[94] Die funktionelle Seite der Konstruktionen lässt einen solchen Vergleich nicht zu. Es liegt dagegen ausser jedem Zweifel, dass das vorliegende Material aus der Wikingerzeit und späten Vendelzeit mit den oben beschriebenen rezenten Zugvorrichtungen verglichen werden kann und soll. Die späte schwedische Zugvorrichtung mit Radnabenzug und Mittelstangen geht demnach bis zum 8. Jahrhundert zurück.

Dass die wikingerzeitlichen Funde den Radnabenzug mit Ketten und nicht mit hölzernen Zugstangen zeigen, macht im Prinzip nichts aus. Es soll auch in Betracht gezogen werden, dass die Kettenbeschläge, soweit es Gräberfunde betrifft, aus Bestattungen vornehmer Leute stammen. Inwieweit die äusseren hölzernen Zugstangen etwa in den alltäglichen Verhältnissen auch in der Wikingerzeit im Gebrauch waren, lässt sich nicht direkt beweisen. Wir haben oben gesehen, dass sie in Rinkaby in Skåne um etwa 1450 bei einem Erntewagen vorkamen. Schon mehr als ein Jahrhundert früher, um 1330, ist der Radnabenzug mit hölzernen Zugstangen von derselben Konstruktion wie in Rinkaby durch Miniaturen in der Wiener Nationalbibliothek bezeugt.[95] Es handelt sich um einfache Wagen mit einem viereckigen Kasten, von denen einige Einspänner zu sein scheinen. Doch ist wenigstens der eine der dargestellten Wagen zweispännig angeschirrt (fol. 145). Von der Zugvorrichtung ist nur eine der äusseren Zugstangen sichtbar, welche vorn direkt am Kummet befestigt ist. Der Anspann ist ohne irgendwelche Mittelstangen nicht als funktionsfähig vorzustellen.

Der eben angeführte Beleg aus dem mittelalterlichen Bilderbuch in Wien, sowie die Funde der Radnabenbeschläge in Dänemark aus dem 10. Jahrhundert erweisen, dass die Zugvorrichtung mit Radnabenzug und Mittelstangen

Abb. 14. Radnabenbe-
schläge aus Mästermyr,
Gotland. Sammlungen
von SHM. Photo ATA,
Stockholm.

einst allgemeineuropäisch verbreitet gewesen sein muss. R. Freudenberg
nimmt an, dass das Aufkommen des langen Zugholzes oder Waagbalkens am
Wagen (und damit auch der Koppeldeichsel und Stränge) mit der Entstehungszeit der oben zitierten Wiener Handschrift ungefähr übereinstimme,
da die Wagen vornehmlich der ersten Blätter der Handschrift ohne Zugholz,
die der letzten dagegen mit Zugholz angeschirrt seien.[96] Obschon wir oben
gesehen haben, dass der Koppeldeichselanspann beim Wagen auf dem Kontinent schon etwa zwei Jahrhunderte vor der Entstehung dieser Handschrift
bewiesen ist, ist es immerhin chronologisch bedeutungsvoll, dass die aus
Skandinavien bekannte Konstruktion noch im frühen 14. Jahrhundert konti-
nental vorhanden war.

Die in Schweden und sporadisch auch in Finnland noch bis zur Gegenwart
fortdauernden Konstruktionen mit Radnabenzug und Mittelstangen sind nach
dem oben Angeführten als die ältesten, noch bekannten europäischen Zugvor-

219

richtungen für Zweispännerwagen moderner Pferdeanschirrung zu bewerten. Geht man von der Mittelstangenkonstruktion beim Osebergswagen aus, welche mit unserer Variante B identisch ist, ist nicht mit der uralten Jochdeichsel als einem grundlegenden Bestandteil dieser Zugvorrichtungen zu rechnen. Es handelt sich dagegen augenscheinlich um einen verdoppelten, einspännigen Zug mit den direkt am Gefährt befestigten Zugstangen, welcher in Europa zuerst durch das etwa im 6. Jahrhundert aufgekommene Sielengeschirr anstatt der antiken Jochanspannung möglich wurde.[97] Der Waaganspann bzw. der Waagbalkenanspann mit Koppeldeichsel wäre demnach als eine mittelalterliche Novation aufzufassen. Unsere Variante A weicht von B nur unbedeutend ab, während die Variante C, wie schon oben angedeutet wurde, wahrscheinlich direkt von der Variante A herzuleiten ist. Erst die Variante D erweist eventuell einen konstruktiven Einfluss der Jochdeichsel, welche in Schweden beim Ochsenwagen bis zur jüngsten Zeit im Gebrauch war. Das späte Verbreitungsbild der Varianten, wie es aus der Karte hervorgeht, scheint im allgemeinen für die angenommene Entwicklungsfolge zu sprechen.

Es steht noch aus, die Variante E, welche mit einem langen Zugholz konstruiert ist, kulturhistorisch zu bestimmen. Die Variante ist in Schweden schon ziemlich früh bildlich dokumentiert: bei einem Lastwagen aus Stockholm im Jahre 1691,[98] und durch die Kalkmalereien von der Himmelfahrt des Elias in zwei Kirchen in Uppland, namentlich in Spånga etwa vor der Mitte des 15. Jahrhunderts[99] und in Dänemark gegen das Ende desselben Jahrhunderts.[100] Es ist wahrscheinlich, dass sich bei dieser Variante der Einfluss des frühen kontinentalen Koppeldeichselanspannes mit dem langen Zugholz, aber ohne Ortscheite geltend macht.[101] Ebenso deutlich ist es aber auch, dass jener Einfluss sich solchenfalls nur auf den Waagbalken beschränkt, während die Konstruktion der Zugstangen auf die älteren bodenständigen Formen zurückgeht und die Variante demzufolge eine Kontamination darstellt.

Wie schon oben erwähnt, ist die Variante E ausser Schweden und Finnland beim Kutschwagen in Norwegen im Gebrauch gewesen. Es liegt darüber eine mündliche Traditionsüberlieferung[102] sowie gegenständliches Material aus dem 18. Jahrhundert vor.[103] Auch in Schweden ist eine Zugvorrichtung mit hölzernen Zugstangen für den zweispännigen Kutschwagen durch die adligen Nachlassverzeichnisse aus dem 18. Jahrhundert und noch am Anfang des vorigen Jahrhunderts bezeugt. Die Konstruktion jener Zugvorrichtung lässt sich nicht näher bestimmen. Sie sticht aber in der Nomenklatur der Verzeichnisse vom Koppeldeichselanspann markant ab[104] und dürfte ohne ein grösseres Risiko als Variante E zu identifizieren sein. Dieselbe Konstruktion ist in Schweden vor dem Waaganspann mit Koppeldeichsel auch beim zweispännigen Arbeitsschlitten im Gebrauch gewesen[105] und wird noch gegen das Ende des 18. Jahrhunderts als normale Zugvorrichtung für gewisse zwei-spännige Ackergeräte bezeichnet.[106] Dies ist jedoch schon eine neue und ganz komplizierte Frage, worauf ich in diesem Zusammenhang nicht eingehen kann.

Anmerkungen

1. Gösta Berg, Sledges and Wheeled Vehicles. Stockholm 1935, S. 150–151 u. Abb. 46.
2. Im südl. Bohuslän doch der sogen. stockvagn von einer älteren Proveniens zum Transport von Baumstämmen u. Brettern bezeugt: Stala, IFF 17886; Torsby, NM 204960; Väster-landa, EU 4230.
3. Atlas of Finland. Helsinki 1925, Karte 23:10.
4. *Eigentl. Finnl.*: Kisko, Marttila, Mynämäki, Paimio, Paattinen, Pertteli, Pöytyä, Raisio, Sauvo, Yläne. – *Satakunta*: Huittinen, Loimaa, Köyliö, Soini, Säkylä, Tottijärvi, Vilppula. – *Häme*: Kalvola, Tammela. KMK, Antworten auf Fragebogen Nr. 6.
5. Beweise dafür aus dem 18. u. 17. Jh., vgl. Kustaa Vilkuna, Varsinaissuomalaisten kan-sanomaisesta taloudesta. Varsinaissuomen historia III:2. Porvoo-Helsinki 1935, S. 219–220.
6. Auf die verhältnismässig späte Verbreitung des Einspännerwagens in Südost-Finnland wird hier nicht Rücksicht genommen. Vgl. Atlas of Finland, a.O. und Berg. S. 156.
7. Berg, S. 110.
8. Berg, S. 156, 165.
9. Quellen. *Dänemark.* Archivsammlungen: DFM (Bildarchiv), IDD, JO, NEU. – Ein-schlägige Literatur. – *Schweden.* Archivsammlungen: EU, GMA, IFF, LLMA, LUFA, ULMA. – Gerätschaftssammlungen: Borås Museum, Göteborgs Museum, Nordiska Museet, Västergötlands Museum. Heimatmuseen: Bergets Kvarn (Halland); Gällersta (Närke); Billinge, Göinge, Loshult, Simrishamn (Skåne); Gränna, Hånger, Lenhovda, Ljuder, Markaryd, Moheda, Nässjö, Sjösås, Svenarum, Virestad, Västervik, Yxnäs, Älghult, Ödestugu, Ölmstad (Småland); Gräfsnäs, Sexdrega, Skövde, Vara (Väster-götland); Malexander, Regna, Ringarum (Östergötland). – Feldaufzeichnungen u. Photos von Verf.
10. Ich schliesse mich der Terminologie R. Freudenbergs an und brauche für das lange, am Hinterende der Deichsel angebrachte Zugholz die Bezeichnung *Waagbalken*, für die klei-nen Zughölzer *Ortscheit*, und für die drei Zughölzer insgesamt *Waage*. Rudolf Freuden-berg, Ortscheit und Waage. Hessische Blätter für Volkskunde 51/52. Giessen 1960, S. 29–61.
11. In Finnland kommen auch andere Geschirrkonstruktionen vor. Vgl. Artikel »Seldon« vom Verf. im Kulturhistoriskt lexikon för nordisk medeltid XV. 1970.
12. Västerstad, Skåne, abgeb. bei Berg, Taf. XXVIII:3; Vemmenhög, Skåne, NM 14854; Torsby, Bohuslän, NM 204960.
13. Kalvola, KMK, Frageb. Nr. 6.
14. Otterstad, Västergötland, EU 1720.
15. A.O. – Vgl. auch den Wagen aus Rackeby, Västergötland, NM 115352, abgeb. bei Berg, Taf. XXX:1.
16. Gårdby, Öland, LUFA 1220.
17. Z. B. Köla, Värmland, IFF 17844.
18. Berg, a.O., S. 162.
19. Tottijärvi, KMK, Frageb. Nr. 6.

20. Vgl. hierzu Sigurd Erixon, Skultuna Bruks historia II. Stockholm 1935, S. 101, Abb. 46.

21. Zwei von den drei Belegen aus Småland sind durch Abb. 10 u. 11 dargestellt. Der dritte aus Gullabo hat eine Mittelstangenkonstruktion wie Var. C und am Zugholze zwei nach hinten gerichtete kurze Riegel, die mit je einem horizontalen Loch zur Befestigung zwischen zwei Paar Deichselarmen versehen sind, IFF 17777. – Die Belege aus Uppland, östlichem Västmanland und Västergötland sind der Abb. 9 gleich. Über den Beleg aus südl. Västmanland nur bekannt, dass die Mittelstangen von derselben Konstruktion wie bei Var. C waren.

22. Der andere Beleg ist von derselben Konstruktion, SLS 547:645. Für diese Belege bin ich Herrn Bo Lönnqvist, Folklivsarkivet in Helsingfors, zum Dank verpflichtet.

23. Z.B. Enebakk u. Kråkstad, Akershus, NEG 438, 15548; Gol u. Nore, Buskerud, a.O. 15564, 15810; Onsøy, Östfold, a.O. 1055; Elverum, Hedmark, a.O. 15855.

24. Lom u. Spydberg, Oppland, a.O. 15427, 15503.

25. Sauvo, KMK, Frageb. Nr. 10.

26. Fors u. Gällstad, IFF 17673, 18035.

27. Stoby, LLMA 1676.

28. *England*: J. Geraint Jenkins, The English Farm Wagon. Hull and London 1961, S. 36. – *Holland*: Th. C. Oudemans, Die Holländischen Ackerwagen. Wageningen 1926, Abb. 26, 32, 35, 45. – *Deutschland*: Belege aus allen Teilen des Landes durch verschiedene Quellen erhältlich, z.B. Ostpreussen: Walter Ziesmer, Preussisches Wörterbuch II. Königsberg Pr. 1940, S. 37 (*Deichsel* u.s.w.); Photos aus Moosbruchgebiet u. Masurien, J. G. Herder-Institut, Marburg/Lahn. – Mecklenburg: Wossidlo-Teuchert, Mecklenburgisches Wörterbuch 2. Berlin 1957, Sp. 179–180. – Schleswig-Holstein: Otto Mensing, Schleswig-Holsteinisches Wörterbuch (Volksaugabe) II. Neumünster 1929, Sp. 588 (*Halskoppel*). – Niedersachsen: Kurt Heckscher, Die Volkskunde des Kreises Neustadt am Rübenberge. Die Volkskunde der Provinz Hannover I. Hamburg 1930, S. 807. – Westfalen: Archiv für Westfälische Volkskunde, Münster, Westf., 1792 (Kreis Unna); Bernhard Heiermeier, Die Landwirtschaftlichen Fachausdrücke auf Grund der Mundart des Kreises Wiedenbrück. Bielefeld 1914, S. 20, 34; Jos. Bröcker, Die Sprache des Schmiedehandwerkes im Kreise Olpe auf Grund der Mundart von Rhonard. Inaugural-Dissertation ... Berlin 1907, S. 31–32. – Rheinland: Josef Müller, Rheinisches Wörterbuch IX, Lief. 2/3. Berlin 1965, Sp. 190–191. – Pfalz: Julius Krämer, Pfälzisches Wörterbuch II, Lief. 9. Wiesbaden, Sp. 185, 189, 191 (*Deichsel, -kette, -waage, -wagen*). – Hessen: Rudolf Mulch, Südhessisches Wörterbuch I. Marburg 1965–1968, Sp. 1453–1455 (*Deichsel*). – Schlesien: Breslau, Hirschberg, Liegnitz, Ratibor, J. G. Herder-Institut, Bildarchiv 4d: 4953, 4c: 187, 4d: 8027, 4f: 302. – *Schweiz*: N. Brockmann-Jerosch, Schweizer Volksleben I. Zürich 1929, Abb. 43, 83, 322. – *Polen*: Louise Boyd, Polish Countrysides. New-York 1937, Abb. 5, 318, 353, 393, 444–445. – *Tschechoslowakei*: Ján Podolák, Pastierstvo v oblasti Vysokých Tatier. Bratislava 1967, Abb. 25, 27. – *Ungarn*: Iván Balassa, Földmünelésa Hegyközben. Budapest 1964, Abb. 76; István Balogh, A lofogatok Debreceben a XVIII–XIX. században. Etnographia LXXVII, evf. 1, Budapest 1966, S. 74–92, Abb. 27, 31. – *Jugoslavien*: Olive Lodge, Peasant Life in Jugoslavia. London [1942], Taf. zwischen S. 80–81. – *Rumänien*: Kurt Hielscher, Rumänien. Leipzig 1933, Abb. 169. – *Ukraine*: Dmitrij Zelenin, Russische (ostslavische) Volkskunde. Berlin u. Leipzig 1927, S. 131; J. G. Herder-Institut, Bildarchiv 4b: 462, 464 (Volhynien).

29. S. Bernotienė, Valstiečių sausumos susisiekimas. Lietuvu etnografijos bruožai. Vilnius 1964, S. 641, Abb. 240: 3–4.

30. A. Bielenstein, Atlas der ethnologischen Geographie des heutigen und des praehistorischen Lettlands. Beilage zu den Grenzen des lettischen Volkstammes und der lettischen Sprache in der Gegenwart und im 13. Jahrhundert. St. Petersburg 1892, Karte VI: 18. – Ders., Die Holzbauten und Holzgeräte der Letten II. Petrograd 1918, S. 562.

31. Ernst Klein, Runö. Folklivet i ett gammalsvenskt samhälle. Stockholm 1924, S. 294–295.
32. Ants Viires, Piirteitä Baltian kansojen vetojuhtien ja vetovälineiden historiasta. Kotiseutu 1965/3–4. Forssa 1965, S. 48, Karte Abb. 2, Abb. 4.
33. Freudenberg, a. O. Das auf der S. 42 genannte 13. Jh. dürfte ein Druckfehler sein. Vgl. die Zusammenstellung der Quellen S. 36–38.
34. Adolph Goldschmidt, Die Bronzetüren von Nowgorod und Gnesen. Die frühmittelalterlichen Bronzetüren II. Marburg a. L. 1932, S. 7 u. Taf. II: 26. – Vgl. auch ein Relief über dasselbe Motiv aus der zweiten Hälfte desselben Jh. bei Józef Matuszewski, Początki nowożytnego zaprzęgu konnego II. Materiały do sprawy pojawienia się zaprzęgu nowożytnego w Polsce. Kwartalnik Historii Kultury Materialnej, rok II, Nr. 3. Warszawa 1954, Taf. II.
35. Wilhelm Treue, Achse, Rad und Wagen. München 1965, S. 216 (Repr. einer allegorischen Szene von Piero della Francesca).
36. J. J. Bagley, Life in Medieval England. London 1960, S. 8. – Es ist schwer zu entscheiden, ob man hier eine Halskoppel oder Brustkoppel abgebildet hat.
37. Vort folks historie i billeder, 3. udgave. København 1955, Abb. 134.
38. Dagligliv i Danmark i det syttende og attende århundrede. Redaktion Axel Steensberg. København 1969, S. 670.
39. Otto Kalkar, Ordbog til det aeldre danske sprog I–V. København 1881–1918. V, S. 404.
40. A. O., IV, S. 855.
41. A. O.
42. A. O., II, S. 138.
43. A. O., V, S. 1182.
44. Danske middelalderlige Regnskaber. 1. Række. I. Bind. Hof og centralstyre. Udgivet ved Georg Galster af Selskabet for Udgivelse af Kilder til Dansk Historie. København 1944–1953, S. 355, 332.
45. Kalkar, a. O., IV, S. 107.
46. Z. B. Barkåkra u. Östra Broby, Skåne, IFF 28954, LLMA 2784. – Edsberga, Halland, LLMA 1702. – Ekeby, Fivelstad u. Hogstad, Östergötland, EU 3621, 2969.
47. Z. B. Småland: Gullabo u. Torsås, IFF 18678; Kalvsvik, EU 51160; Kråkshult, IFF 17749; Fryele, EU 50963. – Västergötland: Fors, IFF 17673; Gällstad, IFF 17771; Istorp, IFF 17668; Tengene, IFF 17880 u.s.w.
48. Die genannten Phasen erhellen aus Skåne: Burlöv u. Everlöv, LUFA 14909, 15043; Hörup, IFF 17812. – Småland: Kulltorp, Säby u. Älmeboda, EU 52328, 50957, 51074. – Västergötland: Husaby u. Väne-Åsaka, IFF 1144, 17983. – Östergötland: Horn, Hällstad u. Östra Ryd, IFF 17610, 17998, 18695. – Södermanland: Enhörna u. Floda, IFF 17881, 17874. – Närke: Bo, IFF 18585. – Uppland: Agarn, Film, Nora, Vittinge, IFF 17765 c, 18042, 17887, 18512. – Västmanland: Kumla EU 11359; Medåker, IFF 17843.
49. Ich nenne nur einige Beispiele: Herrenhof Tistad, Södermanland, d. 18.7.1738: *1 par gl: swarta stångsehlar*, SRA, Svea Hovrätts arkiv. Bouppteckningar. – Herrenh. Grensholmen, Östergötland, d. 9.3.1745: *1 par Stora stångsehlar med ... linor*, a. O. – Herrenh. Kåsäter, Närke, d. 4.5.1759: *1 par gamla stång selar*, a. O.-Herrenh. Hammar, Värmland, d. 12.12.1745: *1 st Stång sehlar*, Göta Hovrätts arkiv. Bouppteckningar im Jahre 1746, Nr. 4.
50. In Finnland sind die hölzernen Zugstangen vorherrschend, z. B. Eigentl. Finnland: Kisko, Paattinen, Paimio, Pöytyä, Yläne, KMK, Frageb. Nr. 6; Satakunta: Huittinen, a. O., Kokemäki, KMK, Bildarchiv 2884: 653.
51. Die Halskoppel in speziellen Fällen auch in Schweden schon früh belegt: Inventar der Schlossartillerie zu Kalmar im Jahre 1555, SRA, Smålands handlingar 1554: 4, fol. 3 v. – Auch im Jahre 1728 im Inventar des königlichen Marstalles, Stockholms slottsarkiv, hovstallet, inventarier.
52. IDD, JO.

53. Eigentl. Finnland: Kokemäki, KMK, Bildarchiv 2884: 653, Raisio, KMK, Frageb. Nr. 10, Yläne, a.O., Frageb. Nr. 6; Satakunta: Säkylä, a.O.
54. Carl von Linnés Gotländska Resa förrättad 1741. Stockholm 1958, S. 17.
55. Landsarkiv in Visby, Gotlands Södra domsaga. Bouppteckningar 1680–1750, Nr. 1.
56. *Rep til 3 wagnar.* A.O., Gotlands Norra domsaga. Bouppteckningar 1644–1700, Nr. 46 b.
57. [de Garsault], Traité des voitures, pour servir de supplement au nouveau parfait maréchal. Paris 1756, S. 40–42, Taf. VII: B–C.
58. Johann Christian Ginzrot, Die Wägen und Fuhrwerke der Griechen und Römer und anderen alten Völker; nebst der Bespannung, Zäumung und Verzierung ihrer Zug- Reit- und Last-Tiere I. München 1817, S. 54.
59. R. Braungart, Uralter Ackerbau im Alpenlande und seine urgeschichtlich-ethnographischen und anthropologischen Beziehungen. Landwirtschaftliche Jahrbücher, Bd. 26. Berlin 1897, S. 24. – Vgl. auch ders., Die Südgermanen. Heidelberg 1914, S. 193.
60. Kazimierz Moszyński, Kultura ludova Słowian I. Kraków 1929, Abb. 528: 10.
61. Jan Falkowski – Bazyli Pasznycki, Na Pograniczu Łemkowsko – Bojkowskim Zarys etnograficzny. Lwow 1935. Prace Etnograficzne. Wydawnictwo Towarzystwa Ludoznawczego we Lwowie Nr. 2, S. 71, Abb. VIII: 4.
62. Kreis Lingen: »halsol ... eiserne oder hölzerne Stange mit einem Bügel, in dem die Deichsel ruht«. Aloys Beestermöller, Technische landwirtschaftliche Ausdrücke aus dem Kreise Lingen. Inauguraldissertation ... 1916, S. 83. Manuskript, Volkskundliche Kommission, Abt. Mundart- und Namenforschung, Münster, Westf. – Kreis Lübecke: »Halsdragen oder Halskoppel ist das Halsjoch, das unten den Koppelbaum trägt.« A.O., Archiv des Westfälischen Wörterbuches.
63. Ginzrot, a.O. – K. Ter Laan, Nieuw Groninger Woordenboek. Tweede druk. Groningen – Djakarta 1952, S. 288.
64. Symeon Ławrynowicz, O rolnictwe powiatu Kowieńskiego w Gubernii Wileńskiey. Dziennik Wileński. Tom I, Numer 6. Wilno 1819, S. 650, Abb. 2, E. – Für den Quellenhinweis bin ich Herrn A. Viires, Tallinn, zum Dank verplichtet.
65. Klein, a.O., S. 295.
66. Viires, a.O., Abb. 4.
67. John Philipson, Harness: As it has been, as it is, and as it should be ... with Remarks on Traction, and the Use of the Cape Cart. Newcastle-on-Tyne 1882, S. 49–54, Taf. XV, XVII–XVIII.
68. Peter Michelsen, Den sjællandske krog. Budstikken 1958, Abb. 3 u. 4. Vgl. auch Abb. 15, welche dieselbe Einrichtung aus den 1880-er Jahren darstellt.
69. Landbrugsmuseet, Lyngby: 1596, 1598, 1599, 1600, 11556. – DFM: 562/1956, 632/1938. – Herning Museum: 188/38, 110/57. – Vendsyssels Historiske Museum: 10192.
70. J. Kramařík, Zur Frage der Rinderanspannung bei den Westslawen. Origine et débuts des Slaves VI. Prague 1966, S. 329–331. – Vgl. hierzu Wolfgang Jacobeit, Jochgeschirr- und Spanntiergrenze. Deutsches Jahrbuch für Volkskunde. Dritter Band, Teil I. Berlin 1957, S. 119–144.
71. Das Halskoppeljoch mit Halsriemen derselben Konstruktion wie in Dänemark beim Ochsengespann auch aus Bissendorf, Niedersachsen, belegt. Bildarchiv des Niedersächsischen Heimatmuseums in Hannover. – Das Paarjoch durch die dänischen Museumssammlungen ausser den bekannten jütländischen Moorfunden nicht belegt. Ein Widerristjoch von der Insel Als (DFM 581/1940) ist eine zufällige Ausnahme und wahrscheinlich ein später Import aus Schweden.
72. Lillkyrka, Uppland, EU 4066. – Vgl. auch Erixon, a.O., S. 101.
73. Z.B. Enhörna, Södermanland, IFF 17866; Hällestad, Östergötland, IFF 17998 u.s.w.
74. Belege in Sammlungen von EU, IFF u. LUFA.
75. Helmut Hagar, Bidrag till dragoxhandelns historia i Sverige. Folk-Liv 1966, S. 23–31. –

Rezente Angaben betr. Pferde- und Ochsenbestand in EU u. IFF. Der Pferdebestand besonders in West-Småland schon am Ende des ersten Drittels des 17. Jh. sehr herabgesetzt. SRA, Steuerverlangungslisten über Vieh- u. Pferdebestand.

76. C. Forsell, Ett år i Sverige. Stockholm 1827, Torna härad. IV.

77. Hans Wåhlin, Scania antiqua. Malmö 1931, Abb. 97.

78. Nils G. Bruzelius, Allmogelifwet i Ingelstads Härad i Skåne under slutet af förra och början af detta århundrade. Malmö 1876, S. 46.

79. Harry Runqvist, Österhaninge socken. Södermanlands hembygdsförbunds sockenbeskrivningar för hembygdsundervisning nr. 16. Nyköping 1961, S. 40–41.

80. Jacob Richardson, Hallandia antiqua & hodierna I. Stockholm 1752, Taf. II.

81. E. Dahlberg, Svecia antiqua et hodierna. Stockholm 1924, III: 82.

82. Wåhlin, a.O., Abb. 31.

83. Sture Bolin, Skånelands historia II. Lund 1933, S. 51, Abb. 20.

84. Sigurd Grieg, Osebergsfundet II. Oslo 1928, Taf. I u. S. 21–23.

85. Wilhelm Holmqvist, Germanic Art during the First Millennium A.D. Lund 1955, Taf. LX.

86. Sune Lindqvist, Gotlands Bildsteine I. Stockholm 1941, Taf. 56: 135, S. 84 u. 120. – Vgl. auch Bertil Almgren, Om vagnåkarnas färder. Gotländskt Arkiv 1946. Lund 1946, S. 88.

87. Almgren, a.O., S. 89–90 u. Abb. 5.

88. SHM 21952. Stockholm.

89. SHM 2110. – Vgl. Almgren, a.O., S. 92–93.

90. SHM 8047. Vgl. Märta Strömberg, Untersuchungen zur jüngeren Eisenzeit in Schonen II. Lund 1961, Taf. 51: 6–7.

91. DNM 3893. – Vgl. Johannes Brøndsted, Danish Inhumation Graves of the Viking Age. Acta Archaeologica VII, S. 144–145.

92. DNM 25581. – Vgl. Brøndsted, a.O., S. 143–144.

93. Vgl. Brøndsted, a.O. und dort angeführte Literatur.

94. Almgren, a.O., S. 90.

95. Cod. 370, Liber pictus, fol. 43, 102, 145.

96. Freudenberg, a.O., S. 42.

97. Über die Chronologie der modernen Pferdeanspannung in Europa vgl. Joseph Needham, Science and Civilisation in China IV. Cambridge 1965, S. 327.

98. Dahlberg, a.O., I: 54.

99. Armin Tuulse och Gunnar Lindqvist, Spånga och Hässelby kyrkor. Sveriges Kyrkor VIII. Stockholm 1959, Abb. 105; vgl. S. 203.

100. Henrik Cornell och Sigurd Wallin, Uppsvenska målarskolor på 1400-talet. Stockholm 1933, Taf. 110; vgl. S. 124.

101. Vgl. Anmerkung 34 und Freudenberg, a.O., S. 43.

102. Akershus: Kråkstad, NEG 15548; Buskerud: Nes, a.O. 15494; Sogn og Fjordane: Jølster, a.O., 15878; Hordaland: Odda, a.O. 15440.

103. Haakon Schetelig, Gammelt kjøre og ridetøj. Bergens Museums Årbok 1910. Bergen 1911, Taf. XIV; S. 118. – Nils Jahrmann, Hestekjøretøyer. By og Bygd 13. Oslo 1960, S. 123.

104. Z.B. Stockholm d. 3.4.1739: *Ett par wagns Stång Sehlar : Ett par bruna wagns Schackel Sehlar*, SRA, Svea Hovrätts arkiv. Bouppteckningar. – Gutshof Grensholmen, Östergötland d. 4.3.1746: *Stora stång sehlar med ...linor : skackel Sehlar swarta*, a.O.

105. Z.B. Heimatsmuseen in Trollhättan, Västergötland; Östervåla in Västmanland; Nässjö in Småland; Gällersta in Närke u.s.w.

106. Profess. Doct. Lostbom, Utkast til Kunskap om Swenska Landtmanna Redskaper. Om Anspann. Hushållnings Journalen, Februarius. Stockholm 1780, S. 35–36.

Abkürzungen

DFM	=	Dansk Folkemuseum
DNM	=	Nationalmuseet, Kopenhagen
EU	=	Etnologiska Undersökningen, NM
GMA	=	Göteborgs Museum, Archiv
IDD	=	Institut for Dansk Dialektforskning, Kopenhagen
IFF	=	Institutet för Folklivsforskning, Stockholm
JO	=	Jysk Ordbog, Archiv. Institut for Jysk Sprog- og Kulturforskning, Aarhus
KMK	=	Finnlands Nationalmuseum, Volkskundl. Abt.
LLMA	=	Landsmålsarkivet, Lund
LUFA	=	Lunds Universitets Folklivsarkiv
NEG	=	Norsk Etnologisk Gransking, Bygdøy
NEU	=	Nationalmuseets Etnologiske Undersøgelser, Kopenhagen
NM	=	Nordiska Museet, Stockholm
SHM	=	Statens Historiska Museum, Stockholm
SLS	=	Svenska Litteratursällskapet, Helsingfors
SRA	=	Riksarkivet, Stockholm
ULMA	=	Landsmåls- och Folkminnesarkivet, Uppsala

Fahrzeuge der obersteirischen Bergbauern

Von KARL HAIDING

Vorbemerkung

Die folgenden Betrachtungen beschränken sich mit wenigen Ausnahmen auf das Einzugsgebiet des Landschaftsmuseums Schloß Trautenfels, einer Abteilung des Steiermärkischen Landesmuseums Joanneum. Mit geringen Ausnahmen ist das Museumsgut erst seit dem Herbst 1955 zusammengetragen worden. Der Sammelbereich erstreckt sich auf den politischen Bezirk Liezen (mit 7 Gerichtsbezirken), der an die Bundesländer Salzburg, Ober- und Niederösterreich grenzt. Die Landesgrenzen bilden keineswegs Kulturgrenzen, vielmehr gliedert sich der Bezirk, vom Volkskundlichen gesehen, in mehrere Kulturlandschaften, die größtenteils über das Land Steiermark hinausreichen. Der Bezirk umfaßt mit 3270 km² fast 20% der Landesfläche, bei rund 75.000 Einwohnern ergibt dies eine Bevölkerungsdichte von 23/km², berücksichtigt man jedoch nur die bewohnbare Fläche, so sind es 103/km². Schon dieses Verhältnis läßt das Ausmaß des Gebirgsanteiles erkennen, dem unter anderem auch das Weiterleben urtümlicher Fahrzeugtypen zu verdanken ist. Bei der Durchreise macht die Landschaft (auch durch den "Ennsboden", größtenteils Überschwemmungsgebiet des Hauptflusses, der Enns) einen vorwiegend bäuerlichen Eindruck, doch gehört nur noch ein Fünftel der Bewohner der Land- und Forstwirtschaft an. Bodenverhältnisse und Wirtschaftslage bedingen ein ungleichmäßiges Vordringen von Neuerungen, so daß wir derzeit ein buntes Gemisch an Kulturerscheinungen und somit auch an Fahrzeugen aller Art antreffen. Der Rückgang des Getreidebaues von über 10.000 ha um die Jahrhundertwende auf 690 im Jahre 1965 bewirkt ein Ausdehnen der Grünlandwirtschaft, gleichzeitig nimmt jedoch infolge des Mangels an Arbeitskräften und der Benachteiligung der Landwirtschaft bei Arbeitszeit und Preisen der Verlust tausendjährigen Kulturbodens nicht nur im Almenbereiche zu.

Das Bergen der Museumsobjekte ging von Anfang an Hand in Hand mit dem Beobachten ihrer Geltung und Wirksamkeit innerhalb eines vom Herkommen und der bewährten Daseinsform einer Gemeinschaft bestimmten Lebensbereiches. Die Art und Weise, wie die einzelnen Höfe Neuerungen aufnehmen und verarbeiten, ist dabei besonders aufschlußreich. Diese Lebensbezogenheit der Museumsgegenstände zu berücksichtigen, ist auch für die Schausammlung von Nutzen, wenn es etwa darum geht, die ausgestellten Objekte durch Lichtbilder zum Sprechen zu bringen. Die Schauräume konnten jedoch nur allmählich von zweckfremder Verwendung befreit werden. Erst seit 1962 war es möglich, daneben einen Lagerraum zu erhalten und nun auch größere Geräte einzubringen. Aus Raummangel mußte die Sammeltätigkeit und eine Aufsatzreihe wieder abgebrochen werden.[1] Die Aufnahmen im Gelände stoßen oft auf große Schwierigkeiten. Manches längst außer Gebrauch stehende Fahrzeug liegt unzugänglich in Gebäuden verstaut und kann weder vermessen noch abgebildet werden. Das Zerlegen der nicht mehr verwendeten Fahrzeuge und das Entfernen der eisernen Beschläge kostet so viel Arbeit, daß vor allem immer wieder Schlitten zu Haufen getürmt und verbrannt werden, um Platz für neue Fahrzeuge zu gewinnen oder unversehens Gebäude abreißen zu können. Allein etwa 30 Abarten von Gestellschlitten wären derzeit noch sicherzustellen und für die vergleichende Forschung auszuwerten.

Aus diesen und anderen Gründen kann hier – wie übrigens in großen Teilen der Ostalpen – nichts geboten werden, was an Ausgeglichenheit an die bewundernswerten, auf umfangreiche Museumsbestände und weitgespannte Feldforschung gegründeten Arbeiten von Béla *Gunda*[2] und Gösta *Berg*[3], um nur zwei der wichtigsten zu nennen, heranreicht. Doch ermutigt das Urteil, das der maßgebliche Erforscher bäuerlichen Arbeitsgerätes, dem diese Festschrift gewidmet ist, bei Besichtigung der Trautenfelser Bestände abgab, hier wenigstens die Vielfalt von Fahrzeugen anzudeuten, deren sich obersteirische Bergbauern und Waldarbeiter bis in jüngste Zeit bedienten. Einzelne, wenig bekannte Geräte, sollen dabei besondere Berücksichtigung finden.

Teilkräfte, die Art und Verwendung eines Fahrzeuges mitbestimmen

Bauart und Einsatz eines behelfsmäßigen wie eines dauerhaften Fahrzeuges ergeben sich aus dem Zusammenwirken verschiedener Voraussetzungen. Ändern sich diese, so kann selbst innerhalb eines Arbeitsvorganges ein Wechsel der Zugkraft oder des Geräts erfolgen. Auf diesen Wechsel wollen wir bei den einzelnen Fahrzeugen im Zusammenhange mit ihrem Gebrauch eingehen, der auch zeigen wird, daß die Einteilung nach menschlicher, tierischer oder motorischer Zugkraft den gleichen Fahrzeugtyp an verschiedenen Stellen einreiht, genau so, wie Sommer- und Winterschlitten oder -schleifen nicht ohneweiteres zu trennen sind. Als wichtigste Grundzüge, die die Art eines Fahrzeuges bedingen, seien genannt:

    a) *Die Beschaffenheit des Bodens.* Tragfähigkeit (festes Erdreich, Moor-boden, aufgeweichter Boden, Schneeharsch, Eis). Glätte (nasser Waldboden, Rasen, Schnee, Eis, Fels). Rauhheit (trockener Erdboden, steiniger Grund). Unebenheit (durch wechselnde Neigung, Steine, Wurzeln). Unwegsamkeit (Gestrüpp, Baumstümpfe, Stämme, Felsbrocken). Künstlich angelegter Schleif- und Fahrweg. Fahrverbot für Schleifen auf den Straßen, Schneeräumung verdrängt Schlittenfuhren.

b) *Geländeneigung.* Unterschiede, je nachdem, ob eine Last bergauf oder bergab geführt wird. Es läßt sich eine Kurve zeichnen, die von der größten Steilheit bis in die Ebene verschiedene Arten des Fortbewegens erfordert und ermöglicht: Bei größtem Gefälle etwa Abwerfen des Bergheus in einem Netz über den Felshang, dann Tragen auf dem Rücken, auf dem Kopfe, Befördern mit einer Astschleife oder ähnlichen, dauerhafteren Gebilden, Schlitten mit Holzkufen, mit einer angehängten Astschleife als Bremse, ohne Anhängsel, mit schleifender Last bis zum vierrädrigen Wagen.

c) *Last.* Es bestimmen a) und b) mit, ob eine Last getragen oder geführt wird, z. B. unterwegs Umladen auf Saumtiere, Heraustragen des gemähten Schilfrohrs aus dem Wasser zum Schlitten. Maßgeblich auch Schwere, Größe und Form der Last, Lade- und Entladehöhe und Zahl der Arbeitskräfte.

d) *Zugkraft.* Von a) bis c) und von e) abhängig. Gleiche oder ähnliche Fahrzeugtypen bei menschlicher und tierischer Zugkraft, Bewertung von Kuh, Ochs, Schnitzkalb[4], Stier, Einhufer (Roß, Esel, Maultier), Motor. Bodenflächen, die für Neuerungen nicht zugänglich sind.

e) *Wirtschaftskraft und Wirtschaftlichkeit.* Behelfsmäßige Fahrzeuge, die nach der Talfahrt als Stallstreu, Brennholz oder anders verwertet werden. Vom Bauern oder Holzknecht (Waldarbeiter) hergestellt, vom Störhandwerker auf dem Hofe gefertigt, beim Handwerker teilweise oder ganz gekauft. Wahl der Zugkraft von der wirtschaftlichen Leistungsfähigkeit mitbedingt. Vor- und Nachteile der Motorfahrzeuge.

Die Fahrzeuge und ihre Verwendung

Bis in unsere Tage, wo sich der Bergbauer mehr und mehr auf Grünland- und Waldwirtschaft beschränkt, von weit her über die Genossenschaft Stroh als Einstreu für das Vieh kauft, Kunstdünger streut und seine technische Begabung beim Einsatz der Motorkraft zeigt, ist hie und da die alte Gewinnung von Stallstreu üblich geblieben. Gewiß schätzte man auch in früheren Zeiten dessen Wert für die Düngergewinnung entsprechend ein, doch zwang das Selbstversorgertum die einzelnen Höfe, die Bedürfnisse auf das einzustellen, was der eigene Grund und Boden bot oder dank herkömmlichen Nutzungsrechten darüber hinaus ohne Kauf durch vielfältige und oft mühevolle Arbeit zu gewinnen war. Der Spruch

Lab und Fòrm
Mòcht in Ocka òrm,
Stroh und Holz
Mocht 'n stolz[5]

zeigt die verschiedene Bewertung dessen, was "Mist" bringen soll. Laub und Farn machen den Acker arm, das heißt, der damit erzeugte Dünger ist minderwertig. Stroh und Holz machen ihn stolz, er trägt danach reiche Frucht.

Mit dem "Holz" ist *"Graß"* gemeint, Tannen- oder (hauptsächlich) Fichtenreisig, von Sprossen und Zweigen bis zu größeren Ästen[6]. Die kleingehackten zarteren Zweige dienten sowohl als vom Vieh gern aufgenommenes, winterliches Futter wie auch als Stallstreu. Auch zu Zeiten des Getreidebaues trat auf vielen Höfen das Stroh als Einstreu völlig zurück, es wurde, kurz gehackt, dem Futter beigemischt, ein Gutteil des Winterstrohs diente zum Füllen der Strohsäcke in den Betten und dem Sattler beim Anfertigen der Kummete.

Umso wichtiger war das Graß, das im Oktober und November von den stehenden Nadelbäumen, hauptsächlich Fichten, geschnaitet ("gschnoat") wurde. Mit Steigeisen versehen, stiegen die Männer an den Baumstämmen immer höher und hackten mit dem leichten "Schnoathackl" die Äste ab. Heute ist das Schnaiteln verboten, weil der Holzwert leidet.[7] In der Gegend von Mitterndorf hatten die Wirtschaften keinen Eigenwald sondern nur Nutzungsrecht im Staatswalde. Sie erhielten zum Schnaiteln Bäume zugewiesen, waren aber auch verpflichtet, beim Holzbezug diese Bäume zu fällen.[8]

Das eingebrachte Graß war vor allem in der Zeit des Tiefstalles[9], mundartlich "Miststall" genannt, unentbehrlich. Neben jedem Stalle gab es eine eigene "Graßhütte" (bei großen Höfen), auf einem Hofe waren gar drei Arbeitskräfte den ganzen Winter über Tag für Tag mit dem "Graßhacken" beschäftigt. Die Zweige mussten kurz gehackt werden, damit sie später beim Düngen ohne Schwierigkeit einzuackern waren. Doch nur bis Fingerdicke eigneten sie sich, was stärker war, verarbeitete man zu Brennholz. Die Rinder (die in manchen Gegenden bis in jüngste Zeit frei im Barren herumgingen) bekamen auch im Anhängstalle häufig Graß eingestreut, so daß der Futtertrog wiederholt gehoben werden mußte, und die Stalldecke immer näher rückte. Noch heute ist der Umbau alter Stalltüren zu erkennen, die ehemals so breit waren, daß ein Wagen durchfahren konnte, wenn – zumeist zweimal im Jahre – der Dünger weggebracht wurde. Das Ausführen des Düngers geschah vor dem Getreideanbau im September (Winterroggen, auch Weizen),

230

auf Steilflächen, wo man den Schlitten benötigte, im Winter, wofern nicht ein schräg abwärts gehendes Tier über ein Umlaufrad den Mistkarren hochzog und dann vor dem Frühjahrsanbau[10].

Wir können das stufenweise Zurückgehen des Stallstreus aus Nadelreisig beobachten. Auf dem Heimhofe aufgelassen, wird es im Sommerstall, den der Talbauer in einem ehemaligen, von ihm erworbenen Bergbauernhofe einrichtet, noch beibehalten, weil die Zubringung von Graß einfacher ist als die von Streu aus dem Tale[11]. In anderen Fällen bleibt Graßstreu nur bei den in Abteilungen sich frei bewegenden Schafen, die sozusagen weiterhin in einem Umlaufstalle sind, und ergibt dort besseren Dünger als die Rinderstände. Allerdings muß es dazu lang durchgetreten werden, weshalb immer wieder Nadelreisig darüber kommt, und die in der Mitte stehende Futterkrippe von Zeit zu Zeit gehoben wird. Mit dem Tode eines alten Mannes, der in den letzten Jahren allein noch das Graßhacken fortsetzte, kann das Graßstreu auch bei den Schafen plötzlich für immer ausfallen.[12] Ein Rückzugsgebiet läßt sich auch auf einigen Almen feststellen, so unterhalb von Admont, wo drei verschiedene Zugkräfte die urtümlichste Art des "Fahrzeuges" in Bewegung setzen[13].

A. Die Astschleife

Um das Graß ins Tal zu bringen, nützt man die Geländeneigung aus, die neben der Größe der Last auch bestimmt, ob Mensch oder Tier und neuerdings der Schlepper (Traktor) zum Einsatze kommen. Auch bei der sogenannten "Graßzig"[14] genügt das "Schleifen der Sache selbst", das *Koren* als Urform des Fortbewegens am Beispiel des Ziehens vom Baumstämmen erwähnt[15]. Allerdings dienen nur die untersten Äste als Fahrzeug, die übrigen, gleich gearteten, bilden die Last. Selbst dieser einfache Behelf muß sachgemäß aufgebaut werden, soll ohne Ärgernis die Fuhre ans Ziel gelangen. Der Zieher legt zwei oder mehrere Äste schräg gekreuzt auf den Boden, schlingt um die Gabelungen der Aststümpfe einen Strick und baut je nach den örtlichen Gewohnheiten nun die Last auf. Entweder kommen die Zweige unmittelbar übereinander oder man staffelt sie nach hinten zu, wobei die Seilschlingen zumeist wiederholt Kreuzungen zusammenfassen. Der sachliche Unterschied von schleifenden und zugleich tragenden Ästen und der Last gleicher Herkunft wird deutlicher im Ausseerlande, wo der Gebrauch von Hülltüchern auch bei der Heu- und Laubzufuhr üblich ist. Dort hackt man sogleich im Walde an Ort und Stelle das Nadelreisig klein, füllt es in Tücher und ladet diese auf Fichtenäste, die etwa einen halben Meter hoch geschichtet werden. Dieser Gròßzug, wie er hier heißt, wird ohne tierische Hilfe von Menschen gezogen.

Kleinere Astschleifen mit händischem Zug heißen um Admont "Graßzigl" sonst "Graßzig". Noch 1965 konnte ich dort auf einem leicht geneigten Waldwege eine achtzigjährige Frau beobachten, wie sie sich mit ihrer Last abmühte. Von der menschlichen Zugkraft, die allerdings auch mit der Geländeneigung wächst, hängt die *Größe des "Fahrzeuges"* ab. Im Osten des Bezirkes, wo statt "Zig" die Bezeichnung "Reis"[16] gilt, legte man vier bis fünf "Graßtatschen" schräg gekreuzt übereinander, verband sie mit einer Seilschlinge und staffelte nach hinten so viele Kreuzungen von Ästen, als man mit Rücksicht auf die Hanglage zu ziehen vermochte (z. B. Gegend von Palfau).

Nicht nur Größe der Last und Geländeneigung sondern auch *Rauhheit oder Glätte der Gleitfläche* sind von Bedeutung. Bei menschlicher wie tierischer Zugkraft bot eine Schneeunterlage Erleichterung. Stand ein ausgefahrener Schlittenweg zur Verfügung, so wurden die vordersten Äste gekreuzt aufgelegt und mit einem Stricke zusammengebunden, die Last darauf nur wenig zurückgestaffelt, hauptsächlich übereinander bis zu 80 cm hoch ohne Bindung gelagert. Mit dem über die Schulter genommenen Strick ziehend, überläßt der Mann die Hauptlast dem Boden, die Ladung schleift fast in ihrer ganzen Länge auf dem geglätteten Schnee. Bei unebenem, schneefreiem Boden bleibt der Strick weg, die zwei längsten Äste, die die Hauptunterlage bilden, werden vorne so weit gekreuzt, daß sich der Zieher dazwischen stellen und die Enden der Äste mit den Händen fassen kann. Dadurch hebt er beim Ziehen die schleifenden Äste teilweise hoch, übernimmt mehr vom Gewicht, vermindert jedoch stark die Reibung (Gemeinde Donnersbach).

Dient die Astschleife von Nadelbäumen zum *Befördern anderer Lasten,* so nimmt man nur so wenig Äste, als für die Schleifunterlage notwendig sind. Als Stallstreu findet stellenweise bis in die Gegenwart auch *Laub* Verwendung. Man kann dessen bevorzugte Nutzung für diesen Zweck (wobei allerdings auch Wirtschaftsgröße und anderes mitspielen) fürs erste schon aus Waldkarten ablesen, die den Anteil der einzelnen Holzarten wiedergeben[17]. Zum Herabführen wird das Laub in große Tücher gebunden. Man legt nur so viel Graß auf, daß die Laubbündel nicht auf der Erde streifen. Unten auf dem Wege erfolgt das Umladen der Bündel, und zwar, falls ein Zugtier zur Verfügung steht, auf eine "Schloapfn", sonst auf eine "Heubudl", zwei Fahrzeuge, die wir noch kennen lernen werden. So ist das Herabschleifen von Laub im Gerichtsbezirk St. Gallen des Bezirkes Liezen üblich, aber auch im Gerichtsbezirk Aussee erfolgt die Bringung ähnlich.

Bis in die Gegenwart wird auch *Farn* im Stalle eingestreut, das auf ver-

Abb. 1. Zig aus Erlenstauden zum Heuführen mit Roßvorspann.

schiedene Weise ins Tal kommt, je nach Wirtschaftsgröße, Lage des Hofes und Jahreszeit. Im Untertal bei Schladming trägt es der Bauer zum Sommerstall auf einer Tragstange herunter, die dem von *Goldstern*[18] abgebildeten "Riedlstock" gleicht, in der Kleinsölk konnte ich im Lichtbilde festhalten, wie Farn einfach auf Fichtenäste aufgelegt und ohne Niederschnüren auch von der Bäurin den Hang herab zum nahen Heimathof gezogen wurde. In der Ortschaft Reith der gleichen Gemeinde bringen einzelne Bauern, die dank der Kinder im leistungsfähigen Alter große Mengen verarbeiten können, diese im Winter auf sorgfältig ausgelegten Fichtenästen bei günstiger Schneelage herab. Die Ladung abwechselnder Schichten von Graß und Farn wird ähnlich, aber einfacher mit dem Seilholz[19] und Strick gebunden, als das Gebirgsheu[20]. Auch Legföhren treten an die Stelle der Fichtenäste. In der Gemeinde St. Nikolai im großen Sölktale wird Farn im Sommer gleichfalls nur lose aufgelegt, die Graßunterlage beschreibt der Bauer als "dreieckigen Stock", den er mit einem Strang zusammenbindet. In Mitterndorf dagegen können sich nur noch ältere Leute an die Zig aus Graß für Farn erinnern. Hier tritt der Laubwald gegenüber dem benachbarten Ausseerland zurück, was die Wahl des Einstreus beeinflußt.

Es liegt nahe, auf die Graßunterlage nicht nur Äste mit Nadelreisig, sondern auch *Fichtenknüttel* und größeres *Prügelholz* zu lagern, wenn der Hang für ein Fuhrwerk zu steil ist. Bei entsprechendem Gefälle oder geringerer Last genügt die menschliche Zugkraft. Prügelholz wird aus dem angeflogenen Baumwuchs, etwa bei Zäunen, gehackt, dickere Stämme werden vor der Abfahrt zu *Scheitern* gespalten. Im Almenbereich erweisen sich Astschleifen zum Befördern verschiedener Lasten als nützlich, so für *Almgerät*, für täglich geschnittenes *Einstellfutter* und für *Bergheu*[21].

Wenn die beim winterlichen Herabführen von Gebirgsheu auf Heuziehbrettern beförderte gebundene Fuhre ebenfalls "Zig" heißt, so erinnert das daran, daß in Nordtirol (Ötztal) Fichtenäste als Unterlage gebraucht werden[22], in Südtirol der Stangengleiter "Reis" heißt[23] und in Kärnten "Heubur'n" auf Fichtenästen gezogen werden[24]. Allerdings gilt der Ausdruck Zig auch für das noch ursprünglichere Ziehen des Bergheus ohne jede Unterlage, wobei es durch einen Strick zusammengehalten wird. Nur wenn der Boden zu "rauh" ist, legen die Mäher Äste unter. Die Bergheugewinnung hat wegen des Mangels an Arbeitskräften seit einem Jahrzehnt ein Ende gefunden.

Schon länger ist es mit dem talwärts Führen der *Rinde,* im mittleren Ennstale "Lafn", im unteren "Loh" genannt, vorbei. Die einstigen Lohstampfen sind längst verstummt, und bei den Gerbern ist Rinde heute nicht mehr begehrt. Auch das Ledergerben auf einzelnen Bauernhöfen lebt nur noch in der Erinnerung fort. Auf Steilflächen, für die selbst der "Lohschlitten", von Menschenhand gesteuert, sich nicht eignete, führten die Waldarbeiter wie die Bauernknechte die Rinde mit Hilfe der Astschleifen bergab. Die Fichtenäste wurden wie sonst im spitzen Winkel gekreuzt, die von zwei Seiten her brillenförmig zusammengerollten Rindenstücke quer aufgelegt, entweder mit einem Seil gehalten oder mit einem zugespitzten Ast niedergespießt.

Das Heimführen von *Heu* unterhalb des Almenbereiches geschah im Ausseerlande ebenfalls auf Fichtenästen. Der untere Strickteil diente zum Ziehen, wodurch die Äste vorn gehoben wurden. Wo es sehr steil bergab ging, mußten zwei zurückhalten, weil sonst die Fuhre leicht seitlich bergab rutscht. Das Umladen auf Wagen ersparte man sich im Tale, wenn man das Heu nicht locker auflud, sondern in Hülltücher band, die unten nach der Ankunft eingetragen wurden. Im Paltental (Gemeinde Rottenmann) holten früher einzelne Bauern von hoch gelegenen Hängen das Heu auf einer Zig herab, allerdings mit Zugvieh.

Wenn aus der Sölk berichtet wird, daß bei einem Unfall auf der Alm oder im Holzschlage beim Fällen der Bäume der Verletzte auf einer Graßzig herabgeführt wurde, die mit Rücksicht auf die menschliche Last höher aufgeschichtet war, als es das Gleiten erforderte, damit die Unterlage federte oder wenn

Abb. 2. Mistzig, händisch gezogen.

etwa eine Kuh hoch oben kälberte und das frisch gefallene Kalb ebenfalls auf
einer Zig zutal kam, so sind das im Augenblick zu schaffende Behelfe.
G. *Berg* erwähnt in der meines Wissens ersten Übersicht der Astschleifen[25]
damit übereinstimmend aus Norwegen das Heimbringen eines verletzten
Stücks Vieh vom Gebirge. Das Herabführen von Hochwild auf "Graßästen"
(sofern es nicht einfach über den Schnee geschleift wird) ist an vielen Stellen
noch üblich.

Selbstverständlich gibt es für diese einfachen Schleifen keine Beschränkung
auf Nadelholz, das hier nur ausführlicher berücksichtigt ist, weil seine Zweige
selbst einst in großen Mengen eingeholt wurden. *Laubäste*, vorwiegend Erlen
und Birken, "Stauden"[26] genannt, dienen je nach Vorkommen dem gleichen
Zweck. Auf steilere Ackerflächen führten sie in Johnsbach zur Zeit des Getreidebaues und des Tiefstalles im Winter bei Schneelage den Mist mit Schlitten hinauf. Im Frühjahre wurde einen Tag vor dem Anbau gedüngt. Der
Mistkarren eignete sich hiefür schlecht, man hätte "einsperren" müssen (einen
Prügel zwischen die Speichen stecken, damit das Rad sich nicht drehen kann,
sondern schleift). Sie hackten daher 2–3 m lange Erlenstauden ab oder nahmen Fichtengraß und machten eine Zig, ein Zugtier wurde vor die Streifkette
gespannt, und so konnten sie oben auflegen und bequem den Dünger abwärts

Abb. 3. Zwei Mistreise für Roßgespann.

führen. Übergangsstufen konnte ich in der Kleinsölk beobachten. Vom Bauern-
hof geht es steil aufwärts, in größerer Höhe sind Mähflächen. Je nach deren
Neigung kam das Heu auf eine "Sprisselrummel", bei stärkerer Hanglage
wurde an diese als Bremsvorrichtung eine Zig aus kürzeren Stauden ange-
hängt und ebenfalls mit Heu beladen. Als schließlich die Steilfläche zum
Hofe hinunter geheugt wurde, fertigte ein Bauernsohn aus größeren belaubten
Ästen eine längere Zig an, die beim Bergabfahren mit Heu beladen wurde.
(Abb. 1). Von der Neigung des Geländes hängt fallweise auch die Wahl des
Zugtieres ab: ist es für ein Roß zu steil, so fährt man mit dem Ochsen.

Wie schon wiederholt angedeutet, erfolgt unterwegs manchmal ein Wechsel
der Zugkraft. Das steilere Stück vermag am besten ein Mensch die "Zig" oder
das "Reis" herabzusteuern, auf der letzten Strecke muß ihn ein Zugtier ablösen. Hie und da kann man die Verbindung dieser urtümlichen Astschleifen
mit einem Traktor sehen[27], der zum Heimhofe oder über den Almboden
größere Lasten zu befördern vermag als jemals ein Roß. Wenn wir bedenken,
wie erst meine in großer zeitlicher Bedrängnis gemachten Beobachtungen der
letzten Jahre zeigen, daß wir aus Gegenwart und Erinnerung die Astschleife
im Einzugsgebiet des Museums und darüber hinaus in Nachbarlandschaften
hundertfältig nachweisen können, während vorher die volkskundliche Lite-

Abb. 4. Anfertigung eines Mistreises.

ratur dieses Gebietes davon keine Erwähnung enthält, läßt sich das Ausmaß der Versäumnisse ahnen, die zum guten Teile nicht mehr gutzumachen sind. Rechtzeitig hat Erika *Hubatschek* Bestandsaufnahmen durchgeführt, in später Stunde Maria *Hornung* vieles sowohl sach- als auch sprachkundlich festgehalten. Erstaunlich ist, was Maria *Kundegraber* noch über die Siedlungen der ehemaligen deutschen Sprachinsel Gottschee in Erfahrung bringen konnte.[28]

B. Staudenjochschleifen

Zum Unterschiede von den jeweils rasch an Ort und Stelle zugehackten Astschleifen gibt es vor allem für das Verteilen des Düngers Geräte mit einem dauerhaften Teil, in dem die Äste oder Zweige, die nach längerem Gebrauche abgeschliffen sind und erneuert werden, einen Halt finden. Wir haben hier eine Weiterentwicklung der üblichen "Zig" vor uns, was auch der Name "Mistzig" oder "Mistreis" andeutet. Das erinnert an andere, von der gleichen Grundlage ausgehende dauerhafte Geräte, die besonders für die Bergheubringung gefertigt werden, wie etwa das südtiroler "Reis" aus drei Gleitstangen, die mit Jochen verbunden sind[29].

237

Abb. 5. Mistzig in steilem Gelände.

Eine "Mistzig" aus Aigen im Ennstal, die früher auf den steilen Hängen des "Boaringer-Lehens" Verwendung fand, besteht aus einem 80 cm langen "Joch" aus einem Birkenkrümmling gefertigt[30]. In den Stamm sind 8 Löcher gebohrt, in diese 8 Birkenruten eingekeilt. Diese haben nur noch eine Länge von 1,50 m, die Enden und die Unterseite sind deutlich abgeschliffen und bezeugen den längeren Gebrauch. Das Joch hat ein Störhandwerker, der auf den Hof zur Arbeit kam, sorgfältig hergestellt und an beiden Enden mit einem Eisenbeschlag verstärkt. Der Eisenbeschlag in der Mitte hat eine Öse für den Eisenring, an den ein Zugstrick von 90 cm Länge geknüpft ist. Am vorderen

238

Abb. 6. Graßdaufel.

Ende des Strickes ist ein 54 cm langes Querholz eingeknotet. Das Gerät ist auf die Kraft des Arbeitenden abgestimmt, es gibt auf dem Berggut des Talbauern auch eine größere Ausführung mit breiterem Joche und 9 Löchern und Ruten für besonders kräftige Männer und eine kleinere mit 7 Ruten für Jugendliche.

Der Dünger wurde zuerst mit einem Fuhrwerk auf den oberen Rand des Feldes geführt, ursprünglich zogen zwei Rosse in Schlangenwindungen den "Schna'lgo'n" mühsam hinauf, erst spät stellte sich der Bauer auf den Ochsenzug mit Seiltasche (Umlenkrolle) um. Das Gefälle des heute nicht mehr genutzten Feldes ist so stark, daß selbst für die Rutenschleife vor dem Joch ein Ast zum Bremsen eingesetzt werden mußte. Es ging rasch bergab, durch eine plötzliche Schwenkung zur Seite wurde die Fuhre abgeleert. Erst wenn das ganze Feld mit diesen kleinen Haufen überzogen war, folgte das "Mistbroatn", das gleichmäßige Ausbreiten des Düngers mit Hilfe von Gabeln. Die Knaben vergnügten sich beim Bergabfahren öfters und fuhren so rasch, daß sie nicht mehr zu bremsen vermochten und die ganze Ladung unten am Zaun landete. Der Vater schimpfte, und der Mist mußte bergauf geworfen werden. Mit dem Strick über die Schulter trugen sie das leere Gerät wieder nach oben.

Selbst die Handhabung eines so einfachen "Fahrzeuges" und die Arbeits-

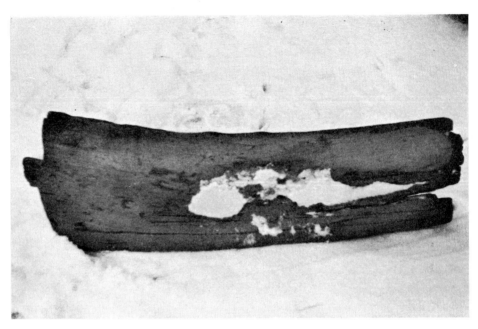

Abb. 7. Graßlöffel.

weise sind vom Gelände abhängig. Im Herbst 1970 konnte ich die Verwendung einer Mistzig in der gleichen Gemeinde, jedoch auf einem weniger stark geneigten Hange des Hofes Fritz beobachten. Im Boaringer-Lehen war es vorteilhaft, wenn die Mistzig frisch "einbirchnt" (mit neuen Birkenruten versehen) wurde und dies samt dem Laube geschah, wobei nur die unnützen Zweigspitzen abgestutzt wurden, weil es beim Bergabführen nicht so "anschob" ("Bal s' neu is, schiabt s' nit a so an"). Auf dem Hofe Fritz müssen sie nicht bremsen, sondern auch bergab kräftig ziehen (Abb. 2). Daher ladet ein zweiter, nicht so kräftiger Arbeiter, der streckenweise auch ziehen hilft, unterwegs mit der Gabel ab. Um das Mistführen zu erleichtern, hat sich der Kleinbauer, der die Landwirtschaft neben einem anderen Berufe betreibt, im Jahre 1970 ein neues Fahrzeug, das er "Rümperl"[31] nennt, gebaut: eine Bretterfläche, unter die vorn als Gleitkufe eine ehemalige "Knittlschloapfn" (darüber unten) genagelt ist, die zugleich dem Zugstrick Halt gibt. Die geringere Reibung erfordert viel weniger Zugkraft.

Auf dem Hofe Gerg der gleichen Gemeinde fand ich an der Wand des ehemaligen Getreidespeichers zwei größere Staudenjochschleifen (Abb. 3), die der Eigentümer J. Radlingmaier dem Museum spendete, weshalb er sich zwei neue Stücke bauen mußte, was ebenfalls Gelegenheit zu Aufnahmen bot (Abb.

240

Abb. 8. Knittelschloapfm mit
Roatlkette.

4). Er nennt dieses Gerät "Mistreis", wie es auch in der benachbarten
Gemeinde Oppenberg heißt. Es wird seiner Größe entsprechend meist von
einem Rosse gezogen. Das Mistreis ist nur auf Feldern des zugehörigen Berg-
gutes in Verwendung. Das Joch, hier "Trackl" genannt, ist zugehackt. Inv. Nr.
5960 des Museums Trautenfels hat einen Tracklquerschnitt von 8 mal 6,5 cm
und eine Länge von 1,11 m, Nr. 5961 die Maße 8,5 mal 6,5 und 1,18 m. Je 6
Ruten sind in die Trackllöcher eingekeilt, die Rutenlänge beträgt rund 3 m,
quer über die Stauden ist mit Draht ein Brett befestigt, das dem Mist besseren
Halt gibt. Die neuen Mistreise waren kurz nach dem Anfertigen im Herbst
1970 schon in Gebrauch.

Abb. 9. Knüttelholz mit der Schloapfm geführt.

Auf einem Fahrweg kann der Dünger oberhalb des Feldes zugeführt und dadurch leicht gelagert werden. Während ein Sohn mit dem Beladen eines Mistreises beschäftigt war, führte eine Tochter das Roß mit dem beladenen zweiten Reis bergab, und der Bauer, der nebenher ging, lud zwischendurch den Mist ab (Abb. 5). Mit dem leeren Reis ging es wieder hinauf zum großen Haufen. Die zweite Tochter breitete mit einer Gabel unterdessen den ausgeführten Dünger gleichmäßig aus. Ein jüngerer Sohn, der uns heraufgeleitet hatte, noch ein Schulknabe, konnte sich, ledig jeder Pflicht, auf seine Weise zwischen den Arbeitenden tummeln.

An dem Trackl der beiden Mistreise sind vorn zwei eiserne Bügel von etwa 16 cm Länge befestigt. Kommt im Gelände eine Stelle, die für das Roß zu steil ist, so wird es ausgespannt, zwei Männer fassen die Eisenbügel an und ziehen selbst weiter, bis das Roß wieder seinen Platz einnehmen kann. Die geänderte Hanglage bewirkt bei gleichem Fahrzeug und gleicher Last den vorübergehenden Wechsel von menschlicher und tierischer Zugkraft!

Auch andere Ursachen können diese Wirkung haben. Die Altbäuerin des Kreistner-Hofes (Treglwang im Paltental) erzählte von der "Miststroaf", einem Trackl mit Löchern, in denen Staudenäste verkeilt sind. In ihrer Jugend zog sie mit ihrem Bruder zu zweit den Dünger vom Hofe feldabwärts, weil das Roß sich dazu nicht recht anschickte ("es war so zuwider"). Sie nahmen zum Ziehen einen Strick um den Bauch.

Die Mistzig ist sicherlich weiter verbreitet gewesen, als wir im Augenblick festzustellen vermögen, wobei auch die Namen, wie in Aigen, sich nicht an den Ortsgrenzen sondern mitten in der Gemeinde ändern können. So heißt sie in Teilen von Donnersbach "Gstauda-Zig", für menschliche Zugkraft genügt auch hier ein Strick, auch Ochs oder Roß werden vorgespannt. Die gleiche Bezeichnung gilt, wenn das Gerät an einen Flachschlitten, die Rumpel, angehängt wird. Von der Mistzig hören wir auch aus der Kleinsölk. In der Großsölk war vor Jahrzehnten eine Staudenjochschleife unter dem Namen "Schloapfm" bekannt, der sonst stärkeren Fahrzeugen vorbehalten ist. Nach der Beschreibung alter Leute waren in dem leicht gekrümmten Joch in vier eingebohrte Löcher Birkenstauden eingesteckt. Das Gerät diente zum "Mistòschloapfm", also zum Hinunterschleifen von Mist. Es wurde damit auch "Dòchzogn". Zu diesem Zweck bohrte man in der Mitte des Joches ein zusätzliches Loch, in dem eine Stange befestigt wurde, in gleicher Lage wie die Ruten. Quer darauf schichteten sie sorgfältig Dachschindeln, ein vorn an der Stange befestigter Strick wurde über die Schindel gelegt und hinten an der Stange niedergebunden. In gleicher Weise konnte auf der "Schloapfm" Heu niedergebunden und geführt werden.

In Oppenberg hängt man das Mistreis an eine Mistrumpel an, um auf diese Weise bergab zu bremsen und gleichzeit mehr Dünger befördern zu können, einzelne Bergbauern begnügen sich für den gleichen Zweck mit Fichtenästen.

Eine ähnliche Entwicklung aus der Astschleife wie die "Schloapfm" aus Groß-Sölk unter Einfügung einer mit den Ruten gleichlaufenden Stange hat in Savoyen über das Gerät *arné* zum "bayard" geführt.[32] E. *Goldsterns* Aufnahmen von 1913/14 haben A. *Niederer* zu einer vergleichenden Untersuchung im Jahre 1967 veranlaßt. Dabei fand er, daß die Gebirgsheubringung heute weniger gefahrvoll mit Seilbahnen erfolgt, das einstige Gerät bayard aber nur noch in Kleinstausführung als Reiseandenken verkauft wird[33].

C. Einfache Gleiter

Es erübrigt sich, hier auf die *Stangenschleifen* einzugehen, die übrigens ortsweise "Schloapfn" oder verkleinert "Schleapfl" heißen, da auch hierüber eine eingehende Bestandsaufnahme fehlt.[34] Die Untersuchung über *Heuziehbretter* wird an anderem Ort fortgesetzt. Nur auf den "Graßlöffel" (Abb. 6) sei kurz eingegangen, den ich im Zusammenhange mit der "Graßdaufel" und dem

Abb. 10. Bretterrumpel nach dem Abladen, fährt zum Heuführen.

waghalsigen Schnoaten fünfzig- bis sechzigjähriger Fichten schon beschrieben habe[34]. Seither ist es uns gelungen, einen Graßlöffel (Abb. 7) für das Museum zu erhalten[35]. Das Gerät ist länger als das von mir nach Angaben erwähnte, weil es sich um ein Stück handelt, das nicht zum händischen Ziehen, sondern vorwiegend für Zugtiere gebraucht wurde. Der Löffel ist aus einem gekrümmten Ahornbaume herausgehackt (Krümmlinge wurden hiefür bevorzugt), die Gesamtlänge beträgt samt der Nase mit dem Führungsloch 1,40 m, die Krümmung ergibt eine Höhe des Kreisabschnittes von 10 cm. Der Löffel ist 45 cm breit. Eine gekrümmte Gleitbahn fand *Schmolke* bei Kufen von "Heuschleifen", urtümlichen Flachschlitten in den Pyrenäen[36]. Gegenüber den geraden Gleitbalken soll die Reibungsfläche verringert werden. Soweit festzustellen ist, dürfte im Einzugsgebiet des Museums heute nur noch ein Graßlöffel in Verwendung sein – allerdings als Wildschleife!

Der Graßlöffel wurde beim "Graßreisen" nur verwendet, so lange der Schnee nicht niedergefahren war. Der Bauer setzte sich auf den Löffel und ließ sich vom Ochsen bergauf ziehen, bis zur Stelle, wo er das Graßreis auflegte, für das der Graßlöffel Kufe und Unterlage bot. Bei genügendem Gefälle für die Talfahrt oder sobald die Schneebahn der Belastung standhielt, blieb die Gleithilfe weg. Wir erinnern uns bei diesem Anlasse an die Führung

244

Abb. 11. Ableeren des Heufuhre von der Sprisselrummel.

der Donnersbacher Graßzig je nach Bodenbeschaffenheit. Verschiedener Schnee kann auch die Benützung verschiedener Schlittenarten zur Folge haben. In der Nähe des Grundlsees konnte ich beobachten, wie von einer höher gelegenen Hütte das Heu (in Tücher gehüllt) auf einem Handschlitten von einem Manne herabgeführt wurde, der samt dem Schlitten über die verharschte Schneedecke kam, ohne einzusinken. Auf dem Fahrweg lud er um, hier konnte der Ochse den schweren Schlitten mit einer größeren Last ziehen.

Wenn ein Gewährsmann berichtet, daß er in der Jugend einen Gefährten beredete, den händisch gezogenen Graßlöffel zur Talfahrt zu benützen und der Genasführte den verschneiten Hang hinabsauste, daß ihm Hören und Sehen verging, so erhebt sich die Frage nach dem Aussehen der "Löffelschlitten", die wir in alten Nachlaßinventaren verzeichnet finden[37].

D. Die Zwieselschlaipfe

Seit dem Bericht über die Ennstaler Stoanschloapfn[38] habe ich aus den Nebentälern der Sölk und des Johnsbaches Nachrichten über das frühere Vorkommen erhalten. Vor einigen Jahrzehnten war der aus einer gewachsenen Ast-

Abb. 12. Sprisselrummel mit angehängter Zig.

gabel gestaltete Vorläufer der Flachschlitten in der Kleinsölk noch allgemein üblich. Man nahm hiezu gern die Zwiesel einer Birke oder Esche und führte damit ausgeackerte Steine an den Feldrand, wo sie allmählich eine noch heute bestehende Mauer bildeten, den "Roan" (Rain).[39] Inzwischen war es möglich, die Arbeit mit einer *"Knittlschloapfn"* aufzunehmen und das Stück für das Museum zu erwerben.[40] Die Beobachtungen erfolgten in einem Waldstück, unmittelbar hinter der Grenze meines Wohnortes. Auch in Aigen ist der gleiche Gleitbehelf für das Herabbringen etwa armdicker Stämme üblich, desgleichen in der Sölk und anderwärts. Wie aus Abb. 8 zu ersehen, ist vorn an einem Ring eine Eisenkette befestigt, an der über flachere Stellen gezogen wird, hie und da dient sie auch zum Bremsen. Beim Auflegen der Fuhre verhindern zwei vor dem Querholz in den Erdboden gesteckte Hölzer das vorzeitige Abgleiten. Wer bei der Arbeit zusieht, merkt, daß es kaum auf geschicktere Weise möglich ist, die Stämme aus dem gelichteten Birkenbestand ins Tal zu führen (Abb. 9), woraus sich das Beibehalten dieses einfachen Fahrbehelfes erklärt – soweit kein Fahrweg zur Verfügung steht und nur Arbeit und keine Lohnkosten aufzuwenden sind.

Ein "Stoanschleapfl" war einst auch in der Raumsau bei Schladming in Gebrauch, die sorgfältige Erhebung würde noch jetzt ein schütteres Belegnetz

246

Abb. 13. Schwere Schloapfm für Forstbauten.

des einstigen Vorkommens im Bezirk erbringen. Darüber hinaus berichteten Museumsbesucher von "Stoanschloapfn" in der Gegend von Wels und von Grieskirchen in Oberösterreich, von einer "Fòßschloapfm" zum Führen großer Mostfässer am Ufer des Attersees in Oberösterreich und von einer ähnlichen "Schleife" für Steine aus Heiligenlinde am Rande des Ermlandes im ehemaligen Ostpreußen. Ein Beispiel mehr für Versäumnisse, die nur zum geringen Teil noch gutgemacht werden können.

E. Flachschlitten

Von den aus derartigen naturgewachsenen Stücken hervorgegangenen Flachschlitten ist die Gruppe der Holz-, Heu-, Räder-, Mist- und Steinrumpel schon behandelt worden[41]. Im Museumsbereich sind bisher keine Beispiele von Flachschlitten oder Gestellschlitten mit vorn zusammenlaufenden Kufen festgestellt worden. Einiges sei hier nachgetragen und zwar über die Heurumpel mit Brettern oder Sprossen, über die Räderrumpel und eine mit Hilfe der motorischen Zugkraft bewegte, ungewöhnlich große Lastschleppe für den Bau im gebirgigen Waldgelände.

Abb. 14. Bau der Räderrumpel: Messen der »Weite« von der Mitte aus.

E 1. Die Bretterrumpel

Das Zuführen von Heu etwa aus den Heustadeln des Ennsbodens, die im Sommer rasch mit Hilfe der Bretterrumpel gefüllt werden konnten, ist in der alten Art nicht mehr möglich. Die Rumpel hat eine geringe Ladehöhe, das Heu wird nur aufgelegt und nicht durch eine auf der Fuhre stehende Arbeitskraft gefaßt und niedergetreten, so daß weniger Menschen erforderlich sind. Mit einer Stange, die quer zur Ladung gegen die Wand der Heuhütte gestemmt wird, ist das Heu leicht und rasch abzuladen, weil der Roßhalter, meist ein Schulkind, das Tier mit dem Fahrzeug wieder in Bewegung setzt, die Ladung herabgleitet und vor der Hütte liegt. Die geringe Entfernung von der Heuwiese erleichtert das rasche Einbringen bei drohendem Gewitter. Bei einem Brand auf dem Hofe ist ein Gutteil des Winterfutters außer Gefahr, es wird bei günstiger Schneelage nach und nach eingeholt, sobald Raum und Bedarf dafür ist.

Der große Mangel an Arbeitskräften, die Schneeräumung auf den Zufahrtsstraßen und der Rückgang des Getreidebaues zwingen zu Änderungen. Auch die seit einem Jahrhundert in Gang befindliche Ennsregulierung wirkt sich aus. Die Rumpel eignet sich auch für das Einholen des Schilfs, wo vor der Ennsregulierung und der Ausbaggerung des Flußbodens der Wasserstand die

Abb. 15. Zusammenschlagen der beiden Rumpelladen.

Erntenden manchmal zwang, das Schilf eine Strecke auf der Gabel zur Rumpel zu tragen.[42] Zum "Außarumpeln" nahm man da lieber einen Ochsen – selbst wenn man ihn entleihen mußte – als ein Roß. Die Ablöse der Pferde durch Motorfahrzeuge hat zur Folge, daß Wiesen, die nur Roßheu lieferten und auch heute keinen besseren Ertrag bringen, nicht mehr gemäht werden und schon binnen wenigen Jahren dort Schilf auftaucht. An anderen Stellen wirken sich die Flußarbeiten günstig aus, die ehemals sauren Wiesen tragen nun Heu für das Milchvieh. In früherer Zeit wurde im Winter das Heu von den Hütten der Ennswiesen auf sogenannten "Ganzschlitten" durch Zugtiere eingeholt. Heute ist dies vielen Höfen nicht mehr möglich, weil die Fahrt ein

249

Stück auf der Betonstraße entlang geht, die ständig mit Rücksicht auf den starken Fernverkehr der Motorfahrzeuge schneefrei gehalten wird. Der Traktor mußte daher Roß und Rind ablösen, doch ist die Entwicklung inzwischen noch weiter gegangen. In den Scheunen des Hofes ist durch den Ausfall des Getreidebaues Lagerraum frei geworden, andererseits fehlen die vielen helfenden Hände von einst, Bauer und Bäuerin müssen sich mit Hilfe der Alten und der Kinder durchkämpfen. Dadurch bedeutet die *Erfindung des Ladewagens* für so manchen Hof überhaupt die Möglichkeit, weiter wirtschaften zu können. Das Heu macht daher nicht mehr den Umweg über die kleinen Hütten, sondern kommt sogleich in die Stallscheune des Hofes. In kürzester Zeit hat sich eine Neuerung durchgesetzt und ein seit Jahrhunderten bewährtes Gerät hauptsächlich auf bäuerliche Wirtschaften in leichter Hanglage beschränkt, die ohne Benützung einer Straße auch zwischendurch zuführen können und über genügend Arbeitskräfte verfügen. Die Heuernte erfolgt dort zuweilen bei gleichzeitigem Einsatz von Zugtier und Traktor, wobei zwei Bretterrumpeln in Verwendung sind. Ein Knabe führt das Roß stückweise weiter, während Jugendliche und Erwachsene das Heu aufladen, ein Helfer bringt von der Heuhütte mit dem Traktor eine leere Rumpel herauf zur Heureihe und holt die volle ab (Abb. 10).

E 2. Die Sprisselrumpel

Die Sprisselrumpel, im oberen Ennstale Sprisselrummel genannt, habe ich im zweiten Teile meines wiederholt erwähnten Aufsatzes ausführlich besprochen. Hier sei nur die Art des Abladens auch im Bild gezeigt (Abb. 11). Während bei der Bretterrumpel der Roßhalter darauf achten muß, daß er das Tier langsam in Bewegung setzt, weil sonst bei einem zu starken Ruck das Fahrzeug unter der Last hinweggleiten könnte, muß auf steileren Hängen von vorn herein die Ladefläche durch Sprossen aufgelockert sein. Das Heu stopft ein Mann sachkundig zwischen die Sprossen und faßt es beim Höherschichten sorgfältig auf, wodurch eine Arbeitskraft mehr erforderlich ist, als bei der Rumpel im Tal. Ein Abstreifen der Ladung kommt nicht in Betracht, am schnellsten geht es mit dem seitlichen Kippen, das verschiedene Bezeichnungen hat. Für das Ziehen durch Menschenkraft gibt es Sprisselrummeln mit nur anderthalb Meter Länge, doch sind dies Ausnahmen, denn auf Steilhängen zogen Ochsenpaare, wofür Rummeln mit einem "Schnabel" gebaut wurden, der meistens aus einem natürlichen Krümmling (Hangbaum), sonst aus einem Stamm mit Hakenende bestand, wo die Verbindung zur Zugstange ansetzte.[43] Die Zugstange verhinderte beim Bergabfahren eine Verletzung der

Abb. 16. Sattelschleife mit Düngerladung, statt auf dem Schlitten, jetzt auf dem Traktor.

Tiere durch das nachschiebende Fahrzeug. Pferde werden mit Zugscheit vorgespannt, wodurch der Schnabel entbehrlich ist, jedoch für steilere Hangfahrten eine "Zig" angehängt werden muß, die – ebenfalls beladen – bremst und bei der leeren Bergfahrt keine Last bedeutet (Abb. 12). In gleicher Weise hängen die Oppenberger Bauern das Mistreis an, fallweise fand ich selbst für das Mistführen einfach Nadelholzäste als ausgleichendes, zusätzliches Fahrzeug. Neuerdings nützen die Bergbauern den Traktor als beweglichen Motorseilzug aus. So konnten wir im Sommer 1970 Filmaufnahmen machen, wie von einem Hofe in 1250 m Seehöhe der Traktor fast waagrecht zum oberen Rande eines Feldes hinausfuhr und von dort aus in der Fallinie an einem Seil die Sprossenrumpel herabließ und nach dem Beladen wieder hochzog. Die sonstige Arbeit des Zusammenrechens und Beladens unterschied sich nicht von der herkömmlichen, nur daß das Fahrzeug einst beim Ochsenfuhrwerk schräger zum Hang stehend beladen wurde.[44]

E 3. Schloapfn (für Forstbauten)

Auch für große Bauvorhaben benützte man bis in jüngste Zeit die bodenständigen einfachen Geräte, die nur für den bestimmten Zweck fallweise etwas

Abb. 17. Sattelschleife (Schloapfm) auf dem Halbwagen, einfache Ausführung.

umgestaltet wurden. So dienten noch vor wenigen Jahren sogenannte "Stein-leitern", die grundsätzlich der in dem 2. Teil meines Fahrzeugaufsatzes abge-bildeten Steinrummel entsprechen, als bewährte Mittel zur Fortbewegung der schweren Steine bei der Uferverbauung der Enns. Heute nehmen Hebema-schinen, die viel rascher arbeiten, den Menschen viel Mühe ab.

Gelegentlich kommt es noch jetzt zu erstaunlichen Umsetzungen alter Vor-bilder. Auf einem neuen Forstaufschließungswege nahe der Finsterberger-Hochalm im Gemeindegebiet von Johnsbach fand ich 1964 ein Ungetüm an Fahrzeug, etwa 6 m lang, die Kufen aus zwei stattlichen Baumstämmen (Abb. 13). Nachträglich stellte sich heraus, daß darauf Betonröhren befördert wurden, wobei ein Caterpillar die gewaltige Last zog. Nach den bäuerlichen Vorbildern nannten die Forstarbeiter das Gerät "Schloapfn".[45]

E 4. Die Räder-Rumpel

Anläßlich der Beschreibung des Johnsbacher "Heukarrens" habe ich die Donnersbacher "Radlrumpl" erwähnt, die auch in der einfachen Form, ohne seitliche Leitern, nirgends mehr aufgefunden werden konnte.[46] Das Gerät ist vielen Bergbauern noch gut in Erinnerung, weshalb es möglich war, daß

252

Abb. 18. Sattelschleife, festere Ausführung Hartholzsohle auf den Schleifstellen.

einer von ihnen, J. Schweiger, insgemein Hörmann, der – wie einst sein Vater – als der "heimliche Wagner" des Erlsberges gilt, für das Museum ein Stück in der herkömmlichen Bauweise, mit dem Schnabel aus einem Birkenkrümmling, mit birkenen Rumpelladen und Sprossen aus Fichte, im Jahre 1970 anfertigte. Die Kufen (Rumpelladen) sind 3,12 m lang, die Spurweite beträgt 1,16 m, die hölzernen Radachsen stehen auf jeder Seite noch 30 cm darüber hinaus. Die Herstellung gab Gelegenheit zu Lichtbildaufnahmen, der siebzehnjährige Sohn erwies sich als anstelliger und gewandter Helfer, der die Werkstradition des Hofes einst fortzusetzen vermag (Abb. 14 und 15). Anscheinend war die Räderrumpel doch nicht der Sprisselrumpel gleichwertig, die zudem viele Bauern selbst herzustellen vermögen, während sie keine Räder anfertigen können. Außerdem ist die Verbindung von Seilzug und "Hatschrumpel"[47], wie die Rumpel ohne Räder gelegentlich zur Unterscheidung von der mit Rädern genannt wird, der alten Arbeitsweise überlegen.

Verbindungen von Rad und Schlitten in der Art, daß die Achse hinter dem Schwerpunkt des Gefährts liegt, so daß die Kufen nur bei stärkerem Ziehen nicht schleifen, bildet G. *Berg* aus Jämtland und Västerbotten ab, wobei das erste Beispiel an die Schna'lgorn (Schnabelkarren) erinnert, mit denen der Dünger einst hochgezogen wurde.[48]

F. Zweirädrige Fahrzeuge

In diesem Zusammenhange können Gestellschlitten, deren Bergung hoffentlich doch noch gelingen dürfte, ehe fast alles vernichtet ist, keine Berücksichtigung finden. Es seien nur jene beiden zweirädrigen Fahrzeuge kurz hervorgehoben, auf die nach dem Bericht über das Zutalbringen von Laubbündeln auf Astschleifen die Last nachher für das flachere Wegstück umgeladen wird. Selbstverständlich dienen die gleichen Fahrzeuge auch zu anderen Fuhren, wie schon der Name des einen, "Heubudl" sagt. Die zwei Beispiele gehören zwar verschiedenen Gruppen von Fahrzeugtypen an, werden hier aber der Einfachheit halber hintereinander gebracht.

F 1. Die Ròdschloapfm (Sattelschleife auf Rädern)

Zum sommerlichen wie zum winterlichen Bergabführen von Baumstämmen durch Zugtiere sattelt man die Last auf einer kurzen Flöz- oder Holzrumpel, auch "Holzhund" geheißen, auf. Für krumme Waldwege gibt es eine um einen senkrechten, starken Eisennagel schwenkbare Auflage, den Reibsattel.[49] Einen Flachschlitten aus Jämtland, für die gleiche Aufgabe, jedoch mit ganz anderer örtlicher Ausbildung finden wir bei G. *Berg* Pl. XII/2, während die Formen Pl. XIII/1–3 schon zu dem alpenländischen "Halbschlitten" überleiten, denen Pl. XXII an die Seite zu stellen ist.

Die Stämme ruhen mit ihrem schweren Ende auf dem Fahrzeug auf, das leichtere gleitet über den Boden und bremst, wozu die Ladung hinten fallweise auch mit einer Kette umschlungen wird. Unten, auf besseren Wegen, wird "aufgerumpelt", das heißt, auch die Stammenden hebt man auf eine Rumpel, die darunter geschoben wird. Mit dieser Fahrweise ist G. *Berg* Pl. XIV zu vergleichen. Die Holzknechte, in diesem Fall "Zieher" geheißen, verwenden nicht derartige Flachschlitten, sondern Gestellschlitten für die winterliche Schlittenbahn, wobei sie vorn in die Unterseite der Stämme einen "Sattel" hacken, damit sie gut aufliegen. Sie begnügen sich für ihre gefährliche Arbeit ortsweise bis heute mit "Böckeln", Schlitten ohne Bremskralle.

Statt der Last als aufgesattelte Schleife gibt es eine aus zwei schwächeren Baumstämmen gefertigte Schleife, die sozusagen eine Verlängerung des Fahrzeuges – Halbschlitten oder Halbwagen – bildet. Wir können die verschiedensten Übergangsformen vom jeweils neu gebildeten Stück bis zu dauerhaften Gebilden noch bis ins letzte Jahrzehnt beobachten. Früher waren die Wege so steil und schlecht, daß es nicht möglich war, darauf mit einem vierrädrigen Wagen zu fahren. Die "Bergschloapfen" auf dem Räderpaar des Vorwagens – als Zwischenstück ein "Trackl" oder "Reibeisen" als Sattel – bot Abhilfe.

Abb. 19. Heubudl für händischen Zug.

Bei Fahrten im Tale tritt heute an Stelle des von Roß oder Ochsen gezogenen Schlittens der Traktor, und nur die Sattelschleife trägt die Last (Abb. 16), den Dünger.

Zum Rindenführen vom Berg herab nahm der Bauer früher in Treglwang (Paltental) nur den Halbwagen und das Querholz, Trackl genannt, mit. Die Schloapfn fertigte er oben im Walde an. Das kostete weniger Zeit, als wenn das Roß sich mit der Schloapfe hätte langsam bergauf mühen müssen und dadurch eine Verzögerung eingetreten wäre. Auch in Stainach fuhr man mit dem Halbwagen auf den Berg und führte als Verbindungsstück ein "Reibeisen" (Ablöse des hölzernen Reibsattels), einen Bohrer und "Schlittäugeln"

255

mit sich. Oben angekommen nahm man zwei schwächere Baumstämme, durchbohrte sie etwa 1 m vom vorderen Ende und schob rechts und links auf die zylindrischen Enden des Reibeisens eine Stange auf, die das Schlittäugel vor dem Herausrutschen sicherte. Nur wenn eine Anzahl von Fuhren hintereinander vorgesehen war, beließ man die Schloapfn, die hinten als Verbindung ein Trackl erhielt, ansonsten wurde sie zerschnitten und beim nächsten Anlasse neu hergestellt. Die Holme der Schloapfen ragten etwa 1 m nach vorn auf den Schlitten, damit auch er belastet wurde. Die auf einen Halbwagen oder "Zwoaradla-Gorn" (Zweirädlerkarren) aufgesattelte "Bergschloapfn" hatte eine Länge von etwa 3 m, das Querholz hinten war so lang, daß die schleifenden Enden den Abstand der Spurweite hatten. Scheiter und Lafn (Rinde) wurden quer aufgelegt, Knüttelholz der Länge nach.

Auf dem Erlsberg (Gemeinde Donnersbach) kam auf den "Halbwagenbock" eine "Schwinge" als Sattel, an der zwei schwache "Bäume" über Bohrlöcher befestigt wurden, dazwischen ruhten kleinere Stämme, als Auflager für Graß und anderes Streu, das man im Herbst nach Hause holte.

Hie und da finden wir die Sattelschleife auf Rädern, die *Koren* für 1838 als althergebracht nachgewiesen hat[50], auch im flach geneigten Gelände noch in Gebrauch, etwa zur Fahrt auf den Acker oder zum Heuführen (Abb. 17). Bei sorgfältigerer Ausführung sind die schleifenden Enden gesohlt (Abb. 18). Vor allem in Gebirgsgegenden können wir das Vorhandensein der Sattelschleife auf Rädern sicherlich öfter annehmen, als es bisher den Anschein hatte. Hier sei beispielsweise auf die Vorkommen in Graubünden, Salzburg, Kärnten und Südtirol hingewiesen[51]. Wenn auch stark verschieden, so gehört grundsätzlich auch eine Räderschleife dazu, die *Schmolke*[52] abbildet und der er Stücke aus dem Tessin und dem Wallis an die Seite stellt. Im steirischen Ennsbereich hätte eine Bestandsaufnahmen noch vor zwei Jahrzehnten ein dichtes Belegnetz erbracht.

F 2. Die Heubudl

Anläßlich der Suche nach dem "Graßlöffel" brachten sie mir beim "Veitlbauern" in Weißenbach a.d. Enns ein Bündel Hölzer vom Dachboden und fragten, was dies wohl sei. Auch der immerhin nicht mehr junge Bauer kannte sie nicht. Ich sagte, daß diese Hölzer zweifellos zum Seilspannen gedient hätten, allerdings hätten sie eine Form, die sich von den zahlreichen Stücken des oberen Ennstales unterschied und mir noch nicht begegnet sei. Kurz danach fand ich das Seilholz – unter dem Namen "Keil" – noch in Gebrauch. Es gehört zur Heubudl, jenem zweirädrigen Fahrzeug, das Kleinbetriebe verwenden, die über kein Zugvieh verfügen. Die Heubudl (Abb. 19) aus St. Gallen ist 4 m lang, hat eine Spurweite von 1,14 m und einen Raddurchmesser von 78 cm. Gegen das Kippen während der Ladetätigkeit schützen sie zwei einfache Stöcke mit Astgabeln. Beim Hereinführen von der Heuwiese geht der Ziehende zwischen den beiden Längsstangen, die Hände an der vorderen Querstange. Die Heufuhre wird der Länge nach mit einem Seil niedergebunden, dessen Spannung hinten mit Hilfe des Keils in einfachster Weise erfolgt.

Was hier geboten werden kann, sind nur Streiflichter, die den Blick auf einige Erscheinungen lenken, ohne sowohl im Einzelfall (Belegnetz) als für Gruppen (Gesamtheit der zum Typ gehörigen Formen) Vollständigkeit anzustreben. Am Beispiel der Graßzig ist zu ersehen, wie eng Stallwirtschaft, Waldpflege und Bringungsweise zusammenhängen, weshalb darauf einleitend ausführlicher eingegangen wurde. Immer wieder zeigte sich die gegenseitige Abhängigkeit von Bodenbeschaffenheit, Hanglage,[53] Wirtschaftsweise und Last. Wenn wir die immer rascher um sich greifenden Neuerungen im Auge behalten, so wird deren Übernahme uns auch über die alten Geräte, deren Bestandsaufnahme und Bergung ein Gebot der Stunde ist, vieles auszusagen wissen.

Anmerkungen

1. *Haiding*, K., »Fahrzeuge des steirischen Ennsbereiches und des Ausseer Landes«, 1. Teil, Zeitschrift des Historischen Vereines für Steiermark LX (1969) S. 173–198. 2. Teil LXI (1970) S. 127–149. Es werden zwar erhebliche öffentliche Mittel für die Erhaltung des Schlosses Trautenfels ausgegeben, die Hausherrenrechte übt jedoch ein Jugendherbergsverein aus, der Platzmangel verhindert sogar die Beschäftigung von Hilfskräften im Museum – auf Kosten der wissenschaftlichen Tätigkeit.
2. *Gunda* Béla, Gaffeldrögen i Karpaterna. In: Kulturspeglingar. Studier tillägnade Sam Owen Jansson, 19 mars 1966. Karlshamn, 1966. S. 109–123.
3. *Berg* G. Sledges and wheeled vehicles. Ethnological studies from the view-point of Sweden. Stockholm-Kopenhagen 1935.
4. Verschnittenes weibliches Kalb; flinker als ein Ochse. Im Ennstale nicht üblich, jedoch im nächsten großen Haupttal südlich der Niederen Tauern (Murtal).
5. Noch 1970 aus dem Munde des Bauern Hans *Kerschbauer* in Stainach aufgezeichnet.
6. Die Minderwertigkeit von Laubstreu hebt *Waldmeier-Brockmann* A., Sammelwirtschaft in den Schweizer Alpen, Eine ethnographische Studie, Basel 1941, S. 137 hervor; über Farnstreu S. 142, Grass, Grasseln, Grisen S. 139 f. *Schmeller* J. A., Bayerisches Wörterbuch. Neudruck der zweiten Auflage (1872–77) von *Fromann* G. K., Aalen 1961 Bd. I Sp. 1008 stellt zu zahlreichen deutschen Belegen auch dänisch »krat«, Buschwerk. *Levan-*

der, Lars, Övre Dalarnes bondekultur, I. Sthlm. 1943, bezeichnet S. 282 gehacktes Fichtenreisig als gebräuchlichste Streu.

7. *Waldmeier-Brockmann* erwähnt S. 129 »grasseln« und »schneiteln« im Berner Oberland, Grotz im Maderanertal und das Verbot des »grotzen und grasseln hauens« in alten Waldordnungen, weil das Notfutter ursprünglich nicht von gefällten, sondern von lebenden Bäumen genommen wurde. Im Ennstal lebt die Erinnerung an das Schnaiteln noch allgemein, das Landschaftsmuseum besitzt eine größere Anzahl von Steigeisen.

8. Nähere Angaben von dem im neunzigsten Lebensjahre stehenden »*Wolfbauern*« in Johnsbach und L. *Pürcher* in Mitterndorf.

9. Über den Tiefstall oder Tretstall siehe *Haberlandt* A., Taschenwörterbuch der Volkskunde Österreichs I, Wien 1953 S. 133 f.; über den »Umlaufstall« mit der Einrichtung des Dauermistes: *Schier* Br., Hauslandschaften und Kulturbewegungen im östlichen Mitteleuropa, 2. Aufl. 1966, Göttingen, S. 320. Den Umlaufstall im Ennstale erwähnt *Rhamm* K., Ethnographische Beiträge zur germanisch-slawischen Altertumskunde, 2. Abt., Urzeitliche Bauernhöfe in germanisch-slawischem Waldgebiet, 1. Teil, Braunschweig 1908, S. 930 f.

10. Über den Dauermist im Anhängstall wissen bejahrte Bauern noch zu berichten. Das Hochziehen des Schnabelkarrens mit dem über das Umlenkrad laufenden Seil wird auf Grund von Lichtbildern aus jüngster Zeit und in Zusammenhang mit den daraus hervorgegangenen Neuerungen an anderer Stelle behandelt. Zu dem Arbeitsvorgang vgl. *Haberlandt* M. und *Haberlandt* A., Die Völker Europas und ihre volkstümliche Kultur, Stuttgart 1928 S. 397. *Moro* O., Nockgebiet, Klagenfurt 1965, S. 250–253.

11. *Haiding* K., Fahrzeuge 1. Teil S. 178 Fußn. 25, Höfe des Murbereiches.

12. So kürzlich beim Tode des Windbacher-Altbauern im Obertal bei Schladming.

13. Auf der Niederscheibenalm, Bezirk St. Gallen.

14. Zig, mhd. züge stf. (*Lexer* M., Mittelhochdeutsches Taschenwörterbuch, 21. Aufl., Leipzig 1936). Statt »die Züge« heißt es in Aussee und um Schladming »der Zug«.

15. *Koren* H., Altertümliche Schlitten in Steiermark. Z. d. Hist. Ver. XXXVI (1948) S. 133.

16. Reis n., mhd. ahd. ris, frühahd. asächs. ags. hris, anord. hris »Gebüsch«. *Kluge* Fr. Etymologisches Wörterbuch der deutschen Sprache. Elfte Aufl. bearb. v. *Götze* A., Berlin 1934.

17. Karten entworfen anläßlich der Trautenfelser Ausstellung »Wald und Holz« von *Eckmüllner* O., dazu dessen Beitrag »Der Ennstaler Wald – einst, jetzt und in der Zukunft« im Ausstellungsheft »Wald und Holz«, hg. v. *Haiding* K. S. 7 ff., Gröbming 1958 (vergriffen).

18. *Goldstern* Eugenie, Beiträge zur Volkskunde des Lammertales. Sonderdruck aus der Zschr. f. österr. Volkskunde XXIV (1918) S. 16. Ganz ähnlich bei *Schmolke* W., Transport und Transportgeräte in den französischen Zentralpyrenäen, Hamburg 1938, S. 9 und Abb. 1 c.

19. Über dessen Arten und Verbreitung *Wildhaber* R., »The ‚Rope-wood‘ and its European Distribution«, Offprint from Studies in Folk Life, chapter 15, London 1969.

20. *Haiding*, Fahrzeuge I Abb. 2 S. 181.

21. *Haiding* K. Almleben in der Obersteiermark. S. 72 u. 73. In: Haiding, Almwirtschaft in der Steiermark, Gröbming 1962.

22. *Gstrein* F. J., Die Bauernarbeit im Ötztal einst und jetzt. Innsbruck o. J., S. 54.

23. *Rehsener* M., Die Gebirgsnatur in Vorstellung und Sage der Gossensasser. Zschr. f. Volkskd. I, Berlin 1891 S. 429 f.

24. *Prasch* H. Bäuerliche Volkskunde Kärntens auf Grund mündlicher und sachlicher Überlieferung. Klagenfurt 1965 S. 86. Mit vorzüglichen Zeichnungen hat schon *Moro* O., Hof und Arbeit in Kleinkirchheim 1939 (jetzt in seinem Sammelband »Volkskundliches aus dem Kärntner Nockgebiet«) Fahrzeuge behandelt.

25. *Berg* G. (Fußn. 3) S. 33. Das seltene Werk G. Bergs konnte ich erst nach Abfassung meiner

beiden Aufsätze über Fahrzeuge und nur durch die gütige Vermittlung von Herrn Bibliothekar Sam Owen *Jansson* kennenlernen.

26. »Staude« ahd. studa, mhd. stude »Strauch, Busch«, zu einer mit »stehen« verwandten idg. Wurzel gehörig. *Kluge-Götze* (Fußn. 16) S. 588. *Schmeller-Fromann* II 733; *Lexer* M., Kärntisches Wörterbuch Sp. 239; *Unger* Th. und *Khull* F., Steirischer Wortschatz als Ergänzung zu Schmellers Bayerischem Wörterbuch, Graz 1903, S. 570 f.
27. *Haiding*, Fahrzeuge I S. 198, Abb. 7.
28. Diese Literatur siehe *Haiding*, Fahrzeuge I, S. 174 f., 197 und Fahrzeuge II S. 127 f.
29. *Rehsener* M. (Fußn. 23) S. 429 f. und meine Ausführungen, Fahrzeuge I S. 175 ff.
30. Landschaftsmuseum Trautenfels, Inv. Nr. 5300.
31. Kleine Rumpel. Über diese siehe unten »Flachschlitten«.
32. *Goldstern* E. (Fußn. 18): Arné S. 42 f., Tafel VII Bild 7; bayard Tafel IX Bild 1–4.
33. *Niederer* A., Kurzbericht von der Forschungsexpedition nach Bessans (Haute-Maurienne), 9. bis 19. Oktober 1967. Österr. Zschr. f. Vkd. 73 (1970) S. 301 f.
34. *Haiding*, Fahrzeuge I S. 187. *Levander*, S. 239. *Kothe*, H., Verbreitung u. Alter d. Stangenschleife. In: Ethnogr. – Archäolog. Fschgn. I, Berlin 1953.
35. Weißenbach b. St. Gallen, Inv. Nr. 6164.
36. *Schmolke* S. 46, *Scheuermeier* II S. 121.
37. *Unger-Khull* (Fußn. 26) S. 441.
38. Zu »schlaipfen« *Schmeller-Fromann* II Sp. 531, 507 f., 509 f. *Haiding*, Fahrzeuge II S. 148 f.
39. Für so erfolgreiche Erhebungen, wie die B. *Gundas* im Karpathengebiet ist es in der Steiermark zu spät, die schwere Zwieselschlaipfe ist zumeist längst abgekommen. Siehe Fußnote 2.
40. Inv. Nr. 6165
41. *Haiding*, Fahrzeuge II S. 133 ff.
42. Auch auf den feuchten Wiesen wäre ein Wagen zu tief eingesunken. Man vergleiche dazu, was *Scheuermeier* II S. 127 über den »mächtigen Schlitten der Poebene« sagt, mit dem man nicht nur im Winter auf dem Schnee sondern auf schlammigem, von Wasser durchtränktem Gelände fährt, wo die Räder eines Wagens einsinken würden.
43. *Haiding*, Fahrzeuge II, Abb. S. 140.
44. Der Bergbauer Karl *Lackner* verbindet den Sinn für die kulturgeschichtlichen Werte des Bauerntums mit der Fähigkeit, Neuerungen aufzunehmen und zu verwerten. Dementsprechend ist er als Vertreter des Bauernstandes an zahlreichen Stellen führend tätig.
45. Auskunft von Förster August *Dietl*, Admont.
46. *Haiding*, Fahrzeuge II S. 142.
47. *Schmeller-Fromann* I, Sp. 1191: schleppenden, schleifenden Gang haben = hatschen.
48. G. *Berg* Plate XXIV, 2 und XXV, 1; W. *Schmolke*, Abb. V a, b, zu S. 52, Räderschleife, hauptsächlich für Heu und Getreide.
49. *Haiding*, Fahrzeuge II Abb. S. 136. Der angekündigte Aufsatz über »Holzgewinnung im steirischen Ennsbereich und im Ausseerland« wird 1972 in der Festschrift für M. Zender, Bonn, veröffentlicht.
50. *Koren* wie Fußn. 14, als Ochsenfuhre zum Abwärtsschleppen des schwer zu bindenden Alpheus.
51. *Scheuermeier* I S. 65 f. u. Abb. 82–84. Richard *Weiß*, Das Alpwesen Graubündens. Wirtschaft, Sachkultur, Recht, Älplerarbeit und Älplerleben, Erlenbach-Zürich 1941, erwähnt S. 147 die für den Heutransport verwendete Schleife und zeigt auf Abb. 45 eine aus dem Bündner Oberland am Tage der Molkenverteilung. Siehe auch E. *Hubatschek*, Lungau S. 78 (wenn der Weg flacher wird, werden auch hinten Räder untergeschoben!). O. *Moro*, Nockgebiet S. 278 f. gibt es beim Übergang zum flacheren Weg eine Vorrichtung zum »Aufwagnen«, bei der die »Schloafn« gehoben und ein zweites Räderpaar untergeschoben wird. Eine Steinleiter, die mit den Krümmlingen der beiden Holme auf die Wagenachse

kommt, während das andere Ende nachschleift, bei *Ligers* Z., Die Volkskultur der Letten I, Riga 1942, S. 211.

52. *Schmolke*, S. 53 und Abb. VIc.
53. Vgl. dazu auch *Schmolke*, S. 1 ff.

Sledges and Wheeled Vehicles in Wales

By J. GERAINT JENKINS

Sleds, Carts and Wagons

Within the boundaries of Wales, many stages in the evolution of transport are still represented and many vehicles of considerable antiquity have persisted to this day. Undoubtedly the earliest method of carrying goods was on the backs of human beings, and the burden rope which is still used by small-holders, particularly in north Wales, represents this ancient tradition. The persistence of the burden rope is an example of a primitive device, adapted perfectly to modern conditions, for undoubtedly it forms by far the most efficient means of carrying the limited quantity of hay grown on the *tyddyn-nod* (smallholdings) in many parts of the Principality. In Caernarvonshire, for example, the burden rope, *rhaff gario,* is still universal among the quarrymen-smallholders who have to harvest perhaps only half an acre of inferior hay. In those districts of small, upland fields, wheeled transport would be uneco-nomic, even if the smallholder owned draught animals. The hayfields are more often than not in close proximity to the farmstead and the harvest when it comes, usually in August, is a communal affair that still depends on the co-operative effort of relatives and neighbours. While the women collect the hay into cocks, the men, each with his burden rope, carry the bundles on their heads to the adjacent rick yard, and in a very short time a field is harvested. This method of carrying was once very common in all parts of Wales where the smallholding predominated and draught animals were rare.

Another device for human porterage that has persisted in Wales is the hand barrow used for carrying such loads as peat from inaccessible places (Peate 1934.54). In the nineteenth century hand barrows were common for general farm duties particularly in hilly districts. In 1850 in the Llanuwchl-lyn district of Merioneth, for example, Charles Ashton describes how dung was carried to upland fields by means of barrows (Ashton 1890.58–9). Each farm in the district, he says, specified a day for dung carrying and all the neighbours would congregate at the chosen farm with their barrows. The carrying was performed by means of a shuttle service; the load changing hands many times before it reached the upland fields. Hand barrows may still be seen in use in some parts of the country particularly on the peat beds

Fig. 1. A hand barrow from the Hiraethog district of North Wales. By permission of The National Museum of Wales Welsh Folk Museum.

on the moorlands of Central and North Wales. In May 1960 in the Hiraethog district peat blocks were carried for some distance from the beds to a road by means of a hand barrow. This was a home-made affair consisting of two straight side pieces eighty inches (204 cm) long to which were nailed seven flat slats twenty-four inches (61 cm) long. The peat was placed on the cross-pieces and carried over boggy ground to the trackway.

In other districts, peat was harvested by means of a hand-drawn sledge. At the Welsh Folk Museum, for example, there is a sledge seventy inches (178 cm) long and twenty-seven inches (69 cm) wide from the Dinas Mawddwy district of Merioneth which was used for carrying peat from Moel Benddin. This consists of two runners cut from slats of wood seven eighths of an inch (2.2 cm) thick and eight and a half inches (22 cm) deep, joined together by a number of battens which form the carrying surface of the sled. These are tenoned and pegged to the runners which are themselves shod with sheet iron. One of the cross battens is removable and the sled was carried on the

Fig. 2. A slide car from Glyncorrwg, Glamorgan, South Wales. By permission of The National Museum of Wales Welsh Folk Museum.

shoulders. For carrying the peat to a farmstead, the sled was dragged by means of a cord attached to the runners by a set of withy loops. The great advantage of the hand drawn sled over other means of transport in this case was the fact that the sled was easily portable in an upland district where it would be difficult to use any form of draught animal. In addition the sled being a dead weight would be self-braking on the long steep descent to the farmstead.

Sledges

Animal drawn sledges are still widely used in the upland districts of Wales. They have persisted because they are still the most efficient method of transport in those districts where any form of wheeled vehicle would be difficult to operate. They have persisted too because they are cheap to produce, for unlike the lowland farmer who was in the past always able to call on the services of numerous village craftsmen to make and repair the tools and implements of the farm, the upland agriculturist often living in an isolated homestead was some distance from a village. He was forced by circumstances to make a great deal of his own equipment for in many parts of upland Wales the specialized craftsman was a rarity. In many parts of Wales, therefore, simple transport devices made by farmers for their own use may still be found and the design and construction of those devices is varied in the extreme. Nevertheless, as far as sledges are concerned, there are two basic types: the slide car and the sled.

The slide car is a very simply constructed vehicle consisting of two stout side timbers some twelve feet (3.6 m) long joined together by a number of cross-bars which carry the load. The side pieces project at one end to form a pair of shafts which are attached to the horse high up on the collar. The vehicle is dragged along the ground at a tilt, hence it is necessary to fit a wooden framework or ladder at the back so that the load does not fall out. A smaller ladder is also fitted at the front, while the load can be made more secure by tying it down with ropes—a necessary procedure when carrying hay, fern, peat or wood on steep mountain slopes. In some districts, notably in Glamorgan and Carmarthenshire, it is customary to equip slide cars with railed sides, but in other areas further north the side rails are absent. The dragging ends of the slide car are protected from wear by wooden shoes, each some eighteen inches (46 cm) long and cleft to an elliptical shape. These, which are easily replaceable, are fitted to the beams by means of an iron ring and bolt.

Although in the nineteenth century slide cars were well known in most of the hilly parts of Wales (Davies 1815.205), in more recent times they were far more common in the southern part of the country, particularly in the counties of Cardigan, Brecknock and Glamorgan. In Montgomeryshire and Radnor the sled was far more common. Davies noted that in South Wales the slide car was widely used. 'In hay or corn harvest', he says, 'it is not uncommon to see half a dozen of these carrying from the same field; one party loading the cars in succession;—a boy mounted on each horse drives full speed—another party attends at the stackyard to receive the loads as they arrive in regular rotation. A stranger', he adds, 'will hardly credit the celerity with which a large quantity will be carried in a short space of time by this simple method' (Davies 1815.205).

It has been suggested (Peate 1935.220) that the slide car developed from the hand barrow; one pair of handles disappeared while the other pair was lengthened to form shafts. Whatever its origins, the slide car was widely used in many parts of the world. In Britain it was never known on the English

264

Plain, while on the European continent the slide car was limited in its geographical distribution to the northern and southern peripheries of the continent. The distribution of the slide car in limited regions is of some significance for there seems to be a close relationship between its distribution and that of the more elaborate one-horse cart. Those districts which from time immemorial possessed the slide car, later possessed the one-horse cart and, as a general rule the four-wheeled wagon was unknown to them (Jenkins 1959. 162 ff). In eighteenth century Scotland, for example, the slide car was universal and the sled was almost unknown there. This is very significant when one remembers that Scotland was the scene of a very important development in the design of the one-horse cart, for in the late eighteenth and early nineteenth centuries the well known Scotch cart was made by a number of renowned Scottish wheelwrights and exported to other parts of Britain. The design of the cart was copied by wheelwrights throughout the world, but nevertheless, the Scotch cart must be regarded as a 'super slide car on wheels' and the direct successor of a vehicle known in Scotland from time immemorial.

The sled differs from the slide car in that the whole body of the vehicle or the runners fitted to that body is dragged along the ground. While the slide car is essentially a one-horse sledge fitted with a pair of side shafts, the sled can in theory be drawn by any draught animal for it is fitted with chain traces.

The sled has a very much wider geographical distribution than the slide car. In Britain it was never limited to the mountainous regions of the west and north, for it was equally well known in the marshy districts of Somerset and Wiltshire. It was even known in the Fens and East Anglia, while throughout the North of England it was commonplace. In East Anglia, for example, the sled which was used as recently as 1957 (Green 1957) for carrying ploughs over flinty roads to the fields, consisted of two side pieces joined together by a number of cross-pieces. The *slod*, as it is known in East Anglia, was fastened to the harness of the horse by chain traces. Simple vehicles of this type were well known in other parts of England until recent times. Unlike their English counterparts, most of the Welsh sledges are tilted forwards on runners; the angle of the tilt often depending on the slope of the land.

Although a great variety of sleds occur in Wales they may nevertheless be divided into four distinct types:

A. *Harvesting sled* fitted with fore and tail ladders. This is known specifically as a *Car Llusg* in Central and North Wales.

B. *General purpose sled* fitted with four corner poles. This is known colloquially as a *sledge* or *slêd* in Central and North Wales.

C. *Tumbril sled* or *Box sled* for carrying manure and lime. This is known as a *Sledge Fach* in Montgomeryshire, *Trol Deilo* in Caernarvonshire and as a *Car Tail* in Merionethshire.

D. *Wheeled sled* which is an ordinary general purpose sled without the runners but fitted with a pair of small cast iron wheels at the back. This type of vehicle is most common in the Dovey valley of Montgomeryshire.

A. Harvesting Sled

This type of vehicle is used for all harvesting duties on Welsh upland farms, not only for harvesting hay and the limited amount of corn grown on each farm but also for harvesting peat and ferns which are still widely used for bedding animals. In Central and North Wales a great variety of sleds occur, mainly due to the fact that sleds are made by the farmers themselves. Their ultimate form depends, therefore, on the farmer's skill and the availability of raw material. The harvesting sled is known throughout the mountainous districts of Central and North Wales as well as in North Cardiganshire, North Pembrokeshire and in the Black Mountains of Carmarthenshire. In Brecon and Radnor as well as in Central Cardiganshire the slide car has always been far more common.

The most common type of harvesting sled is shown in Figure 3. This consists of two side pieces eighty inches (203 cm) long joined together by eight or more cross pieces which are mortised to the side frames to give the vehicle a width of twenty-eight inches (70 cm). The chain traces are attached to a pair of iron brackets at the front of the side frames, and as the vehicle is designed for use in hilly country the harvesting sled is equipped with fore and tail ladders as well as with side rails. In most districts the rails of the end ladders are horizontal, but in the Dolgelley district of Merioneth they are perpendicular. Both ladders stand some thirty inches (76 cm) high, and each one is mortised to the side frame of the vehicle. In addition a pair of rails joins the two end ladders, each one being pegged to the ladders. Vertical spindles eighteen inches (47 cm) long join the side rails to the frame.

Unlike the *slods* of East Anglia (Green 1957) some of the *slipes* of Ulster (Thompson 1958. Fig. 2) and the sleds of Westmorland (Garnett 1912.32), Welsh harvesting sleds are almost invariably tilted forwards on runners which take the heavy wear of the dragging vehicles. Worn runners are replaced at

Fig. 3. Harvesting slide from Llanbryn-Mair, Montgomeryshire, Mid-Wales. Photo G. H. Peate. By permission of The National Museum of Wales Welsh Folk Museum.

regular intervals by the farmers themselves. In some cases the runners are nailed directly to the side frames of the sled, but in others the body of the vehicle is tilted away from the runners and attached by means of pegs.

One of the main advantages of the sled over wheeled vehicles in hilly districts is its braking qualities. The vehicle is a 'dead weight' so that there is no great danger of its sliding on to the horses' hoofs. But on very steep slopes the most common method of braking is to place a piece of wood attached by chains crosswise under the front of the runners. On the very steep slopes of Snowdonia it was customary to harness two horses to a sled; one in front, the other behind the vehicle. While the front horse was equipped with ordinary trace harness, the rear animal was equipped with cart harness (Information from the late Mr. T. P. Jones).

B. General Purpose Sled

In its basic construction this vehicle is similar to the harvesting sled, but it differs from it in that it does not have side rails or end ladders but is equipped with four corner poles. These are usually fitted to pairs of rings bolted at the

267

Fig. 4. Tumbril sled from Llanbryn-Mair, Montgomeryshire, Mid-Wales. By permission of The National Museum of Wales Welsh Folk Museum.

top and bottom of the side frames. An example seen in the Cwmlline district of Montgomeryshire in 1960 measured seventy-two inches (183 cm) long and twenty-eight inches (71 cm) wide. The carrying surface was formed by six pieces of three inch (8 cm) by two inch (5 cm) timber mortised to the side frames, while the pair of runners were bolted to the front end of the frames and kept some three inches (8 cm) away from the frame at the back by a pair of wooden blocks, ten inches (25 cm) long. This type of home-made sledge is mainly used for carting moor gorse and other material that can quite easily overlap the edge of the vehicle.

C. Tumbril Sled

This type of vehicle, again equipped with runners, is used for carrying manure or lime to the fields. Again the tumbril sled was used in all parts of Britain but it persisted longer in the Celtic West. In Cornwall, for example, the *drag* and its smaller version the *slide butt,* were still used in recent years for carrying compost, earth or fertiliser (Worgan 1815.37–8). In Wales, the tumbril sled is still used, particularly in the hilly north and centre; indeed, some mid-Wales farmers consider it superior to the box cart for liming as the lime can be used in a less slaked condition. With the ordinary wheeled cart, the lime has to be shovelled out at the level of the worker's eyes, but as the body of the tumbril sled is no more than a few inches from the ground, there is no such danger to the worker's face. Although there is a considerable variation in the size and construction of tumbril sleds in Wales, the most common type consists of a box-like body some forty-eight inches (122 cm) long, thirty-two inches (81 cm) wide and eighteen inches (47 cm) deep. A pair of runners is pegged to the side frames but they are not fitted in any way. As the manure or fertiliser has to be shovelled out of the body of the vehicle, the floorboards are laid lengthwise, parallel to the side frames of the vehicle. Manure carrying vehicles of all types have this construction as the carter needs a smooth surface for his shovel to slide along. Sturt says 'one board a shade thicker than the one next to it will lift a low but exasperating ridge ... stones may get wedged in between two cross boards' (Sturt 1923.63). Providing the vehicle with long boards overcomes these difficulties.

D. The Wheeled Sled

As far as can be ascertained, the wheeled sled is unknown in other parts of Britain, but in Wales, particularly in the Dovey Valley, it was widely used until recently. The wheeled sled is a development from the general purpose sledge so common in this central region of Wales. Like the sledge, the wheeled version of it has a simple rectangular body, generally equipped with four corner poles. It differs from it however in that the runners are pegged to the front of the side frames only, while at the back a pair of small wheels with a diameter of between nine and fifteen inches (38 cm) is attached to a wooden or an iron axle. On the older examples of the wheeled sled these wheels are solid discs with iron tyres, but in the later vehicles the wheels are cast iron. An example seen at Llanbrynmair, Montgomeryshire, in the summer of 1960 measured ninety-six inches (244 cm) long, and forty-eight inches (122 cm) wide, while the five spoked cast-iron wheels had a diameter of nine inches (23 cm). This vehicle is used primarily for carrying ferns for animal bedding from the uplands. With a heavy load the runners at the front act as brakes when the vehicle is brought downhill, while the wheels are locked with a chain passed around them.

Fig. 5. Wheel car from Llanbister, Radnorshire, Mid-Wales. By permission of The National Museum of Wales Welsh Folk Museum.

Two Wheeled Carts

In very sharp contrast with the English plain, where a heavy, two-horse cart predominates, the two wheeled vehicles of Wales and of Western and Northern Britain generally are varied in the extreme. There are *gambos* and *wains*, *trottle cars* and *low back cars*, *butts* and *long carts* and a great variety of other local types. Yet, despite the miscellaneous nature of 'oceanic' carts, they all display a number of common features. Whether a cart comes from Donegal or Inverness, Cornwall or Cardigan, it is always very light, while the fact that it can be drawn by one horse clearly distinguishes it from the English tumbril. In construction 'oceanic' carts generally show two very distinct influences which are present in all of them, to a greater or lesser extent. Before describing the carts of Wales in any detail, one must look at these influencing factors which are firstly, the slide car and secondly the Mediterranean ox cart.

270

Fig. 6. Y-Frame of an ox cart from Whitland, Calmartten-shire, West Wales. By permission of The National Museum of Wales Welsh Folk Museum.

1. The Influence of the Slide Car on Welsh Carts

The slide car has been described in detail in an earlier section. Its most significant feature is that it is specifically a one-horse vehicle, where the timbers forming the side frames are extended forwards to form a pair of shafts. Its geographical distribution, as has been said, is of some significance for those areas on the European periphery which possessed the slide car, at a later date possessed the two wheeled one-horse cart. The *Car Gwyddelig* (Irish Car) and the *Truckle Carts* of Wales, which will be described at a later stage, are very definitely simple wheeled versions of the slide car. The more elaborate *gambos*, 'Scotch' carts, long carts and others also show the unmistakable traces of the slide car in their design, more particularly in the fact that they are all one-horse vehicles, while on all pre-nineteenth century examples, and on many after that date, the shafts were rigid extensions of the side frames and not independently constructed members.

271

2. The Influence of the Mediterranean Ox Cart on Welsh Carts

Undoubtedly the earliest vehicle known to mankind was the forked slide car; a simple vehicle that has persisted to this day in many parts of the world. Czekanowski for example writes that in his childhood days in the Grojec district of Poland drags made of forked tree trunks ... were used for removing boulders from fields, while similar ox-drawn sleds were also used for carting hay from marshy meadows in which horses and wagons would sink (Czekanowski 1952.114). The forked slide car was well known before 5000 B.C. and it is almost certainly the predecessor of the earliest form of wheeled vehicle—the triangular ox cart. This type of vehicle was in general use among the urban community of the Near and Middle East from around 3500 B.C. (Childe 1954.207) and consisted of two long poles forming the frame of the carrying platform converging at the front to form a central draught pole which was lashed to the yoke of a pair of oxen. This simple vehicle of great antiquity has persisted in many parts of Southern Eurasia from Portugal to the Philippine Islands (Haudricourt 1948.54–64) while a slightly more advanced version of the triangular ox cart is universal throughout this vast area. This southern ox cart consists of a rectangular body frame and an independently constructed draught pole running back under the floor to provide extra support under the carrying platform. This construction was well known in Wales and Western Britain generally for as long as ox draught remained in vogue, while the earlier transitional stage between the triangular cart and the modern Mediterranean vehicle was also very common. Here the apex of the triangle was extended forwards to the shape of a Y. An ox cart from Whitland, preserved at the Welsh Folk Museum, for example is provided with a body consisting of a central draught pole 'to which at the rear end are fixed timbers in a V-formation with a cross strut to complete the body framework. The complete structure is of Y formation and is fixed to the axle by two iron pins through the twin ends of the Y' (Peate 1935.226–7).

In addition to structural similarities between the vehicles of Wales and those of Mediterranean Europe there are also similarities in general appearance. At the Basque Museum in Bayonne, for example, a typical modern Mediterranean harvesting ox cart is preserved. Basically this vehicle consists of a rectangular platform some twelve feet (366 cm) long placed on a pair of slightly dished spoked wheels. It has low sides which curve over the wheels in an arch, while it is equipped with a central draught pole to which a pair of oxen is yoked. In appearance the body of this vehicle is almost identical to the *wain* of Cornwall, the Scotch harvest cart and the *gambo* of Wales, particularly the *gambo* of the Gower Peninsula. Although these British vehicles are at present equipped with side shafts for horse draught, ox traction was well known in Western Britain and vehicles equipped with central draught poles were very common.

Throughout Southern Eurasia ox drawn carts equipped with bodies of basketwork have been known from time immemorial. An ox drawn vehicle from present day Macedonia, for example (Jenkins 1959. Plate 2 D), has a Y shaped body with five upright stakes fitted into each side of the frame. Osiers are interwoven between these stakes to provide solid basketwork sides. In the past this construction was well known in Celtic Britain. Peate quotes the sixteenth century poetry of William Llŷn (Peate 1935.230) where the body of a Welsh ox cart is described as a *cawell* (basket). Though the reference is scant, the *cawell* construction of Mediterranean Europe must have been known in Wales at that time. Indeed it is possible that the intricately spindled and balustered wain of the Vale of Glamorgan is a highly sophisticated development of the simple basket work construction, as is the spindled construction of such wagons as those of Gloucestershire, Somerset and Devon (Jenkins 1961.182 ff).

The Truckle Cart

One of the simplest of all wheeled vehicles is the Truckle Cart which was particularly prevalent in the Gower Peninsula of South Wales. This is a very simple horse-drawn vehicle, which is basically a slide car placed on an axle and a pair of wheels. In some cases these wheels are spoked, but most of the Gower truckle carts were equipped with solid, tripartite disc wheels. These simple wheels, rarely more than two feet six inches (76 cm) in diameter, bound with an iron tyre two and a half inches (6 cm) wide, are of great antiquity having been invented by the inhabitants of the Near East somewhere around 3500 B.C. Although the disc is certainly earlier than the spoked wheel, the earlier wheeled vehicles represented in the archaeological records north of the Alps already had spoked wheels. It may be imagined therefore that although disc wheels were perfectly strong and durable for the carriage of heavy goods they were far from efficient at times when speed and manoeuvreability were required. From around 2000 B.C. spoked wheels are represented in the archaeological records of Mesopotamia and by 500 B.C. the technique of building both disc and spoked wheels was known to people from China to Western Europe (Childe 1954.208). Until recent times solid wheeled carts remained in vogue in many isolated districts of the world, particularly on

Fig. 7. A truckle cart from Llangennith, Gower, Glamorgan. By permission of The National Museum of Wales Welsh Folk Museum.

carts and wagons designed for carrying heavy goods locally. It has been suggested that the occurrence of disc wheels has influenced the shape and design of the spoked wheel (Evans 1942.110). Spoked wheels fitted to post-nineteenth century truckle carts in Gower are rarely more than two feet six inches (76 cm) in diameter, and are never more than two and a half inches (6 cm) wide and display hardly any dish.

The axle of the truckle is either of iron, sometimes encased in a wooden bed, or consists of a wooden axle bed with iron arms no more than two inches (5 cm) in diameter. This is bolted to the side frames, while the wheels, the centre of which are bored to accommodate iron bearings are fastened to it by a linch pin. The wheels are usually of softwood, consisting of three planks mortised together, rounded and bound with iron.

The frame of the body is a rigid extension of the shafts, giving the whole vehicle a length of some thirteen feet. One example preserved at the Welsh Folk Museum consists of nothing more than a pinewood pole split down the

274

Fig. 8. Irish car from Llanharran, Glamorgan, South Wales. By permission of The National Museum of Wales Welsh Folk Museum.

centre to form the side pieces of a truckle car. These decrease in width from four feet (120 cm) at the back to two feet six inches (77 cm) at the front. The carrying platform simply consists of a number of wooden slats nailed to the side frames.

Like its predecessor, the slide car, the truckle is equipped with a tail ladder. This is some four feet (120 cm) high and consists of six or more vertical rails mortised to the rear cross bar and the side frames. A pair of side ladders runs from the front of the carrying platform at an angle of forty-five degrees to be bolted to the tail ladder.

In construction the light and manoeuvreable Gower truckle, like its Irish counterpart (Thompson 1958. Section 4) shows the unmistakable influence of that ancient vehicle, the slide car. Indeed, the truckle is nothing more than a slide car placed on a simply constructed axle and small disc wheels. As such it must be considered as a typological ancestor of all Welsh two wheeled vehicles.

The Irish Car

In many ways the so-called Irish car *(Car Gwyddelig)* is a close relative of the truckle cart, and like the truckle it was mainly used in South Wales, more particularly in the Vale of Glamorgan and in Brecknockshire. Walter Davies, writing in 1815, describes the Irish car of Brecknockshire as 'Convenient to carry grain to the market or mill or small loads of any kind. In peculiar situations they are recommendable for harvest work on account of the expedition and lightness of roping. We have seen it', he adds, 'used as a sociable covered with a tarpaulin and chairs placed inside it by a farmer conveying his family to town in rainy weather' (Davies 1815.210).

Unlike the truckle which is usually equipped with small disc wheels, the Irish car is equipped with stout, slightly dished spoked wheels each one of no more than thirty-six inches (91 cm) in diameter. The tyre is either two and a half inches (6 cm) or three inches (8 cm) wide. The chief characteristic of the Irish car is the shafts which continue in a straight line from the side frames of the body in the manner of a slide car. On some of the late Irish cars, however, the shafts are constructed independently of the body framing, but are firmly bolted on the inside of the frames and again project in a straight line from them. Davies again quotes that in 1815 separately constructed shafts were occasionally replacing the old slide car method of continuing body frames to form shafts. 'The new method was gaining ground on account of timber of short lengths being cheaper to make them' (Davies 1815.211). Nevertheless on the Irish car as well as on more sophisticated Welsh vehicles the shafts do present the appearance of being part of the body framing; a feature of construction which clearly distinguishes the 'oceanic' cart from the 'continental'. In the latter, as for example in the East Anglian tumbril, the shafts are very clearly separate and removable members.

An example of a late nineteenth century Irish car preserved at the Welsh Folk Museum which was used in the Llanharran district of Glamorgan until 1935, is some fifteen feet (458 cm) in length. The carrying platform, which is cross-boarded, is six feet (183 cm) long and three feet seven inches (107 cm) wide. It is equipped with a tail ladder four feet (122 cm) high and four feet seven inches (137 cm) wide bolted to the rear cross bar of the body. A stout cross piece is bolted at right angles to the vertical slats of the tail ladder about half way up its length. Behind this is a revolving cylinder which is firmly fixed to the bar. This is a rope roller used for tightening the ropes passed around a load of hay or other material; a necessary procedure when traversing

Fig. 9. Gambo from Llanwnnog, Montgomeryshire, Mid-Wales. By permission of The National Museum of Wales Welsh Folk Museum.

steep hill slopes. Rope rollers are not often found on British farm vehicles; indeed outside Wales, the only vehicles that possess it are the harvesting wain of Cornwall and the four-wheeled wagons of South-Eastern England.

On the Irish car a railed side-board leaning out at an angle of forty-five degrees over the wheels form the sides of the cart. The eight or more spindles that form this are not boarded in any way. A removable fore ladder or cratch is also fitted 'opening and closing by means of pivots turning in the shaft or frame of the car' (Davies 1815.210).

It has been suggested that the description 'Irish' does not of necessity mean that the cart originated in that country, but that the word *Gwyddelig* (Irish) 'may be used as a term to indicate anything old fashioned, native or strange to the present generation' (Peate 1935.226–7). The Irish car may therefore be an indigenous development of the slipe which has been in existence in Wales from time immemorial. It is on the other hand almost certainly an improved version of the truckle car; a vehicle well known not only in Wales but in Ireland as well. Thompson suggests that the existence of the truckle in

277

both countries 'may even indicate that the Welsh and Irish vehicles have a common origin in Ireland', but there is no literary evidence to prove or to disprove it (Thompson 1958. Section 1).

The Wheel Car

The wheel car is a long bodied two-wheeled vehicle unknown outside Wales. Until recently it was widely used on the hill farms of Central Wales, particularly in the county of Radnor. It may be regarded as the direct successor of the sled, rather than in the same category as the truckle and Irish cars which are wheeled versions of the slide car. Unlike the simple wheeled sleds of Central Wales, the Radnorshire wheel car is equipped with spoked, dished wheels of relatively large size placed in the middle of the vehicle's body. In the early nineteenth century these wheel cars or long bodies were equipped with small, possibly solid disc wheels attached to an axle placed underneath the body (Davies 1815.205). The more recent versions of it are equipped with larger spoked wheels placed above rather than underneath the body framing. The horse is attached to the vehicle by chain traces, not at the lighter, but the heavier end of the body. When loaded with bracken or hay the load is so disposed that a large proportion of it is accommodated in front of the wheels. This makes the front end even heavier and since the bottom of the side frames are bulged and lined with iron the front acts as a brake on descending a hill.

The floor of the vehicle which measures some thirteen feet six inches (398 cm) long and three feet two inches (96 cm) wide consists of a number of regularly spaced wooden slats mortised to the side frames. As the vehicle is designed for carrying such material as hay or grain in sacks, a solid, boarded floor is unnecessary. At each corner of the vehicle a great deal is carried in the front half of the car, it is equipped with a short non-removable fore ladder. In addition, a pair of railed ladders or cratches prevent the load from spilling outwards over the wheels.

One of the most distinctive features of the wheel car is the overslung axle, which has the effect of keeping the body low to ensure efficient braking and stability on steep hill slopes. On an example made at Llanbister Road, Radnorshire in 1929, the all wooden axle, five inches (13 cm) square, is firmly bolted to the frame of the car. A metal rod is bolted underneath it to give the axle added strength. Since the arms are only very slightly canted, the wheels display only a slight amount of dish (Jenkins 1961.82). They can be linked for descending particularly steep hills by means of a chain fixed to the frame of the car. The wheels in the traditional manner of the West Midlands and

Central Wales are equipped not with one piece tyres, but with a series of crescent shaped pieces of iron called *strakes*.

The wheel car with its long commodious carrying platform, its large wheels and overslung axle, is a remarkable and unique vehicle. Its design owes a great deal to Radnorshire craftsmen who wished to make a vehicle as easy to pull as a *gambo* and as stable and controllable on mountain slopes as a sledge. Its persistence in Radnorshire suggests that the wheel car is by far the vehicle best suited to the topography of the area.

Ox Carts

Ox traction has been well-known in Wales for countless centuries and examples of ox equipment and ox-drawn carts from many parts of the country are preserved at the Welsh Folk Museum. The influence of these ox-drawn carts, which go back in time to the prehistoric Middle East, is very clearly seen on the more elaborate horse-drawn vehicles of present day Wales.

Payne, in his paper, *Cwysau o Foliant Cyson* (Payne 1947.1–24), has drawn on literary evidence to show the importance of the ox as a draught animal in medieval Wales. Unfortunately, there are only very scanty references to the types of vehicle that these drew. One of the few *Cywyddau* which describes a vehicle in anything but fanciful terms is that written by William Llŷn, sometime between 1534 and 1580. William Llŷn was either a native of the Llŷn Peninsula or he was a descendant of a Llŷn family. For many years he lived in the Oswestry district, but he also dwelt for short periods in Denbighshire and Merioneth (Peate 1935.230). In his *cywydd* to solicit a wain from Edward ap Huw Conway of Bryneithin, Llandrillo-yn-Rhōs, Denbighshire, in 1562, there is an elaborate and fanciful description of the vehicle.

Dwy olwyn aur ar dâl nant
Drwy oglais yr ymdreiglant.
Certwain arw i sain ar sarn
Cloch cywydd cylchog haearn.
Oes man hwnt sy o'i mewn hi,
A lle i dreiddio llyw drwyddi?
Oes bogel ac ysbigod,
A rhwyll ynghanol pob rhod?

Two golden wheels rolling along the brow of the valley. A wain with grinding sound on the paved road, the bell that sings the song of the wain hoop. Has it room beyond to place the draught pole? Has it a nave and axle and latticed spokes in each wheel?

The body of the vehicle William Llŷn describes as a *cawell* (basket) and the description ends with the line

Wich wach yn ôl chwech ychen
(Wich wach behind six oxen)

Unfortunately the remainder of the poem as well as another *cywydd* written by the poet on the same subject (Morrice 1908.21) is concerned only with fanciful descriptions of the wheels and has little to say about the technical detail.

What then does one learn of the construction of the medieval wain from William Llŷn's description?

a. The wain was a two-wheeled vehicle equipped with spoked wheels. These wheels were probably tyred with a single hoop *(cylchog haearn)*, and this feature of construction was unusual in medieval farm vehicles for in most parts of the country agricultural vehicles were equipped either with solid disc wheels or with roughly shaped spoked wheels, which were left unshod or tyred with strakes.

b. Like all ox-drawn vehicles the wain was equipped with a central draught pole or *neb* bolted to the framework of the body. This passed between a pair of draught animals and was attached to them by a yoke. Paired draught was essential when using oxen, for the draught pole can not be used when only one animal is required.

c. From the scant reference to *cawell*, the wain had either basket work sides or the intricately spindled and balustered wooden sides which had the appearance of wicker work. The well known illustration from the Luttrell Psalter of the fourteenth century shows a two-wheeled harvest cart with an open framework body. The spindles forming the body area are apparently mortised to the side frames and the top rails. Going back even further the Cottonian manuscript illustration of the eleventh century presents very much the same appearance, but in this case the body is formed of horizontal rods woven through upright stakes. The Welsh wain of medieval times had one or other of these methods of construction.

d. Although the wain was a two-wheeled vehicle, it must have been rela-

Fig. 10. Radnorshire wagon from Newchurch. By permission of The National Museum of Wales Welsh Folk Museum.

tively large for it required the tractive power of six oxen. While a pair of these oxen would be yoked to the draught pole, the other two pairs would probably be yoked to chain or rope traces.

At the Welsh Folk Museum is preserved an eighteenth century ox wain of great significance. It came from Wallas Farm, Ewenni, in the Vale of Glamorgan and seems to be very near the design of the medieval ox cart. The vehicle was built between 1750 and 1770 by a certain Thomas Thomas, a Glamorgan wheelwright whose initials appear on the front-board of the wain. Although the wheels are missing, their diameter must have been somewhere in the region of six feet (184 cm). The body itself consists of light, considerably chamfered side frames to which is mortised a large number of round wooden spindles. The inner top rails curve into arched guards which pass over the wheels, and the whole vehicle very closely resembles the ox carts of Mediterranean Europe. In addition the vehicle is equipped with horizontal side-boards and the floorboards are laid lengthwise, which suggests that the

281

wain was used for other than harvesting duties. The significance of the Ewenni wain arises from the fact that not only does it seem to be the direct descendant of the medieval wain and the wains of Mediterranean Europe, but also it seems to be the immediate predecessor of the well known bow wagon. This remarkable four wheeled vehicle was known not only in South Wales but also in the West of England. From Cornwall to Berkshire and from Pembrokeshire to Hampshire the bow wagon was once a familiar sight; indeed wains resembling the Ewenni type were also known throughout this vast region (Jenkins 1961.200–4).

Unlike the Ewenni wain, the Cornish wain and the harvesting carts of the West of England (Jenkins 1961. Plate 2 B) the ordinary harvesting ox carts of South Wales did not have the overlapping sideboards which were curved over the wheels. Like the familiar *gambo*, these ox carts had railed, open sides though they still retained the draught pole of their English and Mediterranean counterparts. In construction, the ox cart showed little variation throughout South Wales and it seems to have been used, particularly in west Carmarthenshire, until the early years of the present century. An ox cart from Whitland, preserved at the Welsh Folk Museum, is equipped with slightly dished hoop-tyred wheels some sixty inches (152 cm) in diameter. The framework of the cart body consists of two side pieces fixed to the all wooden axle by a pair of bolts. The builder of this vehicle used a balk of timber with a bulge in it in the necessary position. This was sawn in two, shaped and used as side timbers. The bulge was then bored to take the pins which connected the body to the undercarriage. This method of construction was also widely practised in East Anglia where wheelwrights used naturally bulged timber for the pillows and bolsters of four-wheeled wagons, which were pierced by the all important king-pin (Jenkins 1961.122). The vehicle which has a long-boarded floor, is equipped with a draught pole that runs parallel to the side frames. This is bolted to the cross bars. The body itself consists of four upright stakes mortised on either side of the frame. Near the bottom of these uprights a horizontal rail that runs the whole length of the vehicle is bolted while another parallel rail is bolted some half way up the stakes.

By removing the two bolts that attach the frame to the axle, the whole body of the cart can be removed. This can be replaced by a Y-shaped draught pole *(fforchwan)* and can be used for carrying timber or sacked grain. The Y-body which resembles the coupling pole of a four-wheeled wagon (Jenkins 1961.88) can be fixed to the axle and wheels by a pair of bolts that pass through the ends of the Y. The significance of the Y shape in the development of wheeled transport has already been discussed.

The Gambo

In most parts of Wales, the well-known cart, the gambo, was used until recently for all harvesting duties. Not only was this vehicle found in all parts of Wales, but it occurred widely in the border counties of Herefordshire, Shropshire and West Gloucestershire. It is a close relative of the Cornish wain, the Scotch harvest cart and the North of England long cart, and undoubtedly is a development from the Mediterranean ox cart.

The harvesting vehicle used in the Gower Peninsula and occasionally in South Pembrokeshire is virtually the same vehicle as the Cornish wain, although it is still known as a 'gambo' (Jenkins 1959. Fig. 2; Worgan 1815. 37–8). The body of the Gower gambo consists of a flat platform some eight feet (244 cm) in length and five feet two inches (155 cm) in width at the front. The dished spoked wheels, each some four feet (122 cm) in diameter are set in the body, so that the width of the carrying platform is no more than four feet (122 cm) behind the wheels.

Above the wheels a section of a hoop or a curved piece of wood is fitted to act as a guard, preventing the load of hay or corn from spilling over the wheels. The top of this arch is connected to the side frame by a bar of iron or timber bolted to the frame and hoop. A wooden slat which runs the length of the body is also fitted to the carrying platform acting as a side plank. At the back a small windlass is fitted to the crossbar and this is used for tightening the ropes passed over the load.

Like the wain, the Gower gambo could be used for horse or ox traction. When oxen were used, and they were used in Gower until the third quarter of the nineteenth century, the gambo, like the wain, was equipped with a central draught pole firmly bolted to the frame of the cart.

The gambo used in the remainder of Wales differs from the Gower cart in that it does not possess the characteristic wheel arches of the latter. In order to prevent the load of hay or corn from spilling over the wheels and clogging them, the gambo is equipped with a pair of ladders which are fitted in the body frame in an upright position behind the wheels. Each side-ladder consists of two vertical standards two feet (61 cm) high to which are mortised a pair of horizontal rails some three feet (91 cm) long. The ladders either fit into slots in the frame or are mortised to it. In addition, the gambo is either equipped with fore and tail ladders, or with four poles, one at each corner of the vehicle. The body itself consists of a flat rectangular platform some ten feet (305 cm) long and five feet (152 cm) wide. The two heavy side frames are continued beyond the body to form a pair of shafts. The wheels are approximately four feet (122 cm) in diameter. In early nineteenth century Wales, it is noted that many gambos were ox-drawn (Davies 1815. I. 201) and, like the Cornish wain, these were equipped with central draught poles.

Long Carts

Throughout Western and Northern Britain a native development from the simple and ancient harvest cart is the long bodied cart. In the West of England a cart which may be regarded as the direct successor of the wain is found. This vehicle possesses a built up body rather than a simple platform and it has wide solid sideboards that curve archwise over the wheels (Jenkins 1961. 201). In the North of England too, the long cart with its planked sides leaning out over the wheels may be regarded as the direct successor of the ox wain 'with an open body furnished with shelvings' (Marshall 1788.254). In Scotland and in Ireland (Smith 1813.101; Thompson 1958. Section IV) the same development can be traced, while in West Wales, particularly in the counties of Cardigan, Pembroke and West Carmarthen the long cart virtually replaced the traditional gambo in the last quarter of the nineteenth century. In South Cardiganshire the side-less gambo is not remembered and it is the long cart that bears the name 'gambo'. In North Cardiganshire, in the Talybont district, the flat gambo was replaced by the long cart some sixty years ago. Here these long carts are known as 'longbodies'. The boundary between the traditional flat gambo in Carmarthenshire occurs along the River Cothi. East of that river most of the harvest carts are of the gambo type, while west of it the long cart predominates.

The framework of the long cart is similar to that of the gambo, the shafts being rigid continuations of the frame. A single width of planking some twelve inches (30 cm) deep caps the frame and this is held in place by three or four pairs of wooden standards or side supports. Each standard is bolted to the side plank, while above each side plank are two railed sideboards which run the whole length of the vehicle.

Both the gambo and its successor, the long cart, are specifically harvest vehicles and apart from undertaking a few days' work in summer and autumn, they are laid up for the remainder of the year. Like most Celtic carts, the gambo and long cart are light, one-horse vehicles whose origins may be traced back to Mediterranean Europe and to the native slide car.

Fig. 11. Montgomeryshire wagon from Llanwnnog. By permission of The National Museum of Wales Welsh Folk Museum.

Box Carts

Over the major parts of Wales, simple sledges and wheeled versions of those sledges have been used for countless centuries to meet all the transport requirements of the farm. Davies, writing in 1815 for example, noted that 'within the memory of a person now eighty years of age, there were only two carts in the parish of Penbryn, near Cardigan; sledges were the only carriages' (Davies 1815. I. 205). This could well apply to many other parishes in eighteenth century Wales, but nevertheless in the relatively level districts of the country there must have been some kind of box cart, in addition to truckles, wheelcars and gambos. These were used for carrying loose material in bulk, such as loads of dung, sand or gravel. Unfortunately there is very little evidence to show what pre-nineteenth century box carts were like. Prints and drawings show very little of their construction and literary evidence is negligible. Davies however describes the carts of Pembrokeshire as long and narrow; those of Cardiganshire he describes in the same terms. The wheels of the latter were four feet six inches (137 cm) in diameter, the body five feet ten inches (178 cm) long, two feet ten inches (86 cm) wide and one foot

285

Fig. 12. Denbighshire wagon from Ruthin. By permission of The National Museum of Wales Welsh Folk Museum.

three and a half inches (39 cm) deep. The cart could carry sixteen bushels and had a track of four feet three inches (127 cm) (Davies 1815. I. 206). Little else is known of these vehicles.

Most of the carts that have persisted in Wales are of the Scotch variety (Jenkins 1959.173–5). Whether these carts are native developments of an earlier type or whether as in Lowland England the pattern had been imported from Scotland (Young 1813. I. 161) it is impossible to tell. In early nineteenth century Wales the one-horse cart was established on estates in the Vale of Towy, in Brecknockshire and North Cardiganshire, but they were gaining in popularity only very slowly (Davies 1815. I. 208). Agricultural writers of the time were quite convinced of their superiority over other vehicles. Sir Edward Hamilton, a landowner of Brecknockshire for example, said 'My one horse carts ... are certainly admirable things ... the general introduction of these would be both an improvement and a great saving' (Davies 1815. I. 208). In England and in Scotland too agricultural writers were equally enthusiastic about the virtues of the one-horse cart.

Whatever its origin the one-horse box cart has been well known in Wales

286

for the last hundred years and occurs with little variation in design throughout the country. The box cart is a relatively light vehicle, usually equipped with all iron axles and slightly dished wheels some four feet (122 cm) in diameter. In many cases the slight dish is compensated by the fact that the spoke mortises are staggered. The wheels are usually narrow tracked and shod with hoops rather than strakes. On some vehicles the shafts are rigid continuations of the body framing but, in the later examples, the whole body is designed to tip, and in this case the shafts are continuations of the underframing. This is fixed to the axle. The body consists of one or more planks, often of deal which on many carts are bolted to one or more upright ribs. The sides of the cart in this case present a panelled appearance. When the cart is required for harvesting, a wooden framework can be fitted to the top rail, thus greatly enlarging the carrying surface of the vehicle. In addition, on some carts a pair of solid sideboards can be slotted into the top rail, particularly for carrying root crops. On some carts the width of the floor at the front is less than the width at the back. This facilitates the tipping of loose material.

A typical example of a late nineteenth century cart from Llanwnnog in Montgomeryshire has the following measurements:

Diameter of wheels = 48" (122 cm)
Length of body   = 75" (191 cm)
Width of body   = 51" (130 cm)
Depth of body   = 18" (46 cm)

Four Wheeled Wagons

Over much of Wales the four-wheeled wagon is unknown for it is unsuited for work in a hilly country and on high moorland (See Jenkins 1961.47–58 for a full discussion of the distribution of wagons in Britain). It does occur however in those districts which from time immemorial have acted as geographical and cultural extensions of the English Plain. In the south the Vale of Glamorgan, that region of trim, thatched villages, represents an extension of English lowland culture into Wales. As an element in this cultural extension one finds a bow wagon of superb design and elegance which is closely related in type to the panel-sided wagons of the Vale of Berkeley and Wessex (Jenkins 1961.188–204). The broad eastern face of the Welsh Massif overlooks the wide curve of the Severn Valley and is entered by several broad vales. Along these valleys of the Wye, the Usk, the Severn and others, countless invaders have made their way and countless ideas from the English plain

Fig. 13. Glamorgan wagon from Pyle. By permission of The National Museum of Wales Welsh Folk Museum.

have passed, penetrating the very heart of the highlands. Along the Severn Valley, for example, cultural elements like the short handled shovel and the half timbered house have penetrated almost as far as the shores of Cardigan Bay as has the four-wheeled wagon based on Shropshire design. In the north too, wagons of West Midland design occur as far westwards as the county of Anglesey.

Wagon types in Wales therefore, must be regarded as intrusions into the country from the English Plain. In the south there is an intrusion from the West of England along the Monmouthshire Coastal Plain to the Vale of Glamorgan and even into South Pembrokeshire. From Hereford and Shropshire there are intrusions along the valleys of the eastward flowing streams and in the north intrusion from Shropshire as far westwards as Anglesey.

Welsh farm wagons may be divided into six distinct types:

(a) *The Glamorgan Bow Wagon* which is a panel sided bow-wagon related to the wagons of Wessex and the Vale of Berkeley (Jenkins 1961. 198–200).

288

(b) *The Monmouthshire,* which is a simplified version of the traditional Hereford box wagon (Jenkins 1961.134 ff.).

(c) *The Radnor Wagon,* which is also closely related to the box-wagon of Hereford.

(d) *The Montgomeryshire Wagon,* a medium sized box wagon closely related to the Shropshire wagon (Jenkins 1961.146 ff.).

(e) *The Denbighshire Wagon,* a heavy vehicle closely related to the box wagons of the North Midlands (Jenkins 1961.152 ff.).

(f) *The Trolley* which is widely used in the southern Border Counties of Radnor, Brecon and Monmouth is a type that has been known in the West Midlands from at least the mid-eighteenth century.

(a) *The Glamorgan Bow Wagon*

From the Vale of Berkeley in Gloucestershire, the bow wagon can be traced along the western banks of the Severn, through South Monmouthshire to the Vale of Glamorgan. In a greatly degenerated form it is found even in South Pembrokeshire, an area historically and culturally associated with Lowland Britain.

Although in shape and design the Glamorgan wagon is similar to the Wiltshire, the West Berkshire, the North West Hampshire, the Dorset, and the North Somerset Vale of Berkeley (Jenkins 1961.189–200) bow wagons, in detailed construction it is somewhat different. Of all the panel-sided bow wagons, the Glamorgan wagon is the most elegant, possessing 'the seemingly inevitable beauty and fitness of the last phases of the sailing ships and of other specialized creations which have been perfected by generations of men content to work in one tradition' (Fox 1931.154). Undoubtedly, the wheelwright's craft in Glamorgan had been developed into an art which displayed itself not only in the four-wheeled wagons built by craftsmen in the later nineteenth century but also in earlier vehicles such as the Ewenni ox wain. In Glamorgan, wagons were regarded almost as family heirlooms and in the Cowbridge district their first journey after delivery from the wheelwright was to take the family to a place of worship on Sunday. As in Gloucestershire wagons too were widely used as hearses to carry the bodies of their deceased owners to the cemetery.

It is probable that the distinct regional type of wagon became fixed in the early years of the nineteenth century. Davies notes that bow wagons 'similar to those used in many English counties' were used in many parts of the

Fig. 14. A late example of a trolley. By permission of The National Museum of Wales Welsh Folk Museum.

country in 1815 and, he says, they were advantageous for carrying hay or corn from upland fields 'where carts with half the loads would hardly stand'. Undoubtedly the wagon was a fairly recent innovation at that time, for as Davies says 'In many parishes in the hills, where twenty years ago only carts were to be seen, now almost every farmer ... has a wagon' (Davies 1815. I. 208–9; details of Glamorgan and other wagons are given in Jenkins 1961. Chapters V–VI).

(b) *The Monmouthshire Wagon*

The Monmouthshire wagon is a rare type of panel-sided box wagon which came into existence in the last quarter of the nineteenth century. It is found in rural North Monmouthshire, North West Gloucestershire and in the Forest of Dean and it may be regarded as a greatly simplified version of the traditional Hereford box wagon, showing many features of construction, particularly in the design of the under-carriage of that heavy, durable box wagon.

290

(c) *The Radnor Wagon*

Despite the hilly nature of much of Radnorshire, four-wheeled wagons were extensively used there mainly for carrying root crops, gravel and for journeys to Hereford cider orchards. The wagon displays many characteristics of the traditional Hereford box wagon, but in design and construction it is definitely a degenerate type. This degeneration becomes far more accentuated as one moves westwards into the heart of the county.

(d) *The Montgomeryshire Wagon*

The Shropshire wagon in its pure form is found in much of the eastern part of the country, but as one moves westwards the type gradually degenerates. In the valleys beyond Welshpool the type of wagon forms, although closely related to the medium sized Shropshire box wagon, is much plainer in design and less elaborately built. They are generally plank sided rather than panelled while the planks themselves are thicker, making the wagon more suitable for stone and gravel carting. In Montgomeryshire, the wagon is a general purpose farm vehicle used alongside carts and sledges for a great variety of purposes. In West Montgomeryshire it seems likely that the wagon did not develop until relatively late, for vehicles predating 1880 from the area are rare.

(e) *The Denbighshire Wagon*

The heavy, straight-lined Denbigshire wagon is found on many of the larger farms of Denbigh and Flint. Its use extends westwards and a few wagons are still found on the farms of the North Wales Coastal Plain, the lower Conway Valley and occasionally in Anglesey.

While in the east of the region the wagons are well constructed and in general design resemble those of Staffordshire, North Warwickshire and Cheshire, towards the West there is a distinct deterioration in style and construction. The controlling factor in the design of the Denbighshire wagon is that it is designed for heavy non-harvest work, and so the side planks, the under-carriage and floor-boards are much heavier and thicker than is normal in farm wagons. It should be noted that despite a very thorough search of Cheshire and South Lancashire in 1955–6 no traditional wagon of any kind was found. Indeed, many of the farmers expressed the opinion that wagons were unknown in the county. Holland (1808.117) does say that a few wagons were used in the arable district around Northwich. Undoubtedly these wagons were of the Staffordshire-North Warwickshire type. (For a full discussion of the vehicles of Cheshire, see Jenkins 1961.230).

(f) *The Trolley*

In Hereford and the adjacent counties the box wagon is a general purpose farm vehicle used not only for harvesting but in the cider orchards and for carting gravel as well. In this region however, the flat bedded wagon or trolley has been known for many centuries specifically as a harvesting vehicle. This four-wheeled vehicle was also known in eastern Radnor and Brecon.

In the last decade of the nineteenth century the design of the trolley was taken over by the large scale manufacturers and the vehicle became a common sight in many parts of the country. But in the Southern Border Counties the trollies were village built and date back at least to the last quarter of the eighteenth century. These older trollies can be distinguished from the later mass produced type by the high loading platform and the large diameter of the wheels. Often all four wheels of the later trolley are of the same size but the rear wheels of the older variety are much larger than the fore-wheels.

In Wales, therefore, examples of sledges and wheeled vehicles representing most of the evolutionary stages in the development of transport are represented. Most of the vehicles were in use until recent times and have only disappeared during the era when the horse ceased to be the main motive power on Welsh farms.

Bibliography

Ashton, C.: Bywyd Gwledig yng Nghymru; in *National Eisteddfod Transactions*, 1890.
Childe, V. E.: in *A History of Technology*, 1954, I.
Czekanowski, Jan: Z Dziejow Wozu i Zaprezegu, in *Lud*. 1952; translated from the Polish by C. Z. Sliwowski (unpublished).
Evans, E. E.: *Irish Heritage*, 1942.
Davies, W.: *A General View of the Agriculture of South Wales*, 1815, I.
– *A General View of the Agriculture ... of North Wales*, 1815.
Fox, C. L.: Sledges and Wheeled Vehicles, in *Antiquity*, 1931, V.
Garnett, F. W.: *Westmorland Agriculture*, 1912.
Green, Charles: The Prehistoric Slod, in *Eastern Daily Press*, 11 May, 1957.
Haudricourt, A. G.: Contribution a la Géographie et L'Ethnologie de la Voiture, in *La Review de Géographie Humaine et d'Ethnologie*, 1948, No. 1.
Holland, H.: in *General View of the Agriculture ... Cheshire*, 1808.
Jenkins, J. G.: Two Wheeled Carts, in *Gwerin*, 1959, II/4.
– *The English Farm Wagon*, 1961.

Marshall, W.: *Rural Economy of Yorkshire*, 1788, II.
Morrice, J. C.: *Barddoniaeth William Llŷn*, 1908.
Payne, F. G.: Cwysau o Foliant Cyson, in *Llenor*, 26. 1947.
Peate, I. C.: *Diwylliant Gwerin Cymru*, 1934.
– Some Aspects of Agricultural Transport in South Wales, in *Archaeologia Cambrensis*, 1935.
Smith, S.: *General View of the Agriculture ... Galloway*, 1813.
Sturt, G.: *The Wheelwright's Shop*, 1923.
Thompson, G. B.: *Primitive Land Transport of Ulster*, 1958.
Worgan, G. B.: *General View of the Agriculture ... Cornwall*, 1815.
Young, A.: *General View of the Agriculture ... Essex*, 1813, I.

Les types de chars utilisés en Pologne féodale, du X au XVIIIe siècles

B. JEWSIEWICKI

Avant d'analyser les différents types de moyens de transport terrestre utilisés en Pologne féodale, il y a lieu, en guise d'introduction, d'esquisser l'évolution du transport économique par terre de "l'Entre-Oder-et-Bug". La position géographique du pays est intermédiaire par excellence. Tout au long de son histoire, la Pologne recevait et transmettait les influences culturelles venant des deux sens (l'est-l'ouest), non sans conserver pour elle-même plusieurs de ces nouveaux éléments. Liée par sa culture intellectuelle avec l'Europe latine, elle ne demeure pas moins héritière de l'est dans sa culture matérielle. Enfin jamais ni la mer Baltique ni la chaîne des Carpathes ne l'ont soustraite aux influences venant de la Scandinavie, ou de la zone méditerranéenne ou occidentale.

Les différents types de moyens de transport utilisés dans "l'Entre-Oder-et-Bug" reflètent bien cette situation médiane : la Vistule constitue la limite occidentale de l'attelage à brancards *(holoble)*. A l'est de cette ligne, l'application du métal dans les chars paysans est de plus en plus rare, l'attelage à boeufs de plus en plus fréquent.[1]

L'apparition en Pologne des moyens de transport à roues doit être liée avec la culture archéologique dite lusitanienne, considérée de plus en plus souvent, comme proto-slave.[2] La première roue découverte à Biskupin, datée du VIIIe siècle av.n.è., est suivie par d'autres découvertes affirmant l'utilisation économique du char.[3] D'ailleurs les conditions avancées par Childe[4] comme étant *sine qua non* pour l'apparition et l'application du char s'y trouvent parfaitement réunies. Rapidement ce moyen de transport devient relativement important, comme le prouvent les résultats des fouilles en Poméranie,[5] qui attestent aussi son haut niveau technique. L'expansion au sud de la branche poméranienne de culture lusitanienne, enrichie d'éléments scandinaves (germaniques), a permis non seulement une plus large extension du char, mais aussi d'importants contacts avec la culture celtique. Les influences celtes, sinon la présence des celtes au nord des Carpathes, sont attestées par les archéologues polonais. Le très haut niveau technique de leurs chars funéraires découverts en Tchécoslovaquie, prouve que le contact ne pouvait être que fécond.[6] Il nous est très difficile de dire si au sud-est se forme un type différent, héritant

294

de la culture scythe son char massif et résistant.[7] Certes, avec l'expansion de la culture lusitanienne vers le sud-est, de nouveaux éléments ont pu y être amenés, mais les quelques rares découvertes ne permettent de rien affirmer.

Le déferlement des nomades asiatiques sur l'Europe orientale et centrale apporte ces éléments incontestablement nouveaux dans le domaine du transport. Le plus important a été certainement l'attelage moderne, dont l'Europe médiévale a largement bénéficié.[8] L'autre apport est constitué par le char léger, très maniable, permettant les déplacements brusques. Ces deux éléments mis ensemble ont profondément modifié la technique du transport.[9] Les Slaves participant au grand mouvement des migrations adoptent non seulement la technique de l'attelage et de la construction qu'ils transmettront après à l'Europe occidentale mais aussi celle du camp fortifié construit de chars. Quelques siècles après, ce dernier, perfectionné par les Taborites, leur assurera quelques victoires éclatantes.[10] La troisième étape de l'évolution en question se place entre le moyen âge et les XVI/XVIIe siècles. Deux facteurs y paraissent déterminants : a. le développement économique de la Pologne féodale et plus spécialement l'essor des villes ; b. à partir des XI/XIVe siècles, l'établissement de la route commerciale Est-Ouest par la Pologne du Sud et la Russie du Sud vers Constantinople et la Mer Noire. Le transit ne disparaîtra tout à fait qu'au XVIIe siècle quand il sera remplacé par celui de la plaine centrale (Varsovie) qui aura d'ailleurs moins d'envergure et d'importance.[11]

Entre le Xe et le XIVe siècle se fixe définitivement la forme du char ainsi que les modes d'organisation du transport commercial en Pologne. C'est à cette époque que se réalise la synthèse des apports des deux périodes précédentes. Elle est heureusement secondée par la prospérité économique. Le char polonais du XIVe, XVe ou XVIe siècle largement pourvu d'éléments métalliques, robuste mais n'étant pas massif, représente le haut niveau technique européen. Son équipement permet de longs voyages commerciaux relativement confortables. L'apparition de grands entrepreneurs-voituriers qui disposent de nombreux chevaux, chars et conducteurs et louent leurs services aux commerçants, consacre l'importance de cette activité économique en Pologne.[12] Il semble bien que les mêmes voituriers et conducteurs assurent le service du transport de l'armée polonaise. Le char s'y perfectionne et s'y enrichit d'éléments métalliques empruntés à l'affût de canon. En même temps, l'apparition des marchés régionaux et le développement de l'exploitation agricole permettent le progrès du transport agricole qui se perfectionne au contact du transport commercial. Enfin, l'artisanat spécialisé aussi bien dans les villes que dans les villages fleurit. Le long des routes commerciales se développent des villages spécialisés dans les réparations des chariots.

Fig. 1. Attelage à bœufs au repos. Aquarelle de J. H. Muntz, fin du XVIIIe siècle, Album, Cabinet de Gravures de la Bibliothèque de l'Université de Varsovie.

Dans cet état de choses, la multitude et la spécialisation des différents moyens de transport routier ne doivent pas surprendre. Suivant sa fonction, le char est non seulement équipé différemment mais aussi différemment construit. C'est aussi à cette époque qu'apparaît la voiture assurant le transport des personnes grâce au coffre suspendu sur quatre ceintures en cuir en guise d'amortisseurs (ill. 25 et 26). Ce système était connu à la fin de l'époque romaine en Thrace. Au moyen âge, les princes russes ont voyagé dans des chars pourvus d'une telle suspension. L'Europe occidentale reçoit ce système probablement de la Hongrie, mais rien ne prouve que le *coach* n'a pas évolué indépendamment en Europe orientale à partir d'un type de voiture comme celui qui nous est connu par les enluminures russes. Les deux d'ailleurs sont probablement tributaires de la voiture thrace.[13]

Le recul général à partir de la deuxième moitié du XVIIe siècle est aussi très sensible dans le domaine du transport, qui suit le sort du commerce des villes. Le succès définitif de la noblesse et la reféodalisation du pays accentuent les difficultés ressenties aussi bien par le commerce transitaire que par le transport à longue distance. Les transformations économiques à l'échelle atlantique et européenne entraînent la mutation de la structure du commerce polonais, en faveur des produits agricoles et forestiers. Après les grandes

296

Fig. 2. Transport de la colonne de Sigismonde de Checin à Varsovie, gravure de W. Hondius du XVIIe siècle, Z. Gloger, Encyklopedia Staropolska Illustrowana, Warszawa 1903, t. IV, il. 23.

découvertes, le transit asiatique ne passe plus par la Pologne et le commerce russe emprunte de plus en plus la voie maritime ouverte encore par la Hanse Teutonique. L'instabilité politique en Europe centrale (guerre de 30 ans) et la crise économique de la seconde moitié du XVIIe siècle lui portent les derniers coups. Le commerce extérieur de Pologne, qui se borne au blé et aux produits forestiers, suit presque exclusivement la voie fluviale et cela pour deux raisons : a. les produits dont la valeur commerciale est peu élevée par unité de poids empruntent de préférence la voie d'eau; b. le passage à la mer se fait du sud au nord et dans ce sens la Pologne dispose d'importantes voies d'eau. Enfin, avec la reféodalisation du pays, le commerce extérieur échappe aux villes par suite de la politique anti-urbaine de la noblesse. Le marché national en train de se former aux XVe et XVIe siècles disparaît et les domaines redeviennent autarciques. Le grand voiturier disparaît et le transport pour les besoins du commerce local et régional passe entre les mains des simples conducteurs qui sont souvent en même temps des commerçants ambulants. Le transport pour les grands domaines est assuré par leurs paysans dans le cadre de la corvée. Les conséquences de cet état de choses sont évidentes : la régression est totale et la stagnation ne sera rompue que vers la moitié du XVIIIe siècle. Le transport commercial connaîtra encore une courte période de montée en desservant les stations de chemin de fer, avant de lui céder totalement sa place.[14]

Le progrès dans la construction du char est représenté par les graphiques

Fig. 3. Transport du sel des mines de Wieliczka, M. Zywirska, Saliny wielickie w sztychach Wilhelma Hondiusa, « Biuletyn Historii Sztuki », XVI, 1954, N⁰ 4, il. 23.

ci-joints. Les grandes lignes ainsi que les causes de cette évolution étant exposées en résumé ci-dessus, voyons donc maintenant quels sont les types de chars utilisés.

La classification naturelle, c'est-à-dire suivant les catégories qui apparaissent dans les sources, me paraît la plus heureuse. Elle reflète, en effet, les valeurs qui sont importantes aux yeux des usagers.

La distinction entre l'attelage à boeufs et celui à chevaux apparaît le plus souvent, notamment dans les documents concernant le transport agricole (inventaires, testaments, etc). Elle reflète principalement les différences d'attelage, lesquelles entraînent certains caractères spécifiques dans la construction. A l'époque et dans les genres de sources mentionnés ci-dessus, la distinction en question marquait premièrement la différence de valeur : le char à boeufs étant toujours plus rudimentaire, donc moins cher.[15] Le caractère même de la traction bovine permet l'utilisation du char robuste, grossièrement travaillé. A cette époque, il est d'habitude dépourvu de tout élément métallique et constitue l'oeuvre de l'artisan du village. Les frais de confection étant relativement bas, ils sont à la portée de la plupart des paysans. Malheureusement les sources ne disent presque jamais s'il est attelé de boeufs ou de

298

Fig. 4. Char à deux roues – enluminure du manuscrit du XVe siècle de la Chronique d'Urich von Richentale, J. Matuszewski, op. cit., il. 3.

vaches. La vache était sûrement utilisée par les paysans pauvres pour le transport à courte distance. La tradition d'un tel attelage est encore vivante dans toute la région des Carpathes.[16] L'avantage de l'attelage bovin réside dans la simplicité relative du char et de l'attelage même, le joug est jusqu'à dix fois moins cher que le collier de cheval et nettement plus simple à confectionner.[17] Tandis que le boeuf peut se nourrir presque tout seul pendant le trajet, le cheval exige de l'avoine. Cela nous explique l'importance de l'attelage bovin au sud-est de la Pologne actuelle et en Ukraine, qui est la seule région de l'Europe centrale et orientale à avoir connu le char à boeufs dans le transport commercial à grande distance (Czumacy du XIXe siècle, ill. 1). Profitant de nombreux terrains vagues, les conducteurs laissaient les animaux paître pendant la nuit.[18] Cela non seulement diminuait sensiblement le prix de revient mais permettait aussi de charger des marchandises au lieu d'avoine. Ce dernier avantage compensait la petite différence entre la

299

Fig. 5. Char à deux roues, bâché, du XVIIe siècle, aquarelle de Dolabella, Musée National Varsovie, collection de Witke-Jezewski.

charge utile du char à chevaux et celui à boeufs. En montagne, le boeuf ou la vache tenaient et tiennent encore aujourd'hui lieu d'âne. Dans cette optique, il est compréhensible que chaque régression économique augmente considérablement le rôle des bovins dans le transport.[19]

A propos de l'attelage bovin, un dernier point reste encore à élucider : le transport des charges extrêmement lourdes.[20] Le boeuf étant plus lent mais aussi plus calme et plus assidu que le cheval, permet la coordination efficace des attelages à unités nombreuses. Cependant, il est impossible de parler dans ces cas de moyens de transport spécialisés, vu qu'on a presque toujours affaire à des constructions de fortune, fort primitives, conçues pour un seul usage et abandonnées ensuite (ill. 2).

Passant à l'attelage à chevaux, il faut s'arrêter un moment sur la question de leur nombre. La distinction établie suivant ce critère recouvre une partie de la typologie des moyens de transport. Dans les sources de l'époque féodale, on rencontre les attelages de un à dix chevaux (ill.3), avec une nette préférence pour les attelages pairs.[21] L'analyse de la construction ainsi que de l'utilisation permet de dégager 4 types distincts : a. le char léger à un cheval assez répandu, particulièrement au nord-est de la Vistule où l'utilisation de

300

Fig. 6. Charbonnier dans une rue de Varsovie en 1869, gravure d'après le dessin de W. Gerson, « Klosy », VIII, 1869, p. 108.

brancards accentue une certaine préférence pour les attelages impairs. Cette forme *(holoble)* diffère des brancards médiévaux ainsi que de ceux qui servent encore actuellement à l'attelage des chars à deux roues. Ces derniers constituent une prolongation du char même et (ill.4) sont par suite immobiles.[22] Au moyen âge, le collier de cheval était par les cordes attaché à ces brancards. Au nord-est de la Pologne et en Russie, les brancards sont mobiles (ill.5 et 6) et au moins à partir du XVIe siècle liés entre eux par une sorte d'anse *(duha)*. Cette forme mobile découle probablement directement du traîneau asiatique recopié à l'usage du cheval et dont la forme était connue précédemment pour le chien, le cerf et le renne à la saison sans neige. Les nomades asiatiques ont été probablement les premiers à introduire l'attelage à brancards mobiles et l'attelage à timon et à cordes (ill. 7). L'Europe adopte et améliore cette forme au moyen âge[23]; b. le char à deux chevaux (ill. 8 et 9) est presque classique dans le transport agricole et dans le transport à courte distance.[24] Son rôle économique augmente au XVIIe et au XVIIIe siècle avec la disparition du commerce de transit et des grands voituriers. La longueur de ce char est de

301

Fig. 7. Char de la Poméranie du XVIIIe siècle *(kolasa)*, dessin de D. Chodowiecki. Daniel Chodowiecki, éd. A. Ryszkiewicz, Warszawa 1953, tabl. I.

160 à 180 cm et sa charge utile varie entre 400 et 600 kg ; c. le char à quatre chevaux paraît représenter la catégorie typique pour le transport commercial.[25] Ce char plus robuste que le précédent est encore utilisable aussi sur les mauvaises routes. Sa charge utile est déjà considérable, 1000 kg de marchandises (la moyenne aux XVIe et XVIIe siècles). Les 4 chevaux sont encore facilement maniable, et leur approvisionnement n'exige pas d'organisation spéciale. La longueur du char à 4 chevaux varie entre 250 et 350 cm suivant l'équipement supplémentaire et les marchandises transportées ; d. le dernier groupe est constitué par les chars lourds (ill.10) attelés le plus souvent à 6 chevaux ou 8. Leur longueur varie entre 3 et 4 mètres, la charge utile entre 1200 et 2000 kg. Ce sont les chars typiques pour le transport de transit Est-Ouest, desservi par les grands voituriers.[26] Le ravitaillement et l'entretien demandés par ce char et son attelage ont nécessité une organisation spéciale, dont l'existence nous est assurée par les documents du XVIIe siècle.[27] La robustesse de sa construction, l'utilisation abondante de renforcements métalliques et la largeur de ses roues qui diminue la pression au cm² (important sur les routes humides ou sablonneuses), sont ses principales caractéristiques.

Ces trois derniers groupes sont des catégories typiques de la production

Fig. 8. Char agricole du XVIe siècle, gravure anonyme, J. Banach, Tematy muzyczne w plastyce staropolskiej, cz. II, Grafika i rysunek, Warszawa 1962, ryc. 24.

Fig. 9. Marché à la fin du XVIIIe siècle, J. P. Norblin, Musée National, Varsovie, Département de Documentation, Nᵒ 10673.

artisanale. Entre le XIVe et le XVIIIe siècle, leurs prix de vente sont réglementés par l'Etat.

L'importance du nombre de chevaux dans l'attelage du char est attestée aussi par les documents fiscaux de la Pologne féodale.[28] Il y avait deux manières de taxer les chars : a) suivant le nombre de chevaux attelés, avec un cheval comme unité ; b) suivant deux catégories : char à deux chevaux et char à plus de deux chevaux. Cette dernière distinction marque la différence entre le transport pour les propres besoins du propriétaire ou pour ceux du petit commerce et le transport pour les besoins du grand commerce.

L'attelage à cheval domine dans le transport et spécialement dans le transport commercial en Pologne depuis l'apparition du char. Le nombre des chevaux attelés permet de dégager, comme nous venons de le voir, des sous-types importants. L'usage du char à quatre roues à brancards *(holoble)* suit la frontière ethnographique. Ce genre d'attelage est aussi bien applicable au char qu'au traîneau (cf. la fameuse troïka russe où le cheval central est attelé entre brancards *(holoble).*

La distinction, très utile ailleurs, entre le char à deux roues (charrette) et celui à quatre roues a, en Pologne, relativement peu d'importance. Le char

304

Fig. 10. Chars commerciaux de la Silésie du XVIIIe siècle, Al. Brückner, Encyclopédia staropolska, Warszawa 1939, t. I, p. 409.

classique à deux roues avec brancards, lesquels constituent la prolongation du cadre du char (ill. 11), est assez peu employé sauf pour le transport de personnes à courte distance. Son rôle paraît augmenter au XVIIIe et au XIXe siècle dans les moyens et grands domaines.[29]

On utilise, particulièrement à la campagne mais aussi pour le transport du bois en forêt et dans les travaux de construction, la charrette qui est tout simplement l'avant du char à quatre roues.[30] Le plus souvent on se sert seulement de sa plateforme en y fixant les objets à transporter. Si c'est un tronc d'arbre, on laisse traîner l'autre bout par terre. Dès que la route n'est plus abrupte, on glisse sous le bout traînant l'arrière du char. De cette manière, on reconstitue le char en se servant du tronc comme lien entre l'avant et l'arrière. Cette technique du transport du bois après l'abattage est très répandue. Son avantage principal est que l'avant du char est plus maniable sur les étroits sentiers et que le bout du tronc qui traîne par terre sert de frein. L'avant du char équipé d'une petite caisse ou de petites ridelles sert occasionnellement au transport à la campagne. Ce même mode est très répandu en haute montagne et se combine parfois avec le traînage.[31] Vu le peu d'importance de la charrette en dehors du transport de personnes, le char à deux roues (c'est-à-dire l'avant du char à quatre roues) ne peut pas être considéré comme une catégorie technique différente. Son application revêt tout de même un caractère spécial.

Le troisième critère qui pourrait être, suivant les sources, interprété comme

Fig. 11. Chars à deux roues de l'armée moscovite, prob. gravure de W. Hondius, Musée National, Varsovie, collection de Witke-Jezewski.

permettant de distinguer les deux types généraux, c'est : char "ferré" et char "non-ferré". Le terme char "non-ferré" signifie que ses roues ne sont pas cerclées, sans que soit mise en cause la présence d'autres éléments métalliques tels que : les anneaux à l'intérieur du moyeu, les bandes en fer reliant de l'intérieur les jantes de roue entre elles, les bandes renforçant les bouts d'axe, etc. La distinction ci-dessus apparaît le plus souvent dans les inventaires ruraux.[32] Nous ne la trouvons presque jamais dans les documents concernant le transport commercial. L'explication est simple : les cercles qui renforcent la roue permettent en même temps qu'elle soit moins massive et donc aussi moins lourde. Si le cercle est bien placé, la roue devient plus résistante aux chocs. Mais le cercle est aussi le plus coûteux de tout l'équipement métallique du char et pour remplir ses fonctions il doit être posé par un forgeron qui s'y connaît. Par suite le prix du char passe presque au double. Il est donc compréhensible que les paysans se servent très souvent du char "non-ferré" et que le nombre de ces derniers augmente considérablement avec le recul économique à partir de la seconde moitié du XVIIe siècle.[33] Pour diminuer leurs frais et faciliter la production on a, de temps en temps, attaché de petites bandes en guise de

Fig. 12. Char de guerre du XVIe siècle, gravure anonyme, J. Muczkowski, Zbior odciskow drzeworytow w roznych dzielach polskich w XVI i XVII wieku odbitych a teraz w Bibliotece Uniwersytetu Jagielonskiego zachowanych, Krakow 1849.

cercle (ill. 12) sur les joints extérieurs des jantes, ou pourvu de cercles seulement les roues de derrière qui sont toujours plus chargées. La valeur élevée des roues pourvues de cercles est attestée par les testaments dans lesquels les cessions d'une ou de quelques roues ferrées sont fréquentes.[34]

L'absence presque totale du char "non-ferré" dans le transport commercial, son usage alternatif à la campagne et l'absence d'importantes différences de construction entre le char "ferré" ou "non-ferré" (sauf que le dernier est plus massif et plus rudimentaire) ne permettent pas d'ériger cette différence d'équipement en critère distinctif.

Après avoir vu les distinctions de caractère général, nous pouvons passer aux types particuliers qui diffèrent, par leur construction, leur utilisation et leur équipement.

Le *rydwan* (ill.13) (peut-être de l'allemand *Reitwagen)* n'est pas le char de guerre mais plutôt le char pour le transport de personnes et de marchandises.[35] Bien connu déjà au moyen âge, il est en partie la continuation du char romain. Très répandu au XVIe et au XVIIe siècles, il a été construit en trois dimensions : le petit – long de 162 à 189 cm, le moyen – long de 212 à 243 cm et le grand – long de 270 à 279 cm. Sa caisse en planches ou plus sou-

Fig. 13. Rydwan du XVIe siècle, gravure anonyme, ibidem.

vent en planches et en vannerie était peinte en rouge ou en vert. Elle était surmontée d'une armature de lattes croisées formant une voûte. D'habitude, elle était couverte de toile ou plus souvent de feutre. Les ouvertures étaient placées en avant et en arrière ainsi que des deux côtés. La caisse était souvent embellie d'enjolivures. De construction solide mais légère, ce char a dominé probablement en ce qui concerne le transport de personnes et le transport de petites quantités de marchandises, quand le marchand accompagnait le fret. Au XVIe siècle, il est le plus souvent acheté par la noblesse et par conséquent son prix d'achat est imposé par le wojewoda. Il était de loin plus cher que le char ordinaire et rien que le coût de ses éléments métalliques dépassait d'un tiers celui du char ordinaire. Les *rydwany* ont très souvent

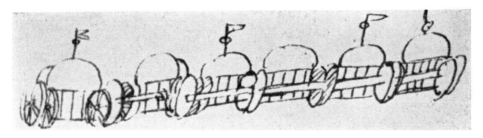

Fig. 14. Camp de chars du XVIe siècle, Al. Brückner, op. cit., t. II, p. 682.

accompagné l'armée polonaise et en cas de nécessité ont servi à la constitution du camp en chars (ill. 14). De là peut venir son nom, dérivant de l'allemand *Reitwagen*. Il disparaît au XVIIIe siècle, devant l'expansion des voitures avec ressorts.

Dans le même genre mais plus massif et plus grand était le char appelé en latin *currus stipendiariorum* (ill.15) et aussi de temps en temps en polonais *char de guerre*.[36] Long d'environ quatre mètres, sa plate-forme était surmontée d'une caisse en vannerie *(wasag)* posée entre les ridelles. Il était bâché de toile, attachée à une armature en voûte. Ils étaient fournis gratuitement par les villes royales à l'armée et accompagnaient celle-ci dans tous ses déplacements. En cas de nécessité, ils servaient à constituer le camp de chars. Il faut dire que contrairement au camp hussite, celui de Pologne n'a jamais eu de caractère offensif, d'où l'absence de char de guerre "blindé" de planches épaisses comme celui des Hussites. La charge utile de ce char a été officiellement déterminée à *5 centnar*, c'est-à-dire 250 kg par cheval d'attelage. Sa valeur d'achat était un peu plus élevée que celle d'un char de charretier.

Il semble qu'à partir de ce char se forme un char utilisé dans le transport à longue distance et nommé *frachtowy* (char de fret) (ill.17). Il apparaît probablement vers le XVIIIe siècle et prend de l'importance au XIXe siècle, quand il est produit par des manufactures spécialisées. Construit comme le *currus stipendiariorum* et couvert comme lui de toile, il possède dans une de ses parois l'ouverture permettant la manutention aisée.

Le transport commercial et plus spécialement celui à longue distance a utilisé généralement le char à plateforme (ill. 3, 10, 18, 19) appelé *"char de transport"*, *"char de commerçant"*, *"char de charretier"*, *"char lacé"* (parce que sa charge bâchée était entourée de cordes la fixant à la plateforme).[37] Le transport des marchandises sur la plateforme est considéré comme d'invention médiévale. Les marchandises posées sur les planches reposant sur les essieux avant et arrière étaient ligotées à celles-ci. Par suite

309

Fig. 15. Transport militaire au XVIIe siècle, Pufendorf, De rebus a Carolo Gustavo ...
gestis ..., 1696, Musée National, Département de Documentation, Nᵒ 64902.

le char constituait un tout avec sa charge et les versements très fréquents, compte tenu de l'état des routes de l'époque, étaient moins ennuyeux. Un tel char était d'ailleurs moins sujet à verser, plus stable, parce que les marchandises étant posées directement sur la plateforme, le point de gravité se trouvait assez bas. Ce char n'étant pas pourvu de caisse, le charretier pouvait suivant ses besoins éloigner ou rapprocher l'avant et l'arrière et obtenir un chariot plus ou moins long. Seulement, pour le transport de marchandises en vrac, par exemple le sel des mines de Wieliczka, les charretiers utilisaient des caisses en planches bien couvertes de toile posée directement sur celles-ci.

Parce que d'habitude il n'y avait pas de caisse, il est difficile de déterminer la longueur de ce genre de char. Elle dépend chaque fois du caractère des marchandises transportées, de l'état des routes, etc. L'absence de caisse rendait possible l'élévation de la hauteur des roues, qui d'habitude dépassaient le rayon des roues de chars ordinairement utilisés. Cet élément, en complétant les autres avantages déjà mentionnés : le centre de gravité placé fort bas et la construction massive mais compensée par le riche équipement en éléments métalliques et le bon graissage, a permis le transport de quantités impressionnantes de marchandises. En 1538, sur la route Cracovie-Chocim, un char à

310

Fig. 16. Camp de chars du XVIe siècle, gravure anonyme, J. Muczkowski, op. cit.

4 chevaux a transporté 1700 kg de marchandises plus 2 peaux de vaches pour les couvrir, un char à 8 chevaux 2200 kg plus quatre peaux. Ces charges ne sont pas exceptionnelles pour le XVIe siècle. Encore au début du XVIIe siècle, sur la route Wilno-Smolensk, les charges sont pareilles. Vers la fin du siècle, avec le recul du transport commercial professionnel, les charges utiles diminuent sensiblement. La vitesse du transport est plus difficile à déterminer mais d'après les rares renseignements qui sont à notre disposition, on peut avancer pour ce genre de transport le chiffre de 30 à 40 km par jour sur une bonne route. Le prix du char en question y compris l'attelage de 4 chevaux était, à la fin du XVIe siècle, d'environ 2000 groszy, qui équivaut aux deux tiers du profit annuel net d'un voiturier.[38]

Un autre char utilisé dans le transport commercial à moyenne distance ayant un caractère moins professionnel et utilisé aussi pour le transport de gens, est la *kolasa* dont le nom vient peut-être du russe *kolà* (la roue) ou de *koliesnica*, une voiture.[39] Son champ d'application est proche de celui du *rydwan*. La *kolasa* était ouverte, le voyageur n'était donc pas protégé contre les intempéries. Ce char est assez léger et son attelage ne dépasse pas 4 chevaux. Sa caisse est d'habitude tressée, les marchandises, en vrac, sont

311

Fig. 17. Chars commerciaux *(frachtowe)* du XIXe siècle, du tableau de M. Zalewski, Widok Kowna, Musée National, Varsovie, Département de Documentation, N° 29868.

couvertes d'une peau ou d'une toile, les passagers s'asseyent devant. La *kolasa* est assez souvent mentionnée dans les registres de douanes, ce qui atteste son caractère mixte : transport et communication (ill.7). Nous pouvons supposer qu'on pouvait parcourir à la fin du XVe et au début du XVIIe siècles environ 40 à 45 km par jour en *kolasa*. Les quantités de marchandises transportées, vu le caractère non professionnel de ce char, étaient le plus souvent inférieures à la norme militaire de 250 kg par cheval.

Currus lignorum ou *currus ligato* (ill.20) représente probablement le char médiéval qui disparaît vers la fin du XVe siècle.[40] Son usage était probablement multiple aussi bien dans le transport que dans la communication. Ce char paraît petit et fort primitif dans sa construction. Son élément le plus caractéristique est, me semble-t-il, l'attachement rigide de l'essieu avant et de l'essieu arrière à la caisse en bois. Il est donc normal que ce char handicapé par la tradition technique du haut moyen âge européen ait été remplacé par d'autres types, plus efficaces.

Il nous reste encore quelques mots à dire à propos des chars utilisés pour le transport agricole.[41] Comme on a pu le constater déjà, ces chars étaient

Fig. 18. Char commercial du XIVe siècle, J. Rohr, Jahre deutsche Leben, Berlin 1931, p. 303 de la collection iconographique du Musée d'Ethnographie de Crakovie, N° 102.

Fig. 19. Char pour le transport de tonneaux de la fin du XVIIIe siècle, du tableau de B. Belotto Canaletto, Plac za Zelazna Brama, Musée National, Varsovie, Département de Documentation, N° 14689.

Fig. 20. Currus lignorum du XIIe siècle, prophète Elie de la porte en bronze de Plock, J. Matuszewski, op. cit., ryc. 2.

d'habitude plus simples, moins soignés, plus petits et enfin moins coûteux que les autres. Souvent ils sont "non-ferrés" et le nombre d'éléments métalliques varie sensiblement suivant la conjoncture. Avec la reféodalisation, le paysan se désintéresse de ses outils. Voulant éviter la corvée du transport considérée comme très lourde et d'habitude supplémentaire au travail des champs, le paysan n'entretenait pas convenablement son char.

Ce char paysan est assez bas : le diamètre des roues arrière ne dépasse pas 1,20 m et les roues avant sont plus petites. Il est attelé le plus souvent de deux chevaux. L'attelage à un cheval devient plus fréquent au XVIIe siècle, mais dans le transport hors village, deux chevaux dominent toujours.

L'équipement en éléments métalliques varie très fort suivant les possibilités du propriétaire, l'époque et la région. Au sud-est et dans la région montagneuse de Gory Swietokszyskie, on rencontre le char fait sans un morceau de métal. Le plus souvent le métal intervient seulement dans la construction de l'axe et du moyeu. Les chars ayant quatre roues cerclées sont assez rares. Relativement souvent et plus spécialement dans les régions forestières, les roues ne sont pas composées de jantes assemblées mais formées du tronc d'un jeune arbre courbé. Une telle roue est plus élastique, et tient mieux,

Fig. 21. Une rue de Varsovie de la fin du XVIIIe siècle, au second plan le char á foin. –
B. Belotto Canaletto, Krakowskie Przedmiescie w strone Kolumny Zygmunta, Musée National,
Varsovie, Nᵒ 128658.

étant dépourvue de cercle, mais par contre la charge utile du char ne peut
pas être trop grande (pour pouvoir former un cercle la tige d'arbuste ne peut
pas être trop épaisse et par conséquent la roue est assez légère). L'autre
avantage d'une telle roue est qu'étant très élastique elle donne un petit effet de
ressort.[42] A cause de ces caractères, elle était assez souvent utilisée pour la
construction des voitures.

Les charges utiles transportées par le char paysan n'étaient pas fort élevées,
vu la simplicité de sa construction et l'état des routes. Les renseignements
concernant les transports effectués par les paysans dans le cadre de la corvée
nous permettent d'avancer le chiffre de 400 kg pour la seconde moitié du
XVII siècle et de 450 à 500 kg par char au XVIIIe siècle. La vitesse de ce
transport variait fort, mais la moyenne ne dépassait probablement pas 25 km
par jour et était très souvent de 20 km.[43] Dans nos sources, le char en question
porte le nom de *currus parvus, currus simplicus, woz prosty* – le char simple
ou *woz roboczy* (ill. 9), le char de besogne.[44] Souvent, suivant l'équipement
utilisé, son nom varie : le char avec de simples ridelles est appelé *drab* (ill.

315

Fig. 22. Char dit *wasag* du XVe siècle, polyptyque de l'église de Mikuszowice, J. Matuszewski, op. cit., il. 4.

Fig. 23. Char dit *wasag* à bœufs, du tableau de B. Belotto Canaletto, Widok Placu Zamkowego od strony Pragi w Warszawie, Musée National, Varsovie, Département de Documentation, | No 14678–9.

Fig. 24. Char dit *z polkoszkami* du XIVe siècle, enluminure du manuscrit dit de Ostrow de la Légende de Sainte Jadwiga, Musée National, Varsovie, Département de Documentation – Iconographie.

21) et utilisé pour le transport de la paille ou du foin, le char dont la caisse est tressée sur une armature de bois porte le nom de *wasag* (ill. 22 et 23), le char équipé de petites ridelles entre lesquelles on met deux demi-caisses de vannerie (genre de demi-paniers) est appelé *woz z polkoszkami* (ill. 24). Les deux derniers servent le plus souvent dans le transport hors village. La caisse en vannerie est toujours considérée comme plus élégante. Elle est souvent embellie de petites enjolivures, parfois peinte. Ce char se place d'ailleurs non loin de la *kolasa* déjà mentionnée.[45]

Pour les travaux agricoles, le char est le plus souvent équipé d'une caisse dont les quatre parois et le fond sont en planches[46] – *currus asserus* (ill. 8).

Le char agricole présenté ici domine dans le transport agricole paysan jusqu'à la fin du XIXe siècle. Les grands domaines modernisent leurs moyens de transport à partir de la seconde moitié du XIXe siècle. La petite exploitation continue l'usage du char décrit ci-dessus, mais en l'équipant de tous les éléments métalliques nécessaires.[47]

Fig. 25. *Coach* du XVe siècle, « Speculum », XXXIV, 1959, pl. II.

Notes bibliographiques

1. K. Moszynski, Kultura ludowa Słowian, cz. I, Krakow 1929; id., Pierwotny zasieg jezyka praslowianskiego, Wroclaw-Krakow 1957.
2. cf. L. Musset, Les invasions. Le second assaut contre l'Europe chrétienne (VIIe–XIe siècles), Paris 1965, Bibliographie: Travaux modernes, III. Les migrations des peuples slaves et p. 76; en polonais: J. Kostrzewski, Kultura prapolska, Warszawa 1962; K. Jazdzewski, Atlas do pradziejow Słowian, Lodz 1949; Historia Polski, Instytut Historii PAN, t. I, red. H. Lowmianski, Warszawa 1957; H. Lowmianski, Poczatki Polski, t. I, Warszawa 1967, etc.
3. J. Kostrzewski, Osada bagienna w Biskupinie, « Przeglad Archeologiczny », V, 1935, pp. 136–137 et A. Bechczyc-Rudnicki, Biskupinskie kolo tarczowe, « Z Otchlani Wiekow », X, 1935, p. 86 et suiv.
4. G. Childe, The First Waggons and Carts – from the Tigris to the Severn, « Proceedings of the Prehistoric Society » (nouvelle série), XXVI, 1960, pp. 63–84; id., The Diffusion of Wheeled Vehicles, « Ethnographisch-Archäologische Forschungen », II, 1954, pp. 1–17; id., Wheeled Vehicles, in A History of Technology, t. I, Oxford 1958, pp. 716–30.
5. W. La Baume, Wagendarstellungen auf Ostgermanischen Urnen der frühesten Eisenzeit und ihre Bedeutung, « Blätter für deutsche Vorgeschichte », 1924, No I, pp. 15–20; id., Urgeschichte der Ostgermanen, Danzig 1934, pp. 83–5; J. Kostrzewski, Od mezolitu do okresu wedrowek ludow, en, Encyklopedia Polska, V, t. 4, I, Krakow 1939, p. 276, 295;

318

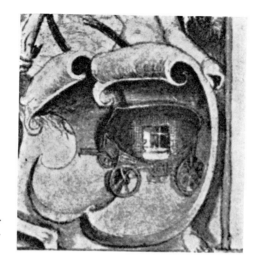

Fig. 26. Voiture du XVIe siècle – genre *coach*, enluminure du Kodeks Behema, Musée National, Varsovie, collection de Witke-Jezewski.

K. Tymieniecki, Ziemie polskie w starozytnosci, Poznan 1951, pp. 297–8; H. Seger, Die Deichselwagen von Gross Perschnitz kr. Militsch, « Altschlesien », III, 1931, pp. 185–204.

6. J. Filip, Die Keltische Zivilisation und ihre Erbe, Prag 1961, pp. 28–43; F. Dvorak, Knizeci pohrby na vozech ze starsi doby zelezne, Praha 1938; cf. aussi T. Powell, The Celts, London 1963.

7. P. Bienkowski, Über skytische Wagen, « Wiener Studien », XXIV, 1902, No 2, pp. 394–7; H. Mins, Scythians and Greeks, Cambridge 1913, pp. 50–2.

8. cf. la thèse de R. Lefebvre de Nöettes, L'attelage, le cheval de selle à travers les âges. Contribution à l'histoire de l'esclavage, Paris 1931, modifiée par A. G. Haudricourt, De l'origine de l'attelage moderne, « Annales d'Histoire Economique et Sociale », VIII, 1936, p. 519 et suiv.; id., Contribution à la géographie et à l'ethnologie de la voiture, « La Revue de Géographie Humaine et d'Ethnologie », I, 1948, pp. 54–64; id. et M. Daumas, Utilisation de l'énergie naturelle, en Histoire générale des techniques, t. I, Paris 1962, pp. 95–7.

9. A. G. Haudricourt, travaux cités et J. Czekanowski, Wstep do historii Slowian, Poznan 1957, pp. 380–409 et J. Matuszewski, Poczatki nowozytnego zaprzegu konnego, « Kwartalnik Historii Kultury Matrialnej », I, 1953, No 1–2 et No 4.

10. cf. L. Niederle, Zivot starých Slovanu, dil. III, sv. 1 et 2, Praha 1923–1925 et id. Rukovet slovanskych starozytnosti, Praha 1954; données techniques cf. E. Wagner, Z. Drobna et J. Durdik, Kroje, zbroj a zbrane v dobe predhusitske a husitske, Praha 1957; organisation et tactique cf. J. Durdik, Sztuka wojenna husytow, Warszawa 1957.

11. cf. B. Jewsiewicki, Organizacja wolnonajemnego transportu kupieckiego w Polsce w okresie gospodarki feudalnej, « Zeszyty Naukowe Uniwersytetu Lodzkiego », série I, fasc. 53, 1968, pp. 11–12 et id., Koszty gospodarczego transportu kolowego w Polsce XVI–XVIII wieku, « Roczniki Dziejow Spolecznych i Gospodarczych », XXXI, 1970, pp. 1–2 et la littérature y citée.

12. id., Organizacja . . ., pp. 13–26.

13. M. Boyer, Mediaeval Suspended Carriages, « Speculum », XXXIV, 1959, pp. 359–66; T. Venedikov, Trackaja povozka, Sofia 1968; autre littérature cf. B. Jewsiewicki, Stan i problematyka badan nad tradycyjnym transportem kolowym, « Zeszyty Naukowe Uniwersytetu Lodzkiego », série I, fasc. 45, 1966, pp. 136–7, voitures russes et discussion cf. id.,

Les graphiques présentent la fréquence des renseignements sur l'usage des éléments ci – dessous d'après les sources de l'époque.

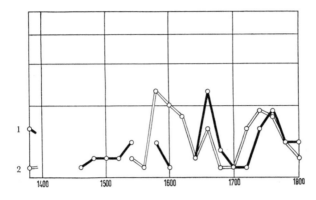

1. Améliorations de l'attelage à corde et à timon. 2. Collier et harnais.

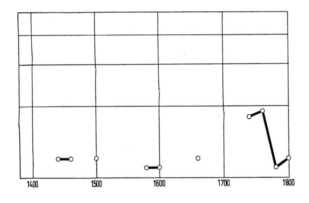

Renforcements des montants entre lesquels sont placés la caisse, cf. ill. 23.

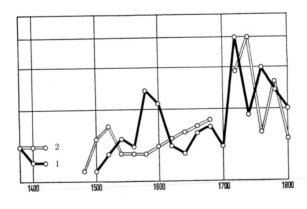

1. Cercle. 2. Renforcements métalliques du moyeu.

Powstanie, rozwoj i znaczenie gospodarcze transportu kolowego w Polsce do konca XVIII wieku, Lodz 1967, thèse de doctorat non publiée.

14. cf. id., Organizacja . . ., pp. 23–6; sur le plan général: H. Kollenbenz, Der kontinentale Handel zwischen Ost- und Westeuropa vom 15. Jahrhundert bis zum Beginn des Eisenbahnzeitalters, rapport présenté au Ve Congrès International d'Histoire Economique, 1970; J. Topolski, La reféodalisation dans l'économie des grands domaines en Europe centrale et orientale (XVIe–XVIIIe siècles), ibidem.

15. B. Baranowski, Podstawowa sila pociagowa dawnego rolnictwa w Polsce, Warszawa-Wroclaw-Krakow 1966; A. Keckowa, Inwentarz zupy solnej z 1559 r, « Kwartalnik Historii Kultury Materialnej », I, 1954, p. 705; Inwentarze dobr szlacheckich powiatu kaliskiego, t. I, od XVI do polowy XVIII wieku, wyd. S. Rusinski, Wroclaw 1955, p. 522, 534; J. Rutkowski, Podzial dochodow w zupach ruskich za Zygmunta Augusta, Poznan 1927, pp. 51, 193; Instrukcje gospodarcze dla dobr magnackich i szlacheckich z XVII–XIX wieku, éd. B. Baranowski, J. Bartys, T. Sobczak, t. I, Warszawa 1958, p. 101; Rejestr wydatkow na budowe kosciola w Biskupicach (1711–1733), éd. J. Kowalczyk et J. Zawadzka, « Kwartalnik Historii Kultury Materialnej », V, 1957, N° 3/4, l'année 1711.

16. cf. les enquêtes effectuées en 1967 par E. Hans, W. Baranowski et B. Jewsiewicki dans toute la région des Karpates polonaises – Archives du Département d'Ethnographie de l'Université de Lodz. Cf. les chars à bœufs fournis par les villes Dolina et Zydaczow – Rejestr wozow skarbnych od miast i miasteczek Rzeczypospolitej koronnych na wyprawe wojenna roku 1521 dostarczonych, éd. C. Biernacki, « Archiwum Komisji Historycznej », III, 1886, pp. 494–5.

17. cf. par exemple Rejestr wydatkow . . ., l'année 1711 et l'année 1712: le joug coûte 15 gr tandis que deux colliers et harnais en coûtent 90. Même à l'est où le harnais est souvent en chanvre, il est plus cher que le joug – Polska Stanislawowska w oczach cudoziemcow, éd. W. Zawadzki, Warszawa 1963, t. I, pp. 700, 728, 729.

18. Czumaki na Zwyrohodszczini, s. l., s. d., p. 15.

19. B. Baranowski, op. cit., pp. 30–65.

20. Z. Gloger, Encyklopedia Staropolska Ilustrowana, Warszawa 1903, t. IV, p. 81.

21. Kodeks dyplomatyczny Malopolski, t. IV, éd. F. Piekosinski, Krakow 1905, p. 486; K. Gorski, Historya artyleryi polskiej, Krakow 1902, p. 286; Lustracje wojewodztwa krakowskiego 1789, éd. A. Falniowska-Gradowska, I. Rychlikowa, Warszawa 1962, I partie, p. 64; Lustracje wojewodztwa lubelskiego 1565, éd. A. Wyczanski, Wroclaw-Warszawa 1959, p. 99; Lustracja wojewodztwa wielkopolskich i kujawskich 1564–1565, II partie, éd. A. Tomczak, Bydgoszcz 1963, pp. 28, 85, 87, 117; A. Sucheni-Grabowska, Materialy do dziejow kultury materialnej chlopow wojewodztwa sieradzkiego i ziemi wielunskiej w XVI w., « Studia z Dziejow Gospodarstwa Wiejskiego », II, 1959, p. 254; Inwentarze mieszczanskie z lat 1528-1635 z ksiag miejskich Poznania, éd. S. Nawrocki, J. Wislocki, Poznan 1961, pp. 99–433; Inwentarze mieszczanskie z ksiag miejskich i grodzkich Poznania, t. I 1700–1758, éd. J. Burszta, Cz. Luczak, Poznan 1962, pp. 257–8. Même type de renseignements dans les taxes de woyewodas. Cf. aussi « (. . .) currum vel vehiculum medium grossum, a duebus equis (. . .) » – Kodeks Dyplomatyczny Malopolski, éd. F. Piekosinski, t. II, Krakow 1886, p. 486. Entrent probablement dans les mêmes catégories les termes: « *super currus* », « *magni currus* » – A. Keckowa, Saliny ziemi krakowskiej do konca XIII wieku, Warszawa-Wroclaw-Krakow 1965, pp. 58–9.

22. Ils ressemblent probablement à l'équipement des moyens de transport connus des publications suivantes: W. Stöetzner, Der dahurischen Karren, « Zeitschrift für Ethnologie », LXII, 1930, p. 316; H. Minns, op. cit., pp. 50–2. Cf. également A History of Technology, red. Ch. Singer, E. Holmyard, A. Hall and T. Williams, t. II, Oxford 1958, pp. 498–9; Histoire générale des techniques, t. I, Paris 1962, pp. 93–104.

23. Il est significatif qu'on rencontre souvent dans les documents l'appellation « char russe

à un cheval » cf. p. ex. – Lustracja wojewodztwa wielkopolskich i kujawskich 1564–1565, I partie, éd. A. Tomczak, C. Ochrysko-Wlodarska, J. Wlodarski, Bydgoszcz 1961, p. 1 et suiv. Egalement Lustracja wojewodztwa lubelskiego 1565, op. cit., p. 98.

Pour le passage du traîneau au char cf. C. Fox, Sleds, Carts and Waggons, « Antiquity », V, 1931, pp. 185–99; R. Lane, Waggons and their Ancestors, ibid. IX, 1935, pp. 139–50; G. Berg, Sledges and Wheeled Vehicles, Stockholm 1935; A. G. Haudricourt, travaux cités et également les travaux de J. Voracek, Nekolik poznamek k studiu evropskeho vouzu a prezitku po starsich formach u nas, « Narodopisny Vestnik Ceskoslovensky », XXXI, 1950, pp. 239–48; L. Baran, Doprava na smycich i poznamky k jej kulturni historie, « Cesky Lid », XXXV, 1948, pp. 71–4, en URSS A. Ibragimova, Niekotoryje matierjaly k voprosu o koliesnom dwizenii u koczevnikov sredniej Azii, « Trudy Instituta Istorii, Archeologii i Etnografii im. Walichanowa, XV, 1962, pp. 137–8 et M. Artamonov, K istorii sredstw pieredwizenija, « Problemy Istorii Matierialnoj Kultury », 1933, No 5/6, pp. 23–32. Sur l'introduction de l'attelage moderne en Europe cf. A. G. Haudricourt, Lumière sur l'attelage moderne, « Annales d'Histoire Sociale », VIII, 1945, pp. 117–99 et autres travaux cités; W. Lec, Travel and Transport through the Ages, Cambridge, p. 187; L. White, Mediaeval Technology and Social Change, Oxford 1963, pp. 57–66; A History of Technology, op. cit., art. de M. Jope, p. 554; L. Gyula, Beiträge zur Volkskunde der Avaren, « Archeologai Ertesitö », III, 1942, pp. 341–6. Pour les territoires slaves cf. J. Matuszewski, op. cit.; J. Zak, Rogowe czesci uprzezy konskiej, « Slavia Antiqua », III, 1951/1952, pp. 195–201; H. Wiklak, Chomonta z XII wieku odkryte w Gdansku na stanowisku I, « Wiadomosci archeologiczne », XXIII, 1956, pp. 267–8; N. Voronin, G. Rabinovicz, Archeologiczeskije raboty na Moskovskom Kriemle, « Sovetskaja Archeologija », VII, 1963, No 1, p. 226; M. Sole, Knizeci pohrebiste na Stare Kouremi, « Pamiatky Archeologicke », L, 1959, p. 1959; J. Filip, Vuz praveky a vznik vozu moderniho, « Vestnik Ceskoslovenskeho Zemedelskeho Muzea », IX, 1936, p. 98.

24. Ksiegi sadowe wiejskie, éd. B. Ulanowski, dans Starodawne prawa polskiego pomniki, t. XII, Krakow 1926, No 574; K. Gorski, op. cit., pp. 48–9, 237, 250; Rejestr wozow skarbnych ..., op. cit., pp. 477–96 – les chars à 4 chevaux ont constitué 85% du total. Aussi Lustracja wojewodztwa rawskiego 1564 i 1570, éd. Z. Kedzierska, Warszawa 1959, pp. 6, 30, 96, 101; Lustracje wojewodztwa sandomierskiego 1564–1565, éd. W. Ochmanski, Wroclaw-Warszawa-Krakow 1963, pp. 205, 208, 298; Lustracje wojewodztwa plockiego 1565–1789, éd. A. Sucheni- Grabowska, S. Szadurska, Warszawa 1965, pp. 9, 174 et autres déjà cités.

25. cf. J. Tarnowski, Consilium tarionis bellicae, éd. J. Turowski, dans, Dziela Jana Tarnowskiego Kasztelana Krakowskiego i Hetmana Wielkiego Koronnego, fasc. I, Krakow 1858, p. 44.

26. B. Jewsiewicki, Powstanie ..., tableau de prix du transport.

27. id. Organizacja ..., op. cit. et id., Koszty ..., op. cit.

28. Lustracja wojewodztwa wielkopolskich ..., op. cit., pp. 28, 85 et B. Jewsiewicki, op. cit., tableau de charges utiles.

29. Inwentarze dobr biskupstwa chelminskiego (1646 i 1676), éd. J. Mienicki, Torun 1955, p. 63; Inwentarze dobr szlacheckich ..., op. cit., p. 233; instrukcje gospodarcze dla majatkow wielkopolskich w pierwszej polowie XIX wieku, éd. J. Bielecka, Poznan 1959, p. 153, Archives d'Etat de la province de Lublin, Archiwum Ordynacji Zamojskiej, No 4285, f. 69.

30. Materialy archiwalne do budowy zamku warszawskiego. Rachunki budowy z lat 1569–1572, éd. M. Halowna, J. Senkowski, « Teki Archiwalne », II, 1954, p. 304; Inwentarze dobr szlacheckich ..., op. cit., p. 360; Ksiega lawnicza wsi Kargowa w powiecie Koscianskim 1617–1837, éd. A. et A. Walawderowie, « Studia z Dziejow Gospodarstwa Wiejskiego », III, 1960, fasc. 3, No 279, No 430.

31. cf. note 16.

32. Inwentarze dobr biskupstwa chelminskiego (1646 i 1676), op. cit., pp. 135, 233, ibid. (1723–1747), t. II, éd. J. Mienicki, Torun 1956, pp. 42, 61, 64, 73, 88, 89 etc.; Inwentarze dobr szlacheckich ..., op. cit., pp. 22, 125, 135 etc.; B. Baranowski, Gospodarstwo chlopskie i folwarczne we wschodniej Wielkopolsce w XVIII wieku, Warszawa 1958, pp. 112–3; J. Topolski, Gospodarstwo wiejskie w dobrach arcybiskupstwa gnieznienskiego, od XVI do XVIII wieku, Poznan 1958, pp. 224–5; Ksiegi sadowe wiejskie, op. cit., t. II, N° 94, 109, 239 etc.; Instrukcje gospodarcze ..., op. cit., p. 21.

33. Inwentarze dobr biskupstwa chelminskiego ..., tomes cités; M. Grosser, Krotkie i bardzo proste wprowadzenie do gospodarstwa wiejskiego, éd. S. Inglot, Wroclaw 1954, pp. 317–9. Cf. B. Jewsiewicki, Powstanie ..., op. cit., tableau de prix – le char ferré est de 50% plus cher que le char non-ferré.

34. Cf. K. Dobrowolski, Wloscianskie rozporzadzenia ostatniej woli na Podhalu w XVII i XVIII w., Krakow 1933, p. 202; Inwentarze dobr szlacheckich powiatu kaliskiego, op. cit., p. 207 et suiv., Archives Centrales des Documents Anciens, Brzesko-Kujawskie grodzkie inscr. 39, f. 207.

35. Rachunki dworu krola Wladyslawa Jagielly i krolowej Jadwigi z lat 1388 do 1420, éd. F. Piekosinski, Krakow 1896, pp. 157–8; Archives d'Etat de Poznan, Kaliskie grodzkie 346, f. 1432; Prawa, przywileje i statuty miasta Krakowa (1507–1795), éd. F. Piekosinski, t. I, Krakow 1885, pp. 586, 632; Cennik wydany dla rzemieslnikow miasta Ksiaza przez Piotra Kmite wojewode krakowskiego w r. 1538, éd. B. Ulanowski, « Sprawozdania Komisji Jezykowej Akademii Umiejetnosci », III, 1884, pp. 358–9; Inwentarze mieszczanskie z lat 1528–1635 z ksiag miejskich Poznania, éd. S. Nawrocki, J. Wislocki, Poznan 1961, pp. 140, 167; Inwentarze dobr szlacheckich powiatu kaliskiego, op. cit., pp. 122, 209; Kilka zabytkow ustawodawstwa krolewskiego i wojewodzinskiego w przedmiocie handlu i ustanawiania cen, éd. B. Ulanowski, « Archiwum Komisji Prawniczej », I, 1895, pp. 109–19.

36. Opisy i lustracje Poznania z XVI–XVIII wieku, éd. M. Mika, Poznan 1960, p. 16; Lustracje wojewodztw wielkopolskich ..., op. cit., pp. 127, 156, 217 etc.; cf. aussi la discussion entre O. Balzer et C. Biernacki in « Kwartalnik Historyczny », I, 1887, p. 295 et 586. Aussi Rejestr wozow skarbnych ..., op. cit.; J. Tarnowski, op. cit., p. 45; Inwentarze dobr szlacheckich powiatu kaliskiego ..., op. cit., pp. 129, 209, 294 etc. Le char hussite cf. Durdik, op. cit., p. 75; E. Wagner, Z. Drobna, J. Durdik, op. cit.; Z. Spieralski, Z problematyki wzajemnych kontaktow miedzy polska a husycka sztuka wojenna, « Wojskowy Przeglad Historyczny », I, 1957, N° 2, p. 280. L. Niederle, Slowianskije driewnosti, Moskwa 1955, p. 359 atteste d'après Ipatievskaja Lietopis l'usage de tels chars (bâché) en Russie, en 1208 pour construire le camp de chars. Pour char dit « *frachtowy* » cf. H. Cegielski, Praktyczna mechanika rolnicza w zastosowaniu do potrzeb ziemian polskich, Warszawa 1863, p. 141.

37. Lustracja wojewodztwa lubelskiego ..., op. cit., p. 99; Lustracja wojewodztwa plockiego ..., op. cit., pp. 25, 26, 52, 79; Kodeks Dyplomatyczny ..., op. cit., p. 221; M. Wolanski, Zwiazki handlowe Slaska z Rzeczypospolita w XVI wieku, Wroclaw 1961, p. 66; A. Keckowa, op. cit., p. 57. Sur l'introduction de ce char cf. A History of Technology, op. cit., p. 496.

38. B. Jewsiewicki, Powstanie ..., op. cit. et id., Koszty ..., op. cit.

39. Liber quitantiarum regis Casimiri ab a. 1484 ad a. 1488, dans, Teki A. Pawinskiego, t. II, Warszawa 1897, p. III – « *colassa salis* »; Polskie ustawy i artykuly wojskowe od XV do XVIII wieku, éd. S. Kutrzeba, Krakow 1937, p. 154 et suiv. M. Wolanski, op. cit., p. 63; J. Burszta, Das ostpomersche Dorf um 1600. Die wichtigsten Merkmale seiner Kultur, dans Visby – symposiet för historiska vetenskaper, 1965, p. 179; Pamietniki o Koniecpolskich, éd. S. Przylecki, Lwow 1842, p. 258.

40. Ksiega ziemska plonska, dans, Najdawniejsze ksiegi sadowe mazowieckie, t. I, Warszawa 1920, Nº 215, 415, 438, 441; Antiquissimi libri indiciales terrae cracoviensis, éd B. Ulanowski, dans, Starodawne Prawa Polskiego Pomniki, t. VIII, 1–2, Krakow 1886, Nº 5143; Kodeks Dyplomatyczny Wielkopolski, t. I, Poznan 1877, Nº 50; Inwentarze mieszczanskie . . ., op. cit., pp. 59, 140, 188, 433; la distinction entre ce char et celui non-ferré: ibid. p. 99.

41. Instrukcje gospodarcze . . ., op. cit., t. I, p. 128.

42. Souvent les deux bouts de cercle n'étaient pas fixés l'un dans l'autre et le petit espace entre eux assurait l'élasticité de la roue.

43. B. Jewsiewicki, Powstanie . . ., op. cit.

44. Lustracje wojewodztwa lubelskiego 1565, op. cit., p. 74; Kodeks dyplomatyczny Wielkopolski, t. V, Poznan 1908, Nº 134 – *currus parvi kmethones*.

45. S. Morawski, Sadecczyzna za Jagielonow z miasty spiskimi i kiestwem oswiecimskim, Krakow 1865, t. II, p. 342; Archives Centrales de Documents Anciens, Brzesko-Kujawskie grodzkie inscr. 39, f. 207; J. Majewski, Gospodarstwo folwarczne we wsiach miasta Poznania w latach 1528–1644, Poznan 1957, pp. 63–4; B. Baranowski, op. cit., pp. 108, 113; Inwentarze mieszczanskie . . ., op. cit. pp. 188, 433.

46. Akta radzieckie poznanskie, éd. K. Kaczmarczyk, Poznan 1931, t. XI, p. 328.

47. F. Bujak, Zmiaca, wies powiatu limanowskiego, Krakow 1903, p. 92; I. Rychlikowa, Klucz wielkoporebski Wodzickich w drugiej polowie XVIII wieku, Warszawa-Wroclaw-Krakow 1960, p. 97; S. Cackowski, Gospodarstwo wiejskie w dobrach bis kupstwa i kapituly chelminskiej w XVII–XVIII wieku, II partie, Torun 1959, pp. 38–9; J. Wojtowicz, Narastanie kapitalizmu w rolnictwie ziemi chelminskiej, Torun 1962, pp. 80, 81, 184.

Wollene Hirtentaschen in den Karpaten – ein Beitrag zur Kenntnis der Transportmittel und Transportarten in der Almwirtschaft in den Karpaten

B. KOPCZYŃSKA-JAWORSKA

In der Gebirgswirtschaft sind die Transporttaschen zum Teil durch die naturelle Umwelt bedingt. Besonders deutlich ist diese Abhängigkeit in der Almwirtschaft ersichtlich. Von den höchstgelegenen Almen kann man Milcherzeugnisse nur mit Hilfe von Tragtieren (auf dem Rücken des Tieres) oder mit Hilfe von Menschenkräften (Fusstransport) oberschlächtig befördern. Sogar in den niedrigeren Bergen, wo die Möglichkeit besteht mit dem Wagen auf die Alm zu gelangen, sind die Zufahrtswege meistens länger und schwer durchfahrbar, so dass der Fusstransport (auf dem Rücken tragen) immer noch von grosser Bedeutung ist. Aus diesem Grunde konnte man in den Bergen bis in die letzte Zeit auch vielen archaischen und primitiven Transportarten begegnen[1].

Unter den Transportarten, die in der Almwirtschaft in den Karpaten den ersten Platz einnehmen, ist der Fusstransport (oberschlächtig). Neben der oberschlächtigen Transportart war in der Vergangenheit auf weiten Gebieten der Packtransport verbreitet, augenblicklich im Zusammenhang mit der Verbesserung der Transportwege durch den Radtransport verdrängt.

Ausser den Umweltbedingungen hat für die Transportorganisation ebenfalls die Art der transportierten Gegenstände und Produkte ihre Bedeutung[2]. In der Almwirtschaft in den Karpaten waren und sind Transportartikel weicher und harter (geräucherter und getrockneter) Käse, manchmal das hinterbliebene Milchwasser, seltener Sahne oder Butter, wie auch Käseprodukte, mit Brimsen an der Spitze.

Als Hilfstransportmittel für den Transport von Flüssigkeiten (Sahne und Milchwasser) benutzte man in den Ostkarpaten schmächtige Fässlein im rum. *berbenţe*[3], (Ţara Ardealului), *bărbînţa*[4] (Maramureş), ukrain. *berbenica*[5] (бербениһа) genannt, in den überwiegenden Gebieten der Westkarpaten wiederum flache Fässlein im poln. *baryla*, *ụobońka* (Schlesien), *obońka* (Bezirke von Żywiec, Orawa[6], Hohe Tatra Vorland – Podhale), slow. *l'agvica* (Hohe Tatra[7], Gebiet am Poprad[8], Horehronie, Pohronie), *obońka* (Hohe Tatra[9], Kisuce), *obuňka* (Liptów), *l'ahvica* (Detva[10]). Neben den letzten wurden hie und da (z.B. in Gorce und in den Hohen Beskiden in der Gegend von Żywiec, Ostkarpaten, Bukowina) ebenfalls hölzerne Krüge, von Böttchern gemacht, mit einem Henkel, im poln. *konewka* (Podhale, Żywiec),

Fig. 1. Eseltransport. Rumänien, Munţi Apuseni, 1959. Aufnahme B. Jaworska.

kunewka (Gorce), slow. *kop, krhla*[11], ukr. *konovka* (конобка)[12], rum. *cofa* genannt. Diese Kannen sind in den ganzen polnischen Karpaten als Vorratsgefässe für Milch, vor allem Kuhmilch, bekannt. Nur in Gorce und in der Umgebung von Żywiec dienen sie zum Transport und aus diesem Grunde haben sie dichtschliessende Deckel[13].

Fässlein, mit Schnüren an den Sattel befestigt, beförderte man mit Pferden. Aus diesem Grunde [hatten die sog. *oboñki* in vier symmetrisch dislozierten, dickeren Dauben Deckel, durch die Schnüre durchgezogen wurden, oder auch wurden sie in Doppelpacksatteltaschen hineingelegt, die im poln. *bisagi, bisaki,* slow. *bisahi* (Hohe Tatra[14], Detva[15]), *sajdak* (Liptów, Niedrige Tatra), ukrain. *besaha* (Huzulerland[16]), rum. *disag,* bulg. *disagi* (дисаги), serb. *bisagi* (бисаги) gennant werden.

Doppelpacksatteltaschen kann man am Sattel befestigen; in diesem Falle haben sie einen besonderen Ausschnitt, der es ermöglicht, sie am Sattelbogen zu befestigen, oder auch werden sie unmittelbar auf den Rücken des Tieres gelegt.

Es ist interessant, dass die Traditionen des Packtransports in den polnischen Karpaten nur im Gebiet des Hohe Tatra Vorlandes (Podhale) bekannt sind. Der Packtransport in der Hohen Tatra wurde schon in der zweiten Hälfte des XIX Jhd. durch

Fig. 2. Molketransport in der
Milchkanne (poln. *konewka*).
Polen, Dorf Żabnica, Kr. Żywiec, 1961. Aufnahme B. Jewsiewicki.

den Radtransport verdrängt. In den Ostkarpaten im Huzulerland wurde er noch
nach dem 1. Weltkrieg angewandt. In der Slowakei und in Rumänien konnte man
ihm noch sporadisch nach dem 2. Weltkrieg begegnen. In Bulgarien und im östlichen
Serbien wird er bis heute praktiziert, nur werden zum Transport im allgemeinen
nicht Pferde, sondern Esel benutzt.

Kannen werden auf kurzen Entfernungen in der Hand getragen, wenn man sie
aber auf weitere Entfernungen befördern muss, werden sie in Tücher gewickelt und
auf den Rücken gebunden. Auf ähnliche Art werden manchmal auch einzelne
obońki (Hohe Tatra und Podhale, Teschener Schlesien) transportiert.

In der letzten Zeit werden sowohl Fässlein wie auch Kannen (Krüge) durch
Metallkannen, fabrikmässig hergestellt, ersetzt. Grosse Milchkannen werden mit
Wagen befördert, kleinere, emaillierte, in Händen getragen, oder manchmal, gleich
hölzernen Krügen, im Tuch auf dem Rücken.

Als in der polnischen Tatra der Packtransport aufhörte, begann man von einigen

Fig. 3. *Cedilka* (bulg. *цедилка*). Bulgarien, Dorf Malka Ribarica. (Ethnographisches Museum, Sofia, Nr. 33956). Aufnahme N. Nikolov.

entfernteren und hochgelegenen Almen, mit schwer zugänglichen Zufahrtswegen, Gefässe mit Milch auf zwei vorderen Wagenrädern sog. poln. *kara* herabzutransportieren, auf die zwei Tannenstämmchen, poln. *smyki*, mit gelichteten Ästen gelegt waren. Die Tannenstämmchen werden auf dem Boden geschleift und bremsen auf diese Art bei der Herabfahrt. *Oboñki* oder Milchkannen werden mit Ketten an den Tannenstämmen befestigt[17].

Zum Befördern von Schafkäse[18] sind im allgemeinen keine speziellen Vorratsgefässe nötig. Weicher Käse wird auf weiten Gebieten der Ostkarpaten und in den ganzen Westkarpaten unmittelbar von der Wirtschaft abgeholt, einige Tage nach der Herstellung entwässert und abgetrocknet, leicht fermentiert, in Form einer Kugel (Durchmesser 25–45 cm), deren Grösse von der Menge der gemolkenen Milch abhängig ist. Der Käse ist im tschech. *hrudka*[19], poln. *grudka*, *gruda* (Schlesien, Bezirk von Żywiec, Orawa[20], Podhale, Gorce[21]), *buła* (Bezirk von Żywiec), *hrudka* (Bezirk von Sącz[22]), slow. *hrutka* (Liptów), *hruda*, *hrudka* (Kisuce, Čaca[23], Horehronie, Detva[24]), bulg. *gruda* (Umgebung von Sofia[25]), oder ganz einfach *syr* bzw. *bundz* (Bezirk von Żywiec, Podhale), *bonc* (Orawa[26]), *budz*, *bundz* (Huzulerland)[27] genannt.

Ausschliesslich im südlichen Teil der Ostkarpaten wird eine Art Weichkäse her-

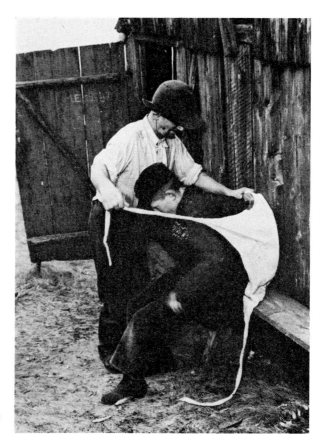

Fig. 4. Molketransport in der *baryła*. Polen, Dorf Brenna, Kr. Cieszyn, 1957. Aufnahme S. Deptuszewski.

gestellt, der im rum. *cas de telemea* genannt wird und dem bulgarischen *sirene* (сирене) ähnlich ist, und der nach dem Auspressen des Milchwassers nicht getrocknet, sondern nur mit Salz bestreut und in Handzubern aufbewahrt wird. In ähnlichen, runden Gefässen, nach oben hin enger werdend, manchmal mit zwei Henkeln und dicht schliessendem Deckel, wird Brimsen befördert, wenn er von Hirten in den Bergen und nicht im Dorf erzeugt wird. Diese Gefässe werden genannt: poln. *sądek* (Schlesien), *faska* (Orawa[28]), *dzieżka, dzizka* (Gorce, Bezirk von Sącz[29]), slow. *dieżka* (Hohe Tatra), *džeska* (Gebiet am Poprad[30]), *pucinka na bryndze* (Gebiet am oberen Poprad[31]) oder *gieleta* (Horehronie[32]), bulg. *kače* (каце).

Ausnahmsweise wird in einigen Gegenden Rumäniens oder Bulgariens Brimsen in Schafleder (Schlauche) genäht, aufbewahrt und transportiert: rum. *cas de burduf* genannt.

Ähnlich werden keine Gefässe benötigt zum Befördern von Hartkäse, geräuchert oder getrocknet, bzw. zu grossen Scheiben geformt, genannt: poln. *brusek*, rum.

Fig. 5. Die Wiege (bulg. *люлка*). Bulgarien, Dorf Vyrbica, Kr. Pleven, 1970. Aufnahme Bagra Georgieva, Ethn. Mus., Sofia.

kaşkaval, bulg. *kaškaval* (кашкавал), bzw. für kleine Käse in Spindelform, poln. *oscypek*, slow. *oštiepok* oder Käse in Form von Tieren oder Herzchen[33].

Von Hirten in den Bergen erzeugte Käseprodukte werden in Tüchern, Taschen, seltener in Körben[34], in letzter Zeit öfters in Touristenrucksäcken transportiert.

Die einfachste Transportart ist das Befördern von Käse, in Leinwandtuch gebunden, poln. *chustka*, slow. *chustočka*. Wenn das Tuch klein ist, werden die gegenüberliegenden Ecken, je zwei in Knoten gebunden und der darin gepackte Käse in der Hand oder auf dem Stock oder Tragjoch auf die Schulter gestützt[35].

Wenn das Tuch, poln. *plachta*, *obrus*, *loktusa* (Gorce), *syrzyna* (Podhale), slow. *obrus*[36], grösser ist, kann man die zu tragende Last in zwei Ecken wickeln, sie auf den Rücken hängen und die beiden anderen Ecken über die Achseln legen und auf der Brust in Knoten binden (auf diese Art werden die schon erwähnten Kannen und *oboñki* transportiert). Nicht bedeutungslos ist, dass sich mit dem Transport von Milchprodukten hier nur Frauen befassen, die gewöhnlich Lasten im Tuch auf dem Rücken tragen.

Um das Binden und Befestigen der Last an dem Tragjoch, an der Seite oder auf

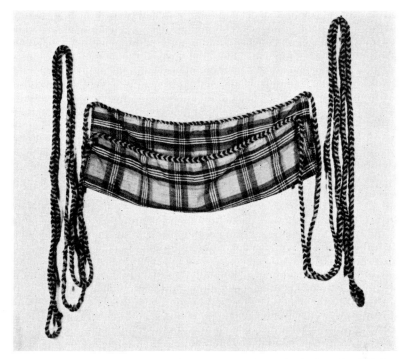

Fig. 6. Die Wiege. Bulgarien, Dorf Kostičovci, Kr. Beogradčik. Aufnahme N. Nikolov, (Ethn. Mus., Sofia, Nr. 34400).

dem Rücken des Tragenden zu erleichtern, sind an die Ecken des Tuches manchmal Strippen gebunden. In einem solchen Leinentuch, dessen Ausmasse 70 × 70 cm betragen, im poln. *dzichówka, dzichta, dziechytka,* genannt, wird im polnischen Teschener Schlesien das Fässlein mit Milchwasser ins Tal hinab getragen. Die obere und untere Strippe von jeder Seite des Tuches, das die Last auf dem Rücken des Tragenden anhält, sind vorn an seinen Schultern in einen Knoten und ausserdem noch auf der Brust in einen zusätzlichen Knoten gebunden. Diese Art von grösseren Tüchern ist in den Karpaten allgemein zum Tragen von Heu auf dem Rücken, zum Transport auf Wagen oder Schlitten benutzt. Sie sind mit Strippen aufs Kreuz geschnürt[37]. Im poln. *chusta, płachta, trawnica,* slow. *travnica, płachta, plachietka*[38] genannt. Ein solches Tuch an einen waagerechten Stock gebunden, kann im Felde als primitive Wiege dienen[39].

Manchmal haben die Strippen die Form zweier langer Henkel. Ein solches Tuch wird dann in der Mitte gefaltet, und mittels der Doppelstrippen wird es auf den Rücken oder die Brust des Tragenden gebunden. Diese Art von Tüchern, *cedilka* (цедилка) genannt, werden allgemein in Bulgarien zum Tragen verschiedener

331

Fig. 7. Die Tasche. Bulgarien, Dorf Wraždebna, Kr. Sofia, 1912. Aufnahme N. Nikolov, Ethn. Mus., Sofia.

Lasten benutzt. Sie werden aus Wollgarn, meistens zu farbig kariertem, seltener gestreiftem Zeug, gewebt. Im allgemeinen haben die Tücher ein Quadrat mit den Ausmassen 50 × 50 cm und sind kariert. Die Lasten werden in ihnen auf dem Rücken getragen und die Strippen (bulg. *vrăzki*, бръзки) werden auf der Brust gebunden, oder die Last wird auf der Hüfte getragen und die Strippen schräg über die Brust gebunden. In solchen Tüchern tragen Frauen oft Kinder. Grössere Tücher (*cedilka*) werden als Wiegen (bulg. *ljulka*, люлка) sowohl im Felde wie auch zu Hause angewandt.

Im östlichen Serbien verzeichnete man den Brauch, Käse in einem ähnlichen Wolltuch zu tragen, hier serb. *cedilo* (цедило) genannt.

Ein zusammengelegtes Tuch kann man leicht in eine Tasche umwandeln, indem man sie an den Seiten zusammenäht. Eine solche Tasche wird nach allgemeinem

Fig. 8. Taschentransport auf die *kobilka* (bulg. *кобилка*). Bulgarien, Dorf Gramada, Kr. Vidin, 1966. Aufnahme B. Jaworska.

Brauch auf der Hüfte des Tragenden getragen, wobei man den Henkel der Tasche quer über die Schulter hängt. Taschen, vor allem leinene, waren in allen slawischen Ländern im Gebrauch und wurden für verschiedene Zwecke angewandt. Einen weit kleineren Bereich des Auftretens hatten Wolltaschen, die vor allem in den Karpaten und in den Balkanländern verbreitet sind[40].

Wolltaschen: bulg. *torba* (морба), serb. *torba wynena* (морбаьпнена), wlach. *trašta* werden zum Transport verschiedener Lasten, vor allem auch zum Transport von Käse, Wolle und anderen Produkten der Hirtenwirtschaft benutzt.

Aus einem Stück rechteckigen Tuches, in der Mitte gefaltet, in verschiedenen karierten Mustern gewebt, unterscheiden sich die Taschen in Dimensionen (im allgemeinen hat eine Seite der Tasche etwa 50–60 cm) und in der Art der Befestigung der Strippen. Bulgarische Taschen haben oft keinen Henkel nur zwei Strippen, die,

Fig. 9. Taschentransport auf die *obramica* (serb. *обрамица*). Ostserbien, Dorf Žagubice, Kr. Požarevac, 1963. Aufnahme B. Jaworska.

abhängig davon zu welchem Zwecke sie benutzt werden sollen, nach Belieben gebunden über die Schulter gehängt werden, an den Sattel oder das Tragjoch gebunden werden: bulg. *kobilka* (кобилка), wlach. *kobyłka*, serb. *obramica* (обрамица). Ostserbische Taschen haben zwei Henkel, an den vier Ecken der Tasche befestigt, ähnlich wie die Henkel an der *cedilka*.

Ausser einzelnen Taschen sind in Bulgarien und besonders in Rumänien wollene oder leinene Doppeltaschen: bulg. *disagi* (дисаги), rum. *desag* im Gebrauch. Diese Taschen werden so über die Schulter gehängt, dass eine vorn, die andere hinten über der Schulter des Tragenden herabhängen. Diese Taschen sind ebenfalls buntkariert oder gestreift gewebt. Sie werden auf einem Webstuhl mit 4 Fäden angefertigt.

Ähnliche Taschen, nur in grösserer Ausführung werden auch als Packsatteltaschen für Pferde oder Esel benutzt[41]. Packsatteltaschen wurden früher in Bulgarien, Mazedonien und im östlichen Serbien oft aus Ziegenwolle hergestellt (bulg. *kozina*, козина). Sie wurden auf besonderen senkrechten Webstühlen gewebt.

In den Westkarpaten, in Polen (Hohe Tatra, Orawa), in der Slowakei und in der

Fig. 10. Die wollene Tasche (serb. морбаьпнена). Ostserbien, Dorf Žagubice, Kr. Poža-revac, 1963. Aufnahme B. Jaworska.

Vergangenheit ebenfalls in der Mährischen Walachei benutzten Hirten zum Transport von Käse und verschiedenen Gegenständen, und manchmal auch zum Aufbewahren von Privatgegenständen auf der Alm[42] spezielle Wolltaschen, ab-weichender Art als die in Rumänien und Bulgarien: in poln. *torba bacowska*, slow. *cedilo, cedidlo*[43], tschech. *zajdak, sajdak*[44] genannt.

Diese Taschen wurden aus hausgewebtem Wolltuch hergestellt, in einfachem Webmuster auf zweifädigem Webstuhl gewebt. Einschlag und Kette sind wollen, wobei der Einschlag in der Regel in zwei Farben, braun und schwarz, gewebt wird. Ausser Henkeln hatten die Taschen auf der Klappe gestickte Ornamente, aus dickem Wollgarn, in Kettenstich ausgeführt. Das Klappenornament bestand aus einigen Franzen, aus den Fäden der Kette und den hinzugefügten Fäden, durch den Rand des Tuches hindurchgezogen und zusammengedreht. Der Faden, der die Verläng-erung des Einschlages bildet, war weiss, die zusätzlichen Fäden dagegen, oft dun-kel, weswegen die Franzen nach dem Zusammendrehen zweifarbig waren[45].

Nach dem Weben, dem Zusammendrehen der Franzen und dem Sticken des Or-naments wurde das Tuch für die Tasche gewalkt. Unter der Einwirkung von heissem Wasser und Stampfen verfilzte sich das Tuch, wurde dichter und die Struktur des Tuches wie auch des Stickornamentes verwischte sich. Nach dem Herausnehmen

Fig. 11. Die doppelte Tasche (rum. *desag*). Rumänien, Dorf Feleac, Kr. Cluj, 1959. Aufnahme B. Jaworska.

aus dem Walk ähnelte das Ornament des Tuches fast dem Aussehen des Gewebes. Den zubereiteten Stoff, etwa 60 cm breit und etwa 150 cm lang (die Franzen nicht miteinbegriffen) legte man zusammen und nähte die Seiten in lichtem Stich, mit wollenem Zwirn, zur Tasche auf diese Art zusammen, dass eine kleine Klappe mit Franzen verziert entstand. Die Klappe diente nur dekorativen Zwecken, da sie nicht die Öffnung der Tasche bedeckte.

Die Tasche hatte etwa 130 cm lange Träger in Form von Strippen, die ähnlich wie in serbischen Taschen an den Ecken befestigt waren.

Gefüllte Taschen trug man wie den Rucksack, auf dem Rücken, und die langen Träger band man auf der Brust in einen Knoten. Die leere Tasche, zur Hälfte zusammengelegt, trug man auf einer Schulter, indem man die Strippen quer über die Brust band, ähnlich wie beim Tragen der *cedilo*.

Die Benutzung von wollenen Taschen ausschliesslich durch die Gebirgsbewohner Polens, der Slowakei und Mährens, besonders durch Hirten, sowie die Ähnlichkeit im allgemeinen mit den in den Balkanländern benutzten Taschen scheint auf das karpatisch-balkanische Herkommen dieser Taschen hinzuweisen. Davon zeugt auch

336

Fig. 12. Die doppelte Tasche (bulg. *gucazu*). Bulgarien, Kr. Botevgrad. Aufnahme N. Nikolov, (Ethn. Mus., Sofia, Nr. 39649).

eine ähnliche Tasche auf der bekannten und oft reproduzierten Zeichnung, die einen walachischen Hirten aus dem XVII Jhd. darstellt[46]. Ein weiteres Argument dafür scheint unseres Erachtens nach die slowakische Benennung der Tasche – *cedidlo, cedilo* – zu sein.

Das Wort *cedilo* hängt zweifellos mit dem Wort: seihen, poln. *cedzić*, tschech. *cediti*, altkirchenslawisch *čediti* zusammen. A. Brückner leitet das Stammwort von der Bezeichnung *czysty* (sauber) ab, der das präslawische *cěsta* oder »gesäuberter Weg« entspricht. Es ist desshalb nicht sonderbar, dass die Geräte zum Seihen in allen slawischen Ländern davon abstammende Bezeichnungen haben; z.B. poln. *cedziłka*, slow. *cedilko, cedzak*, tschech. *cez, cidice* usw.[47], sowie auch das Tuch zum Seihen von Schafmilch in Mähren *cedilko, céčka*[48], Kisuce: *cecka*, Bezirk von Sącz: *cieczka*[49], am Poprad: *cietka, ced'ienka, cecka, cička*[50], Liptów: *ciecka*, Horehronie: *cietka, ced'ielko*[51], Pohronie: *ciecka*, słow. Orawa: *ciečka*[52], Huzulerland: *cidylo* (цидило)[53], bulg. *cedka, cedilka, cedak, cedilo*[54], karakasch. *candila*[55] und serb. *cedilo* (цедило).

Das gegenwärtig zum Seihen von Schafmilch benutzte Tuch ist überwiegend in Gebieten der Karpaten aus einem quadratischen Leinentuch (ausnahmsweise nur Hanftuch) hergestellt, das keine Strippen hat. Beim Milchseihen wird es mit den Händen festgehalten oder mit einem hölzernen Ring befestigt. Nur das serbische

Fig. 13. Der Hirt mit Tasche.
Slowakei, Gebiet Detva.
Aufnahme K. Plicka.

cedilo zum Seihen der Milch ist aus scharfer, ungewalkter Wolle hergestellt und hat angenähte Strippen. Nach Informationen von Nutzniessern sind die Strippen zum Binden des *cedilo* nötig, wenn es zum Transport von Käse dient.

In Bulgarien wird *cedilka* ausschliesslich von Frauen getragen[56]. Sie tragen in ihnen event. Milchprodukte. Es ist nichts Sonderbares, denn obwohl sich Männer mit dem Weiden von Schafen und Ziegen beschäftigten, so ist doch die Almwirtschaft in Bulgarien und Serbien (ebenfalls im südlichen Rumänien) durch viele Bande mit der Haushaltswirtschaft verbunden. Sie trägt oft den Charakter einer Filialwirtschaft. In Hirtenhütten verbleiben periodisch ganze Familien; Frauen nehmen Teil an Arbeiten, die mit der Verarbeitung der Milch verbunden sind. Hier ist zu bemerken, dass in den Balkanländern bis in die Zwischenkriegsjahre fast ausschliesslich Schafmilchprodukte konsumiert wurden[57].

Fig. 14. Die Tasche des Heiratsvermittlers (bulg. *gebenoba
mopδa*). Bulgarien, Dorf Raj-
kovo, Kr. Smoljan. Aufnahme
N. Nikolov, Ethn. Mus., Sofia.

In Bulgarien erfüllen die obengenannten *cedilka* heute ausschliesslich die Funktion eines Transportmittels, jedoch ist die Tradition lebendig, dass in der Vergangenheit auf diesen Gebieten zum Seihen von Schafmilch nicht nur wie heut Hanftücher als Seihtücher benutzt wurden, sondern ebenfalls wollene. Aus serbischen Analogen schliessend konnten die Seihtücher dieselbe Form wie die heutige *cedilka* haben, die wie das serbische Seihtuch aus ungewalktem Wolltuch hergestellt ist und sich zum Seihen eignet.

Sobald sich auf dem bulgarischen Gebiet ein Transportmittel verbreitet hatte, dessen Benennung nicht mit seiner Hauptfunktion übereinstimmend war, ist es nicht erstaunenswert, dass die Benennung eines Gegenstandes mit ähnlicher Funktion und ähnlichem Aussehen wie die Wolltasche, die bis heut von slowakischen Hirten benutzt wird, übertragen werden konnte. Um so mehr als das walachische Volk, das

Fig. 15. Wolltasche. Polen, Dorf Ciche, Kr. Nowy Targ, 1952. Aufnahme W. Tomaszkiewicz.

nicht der slawischen Sprache mächtig war, diese Übertragung der Benennung vermitteln konnte.

Die Übertragung der Benennung auf einen neuen Gegenstand konnte zusätzlich dadurch verursacht sein, dass in den Westkarpaten fast ausschliesslich Männer sich mit der Hirtenwirtschaft befassten, die wiederum niemals gebundene Tücher, sondern Taschen zum Lastentragen benutzten[58]. Es fehlt dagegen die Antwort auf die Frage, warum die Benennung *cedilo* und ihre Ableitungen für die Bezeichnung von Wolltaschen (wie auch leinenen) sich in den Westkarpaten auf das Gebiet der Slowakei begrenzt und in seinen Bereich weder die polnischen Karpaten noch die Mährische Wallachei einbegreift. Mag sein, dass dies von einem längeren und intensiveren Kontakt der ersten Gebiete mit den südlichen Slawenländern zeugt.[59].

Die Tasche aus den Westkarpaten, in ihrer jetzigen Form, konnte nicht, wie manche es annehmen[60], zum Seihen der Milch dienen, da sie im Gegensatz zu Ta-

340

Fig. 16. Der Hirt mit der wollenen Tasche auf dem Rücken. Dorf Ciche, Kr. Nowy Targ, 1952. Aufnahme W. Tomaszkiewicz.

schen, *cedilka*, und zum balkanischen Seihtuch aus unhygroskopischem, gewalktem Tuch hergestellt ist[61].

In der ersten Phase des Umwandlungsprozesses beobachten wir bei unveränderter Benennung und Form eine Begrenzung der Funktion des Gegenstandes (vom Tuch zum Seihen und Transport eine Begrenzung ausschliesslich zur Funktion des Transportmittels), in der zweiten Phase eine Verschiebung der gleichen Benennung auf einen anderen Gegenstand mit analogischer Funktion (Transportmittel zum Tragen).

Am Schluss der Erwägungen über den Gebrauch und das Aufkommen von Wolltaschen kann man noch ein Problem vorlegen, das wert ist, geklärt zu werden: warum, im Gegensatz zu den übrigen Gebieten, benutzen die Hirten in den polnischen Karpaten nicht die sowohl in der Slowakei als in Ungarn[62] verbreiteten Ledertaschen (slow. *kapsa, tanistorka, tanistra*)? Das Tragen einer solchen Tasche mit einem entsprechend breiten Gürtel und Ornamenten war das Vorrecht des Oberhirten, dem Leiter der Almwirtschaft. In der polnischen Tatra war die Wolltasche mit Franzen Symbol des Hirtenberufes. Sie wurde an der Seite (leer) oder auf dem Rücken (voll) getragen und war ein Element der festtäglichen Kleidung des Hirten[63].

341

Fig. 17. Die Art der Verbindung der Tasche. Polen, Podhale. Aufnahme J. Darowski. (Archiv Ethn. Mus., Zakopane).

Fussnoten

1. GUNDA, 1955, 152.
2. GUNDA, 1955, 151.
3. VIEHZUCHT, 1961, 358.
4. Überall dort, wo die Quelle nicht angeführt ist, beruhen die Informationen auf Feldforschungen der Verfasserin; das Material von den Feldforschungen befindet sich im Archiv des Lehrstuhls für Ethnographie an der Universität in Łódź.
5. MOSZYŃSKI, 1967, 308; VIEHZUCHT, 1961, 370.
6. JOSTOWA, 1968, 212.
7. PODOLÁK, 1967, 125.
8. PODOLÁK, 1961, 59.
9. PODOLÁK, 1967, 125.
10. MEDVECKÝ, 1906, 223.
11. GUNDA, 1955, 197.
12. MOSZYŃSKI, 1967, 308; VIEHZUCHT, 1961, 368 u. 369.
13. Marginell ist anzuführen, dass B. Gunda nach K. Moszyński der Meinung ist, dass

342

Fig. 18. Tuch zum Seihen der Milch (serb. *цедило*). Ostserbien. Aufnahme B. Jaworska. (Ethn. Mus., Pozarevac, Nr. 703).

Holzkannen in slawischen Ländern nicht heimischer Herkunft sind (MOSZYŃSKI, 1967, 308.) Es ist zu erwägen, ob zu ihrer Verbreitung in den Karpaten nicht wandernde Händler und rumänische Hirten beigetragen haben: GUNDA, 1955, 196–197.

14. PODOLÁK, 1967, 125.
15. MEDVECKÝ, 1906, 149.
16. HARASYMCZUK u. TABOR, 1938, 41.
17. GUNDA, 1955, 153.
18. Eine Anzahl von Beschreibungen über die Herstellung von Milchprodukten siehe: VIEHWIRTSCHAFT und HIRTENKULTUR. Ethnographische Studien, Budapest 1969.
19. BARTOŠ, 1891, 203.
20. JOSTOWA, 1968, 217.
21. WODZOWA, 1962, 63.
22. Materialien aus den Feldforschungen von A. Kowalska-Lewicka; Archiv der Ethnographischen Arbeitsstelle des Instituts für Geschichte der Materiellen Kultur der Polnischen Akademie der Wissenschaften in Łódź.
23. MAŁECKI u. NITSCH, 1934.
24. MEDVECKÝ, 1906.
25. WAKARELSKI, 1969, 50.
26. JOSTOWA, 1968, 217.
27. SZUCHIEWICZ, Bd. 1, 1902, 223; SCHNEIDER, 1899, 60.
28. JOSTOWA, 1968, 212.

29. KOWALSKA-LEWICKA, Materialien.

30. PODOLÁK, 1967, 120.

31. PODOLÁK, 1956, 116.

32. PODOLÁK, 1961, 63.

33. Ledersack zum Transport benutzt, bulg. *mjach* (*мях*).

34. Dem Transport von Käse in Rückenkörben begegnen wir z.B. in Myto bei Dumbier, Bez. Brezno (KOPCZYŃSKA-JAWORSKA, 1959, 396, Abb. 1). Auf slawischem Gebiet ist der Transport in Rückenkörben als vermutlich neue Transportart angesehen (GUNDA, 1955, 203), auf jeden Fall ist er ausser dem Grantal nicht verzeichnet.

35. Das Tragjoch, als Hilfsgerät zum Tragen von Lasten benutzt, hat einen sehr weiten Bereich des Auftretens. Auf dem Gebiet der östlichen und westlichen slawischen Länder, mit Haken versehen, dient es gewöhnlich zum Tragen von Wassergefässen. Es wird auf beiden Schultern getragen, wobei die Gefässe mit den Händen gehalten werden. Die Gewohnheit, andere Lasten (Wäschebündel, Körbe, Säcke usw.) mit dem Joch zu tragen, ist bis heut in den Balkanländern allgemein, in der Vergangenheit wurde es sporadisch zum Tragen von Wäsche in Grossrussland und der Ukraine (MOSZYŃSKI, 1967, 632) benutzt. In den Balkanländern (Serbien, Bulgarien) wird das Tragjoch gewöhnlich auf einem Arm getragen.

36. Nach A. Brückner haben die Benennungen *obrus* und *płachta* einen allgemein slawischen Charakter. Das Wort *płachta* ist abgeleitet von der Bezeichnung: *płaski* (platt, flach), *obrus* ist abgeleitet von *brusić*, d.h. abwischen, schleifen (hiervon *brus*-Schleifstein, Wetzstein). Bis zum XIV Jhd. diente *obrus* (Tischtuch) als Handtuch zum Abwischen: BRÜCK-NER, 1957, s.v. obrus, płachta. Vergleiche auch: GUNDA, 1955, 203.

37. Siehe Abbildung: DORYWALSKA, 1969, 92 u. KOPCZYŃSKA-JAWORSKA, 1969, 87.

38. GUNDA, 1955, 190–191.

39. GUNDA, 1955, 168.

40. MOSZYŃSKI, 1967, 633–634.

41. Im Dorftransport wurden allgemein Esel benutzt. Pferde gebrauchten nur reichere Landwirte und Kaufleute.

42. PODOLÁK, 1966.

43. Vergleiche auch PODOLÁK, 1956, 112.

44. ŠTIKA, 1959, 82.

45. Taschen mit Franzen sind charakteristisch für die Umgebung von Skopje in Mazedonien. In diesem Gebiet hat der Mantel des Heiratsvermittlers (mazed. *deverska gunie*, деверска гуня) Franzen. Mit Franzen werden auch rituelle Taschen in Bulgarien geschmückt z.B. die Tasche des Heiratsvermittlers während der Hochzeitszeremonie (bulg. *deverova torba*, деверова торба). Diese Franzen sind aber an die genähte Tasche angeknüpft, und nicht mit der Tasche mittels Webetechnik verbunden: Inf. Dr M. Veleva, Sofia.

46. REINFUSS, 1949, 114.

47. BRÜCKNER, 1957, s.v. cedzić. Vergleiche auch KALAL, 1924, s.v. cedzak.

48. BARTOŠ, 1891, 203.

49. KOWALSKA-LEWICKA, Materialien.

50. PODOLÁK, 1967, 115.

51. PODOLÁK, 1961, 55.

52. ČAPLOVIČOVA, 1962, 128.

53. SIMONJENKO, 1961, 384.

54. WAKARELSKI, 1969, 559.

55. MARINOV, 1961, 188.

56. Informationen nach M. Veleva und M. Čerkiesova aus dem Museum der Bulg. Ak. der Wissenschaften in Sofia.

57. KOPCZYŃSKA-JAWORSKA, 1971.

58. GUNDA, 1955, 184.

59. Laut der Volkstradition war auch in der Slowakei in dem Gebiet Zvolen das Seihentuch aus Schafwolle gefertigt und wurde *cedilko, odzciezka* genannt. Inf. Dr. Pavol Kuka, Mus. Zvolen.

60. ČESKOSLOVENSKA VLASTIVEDA, 1968, 824.

61. Gewalkte *cedilka* werden hauptsächlich in der Rhodopen hergestellt. Das Tuch für die *cedilka* wird im allgemeinen in einfacher Geflechttechnik gewebt (bulg. *lita*): Inf. M. Veleva.

62. POLONEC, 1961, 163–195; GUNDA, 1955, 195.

63. Vergleiche auch GUNDA, 1955, 187–188.

Literatur

BARTOŠ, F. 1891: Lid a národ (Volk und Nation). Velke Meziřici.

BRÜCKNER, A. 1957: Słownik etymologiczny języka polskiego (Etymologisches Wörterbuch der polnischen Sprache). Warszawa.

ČAPLOVIČOVA, Z. 1962: Zo zázrivského salašnictva (Die Almerei in Zazriva). »Sbornik Slovenského Národného Múzea«, Bd. 56, Martin.

ČESKOSLOVENSKA VLASTIVEDA. 1968: Bd. 3. Lidova kultura (Volkskultur). Praha.

DORYWALSKA, E. 1969: Gospodarka na polanach i wypas szałaśniczy w Żabnicy pow. Żywiec (Weidewirtschaft und Salaschenwirtschaft im Dorf Żabnica, Kr. Żywiec). »Prace i Materiały Muzeum Archeologicznego i Etnograficznego w Łodzi«, Seria etnograficzna, Nr 13, Łódź, S. 65–130.

GUNDA, B. 1955: L' údový transport v Żakarovciach (Volkstransport in Zakarovce). »Slovenský Národopis« Jg. 3, Nr 2, Bratislava, S. 150–212.

HARASYMCZUK, R. W. und TABOR, W. 1938: Etnografia połonin huculskich (Die Ethnographie der Huzuler Almen). Lwów. Abdruck aus »Lud«, Bd. XXV, 1937.

JOSTOWA, W. 1967: Tradycyjne pasterstwo na Orawie polskiej (Traditionelles Hirtentum in der polnischen Orawa). Łódź, Manuskript im Lehrstuhl für Ethnographie an der Universität in Łódź.

KALAL. 1924: Slovenský slovnik (Slowakisches Wörterbuch). Banska Bystrica.

KOPCZYŃSKA-JAWORSKA, B. 1951: Gospodarka pasterska w Beskidzie Śląskim (Hirtenwirtschaft in den Schlesischen Beskiden). »Prace i Materiały Etnograficzne« Jg. VIII-IX, Łódź-Lublin, S. 155–322.

 - 1959: Materiálie k študiu pastierstva na Slovensku (Beiträge zur Untersuchung des Hirtenwesens in der Slowakei). »Slovenský Národopis« Jg. VII, Nr 3, Bratislava, S. 387–433.

 - 1960: Z wędrówek po szałasach rumuńskich (Aus Wanderungen in rumänischen Salaschen). »Wierchy« Jg. XXIX, Kraków, S. 52–77.

 - 1961: Das Hirtenwesen in den Polnischen Karpaten, /in/ Viehzucht und Hirtenleben in Ostmitteleuropa, Budapest, S. 389–438.

 - 1962: Gospodarcze i społeczne podstawy pasterstwa tatrzańskiego (Wirtschaftliche und soziale Grundlagen des Hirtentums in der Hohen Tatra) /in/ Pasterstwo Tatr Polskich i Podhala (Hirtentum der Polnischen Hohen Tatra und des Hohe Tatra Vorlandes), Bd. IV, Wrocław, S. 107–162.

 - 1971: Warunki bytowe i budżet rodziny wiejskiej w Gramadzie (Existenzbedingungen und Budget der Landfamilie im Dorf Gramada /Bulgarien/). »Etnografia Polska«, Bd. XV, H. 1.

MAŁECKI, M. und NITSCH, K. 1934: Atlas językowy polskiego Podkarpacia (Der Sprachatlas der polnischen Vorkarpaten). Kraków.

MARINOW, W. 1961: Die Schafzucht der nomadisierenden Karakatschanen in Bulgarien, /in/ Viehzucht und Hirtenleben. Budapest, S. 147–196.

MEDVECKÝ, K. 1906: Detva. Detva.

MOSZYŃSKI, K. 1967: Kultura ludowa Słowian. T. 1. Kultura materialna (Die Volkskultur der Slawen, Materielle Kultur) II. Ausgabe, Warszawa.

PODOLÁK, J. 1961: Letné salašnictvo oviec v oblasti Horného Hrona (Salaschenwirtschaft im Bezirk von Ober Hron), »Sbornik Slovenského Národného Múzea«, Bd. LV. Martin, S. 5–76.

— 1956: Poľnohospodarstvo (Die Landwirtschaft) /in/ Banicka dedina Žakarovce. Bratislava, S. 63–126.

— 1967: Pastierstvo v oblasti Vysokých Tatier (Hirtentum im Bezirk der Hohen Tatra). Bratislava.

POLONEC, A. 1961: Slovenské opasky a iné remenné odevné súčiastky (Slowakische breite Gürtel und andere lederne Bekleidungszutaten) »Etnografia Polska«, Bd. V, Wrocław, S. 163–195.

REINFUSS, R. 1949: Wełniane torby góralskie (Wollene Taschen der Bergbewohner), »Polska Sztuka Ludowa«, Nr 3–4. Warszawa, S. 112–119.

SCHNEIDER, J. 1899: Z kraju Huculów (Aus dem Huzulerland), »Lud«, Jg. V. Lwów, S. 57, 147, 207, 336.

SZUCHIEWICZ, W. 1902: Huculszczyzna (Huzulerland). Bd. 1, Lwów.

SIMONJENKO, I. 1961: Almenwirtschaftliche Schafzucht der ukrainischen Bevölkerung in den Waldkarpaten im 19. und zu Beginn des 20. Jahrhunderts /in/ Viehzucht und Hirtenleben, Budapest, S. 363–388.

ŠTIKA, J. 1959: Odivani salašnických pastevcu na Valašsku (Bekleidung der Schafhirten in der Walachei) /in/ Lidova kultura východni Moravy, Gottvaldov.

WAKARELSKI, Ch. 1969: Milchverarbeitung und Milchprodukte bei den Bulgaren /in/ Viehwirtschaft und Hirtenkultur. Ethnographische Studien. Budapest, S. 547–573.

WODZOWA, K. 1962: Wypas i gospodarka polaniarska we wsi Obidowa, pow. Nowy Targ (Weiden und Weidewirtschaft im Dorf Obidowa, Kreis Nowy Targ). Łódź, Manuskript im Lehrstuhl für Ethnographie an der Universität in Łódź.

Traditionelle Transportmittel in Bulgarien

Von VASIL MARINOV

Ethnologische Untersuchungen der traditionellen Transportmittel in Bulgarien sind bisher nur im Rahmen von allgemeineren Untersuchungen der Lebensweise und der Kultur der bulgarischen Bevölkerung[1] oder einzelner ethnischer Gruppen in verschiedenen geographischen Gebieten[2] durchgeführt worden. Wir finden historische Angaben über die Transportmittel in den bulgarischen Ländereien in den "Quellen der bulgarischen Geschichte"[3], herausgegeben von der BAW, in einzelnen Untersuchungen von Historikern[4] und Archäologen[5]. Eine einheitliche ethnologische Untersuchung dieser Frage ist jedoch bisher in Bulgarien nicht durchgeführt worden. Einen ersten Versuch über "Die ethnologische Charakteristik der Transportmittel in Bulgarien" werden wir im Rahmen des Sammelbandes zu Ehren von Prof. Dr. Béla Gunda ausführen.

1. *Historische Übersicht.* Bei den archäologischen Ausgrabungen von prähistorischen Grabhügeln in Bulgarien aus der Epoche des Neolithikums und Eneolothikums[6] wurden keine konkreten Angaben über die Transportmittel und -arten entdeckt, jedoch können wir indirekte Schlußfolgerungen ziehen. Bei diesen Ausgrabungen sind nicht nur Fragmente von handgearbeiteten keramischen Gefäßen, sondern auch eine große Anzahl von vollkommen bewahrten Gefäßen zur Aufbewahrung von Getreide und Wasser, Kannen und Wasserkrügen mit ein, zwei oder mehr Griffen, von denen einige Öffnungen besitzen, um eine Schnur zum Tragen durchzwängen zu können, aufgefunden worden. Während der Bronzeepoche (4.–3.Jh.v.u.Z.) waren den Thraken der Bronzekessel mit beweglichem Henkel, genannt "prevezlo"[7] (Abb.1), bekannt. Dieser Kessel ist seiner Form nach dem heutigen Kupferkessel (Abb.10) und dem Kupferkessel *(haranija)* für Wassertransport fast gleich. Die Thraken haben für Kriegszwecke einen zweirädrigen Bronze-Streitwagen, mit künstlerischen Figuren verziert, verwendet.[8] Es wurden damals auch vierrädrige Pferde-Bronzewagen verwendet. Aufgefunden wurden auch versilberte und vergoldete, dünne Platten, verziert mit Pferdeköpfen oder ganzen Pferden mit Zügeln und Halfterstricken[9], die als Schmuck der Pferderiemen dienten (Abb. 2). Die Thraken haben die Pferde auch geritten und beladen, wie aus den

Abb. 1. Bronzekessel mit beweglichem Metallgriff, gefunden in der thrakischen Kuppelgruft bei Mal-Tepe (Erste Hälfte des IV. Jh. v. Chr.), den heutigen Kupferkesseln in Bulgarien ähnlich.

herrlichen farbigen Zeichnungen auf den Wänden und der Kuppel des einzigartigen thrakischen Grabmals bei Kasanlak[10] ersichtlich ist (Abb.3). Auf den thrakischen Moneten (Deronen) ist ein thrakischer Wagen mit vier Rädern dargestellt.[11] Die Römer haben ebenfalls einen schweren vierrädrigen Pferdewagen für den Tansport von Menschen und Lasten verwendet, wie aus der vorgefundenen Grabmalplatte, einen solchen Transport darstellend, ersichtlich ist.[12] (Abb.4).

Die Slawen, die bei ihrer Ankunft in den heutigen bulgarischen Ländereien romanisierte und nicht romanisierte Thraken vorfanden, haben ebenfalls Pferde verwendet, wie aus den Pferdebegrabungen ersichtlich ist.[13] Jedoch wurden die Pferde nicht als Zug- oder Lasttiere, sondern nur zum Reiten gebraucht. Die Khans und Könige des bulgarischen Reichs (7.–10.Jh.) haben die Reiterei im Krieg und in Feldzügen verwendet, doch kann heute noch nicht mit Sicherheit gesagt werden, ob die Troßwagen von Pferden gezogen

Abb. 2. Dünnes, versilbertes Plättchen mit Abbildung eines Reiters auf einem Pferd, zur Verzierung der Lederriemen des Pferdegeschirrs verwendet, im thrakischen Hügelgrab bei Vratza (Nordwest-Bulgarien) (4.–3. Jh. v. Chr.) gefunden.

wurden. Nach Angaben von Simeon Magister aus dem Jahre 812 ist bekannt, daß nach dem Sieg des bulgarischen Khans Krum über die Byzantiner bei Adrianopel 5.000 Byzantiner mit Frauen und Kindern gefangen genommen und auf Wagen geladen wurden, während alle Kühe, Ochsen und Schafe eingefangen und nach Bulgarien gebracht worden sind.[14] Bulgarische Reiter sind auf mehr als 20 farbigen Miniaturen der Chronik von Manasij aus dem 14. Jh. dargestellt.[15] Das Pferd diente für den Transport auf schlechten Wegen[16] und der König verfügte über viele Pferde.[17]

In Bulgarien blühen im Mittelalter (11.–14. Jh.) die Gewerbe: Sattlerei, Wagenbauerei usw.[18] Der Historiker Joan Kinam schreibt Mitte des 12. Jh., daß die byzantinische Regierung von der Bevölkerung in Thrakien eine große Anzahl von "Karren" requiriert hat.[19] Wir können annehmen, daß es sich um Pferdekarren handelt, obwohl wir dies nicht mit Bestimmtheit behaupten können. Damals bestand ein stark entwickelter Warenhandel, der mit Wagen, kleinen Karren, Pferden und Eseln ausgeführt wurde. Es gab zwei-[20] und vierrädrige Wagen[21]. In der mittelalterlichen bulgarischen Malerei sind der Hlg. Georg und der Hlg. Trifon sehr oft als Reiter auf Pferden mit reich-

349

Abb. 3. Szene aus den Abbildungen in der Kuppel des thrakischen Grabmals bei Kazanlak, ein beladenes Pferd und zwei Reitpferde mit Sätteln darstellend (4. Jh. v. Chr.).

verzierten Sätteln, breiten vielfarbigen Bauchriemen, ledernem Unterschwanz und reich verzierten Lederzügeln abgebildet[22] (Abb.5). Es wurden auch Pferdepostwagen benutzt. Die in den bulgarischen Ländereien Reisenden beschreiben in ihren Reisenbeschreibungen die während der osmanischen Herrschaft (14.–19.Jh.) von ihnen benutzten Wagen, von denen einige mit Wagenplanen bedeckt waren. Wir verfügen über Angaben, daß im Bezirk Prilep 1550 zweirädrige und 1650 vierrädrige Wagen sowie 50 vierrädrige Pferdewagen vorhanden waren.[23] Der bulgarische Tschorbadzi Grujolu aus Kasanlak hat im Jahre 1878 dem türkischen Pascha Kabral Mehmed in Adrianopel einen eleganten Wiener Fiaker geschenkt.[24] Der Bulgare Ivan Najdenov und der erste bulgarische Exarch Antim I. haben im Jahre 1878 als Verbannte von Konstantinopel nach Engjur (Kleinasien) zuerst eine Kutsche und später einen vierrädrigen Pferdekastenwagen benutzt.[25] Die Türken haben für ihren Armeetroß Tausende von hölzernen Ochsen- und Büffelwagen von den bulgarischen Bauern requiriert[26].

Nach der Befreiung Bulgariens (1877–78) gab es überwiegend Holztransportwagen ohne Eisenschienen, von Ochsen und Büffeln gezogen. Anfangs fand

Abb. 4. Grabstein mit Abbildung eines vierrädrigen Pferdewagens (5. Jh. v. Chr.), in Bulgarien gefunden.

man nur sehr selten Pferdewagen, die Pferde wurden als Lasttiere, zum Reiten und bei den volkstümlichen Rennen zu Ehren des Hlg. Theodor benutzt, jedoch nicht zum Transport und nicht bei der Feldarbeit. In den Gebirgsgegenden ist der vierrädrige Wagen erst jahrzehntelang nach der Befreiung Bulgariens aufgetaucht, da früher keine geeigneten Straßen vorhanden waren. In den Rhodopen, dem Balkangebirge, der Sredna Gora, dem Rila- und Piringebirge wurden als Lasttiere Esel, Maulesel, Pferde und Kamele (hauptsächlich in den Rhodopen) verwendet. In diesen Gebieten wurde auch der zweirädrige Wagen zum Transport von Menschen und Waren benutzt. Die Ein- und Zweipferdewagen überwiegen in der Donau- und thrakischen Ebene, in Dobrudza und den Talkesseln. Nach dem Ersten und besonders nach dem Zweiten Weltkrieg wurden infolge der Verbreitung der Eisenbahnlinien, der breiten und gepflasterten Straßen und besonders nach der Industrialisierung und Kollektivierung der Landwirtschaft (nach 1945) die herkömmlichen Transportmittel durch den Eisenbahn-, LKW-, See- und Lufttransport verdrängt.

2. *Fußgängertum.* Besonders in der Vergangenheit und manchmal, jedoch sehr selten, auch heute noch werden Gegenstände von Menschen zu Fuß transportiert. Während der heißen und trockenen Sommermonate gehen besonders in den Ebenen die Bauern barfuß vom Dorf zu den Ackerfeldern und zurück, indem sie die landwirtschaftlichen Geräte, ein Bündel mit Nahrung,

Abb. 5. Sankt Georg, auf einem Pferd mit reich verziertem Pferdegeschirr, tötet einen Drachen. Wandmalerei an der Außenwand der Kirche in Dragalevci in der Umgebung von Sofia (14. Jh.).

den vollen Wasserkrug usw. tragen. Die bulgarische Bauernbevölkerung, sowohl in den Ebenen, als auch in den Gebirgsgegenden, trägt selbstgefertigte Lederopanken (Bundschuhe-*carvuli*, Abb.6) aus gesalzenem und getrocknetem Schweins-, Rind- oder Büffelleder[27] zwecks Bewahrung der Füße vor Verletzungen, Kälte und Schmutz. Die *carvuli* sind von den Thraken vererbt.[28] Es wurden auch *carvuli* auf den Märkten gekauft, ausgearbeitet von speziellen Meistern (*carvuldzii*/Bundschuher oder *saraci*/Sattler)[29]. Die Frauen tragen ausserdem verschiedene Arten von Pantoffeln und die Männer Schuhe und Stiefel. Um im Winter nicht in den Schnee einzusinken, tragen hauptsächlich die Hirten und Jäger in den Gebirgsgegenden Schneeschuhe *(zeigari, naputila* oder *napatila)* (Abb.7)[30]. Es handelt sich gewöhnlich um ellipsenförmige oder runde zähe Hölzchen, die am Ende fest zusammengebunden sind und in der Mitte ein Netz haben, das am Holz mit dünnen Lederriemchen oder Stricken angebunden ist. Diese Schneeschuhe werden an den *carvuli* oder Schuhen festgebunden. Um nicht auszugleiten, verwenden die bulgarischen Bauern handgeschmiedete Eisengreifer *(kotki)* (Abb.8)[31], die an den *carvuli*, Schuhen oder Stiefeln befestigt werden und mit Eisenspitzen versehen sind, die beim Gehen ins Eis, in den Schnee oder in den Boden eindringen. Sie werden ebenfalls von einheimischen Meistern angefertigt. In sumpfigen Gegenden und nach schweren Regenfällen verwenden hauptsächlich die Hirten sogenannte Stelzen

Abb. 6. Bulgarischer Bauer in traditioneller Tracht mit weißen Wickelgamaschen und Bundschuhen aus dem Bezirk Jambol. Phot. V. Marinov, 1950,

(kokili, stulce, nastulci, paterici, kataragi)[32], die aus zwei 1,5–2 m langen Stangen bestehen, die etwa einen halben Meter über dem Boden einen kurzen Ast haben, auf den der Mensch seine Füße setzen kann. Es gibt auch eine zweite Variante dieser Stelzen, die Stufen aus gut ineinander geflochtenen Weiden- oder anderen zähen Ruten besitzen, und auf denen der Fuß einen guten Halt finden kann. Die Stelzen werden heutzutage von den Kindern zum Spielen verwendet oder bei einigen Bräuchen und Festen getragen, um Gelächter hervorzurufen.

3. *Transport von Gegenständen durch Menschen.* Sowohl in der Vergangenheit als auch heute noch ist es allgemein üblich, Gegenstände *mit der Hand* zu tragen, besonders auf den Märkten und Jahrmärkten und zwar Brot, lebendes Geflügel usw. In der Hand und auf den Händen werden auch andere Gegenstände wie Kessel und Eimer für Milch, Wasserkrüge, Körbe mit Eiern, Weintrauben, Rosenblüten, Kinder usw. getragen.

Es ist auch üblich und zwar sowohl früher als auch heute, Gegenstände *auf einer Schulter* zu tragen. Wenn der Bauer morgens zur Arbeit geht, trägt er den Holzhammer auf der Schulter und den Wasserkrug in der anderen Hand, die Bäuerinnen tragen Hacken auf der Schulter und einen Korb in der anderen Hand. Der Bauer trägt auch die Sense, Hacke, Schaufel, Harke

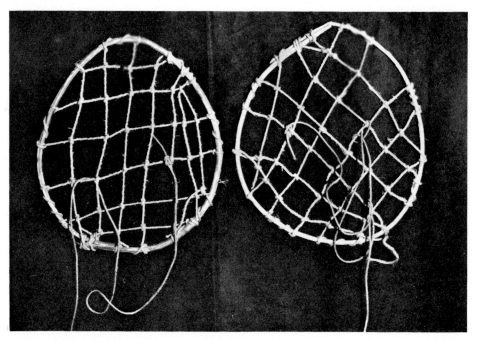

Abb. 7. »Zejgări« zum Anbinden an den Füßen bei Schnee. Dorf Progled, Ostrhodopen. Phot. V. Marinov, 1951.

usw. auf der Schulter (Abb.9). Sehr charakteristisch ist das Tragen eines Schulterjoches *(kobilica)* mit angehängten Kupfer- oder verzinnten Wasserkesseln[33] (Abb.10). In Bulgarien werden verschiedene dialektalische Bezeichnungen für das Schulterjoch verwendet: *kotlovarka, kubilica, vodac, udac, vudacka, tuvaricka.*[34] Wir unterscheiden einige Arten von Schulterjochen: 1. kurze (100–110 cm lang) mit einem Einschnitt am Ende und aus ziemlich dickem rundem Holz, die schwach gebogen sind, wie z.B. die *vodaci* im Rhodopengebirge; 2. in der Mitte und am Ende stark gebogene mit natürlich gebogenen oder zusätzlich angenagelten Hörnchen an den Enden. Sie werden aus dünnerem, rundem und glattem Kornelkirschholz verarbeitet und sind am häufigsten in der Gegend von Sofia anzutreffen. Einige von ihnen haben an den Enden noch je zwei zusätzliche Hörnchen, um gleichzeitig Kessel und Wasserkrüge tragen zu können; 3. aus Buchen- oder Eichenholz in rechteckiger Form, in der Mitte schwach gebogen und mit scharf zugespitzten Enden mit Einschnitten, 150–180 cm lang[35]; 4. mit kurzen Hörnern[36] oder mit stumpfen Hörnern[37]; 5. stark gebogene mit an den Enden aufgesetzten, zähen, gebogenen Hölzchen mit Einschnitten, türkisch *suadzi* genannt[38], die i N. O. Bulgarien aufgefunden werden; 6. ohne Einschnitte an den natürlich geboge-

354

Abb. 8. Eiserne Schneeschuhe (»kòtki«) zum Anbinden an den Füßen bei Schnee und Eis. Dorf Jakoruda, Westrhodopen. Phot. V. Marinov, 1968.

nen Hörnern, die hauptsächlich in der Gegend von Panagjuriste vorgefunden werden.[39]

Auf der Schulter werden hauptsächlich von den Männern übergeworfene Doppelsäcke *(disagi)* getragen, die aus zwei miteinander verbundenen aus Ziegenwolle ausgearbeiteten Säcken bestehen.[40] Diese Doppelsäcke können bequem auch auf einem Esel-, Maulesel- und Pferdesaumsattel getragen werden, wozu der Schnitt in der Mitte des Verbindungsteiles beider Säcke hilft. Die Hirten haben mit diesen Säcken an der einen Seite flache Blechgefäße mit gemolkener Milch befördert. Die bulgarischen Einwohner des Dorfes Karaagac, jetzt Griechenland, haben mit Wasser gefüllte Krüge getragen, "je einen auf jeder Schulter und mit der Hand gestützt". Es handelt sich um Wasserkrüge mit zwei Henkeln und breitem Hals.[41] Auf einer Schulter werden auch Backtröge mit gebackenem Brot getragen, während auf dem Rücken schwere Gegenstände und Lasten wie Holztröge, Backtröge usw., mit Seilen angebunden, zum Verkauf in den Dörfern getragen werden. Auf diese Weise werden auch Säcke, gefüllt mit Weizen, Gerste, Roggen usw. getragen und zwar bis zu den Dorfspeichern oder zur Mühle zum Mahlen. Auf der Schulter und auf dem Rücken werden Mehlsäcke getragen. Die Hirten tragen, befestigt

Abb. 9. Frauen gehen zur Arbeit mit der Hacke auf der Schulter und dem Korb in der Hand. Dorf Vasil Levski bei Karlovo. Phot. V. Marinov, 1968.

an einem Ledergürtel, besondere mit Knochenplatten[42] verzierte Taschen[43] (Abb.11), in denen sie vornehmlich ihre Nahrung, jedoch auch Dudelsack, Hirtenflöte und andere Gegenstände zum Schutz gegen Regen, tragen.

Auf dem Rücken werden verschiedene schwerere Gegenstände wie Kisten und Säcke mit Nahrungsmitteln oder Mehl getragen, die von hinten mit beiden Händen gestützt werden. Die Frauen tragen auf dem Rücken meistens in den Wäldern gesammelte Holzknüppel, mit Seilen angebunden, die über beide Schultern gehen und vorne auf der Brust gekreuzt werden. Auf diese Weise tragen die Frauen auch Wäsche, um sie am Fluß oder Brunnen zu waschen, sowie große Kupferkessel, in denen Wasser zum Waschen erwärmt wird, geflochtene Körbe usw. (Abb.12). Charakteristisch war früher in Bulgarien das Tragen von kleinen Kindern auf dem Rücken in Stoffwiegen *(cedilnik),* mit wollenen Stricken versehen, die auf der Brust gekreuzt und auf dem Rücken festgebunden werden (Abb.13). Die Mütter tragen auf diese Weise ihre Kinder zur Feldarbeit, zum Markt in den Städten und zum Besuch.[44] Früher wurden auf dem Rücken auch Lederschläuche, die mit Wasser, Wein, Milch, Quark

Abb. 10. Wassertragen in Kesseln, an Schulterjochen angehängt. Dorf Glozevo bei Kubrat, Nordost-Bulgarien. Phot. V. Marinov, 1951.

und Käse gefüllt waren, getragen.[45] Kleine Kinder werden auf dem Rücken, auch nur mit den Händen gestützt, getragen.

Auf dem Kopf werden früher und heute Lasten getragen, jedoch ist diese Tragart nicht für Bulgarien charakteristisch. Es werden auf diese Weise Stoffbündel mit Kleidern, Wolle usw. getragen (Abb. 14,15). Felix Kanitz behauptet, daß in Bulgarien Gefäße mit Wasser und Körbe mit Rosenblüten auf dem Kopf getragen wurden. In Sliven, Nessebar und Karnobat wurden Tongefäße auf dem Kopf getragen.[46]

Ein Handtransport mit verschiedenen Tragbahren *(targi)* wird von zwei Personen ausgeführt. Die Tragbahren haben zwei Griffe und es gibt verschiedene Varianten: 1. zum Tragen von Spreu oder Heu für das Vieh von der Scheune bis zum Stall, *targa* (t. *tesgere, alaf targasa,* Abb.16) genannt,[47] die nach den Vergleichsuntersuchungen von Prof. B. Drobnjakovic[48] antiken Ursprungs ist und vornehmlich in N. O. Bulgarien vorgefunden wird.[49] Es gibt auch von dieser Art Tragbahren mit einem Griff;[50] 2. mit flachem Tragboden und 4 Griffen, die von zwei Personen getragen werden; 3. aus zwei parallelen

357

Abb. 11. Beutelförmige Leder-Hirtentaschen, die über die Schulter gehängt oder auf dem Rücken getragen werden. Dorf Zlatar bei Preslav, Nordost-Bulgarien. Phot. V. Marinov, 1952.

Holzstämmen, die von zwei Personen getragen werden. Beide Holzstämme haben durchbohrte Löcher, in denen quer leicht gebogene, runde Äste, mit anderen Holzruten verflochten, eingesteckt sind. Mit ihnen werden Steine, ungebrannte Ziegeln, Ziegelsteine usw. transportiert; 4. die vierte Variante heißt *lesa*.

Um die Lasten leichter auf größeren Entfernungen transportieren zu können, werden *Schubkarren* mit einem oder zwei Rädern benutzt. Die Schubkarren mit einem kleinen Holz- oder Eisenrad haben einen langen Holzgriff, auf dem Nägel eingeschlagen sind, um Wasserkessel, Wasserkrüge, Körbe mit Weintrauben usw. anhängen zu können. Der Schubkarren wird mit der Hand geschoben. Die Schubkarren mit zwei an einer Holzachse befestigten Rädern haben ebenfalls einen Holzgriff, jedoch ragen von der Achse zwei krumme

Abb. 12. Heukorb, auf dem
Rücken zu tragen. Dorf Zlatar,
bei Preslav, Nordost-Bulgarien.
Phot. V. Marinov, 1952.

Hölzer hervor, die an ein und derselben Stelle mit dem Griff verbunden
sind. Die von den krummen Hölzern und dem Griff gebildete kleine Platt-
form wird zum Transport von schweren Lasten benutzt: Säcke mit Weizen,
Gerste, Roggen, Mehl, Gepäck usw. Der Schubkarren wird nicht mit den
Händen geschoben, sondern gezogen.

Fast in jedem Bauernhof findet man einen Holzschubkarren mit einem Rad,
zwei Holzgriffen und einem trapezartigen Holzkasten (Abb. 17).[51] Dieser von
einer Person geschobene Schubkarren dient zum Transport von Erde, Sand,
Ziegelsteinen, Steinen usw. beim Bau von neuen Gebäuden. In den Städten
werden hauptsächlich Plattform-Schubkarren mit zwei Holzhandgriffen zum
Schieben verwendet.

4. *Tragen und Transport mit Lasttieren.* Der Lastentransport datiert aus

Abb. 13. Tragen von kleinen Kindern mit Hilfe von Stoffbeuteln (»cedilnici«). Kotel, Mittelbalkan. Phot. V. Marinov, 1950.

den ältesten Zeiten. Auch in unseren Ländern ist dies durch die archäologischen Funde bewiesen, wie z.B. die erwähnten Wandmalereien im Grabmal von Kasanlak.[52] Anfangs wurden die Lasten auf dem bloßen Rücken der Tiere (Esel, Maulesel, Pferd) transportiert und erst später werden Schwitztuch, Saumsattel und Sattel verwendet, die zum bequemeren Sitzen des Reiters und zur besseren Befestigung der Lasten dienen, sowie das Tier vor Verwundungen infolge langen Tragens schwerer Lasten schützen. Bei uns werden die Ochsen, Kühe und Büffel nicht zum Reiten oder Tragen von Lasten auf dem Rücken benutzt, sondern diese Tiere dienen nur als Zugtiere. Der Esel wird zum Reiten und Transport von leichteren Lasten verwendet, die auf einem speziellen Esel-Holzsaumsattel *(samar, semer)* befestigt werden und zwar Brennholz, *disagi* mit Mehl, Futter, Blechkisten mit frischer Milch, Quark oder Käse sowie Brot für die Hirten im Gebirge. Die Esel-Saumsattel bestehen vorne und hinten aus je zwei leicht gebogenen Holzstücken, die sich oben kreuzen und in Rillen verbunden sind, während sie von beiden Seiten durch drei-vier flache Hölzchen, ebenfalls in Rillen eingesteckt, verbunden werden. Under den Saumsattel wird ein weiches Kissen *(stelja)* gelegt, und er wird durch einen Unterbauchriemen befestigt. Unter dem Schwanz wird er durch

Abb. 14. Tragen von Wasser-
kannen auf dem Kopf. Gra-
vüre von F. Kanitz.

einen "podopasnik, kjustek oder paldǎm" aus Stricken oder Riemen befestigt,
damit er nicht zu den Vorderfüßen und dem Kopf des Tieres herunterrutscht.
Auf den Eselskopf wird ein aus Stricken oder Riemen ausgearbeiteter Esels-
halfter (ohne Mundstück), mit Knöpfen verziert, aufgelegt. Der Halfter hat
einen Halfterstrick aus Seil oder Leder und eine Eisenkette, die zum Führen
und Anbinden des Esels dienen.

Zur Beförderung von schwereren Lasten, zum Reiten und für lange und
steile Wege werden Maulesel *(katǎri)*, und eine spezielle Rasse von Gebirgs-
pferden verwendet.[53] Während des Mittelalters und der osmanischen Herrschaft wurden die Handelswaren mit Maulesel- und Pferdekarawanen ausgeführt, die von Dubrovnik am Adriatischen Meer in östlicher Richtung die
Balkanhalbinsel bis zum Schwarzen Meer kreuzten.[54] Für diesen Warentransport wurden größere Saumsättel, von Handwerksmeistern gearbeitet, benutzt,

Abb. 15. Tragen eines geflochtenen Korbs mit Rosen auf dem Kopf und traditionelle Rosenöl-Destillation. Gravüre von F. Kanitz.

die bequemer zum Reiten und Befestigen von Lasten als die leichteren Esel-Saumsättel sind. Die Maulesel- und Pferde-Saumsättel bestehen aus zwei dünnen, gebogenen Brettern *(oblak)*, vorn und hinten. Es gibt Saumsättel mit Schnitzereien auf dem breiten und oben runden Brett, das an seinem unteren Ende zwei gebogene Füße besitzt. Diese zwei Bretter werden in Rillen mit zwei flachen und gebogenen Sattelhölzchen *(paidi)* verbunden, die die Rolle des Sattels spielen. Von beiden Seiten werden die Füße dieser zwei Bretter durch je zwei flache, in Rillen gesteckte Seitenhölzchen verbunden. Unter dieses Holzteil wird ein dickes, mit Leder umwickeltes Kissen *(stelja)* gelegt und mit einem Unterbauchriemen befestigt, während hinten der "paldăm" aufgesetzt wird. Auf dem hinteren Brett werden zwei Holzhaken *(kalugerki, kukumjavki)* angenagelt, die zusammen mit den zwei vor dem Vorderbrett hervorragenden Teilen der "paidi" zum Umwinden und Befestigen von starken Schafs- oder Ziegenwollstricken dienen. Diese werden zur Befestigung des Gepäcks oder der Lasten am Saumsattel verwendet, insbesondere damit sie nicht beim

362

Abb. 16. Tragbahre aus krummen Holzstäben zum Transport von Viehfutter, die von zwei Männern getragen wird. Dorf Zlatar bei Preslav, Nordost-Bulgarien. Phot. V. Marinov, 1952.

Abb. 17. Zwei Schubkarren mit je einem Rad und zwei Holzfüßen. Dorf Sevar bei Kubrat, Nordost-Bulgarien. Phot. V. Marinov, 1952.

Abb. 18. Pferdesaumsattel mit vorderem und hinterem »òblak« und Pferdegeschirr. Dorf Krumovo bei Topolovgrad, Südbulgarien. Phot. V. Marinov, 1950.

Ersteigen und Hinuntersteigen von steilen und unebenen Wegen lose werden und ins Wanken geraten. Die Steigbügel zum Reiten sind aus Metall oder Stricken. Diese Saumsättel wurden auch zur Versorgung der Bevölkerung in den Gebirgsgemeinden mit Getreide, Futter, Mehl, Salz, Textilwaren usw. benutzt. Auf dem Rückweg wurden auf ihnen Milchwaren, konserviertes Fleisch, Wolle, grobe von den Frauen handgewebte Stoffe und sonstige Waren zum Verkauf auf den Märkten befördert. Solche Saumsättel wurden auch zum Transport von Bauholz in die Täler verwendet. Die Nomadenhirten (Walachen und Karakatschanen) haben früher und sogar bis 1960 in Bulgarien mit diesen breiten und bequemen Saumsätteln, auf Pferde gelegt, ihren Hausrat transportiert (Abb.18).[55] Diese Pferde- und Maulesel-Saumsättel sind im Balkankrieg und im Ersten Weltkrieg auf der Balkanhalbinsel massenhaft vom Armeetroß und zum Transport von Maschinengewehren und Gewehren, besonders in den Gebirgsrayons, verwendet worden. Während der osmanischen Herrschaft und auch unmittelbar nach der Befreiung Bulgariens gab es viele Handwerker, die Saumsättel ausarbeiteten, weil sie sehr gesucht waren. Diese Handwerker bildeten spezielle Handwerkervereinigungen, die

Abb. 19. Kamelsaumsattel, gefunden in Südost-Bulgarien; nach A. Primovski.

eine gemeinsame Kasse hatten und einen Teil des Gewinns für den Bau von Brücken, Brunnen und Kirchen sowie auch für kostbare Geschenke für die Klöster (reich verzierte und geschnitzte Altarwände, Ikonen, große Kerzen usw.) beiseite legten. Nach dem Zweiten Weltkrieg ist dieses Gewerbe schnell verfallen und heute kann man nur wenige Meister in einigen Dörfern und Städten in den Gebirgsrayons Bulgariens finden.

Das Kamel wurde auch in Bulgarien als Lasttier benutzt.[56] Kamelkarawanen, mit Salz, Mehl, Getreide, Futter, Textilwaren und Handwerkserzeugnissen beladen, brachten diese Waren nach den größten Dörfern und Städten in den Rhodopen, um von dort Nahrungsmittel (Käse, Kaschkaval, *pastarma* und *sazdarma*), Fuß- und Bettdecken (*kitenici* und *halista*) aus den Rhodopen, grobgewebte Stoffe, fertige Kleider usw. zurückzubringen. Die Kameltreiber haben aus den Ostrhodopen auch Ballen mit "dzebel"-Tabak für die Tabaklager in Gümürdzina gebracht.[57] Bulgarische Kameltreiber haben auch aus dem Balkangebirge in der Gegend von Sliven Holzkohle zum Gießen von Kanonenkugeln für die türkische Armee transportiert.[58] Während des Balkankrieges wurden "Patronen, Mehl, Reis und anderer Proviant" für die bulgarische Armee bei Adrianopel und Tschataldza auf Kamelen befördert.[59]

365

Auch im Ersten Weltkrieg wurden Kamele zum Transport benutzt.[60] Teilweise wurden auch bei der Vorbereitung des Zweiten Weltkriegs (1939, 1940, 1941) Kamele für Transportzwecke verwendet.[61] In einzelnen Fällen hatte man in Bulgarien Kamele auch als Zugtiere.[62] Der Saumsattel, der von den bulgarischen Kameltreibern gebraucht wurde, unterscheidet sich vom Esel-, Maulesel- oder Pferdesaumsattel. Er wird entweder von den Kameltreibern selbst oder von speziellen Meistern angefertigt. Der Kamelsaumsattel ist unter dem Namen *aut (aute)* bekannt.[63] (Abb. 19). Je nach der Größe der Kamele unterscheidet A. Primovski drei verschiedene Kamel-Saumsättel: 1. großer – 100–120 cm; 2. mittlerer – 80–100 cm; und 3. kleiner – 60–80 cm.[64] Der weiche Teil des Saumsattels besteht aus zwei umgebogenen Teilen, wobei in der Biegung in der Mitte Platz für den Kamelbuckel gelassen wird. Von der Innenseite wird die *stelja* mit Hanfstoff und von der Außenseite mit Ziegenstoff umwickelt und innen mit kleinem "saz" gefüllt. Damit diese Saumsättel schwere Lasten tragen können, werden sie vorn von zwei gebogenen Holzstücken *(atapi)* umspannt, die nahe hintereinander gelegt werden und nicht aus einem ganzen Holzstück, sondern aus zwei einzelnen, gleichen Teilen bestehen, die miteinander durch einen Holzklotz verbunden sind. Diese zwei Holzstücke *(atapi)* werden untereinander durch zwei kurze Seitenhölzchen *(skendzi)*, verbunden, die auf den *atapi* und den hervorragenden Holzklötzen mit festen Schnüren *(sergii)* festgebunden sind.[65] Die Holzstücke *(atapi)* werden mit vier Schnüren *(elika)*, zwei vordere und zwei hintere, die "tief an der Innenseite des Saumsattels"[66] festgenäht sind, verbunden. Ein spezieller Strick *(jureme)*, der beim linken kurzen Seitenhölzchen herauskommt und den Saumsattel zweimal umbindet und quer umkreuzt, hält ihn fest. Der Saumsattel wird mit zwei Unterbauchriemen, die mit zwei Holzschnallen versehen sind, festgebunden. Der vordere *atap* besitzt einen Eisenhaken, an den eine Glocke angehängt ist. Ein breiter Riemen dient ebenfalls zum Befestigen des Saumsattels am Körper des Kamels. Die Kamelhalfter werden aus Stoffbändern und die Halfterstricke aus Seilen gemacht. Die Kamele werden eins hinter dem anderen mit einem 8 m langen Seil an den Saumsätteln angebunden.[67] In Winter werden die Kamele zum Schutz vor Kälte und Regen mit Decken *(cul)* bedeckt.[68]

5.Transportmittel, von Hornvieh, Pferden, Eseln, Mauleseln und Kamelen gezogen. Aus Mitteilungen ausländischer Reisender, die die bulgarischen Ländereien bereist haben, wie z.B. Pierre Lescaloppier (1574),[69] erfahren wir, daß die Braut hoch zu Roß und von einem Ochsenwagen begleitet zum Heim des Bräutigams gebracht wurde. Im Wagen befand sich wahrscheinlich die Aussteuer. General Jochmus teilt in seinen Reisebeschreibungen aus den

Abb. 20. Der kranke F. Kanitz reist durch Bulgarien in einem zweirädrigen Wagen mit Wagenplane, von einem Ochsen gezogen. Gravüre von F. Kanitz.

ostbulgarischen Ländern mit, daß er im Jahre 1847 auf seinem Weg "einigen Karawanen von Ochsenwagen begegnet ist, die Baumaterial und Eichenstämme allerbester Qualität beförderten" und zwar aus dem östlichen Teil des Balkangebirges.[70] Auf seiner Reise ist er "bulgarischen und türkischen Karawanen begegnet, die mit Büffeln vom großen Markt in Uzundzovo Tabak nach Schumen und Bukarest beförderten."[71] Er fährt fort: "Soweit meine Augen reichten, war die Straße von Ochsen, Büffeln, Pferden und Wagen ausgefüllt. Schlanke bulgarische Frauen und scherzhafte Zigeunerinnen ritten auf Eseln und Mauleseln zum Markt in Gorna Orjachoviza . . . Dort gab es mehr als Zehntausend Personen und 2500 Wagen".[72] Er erzählt weiterhin, daß er ". . . vielen Wagen-Karawanen mit Ochsen und Büffeln als Zugtieren begegnet ist, die Nahrungsmittel zur Hauptstadt (Konstantinopel) beförderten."[73] K. Jireček wiederum schreibt, daß "auf der Balkanhalbinsel das Pferd nicht für landwirtschaftliche Arbeit benutzt wird, die von den Büffeln und Ochsen ausgeführt wird, sondern nur zum Reiten und zum Warentransport."[74] Er erwähnt weiterhin, daß "die Büffeln an ganz primitiven Wagen ohne Joche angespannt sind, ihre Köpfe werden durch eine Art von Rahmen, befestigt an beiden Seiten der Deichsel, durchgezwängt, so daß die Zugkraft ausschließlich auf den Hals fällt."[75] Er meint, daß die größten Wagen in der

Marica-Ebene angetroffen werden: "Es waren sehr große viereckige Korb-wagen, ausgearbeitet aus schwarzen Holzstäben, die so hoch sind, daß sie nicht der Größe der Zugtiere entsprechen". Jireček schreibt weiterhin: "Diese langsamen unförmigen Wagen, beladen mit Weizen oder Stroh, zeugen davon, daß das Land fruchtbar ist und keine Abhänge und Felsen hat".[76] Wir ver-danken ihm auch die Mitteilung, daß die Karawanen der serbischen Kauf-leute in 20 Tagen von Belgrad bis Uzundzovo in Südbulgarien gelangten.[77]

Kleine zweirädrige Wagen mit einer Deichsel und einem Fröschlein *(zabka)* zum Einspannen von großen Zugtieren in einem Joch werden in den Gebirgs-gegenden des Landes (Rhodopen, Stara Planina, u.a.) angetroffen und zum Abschleppen von Holzstämmen benutzt, die an der Holzachse angebunden werden, während deren hinterer Teil auf dem Boden schleppt. Sie werden *vraduni (varduni, farduni, kangali)* genannt.[78] Der vordere, viereckige Teil der Deichsel ist von zwei Eisenbändern umspannt, damit das Holz nicht zer-springt. Oben auf der Deichsel ist mit Eisenkeilen an drei Stellen der hin-tere Teil der "zabka" befestigt, indem sein Vorderteil das Ende der Deichsel überragt. Unter der Deichsel ist der zweite Teil der "zabka" unbeweglich be-festigt, während sein Vorderteil ebenfalls vor der Deichsel hervorragt und auf diese Weise den Mund des "Frosches" bildet, der den oberen Teil des Joches anbeißt, der hier mit einem beweglichen Eisenkeil *(teglic)* befestigt wird, der durch die durchbohrten Löcher des oberen und unteren Teils des "Frosches" durchgeht.

Große zweirädrige Holzwagen wurden zur Beförderung von Getreide- oder Gerstensäcken zur Mühle und zum Zurückbringen von Mehl, sowie zum Trans-port von Brennholz, von Dünger zu den Feldern, zu Einkäufen auf dem nahen Marktzentrum usw. verwendet. Da passende Straßen fehlten, wurden in den Gebirgsgegenden lange Zeit nach der Befreiung Bulgariens keine Transporte mit vierrädrigen Wagen durchgeführt. Wir finden schon bei F. Kanitz[79] Angaben über zweirädrige Planwagen, von einem Ochsen gezogen (Abb.20). Diese zweirädrigen Wagen sind heute fast verschwunden, wir haben jedoch 1969 einen solchen Wagen im Bezirk Vraza (Abb.21) und einen zweiten im Dorf Kirkovo (Bezirk Kardzali) aufgefunden. Einige dieser Wagen haben einen rechteckigen, geflochtenen Korb, der in der Mitte des Wagens aufge-stellt ist. In N.W.Bulgarien sind diese Wagen unter dem Namen "gjavolska kola"[80] bekannt; man findet sie auch in Ostthrakien.[81] Die Holzräder hatten anfangs keine Schienen, doch begann man später auch Schienen zu verwen-den. Die Teile des Holzrads sind: "glavina", 12 Speichen *(spici)* und 6 "nap-lati".[82] In den wasserarmen Gegenden des Landes, besonders in N.O.Bulga-rien – Ludogorie (Deliorman) und Dobrudza – werden auch zweirädrige,

Abb. 21. Zweirädriger Wagen, von zwei Ochsen gezogen. Dorf Pavolce bei Vratza, Nordwest-Bulgarien. Phot. V. Marinov, 1968.

Abb. 22. Eselkarren aus dem Bezirk Vidin, Nordwest-Bulgarien. Phot. V. Marinov, 1968.

von Eseln gezogene Wagen verwendet (Abb.22), die zum Transport von Trinkwasser aus den entfernten Dörfern, wo Brunnen oder Quellen vorhanden sind, dienen. Zu diesem Zweck wurden auf die Wagen Fässer oder Kübel aufgestellt. Wenn diese Wagen von zwei Pferden gezogen werden, haben sie eine Wagen-Deichsel *(ok)* und keine Deichsel für Horntiere *(proceƥ)*, während die Einpferdewagen zwei seitliche Holzstangen *(straki)* besitzen, die zwischen der Achse und dem Stuhl herausragen oder an ihnen mit Eisenklammern und -ringen befestigt sind, zwischen denen das Pferd angespannt wird.

Vierrädrige Wagen. Wie schon angeführt, wurde durch archäologische Funde und geschichtliche Angaben festgestellt, daß der vierrädrige Holzwagen in den bulgarischen Ländereien schon seit dem Altertum und bis zu unseren Tagen vorhanden ist. Im Prozeß seiner Entwicklung ist er gewissen Veränderungen und Vervollkommnungen unterworfen worden. Wir werden hier nicht die in den verschiedenen geschichtlichen Epochen stattgefundenen Veränderungen untersuchen, doch möchten wir nur erwähnen, daß die Bulgaren diesen Wagen schon im Mittelalter und besonders während der osmanischen Herrschaft kannten. Ethnographische Daten über den vierrädrigen Wagen in Bulgarien können in dem Buch "Pokasalez" von G. S. Rakovski, herausgegeben 1859,[83] bei Jirecek,[84] D. Marinov,[85] Hr. Vakarelski,[86,87] V. Marinov[88] u.a. gefunden werden. Der vierrädrige Wagen ist in Bulgarien unter dem Namen *kola (kula,* t. *araba)* bekannt. Er besteht aus zwei Teilen:

1. *Der vordere Wagen (presnica,* t. *ilijasi,*[89] *iliasak,*[90] *predna kolesarka,*[91] *predna kolesnica*[92]*).* Er war anfänglich aus behauenen, dicken Holzstücken gearbeitet, die in den einzelnen Gegenden Bulgariens verschiedene Bezeichnungen tragen. Er besteht aus: einer Holzachse *(os* oder *dingil)* mit zugespitzten Enden *(vretena,* t. *kol),*[93] an denen die Räder befestigt sind. In der Mitte der Achse ist ein Loch durchgebohrt, während zwei kleinere Löcher an den Enden durchgebohrt sind, in denen Eisennägel mit breitem Kopf eingeschlagen werden, um die Räder festzuhalten. Auf der Achse werden drei oder vier Einschnitte gemacht, damit die zwei Enden *(rakavi)* der Deichsel festgemacht werden können (Abb. 23a). Ein zweites, behauenes, viereckiges Holzstück von gleicher Länge wird auf die Achse aufgelegt, es hat ebenfalls in der Mitte ein durchgebohrtes Loch und 2–3 Einschnitte und wird *oplen,*[94] *bobotec,*[95] *bojadzik, barzik, bube, bajadzik,*[96] *jastăk,*[97] *proskeval,*[98] *stol, stolnica*[99] genannt. D. Marinov[100] und St. L. Kostov[101] setzen "jastăk" und "bojadzik" gleich, aber unserer Meinung nach ist das falsch. Das zweite behauene Holzstück, das über die Achse gestellt wird und durch Holzkeile mit ihr unbeweglich verbunden wird, ist der sogenannte *bojadzik, bardzik, oplen, bobotec, bube*[102] und soll die "Ärmel" *(rakavi)* der Deichsel festhalten und außerdem ihren Vorderteil heben, da die Vorderräder kleiner als die Hinterräder sind, und ihn in waagerechter Lage halten. Das dritte, viereckige Holzstück mit einem durchgebohrten Loch in der Mitte und zwei seitlichen in zwei Rillen befestigten Stützhölzern *(podporki, klimii)* bewegt sich frei um den mittleren Holz- oder Eisenkeil, genannt *slepec,*[103] *klecka,*[104] t. *orta, bas cuvija,*[105] *sradna* oder *sranna cufija, precnik, gradnjak, gradnik.*[106] Dieses dritte Holzstück wird auch *stol, stolica, stolnina, prag, prak, văzglavnica* (t. *jastăk)* und *proskeval* genannt. Der mittlere Pflock, der durch die Löcher des *stol, oplen* oder *os* durchgesteckt wird, dient dazu, daß sich der Wagen nach links oder rechts wenden und leichter die scharfen Kurven der gewöhnlichen, schwarzen Straßen nehmen kann. Die Stützhölzer, die seitlich vom "stol" herausragen und zum Aufstützen der "kanati" des Wagens dienen, werden *klimii, kol, kulove, kolluk, sjuve* und *sjuvjan* genannt.[107]

2. *Der hintere Wagen (zadna kola,* t. *gerisi*[108,109] genannt) besteht aus zwei Holzstücken: 1. Achse *(os, dingil),* deren Länge der Länge des Vorderteils des Wagens gleich ist, und 2. Stuhl *(stol, văzglavnica, jastăk)* mit zwei *klimii,* aber dieser Stuhl ist im Unterschied zum "stol" des Vorderradgestells des Wagens unbeweglich zur Achse durch Holzkeile verbunden, wie dies auch beim "oplen", "bobtec" oder "bardzik" der Fall ist, der hier fehlt, was zur

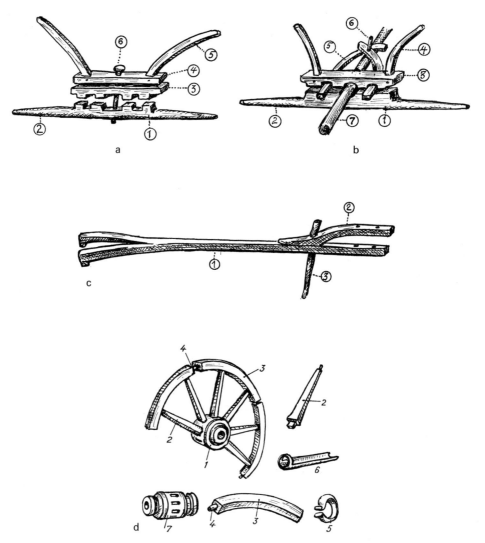

Abb. 23. Zeichnungen der Teile des Holzwagens: a) Vorderwagen, b) Hinterwagen, c) Deichsel, d) Rad.

Ausgleichung des Wagenbodens "potonica" des Vorderteils mit dem hinteren Wagen hilft (Abb.23b). Der Hinterteil des Wagens wird mit dem Vorderteil durch eine lange Holzdeichsel, *rastoka, rastocna*,[110] *rastocnik*,[111] *stărciste*,[112] *opasnica*,[113] *ok*[114] genannt, verbunden, die in ihrem Vorderteil ein durchgebohrtes Loch hat, durch das der mittlere Pflock durchgesteckt wird. Um die Verbindung der Deichsel mit dem Vorderteil zu verstärken, wird oft ein breites Eisenstück, "germe"[115], wie eine "zabka" gebogen, verwendet. Dieses

Eisenstück hat ein Loch und liegt auf dem "stol", damit der mittlere Pflock durch das Loch durchgesteckt werden kann, während der hintere Teil des Eisenstücks mit der Wagendeichsel durch einen eingeschlagenen Haken verbunden wird.[116] In der Mitte des "ok" *(rastok)* befinden sich durchgebohrte Löcher, die eine Verlängerung oder Verkleinerung des Wagens gestatten. Zu diesem Zweck werden zwei krumme Hölzer verwendet, *lesici, lesicini*[117] oder *karlangaci*[118] genannt, die an ihrem hinteren Ende "glavicki" *(cumaljuski)*[119] haben, die die Achse in ihren zwei Einschnitten erfassen, während sie von oben vom "stol" angedrückt werden, außerdem sind sie auch durch einen Holzkeil angenagelt. Die vorderen Teile der "lesici" werden auf dem "ok" gekreuzt und durch einen Holzpflock *(lesicina klecka (klin)* oder *karlangac civisi*[120]*)* in eines der Löcher der Deichsel eingesteckt. Durch ein Vorrücken oder Zurückstellen dieses Holzpflocks wird der Hinterwagen je nach Bedarf, verlängert oder verkürzt. Der hintere Teil der Deichsel ragt über die Achse des Hinterwagens heraus und trägt den Namen "opaska"[121]. Er wird oft zum leichteren Besteigen des Wagens benutzt und an ihm wird auch der Wasserkrug aufgehängt. Zur Steigerung der Widerstandsfähigkeit der Deichsel *(rastok)*, wird sie manchmal verstärkt, indem ein zusätzlicher Holzklotz unter ihr angebunden und angenagelt wird, der bis zum mittleren Holzpflock *(slepec, pastuch*[122]*)* reicht und die mittleren Holzpflöcke vor den Zerbrechen – infolge harten Aufschlagens der Räder auf Steine – bewahrt.[123]

Die Räder (Abb. 23d). An den Spindeln der Holzachsen des Vorder- und Hinterwagens sind vorn kleinere und hinten größere Räder angebracht *(kolela, koleleta, tarkala, tarkaleta, tocila*[124] oder *t. tekerlek).*[125] Das Rad besteht aus folgenden Teilen: 1. *glavina,*[126] *vodilo* oder *kolo,*[127] *baslak*, von den Walachen-Zigeunern *kapacuna* genannt,[128] mit 12 Rillen *(dlabove, glabove, lastovici*[129]*)* und wird mit einem Eisenreifen festgezogen. Die "glavini" werden aus zähem Eichenholz gearbeitet; 2. Zwölf Holzspeichen mit einer Länge von 40–45 cm, *krak, spica, t. ajak, parmak*[130] genannt, die strahlenförmig aus der "glavina" herausgehen und deren dickerer Teil in den Rillen, während der dünnere in zwei Löchern der "naplati" eingesteckt sind. 3. Sechs "naplati"[131] *(t. espidi)*, bogenartige Hölzchen, die 70–80 cm lang und 5–6 cm dick sind, mit einem Loch an dem einen Ende, in dem ein behauener Holzkeil *(cop,*[132] *pisljak*[133]*)* eingesteckt wird. Es gibt aber auch "naplati" mit zwei Löchern und einzelnen Holzkeilen, die in beiden Löchern bei der Verbindung von zwei "naplati" eingesteckt werden. Die auf diese Weise angebundenen "naplati" bilden das Holzrad, das früher nicht mit einem Eisenreifen umgegeben wurde. Die Speichen und die "naplati" werden aus Buchenhölzchen gemacht. Damit die Spindel infolge des Drehens der Räder nicht leicht zerbrechen, werden sie mit Teer eingeschmiert, und eine Eisenunterlage *(blech)*[134] wird an dem einem Ende festgemacht. Um kein Durchreiben der Öffnung der "glavina" zu erlauben, wird in der Öffnung ein Eisenreifen *(zadnivka,*[135] *pojra, purija*[136]) montiert. Damit die Räder nicht von den Spindeln ausfallen, werden sie von außen mit großen Nägeln festgemacht, die in ein dünnes Loch eingesteckt werden.[137]

Wir unterscheiden drei Arten von Teerbehältern *(katranici):* aus Horn, hölzerne und keramische. Am verbreitesten sind die "katranici" aus Büffel- oder Ochsenhörnern, "manda bujnuzu" genannt.[138] Am oberen Ende des Horns wird ein Eisenring eingebohrt oder ein Drahtring befestigt, der zum Anhängen oder Befestigen des Horns an dem Tierschwanz, an den Wagenleitern oder an dem Holz- oder Eisenzugteil des Jochs dient. Die Hornöffnung wird durch ein Holz- oder Blechdeckelchen geschlossen und durch eine Öffnung in diesem Deckelchen wird eine Entenfeder im Teer eingetaucht.[139] Die hölzernen Teerbehälter sind kleine Fässerchen mit Holzdeckeln, die an der Öffnung mit einem Strick umwickelt sind, der einige Haken hat. Sie werden meistens in den Gebirgsgegenden und im Gebirgsvorland verwendet, besonders in der Umgebung von Gabrovo, Teteven und Elena. Als "katranici" werden auch Tontöpfe mit Deckel und Seilhaken benutzt.

Die Deichsel (procep, procap, t. aräz, ok, jok)[140] (Abb.23c) ist ein rechteckiges, behauenes Holzstück von 2,5–3 m Länge, 7–8 cm Breite und 7–8 cm Dicke. Ihr hinteres Ende ist verzweigt oder gespalten und mit Hilfe eines Holzkeils gabelartig geöffnet, indem es zwei "Ärmel" *(rakavi)*[141] bildet, die am Ende "cukanceta", "comaljusgi"[142] haben, um besser die Einschnitte erfassen zu können. Einige dieser Ärmel sind gerade Holzstücke, jedoch sind viele von ihnen gebogen, damit der Wagenlenker leichter aufsteigen und seine Füße stützen kann. Dort wo die Holzkeile eingesteckt sind, werden die Ärmel mit breiten Eisenringen festgehalten, damit sie widerstandsfähiger sind. An ihrem vorderen Ende hat die Deichsel fast immer ein gebogenes Holzstück, *zabka* ("Fröschlein") genannt, *(t. kepce,*[143] *skripusa*[144]). Der gebogene Teil der "zabka" reicht genau bis zum Ende der Deichsel, und das ist die am meisten verbreitete Variante in Bulgarien. Die "zabka" ist mit dem oberen Teil der Deichsel durch ein oder zwei kleine Holzkeile fest verbunden und von oben nach unten ist auch ein 45–50 cm langer und 2–2,5 cm dicker Holzkeil durchgesteckt *(podpor,*[145] *stojalo,*[146] *stojalce,*[147] *stojalka, stojacka, stoeska,*[148] *t. camurluk*[149]), der als Stütze dient, und dessen untere Hälfte breiter als die obere ist. Die Deichsel stützt sich in einer Höhe von 50 cm über dem Boden auf dem breiteren Teil, und der über die "zabka" herausragende Teil wird verkeilt. Der Holzkeil dient demnach sowohl zum Aufrechterhalten in horizontaler

374

Abb. 24. Eisenwagen mit Sitzbrett und seitlichen, vorn hörnerartig gebogenen Holzstücken. Dorf Konjarsko, Westrhodopen. Phot. V. Marinov, 1966.

Lage des vorderen Teils der Deichsel über dem oft feuchten Boden, um ein Verfaulen des Holzes zu verhindern, und zum leichteren Auflegen des vorderen Teils auf den Hälsen der Zugtiere, als auch um die "zabka" an der Deichsel festzuhalten.[150] Bei der zweiten Variante wird die "zabka" durch ein gekrümmtes Holzstück *(samokrivka, stojalo, kukudecka, kukumjavka, t. dajak*[151]*)* mit der Deichsel verbunden. Sie wird hauptsächlich im Gebiet von Sofia angetroffen. Die dritte Variante ist seltener, sie hat eine verhältnismäßig kürzere Deichsel und eine "zabka", die ziemlich weit vor dem Deichselende herausragt. Um die "zabka" befestigen zu können, wird unter der Deichsel ein zusätzliches Holzstück, das die Länge der Deichsel hat, durch Holzkeile angenagelt. Diese Variante hat ebenfalls eine Holzstütze. Die vierte Variante besitzt auch eine "zabka", jedoch aus Eisen, die die gleiche Form wie die "zabka" aus Holz hat. Nach Auflegen des oberen Jochbalkens auf die "zabka", wird ein Holz- oder Eisenkeil durch die in der "zabka", dem Joch und der Deichsel durchgebohrten Löcher durchgesteckt. Dieser Keil wird *teglic,*[152] *tagacka,*[153] *zavran,*[154] *utres,*[155] *sredna klecka*[156]*, t. ceki civisi, cekedzek*[157] genannt. Die Holzzugteile *(teglici)* ragen in einigen Ortschaften hoch über die "zabka" heraus und dienen zum Aufhängen der Halfterzügel. Dieselbe

375

Abb. 25. Ochsenwagen mit Wagenleitern. Dorf Tica bei Kotel, Mittelbalkan. Phot. V. Marinov, 1969.

Rolle spielt der Bogen in Form einer Schnecke oder eines Halbmonds der "teglici" aus Eisen, die auch als Verzierung dienen. Beim Holzwagen wird auch ein Wagenjoch verwendet, *kolarski homot*,[158] *omot, imot, hamot,*[159] *homut,*[160] *humot,*[161] *imot,*[162] *t. bojundruk*[163, 164] genannt.

Der beschriebene Holzwagentyp ist in ganz Bulgarien verbreitet, hat jedoch einige Varianten entsprechend den Funktionen, die er beim Transport von Waren und Personen erfüllen muß. Er besitzt deshalb einen unterschiedlichen Wagenboden *(potonica, t. djuseme).*[165] Der Wagenboden besteht demnach aus: 1. zwei oder drei nebeneinander gelegten, jedoch nicht zusammengezimmerten Brettern, die vorn durch Holzkeilchen festgehalten werden. Dieser Wagentyp dient zum Transport von Holzbalken oder -stämmen; 2. miteinander vernagelten Brettern[166] oder verflochtenen dünnen Ästen oder breiten Lindenrinden *(lesa).*[167] Dieser Wagentyp dient zum Transport von Frauen, Kindern, landwirtschaftlichen Geräten, Nahrung, Kleidern usw. zu den Ackerfeldern; 3. drei dicken Brettern, durch zwei Balken begrenzt, die vorne zwei gewölbte Hörner haben, an deren Innenseite eine hölzerne Scheidewand aus drei Brettern, die bis zur Höhe der Hörner reicht, angenagelt ist (Abb.24). Diese Scheidewand dient zum Schutz gegen das Herausfallen der schweren Lasten und gegen Verletzung der Zugtiere. Der Wagen dient zum Transport

376

Abb. 26. Wagen mit Wagenleitern aus Stäben zum Transport von Garben. Malko Tarnovo, Strandzagebirge, Südost-Bulgarien. Phot. V. Marinov, 1969.

von Steinblöcken aus den Steinbrüchen. Die Wagenteile des Radvor- und -hintergestells werden mit Eisenklammern zusammengehalten, die Räder sind niedriger für eine bequemere Beladung und mit Eisenschienen versehen, die hinteren Seitenhölzer *(klimii)* sind aus kürzeren Holzstücken gearbeitet, und es gibt keine vorderen "klimii". Es gibt auch Wagen mit einem Boden aus krummen Holzstücken *(ljoki, levki,*[168] *t. dajak),*[169] an deren unterem Ende ein Eisenring zum Anhängen an die Spindeln der Achse befestigt ist, während der obere Teil mit den "klimii" gekreuzt und durch einen durchgesteckten Holzstift verbunden wird. Dieser Holzstift bewahrt die Räder vor einem leichten Ausfallen aus den Spindeln und zur Entfernung der Baumäste aus den Radspeichen beim Befahren von Waldwegen.

Die Wagen unterscheiden sich auch durch ihre Seitenteile, "kanati", die entsprechend ihrer Funktion verschieden sind. So werden z.B. zum Transport von Kornsäcken, Mist usw. Kasten benutzt, deren Seitenteile aus dicken Brettern gemacht sind, oder sie sind wie schon erwähnt aus *lesi* (Abb.25). Die Getreidegarben werden von den Feldern mit verlängerten Wagen, mit speziellen Wagenleitern *(litri, ritli)*[170] versehen, transportiert. Die Wagenleitern setzen sich aus zwei parallelen, 3–3,5 m langen, runden Holzstücken zusammen, die an ihren beiden Enden, manche sogar in der Mitte, durch breite, behauene Holz-

377

Abb. 27. Eisenwagen mit Wagenleitern (»manùsi«) zum Transport von Spreu. Dorf Pavolce bei Vratza, Nordwest-Bulgarien. Phot. V. Marinov, 1968.

stücke *(sabica)*[171] verbunden sind, und diese Holzstücke *(litrista)*[172] haben durchgebohrte Löcher, durch die von oben nach unten oder von unten nach oben bis 150 cm lange Holzstäbe durchgesteckt werden, deren Enden zuge-spitzt sind *(sisove,*[173] *reznista, zegli).*[174] Die Holzstäbe, die von oben nach unten durchgesteckt werden, stützen sich auf ihrem breiteren, oberen Teil, während diejenigen, die von unten nach oben durchgesteckt werden, in der Mitte dicker als an beiden Enden sind und Einschnitte besitzen, so daß sie sich auf den unteren und oberen "litrista" anstemmen[175] (Abb.26). Dieser Wagentyp dient nur zum Transport von Garben von den Feldern bis zu den Dreschtennen der einzelnen Landwirte. Die Garben werden zuerst liegend aufgeladen, und nach Beladung des Wagens werden Garben auch von außen auf den Holzstäben aufgehängt und dann von oben wieder mit liegenden Garben zugedrückt.[176] Damit die schwer beladenen Wagen nicht umkippen, wird eine lange Holzstange auf die Garben gelegt und mit einem Seil unter dem Wagen fest angebunden. Die Beladung der Garben erfolgt auch auf Wagenplattformen, die quer auf den Wagenleitern, "litrista", aufgestellt sind[177] (Abb.27). Wenn der Wagen höhere Seitenteile hat, "manusi" ge-nannt,[178] die ein bis zwei Meter hohe Holzrahmen, aus Draht oder Stricken geflochten, darstellen, dann dient der Wagen nur zum Transport von Stroh

Abb. 28. Hölzerne, schlittenartige Bremse (»kùcka«) für schwer beladene Wagen. Dorf Pavolce bei Vratza, Nordwest-Bulgarien. Phot. V. Marinov, 1968.

und Spreu von den Tennen zu den Scheunen. Er ist vorn und hinten mit einem geflochtenen Deckel, ebenfalls aus Draht oder Stricken, verschlossen. Mit diesem verlängerten Wagen werden auch Holzkohlen in großen, geflochtenen Körben, aus geflochtenen Ruten, tranportiert, die von beiden Seiten durch zwei an den "klimii" befestigten Holzstücken gestützt werden.

Um die schwer beladenen Wagen beim Hinunterfahren auf steilen Straßen vor einem Umstürzen zu bewahren, verwenden die Bauern hölzerne oder eiserne Bremsen *(kucki)*.[179] Die Holzbremsen[180] (Abb.28) sehen kleinen, schmalen Schlitten ähnlich, auf die das eine Rad gepresst wird, daß es sich dadurch nicht mehr dreht, wodurch die Geschwindigkeit des Wagens gebremst wird. Die Eisenbremsen sehen ebenfalls kleinen, schmalen Schlitten ähnlich. Diese Bremsen werden am Wagen befestigt. Hinten am Wagen wird auch ein gebogenes Holzstück befestigt, das auf dem Boden schleift und die Geschwindigkeit des herunterfahrenden Wagens bremst.

Beim Zerbrechen der Wagenachse oder eines Rads haben die Bauern zum Emporheben der schwer beladenen Wagen eine hölzerne Hebewinde *(krik)* benutzt (Abb.29), die von den Wagenmeistern sehr gut ausgearbeitet wurde. Es handelt sich um ein Muster der bulgarischen Holzschnitzkunst, sie ist sehr kunstvoll gearbeitet und sieht kleinen Denkmälern oder hölzernen Kirchen

Abb. 29. Hölzerne, hundert-
jährige Winde zum Heben
von beschädigten, schwer be-
ladenen Holzwagen zwecks
Reparatur. Dorf Fakija bei
Burgas, Strandzagebirge,
Südost-Bulgarien. Phot. V.
Marinov, 1968.

ähnlich. Man kann solche hölzerne Hebewinden auch heute noch vorfinden, obwohl sie nicht mehr verwendet werden, und einige von ihnen über 100 Jahre alt sind. Wir haben eine solche Hebewinde im Jahre 1969 im Dorf Fakija im Strandza-Gebirge gefunden und hier abgebildet.

Viele Wagen besaßen früher ein halbsphärisches Gerüst, das aus halbrunden oder geraden Stangen bestand, die auf den hölzernen Wagenleitern oder dem Holzkasten befestigt und mit einer Decke, *cergilo* genannt,[181] bedeckt sind.

Pferdewagen. Die Landwirte, besonders die reicheren, türkischen und bulgarischen Bodenbesitzer haben vor der Befreiung Bulgariens und auch später Pferde zum Reiten und zum Anspannen gehalten. Jedoch werden die Pferde als Anspanntiere in größerem Ausmaße erst ziemlich spät und zwar Mitte und Ende des 19. Jh. und im 20. Jh. verwendet. Es beginnt die Herstellung von eisernen Pferdewagen, *konski karuci* oder *taligi* genannt.[182] Diese Wagen sind sowohl dauerhafter und widerstandsfähiger als auch schneller als die Holzwagen. Solche Wagen konnten jedoch nur gut spezialisierte Eisenwagen-Meister ausarbeiten (Abb.30), die in den Zentren der landwirtschaftlichen Produktionsgebiete ansässig waren, wie Varna, Dobric, Silistra, Ruse, Rasgrad, Provadija, Pleven, Vraza, Sofia, Plovdiv, Pazardzik, Asenovgrad u.a.m. Diese Wagen haben Kasten, die von Laien- und Volkskünstlern mit Ölfarben reich verziert sind. Besonders der hintere Deckel des Kastens war reich verziert und zwar mit geometrischen und Pflanzenornamenten mit Tierszenen (Abb. 31). Diese "bemalten und singenden Wagen" werden hauptsächlich an Feiertagen benutzt, indem mit ihnen die ganze Familie alte Kirchen und Klöster sowie "obrocista" besucht, die sich in schönen Gegenden bei Quellen, Flüssen oder in Wäldern befinden, wo sie den ganzen Tag verbringt. Bei diesen Besuchen wurden Weihtiere geschlachtet, Lämmchen am Spieß gebraten und Lieder gesungen. Diese Wagen werden auch bei Hochzeiten benutzt, besonders in N.O.Bulgarien (Ludogorie und Dobrudza), doch von dort haben sie sich allmählich in ganz Nordbulgarien sowie auch in Süd- und Westbulgarien und im Gebiet von Sofia verbreitet. Nach der Bauart des Kastens und den Verzierungen unterscheidet man einige Typen von singenden und verzierten Eisenwagen und zwar die Typen von Dobrudza, Dobric, Silistra, Varna, Provadia, Schumen, Popovo, Ruse und sonstige.[183] Die Wagenseiten sowie der vordere und hintere Deckel der Kasten werden durch dünne, flache Eisenbänder festgehalten, die außerdem auch als Dekoration verwendet werden und mit verschiedenen bunten Farben bemalt sind. Um den Wagen leichter besteigen zu können, werden an beiden Seiten des Kastens Stufen aus Eisenstäben angebracht. Der Vorder- und Hinterteil des Wagens und seine Ausarbeitung sowie die Bezeichnungen der einzelnen Wagenteile sind denen des Holzwagens gleich.[184]

Die eisernen Pferdewagen werden außer zum Transport von Waren und Personen auch als schnelle Verkehrsmittel zwischen den Dörfern und den Städten benutzt, besonders seitens der reicheren Landwirte. Eine Folge davon war die Verbesserung der Landstraßen. Die ärmeren Landwirte haben jedoch bis nach dem Zweiten Weltkrieg hauptsächlich den Ochsen- und Büffelwagen benutzt, indem dessen Räder von Eisenschienen umzingelt wurden. Auch heute noch werden Pferde-Plattformwagen, jedoch meistens schon mit Gummirädern, zum Transport von Waren verwendet und zwar besonders bei den Güterbahnhöfen der kleineren und manchmal auch der größeren Städte. Doch sind die Pferdekutschen, die in großer Anzahl in Vraza, Pleven, Schumen, Plovdiv, Burgas und Ruse hergestellt wurden, schon fast vollständig aus dem

Abb. 30. Verzierter und »singender« Pferdewagen mit Kastenaufbau. Tolbuchin in der Dobrudza, Nordost-Bulgarien. Phot. V. Marinov, 1968.

Verkehr verschwunden. Die verzierten Wagen, mit einem Pferd oder Esel angespannt, sind jedoch aus den Weingebieten Bulgariens noch nicht vollkommen verschwunden und werden von einzelnen Kooperativbauern für ihren Eigenbedarf benutzt. Heute werden verzierte Eselwägelchen und Pferdekutschen den Kurgästen in den Kurorten bei Varna und Burgas, in Nessebar und Pomorie zur Verfügung gestellt.

Schlitten (sejna, sanja, t. kazak). Sowohl in den Gebirgsgegenden als auch in den Ebenen werden im Winter bei Schneefall gleichzeitig mit den Wagen auch Schlitten als Verkehrsmittel verwendet. Es handelt sich um Holzschlitten, die von einem oder zwei Tieren gezogen werden[185] (Abb.32). Die von einem Pferd gezogenen Schlitten sind kleiner und leichter als die Schlitten, die von zwei Ochsen, Büffeln oder Pferden gezogen werden. Diese Schlitten werden sowohl von den Landwirten selbst als auch von gelernten Eisenwagen-Handwerkern gearbeitet. Der Schlitten besteht aus zwei parallelen, breiten und dicken Holzkufen aus Buchen-, Birnen- oder anderem Holz, *sanki, sanare*,[186] *taban*[187] genannt, die folgende Ausmaße haben: Länge 250 cm, Breite 10 cm und Dicke 8 cm, und deren vordere Enden gebogen und wie Hörner zugespitzt sind.[188] Jedes Holzstück (Kufe) hat zwei Holzfüsse,[189] auf denen quer

382

Abb. 31. Farbig verzierter Hinterteil des Kastens eines Pferdewagens mit Pflanzenornamenten. Tolbuchin in der Dobrudza, Nordost-Bulgarien. Phot. V. Marinov, 1968.

zwei Holzstühle[190] aufgestellt sind, die mit zwei Holzpflöcken befestigt sind.[191] Auf die Stühle wird ein Holzboden[192, 193] gelegt, jedoch werden auf einigen Schlitten auch ganze Holzkasten mit hölzernen oder geflochtenen "kanati"[194] montiert. Bei einigen Schlitten sind die Füsse nicht senkrecht, sondern nach außen gebogen.[195] Zum Anspannen der Zugtiere werden zwei Holzstücke (poteglica,[196] straki)[197] verwendet, die durch seitliche Holzstifte in den Löchern an den beiden Innenseiten der Holzkufen befestigt werden und vorne verbunden sind. Durch die durchgebohrten Löcher wird ein Holzkeil (teglic,[198] t. camurluk)[199] durchgezwängt, an dem ein hölzernes Wagenjoch angehängt wird. Zum Anspannen eines Pferdes wird eine Deichsel mit "zabka" und leicht gebogenen Seitenhölzern, durch Holzkeile an die Innenseiten der Holzkufen angenagelt, während sie vorn direkt oder durch ein krummes Holzstück an beiden Seiten des Pferdejochs befestigt werden. Bei einem Zweipferdeanspann wird eine Holzdeichsel benutzt, die am hinteren Ende gespalten und durch zwei Holzkeile[200] an der Innenseite der Holzkufen nahe am hinteren Stuhl befestigt ist.

Die Schafhirten benutzen in Bulgarien bewegliche, auf Kufen montierte Hütten (Abb.33), von denen die kleineren zum Schlafen und zur Aufbewah-

Abb. 32. Hölzerner Schlitten mit Faß und Schulterjoch zum Aufhängen von Kupfer-Wasserkesseln. Dorf Sevar bei Kubrat, Nordost-Bulgarien. Phot. V. Marinov, 1951.

rung des Hausrats und die größeren als Molkereien *(mandri)* zur Milchverarbeitung und Herstellung von Milcherzeugnissen verwendet werden. Beide Hütten haben aus geflochtenen Gerten oder zusammengenagelten Brettern Wände,[201] die mit Hilfe von Holzkufen und Deichseln von Horn-Zugtieren gezogen werden.

Gleichzeitig mit den Pferdewagen und -kutschen erscheinen auch die Pferde-Eisenschlitten zur Beförderung von Personen in den Städten sowie auch zwischen den Städten und Dörfern, sie sind jedoch heute fast vollständig verschwunden.

Zum Abtransport von Holzstämmen in den Wäldern und Gebirgsgegenden werden sogenannte Holzzüge verwendet.[202] (Abb.34). Der Holzzug besteht aus zwei dicken Kufen *(sanja* oder *plasa)*, die an ihrem hinteren Ende leicht gebogen und dicker sind, während am vorderen Ende die Kufen dünner und gekreuzt sind. Sie haben ebenfalls durchgebohrte Löcher zur Verbindung mit Hilfe von durchgezwängten Holzkeilen (Abb.35). Das untere Zugholz und das zusätzliche Holzstück, das auf die Kreuzung und das zweite obere Zugholz gelegt wird, haben ebenfalls durchgebohrte Löcher. Diese drei durchgebohrten Löcher dienen zum Durchzwängen einer langen Holzstütze *(stojalo)*, die sich auf den Boden stützt. Dieses Holzstück wird durch einen zweiten Holzkeil mit dem unteren Zugholz verbunden und liegt ziemlich hoch über dem

384

Abb. 33. Schlitten mit Schäfer-
hütte. Dorf Jarlovo bei Samo-
kov, Kreis Bezirk Sofia. Phot.
N. Nikolov, 1950.

oberen Zugholz, das zum Aufhängen und Festhalten der Eisenkette dient, die
zum Festmachen der Baumstämme an dem Holzzug verwendet wird. Die vorderen Teile des oberen Holzstücks und der unteren Kufe *(plas)*, die hervor-
ragen, haben zwei durchgebohrte Löcher zum Durchzwängen eines Eisenkeils
(teglic), der durch das obere Holzstück des Jochs und der unteren Kufe durchgezwängt wird und zum Aufrechterhalten des gesamten Jochs und zum Anspannen der Zugtiere durch zwei unbewegliche, innere Schrauben *(burmalii)*
und zwei äußere, bewegliche *zegli* dient. Auf dem hinteren Teil der zwei Kufen
wird ein Stuhl quer aufgestellt, der direkt oder auf zwei dicken Holzunter-
lagen mit Hilfe von zwei dicken Holzstiften oder Keilen befestigt wird. Der
Stuhl dient als Unterlage für dicke Holzstämme, die am Holzzug durch Eisenketten angebunden werden.

Wassertransportmittel. Zum Überqueren von kleineren und größeren Flüssen oder zum Fischfang werden einzelne oder doppelte, ausgehöhlte Baumstämme als Boote benutzt. Während der osmanischen Herrschaft und auch
einige Jahre nach der Befreiung Bulgariens wurden im mittleren und unteren

Abb. 34. Zwei hölzerne »Züge« (»vlak«) zum Abschleppen von Holzbalken aus den Rodhopen. Dorf Belovo bei Pazardzik, Südbulgarien. Phot. V. Marinov, 1956.

Lauf des Flusses Mariza zum Transport von Holzmaterialien und anderen Waren auch Flöße benutzt. Jedoch verschwinden die Flöße nach dem Bau der Eisenbahnlinie Sofia-Istanbul und der Errichtung von besseren Straßen. Aber auch heute werden noch an einigen Stellen entlang der Flüsse Kamtschija und Arda, wo keine Brücken errichtet sind, zur Beförderung von Personen und Wagen, mit Garben, Holz usw., Boote mit flachem Boden, *kaik* genannt, zum Überqueren der Flüsse verwendet (Abb.36). Zur Bedienung dieser Transportart werden Vereinigungen von Bootsführern aus einigen Dörfern gebildet, die sich bei ihrer Arbeit abwechseln. Die Überquerung der Flüsse wird durch erfahrene Bootsführer ausgeführt, welche die Boote mit Hilfe von langen, zugespitzten Stangen, die in den Flußboden eingesteckt werden, zum anderen Ufer lenken. Die Überquerung der Flüsse erfolgt in im voraus festgelegten Stunden. Auf den großen Flüssen, wie die Donau, auf den Seen und Teichen werden Fischerboote zum Fischfang benutzt, während auf dem Schwarzen Meer außer Fischerbooten auch Schiffe für den Fischfang verwendet werden.

Abb. 35. Wagen-Rahmenjoch mit eisernen »zeglì« und »teglìc« und hölzernem »stojàlo«, angehängt durch ein spezielles »Fröschlein« (»zàbka«). Dorf Belovo bei Pazardzik, Süd- bulgarien. Phot. V. Marinov, 1951.

Anmerkungen

1. Г. С. Раковски, Показалец, Одеса, 1859 / *G. S. Rakovski*, Anweisung, Odessa, 1859 /; К. Иречек, Пътувания по България ч. II, Пловдив, 1889 / *K. Jirecéek*, Reise durch Bulgarien, B. II, Plovdiv, 1889/; Д. Маринов, Градиво за веществената култура на България, СбНУ, кн. XVIII – Материали, 1901 / *D. Marinov*, Grundmaterialien über die materielle Kultur in Westbulgarien, Saml. NU, B. XVIII–Materiali. / Йордан Захариев: Кюстендилско краище, БАН, 1918, Каменица, БАН, 1935; / *J. Zachariev*, Küstendilsko kraischte, BAN, 1918; Kameniza. BAN, 1935 /; Хр. Вакарелски, Бит на тракийските и малоазийски българи. ч. I в Тракийски сборник, кн. V, 1935 /.

2. В. Маринов, Принос към изучаването на бита и културата на турците и др. гагаузите в Североизточна България, БАН, 1956 / *V. Marinov*, Beitrag zum Studium der Lebens- weise und der Kultur der Türken und der Gagausen in Nordostbulgarien, BAN, 1954 /; В. Маринов, Произход, бит и култура на каракачаните в България, БАН, 1964 и други / *V. Marinov*, Beitrag zum Studium der Herkunft, der Lebensweise und der Kul- tur der Karakatschanen in Bulgarien, BAN, 1964 /.

3. Извори за българската история, издания на Българската академия на науките: I. Тръцки извори, БАН, 1954; II. Латински извори, БАН, 1958; III. Гръцки извори, БАН, 1958; IV. Турски извори, БАН, 1959; V. Турски извори, БАН, 1960; VI. Гръцки извори, БАН, 1960; VII. Латински извори, 1960; VIII. Гръцки извори, 1961; IX. Гръцки извори,

Abb. 36. Großes Holzboot zum Transport von Personen und Wagen mit Garben vom linken Ufer des Flußes Arda zum rechten Ufer und umgekehrt. Dorf Lisicite bei Kardzali, Südost-Bulgarien, Phot. V. Marinov, 1951.

БАН, 1964; X. Турски извори / XV–XVI в. /, БАН, 1964; XI. Гръцки извори, БАН, 1965; XII. Латински извори, БАН, 1965; XIII. Турски извори / XV–XVI в. /, 1966; XIV. Гръцки извори, БАН, 1968 / Die Quelle über Geschichte des Bulgarischen Volks, Bulgarische Akademie der Wissenschaft: I. Griechische Quelle, 1954; II. Lateinische Quelle, 1958; III. Griechische Quelle, 1958; IV. Türkische Quelle, 1959; V. Türkische Quelle, 1960; VI. Griechische Quelle, 1960; VII. Lateinische Quelle, 1960; VIII. Griechische Quelle, 1961; IX. Griechische Quelle, 1964; X. Türkische Quelle, XV–XVI Jahrhundert, 1964; XI. Griechische Quelle, 1965; XII. Lateinische Quelle, 1965; XIII. Türkische Quelle /, XV–XVI Jahrh. /, 1966; XIV. Griechische Quelle, 1968 /.

4. Г. И. Кацаров, Бит на старите траки, Сб. НУ, кн. I, 1913 / и други /.
5. И. В. Венедиков, Тракийската колесница, БАН, 1960.
6. *G. Georgiev*, Kulturgruppen der Jungstein- und der Kupferzeit in der Ebene von Thrakien /Südbulgarien/. L'Europe à la fin de l'âge de la pierre. Prague-Liblice-Brno, 1959, T. I–XXXI. В. Миков, Техника на керамичното производство през праисторическата епоха в България. ИАИ, XXIX, 1966, стр. 195, обр. 19, стр. 196, обр. 20 и сл.
7. Б. Филов, Куполните гробници при Мезек, ИБАИ, т. XI, 1937, св. I, 1938, с. 62, П. Детев, Характерни черти на глинените съдове от бронзовата обр. 63. епоха. ГМ-Пл. Окръг, II, 1954, стр. 101–109-съд с чучурче, обр. 3, с. 102, чаши с дръжки-обр. 8Б, обр. 10, купи с една и две дръжки-обр. 9, кани-стр. 106, обр. 14.
8. Ив. Венедиков, Тракийската колесница, БАН, 1960 /.
9. Ив. Венедиков, Новооткрито тракийско могилно погребение във Враца, Археология, кн. 1, 1966, с. 7–15 / -могилно погребение от IV в.пр.н.е.-откритата колесница с четири

колела е една от най-старите открита в България /; от същия: Нов голям извор за проучване на тракийското изкуство, Изкуство, год. VI, бр. 2, 1966, стр. 37–42-първата половина на IV в. пр. н. е.

10. В. Миков, Античната гробница в Казанлък, Арх. И-т и музей, кн. I, 1954, с. 34; / *Schefer und Andre*, Die Kunst des alten Orients, Berlin, 1942, S. 545–Zeichn. Ein Pferd mit Last aus dem Palast Assurbanipals / 668–626 vor Chr. / Д. П. Димитров, За датата на стенописите от Тракийската гробница при Казанлък, Археология, кн. 2, год. VIII, 1966, с. 2, обр. 1 /.

11. Г. И. Кацаров, пос. съч., с. 18 /; траките събрали кола и образували вал предсебе си срещу войските на Ал. Македонски, когато преминавал Балкана 5с.

12. Вж. »Изкуство«, год. VI, бр. 1, 1966-на корицата.

13. Ст. Станчев и Стефан Иванов, Некрополът до Нови Пазар, АИМ / БАН /, 1958, с. 27 /; *St. Stančev* und *St. Ivanov*, Nekropol bei Novi Pasar, AIM/BAN/, 1958, S. 27 /.

14. Г. Баласчев, Бележки върху веществената култура на старобългарското ханство и пр., София, 1902, с. 52 / *G. Balasčev*, Bemerkungen über materielle Kultur im bulgarischen Fürstentum u. s.w., Sofia, 1902, S. 52 /. PRISK mitteolen /448/ über slawische: »kola«, »kolesnitza« und »w o z«.

15. Ив. Дуйчев, Миниатюрите на манасиевата летопис от XIV в., София, 1962, Т. 13, 17, 20, 41, 42, 43, 47. 50 и пр. / *Ivan Dujčev*, Miniaturen über Manasievata Chronika XIV Jahrhundert, Sofia, 1962, Tafel: 13, 17, 20, 41, 42, 43, 47, 50 u.s.w. /.

16. Ив. Сакъзов, Скотовъдството в Средновековна България / Страници от стопанско-правната история /, Юрид. Пр., год. XXIX, 7–8, 1928, с. 314, с. 319 / *I. Sakazov*, Die Viehzucht im mittelalterlichen Bulgarien, Üridiceski Pregled, Jahr XXIX, 7–8, 1928, S. 314, S. 319 /; auch Wirtschaftliche Verbindungen zwischen Dubrovnik und Bulgarien während des XVI und XVII Jahrh., Handelsministerium .., Sofia, 1930.

17. Там, с. 319 / es Dort, S. 319 /.

18. Д. Ангелов, По въпроса за стопанския облик на българските земи през XI–XIV в. ИПр., кн. 4–5, 1951, с. 438 / *D. Angelov*, Über die Frage des Gesichtsausdruckes Bulgariens während des XI–XIV Jahrh., IPr., B. 4–5, 1951, S. 438 /.

19. Там, с. 438 / Dort, S. 438 /.

20. Б. Цветкова, Към въпроса за пазарните и пристанищните мита и такси в някои български градове през XIX в. Изв. ИИ, т. 13, 1963, с. 214. / *B. Zvetkova*, Zu Fragen für Markt- und Hafenzoll und Preise in einigen bulgarischen Städtchen während des XIX Jahrh., Izwestia Ist. Inst. B. 13, 1963, S. 214.

21. Там, с. 231 /. Dort, S. 231 /.

22. Ек. Манова, Върху някои иконографски черти в българските стенописи от XV в., Археология, год. IV, кн. 3, бр. 6, 1962, с. 9 / *Ek. Manova*, Über einige Heiligebildenischen Strichen bei der bulgarischen Wandmalereien von XV Jahrh., Archeologie, Jahr. IV, B. 3, num. 6, 1962, S. 2 /.

23. А. Павлов, Икономическо развитие и състояние на гр. Казанлък, Сб. Казанлък, т. I, София, 1912, с. 293 / Wirtschaftliche Entwicklung und Zustand Kazanlǎk, Saml. Kazanlǎk, B. I, Sofia, 1912, S. 293 /.

24. Ив. Найденов, Заточението ми с първия български екзарх блаженопочившия Антим I, Сб. Казанлък в миналото, София, 1912, т. I, с. 117, 119, 121, 125, 128 / *Iv. Najdenov*, Meine Verbannung mit erstem bulgarischen Exarch Antim I, Saml. Kazanlǎk in Vergangenheit, Sofia, 1912, S. 117, 119, 121, 125, 128 /.

25. Там, с. 117 /. Dort, S. 117 /.

26. В. Маринов, Принос ... пос. съч., стр. 304.

27. Ст. Л. Костов, Цървулите в Балканския полуостров, Сб. в чест на Проф. А. Иширков, 1930, с. 221–22.

28. *Fl. B. Floreșçu*, Opincib la Romîni. Studii de arta populara și etnographia, ARPR, II, 1957, S. 138.

29. *Ch. Vakarelski*, Etnografia .., S. 127, Zeichn. 68–1.

30. *V. Marinov*, Archiv materiali.

31. *Ch. Vakarelski*, Etnografia ..., S. 127, Zeichn. 68–2.

32. *Dort, S.* 127, Zeichn. 69 ос. съч., с. 253, 279, 280 / обр. 262, 297 а, б, в, 298, 299 а, б, 300 /

33. В. Маринов, Принос ... с. 253, 279, 280.

34. Хр. Вакарелски, Етнография ... с. 128.

35. В. Маринов ... с. 280, обр. 299.

36. Там, с. 253, обр. 262.

37. с. 280, обр. 299.

38. с. 280, обр. 300.

39. Хр. Вакарелски, Етнография, с. 127, рис. 68-4 а.

40. В. Маринов, лос. съч., с. 302.

41. Хр. Вакарелски ... с. 251.

42. В. Маринов, Украсени костени плочки върху овчарски чанти. Музеи и ы Паметници на култрата, год. IX, кн. 1, 1969, с. 15–19; В. Маринов, Съвременен бит и култура на овцевъди от Казанлъшки Старопланински район, ИЕИМ / БАН /, кн. IX, 1966, с. 15; *V. Marinov*, Die Schafzucht der nomadisierenden Karakatschanen in Bulgarien, in: Viehzucht und Hirtenleben in Ostmitteleuropa, hrsg. L. Földes, Budapest, 1961, S. 162, Abb. 17 a, b; *V. Marinov*, Die Almenwirtschaftliche Schafhaltung in Z. Balkangebirge, in: Viehwirtschaft und Hirtenkultur, hrsg. L. Földes, Budapest, 1969, S. 369.

43. Хр. Вакарелски, пос. съч., с. 128.

44. Там, с. 129, рис. 71.

45. с. 130.

46. Там.

47. В. Маринов, Принос ... с. 119, обр. 77.

48. Б. Дробњаковѣ, Уедно давнашње оруѣ за пренос хране. Гл. Етн. И-та, IV–VI, 1955–57, Београд, 1957, с. 1–28, фиг. 10-тарга ат с. Златар, Преславско; срв. В. Маринов, Миналото на с. Девня, Провадийско с оглед на »арнаутите« в Североизточна България. Езико-етн. изследване в памет на Акад. Ст. Романски, БАН, 1960, с. 614, обр. 4.

49. В. Маринов, Принос ... с. 119, обр. 77.

50. Там, с. 118, обр. 76.

51. Там, с. 223, обр. 205.

52. Д. П. Димитров, пос. съч., с ...

53. Marinov, V., Beitrag zur Untersuchung der Herkunft, Lebensweise und Kultur der Karakatschanen in Bulgarien. – Bulgarische Akademie der Wissenschaften, Institut für Ethnographie und Museum, Sofia, 1964, S. 54–56; Маринов В. Население и бит на Средните Родопи. Рокопска експедиция (1953) Ългареска Академия на науките, София, 1955, стр, 45.

54. Ив. Сакъзов, Скотовъдството в средновековна България / Страници от стопанско-правната история. Юрид. Преглед, год. XXIX, 7–8, 1928, с. 314.

55. В. Маринов, Арх. мат. / *V. Marinov*, Archiv. Mat. /.

56. Ан. Примовски, Камиларството в Беломорска Тракия, ЪАН, 1958, с. 43 / *An. Primovski*, L'élevage des Dromadaires et le métier des Chameliers dans la Thrace méridionale, BAN, 1958, S. 43 /.

57. Там, с. 44 / Dort, S. 44 /.

58. Там / Dort /.

59. Там / Dort /.

60. Там, с. 45 / Dort, S. 45 /.

61. Там, с. 46, фиг. 21, с. 49, фиг. 24, с. 48, фиг. 23 / Dort, S. 46, fig. 21, S. 49, fig. 24, S. 48, fig. 23 /.
62. Там, с. 33, фиг. 12, с. 34, фиг. 13, с. 36, фиг. 15, с. 37, фиг. 16 / Dort, S. 33, fig. 12, S. 34, fig. 13, S. 36, fig. 15, S. 37, fig. 16 /.
63. Там, с. 33 / Dort, S. 33 /.
64. Там, с. 34 / Dort, S. 34 /.
65. Там, с. 35 / Dort, S. 35 /.
66. Там / Dort /.
67. Там, с. 40 / Dort, S. 40 /.
68. Там / Dort /.
69. Б. Цветкова, Един френски пътепис от XVI в. за българските земи, ИБид-во, кн. XXVI, БАН, 1968, с. 265 / B. Zvetkova, Eine französische Reisebeschreibung vom XVI Jahrh. über das bulgarische Land, Nachr. Bulg. Gesch. Gesellschaft, XXVI, BAN, 1968, S. 265 /.
70. Б. Цветкова, Из бележките на генерал Йохмус пътуването му по източните български земи през 1847г., ИБИД-во, кн. XXVII, 1968, с. 284 / B. Zvetkova, Aus Bemerkungen General Jochmus über seine Reisen durch Ostbulgarische Länder während des Jahres 1847, Nachr. Bulg. Gesch. Gesellschaft, XXVII, 1968, S. 284/.
71. Там, с. 285 / Dort, S. 285 /.
72. Там, с. 294 / Dort, S. 294 /.
73. Там, с. 278 / Dort, S. 278 /.
74. К. Иречек, пос. съч., ч. II, с. 177 / K. Jireček ... B. II, S. 177 /.
75. К. Иречек, пос. съч., ч. II, с. 186.
76. Там, с. 187.
77. Там. ч. I, с. 261.
78. Хр. Вакарелск, Етнография . . . с. 133.
79. Ф. Каниц, пос. съч., с. 78.
80. Д. Маринов, пос. съч., с. 120, рис. 114.
81. Хр. Вакарелски, пос. съч., с.–Бит . . ., с. 253, обр. 384.
82. В. Маринов, Принос . . . пос. съч., с. 303, обр. 337–9,10.
83. Г. С. Раковски, Показалец, 1859 . . ., с . . . .
84. К. Иречек, пос. съч., с. 187, фиг. 8, фиг. 9.
85. Д. Маринов, пос. съч., с. 118–26, с. 149–185.
86. Ст. Л. Костов и Е. Петева . . . пос. съч., с. 89, обр. 75.
87. Хр. Вакарелски, Бит . . ., с. 254, обр. 385.
88. В. Маринов, Принос . . . с. 302–315, обр. 330а, б, в, с, обр. 331, 332, с. 305–обр. 333, 334, с. 306–обр. 335, 336, с. 307–обр. 337, с. 308–обр. 338, с. 309–обр. 339, 340, с. 310–обр. 341, 342, с. 311–обр. 343а, б, 344а, б, с. 312–обр. 345, с. 313–обр. 346, с. 315; срв.
В. Маринов – Архивни материали за всички окръзи в България при ЕИМ на БАН.
89. В. Маринов, Принос . . . с. 304, обр. 330а, б, с, с. 305–обр. 331, 332.
90. Хр. Вакарелски, Бит . . . с. 256.
91. Д. Маринов, Градиво . . . с. 122, рис. 116, 117.
92. Ст. Л. Костов . . . с. 90, обр. 75.
93. В. Маринов, Принос . . . с. 304–обр. 330а, б-1; кол-2.
94. Д. Маринов . . . с. 122, обр. 117.
95. Там.
96. В. Маринов, Принос . . . с. 304.
97. Д. Маринов . . . с. 122.
98. Ст. Л. Костов . . . с. 90, обр. 75.
99. В. Маринов, Принос . . . с. 304-още: слепец, слъбец сэеднивка.

100. Хр. Вакарелски, Бит . . . , с. 255.
101. Там.
102. Д. Маринов, Градиво . . . с. 122, рис. 116-още: пречелник, челник.
103. Ст. Л. Костов . . . с. 91, обр. 75.
104. Д. Маринов . . . с. 122, обр. 117.
105. В. Маринов . . . с. 305.
106. Ст. Л. Костов . . . с. 91, обр. 75.
107. В. Маринов . . . с. 304-обр. 330а, б–1, с. 305-обр. 331–4.
108. В. Маринов . . . с. 306-обр. 333, 334, с. 307-обр. 335, 336.
109. Д. Маринов . . . с. 123, рис. 117.
110. Там.
111. Там, с. 124.
112. Там.
113. Там, с. 123.
114. В. Маринов . . . с. 306, обр. 333–7, обр. 334–7,8.
115. Там, с. 304, обр. 330а–6, с. 305, обр. 332.
116. Там, с. 305, обр. 332.
117. Д. Маринов . . . с. 123, рис. 117.
118. В. Маринов . . . с. 307, обр. 333–5, обр. 334–6.
119. Д. Маринов . . . с. 123.
120. В. Маринов . . . с. 306, обр. 333–6, обр. 334–6, още: пъп / пап /, клещи, слепец.
121. Там, с. 306, обр. 333–7, обр. 334–8.
122. Ст. Л. Костов . . . с. 93, обр. 77.
123. Там, с. 91.
124. Д. Маринов . . . с. 118, 120.
125. В. Маринов . . . с. 308, обр. 337.
126. Д. Маринов . . . с. 120.
127. Там, с. 121, рис. 115.
128. В. Маринов, Наблюдение върху бита на цигани в България. ИЕИМ / БАН / кн. V, 1962, с. 270.
129. Д. Маринов . . . с. 120.
130. В. Маринов, Принос . . . с. 308, обр. 337–2,8
131. Там, с. 308, обр. 336–9, с. 309.
132. Там, с. 308, обр. 337–4,6.
133. Ст. Л. Костов . . . с. 89.
134. В. Маринов . . . с. 308, обр. 337–9, с. 309.
135. Ст. Л. Костов . . . с. 89.
136. В. Маринов . . . с. 308, обр. 337–10, с. 309.
137. Там, с. 309.
138. Там, с. 311; срв. Д. Маринов . . . с. 126, рис. 124 А.
139. Ст. Л. Костов . . . 93.
140. В. Маринов, Принос . . . с. 309, обр. 339; у Д. Маринов . . . с. 119, рис. 113-жабка-скрипуша, с. 120, рис. 114; у Ст. Л. Костов . . . с. 91, обр. 74-бабица.
141. В. Маринов . . . с. 310, обр. 339–6; у Д. Маринов . . . с. 119.
142. В. Маринов . . . с. 309; у Д. Маринов . . с. 119.
143. В. Маринов . . . с. 309, 310, 339-обр. 2.
144. Д. Маринов . . . с. 119, рис. 113, с. 120, рис. 114.
145. Г. С. Раковски, Показалец . . . с. 47; срв. у В. Маринов, Етнографска характеристика на ярема в България. Сб. в чест на акд. М. Арнаудов, БАН, 1970, с. 461, също: *V. Marinov*, Zur Ethnographie des Jochs in Bulgarien. Bulletin d'ethnographie Tchéchoslova-

que, III–IV, 1969, Brno /Narodopisná spoleňost Československá PŘI ČSAV /, S. 168.

146. Д. Маринов ... с. 120, рис. 114-г: стояло, стоялце, стоячка, стоешка, с. 119, рис. 114.

147. Ст. Л. Костов ... с. 91, обр. 74-з.

148. Д. Маринов ... с. 120.

149. В. Маринов, Принос .. с. 310, обр. 333-3.

150. В. Маринов, Етнографска характеристика на ярема ... с. 461, обр. 6.

151. Там, с. 461, обр. 7.

152. В. Маринов, Принос ... с. 310; срв. у Д. Маринов ... с. 119, рис. 113.

153. *V. Marinov.* Zur Ethnographie des Jochs ... S. 173.

154. Dort, S. 168.

155. Dort.

156. *V. Marinov*, Zur Ethnographie des Jochs ... S. 168.

157. В. Маринов, Принос ...с. 310, обр. 339-5.

158. *V. Marinov*, Zur Ethnographie des Jochs ... S. 164; В. Маринов, Етнографска характеристика на ярема ... с. 460, Карта I, с. 458 и Карта II, с. 459.

159. *V. Marinov*, Zur Ethnographie. ... S.167, Kart Num. 3 – Verbreitung der volkstümlichen Jochtermini in Bulgarien.

160. Dort.

161. Dort.

162. Dort, S. 167.

163. Dort, S. 167–168.

164. В. Маринов, Принос ... с. 312, обр. 344 а, б.

165. Хр. Вакарелски, Бит ... с. 258.

166. В. Маринов, Принос ... с. 311.

167. Там, с. 310–311, обр. 340, 341.

168. Д. Маринов, Градиво ... с. 124, рис. 119.

169. В. Маринов, Принос ... с. 305, обр. 331-5, обр. 332, с. 306, обр. 334-3, с. 307, обр. 335-4 и обр. 336, с. 309, обр. 338.

170. Там, с. 311, обр. 342.

171. Д. Маринов ... с. 124, рис. 120.

172. Там, още: »пържана«.

173. В. Маринов ... с. 311.

174. Д. Маринов ... с. 124, рис. 120.

175. Хр. Вакарелски, Бит ... с. 259, обр. 388.

176. В. Маринов ... с. 311, обр. 342.

177. Хр. Вакарелски, Бит ... с. 259, обр. 388.

178. В. Маринов, Принос ... с. 311, обр. 343.

179. Хр. Вакарелски, Бит ... с. 259, обр. 390.

180. Там, с. 261, обр. 393.

181. Д. Маринов, Градиво ... с. 128, рис. 128.

182. В. Маринов ... с. 314–315, обр. 346.

183. В. Маринов, Писани и пеещи конски каруци в Североизточна България, Изкуство, кн. 7, 1967, с. 6 -чампари.

184. В. Маринов, Дисертация-Принос към изучаването бита и културата на селата Златар и Драгоево, Преславско, София, 1961.

185. В. Маринов, Принос ... с. 315, обр. 347.

186. Д. Маринов ... с. 127, рис. 126.

187. В. Маринов ... с. 315, с. 316, обр. 347, 348.

188. Хр. Вакарелски ... Етнография, с. 132, рис. 73-2.

189. Там, с. 132.

190. В. Маринов . . . с. 315, обр. 347-4, обр. 348-2, с. 316.
191. Там, с. 316, обр. 347-5, обр. 348-3.
192. Ст. Л. Костов . . . с. 93, обр. 93.
193. В. Маринов, Принос . . . с. 316, обр. 347-6.
194. Там, с. 317, обр. 350а, б.
195. Там, с. 316.
196. Хр. Вакарелски, Етнография . . . с. 132, рис. 73-2.
197. Д. Маринов . . . с. 126, обр. 126.
198. Там, с. 126.
199. В. Маринов, Принос . . . с. 316, обр. 349-2.
200. Там, с. 316, обр. 348-4.
201. П. Петров, Овчарските движими колибки в България, Сб. вчест на Йордан Захариев, БАН, 1964, с. 169–179.
202. Хр. Вакарелски, Етнография . . . с. 132, рис. 73-1.

Transport in Hungary by Canvas Sheets on the Human Back

By ATTILA PALÁDI-KOVÁCS

Transport by human beings can be carried out in greatly varied ways and by means of a variety of equipment. In the Hungarian language area the most important of these ways are transport on the head, on the back and on the shoulders. At the beginning of the 20th century they showed a very significant distribution among the Hungarians. In Transdanubia and the central parts of Transsylvania transport on the head, in Northern parts of Hungary transport on the back by means of canvas sheets and in Transsylvania and in the Eastern parts transport on the shoulder by means of double satchels (Hung. *átalvető*) were the dominant way of transport. As I pointed out in an earlier study (Paládi-Kovács 1971), these ways rarely occur together in the same area. Only in the central part of Transsylvania is there mixed transport on the head and transport on the shoulder by means of double satchels.

In the present study I wish to survey one of the three basic ways of transport, i.e. transport on the back by means of canvas sheets, *batyuzás* in Hungarian. First I wish to show its spread and to draw some conclusions from it. The illustrative maps showing the spread of transport by means of canvas sheets in the Hungarian language area were constructed on the basis of the documentary point-maps of the Hungarian Ethnographic Atlas (Magyar Néprajzi Atlasz, abbr. MNA) now being published. The present author was responsible for the transport themes in it. It is necessary to emphasize that these sketch-maps reflect conditions existing at the end of the 19th and at the beginning of the 20th century.

The 81st theme of MNA investigates the ways of and equipment for transporting small quantities of fodder, hay, and grass. Equipment for carrying fodder includes the canvas sheet, as well as differently shaped baskets, carried on the back or in the hand, and the haybend (Germ. *Heubogen*) which consists of two sticks curved into semicircles and a coarse net stretched over them. I will not enter into the discussion of baskets and haybends this time but it will be worth looking into the matter of transport by means of canvas sheets.

There are two basic ways of transporting hay in sheets:

1. The person carrying hay walks upright with the burden on the head,

2. The person walks with a stoop and carries the burden fastened to the back.

It has become clear already from the German Ethnographic Atlas (Atlas der deutschen Volkskunde) that these ways of transport are segregated in the German language area though not very distinctly (Wiegelmann 1969.214). Similarly though regional differences can be discovered in the Hungarian language area between the two methods of carrying hay, there are no clear borderlines here either. In Transdanubia transport on the head is the primary way of carrying not only hay but also other loads. Here women carry grass and hay wrapped in sheets on their heads from the field to the village. They also carry water- and milk vessels and every other kind of load on their heads. On the other hand, the men of this Transdanubian region do not usually carry things in this way as they do not regularly transport hay or grass from the field to the village. On peasant farms it is the men who carry fodder from the stacks or barns to the stables and sheds, and they also use canvas sheets for this purpose. However, they do not put them on their heads but take them on one shoulder. The same situation can be observed among the people of the Hungarian-speaking pockets in central Transsylvania (Fig.1).

Transport of different kinds of feeding stuffs, hay and grass is done by means of sheets carried on the back in a large contiguous district in the North-East and in smaller but in toto considerable areas in the North-West. In much smaller spots it occurs in Transsylvania and to the east of the Carpathians, in Moldavia. In the greater part of the Great Hungarian Plain— as can be seen on the map—sheets are not used at all for transporting hay. Likewise hay-carrying sheets are not known amongst most Hungarian groups in Transsylvania, and they are totally unknown by the Székelys (i.e. Hungarians of Eastern Transsylvania). These negative data are nearly as important as the positive, in considering the historical background of our subject.

Before investigating the spread of transport by means of sheets carried on the back, which we may call back-sheets, it is necessary to emphasize that there is other equipment for transporting hay e.g. hay baskets, in the areas where canvas sheets are also used. The back-sheet, being primary, does not exclude the presence of other implements, and accordingly it does not imply absoluteness.

The 87th theme of MNA does not investigate a particular method of transport by means of sheets, nor transport equipment in relation to kinds of feeding stuffs, but it inquires into the matter of transport on the back by means of sheets in general, noting the form and name of the sheet but not the sort of load. It asks what is usually transported in this way and on what occasions back-sheets are used. Fig.3, shows the spread of transport on the

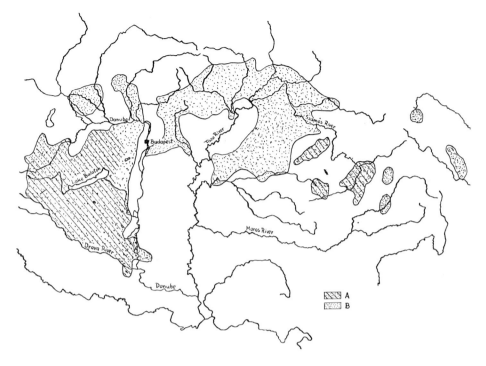

Fig. 1. Distribution of hay-bearing sheets in the Hungarian language area. A: transport on the head. B: transport on the back.

back by means of canvas sheets among Hungarians. Even without thorough investigation it is apparent that this method of transport is unknown in the greater part of Transdanubia, in Transsylvania and most of the Great Hungarian Plain, not to mention smaller patches. On the other hand in the North it forms a large contiguous block that is interrupted only above Budapest, a fact which can be explained by the intensive multi-purpose use of the so-called back-basket there.

Comparing the two sketch-maps at least two statements can be made:

1. Hay-carrying sheets are used in a larger area among Hungarians than back-sheets.

2. Transport on the back by means of canvas sheets is known in certain places on the plain of the river Tisza and in a stretch along the Danube where canvas sheets are not employed at all for transporting hay.

These observations reinforce the conclusion that equipment for load transportation—in this case canvas sheets—does not always coincide with a certain way of transport. On the contrary, there are several possible ways of carrying a certain piece of equipment.

397

It is an instructive fact for European ethnology that the distribution of these ways of transport also shows a certain continental regularity. Transporting hay in sheets is known in the French and Spanish Pyrenees (Krüger 1936.43; Schmolke 1938.11) and it is wide-spread also in the Alps (Stebler 1903.218–20; Weiss 1941.136; Lorez 1943.128). In certain valleys of the Alps hay is wrapped in sheets even if it is to be transported in carts (Stebler 1903.304). However, in these western parts the bundle of hay is carried mostly on the head or shoulders, whereas in the Carpathians and other East European parts it is carried on the back. This significant aspect of the distribution of the two ways of transport in Europe has been recognized by *Béla Gunda* (Gunda 1955. 193). The German Ethnographic Atlas also confirmed the fact of segregation between these two basic ways of transport.

If we try to interpret the transport of hay-bundles among Hungarians in this light, we shall find it natural that it is done on the head in Transdanubia. Although we do not accept *Fr. Krüger's* explanation about the Roman roots of transport on the head, we should like to recall the fact that Transdanubia had been a Roman province for centuries under the name of Pannonia. Cultural and ethnographic history in many cases proved the existence of relations between this territory and the Mediterranean and the Alps in the Middle Ages and in modern times. Transport on the head can also be considered as a proof of these historical contacts.

Transporting hay wrapped in a sheet is only one form of transport on the head. Sheets cannot be found here in any other functions of transport. On the contrary in the northern and central Hungarian areas showed in Fig.3. it may be stated with little exaggeration that "everything is carried on the back in sheets". In this area back-sheets can be found serving many purposes, they are used on various occasions, and according to their function, their form, size and even colour and decoration show great variety.

For transport in the field and round the stables and sheds sheets made of coarse, thick canvas are used. In certain mountain villages manure is carried up in such sheets on the back to high-lying fields. The coarse canvas sheets used by men round stables and sheds are bigger in size and dirtier than the ones used by women to get grass in from the field on their backs. Sometimes pieces of rope are fixed to two or four corners of the sheets used for transport in the field or round the stables and sheds to increase their capacity.

Nevertheless we have to be careful in generalizing because important regional differences can be pointed out in the size, form and terminology of the canvas sheets. In this respect the valley of the River Sajó is the dividing line. East of Sajó as far as the River Tisza the load-bearing canvas sheets

Fig. 2. Man wrapping fodder in a canvas sheet. (Lénárd-daróc, county Borsod). Photo A. Paládi-Kovács, 1960.

are generally 100 cm square, and there are 70–100 cm long pieces of rope fixed to their four corners. In this relatively small area back-sheets have a variety of names: e.g. *korcos, pacókos, trakkos, tracskos.* These names are important for us not only because they are not found to the west of the Sajó but also because they are derivatives of the names of the binding ropes or bands, e.g. *korc, pacók, trak, tracska.*

West of the Sajó canvas sheets used for transport in the field and round the stables or sheds are oblong in most cases. The size of the sheets used by men in stables or sheds is 120 × 200 cm or somewhat smaller. It is called the "canvas for the stable" to distinguish it from the one used by women in the field, the most frequent size of which is 120 × 140 cm. There are rarely binding ropes or bands fastened to the canvas sheets to the west of the Sajó. If nevertheless binding ropes are used, they are usually fixed only to two corners of the sheet, very rarely to all four, and they are short, about 20–30 cm long. The attachment of binding ropes to sheets is not as inevitable as it is to the east of the Sajó. The fact that the names of the binding ropes or bands are often indefinite and in many cases even lacking, emphasizes the occasional nature of their occurrence. There is not any current name of the back-sheet coming from the names of the binding ropes or bands.

Examples so far of transport on the back by means of canvas sheets have related to the hard and dirty toil of the peasants, with their agricultural activity, e.g. transport of hay, straw, grass, manure, wood, etc. The material, state and size of the sheets suit these jobs like the clothes of the people doing them. Another sphere of peasant life is participation in trading and communication by taking goods like eggs, fruit, milk products, etc. to the town or market. Here also belong the transport of e.g. corn to the mill in a village to be ground or hemp to a certain place to be broken. Women of the North Hungarian areas shown in Fig.3 not only put on clean, neat clothes for such occasions but also carried the load on their backs in a cover made of finer, bleached canvas. West of the Sajó bands were never fastened to this type of sheet, and in most of the villages it had a different name from the one used in agricultural labour.

It has to be made clear that the above mentioned transporting activity was exclusively done by women. Men never carried loads on their backs in sheets when going to town or market. To do so would have been considered shameful for men. The same is also true for the third sphere of transport by means of back-sheets, i.e. on the festive occasions. The Roman Catholic peasantry used to visit far-away shrines or other places of pilgrimage several times a year, which usually meant several days' journey. Women carried necessaries and food wrapped up in a bundle on their backs during the journey. To the weddings that were considered similarly festive occasions women took presents and cake in back-sheets too. In the same way food and presents were taken to women in childbed. Women put on their best clothes for these occasions and they used fine, embroidered sheets for transport. The material of these sheets was woven of mixed hempen and cotton yarns. The sides were decorated by borders woven of coloured yarn or by embroidered flowers. In the villages to the west of the Sajó, 20–24 red roses were embroidered on the sheets used on festive occasions.

The homogeneity of the name for the sheets used on journeys, festive occasions and for carrying goods to market is remarkable. They are called *abrosz*, the ordinary name for a tablecloth, in the whole North Hungarian area. For the sake of differentiation it is emphasized only in adjectival phrases that the *abrosz* in question is one for transport.

400

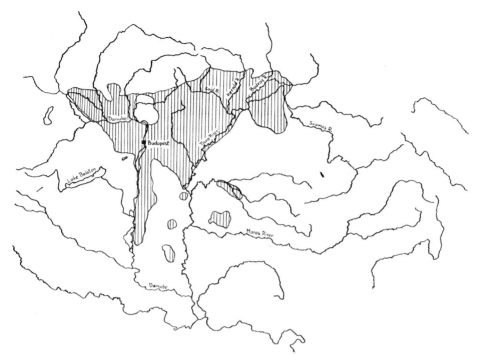

Fig. 3. Distribution of transport on the back by means of canvas sheets in the Hungarian language area.

The important role of canvas sheets for transport in the North Hungarian parts is proved by numerous facts, of which some examples may be given. In the environs of the river Hernád in the villages of Arka, Fóny, Hejce, and Korlát vinegrowers use wooden butts during the grape harvest. These butts are wrapped in sheets and bound to the back. The same method is used with wicker baskets similar in shape to wooden butts. In other parts of the country butts and baskets are fastened to the back by means of two shoulder-bands.

In the area shown in Fig.3, women now 50–60 years old got a small-sized sheet from their mother or grandmother at the age of 8–10, and with its help they learned to carry loads on their backs. In imitation of the older women, they transported small quantities of hay, grass and fruit, and in this way became used to this activity.

Apart from the strict question of transport, sheets of different quality, form and size were indispensable to the peasantry in this area. Women bound their infants with sheets to their body when they took them to the field or elsewhere. In the field they made a temporary hanging cradle for the baby out of some sticks and the back-sheet. At the turn of the century in many places cradles made out of a sheet and hung on the rafters were used in the house too. Women gathered grass in the field, fruit, mushrooms, etc. into a sheet bound to their waist or one shoulder. When sowing men bound a sheet containing small quantities of wheat or other grain round one shoulder and took handfuls out of it. Maize-ears, sunflower-heads, etc. were also gathered into sheets.

Certain items of transport equipment can be found among the bridal presents given by many peoples. For example, the Norwegians, the Swedes and the Serbs of Hungary gave ornamental load-bearing poles for the purpose of transporting water-vessels, the Czechs gave decorated net-bags, and the Hungarians of Transsylvania gave double satchels to the bride as presents (Gunda 1956.128). In the North Hungarian parts—corresponding to the dominant way of transport—canvas sheets meant for transport belonged to the bride's dowry. In the village of Domaháza (county Borsod) in 1911 a wealthy farmer's daughter got 10 coarse canvas back-sheets, 12 fine canvas sheets, *abrosz,* 8 side-satchels made of canvas, 2 back-satchels and 20 sacks. Daughters of not so well-to-do farmers at the same time and place got 2 coarse canvas sheets, 6 sheets of finer canvas, 2 back-satchels and 4 side-satchels. About 1910 in the village of Arka (county Abaúj) the well-to-do farmers' daughters got 3 coarse canvas sheets and 6–7 sheets of finer canvas *abrosz.*

In the North Hungarian area in the first half of this century about half of the home-produced canvas was used for making load-bearing sheets and satchels. It is worth mentioning here that the domestic processing of hemp survived longer in the areas where sheets were used for transport than in other parts of the country. In Transdanubia and in most of the Great Hungarian Plain the domestic processing of hemp was dying already between the two world-wars. On the other hand it was preserved in the North where it vanished gradually only after the second world-war.

Nowadays in Hungary transport on the back by means of canvas sheets is disappearing. Rapid industrial development, urbanization, and the establishment of co-operatives have resulted in changes in the way of living and thinking. Young countrywomen no longer follow their mothers in the traditions of transport. Women belonging to the middle generation use back-transport in their own village but not outside it. Today in the towns, and in trains and buses, only old countrywomen can be seen carrying loads on their backs by means of canvas sheets.

Relatively little is known about the historical background and relationships of the method of transport under discussion. It seems to be certain that trans-

Fig. 4. Old woman carrying
hay on her back in a sheet.
(Kazár, county Nógrád). Photo
A. Paládi-Kovács, 1970.

port on the back is of long standing amongst the western and eastern Slavic
peoples. Among Moravians and Czechs (Václavík 1930.292; Stránska 1936.
219–221) and especially Slovaks it has been frequently noticed and described
(Bednárik 1950; Baran 1952.87). We have data also about the back-sheets
used by Poles and Ukrainians in Galicia and the Carpathians (Moszyński
1929.164; Falkowski-Pasznycki 1935.72). It is not known to what extent it is
spread among the Belorussians (Zelenin 1927.147). *B. Gunda* considers the
back-sheet as an ancient piece of equipment used by the Slavs for transport
(Gunda 1955.193). *G. Wiegelmann's* map No 1. shows that transport on the
back by means of sheets is very common also in the German language area.
He noted that: "Es handelte sich um ein Vordringen, das wohl seine Wurzel
im östlichen Mitteleuropa hatte, sozusagen als "rückläufiger Kulturstrom"
nach den Zeiten der deutschen Ostkolonisation; denn dort, bei den Slawen,

Fig. 5. Women on a journey.
(Ózd, county Borsod). Photo
A. Paládi-Kovács, 1959.

lassen sich die ältesten und vielfältigsten Arten des Rückentragens nachweisen." (Wiegelmann 1969.216).

The area shown in Fig.3 is adjacent to the Slovak and to some extent to the
Ukrainian language area, and the transport equipment here is related to the
ways of transport of the neighbouring Slavs. It is a fact that the Slovaks have
preserved their way of transport by back-sheets also in a strange environment.
The Slovak colonies that came into being about mid-eighteenth century in
certain parts of Transdanubia (Bakony Mountains, Pilis Mountains) have
preserved back-sheet-transport up to the present, though Hungarians and
Germans in the neighbouring areas use head-transport (Vajkai 1941.88–92).

It seems probable that Slavs living in the Northern Carpathians, and the
neighbouring Hungarians, carried loads on the back in canvas sheets already
in the Middle Ages. However, the necessary historical proofs are not yet at
our disposal. Interethnic relations have also not been clarified in relation to

404

Fig. 6. Women with bundles
on their backs in the market-
place. (Ózd, county Borsod).
Photo A. Paládi-Kovács, 1959.

this way of transport. At present we can rely only on certain linguistic data
but there are contradictions even in linguistic opinions.

For example, the load carried on the back is generally called *batyu* 'bundle,
package' by the Hungarians. In the middle-Slovak dialect the word *batoch*,
idem, is known. The genetic relationship between the two words is obvious.
R. Bednárik, the Slovak ethnographer, presumes that the Hungarian word
has its origin in the Slovak one (Bednárik 1950.12). In contradiction to this
opinion, Hungarian linguistics has proved that the Hungarian word was
borrowed by the neighbouring languages (Historical-Etymological Dictionary
1967.260). In the Eastern-Slovak dialect and among the Carpathian Ukrainians
the name of the bundle carried on the back is *zajda, sajda,* and the same word
is used by the Hungarians living between the rivers Hernád and Tisza.
Hungarian linguists trace the Hungarian word from the Slovak language
(Kiss 1965.214–8). The Hungarian word for the back-sheet, *abrosz,* also

405

comes from one of the Slavic languages (Kniezsa 1955.59). On the other hand among the Hungarian names for the back-sheet the word *hamvas* has developed from a Finno-Ugric root (Bárczi 1941.111), and the word *hara* is a Turkish loan-word (Moór 1965.94). The Hungarian terminology for transport on the back by means of canvas sheets extends to about 50 words, so we have no possibility of analysing it here.

The above-mentioned examples illustrate two facts: 1. Linguistics is also able to help in revealing the history of transport-equipment. 2. The history of transport on the back by means of canvas sheets in the Carpathian Basin raises complicated problems, and over-simplified conclusions must be avoided.

It is hoped that the data and facts presented in this study will be useful in revealing the connections among the ways of transport by human beings in Europe.

Bibliography

Baran, L., Zpusob dopravy při senách na Horehroni. *Česky Lid*, XXXIX. Praha 1952.
Bárczi, G., *A magyar nyelv szófejtö szótára*. / Etymological dictionary of the Hungarian language/. Budapest 1941.
Bednárik, R., Systému l'udového transportu. *Časopis Muzeálnej Slovenskej Spolocnosti*, XLI. Turčiansky Sväty Martin 1950.
Falkowski, J. – Pasznycki, B., *Zachodnie pogranicze huculszczyny.* Lwów 1935.
Gunda, B., L'udový transport v Žakarovciach. *Slovenský Národopis*, III. Bratislava 1955.
– *Néprajzy gyüjtöúton.* /Ethnographical fieldwork./ Debrecen 1956.
Kiss, L., Zajda. *Magyar Nyelv*, LXI. Budapest 1965.
Kniezsa, I., *A magyar nyelv szláv jövevényszavai.* /Slavic loan-words of the Hungarian language/. I/1. Budapest 1955.
Krüger, Fr., *Die Hochpyrenäen*. Teil C. Barcelona 1936.
Lorez, Ch., *Bauernarbeit im Rheinwald*. Basel 1943.
A magyar nyelv történeti-etimológiai szótára, I. /Historical-Etymological Dictionary of the Hungarian Language, I./ Budapest 1967.
Moór, E., Hara. *Magyar Nyelv*, LXI. Budapest 1965.
Moszyński, K., *Ethnogeographische Studien in Ostpolen*. Krakau 1929.
Paládi-Kovács, A., Néhány megjegyzés a magyar parasztság teherhordó eszközeiröl. /Some remarks on transport equipment among Hungarian peasantry / *Müveltség és Hagyomány*, XIII. Debrecen 1971.
Schmolke, W., *Transport und Transportgeräte in den französischen Zentralpyrenäen*. Hamburg 1938.
Stebler, F. G., *Alp- und Weidewirtschaft*. Berlin 1903.
Stránska, D., Lidové kroje. *Československá vlastiveda*, II. Praha 1936.
Václavík, A., *Luhačovske Zálesi*. Luhačovice 1930.
Vajkai, A., Adatok a Veszprém vármegyei magyarság és németség teherhordásához. /Data about the transport of loads by Hungarians and Germans in county Veszprém/. *Nép és Nyelv*, I. Cluj-Kolozsvár, 1941.

Weiss, R., *Das Alpwesen Graubündens*. Erlenbach-Zürich 1941.

Wiegelmann, G., *Erste Ergebnisse der ADV-Umfragen zur alten bäuerlichen Arbeit*. Bonn 1969.

Zelenin, D., *Russische /ostslavische/ Volkskunde*. Berlin-Leipzig 1927.

Land Transport in the Ukraine

By MYKOLA P. PRYCHODKO

Archaeological and written data indicate that the origins of land transport in the Ukraine date far back into antiquity. The overland means of transport used by Ukrainians in the past were sledges in winter, and carts in summer.

The sledge is one of the oldest means of transport amongst the Eastern Slavs. Evidence of this is the ancient custom of burying people in sledges. Its proto-type was a dragging sledge, *volokòoshi,* whose original form probably consisted of two small trees pulled out of the ground with their roots and foliage intact, or two smooth poles, used as shafts, pulled by a horse. Across these poles, straw, hay and similar freight was transported. A cross-bar was later added to the smooth poles of the *volokòoshi,* and this gave it a resemblance to a sledge. At the end of the 19th and the beginning of the 20th century the *volokòoshi* was still in use in the Carpathian Mountains *(vlàcky)* and in Pokòotya *(kopanỳtsi).*

Sledges of various shapes and sizes, having different names, were used for different purposes. The simplest type of farm sledge was the one called *ròjni, rijnàti, grinjòly* consisting of two naturally turned up runners connected by two square wooden beams, *oplìny,* which were attached to the small poles, *kòpylỳ,* rammed vertically into the runners. The naturally turned up runners are a characteristic feature of the Ukrainian sledge. There were two or more cross-pieces, depending on the number of *kòpylỳ.* The box or boards put on the cross-pieces depended on what the freight was to be.

Sledges of similar construction, but of smaller dimensions were used to transport loads "by one's own effort" and children used them while at play. These were called *grinjòly.*

Rich peasants possessed high class sledges of light types, *kozyrkỳ, hlabtsì,* etc. with a back and a curved front, which often had intricate ornamentation. Another variant of these sledges, *rozvalni,* had a curved front but no back. It was a transitional form between a big farm sledge and a light sledge for everyday use. In the North-Eastern part of the Ukraine, Hlookhivshtshyna, there existed the *rozvalni,* a hooded sledge with windows, that looked like the Russian *kolymàga* (heavy and unwieldy carriage). A four-runner sledge consisting of two half-sledges was used to transport timber.

408

The most widespread wheeled vehicle was a four-wheeled waggon, *viz*, used in the Ukraine territory from the 5th century B.C. It got its name in the Kiev Rus period. Originally the waggon wheels had revolving axles.

The first cart wheels were sawn out of a log, as was the case with Scythian carts. Wheels of this type were still being used in the Carpathian Mountains at the beginning of the 20th century. Small carts for transporting hay from the mountains, and also barrows and small children's carts had this type of wheel. Wheels made of separate parts, hub, rim, and spokes, appeared not later than the 14th century, as can be seen in the miniature drawing of this date from the Chronicle "Life of Boris and Glebe", where the so-called *kòla* had spoked wheels.

The most widely used waggon in the Ukraine was the type whose front- and back wheel parts were connected by a square wooden beam, *pidtòka*, tightly attached to the rear axle and joined to the front one by means of a coupling-bolt. There also existed the *rozvoròvy* waggon, whose front- and back ends could be moved further apart or nearer, and this was useful for transporting long logs. The construction of a waggon and the names of its parts were the same all over the Ukraine, while the forms varied greatly, depending on the utilitarian purpose and local geographical conditions. The form of the Ukrainian cart differed first and foremost in the type of box that was put on the waggon-frame. Depending on utility needs, the boxes were either made of boards or of interwoven wicker-work. They were ladder-like, *drabynyàsti*, deep, flat, long, and narrow, etc.

Typical for Poltava, Kharkiv and Kiev provinces was a middle-sized cart, having a not very deep, but broad box. Regions bordering Russia had carts that resembled the Russian type; in the woodlands of Polìssya, where narrow roads were common, carts were long and very narrow. In the steppe part of the Ukraine the carts, *harbà, majàra, brỳtshka, khòdy*, were of large dimensions and were used to transport sheaves, straw or hay.

The Ukrainian two-horse *harbà*, with a long ladder-like box, on high wheels, was widely used throughout the Ukraine.

The *hrabàrka* cart was used to transport earth and coal. It had a box made of three loose broad planks, one of which served as a bottom, and the other two as sides that were lifted while unloading. People working on them were called *hrabarì*. These carts were especially numerous in the Donets coal fields (Donbas). Boxes and barrels were transported on *benduhỳ* carts which were used mainly in towns. They had large, broad, wooden platforms, and their drivers were called *bendùjnyky*. A *beztàrka* cart with a high solid box of planed boards was used for transporting grain.

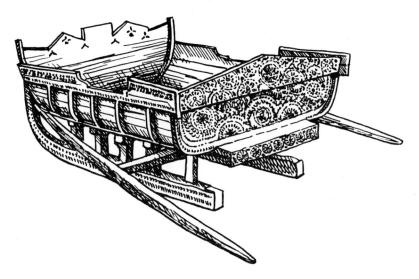

Fig. 1. The *hlabtsì* sledge from Poltava Region.

Shepherds, *chabanỳ*, of Southern Ukraine made use of the *kotỳha* cart. This was a peculiar hut, *koorìn'*, on wheels. Sometimes a big *brỳtshka* with a wattled cabin or a roof made of reeds was used in place of a *kotỳha*.

Characteristic for the Ukraine was the *màja*, a cart used by the *tchoomàks*, Ukrainian ox-cart drivers. Its construction did not differ from an ordinary cart, but because its purpose was to transport loads long distances, it had to be of a larger size and very sturdy, with its deep box being thoroughly finished. These boxes were hollowed or burnt out of big lime-trees and finished accordingly. When making a *màja*, special attention was paid to the use of firm and hard sorts of wood for the manufacture of axles and wheels. It should be noted that up to the second half of the 19th century all parts of the cart were made of wood. Iron parts came into use only later on: rod iron was used as reinforcement for axles, and wheels were shod with iron rings, *rỳkhva*, and tyres. The rims of the *tchoomàk màja's* wheels were broad so as to avoid sinking deep into the mud. A *màja* was often intricately ornamented with fretwork, especially such parts as the detachable front, cross-pieces and *looshnì* (curved pieces of wood attached to the axles and supporting the ladder-like box with their upper parts).

A small hand-pulled cart on two wheels was widely used in the Ukraine.

The simplest type of cart that survived in the Ukraine till the turn of the 19th–20th century was the so-called *bedà (bìdka, bedàrka, paloobtsì)*. This was a one-axled, two-wheeled cart, the back of which lay on the axle, and

410

Fig. 2. The *màja*, a tchoomák cart.

the front on the shafts, used for driving and transporting light loads. This type has come down to us from ancient times. It existed over the entire territory of the Eastern Slavs, and the Mongol—Turkish peoples of Asia had similar carts.

In addition to the types of carts listed above, coaches, large coaches *(ridvàny)*, *pàlooby* (with roofs), cabins, *taradỳky,* carriages and others were also used in the 17th–18th centuries mainly by the gentry and Cossack officials.

Carts were ox- and horse-drawn. An ox-cart had larger dimensions than a horse-cart, and in place of shafts it had a *vìya (dìshel,* a pole) forked at its rear end, and attached to the front-axle. In the Right-bank part of the Ukraine, horse-carts had poles that differed from the *vìya* of an ox-cart by not having forks and by a different way of fastening. In the Left-bank part of the Ukraine, carts, as a rule, had shafts, and the horse-cart harness was the collar, shafts, and bow, which was also found in Right-bank Ukraine (Volỳn', Pokòotya). This type of harness was basically Russian, and found its way into the Ukraine together with the Russian ethnic influence. In Right-bank Ukraine a trace breast-band type of horse harness prevailed.

Carts having shafts were pulled by one horse, and those with a pole were drawn by a pair of horses in breast-bands. The *tròika* (three horses harnessed abreast) and tandem harness *(vstyàj)* were widespread only among landlords in the Ukraine. The harness for ox-drawn carts was the yoke and pole

411

Fig. 3. An ox team.

throughout the Ukraine. A special type of harnessing was the one-ox team, *bovkoonòm*. For faster driving, the most prosperous inhabitants of the Ukraine made use of a lighter means of conveyance, such as the *biỳtshka*, the break (large wagonette), and the *tachànka*, (machine-gun cart), which all had springs. The *tachànka*, which first appeared in the South of the Ukraine, later on spread all over the whole steppe area of Russia and was widely used during the Civil War period.

Pack transport, done mainly by horses, was known in the Ukraine ever since the times of the Old Rus state. The method of transporting loads in saddle-bags, *sàckvy*, *bèssahy*, was especially common in the Carpathians and in woodlands where the roads were narrow. In the 19th and the beginning of the 20th century pack transport had survived chiefly in the highlands.

Horseback riding was very popular in the Ukraine. Short distances were covered without a saddle, and for longer routes, a saddle was used. Often the saddle was well ornamented. In the Carpathians, horsewomen were not unusual.

One of the oldest ways of moving across slippery areas, e.g. across ice, in mountains, etc., was by using the so-called *ràcky* (crawfish) of various shapes, made of iron and wood. These were attached to the soles of high boots.

Walking on stilts, *khodòol'ni*, *klyòotshky*, *kostylì*, was also known. The

Fig. 4. Pack transport in the Carpathians.

stilts were used very rarely, mainly in the Carpathians for crossing unfrozen rivers or while fishing.

There were various ways by which light loads were carried. Loads were carried in bundles wrapped in cloths. Liquids such as milk, water or the like were carried in jugs, *hlèchyky*. Various forms of poles, often decorated with carvings, were commonly used to carry buckets with water, baskets with laundry, etc. In the Western Ukraine such poles were called *nòshi, kilkỳ, shìdy* and so on.

Wicker baskets, *kòshyky*, of various forms, open and with covers, were used, as well as bags, *tòrba*, of all sizes. In Bukovina, Podillya and Galicia the bags were called *bèssahy*. These were carried on a strap of woven braid, *tas'mà*, across the shoulder. Besides linen bags, leather bags were also popular in Polissya.

The practice of carrying bags, baskets etc. on the shoulders was also widespread. Small amounts of hay were carried in bundles; hay from marshes was carried with the aid of woven nets or on two poles. Stretchers, *petel'kỳ* (cord loops), *klyootshì* (part of a thin trunk with a circle of boughs) were also in use.

Women carried baskets, jugs etc. on their head only in Bukovina. For this reason a small cushion, often with beautiful embroidery, or a hoop, *hòmlya*,

413

was placed on the head under a basket or a jug. These were carried without the aid of hands.

Ukrainian women, like other European women, used to carry little children in front of them in their arms, and bigger ones on their backs. In some localities children were suspended in front in a piece of linen, *obròos,* hung over the shoulders.

Such were the traditional means of transportation and conveyance of Ukrainians in the times of feudalism and capitalism.

Drawings by Marian Malovsky

Traditional Ways and Means for Land Transport in the Faroe Islands

By HOLGER RASMUSSEN

In his excellent book The Atlantic Islands Kenneth Williamson gives a vivid description of what travelling is like in the Faroe Islands even after the building of roads and introduction of motor cars (Williamson 1948.185–188). The development of road building and the transformation of land transport which had proceeded slowly in the first decades of this century has been accelerating ever since World War II, but this question will not be dealt with here. We are here confining ourselves to the traditional ways and means of transport from a period when no roads were known and no vehicles used.

At that time all transportation was done by boat or on foot, by walking. Now and then horses could be used for some kinds of work, but not every farm house, and not even every island kept horses. In order to give an impression of the ordinary conditions before the development of roads a few words are necessary on the natural environment and the typical placing of the built-up areas.

The Faroe Islands include 18 smaller and bigger islands, the smallest only 0.82 square kilometres and the biggest 373.47 square kilometres, and a few islets. Seventeen of the islands are inhabited, one of them by only one family. All the islands are hilly, often with precipitous shores. The small villages, *bygdir,* which constitute the main part of the built-up areas, are all placed near the shores, and consequently transport by boat is and has always been predominant, even more so as land transport was not helped by roads. Only narrow paths or tracks, marked by cairns on difficult ground, led from one *bygd* to another, or from the *bygd* into its fields and hills. Those paths and tracks could be used by men and animals on foot, but not by vehicles. Neither sledge nor carriage was known in the traditional Faroese culture.

For this period carrying was the ordinary way of transporting goods of any kind. It could be executed in different ways, and here we will omit the simplest one, by hand, and concentrate on the more characteristic ones, on the human back, and by pack animal.

Fig. 1. Man carrying
fish in *byrðarleypur*.
Photo: F. Børgesen
c. 1900.

Carrying by man power

Two methods are here significant, the first by a carrying-band against the
fore part of the bearer's head, the second by a breast band. In addition some
more unusual methods will be mentioned.

The first method is mainly confined to men. Now and then a woman may
be seen carrying a load in that way, and children, especially boys, are made
accustomed to it through equipment matching their size and age. Normally
they start at an age of about 9 to 10.

The characteristic device for carrying with a head band is a wooden box,
leypur. Recently this implement has had its own monograph (av Skarði 1955),
where all details have been dealt with: construction, dimensions, names, use

416

Fig. 2. Man with *grótleypur* from Sand. Photo:
H. Rasmussen 1947.

etc. Consequently I shall here only give a general description of its main
features.

The box consists of four posts joined by spars set slightly apart, or by solid
boards. The posts protrude both at the top and at the bottom. The box tapers
more or less towards the base. The upper ends of the posts, turning against
the back of the bearer, are joined by a short bearing band of rope, wrapped
around with a cloth band in the middle. In former times this band was made
of a woollen braid, which was broader in that part resting against the
forehead.

The common box for all sorts of transport is called *byrðarleypur* (*byrða* =
burden). The box can be of different sizes, but it is always constructed with
the bars set apart. Sometimes, however, the part resting against the back of

Fig. 3. Carrying hay with *hoyberareip*. a: The hay is placed on the double rope; b: The burden of hay is lashed together; c: The wife is helping to raise the burden; d: The man on his way with the hay burden. Photo: H. Rasmussen 1947.

the bearer is solid in order not to spoil his clothes during the transport of, for instance, fish or seaweed (Fig. 1). In days of old it was also used for the transport of manure, but later on a smaller, solid container, *tøðleypur, (tøð* = manure), was employed for that work. In some places they also used liquid manure for fertilizing the fields. The liquid was filled into a solid wooden box, closed at both ends with a bottom inserted in grooves. In the lid was a hole closed with a plug. Even if such a box evidently differed from the ordinary *leypur* it was still called by that name, *landleypur (land* = liquid manure), and was also carried in the same way. In the last few years people have started transporting manure in zink tubs, *sinkleypur.*

We have seen that the box for liquid manure was of a different construction, and so were other solid boxes for special purposes, for instance for the transport of clothes when civil servants visited different places in their district, or when the clergyman travelled to his parish-of-ease and had his cassock in a *lokaleypur (lok* = lid) or *prestleypur,* always provided with a cover on hinges and sometimes with a padlock. Under the cover there could be a separate compartment for the special Danish clergyman's ruff. But whatever the construction of the box, it was always carried in the ordinary way with a band against the fore part of the head.

A special device for heavy burdens is the so-called *grótleypur (grót* = stone) which consists of an angular frame combined with crossbars. In order to make it extra strong the two L-shaped pieces of the frame are sometimes of solid wood (av Skarði 1955, Fig. 7; Jirlow 1931a, Fig. 39, and Jirlow 1937, Fig. 3). (Fig. 2).

For Faroese agriculture hay is the most important crop. Large quantities of grass are mown on the infields and when dry carried home and placed in ricks, *dés,* on a fenced spot near to or in between the cluster of houses. Special hay houses were introduced very late to the islands and are not in use everywhere. Generally all the hay is transported on the human back from the fields to the hay yard. Both men and women may transport hay, but usually it is done by the men as it is heavy work.

For this transport is used a rope, *hoyberareip,* now of ordinary material, though it may still be possible to find one made of horsehair in the old fashion. The rope is about 15 m long, placed double and with a ring, *held,* attached to the middle of it with a sling-hitch. This ring is made of a ram's horn, the ends of which are cleverly hooked together. Such rings are made by the farm folk themselves, but wooden rings of Norwegian origin could also be got. The diameter of the ring is from 12 to 15 cm. This ring serves as a loop when the bundles of hay are lashed together. When the burden is ready a bend of the

Fig. 4. Milk-maids from Haraldsund carrying pails for milking in the outfields. Photo: Johs. Klein 1898.

rope is kept out, wrapped in hay, and used as the carrying band for the transport (Fig. 3).

The hay-bearing work was a common enterprise where neighbours were invited to help in order to have the carrying finished in one day. If the men invited were not farmers they were paid in kind, traditionally in mutton at Christmas (Rasmussen 1949.65). Farmers, however, were not paid but in turn expected the same kind of help.

The special way of carrying for women was by a breast band. This was always used during the summer when they went to the outfields for milking the cows. A few words are needed to explain the general traits of the care of cattle in the Faroe Islands. The cattle were kept in the byre during the winter and traditionally fed exclusively with hay. As early as possible the cows were let into the outfields for grazing and stayed there all the summer and often far into the autumn. All the daily work with the cattle, such as mucking out and milking which was thought of as unpleasant by the men, was handed over to the womenfolk. It is significant for the traditional view of the role of man's

Fig. 5. Milk-maid from Kvivík carrying pails and knitting stocking. Photo: F. Børgesen c. 1900.

Fig. 6. Milk-maids from Haldorsvík with modern sheet-metal pails. Photo: H. Rasmussen 1947.

and woman's work that the occupation with the cattle was given a low esti-mate. The name for a milk-maid, *neytakona* (*neyt* = cattle), was regarded as invective when applied to a man. Usually the *neytakona* was a servant girl.

Twice a day the milk-maids would have to seek out the animals, which could be a troublesome task involving a lengthy walk, sometimes with a neg-ative result if the cows were far away and fog was making orientation difficult.

The milk pails, *dyllur* or *biðir*, were traditionally made of wooden staves with two vertical ears at the upper half of the pail. A tanned sheepskin tied to the top served as a "lid". Nowadays the pails are mostly of sheet-metal, but of the same form.

The pails were carried on the back by a braided woollen band, threaded through the ears and resting across the bearer's breast and the upper part of her arms. To protect the back against the rubbing of the pails the milk-maid may carry a piece of homespun suspended from the neck, and on the hips a pad, for instance an old sock stuffed with hay. In that way she may transport two or three pails at once on her back and even a few on her bent arms. Possibly she may be knitting a stocking as well (Fig. 4).

As the natural environment of the villages has not changed very much, this

Fig. 7. Man with *kópa-taska* made of sealskin, for clothes. Tjørnavík. Photo: H. Rasmussen 1947.

is still the ordinary means of executing the milking job, as one will have to climb the more or less precipitous hills of the outfield as soon as one leaves the fencing of the infield.

A very old-fashioned device for carrying has been used recently in a few places, but was in more common use when seal-hunting was of importance. It was a bag for clothes, *klæðsekkur*, made of a whole sealskin stripped off the carcass in one piece. Only a few bags of that kind have been preserved. Jirlow illustrated one in his paper on Faroese work (Jirlow 1931b. Fig. 31), but they are repeatedly mentioned in earlier works on the Faroese culture. Svabo, for instance, says that it is the common seal *(Phoca vitulina)* which is treated in that way 'and used for a valise' (Svabo (1781–82) 1959.51). Landt adds to this that what is kept in such bags is transported comfortably well-preserved in damp weather (Landt (1800) 1965.216).

As a successor to the old style of bag one may find a knapsack, *kópataska* (*kópa* = seal), of the same material and for the same use (Fig. 7).

A rather peculiar way of carrying is or, at least, was used when people from villages without a church wanted to have their children baptized. Often the children had to be carried for great distances over hill and dale to the church, and in order to hold and protect the child it was kept in a sheet suspended in front of the bearer and held in position by straps from the corners of the sheet round the neck of the bearer. The custom is mentioned by Svabo, and I have also treated it fully from oral tradition in respect of the beliefs connected with it (Rasmussen 1959.134–139). As the main belief contributes greatly to an understanding of the special conditions for Faroese culture I shall here give a brief summary of it.

Running, or at all events walking quickly with the children has been generally practised in conjunction with this method of carrying, both going to and coming from the church. Most accounts say that it took place when the male child was to be christened, but in one case at least it was done at the baptism of both boys and girls. When a reason for the custom is given—and it is in nearly every instance—it is said to be in order that the child shall be quick on its feet (to be *goður gongumaður*).

Both in order to cross the mountains with the desired speed and because the carrying of a child to and from the church was an arduous task, it was always a godfather who carried. Sometimes it was arranged that an old man bore the baby to the church whilst a younger man carried it back. If several children were baptised the godfathers often ran a race homewards. How deeply rooted this idea is, is shown by the modern change in the custom now that the road net in the Faroes has been developed. If one drives to the church in a car, the chauffeur is often told jokingly to drive fast in order that the child may become 'gongumaður', and when the church is reached the child is lifted out and carried the last stretch at a run.

In my paper of 1959 I have given parallel examples from different parts of Europe. The most striking similarity is from a locality in the Alpine part of Italy, Antronapiana, where an extremely difficult terrain demands endurance and agility in the women who, during the period when the male population was away acting as harvesters in other districts, had to take care of the haymaking at home. Let me quote what Scheuermeier (in his book: Bauernwerk in Italien. Erlenbach-Zürich 1943) says: 'Die Marsch- und Trag-

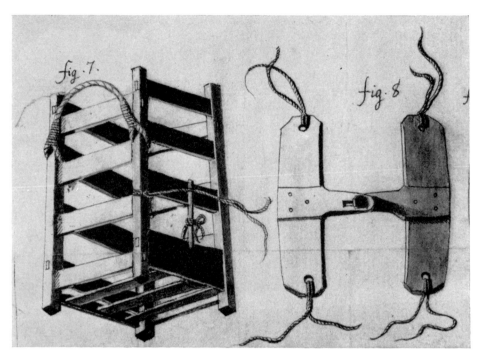

Fig. 8. *Rossleypur* and *klyvberi* from the manuscript of Svabo 1781–82. The device for opening the leypur is clearly seen.

fähigkeit dieser Frauen ist aussergewöhnlich, und sie ist auch nötig. Bezeichnend dafür ist folgender Taufbrauch in Antronapiana. Wird ein Mädchen geboren, so lässt man es an der Taufe von einer leichtfüssigen Jungfrau in möglichst raschem Lauf in die Kirche tragen, und alle, die unterwegs den beiden begegnen, grüssen das Neuangekommene mit dem Wunsche: Santa Maria, *buona gamba!'*

Carrying by pack animal

For transport of heavy weights and large loads, chiefly peat and manure, it was customary to use horses for those able to afford pack animals. The Faroese horse is of a small breed similar to the Icelandic one, sturdy and hardworking, but not such an important part of the traditional Faroese culture as the Icelandic one.

The equipment for transporting by pack-animal is described in detail by Svabo (Svabo (1781–82) 1959.138–140) and it has not changed essentially since then. His description will be given here with additions from information

Fig. 9. Transport of milk to Tórshavn on *klyvberi*. Photo: Generalstaben *c.* 1890.

gathered for a complete set of equipment acquired for the collections in the Danish National Museum in 1937.

All the different parts of the equipment for a pack-horse, without exception home-made, are called by a joint name *týggj* or *rossatýggj (ross* = horse). As a protection a sheepskin covering is put over the back of the horse. This covering could also be a blanket or a thin mattress. The covering is called *bjølgur.* On top of it is placed a mat, made of bands of hay, and over that again a wooden crook saddle, *klyvberi,* consisting of two pieces hooked together at the top by two big horns, called *klakkar.* The saddle is held in position by two woollen strings attached to holes in the vertical board of the saddle. One of the strings is passed round the breast of the horse. It is called *bróstskeri.* The other one passing beneath the tail of the horse is called *bahá-lin.* The part of it resting directly beneath the tail is wrapped round with tangled wool to prevent chafing. This thicker part of the string is called *halatógvi.* Svabo adds that when the horse is descending a steep hill with its load a broad woollen string attached to the wooden boxes and passed behind

425

the hind legs may be used as a means of preventing slipping. Such a string is called *læraband* (*lær* = thigh). Exceptionally, a belly band may be used.

The load is put in wooden boxes, *rossleypar*, of the same basic construction as the *byrðarleypar* mentioned above. Normally they are a bit bigger. In one point they differ from the normal *leypur*, in having a special device for opening at the bottom, so that manure or whatever else is transported can be emptied easily. The bottom of the *leypur* consists of two cross pieces, *nit*, connected with bars. One of the cross pieces has pivots inserted in the lower part of two of the posts, forming in that way a hinge. The bottom is kept closed by a string attached to a small stick, firmly fixed to the outside of the box. For opening, it is only necessary to release the stick and the load will force the bottom open. The pair of *rossleypar* is attached to the saddle by rope loops, *fetlar* (Fig. 8).

Svabo maintains—and all other authors dealing with Faroese conditions are in accordance with him—that the transport of peat and manure was very hard work for the horses, but except for this period of the year the horses were not much used. Lunddahl writing in 1851 (Lunddahl (1851) 1911.446) makes a statement that is representative not only for his own time: 'The periods of the year in which a constant use of horses is necessary is in spring, when the manure is carried to the fields, and in summer when peat is transported home previous to the work with the hay. In many places, however, horses are not used, not even for those tasks. In the Northern Islands only a few are found. The rest of the year horses are only used as an exception, as the people carry out their considerable carriage of loads and almost all their inland travelling on foot . . .'

Conclusions

The archaic and rather limited ways and means for land transport in the Faroe Islands have their great interest in showing the influence of both the natural environment and historical traditions. The Faroe Islands were settled about 825 by people of mostly Norwegian origin. With them they brought their domestic culture and carried it on almost under the same natural conditions as in the country they had left. No wonder that there are great similarities of cultural elements in the two parts of Northern Europe. Even if the Faroe Islands lie isolated in the Northern Atlantic sea, there were nevertheless connections with other parts of the North Atlantic world, as can be seen in many cases (Laquist 1952.49–66; Rasmussen 1955.131–157).

Sticking to our actual theme those similarities have been mentioned several times. In the paper by A. Fenton (Fenton 1973.128) in this volume both the crook-saddle and the *leypur* are taken into consideration under the discussion of the Scottish material, and Jirlow has several times used Faroese material for comparison with for instance Lapp material (Jirlow 1931b.90–95), Central-European material (Jirlow 1935.228) and more general European and non-European material (Jirlow 1937.137–148). It thus reveals a value not only for local but for comparative studies in the field of European ethnology as well.

Bibliography

Fenton, A. Transport with Pack-Horse and Slide-Car in Scotland, in *Land Transport in Europe. Studies of Folk Life* 4, 1973, 121–71.
Jirlow, R. Drag ur färöiskt arbetsliv, in *Rig* 14, 1931, 97–133.
– En lapsk klövsadel och dess ursprung, in *Rig* 14, 1931, 90–95.
– Bärmesen. Ett ålderdomligt bärredskap och dess utbredning, in *Ymer* 1935, 209–235.
– Das Tragen mit dem Stirnband, in *Acta Ethnologica* 1937, 137–148.
Landt, J. *Forsøg til en Beskrivelse over Færøerne* (1800), 1965.
Laquist, B. Lulelapparnas byxtyp en nordisk-arktisk reliktföreteelse, in *Svenska Landsmål och svenskt Folkliv* 1952, 49–66.
Lunddahl, J. A. Nogle Bemærkninger om de færøske Landboforhold (1851), in *Forslag og Betænkninger afgivne af den færøske Landbokommission* 1911, 421–462.
Rasmussen, H. Korntørring og -tærskning på Færøerne, in *Kuml* 1955, 131–157.
– Carrying Children »í kiltingi«, A Faroese Christening Custom, in *Folk* I, 1959, 133–139.
Rasmussen, R. *Sær er siður á landi*. 1949.
Skarði, J. av Føroyski leypurin, in *Fróðskaparrit. Annal. societ. scient. Færoensis* 4, 1955, 32–60; 5, 1956, 108–152.
Svabo, J. Chr. *Indberetninger fra en Reise i Færøe 1781 og 1782*. 1959.
Williamson, K. *The Atlantic Islands. A Study of the Faeroe Life and Scene*. 1948.

Draught Oxen and Horses in the Baltic Countries

By ANTS VIIRES

Today the only draught animal used in the agriculture of the Baltic Soviet Republics is the horse, which is being more and more superseded by motor transport. But not more than a hundred years ago in large parts of Estonia and Lithuania oxen were widely used in the plough and for traction. In earlier days ox draught was still more widespread. On the other hand, in Latvia the horse was the principal draught animal also in the 18th and 19th centuries. The writers of that time firmly underline this fact. They also speak about the repeated unsuccessful attempts of the local Baltic German landlords to teach the Lettish peasants to use draught oxen (e.g. Hupel 1789.340–341, 362, 371; Hupel 1796.26–27; Friebe 1803.75, 90; Mellin 1831.350–357).

Using ethnographic and linguistic argument *K. Vilkuna* has demonstrated that Estonia and south-western Finland make one of the most northern ox-keeping areas in Europe dating from the far past (Vilkuna 1936). The horn yoke as an obvious relic in both the above-mentioned regions as well as in western Lithuania (Žemaitia) shows that the use of draught oxen in Estonia, Finland and Lithuania should be regarded as a genetic whole (cf. Vilkuna 1949.24; Viires 1969). To this background the Estonian-Lithuanian and Lettish dichotomy in the sphere of draught animals becomes especially intriguing, with the Baltic countries comprising the border zone between two large areas where the main agricultural draught animals have probably differed already from the days when agriculture became the leading source of subsistence: the ox in the south, west and south-west, the horse in the north and north-east. The Lithuanian scientists *J. Jurginis* and *V. Dunduliene* have lately come to the conclusion that the horse as a plough animal in Lithuania is more ancient than the ox, the latter beginning to spread not before the 13th century and becoming universal by the 16th century (Jurginis 1955.62–65, 73; Jurginis 1962.51–52, 56; Dunduliene 1956.6, 13, 32–33; Dunduliene 1963.137–138). Might we have here a primeval Balto-Finnic and Baltic difference? But in the eastern and northern Balto-Finnic areas the ox is altogether unknown. Perhaps in Estonia and Finland draught oxen are of a later origin than has been supposed up to now? Or may the Balts yet have used them more widely earlier? This possibility should be taken into serious consideration, when we take into account the general history of draught animals in Europe and in particular the fact that an effective horse harness presumably did not come into use until the middle of the first millennium of our era. We must also consider such early developments as the replacement of oxen by horses for ploughing in western Scotland and Ireland already in prehistoric times (Fenton 1969.18) and in northern Germany, Denmark and Hungary during the Middle Ages (Jacobeit 1957.135–143; Granlund 1969.107–108; Szabó 1966.13). However, there were some opposite developments, e.g. in Mecklenburg in the 16th–18th centuries (Bentzien 1964).

Thus the problem is complicated enough. In the following we shall try to throw some light on this subject making use of the available historical, ethnographic, archaeological and linguistic materials.

Historical data. The first historical source that allows us to draw some conclusions about the draught animals in the Baltic countries is the early 13th century Chronicon Livoniae by Henry of Latvia (Heinrich von Lettland 1959). According to the chronicle, the campaigns and looting raids of the local tribes took place, as a rule, in winter on horseback and in sledges that could be drawn only by horses in case of a quick raid. The loot always included horses and cattle *(equos et pecora)*. But very often the cattle are referred to more precisely. The word *bos* 'ox, cow' appears in the text of the chronicle at least twelve times, nine times in connection with the Estonians, twice with the Livs and once with the Ingrians. It is not easy to determine in which case this word implies the ox only. The rhyming word-pair *oves et boves* repeatedly used as a formula (XX,2, XXVII,2 and XXVIII, 5 Estonia, XXV, 6 Ingria) hardly means anything else than 'sheep and cattle'. Concerning the oxen we cannot rely upon such word-pairs either as *boves et (alia) pecora* (XV, 3 Livs, XVIII, 5 the Sakala Estonians) and *equos et boves* (XXVII, 1 Livs and Letts, XXX, 5 the Estonians of Saaremaa), the meaning of which could also be 'cattle and (other) livestock' and 'horses and cattle'. As to the latter word-pair, there is one exception: when in 1223 the army from northern Estonia and Saaremaa besieged Tallinn and was defeated, the Germans and Danes looted also its *boves et equos* (XXVII, 11). It seems plausible that the Estonian army had taken along only draught animals and mounts, i.e. oxen and horses. When the loot from the raid to Soontagana (West Estonia) in the winter of 1210/11 contained *"boum et vaccarum quatuor milia"* (XIV, 10), it has the unambiguous meaning of 'four thousand oxen and cows'. And when in 1223 insurgent Estonians in Tartu put the fat priest

Hartwig on the back of the fattest ox *(locaverunt super bovem pinguissimum,* XXVI, 7) in the sacrificial ceremony, we can be sure the beast was an ox indeed. In a couple of cases the chronicle mentions 'draught animals' *(iumenta,* XII, 6 Sakala, XVI, 4 in the Livish hill-fort Sattesele). Here also the presence of oxen is most likely. If there had been horses alone, it would have been more logical to say simply *equos.*

Consequently, we can be more or less sure that the chronicle specifies oxen at least five times. Four of these examples indicate the use of oxen practically in the whole area inhabited by the Estonians, while one implies the Livs. On the other hand, the chronicle gives direct references to horses as draught aimals both with the Livs and the Letts. When the Livs in 1211 were subjected to an annual crop tax per horse *(de quolibet equo,* XV, 5) and the Letts of Tolova in 1214 per two horses *(de duobus equis,* XVIII,3), there can hardly be any doubt that it was just the plough animals that were taxed, as was the custom of that time. In 1230 and 1267 the peasants in Courland (Kurzeme) were also taxed on horses as draught animals used in the plough and harrow as directly stated in the respective sources (cf. Doroshenko 1959. 30; Tarvel 1966.29).

Hence the Estonian-Latvian contrast known to us from the 19th century existed already in the 13th century. The Letts used horses in field work while the Estonians made use of oxen too. The Livs seem to have also had oxen although they used the horse in the plough as well.

As to the Lithuanians, we have no such direct data from the 13th century. J. Jurginis (1955.62–65) draws our attention to the fact that in East Prussia in the 13th century both the "German" and "Polish-Prussian" plough were used as the basis for taxation. The former, which was more heavily taxed, he connects with ox ploughing (according to the German example then). Later it may have spread also to the Lithuanian territory where in the 16th century "the ox sokha" or simply "the sokha" (i.e. a sokha drawn by a pair of oxen that Jurginis connects with the Lithuanian ox sokha of the 19th century) was taxed twice as high as the horse sokha. To connect the 13th century "German plough" with the Lithuanian ox sokha of the 16th–19th centuries is quite risky in view of the fact that the latter differs greatly from the ploughing implements used in Germany. Thus the theory presented by Jurginis remains hypothetical and shows us only that the Prussians of the 13th century were most probably acquainted both with the ox and the horse ploughing.

The earliest direct information about the plough animals of Lithuania (esp. of Žemaitia) dates back to the beginning of the 16th century. At that time oxen clearly predominated. Such correlation lasted till the 18th century (Jurginis 1955.62).

The difference between the Estonian and Lettish draught animals continued throughout the further centuries. Yet a number of historical sources, beginning with the 14th century, tell us about oxen being used to some extent in Kurzeme and Vidzeme (Lettish part of Livonia). The Latvian historian *V. Doroshenko* who has made a thorough study of the draught animals of the Latvian peasants in the 13th–16th centuries (Doroshenko 1959.50–53; Doroshenko 1960.108–111), admits that this was partly due to the considerable decrease in the number of horses as a result of the frequent wars. That had become a sore subject in Livonia already in the 15th century. The peasants were to a certain extent forced to use oxen besides horses as draught animals. It is interesting to note that most data about draught oxen come from the Livish area or from the direct vicinity of the Estonians in northern Vidzeme, and from northern Kurzeme where some Livish villages have remained up to the present days (cf. Vilkuna 1936.80–81). In Kurzeme, one of the main centres of ox keeping was the Dundaga Castle territory where in 1387 a number of Livish villages were registered on the northern coast (LUB III, 1248; cf. LUB VIII, 765–the year 1434). In those Livish villages draught oxen were used to some extent even in the second half of the 19th century, in contrast to the neighbouring Lettish villages (Vilkuna 1936.80–81; Kettunen 1938.128–*kiñdš*, 516–*ārga*).

Secondly, many Baltic German landlords began to breed oxen and cows, in smaller quantities also horses, to hire them out to the peasants. The corresponding data are available beginning with the 14th century (Johansen 1928. 151, 152, 155–Virumaa 1330–50; LUB II, 846–Virumaa and Alutaguse 1346; LUB III, 1248–Dundaga 1383). Particularly the hiring of oxen became a custom lasting for centuries. This fact has led some historians to the opinion that draught oxen were introduced to Livonia only by German colonists (Bosse 1933.294). Such was not the case. The need for breeding and hiring draught animals was brought about by the ravages of war and by the frequent epidemics that devastated the herds of the peasantry (cf. Soom 1954. 108–109). Besides, the bulk of the data about the hired oxen come from northern and western Estonia (e.g. Johansen 1925–the surroundings of Tallinn 1435–1507; Stackelberg 1928. 199–201, 250–Läänemaa; Brieflade I, 608–Haljala, 931–Kose, etc.) where ox keeping, as we shall soon see, was rooted very firmly. In many places people still remember that, in the 19th century, peasants got oxen for use from their landlords. In Lithuania the

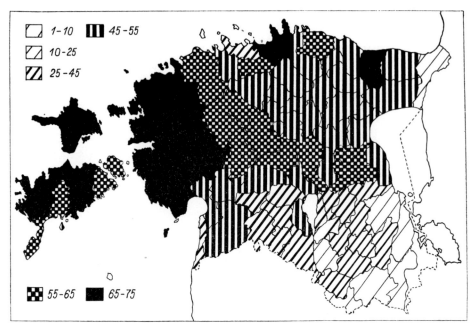

Map. 1. The percentage of oxen in Estonia in 1744.

hiring of oxen was a wide-spread custom as well. Numerous corresponding data are to be found from the 16th–19th centuries (Jablonskis 1937.43; Vaitekūnas 1938.208; Dundulienė 1963.138).

That the German landlords in the Lettish part of Livonia (Vidzeme) really tried to introduce ox labour, achieving even some temporary results (especially after devastating wars), is documented in different sources. But more permanent results were never obtained.

The preference for oxen as against horses on estates was characteristic not only of the Baltic lands. For instance, in the 16th–18th centuries we see the same tendency on the manors of Mecklenburg in northern Germany (Bentzien 1964). Still more noteworthy is the fact that in the 14th–16th centuries oxen were used particularly on the largest estates in the north-eastern area of the Moscow state, the region of traditional horse transport (Gotye 1937.319–320; Gorsky 1959.27–28; Kochin 1965.255–256). That oxen were preferred in large-scale farming, was due to certain reasons. Oxen were much cheaper to feed than horses, and they produced more manure. Their harness, the yoke, was also very simple and cheap. In addition, it was possible to fatten them later and market them as beef cattle. The use of oxen was profitable for

432

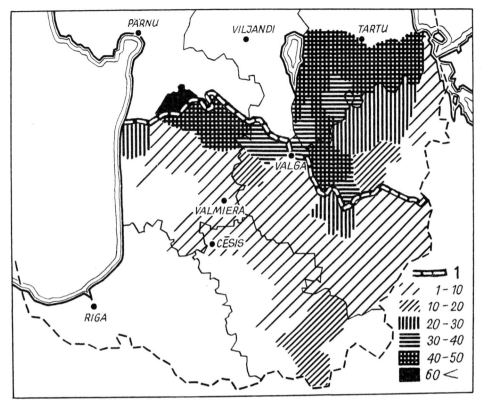

Map 2. The percentage of oxen in South-Eastern Estonia and Vidzeme in 1638. 1 – The border of the Estonian and Lettish settlements.

large-scale farmers, as has been continually emphasized in the literature beginning with the medieval West-European agricultural treatises (e.g. Walter of Henley). In this respect the Baltic authors of the 17th–19th centuries are no exceptions (Gubert 1688.114; Hupel 1796.26–27; Friebe 1803.75–76; Mellin 1831). With small farms strongly inclining to a self-sufficient economy, such considerations carried no weight.

Since the end of the 16th century the repeated revisions of the peasantry and other censuses in Estonia and Livonia give us quite a good view of the local differences and the changes in the number of horses and oxen. The information concerning Estonia till the beginning of the 19th century has lately been analysed in detail by *H. Ligi* (1969). It appears that in the number of draught animals great fluctuations continually took place owing to the frequent wars and requisitions and the devastating effects of epidemics on animals. A more or less normal state of affairs is reflected by the revision of 1744 when those disturbing circumstances had been missing for a longer time.

Concerning our subject, it is most essential to know the correlation between the number of oxen and the number of horses. Further we shall show it with the percentage of oxen in the total number of draught animals. In map 1 we see that in 1744 oxen comprised two thirds, and even more, of the draught animals in western Estonia and in places on the northern coast. In northern Estonia and in the south-west region the number of oxen and horses was more or less the same. In south-eastern Estonia the oxen had a much smaller significance. In the uttermost south-east their percentage practically neared zero. In north-eastern Estonia near the Russian frontier the role of oxen also abruptly decreased.

Turning from the mid-eighteenth century to the farther past, we can observe in south-eastern Estonia in 1591 a rate of oxen (64%) that corresponds to that of western Estonia in 1744. H. Ligi considers this phenomenon a temporary result of the wars that half a century later had already receded. From the 1638 revision we have data about south-eastern Estonia and the whole of Vidzeme (map 2).[1] Taking into consideration the fact that draught oxen in Estonia were most rarely used just in the south-east, the Lettish-Estonian contrast in ox keeping becomes really impressive. In Vidzeme oxen are more numerous in the immediate vicinity of the Estonian border only. This region may have been partly inhabited by Estonians at that time. Still in 1841, for instance, the leivus, a little group of Estonians in north-eastern Vidzeme, are said to have used oxen in ploughing like the other Estonians and unlike their Lettish neighbours (Brackel 1841.376–377). The increase in the relative importance of oxen in Vidzeme from 9% in 1638 to 16% at the end of the century, H. Ligi regards as the restoration of the normal state in more peaceful circumstances. But according to our previous observations, it seems that E. Dunsdorf is more accurate when he says that the increase was the result of the respective efforts of landlords (cf. Ligi 1969.198). Moreover, direct evidence is to be found about oxen being bred by the Swedish potentates among the Lettish peasantry in the middle of the 17th century (Dunsdorfs 1938–1941. DXIV). As a matter of fact, 16% is such a small quantity that we can in no manner speak about a normal and general use of oxen. Such a rate rather implies the accumulation of oxen on a few estates, as it actually was.

Throughout the 18th century the correlation between oxen and horses remains more or less uniform (table 1).[2] As in practical work a pair of oxen has, as a rule, been considered equal to one horse[3], the following relation between ox and horse teams existed in the Estonian districts of that time: 7:6

Table 1

The number of horses and oxen on Estonian farms in the 17th to 19th centuries*

Estonian gub.

Districts	1686–1688			1732			1744			1765			1803			1863		
	Horses	Oxen	% Oxen	Horses	Oxen	% Oxen	Horses	Oxen	% Oxen	Horses	Oxen	% Oxen	Horses	Oxen	% Oxen	Horses	Oxen	% Oxen
Läänemaa......	2487	5872	70	4310	9365	69	2739	6556	70	2691	5398	67	5973	8705	59	12467	9954	44
Harjumaa.......	2868	4320	60	6120 (1739)	8153	57	4698	6105	57	5282	6493	55	4744	4595	49	10932	9915	47
Virumaa.......	1600	1832	53				3681	4496	55	2189	2828	56				13073	5202	28
Järvamaa......	2668	3254	55	3210	2852	47	2399	2438	50	1579	1778	53	1995	1902	46	7381	2275	24

Livonian gub.

Districts	(1721–)1724			1744			1758 (1757)			1805 (on some estates)			1881–1883		
	Horses	Oxen	% Oxen	Horses	Oxen	% Oxen	Horses	Oxen	% Oxen	Horses	Oxen	% Oxen	Horses	Oxen	% Oxen
Saaremaa.......				4218	7787	65	6253	3175	34				6083	710	11
Pärnumaa.......	1766	2335	57	2335	2720	54	3040	3419	53	1540	1069	44	8924	331	4
Viljandimaa.....	3842	3463	47	5175	4676	47	6236	5794	48	841	525	38	13181	188	1
Tartumaa.......	5082	4035	44	8826	5622	39	9735	5745	37	2048	907	31	7403	84	1
Võrumaa........	3018	1363	30	6257	1415	18	6433	1638	20						

* According to: Ligi 1969, tables 3, 4, 6, 8, 10, 12; Jordan 1871, 76–77 (Estonian gub. in 1863); Jung-Stilling 1885, table 11 (Livonian gub. in 1881–1883).

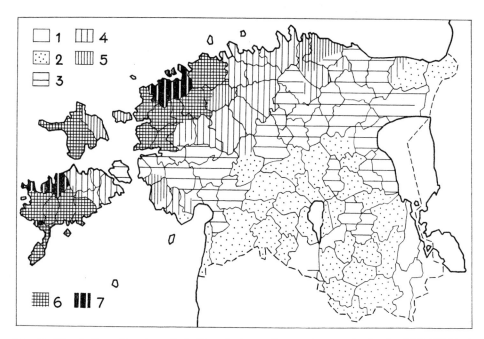

Map 3. The decline of ox draught in Estonia (according to the questioning in 1926; KV 1–4, 47). Draught oxen not remembered (1); ox draught ceased: in the mid-nineteenth century (2), 1860–1885 (3), 1885–1900 (4), 1900–1915 (5); ox draught in 1926: rare (6), usual (7).

in Läänemaa, 1:1 in Saaremaa, 3:5 in Harju-, Viru- and Pärnumaa, 1:2 in Järvamaa, 6:13 in Viljandimaa, 1:3 in Tartumaa, and 1:8 in Võrumaa.

Though the data on draught animals from the beginning of the 19th century are deficient and not quite reliable, they nevertheless indicate a slight decrease in the use of oxen all over the country. During the 19th century this process deepens at an accelerating speed. We are given an idea of this development by the censuses of animals in the second half of the century (table 1). A more detailed picture can be drawn from the all-Estonia questioning of 1926 organized by the Estonian National Museum with the help of country schools (map 3). In southern Estonia where oxen had been of relatively little importance in the previous centuries already, ox keeping came to an end actually by the middle of the 19th century. In most parts of northern Estonia it disappeared during the second half of the century. The estates were much more conservative in using draught oxen (esp. in northern Estonia). There the substitution of statute labour for hired labour in the middle of the 19th century led to a greater quantity of draught animals. For example, in

436

1863 the number of draught horses and oxen on the estates of the Estonian guberniya was as follows (Jordan 1871.76–77):

Table 2

Districts	Horses	Oxen	The percentage of oxen	The percentage of oxen on the farms
Läänemaa............	1314	2889	*69*	*44*
Harjumaa............	1702	2534	*60*	*47*
Virumaa.............	2263	2417	*52*	*28*
Järvamaa............	1299	1358	*51*	*24*

While the importance of oxen on the farms had perceptibly diminished by this time, almost the same ratio persisted on the estates as on the farms of the respective districts during the 18th century. According to the census of 1880 the quantity of draught oxen on the farms had decreased still more (esp. abruptly in Viru- and Järvamaa), while on the estates (excl. Järvamaa) it remained more or less at the same level. The continuance of ox keeping on the estates can be explained mainly by the factors mentioned above. In the last decades of the 19th century it began to recede and came to an end with the elimination of the land possessions of the Baltic German landlords in 1917–1920.

At the beginning of the 20th century draught oxen were still used by the peasantry to a greater extent in north-western Estonia, on the island of Hiiumaa and on western Saaremaa where also the traditional local ploughing implements were substantially preserved. Those were typical relic areas in the once basic region of ox keeping where the tradition of using oxen was rooted most deeply. The vanishing ox keeping in this area was given a final blow by the requisitions of World War I after which oxen were not bred any

Table 3

Rural districts	Horses	Oxen	The percentage of oxen
Harjumaa			
Pakri (islets)..........	82	88	*52*
Vihterpalu............	196	105	*35*
Nõva.................	246	109	*31*
Kloostri..............	1203	323	*21*
Saaremaa			
Kihelkonna...........	1051	187	*15*
Mustjala.............	823	104	*11*

more. According to the census of 1925 the total number of oxen in Estonia was 2575. In a greater quantity they were to be found in the rural districts of north-western Harjumaa and north-western Saaremaa[4] (see table 3).

In 1939 only 530 oxen were counted in Estonia, sporadically all over the country.[5] The last citadel of ox keeping was the Nõva rural district in north-western Estonia where 50 oxen were counted. The two last pairs of oxen were in use here till collectivization in 1950.

On the quantity of oxen and horses in Lithuania there are a few data published only beginning with the first half of the 19th century (Dundulienė 1963.139; Ulashchik 1960.150–152). The data of 1831 give us the following numbers in some of the Lithuanian districts:

Table 4

Districts	Draught horses	Draught oxen	The percentage of oxen
The Vilnius gub.			
Oshmeny............	7501	15604	*68*
Vilnius..............	8466	9350	*52*
Trakai (1839)........	3260	3896	*54*
Braslav..............	5045	–	–
The Kaunas gub.			
Kaunas..............	5560	10017	*64*
Raseiniai............	11106	14416	*56*
Upytė (Panevežys).....	15004	4989	*25*
Šiauliai..............	16617	3379	*17*
Telšiai	22600	–	–

Hence the relative importance of oxen in southern and central Lithuania was far greater than in northern Lithuania. The approximate ratio of ox teams to horse teams was 8:9 in the Kaunas district, 3:5 in the Vilnius, Trakai and Raseiniai distr., 1:6 in the Panevežys distr., 1:10 in the Šiauliai distr. and 0:1 in the Telšiai distr. (north-western Lithuania). On the southern neighbouring territories in Byelorussia the role of oxen was even greater than in southern Lithuania. In the Oshmeny district of mixed Byelorussian and Lithuanian population the ratio was 1:1, and in the Grodno guberniya it was even 9:7 according to the data of 1811 (156 936 oxen and 60 586 horses). On the contrary, in the north-eastern neighbouring region of Byelorussia (the Braslav distr.) oxen were missing altogether.

During the 19th century the use of draught oxen declined in Lithuania as well. Already in 1819 it is said about the Kaunas district that in earlier times mostly oxen were used in ploughing, but then horses came to be used more widely (Ławrynowicz 1819.652). Like in Estonia, oxen finally disappeared from the farm fields of Lithuania during the second half of the 19th century. Here they were also displaced firstly in those areas where their role had already been secondary before, i.e. in northern and western Lithuania. In eastern and southern Lithuania (esp. in the Vilnius and Trakai districts) ox keeping remained quite essential up to the end of the 19th century. In Lithuania oxen were also used on estates longer than on farms (Vaitekūnas 1938. 203; Dundulienė 1963.140–141). The last few draught oxen could be seen in south-eastern Lithuania at the end of the 1940s.

One of the most essential factors that made for the decline of ox draught both in Estonia and in Lithuania obviously was the disappearance of serf and statute labour on the estate fields as a result of the reforms in the middle of the 19th century. As we could see, on estates ploughing with oxen was preferred and propagated even where oxen were not popular (in Latvia). To supply peasants with draught animals, a number of estates raised oxen for hiring. As peasants had to cultivate the estate fields with their own teams till the mid-nineteenth century, these efforts of landlords helped to preserve ox keeping on the farms. Serf labour having been abolished, the peasants had a free hand in choosing their own draught animals. Under the new conditions of capitalist development the ox, not fastidious but slow, was replaced by the quicker and more vigorous horse. Moreover, the horse was universal in all kinds of transport, whereas the exploitation of the ox was much more limited. Such factors as the promotion of dairy herds caused by the rapid growth of towns, the improving of the fodder base, the spread of modern agricultural implements, etc. were also of importance. Ox keeping lasted longest in the areas where it was a deeply rooted tradition and where the development of agriculture was slow, as is quite clear in the case of north-western Estonia and West Estonian islands.

Ethnographic material. In Estonia a rich collection of objects and descriptive material about recent ox keeping has been gathered since the year 1910. Most of it is concentrated in the collections of the State Ethnographic Museum in Tartu (descriptions in the collections EA and KV). In Lithuania the respective material is not so abundant. Most of it has been published by *V. Vaitekūnas* (1938) and *P. Dundulienė* (1963), on whose work we shall greatly rely in the following.

In both countries the ox was first and foremost a plough animal. Regardless of this fact already the oldest available sources from all the Estonian and Lithuanian ox-keeping areas and especially the authors of the 18th–19th centuries report that horses too were used in the plough. Usually a pair of oxen or one horse was harnessed to a plough. From south-western Lithuania (Raseiniai distr.) where the so-called "Lithuanian sokha" was used, there is evidence that a pair of oxen or two horses made a plough-team (Reutovich 1852.5; Afanasyev 1861.367). In ploughing the ox was appreciated because of its even and steady tread. For that reason hard soil (e.g. loam) was preferably ploughed with oxen.

In harrowing as a lighter job horses generally were preferred for their being quicker. Nevertheless, the Lithuanian sources of the 19th century speak about harrowing with a pair of oxen, esp. in Žemaitia, rejecting it as waste of labour (Ławrynowicz 1819; Reutovich 1852.6; Afanasyev 1861.368).

In Lithuania wagons were seldom drawn by oxen and in winter transport oxen seem never to have been used. In Estonia, however, oxen were often employed in short distance haulage. In the marshy meadows of north-western Estonia haycocks were drawn on boughs by a pair of oxen. Elsewhere it was usually done with a horse. Oxen transported dung, hay, corn, wood, faggots, stones, etc. In hauling wood and hay oxen were used in winter too. On a narrow winter road a single ox was preferred. Accordingly the single ox yoke was known as the winter yoke and the double yoke as the summer yoke. In north-western Estonia and on the islands special ox wagons and broad low ox sledges for a pair of oxen were in use. More seldom oxen were used on longer routes. Fishermen from the North-Estonian coast villages carried salt fish inland with oxen to sell.

Thus in Estonia the sphere of ox work was much wider than in Lithuania. On the farms where oxen were kept, the main tasks of horses were long distance haulage, light driving and harrowing. A typical task for the horse was also the treading of corn on the threshing-floor for which in the Mediterranean region traditionally oxen were used. Only from north-western Estonia a few cases of exploiting oxen for this purpose are known.

As a rule, only castrated oxen were employed. Usually, a steer was at first used in mating the cows and then at the age of two or three (in Lithuania two) it was castrated. Already in the 17th century the first agricultural handbook in the East Baltic lands recommends the castrating of oxen not before the age of two (Gubert 1688.152). And, as though taking into account the centuries-long experience of the Estonian peasants, C. *Jordan* writes in a mid-nineteenth century handbook: "Sind diese Thiere sehr jung als Kälber verschnitten, so werden sie sehr hoch, langbeinig, bekommen einen weniger gedrungenen, weniger langgestreckten und weniger breiten Körper und mehr ein kuhähnliches Ansehen. Sie setzen bei der Mast viel Fett an und liefern ein ganz besonders zartes Fleisch, sind aber weniger ausdauernd und zur Arbeit sehr schwach, woher man besser thut, seine jungen Bullen in einem jährigen oder anderthalbjährigen Alter zu schneiden ... Noch älter, mit 2, 2¹/₂ oder 3 Jahren geschnittene Thiere sind noch ausdauernder und stärker bei der Arbeit, jedoch meistens etwas wilder und ungelehriger, geben auch mit dem höheren Alter ein etwas grobfaseriges Fleisch" (Jordan 1852.168).

There is a strange discrepancy between this and the following: in Finland draught oxen were castrated as calves at the age of some weeks till a few months, this being the custom in Sweden as well (Vilkuna 1936.59–60; Granlund 1969.108). A brought-up bull was castrated only in rare cases. "Aber ein dem "Kalbochsen" gleichwertiges Zugtier hat er nicht abgegeben; er war faul und leicht erschöpft" (Vilkuna 1936.60). These diametrically opposing statements about the capacity of oxen castrated at different age show to what an extent such opinions depend on an established tradition among the people.

The earliest way of castration used all over Estonia was beating, described by *C. Jordan* as follows: "Die Bauern in den Ostsee-Gouvernements entmannen ihre Bullen, junge wie alte, oft auf eine den Thieren sehr qualvolle ... Weise, indem sie die Hoden auf einer festen Unterlage zwischen zwei hölzerne Brettchen so lange mit einem hölzernen Klöpfel oder Hammer nicht allzu stark klopfen, bis die Hoden etwas dünner, weich und welk geworden sind, was meistens über eine halbe Stunde dauert" (Jordan 1852.174). Such beating, used in the 18th century also in gelding stallions (Hupel 1777.251), survived in some parts of western Estonia till the last days of ox keeping. Yet in general it was not the testicles that were beaten, as said above, but the spermatic cords. The neck of the scrotum was tied to the hammering-stick and beaten on it with the sharp edge of a wooden hammer or with a round stone till the cords were severed (fig. 1). Beaten oxen were considered stronger than cut oxen.

About this ancient way of castrating there are some earlier reports also from the Finnish and Swedish ox-keeping areas (Vilkuna 1936.60, 95–96). Like the head yoke, this also should be considered a relic in the peripheral area of ox keeping. About the ways of castration in Lithuania we have unfortunately no information. We can only suppose that in the 19th century beating was no longer a custom, otherwise it should have aroused attention.

The training of oxen in Estonia and Lithuania, as usual, was begun at the age of three, in Finland already at the age of 1.5–2 years. The methods of training were principally similar in all three countries. For the time being, the young ox was walked with a stick or a rope tied to the horns. The training itself was done always in pair, preferably with an old ox. First the pair of

441

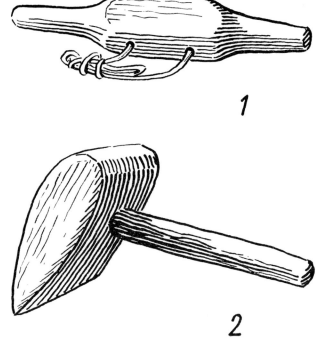

Fig. 1. Castrating instruments: 1) hammering-stick, 2) hammer. South-eastern Estonia (Kambja parish). From the collections of the State Ethnographic Museum, Tartu.

oxen was harnessed to a sledge, then in a few days to a plough. In the beginning the young ox was preceded by a driver who, when necessary, guided it or beat it slightly on the nose if it disobeyed. With a more stubborn ox a rein could be used, tied round the nose and the outside ear. If an ox lay down and would not rise, a fire was made under its tail, a custom known in Estonia and Lithuania.

A trained pair of oxen was together both in work and in the cattle-shed. In the plough and for transport reins were usually not used, and the oxen were driven with certain exclamations and with a whip or a switch. Driving trained oxen with reins occurred in Finland to some extent, the Swedish example being followed here (in Sweden ox reins came into use in the Middle Ages) (Sirelius 1919.419; Granlund 1969.112–114). In Estonia in the 19th century the goad, characteristic of the earlier ox keeping in Europe, was still used sporadically (Viires 1968.158–160). In driving the name of the corresponding ox was called and added to it was an order of one word, in Estonia, for example, *astu!* 'step!' while urging to a quicker pace, *keera!*, *pööra!* 'turn!'

while turning, and *vagu!* 'furrow!' when the ox deviated from the furrow. At the same time the outer side of the ox was beaten slightly not to disturb the other ox. At the end of a furrow oxen turned quicker and more firmly than horses. They also very firmly kept to a furrow or a road. Where there was no way ahead, as in pulling haycocks on a meadow, one had to walk before the oxen.

Oxen were supported at less expence in food than horses. In winter they were fed with rye straw mostly. Before the beginning of the spring ploughing, from March onwards they were given hay and water mixed with chaff and flour. During the summer work period they grazed on a pasture at night, often together with horses, where the village youth watched them.

As usual, oxen were kept till the age of ten (not seldom till the age of 6–7 years only). Then they were fattened or sold without fattening as beef cattle.

On the whole, in using oxen Lithuania, Estonia and Finland had so many features in common that there can hardly be any doubt about ox keeping in these areas being genetically connected. The older elements were preserved longest and in greatest number in Estonia which in recent centuries was isolated from the other ox-keeping areas, whereas Lithuania was in touch with Byelorussia, and Finland was in close relations with Sweden up to the beginning of the 19th century. Some specific features of Finland (e.g. castration at an earlier age and the use of reins) are likely to be connected with Sweden. But in general, the Swedish and East Baltic ox keeping belong to the same culture area.

Archaeological data. Exploitation of horses and oxen as draught animals in the natural conditions of the North-European forest zone can be connected only with agricultural activity. An essential prerequisite for it was the development of plough cultivation, the beginning of which in the forest zone has been by recent studies shifted more and more to a farther past. According to Y. *Krasnov* plough cultivation was known already at the end of the Bronze Age in the southern marginal area of the North-East European forest zone in the Dnieper and Volga-Kama basins. But then it retreated farther south for some time, due to the cooling climate, and began to spread again northward at about the beginning of our era. In the first centuries A.D. it was spread over a large territory including the whole East Baltic area (Krasnov 1968; Moora 1968.241–243). The oldest ard share of north-eastern Europe (from the third or second centuries B.C.) was found in 1961 in the cemetery at Szwajcaria on the territory of the Baltic tribes, now north-eastern Poland, Suwalki (Antoniewicz 1962.208; Gimbutas 1963.114). In his recent monograph on the Early Metal Age in Estonia *V. Lõugas* quite convincingly shows the leading role of plant cultivation beside animal husbandry in Estonia in the first millennium B.C., considering the use of the plough already at that time probable (Lõugas 1970.31–34).

The appearance of the domesticated horse cannot be exactly dated by the archaeological bone finds as there are no established criteria for differentiating the early domestic horse from the wild horse. Using a number of indirect data, different theories on the time and place of domestication have been presented. The best motivated seems *B. Lundholm's* view about the horse having been domesticated in large areas of Europe more or less at the same time, during the period of transition from the Stone Age to the Bronze Age. The first stage of domestication was taking foals from wild or half-wild mare-herds and taming them, as was still customary quite lately on Gotland and in Westphalia (Lundholm 1949.180–182). *K. Vilkuna* has pointed out that similar horse-breeding flourished during the Middle Ages in the Balto-Finnic area in Karelia. At the same time he points to Herberstein's statement that in Lithuania wild horses were still quite usual in the middle of the 16th century (Vilkuna 1967.32–48; cf. Paaver 1965.183).

According to *K. Paaver* the wild horse was common in the whole East Baltic area till the second millennium B.C. But already at the beginning of the first millennium sure bone finds of the domesticated horse make their appearance in the fortified settlements of this area (Paaver 1965.180–182, 364–369, 393; Krysiak 1958.72–74). Unfortunately, by these finds we cannot judge whether the horse was used as a draught animal. The bones are to be found mainly among the remnants of cookery and are often broken, thus implying the use of the horse for food first and foremost, as was also the custom in the neighbouring territories. During the first millennium A.D. the number of horse bones in settlement and hill-fort finds in the whole of eastern Europe considerably decreases. This has been interpreted as the sign of desisting from using horse meat for food, and of the rapidly growing importance of the horse as a draught animal due to plough cultivation becoming the leading branch of economy (Tsalkin 1956.141–143, 146; Tsalkin 1962.66–67; Paaver, Kulikauskas 1965.277). Presumably the tribes of the Chernyakhov culture in the forest steppe west of the middle Dnieper in the second to the fourth centuries A.D. were the first in eastern Europe to use the horse more constantly instead of the ox as a draught animal (Tsalkin 1962.70–71; Tsalkin 1966.79–81; 92). From here the custom of harnessing the horse in the plough may have spread northward to the area of the Baltic tribes. A probable precondition for that was the coming into use of the horse-collar (cf. Viires 1970.288–289).

All this by no means denies the possibility that the horse was used in lighter transport and for riding much earlier (cf. Clark, Piggott 1965.319). Clear evidence is the mouth-pieces of bone found in the Estonian fortified settlements of Asva and Iru dating from the middle of the first millennium B.C. (Lõugas 1970.34; Vassar 1939.81, fig. 46:5). In addition there is a number of engravings representing men on horseback and four-wheeled wagons drawn by two horses to be found on the Early Iron Age face-urns from the area of the West Baltic tribes on the southern coast of the Baltic Sea in Pomorze, esp. in the delta of the Vistula (La Baume 1924; La Baume 1928.32, 34, 38, tables 10, 12, 16; Gimbutas 1963.78, tables 14, 15). Consequently, in the first millennium B.C. the horse was quite widely used in transport on the south-eastern and eastern coast of the Baltic Sea.

Burials with horses in the Prussian and Lithuanian areas beginning from the last centuries B.C. and becoming most popular in the 9th–12th centuries A.D. are usually interpreted as the graves of mounted warriors (e.g. Kulikauskienė 1953.221–222; Gimbutas 1963.164–165). The Polish archaeologist J. Jaskanis recently expressed the view that the numerous horse burials in the "poor" graves (without grave-goods) of the earlier period rather speak about the economic importance of the horse and about its essential role in farming and herding the domestic animals (Jaskanis 1966.60–65).

On the basis of bone finds it can be said that the ancient horse in northern and central Europe was of a small or a middle height (Lundholm 1949.124–127; Vitt 1952.186). The prehistoric domestic horses of the North-East European forest zone were mostly small, with a shoulder height of 120–128 cm, whereas the middle height grew a little greater by the end of the first millennium of our era. This has been explained as a result of a more intensive use of the horse in transport (Tsalkin 1962.45–46; Tsalkin 1966.48). The ancient horse in the Baltic lands was also small. The domestic horses of the Prussian and Lithuanian tribes are unanimously considered the domesticated species of the local sylvan tarpan *(Equus gmelini)*. All this is in accordance with *B. Lundholm's* view on the process of horse domestication in Europe.

In Latvia especially small horses (with an average shoulder height of 122 cm) were spread in Kurzeme and in the Semigallian area of the Lielupe river-basin. Eastward on the Daugava the average shoulder height was 130 cm (Tsalkin 1962.101–102, 105–109). The small but steady horse in the western parts of the Baltic area, in Žemaitia, Kurzeme and on the West Estonian islands is praised in local publications up to the 20th century. And it is quite probable that the wide use of the two-horse team in Žemaitia, Kurzeme and earlier also on western Saaremaa is partly due to the small size of the local horse.

As to draught oxen the archaeological material in the East Baltic area presents very little evidence. By the bone finds only the antiquity and prominence of cattle among domestic animals is proved. But the existing finds do not permit anything to be said about castration as an essential piece of evidence for ox keeping. If in prehistoric times oxen were castrated here when grown-up, like in the 18th–20th centuries, it is difficult to find any traces of it in the bones. On the other hand, the antiquity of ox castration is generally accepted (Clark, Piggott 1965.171). In the central German area, for instance, castrated oxen existed already in the earlier period of the Neolithic Linear Pottery culture (Müller 1964.146).

In the light of *V. Tsalkin's* studies the castration of oxen and, accordingly, the use of draught oxen in the Late Bronze Age and Early Iron Age was widely spread in eastern Europe and in the Urals, including the forested upper Volga basin and the Valdai hills, the area of the Dyakovo culture ascribed mostly to the Finno-Ugric tribes. There farming was probably less developed than in the East Baltic area. True, the percentage of oxen in the forest zone remained quite small if compared with the southward steppes and forest steppes, but nevertheless, Tsalkin considers this the proof of horses being preceded here by oxen as draught animals (Tsalkin 1962.22, 30; Tsalkin 1966. 19, 24, 92). Lastly, the Danish yoke finds from the Early Iron Age, and the images of oxen before the plough or the cart on the South Scandinavian rock-engravings dating from the Bronze Age, are generally known.

On this evidence from the closer and farther neighbouring territories, we must admit that oxen in the East Baltic area were most likely used as plough and draught animals at a very early date.

Linguistic evidence.[6] A large number of words signifying the horse with the local people seem to confirm the view that the wild horse in the Baltic area was actually domesticated on the spot. For instance, Estonian *hobu, hobune*, Livish *e'bbi*, etc. 'horse' meaning originally 'mare', is an ancient word of a descriptive origin, known in all the Balto-Finnic languages and dating most probably from the time before our era (cf. Vilkuna 1967.31, 45). First it was used as a call- and pet-word, and this was possible only in the case of a domesticated horse. Est. *varss*, Liv. *vārza* 'foal', Est. *sälg* 'colt, filly' (originally "slender, slim"), and Finnish *ori* 'stallion' preserved in Estonian only in old folk songs are also old Balto-Finnic common words (Saareste 1924.49; Vilkuna 1967.31). Disputable is the age of the Germanic loanword, Est. *mära*, Finn. *mera* 'mare'. In *K. Vilkuna's* opinion it is also of a quite ancient origin (Vilkuna 1967.42–43).

In the Baltic languages the old name for the horse is Lettish *zirgs*, Lithuanian *žirgas* ('riding horse'), Prussian *sirgis* ('stallion'). To the old original terminology belong also Lett. *kumeļš*, Lith. *kumeliùkas* 'foal', Lith. *kũmelė* 'mare', *kumelỹs* 'stallion'; Lett. *ērzelis*, Lith. *eržilas* 'stallion', Lett. *ķēve* 'mare', Lith. *kèvė* 'jade'.

The current Lithuanian word *arklỹs* 'horse' is connected with the stem *árti* 'to plough' and accordingly has the original meaning of a plough animal. J. Jurginis has considered it an evidence of the long use of the horse as a plough animal in Lithuania (Jurginis 1955.62; Jurginis 1962.51; cf. Dundulienė 1956.6). But against the great age of this name speaks the mere fact that the word is to be found only in Lithuanian. Evidently it is more recent than the other Baltic words for the horse and has come into use in a time when it became necessary to make a difference between the draught horse and the riding horse *(žirgas)*.

As to the words for the ox, it should be mentioned that, as in other languages, they often mean the bull as well. Therefore on the basis of these words it is fairly difficult to draw reliable conclusions about the use of draught oxen. Nevertheless, it must be pointed out that the Balto-Finnic word for the ox, Est. *härg*, Finn. *härkä*, Liv. *ārga*, etc., is most likely an old Baltic loanword, the source being the name for the horse in the Baltic languages, cf. Lett. *zirgs*, etc. It is widely known that the names of animals are easily transmitted from one species to another. In the above case *W. Thomsen* has suggested a more original meaning of 'a pulling draught animal with a stiff neck' (cf. Kalima 1936.103). This supposition has been strongly criticized by *V. Ruoppila* presenting the point of view that the original meaning of the Balto-Finnic word was not 'draught animal' but simply 'big animal' (Ruoppila 1943.114–120). That the Balto-Finnic tribes, after all, have learned much from the Balts in using draught animals is shown by such old Baltic loans as Est. *ais* 'shaft', *regi* 'sledge', *ratas* 'wheel', etc. Finnish *juhta* 'draught animal (a horse, an ox)' is probably also of the Baltic origin, cf. Lith. *jùngti* 'to yoke', Lett. *jūgt* 'to harness'. With such a background the word *härg* 'ox' seems most likely to have been applied originally just to a (big) draught animal.

Seemingly also of Baltic origin is the Est. *värss*, *härjavärss* 'steer, young bull bred to an ox'. The word has been widespread in nearly the whole area of the Estonian language, excluding south-eastern Estonia where draught oxen were less popular. The Baltic equivalent is an old name for the ox: Lett. *vērsis* 'ox, bull', Lith. *veršis* 'ox, bull, steer', Prussian *werstian* 'calf'. The semantic connection is obvious, thus there can hardly be any doubt about the Baltic origin of the Estonian word although it is missing in the corresponding studies of loanwords.[7] The most common word for the ox in Lithuanian, *jautis*, has no direct equivalents in other languages but is connected with an old Indo-European stem having, inter alia, the meaning 'anziehen, anspannen, anbinden, etc.' and thus surely indicating a draught animal.

It should also be pointed out that while the words for the draught oxen both in the Estonian and the Lettish and Lithuanian languages are very old, the most common word for the bull in all the three languages (Est. *pull*, Lett. *bullis*, Lith. *bulius*) is of a much later origin (< Middle Low German *bulle* 'id.'). In the light of the recent Estonian ethnographic material it becomes clear that this word spread with special breeding bulls raised on the estates, while the peasants originally made a difference only by the age: a young bull *(värss)* was used for a year or two in mating cows, then it was castrated and turned into a draught ox *(härg)*. Between Lith. *veršis* and *jautis* there seems to have been a similar difference.

Thus in the Baltic countries (incl. Latvia) the words signifying the ox are quite ancient. The common word for 'to castrate' in the Estonian-Finnish ox-keeping area, Est. *kohitsema, kohima*, Finn. *kuohia*, also dates from the far past. The words for gelding, on the other hand, are much younger as is generally characteristic of a large part of Europe. This only underlines the well-known fact that the use of mares as draught animals is more universal and ancient than the use of cows, owing to which the gelding of stallions was not of vital importance. But to a certain extent it also shows the later origin of the exploitation of the horse in heavy draught when compared with the ox. Est. *ruun*, Finn. *ruuna*, Liv. *rūna* and Lett. *rūnis* 'gelding' come from Middle Low German *rūne*. Of the same origin is the verb, Est. *ruunama*, Finn. *ruunata*, Liv. *rūnə̂*, Lett. *rūnīt*, meaning originally 'to castrate a horse' but having later extended to other animals as well. The etymology of Low German *rūne* points to hammering in castration of the horse (cf. Vilkuna 1936.96). Most words for gelding in the European languages appearing only in the Middle Ages refer to the skill of cutting stallions learned from the more easterly peoples, e.g. Russian *мерин* (< Mongolian), German *Reuss, Wallach*, Swedish *valack*, Finnish *valakka*, French *hongre*, etc. All these words are originally connected with geldings imported from the eastern countries, or with professional wandering gelders coming from these countries who practised cutting instead of beating in castration. In the Baltic lands the corresponding men were mostly Russians which is proved by the North-East Estonian word *kanavaal* 'gelder' (< Russian *конобал* 'wandering horse-curer'). This work was done also by Hungarians (Hungarian gipsies; Jordan 1852. 168; Vilkuna 1936.97), especially on estates. This is suggested by the Baltic-German loan-word Est. *ungur*, Liv. *ūngar*, Lett. *unguris* 'gelder' (< Baltic-German *Ungar, Unger* "Hungarian"; Virányi 1938.857–859; Kettunen 1938. 461). That cutting stallions was known in the eastern neighbourhood of the Baltic countries already at the end of the first millennium A.D. is shown by a bundle of wooden castrating clips found in Staraya Ladoga and dating from the 7th–9th centuries (Orlov 1954.352, fig. 8). Such clips belonged to the gelder's equipment also in Estonia till the recent times.

In the use of draught animals, close Baltic and Balto-Finnic relations are also indicated by some additional linguistic data. For instance, the custom of calling oxen by their colour was common over the whole Baltic and Finnish ox-keeping area (Vilkuna 1936.93–94; Vaitekūnas 1938.209). Both linguistic groups have in common a number of old words specially pointing to the colour of a horse (or a bovine), e.g. Est. *lauk*, Finn. *laukki*, Liv. *laìk̆* ~ Lett. *laùks*, Lith. *laũkas* 'blazed horse (ox, cow)'; Est. *paat*, Finn. *paatti* ~ Lett. *pāt(i)s* 'fawn (horse)'; Est. *hall*, Finn. *halli* ~ Lett. *šaln̂is*, Lith. *šalnis* 'grey (horse, ox)'; Est. *raudjas*, Finn. *rautias, raudakko*, etc. ~ Lett. *raũdis*, Lith. *raũdis* 'chestnut (horse)'; Est. *ruske*, Finn. *rusko* 'red (ox, horse)' ~ Lett. *ruzgs, ruskans* 'rötlich, rotbraun'. The similarity of the two last Balto-Finnic and Baltic word-groups has up to now been regarded as an incidental phonetic parallelism (Kalima 1936. 19–20, 158). But considering the exact semantic accordance and other analogical common names for colour, there can hardly be any doubt about their belonging together.

In another connection I have already pointed out the fact that the terminology concerning the old head yoke of oxen in Estonian and Finnish as well as in Lithuanian and Lettish also dates from the far past, although here no direct mutual relations are apparent (Viires 1969.132–134).

Our linguistic data lead us to conclude that both the horse and the ox in the East Baltic area surely reach back to a far past. At the same time, they do not allow us to say anything definite about the priority of either one or the other. But we can be quite sure that the old names for the ox and the yoke in the Lettish language indicate the prehistoric use of the ox as a draught animal by the Letts also. The linguistic material clearly shows that the use of the tractive power of animals by the Balto-Finnic and Baltic tribes developed in close mutual relationship, the receivers being the Baltic Finns, in the earlier periods at least.

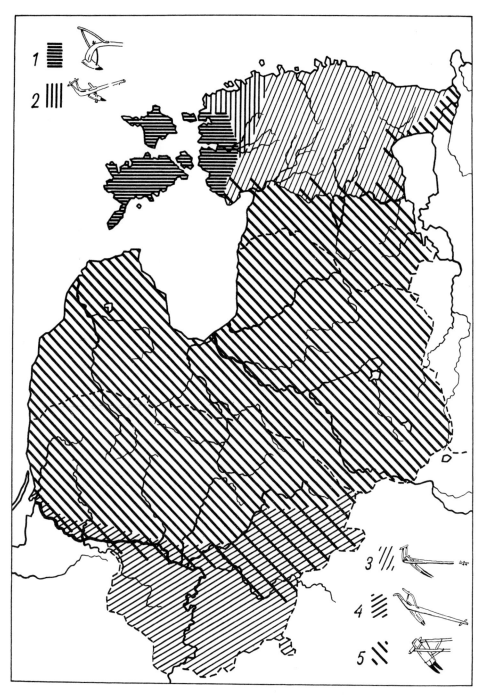

Map 4. The distribution of traditional plough types in Baltic countries in the late 19th century. (After Moora 1968; Dunduliené 1963).

Conclusion. To sum up all the above material, we can say that the Estonian-Lettish horse-ox dichotomy is beyond doubt quite old. It was apparent already in the 13th century. But it would be wrong to state that the Baltic peoples originally employed the horse which was later superseded by the ox in the Lithuanian area.

It seems to be plausible that in ploughing (this as the most typical ox-work is the clue to the problem) both the ox and the horse were used in the whole East Baltic area already in the earliest times. First the ox dominated but then the spread of the horse-collar in the middle of the first millennium of our era made it possible to employ the horse more widely in the plough. The corresponding development of the Chernyakhov culture in the Dnieper area may have served as an example in using the horse.

Yet why did the Letts prefer horses in ploughing while the Lithuanians did not? Here the reason seems to be in the different plough-types. Pointing out the difference of the plough-types in northern and southern Lithuania, *P. Dunduliene* considers the use of oxen in southern Lithuania more general than in northern Lithuania already long ago. She refers also to *A. Guagnini's* remark from the 16th century that the Žemaitians cultivate land with small and steady horses (Dunduliene 1956.32–33; Dunduliene 1963.137–138). Thus the relatively rare use of oxen in northern Lithuania in the 19th century is possibly an old tradition as was also the case in southern Estonia. The long-lasting secondary role of oxen in field work may have led to the preservation of the ancient head-yoke in Žemaitia up to our days although the neighbouring areas used the withers yoke.

On the basis of the Estonian material *H. Ligi* stresses still more explicitly the connection between draught animals and local plough types (Ligi 1969. 218). Comparing the distribution of different plough types in the Baltic countries (map 4) with the distribution of oxen, it is evident that ploughing with oxen in Estonia is connected mainly with the sole ard and the crook ard (1,2) in north-western Estonia and on the islands, to a lesser degree with the North Estonian sokha (3), the hybrid form of the crook ard and the sokha, and in Lithuania with the so-called Lithuanian sokha (4) known in southern and eastern Lithuania and wide-spread also southward, in the Byelorussian ox-keeping areas. The East European light sokha (5) known in the whole Lettish area, in southern Estonia and northern Lithuania, is in its construction a typical horse-drawn implement with two short draught poles. The horse is its natural companion. When used with a pair of oxen as was done in southern Estonia and northern Lithuania, its construction had to be correspondingly adjusted. In each separate area this was done in a different way. In southern

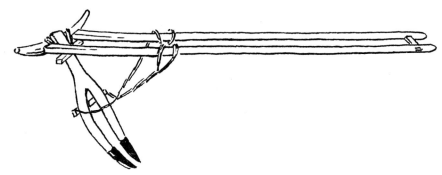

Fig. 2. Ox-sokha, south-western Estonia (Pärnumaa), late 18th century. (After J. Chr. Brotze.)

Estonia the front ends of the draught poles were drawn closer and joined so that they supplied the beam of the ox-plough (fig. 2) (cf. Hupel 1777.276–277). In northern Lithuania the end of the beam was fastened in the forked working part or the handle, or it was split from behind as was done with the North Estonian sokha (Dunduliené 1963.96–97, 100). All these are distinct reconstructions instead of the original two draught poles.

The original ox ploughs, on the other hand, were adjusted for one horse by cutting the beam shorter and fastening to this the pair of draught poles in one or another way. This may be observed on the West Estonian islands and in north-western Estonia as well as in southern Lithuania (Dunduliené 1963. fig. 17 and 38; Hagar 1949. fig. 5 and 6).

In the light of archaeological finds the sokha in eastern Europe came into use during the transition from the first millennium to the second. It soon spread to the East Baltic area where its shares have been found especially on Latvian territory (Moora 1968.247–249). Why did this new horse-plough not spread all over the Baltic area? Partly it was caused by the soil conditions, which is evident especially in Estonia and Latvia (cf. Moora 1968. fig. 1, 6a, 8). Partly the new sokha was stopped by the ethnic, i.e. tribal boundaries. Thus in Lithuania it was distributed especially in Žemaitia, and in southern Estonia its region extended to the South Estonian dialect border, also a former tribal border.

We can state with assurance that besides oxen horses were used with the old local ploughing implements already long ago, as was frequent in the 17th–19th centuries. But it was obviously only with this new plough type that the horse became the main draught animal in the whole Lettish area and superseded to a certain degree the ox in the neighbouring areas of southern Estonia and northern Lithuania.

452

Notes

1. For compiling the map data, the following source publications are summed up: Liivimaa 1638.a. maarevisjon. Eesti asustusala I. Kaguosa. Tartu 1941; Dunsdorfs 1938–1941, tables 43–45, 52, 56, 69.
2. The abrupt decrease in the number of oxen (and cows) and increase in that of horses on the island of Saaremaa in 1744–1757 *H. Ligi* rightly considers a temporary phenomenon, due to the violent epidemics in cattle current on the island.
3. According to calculations the ratio of the tractive power of an average draught horse to that of a draught ox is 1:0.66 (Forbes 1965. 85, table IV).
4. The data from: 1925.a. põllumajandusliku üleskirjutuse andmed, Tallinn 1926, table 12.
5. III põllumajandusloendus 1939.a. Vihk I. Tallinn 1940, table VII-a.
6. Where there are no other references, the etymologies of the Balto-Finnic words come from the following sources: Toivonen, Itkonen, Joki 1955–1969; Ruoppila 1943, and the Baltic etymologies from the following: Fraenkel 1962–1965; Mühlenbach, Endzelin 1923–1932.
7. Saareste 1924. 52 gives to the Estonian *värss* a German etymology (cf. Germ. *Färse* 'heifer'), but as the Baltic equivalent is exact both phonetically and semantically, the Baltic origin is more feasible.

Bibliography

Afanasyev, D. 1861: Д. Афанасьев, Ковенская губерния. (Материалы для географии и статистики России, собранные офицерами генерального штаба.) С.-Петербург.

Antoniewicz, Jerzy. 1962: Odkrycie grobu rolnika jaćwieskiego z narzędziami produkcji z okresu rzymskiego. – Rocznik Białostokí, t. III Białystok, pp. 205–223.

Bentzien, Ulrich. 1964: Pferde und Ochsen als Spannvieh in der mecklenburgischen Landwirtschaft vor dem Dreissigjährigen Krieg. – Zeitschrift für Agrargeschichte und Agrarsoziologie (Frankfurt a.M.), 1964, H. 1, pp. 21–28.

Bosse, Heinrich. 1933: Der livländische Bauer am Ausgang der Ordenszeit (bis 1561). – Mitteilungen aus der livländischen Geschichte (Riga), 24. Bd., 4. H., pp. 281–511.

Brackel, H. v. 1841: Nachtrag zu dem Aufsatze »zur Kenntniss der Alterthümer besonders aus Bronze, die in den Ostsee-Provinzen aus der Erde gegraben werden«. – Mittheilungen aus dem Gebiete der Geschichte Liv-, Ehst- und Kurland's (Riga und Leipzig), II. Bd., 2. H., pp. 340–378.

Brieflade = Est- und Livländische Brieflade. Hrsg. von R. Toll, F. G. Bunge und andere. I–IV. Reval 1856–1887.

Clark, Grahame, and Piggott, Stuart. 1965: Prehistoric Societies. London.

Doroshenko, V. V. 1959: В. В. Дорошенко, Сельское хозяйство феодальной Лифляндии (Видземе) в XIII–XVI веках. Материалы по истории сельского хозяйства и крестьянства СССР. III. Москва, pp. 41–88.

– 1960: Очерки аграрной истории Латвии в XVI веке. Рига.

Dunduliene, P. 1956: П. Дундулене, Земледелие в Литве в эпоху феодализма. – Балтийский этнографический сборник. (Труды Института этнографии, новая серия, т. XXXII.) Москва, pp. 3–47.

– 1963: Žemdirbystė Lietuvoje. (Nuo seniausių laikų iki 1917 metų.) Vilnius.

Dunsdorfs, Edgars. 1938–1941: Die Hakenrevision Livlands 1638 (lettischer Teil). (Quellen zur Geschichte Lettlands, Bd. IV). Riga.

Fenton, Alexander. 1969: Draught Oxen in Britain. – Národopisný věstník Československý, ročník III–IV. Brno-Praha, pp. 17–51.

Forbes, R. J. 1965: Studies in Ancient Technology. Vol. II. Second revised edition. Leiden.

Fraenkel, Ernst. 1962–1965: Litauisches etymologisches Wörterbuch. I–II. Heidelberg-Göttingen.

Friebe, W. Ch. 1803: Grundsätze zu einer theorethischen und praktischen Verbesserung der Landwirtschaft in Liefland. II. Bd. Riga.

Gimbutas, Marija. 1963: The Balts. London.

Gorsky, A. D. 1959: А. Д. Горский, Из истории земледелия в северо-восточной Руси XIV–XV веков. – Материалы по истории сельского хозяйства и крестьянства СССР. Ш. Москва, pp. 5–40.

Gotye, Y. V. 1937: Ю. В. Готье, Замосковный край в XVII веке. 2 изд. Москва.

Granlund, John. 1969: Rinderanspannung und Joche in Schweden. – Národopisný věstník Československý, ročník III–IV. Brno-Praha, pp. 99–118.

Gubert, Salomon. 1688: Stratagema oeconomicum, Oder Akker-Student. [4th impr.] Riga.

Hagar, Helmut. 1949: Zur Geschichte des baltischen Hakenpfluges. – Apophoreta Tartuensia. Stockholm, pp. 119–128.

Heinrich von Lettland. 1959: Livländische Chronik. Neu übersetzt von Albert Bauer. Würzburg.

Hupel, August Wilhelm. 1777: Topographische Nachrichten von Lief- und Ehstland. Zweyter Band. Riga.

– 1789: Die gegenwärtige Verfassung der Rigischen und der Revalschen Statthalterschaft. Riga.

– 1796: Oekonomisches Handbuch für Lief- und Ehstländische Gutsherren. Erster Theil. Riga.

Jablonskis, K. 1937: Arklas ir jaučio jungas praeity. – Gimtasai Kraštas (Šiauliai), Nr. 1 (13), pp. 41–45.

Jacobeit, Wolfgang. 1957: Jochgeschirr- und Spanntiergrenze. – Deutsches Jahrbuch für Volkskunde. Dritter Band, Teil I. Berlin, pp. 119–144.

Jaskanis, Jan. 1966: Human Burials with Horses in Prussia und Sudovia in the First Millennium of Our Era. – Acta Baltico-Slavica IV. Białystock, pp. 29–65.

Johansen, Paul. 1925: Das älteste Wackenbuch des Revaler St. Johannis-Siechenhauses. 1435–1507. (Publikationen aus dem Revaler Stadtarchiv. IV. Folge, 2.) Reval.

– 1928: Beiträge zur älteren estnischen Agrargeschichte. – Beiträge zur Kunde Estlands (Reval), XIII. Bd., 5. H., pp. 144–157.

Jordan, Carl. 1852: Praktisches Handbuch der Rindviehzucht, oder vollständige Anleitung zur Zucht, Pflege und Nutzung des Rindes. Dorpat.

Jordan, Paul. 1871: Beiträge zur Statistik des Gouvernements Ehstland. Zweiter Band. Reval.

– 1889: Beiträge zur Geographie und Statistik des Gouvernements Ehstland nebst einem Anhange: »Ueber die Bauerburgen«. Reval.

[Jung-Stilling, Fr. v.] 1885: Materialien zur Kenntniss der livländischen Agrarverhältnisse mit besonderer Berücksichtigung der Knechts- und Tagelöhner-Bevölkerung. Riga.

Jurginis, J. 1955: Ю. М. Юргинис, Земледедие и техника сельского хозяйства Литвы в XIII–XV веках. – Труды Академии наук Литовской ССР, Серия А, 1 (Вильнюс), pp. 57–73.

– 1962: Baudžiavos įsigalėjimas Lietuvoje. Vilnius.

Kalima, Jalo. 1936: Itämerensuomalaisten kielten balttilaiset lainasanat. (Suomalaisen Kirjallisuuden Seuran Toimituksia 202.) Helsinki.

Kettunen, Lauri. 1938: Livisches Wörterbuch mit grammatischer Einleitung. (Lexica Societatis Fenno-ugricae V.) Helsinki.

Kochin, G. Y. 1965: Г. Е. Кочин, Сельское хозяйство на Руси в период образования Русского централизованного государства, конец XIII–начало XVI в. Москва-Ленинград.

Krasnov, Y. A. 1968: Ю. А. Краснов, О возникновении пашенного земледелия в лесной полосе Восточной Европы. – Советская археология (Москва), № 2, pp. 3–22.

Krysiak, Kazimierz. 1958: Charakterystyka materiału zwierzęcego ze stanowiska w Jeziorku, pow. Giżycko. – Materiały starożytne III. Warszawa, pp. 71–74.

Kulikauskienė, R. K. 1953: Р. К. Куликаускене, Погребения с конями у древних литовцев. – Советская археология XVII. Москва, pp. 211–222.

La Baume, Wolfgang. 1924: Wagendarstellungen auf ostgermanischen Urnen der frühen Eisenzeit und ihre Bedeutung. – Blätter für deutsche Vorgeschichte (Danzig), H. 1, pp. 5–28.

– 1928: Bildliche Darstellungen auf ostgermanischen Tongefässen der frühen Eisenzeit. – IPEK (Leipzig), pp. 25–56.

Ławrynowicz, Symeon. 1819: O rolnictwie powiatu Kowieńskiego w Gubernii Wileńskiey. – Dziennik Wileński (Wilno), t. I, Nr. 6, pp. 647–666.

Ligi, Herbert. 1969: Veloomadest Eestis feodalismi perioodil. – Etnograafiamuuseumi Aastaraamat XXIV. Tallinn, pp. 195–222.

LUB = Liv-, Est- und Kurländisches Urkundenbuch. I–XII. Reval, Riga u. Leipzig 1853–1910.

Lundholm, Bengt. 1949: Abstammung und Domestikation des Hauspferdes. – Zoologiska bidrag från Uppsala XXVII, pp. 1–287.

Lõugas, V. 1970: В. А. Лыугас, Период раннего металла в Эстонии (с середины II тыс. до н.э. до начала н.э.). Автореферат диссертации на соискание ученой степени кандидата исторических наук. Таллин.

Mellin, [Ludwig August]. 1831: Ueber den Gebrauch der Pferde und Ochsen beim Pflügen, wie auch anderweitigen Anspann bei den Bauern. – Livländische Jahrbücher der Landwirtschaft. 6. Bd. 3. St. Dorpat, pp. 341–358.

Moora, H. 1968: Zur älteren Geschichte des Bodenbaues bei den Esten und ihren Nachbarvölkern. – Congressus secundus internationalis fenno-ugristarum, pars II. Helsinki, pp. 239–257.

Mühlenbach, K., Endzelin, J. 1923–1932: K. Mühlenbachs Lettisch-deutsches Wörterbuch. Redigiert, ergänzt und fortgesetzt von J. Endzelin. I–IV. Riga.

Müller, Hanns-Hermann. 1964: Die Haustiere der mitteldeutschen Bandkeramiker auf Grund osteologischer Untersuchungen. – EAZ (Berlin), pp. 145–149.

Orlov, S. N. 1954: С. Н. Орлов, Остатки сельскохозяйственного инвентаря VII–X вв. из Старой Ладоги. – Советская археология XXI. Москва-Ленинград, pp. 343–354.

Paaver, K. 1965: К. Паавер, Формирование териофауны и изменчивость млекопитающих Прибалтики в голоцене. Тарту.

Paaver, K., Kulikauskas, P. 1965: Znaleziska kości zwierzęcych z grodzisk i osad z okresu wczesnożelaznego i rzymskiego na Litwie. – Acta Baltico-Slavica II, Białystok, pp. 261–279.

Reutovich, D. 1852: Д. Реутович, Хозяйство Жмуди. – Библиотека для чтения (С.-Петербург). Т. 114.IV. Промышленность и хозяйство, pp. 1–14.

Ruoppila, Veikko. 1943: Kotieläinten nimitykset suomen murteissa. I. (Suomalaisen Kirjallisuuden Seuran Toimituksia 222.) Helsinki.

Saareste, Albert. 1924: Leksikaalseist vahekordadest eesti murretes. I. (Acta et Commentationes Universitatis Dorpatensis B VI. 1.) Tartu.

Sirelius, U. T. 1919: Suomen kansanomaista kulttuuria. I. Helsinki.

Soom, Arnold. 1954: Der Herrenhof in Estland im 17. Jahrhundert. Lund.

Stackelberg, F. 1928: Das älteste Wackenbuch der Wiek. (1518–1544). – Sitzungsberichte der Gelehrten Estnischen Gesellschaft 1927, Tartu, pp. 78–254.

Szabó, István. 1966: Ungarns Landwirtschaft von der Mitte des 14. Jahrhunderts bis zu den 1530-er Jahren. Die Agro- und Zootechnik. – Agrártörténeti szemle. 1966. Supplementum. Budapest.

Tarvel, E. 1966: Adramaa XIII sajandil. – Eesti NSV Teaduste Akadeemia Toimetised, Ühiskonnateaduste seeria (Tallinn), Nr. 1, pp. 27–40.

Toivonen, Y. H., Itkonen, Erkki, Joki, Aulis J. 1955–1969: Suomen kielen etymologinen sanakirja I–IV. (Lexica Societatis Fenno-ugricae XII.) Helsinki.

Tsalkin, V. I. 1956: В. И. Цалкин, Материалы для истории скотоводства и охоты в древней Руси. (Материалы и исследования по археологии СССР № 51.) Москва.

– 1962: К истории животноводства и охоты в Восточной Европе. (Материалы и исследования по археологии СССР № 107.) Москва.

– 1966: Древнее животноводство племен Восточной Европы и Средней Азии. (Материалы и исследования по археологии СССР № 135.) Москва.

Ulashchik, N. N. 1960: Н. Н. Улащик, Скотоводство в Литве и в западной Белоруссии (1811–1861 гг.). – Материалы по истории сельского хозяйства и крестьянства СССР. IV. Москва pp. 139–172.

Vaitekūnas, V. 1938: Arimas jaučiais. (Etnografijai škicas.) – Gimtasai Kraštas (Šiauliai), Nr. 1–2 (17–18), pp. 203–213.

Vassar, A. 1939: Iru linnapära. – Muistse Eesti linnused. Tartu, pp. 53–100.

Viires, Ants. 1968: Härjarakend Baltimaades. – Etnograafiamuuseumi Aastaraamat XXIII. Tallinn, pp. 134–174.

– 1969: Rinderanschirrung im Baltikum. – Národopisný věstník Československý, ročník III–IV. Brno-Praha, pp. 121–136.

– 1970: Itämerensuomalaisten hevosvaljaiden historiasta. – Kalevalaseuran Vuosikirja 50. Helsinki, pp. 282–309.

Vilkuna, Kustaa. 1936: Verwendung von Zugochsen in Finnland. – Studia Fennica II. Helsinki, pp. 55–98.

– 1949: När kommo östersjöfinnarna till Baltikum? – Folk-Liv XII–XIII. Stockholm, pp. 15–43.

– 1967: Zur Geschichte des finnischen Pferdes. – Studia Fennica XIII. Helsinki, pp. 5–49.

Virányi, Elemér. 1938: Ungari sõnad ja ungari kohta käivad väljendid eesti murretes. – Liber saecularis II (Õpetatud Eesti Seltsi Toimetused XXX), Tartu, pp. 854–859.

Vitt, V. O. 1952: В. О. Витт, Лошади Пазырыкских курганов. – Советская археология XVI. Москва-Ленинград, pp. 163–205.

Die Gleit- und Laufschiene des Seehundfängers

Von KUSTAA VILKUNA

Auf dem Bottnischen Meerbusen – vor allem in der Gegend des Nordkvark und nördlich davon – wird bis in die heutige Zeit eifrig Jagd auf Seehunde gemacht. Das neueste Transportmittel sind die Motorschlitten, die zu Beginn der sechziger Jahre aufkamen. Immer noch braucht der Seehundfänger jedoch ein ganz bestimmtes Gerät, wenn er sich im Spätwinter einem auf dem Eis liegenden Seehund nähert: die sog. Gleitschiene, für die die Finnen den Namen *ajopuu* (*ajo* 'Jagd, Treiben', *puu* 'Holz') haben und die Schweden *skridstång* (*skrida* 'schreiten, gleiten', *stång* 'Stange'). In den schwedischen Diaiekten der finnischen Provinz Ostbottnien gelten die Bezeichnungen *ränn-stången, rännstaandjen* (*ränn* 'Lauf') und *fälstång* (*fäl* < *färd* 'Fahrt').

Die Gleitschiene ähnelt einem grossen Ski, sie ist 3,5–4,5 m lang und 7–10 cm breit. Der Hauptteil besteht aus einer etwas nach oben gewölbten, aus Birkenholz geschnitzten Schiene oder Kufe, deren Vorderteil in einem flachen Bug ausläuft, wie auch hinten die Schiene etwas erhöht ist. Die Gleitschiene ist somit leicht beweglich, sowohl nach vorn als auch nach hinten. Unter der Schiene verläuft heute ein Messing- oder Kupferblech, früher bildete eine Platte aus dem harten Splintteil der Kiefer (fi. *talla*) den Schutz. War eine solche Schutz-"sohle" auf dem schartigen Eis abgenutzt worden, konnte sie durch eine neue ersetzt werden: die eigentliche Schiene blieb die alte. Zwischen dem Metallschutz und dem Holz kann ein Stück Stoff angebracht sein, wodurch das Scharren gedämpft wird, das durch die Bewegung auf dem unebenen Eis verursacht wird. Vom Mittelpunkt aus etwas nach vorn befindet sich der Handgriff, an dem die Schiene bei Bedarf hochgehoben werden kann und in den der Seehundfänger bei Benutzung der Kufe seinen Schuh mit der Spitze hineinschiebt. Dahinter liegt heute eine Korkplatte als Unterlage für die Sohle. Die älteren Gleitschienen hatten hinten zwei aus Holz geschnitzte Widerhaken, um die die Harpunenschnur gewickelt und wo die Harpunen-spitze befestigt war (Abb. 2); vorn befand sich ein Ständer für die Büchse und ein Loch für die Errichtung eines Schutzschirms. Die ältesten bekannten Laufschienen mit Holzsohle sind schmal wie Skier, die neueren dagegen breiter, wie S. Ekman bemerkt hat.[1]

457

Abb. 1. Zweiteilige Gleitschiene älteren Musters aus Replot (Raippaluoto), 4,24 m lang und 9,5 cm breit. Finn. Nationalmuseum.

Diese Laufschiene fand nur im Spätwinter Verwendung, von Ende März bis zum Mai, in welche Zeit der längste und ertragreichste Fangzug fiel, der den ganzen inneren Bottnischen Meerbusen zwischen Tornio und dem südlichen Nordkvark erfasste. Im April/Mai d.J. 1939 hatte ich Gelegenheit, den Seehundfang vor Kalajoki mitzumachen. Wir kamen dabei 50–60 km von der Küste nach Westen.

Die Fahrt beginnt mit einem Grossboot, das, auf einer besonderen Kufe stehend, das Eis entlang bis zu offenen Stellen geschoben wird. Dabei nahm man manchmal auch ein Segel zu Hilfe: die Männer liefen dann an den Seiten des Bootes und hielten mittels einer Querstange das Gleichgewicht aufrecht. Auf dem Meer bildet das Boot dann gewissermassen das Wohnlager, das nach Bedarf verlegt wird. Jeden Tag werden vom Boot aus mit der Gleitschiene Fangzüge in die Umgebung gemacht; der Name in den schwedischen Dialekten von Ostbottnien, Laufstange *(rännstång)*, wäre im Hinblick auf die Funktion vielsagender. Ich habe im Laufe dieser Forschungsreise u.a. die folgenden Aufzeichnungen über die Verwendung dieser Schiene gemacht.

Für den Seehundfänger, der vom Lagerboot aus allein auf dem Eise wandert, ist die Gleitschiene heute von einzigartiger Wichtigkeit. Es ist eine Freude und ein Genuss, den Männern auf ihren grossartigen Eisfahrten zu folgen. Auf ebenem Eis gleiten sie ebenso rasch dahin wie ein Fahrrad auf glatter Strasse. Der Seehundjäger steht mit dem einen Fuss auf der Gleitschiene und stösst sich mit dem anderen in sicherem Gleichtakt ab. Dabei beschleunigt er seinen Lauf noch mit dem als Skistab dienenden Robbenstaken.

Auf dem Vorderteil der Laufkufe ist in einem Futteral aus weissem Kalbsfell mittels zweier Krampen die Seehundbüchse befestigt. Daneben ist eine kleine, auf einem Stock aufgewickelte Leinenrolle angebracht, die bei Bedarf als Tarntuch beim Anschleichen dient. Griffbereit hängt das Fernrohr am Hals des Jägers. Es dauert nicht lange, und der gegen den Wind vom Lager aufbrechende Fänger ist in der Eiswüste dem blossen Auge entschwunden. Ist

Abb. 2. Hinterer Teil einer alten Laufschiene mit Spitze und Schnur der Harpune. Der Stiel, der am einen Ende eine Eisenspitze mit Widerhaken trug, diente dem Jäger als Stab. Finn. Nationalmuseum Nr. 1475: 1, Helsinki.

er ins Packeis gekommen, springt er ab von der Laufschiene und zieht sie hinter sich her. Die Zugleine ist so kurz, dass sie gerade von der Hand bis zur Kufenspitze reicht, ohne dass man sich zu bücken braucht. Die Schiene, die auf diese Weise fast senkrecht von oben gezogen wird, kippt dann nämlich auch im schlechtesten Brucheis nicht um, was wiederum wegen der wertvollen Büchse unbedingt nötig ist. Stösst man auf eine schmale Rinne, dient die Laufkufe als Brücke.

Von Zeit zu Zeit bleibt der Seehundjäger stehen und hält Ausschau. Er hebt das Fernrohr vor die Augen und stützt es dabei auf den langen Stab des Seehundstakens. Hat er das Packeis erreicht, klettert der Jäger sogleich auf den höchsten Eiswall und späht mit dem Fernglas in die Runde. Fern am Horizont hebt sich ein kleiner schwarzer Punkt ab. Darauf nimmt er jetzt mit der Laufschiene Kurs, obwohl der Punkt beim Herunterkommen vom Eiswall aus dem Sichtkreis verschwunden ist. Endlich zeigt er sich wieder. Wenn es zwischen Jäger und Seehund gegen den Wind geeignete Eisbuckel gibt, nutzt

Abb. 3. Seehundjäger in voller Fahrt auf dem Eis. Von der Reise des Verf.s 1939 in Kalajoki, Kalla. Aufnahme von Eino Mäkinen.

der Fänger sie als Deckung aus, indem er sich vorsichtig vorwärts arbeitet. Wo dergleichen nicht existiert, muss sich der Jäger bald tiefer herabbücken und den Seehundstaken an der Spitze der Laufschiene befestigen. Er stützt sich nun mit dem linken Knie auf der Kufe auf und stösst sich mit dem rechten langsam vorwärts. Bald geht auch das nicht mehr: nun geht es auf allen Vieren weiter. Vorsichtig öffnet er das Bugsegel als Tarnschutz, nimmt die Büchse aus dem Behälter und arbeitet sich – den Bauch auf der Kufe – weiter heran. Auf den Ellbogen robbt er sich auf den Seehund zu; die Laufschiene steuert er dabei mit den Fussspitzen. Mitunter stösst er unterwegs auf Wasserlachen, die die Sonne auf dem Eis hat entstehen lassen. Sie hindern ihn nicht:

Abb. 4. Der Seehundfänger zieht seine Eisschiene durchs Packeis.

er kriecht weiter, auch wenn das eisige Wasser seine Kleider durchtränkt und er vor Kälte schaudert. Im Spätfrühling kann das sonnenbeschienene Eis so schwach sein, dass hinter der Laufschiene das blanke Meerwasser hochquillt und der Seehundjäger an den dünnsten Stellen seine Arme ausbreiten muss, um eine grössere Tragfläche zu erhalten. Sein Blick lässt nicht vom Seehund. Manch ein alter "Herr", manch eine alte "Dame" schlummern so sorglos, dass der Jäger bis auf 50 m herankommen kann, um dann mit Sicherheit den tödlichen Schuss anzubringen. Die meisten der auf dem Eise liegenden Tiere werden allerdings unruhig, heben den Kopf und machen andere Bewegungen. Die Seehundjäger sind gute Scharfschützen und noch auf dreihundert Meter treffen sie den Seehund in seinen kleinen Schädel. Ihn

461

Abb. 5. Man nähert sich hinter dem Tarnschirm kriechend dem Seehund.

anderswo zu treffen ist zwecklos: die Beute muss sofort tot sein. Ein Todes-
kampf von nur wenigen Sekunden genügt, und der Seehund wälzt sich vom
Eis ins Meer.

Kaum ist der Schuss verhallt, da richtet sich der eben noch am Boden
liegende Schütze auf und rast in schneller Fahrt mit dem Staken in der Hand
auf die Beute zu, damit sie ja nicht unter dem Eis verschwindet. Das Blut des
toten Tieres färbt das Eis rot. Wie viele seiner Vorväter saugt auch noch der
heutige Robbenjäger das Blut aus der Wunde: es schmeckt und gibt neue
Kräfte. Schnell und geübt zieht er die Speckschicht mit dem Fell und der
Schwimmhaut ab und stopft die übrigen Teile unter das Eis. Dann erhält die
Laufschiene neue Arbeit. Aus der 30–40 Kilo wiegenden Speckhaut formt

Abb. 6. Die Beute wird zum Lagerboot gebracht. Der Jäger zieht rasch das Fell mit der dicken Fettschicht ab und schiebt sogleich alle übrigen Teile unter das Eis. Von alters her war es ein ständig befolgter Brauch, keine dunklen abgehäuteten Körper auf dem Eise liegen zu lassen, damit nicht ein anderer sie von ferne erspäht und sich mühsam auf Schussweite heranarbeitet. In seiner Mütze hat der Seehundfänger stets eine Segelnadel und Segelgarn, womit er mit einigen groben Stichen die beiden Flanken der Speckhaut zusammenzieht und diese – wie auf dem Bild zu sehen – auf der Gleitschiene befestigt. Damit sie sich auf der schmalen Kufe besser hält, wird hinten das Puukko-Messer aufrecht hineingehauen.

der Jäger ein Paket und legt es auf die Kufe, die er jetzt wie einen Schlitten auf das Lager zu zieht. Manche Laufschienen besitzen in der Mitte aufklappbare Seitenbretter, die unterhalb der Last gleichsam als Leisten dienen und verhindern, dass die Speckhaut mit ihren Seiten gegen das Eis scheuert und damit die Reibung vergrössert.

463

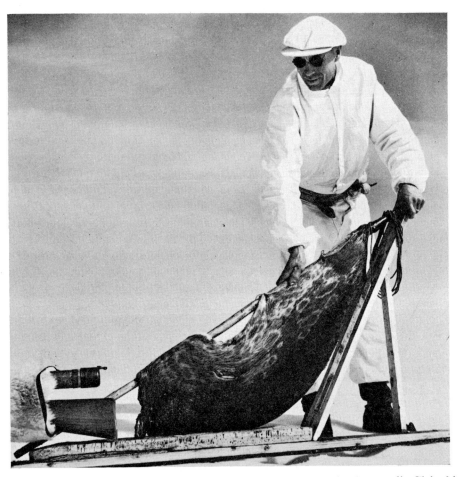

Abb. 7. Der Seehundjäger hat mit Hilfe des Stakens und der Seitenbretter die Gleitschiene umfunktioniert in einen sog. Tretschlitten.

Unterwegs entdeckt der Fänger einen zweiten Seehund: ihm ergeht es wie dem ersten. Die Last wird immer schwerer, der Jäger hat noch viele Dutzend Kilometer vor sich und seine Kräfte lassen allmählich nach. Siebzig oder achtzig Kilometer mit der Laufschiene an einem Tage sind nichts Aussergewöhnliches. Die Tage sind schon lang, die Nächte kurz. Vom Steven des Lagerbootes aus verfolgt der "Posten" mit dem Fernrohr aufmerksam die Bewegungen der Jäger, solange sie in Sichtweite sind. Hat er die schwere Beutelast erspäht, eilt er als Ausgeruhter vom Boot aus helfend entgegen.

Eine fast ebenso ausgerüstete, oft jedoch etwas längere Gleitschiene begegnete noch zu Beginn unseres Jahrhunderts im mittleren Teil des Finnischen

Meerbusens an der Küste von Ost-Uusimaa, auf Suursaari (Hogland), in Seis-
kari und an der estnischen Küste westlich von Narva (Allentaken) sowie auf
der Insel Prangli (Wrangel) in der Nähe von Tallinn (Reval). Die Schweden
in Ost-Uusimaa verwendeten dafür die Bezeichnung *skridstang* und *sälastang*
(*säl* 'Seehund'), die Finnen den Namen *tanko*, die Esten *tang*, entlehnt also aus
den nächsten schwedischen Dialekten.[2] Über die im Ethnographischen Museum zu Tartu (Dorpat) aufbewahrte Gleitschiene schreibt I. Manninen folgendes: "In den Sammlungen befindet sich nur eine Schiene *(tang)*, von der
Insel Prangli. Sie ist 4 m lang, in der Mitte 10 cm breit und wird ganz allmählich nach beiden Seiten zu schmäler. Mit dem Bauch auf der Schiene
liegend stösst sich der Jäger auf die auf dem Eise liegende Robbe zu vorwärts. An dem vorderen Ende der Schiene ist ein Schirm aus weissem Tuch
befestigt, in dessen brettartigem Halter sich ein Loch zum Beobachten und
für die Büchse befindet. Der untere Rand des Schirmtuches ist mit Gewichten
versehen. Nicht weit vom hinteren Ende der Kufe ist eine Öse sichtbar und
weiter nach dem Schirm zu in gewissem Abstand voneinander zwei Schnur-
schleifen. Es ist offensichtlich, dass diese Kufe mit ihrem Segel an der Nord-
küste Estlands aus Finnland entlehnt ist, wo sie bei den Robbenfängern sowohl des Finnischen wie des Bottnischen Meerbusens in Gebrauch ist."[3]

Keine Angabe berichtet darüber, dass die Gleitschiene im Bereich des
Finnischen Meerbusens wie ein Ski in der Art der diesbezüglichen Kufe vom
Bottnischen Meerbusen verwendet worden wäre. Auf dem Finnischen Meerbusen zog man sie nur hinter sich her und – wenn man sich an einen Seehund heranschlich – kroch man mit ihrer Hilfe möglichst nah an die Beute
heran. Ferner diente die Gleitschiene als Brücke über Eisspalten. In einem
ausgedehnten Zwischengebiet im südlichen Teil des Bottnischen Meerbusens,
auf Åland und im Norden der Ostsee sowie auf dem Ladoga benutzte der
Seehundfänger anstelle einer Gleitschiene einen leichtgebauten Schlitten.[4]

Bei der Erörterung von Alter und Funktion der Gleitschiene ging K. B.
Wiklund davon aus, die Gleitschiene gehöre zu den allerältesten Geräten der
"Eisjagdkultur", ähnlich wie die Harpune, der transportable Schirm und die
weisse Tarnkleidung; sie könne somit älter sein als die Skier.[5] Ernst Klein und
Ilmari Manninen waren dagegen der Meinung, die Gleitschiene sei relativ
jung, erst im Zusammenhang mit dem Gewehrfang entstanden.[6] Wie spät
diese Laufkufe in den Süden des Nordkvark gelangte – nach dem 18. Jh.
nämlich – ist auch von Edvin Brännström betont worden.[7] Für den Finnischen Meerbusen kann Manninens Schlussfolgerung durchaus zutreffen, denn
die ältere winterliche Seehundjagd im Finnischen Meerbusen war ganz anders geartet als die im Bottnischen Meerbusen: die Seehunde und ihre Jungen

wurden in ihrem Lager und an den Atem- bzw. Luftlöchern erlegt, zu deren Auffindung Hunde mitgenommen wurden,[8] so dass die Gleitschiene zum Anschleichen unnötig war. Im Bottnischen Meerbusen dagegen suchte man später im Frühjahr und ohne Hund nach auf dem Eise liegenden, sich auf die Brunft vorbereitenden Seehunden, wobei das Gerät zum Anschleichen unumgänglich war. Ferner war das Eis zu dieser Jahreszeit schon gebrochen, so dass die Gleitschiene zur Überquerung von Rinnen und Spalten nötig war. Der Jäger konnte auf diese Weise auch ein grösseres gebrochenes Eisfeld überwandern, indem er mit dem Staken eine kleinere Eisscholle an eine grössere heranruderte usw. Als die Schusswaffe auch beim Seehundfang in Gebrauch kam, verlängerte sich die alte winterliche Jagdperiode auf Seehunde bis in die Zeit des brüchigen bzw. Treibeises, wo die Seehunde ihre Jungen bereits verlassen haben und keine Atemlöcher mehr brauchen, sondern meist auf grossen Eisschollen liegen. In diesem Fall war die Gleitschiene nützlich, ja sogar notwendig. Ihr spätes Erscheinen im Finnischen Meerbusen wird auch durch die finnische Bezeichnung *tanko* bezeugt, eine späte Entlehnung aus dem lokalen schwedischen Dialekt, sowie durch den Tatbestand, dass die Gleitschiene hier nicht als schnelles Transportmittel diente, was im nördlichen Bottnischen Meerbusen ein so charakteristischer Zug war und wodurch diese Kufe gewissermassen verbunden ist mit einem anderen uralten lappisch-finnisch-nordskandinavischen Beförderungsmittel auf dem Schnee: den unpaarigen Skiern.[9] Man kann nämlich sagen, dass die Laufschiene der Seehundjäger im inneren Bottnischen Meerbusen das Ergebnis der Weiterentwicklung des Gleitskis des linken Fusses vom verschieden langen Skipaar darstellt. Da die Laufschiene nur im Frühjahr auf dem Meereis verwendet wurde, wo kein Schnee mehr lag, war der Stossski des rechten Fusses nicht nötig, da die Schuhsohle auf eine harte Oberfläche traf. Die Fortbewegungstechnik ist in beiden Fällen dieselbe: der linke Fuss steht auf dem biegsamen, langen Ski, der rechte stösst ab und sorgt damit für die Geschwindigkeit. In der Hand hat der Skiläufer nur einen Stab, der im Wald auf der Jagd gleichzeitig als speerartige Waffe dient. Für den Seehundfänger auf dem Eis war der Stab gleichzeitig Harpunenstock und Speer mit wenigstens einem Widerhaken.

Die ältesten Verbreitungsgebiete der unpaarigen Skier und der nördlichen Gleitschiene liegen ebenfalls nahe beieinander. In seinen ausführlichen Untersuchungen ist T. I. Itkonen zu dem Ergebnis gekommen, dass das verschieden lange Skipaar schon in vorhistorischer Zeit "namentlich im Zusammenhang mit dem Jagdskilauf im äussersten Winkel des Bottnischen Meerbusens von den dort lebenden Lappen" entwickelt worden sei; von dort habe es sich

466

einerseits nach Schweden, andererseits nach Finnland und Ostkarelien ausgebreitet.[10] Gestützt wird diese Annahme durch die späteren Untersuchungen von Terho Itkonen über die finnische Skiterminologie.[11] Die Schnelligkeit war für beide Transportmittel eine unbedingte Eigenschaft. Der Seehundjäger musste tagsüber während der kurzen Jagdsaison grosse Eisflächen "durchkämmen" können; auf dem Lande wurden, wie alte schriftliche Quellen berichten, unpaarige Skier vor allem bei der Rentierjagd verwendet, denn wer nur langsam vorwärts kam, machte keine Beute. Wirkungsvoll konnten unpaarige Skier natürlich erst im Spätwinter eingesetzt werden, wenn der mit dünner Eiskruste überzogene Schnee einen auf langem Ski stehenden Mann trug, während das Rentier einsank.

Doch für den Seehundfänger, der sich der Robbe ohne Feuerwaffe näherte, war die Gleitschiene auf dem Frühjahrseis unumgänglich: ungeschützt mit dem Bauch auf der Laufkufe liegend ahmte er mit seinen Bewegungen eine auf dem Eise kriechende Robbe nach. Eine gute Schilderung dieses Heranrobbens verdanken wir Chr. Salmenius aus d. J. 1754. Er war in der Provinz Mittelostbottnien, in Kalajoki, geboren und aufgewachsen, einem ganz besonders für seinen Seehundfang bekannten Gebiet. Als sein Vater (geb. 1706) Pfarrherr in Kalajoki war, bekam er Robbentribut, so dass er und sein Sohn oft in Kontakt mit den Seehundfängern waren. Salmenius berichtet folgendes: "Wenn sie einen Seehund erblicken, begeben sie sich zu ihm mit einem zu diesem Zwecke gemachten Ski bzw. einer Kufe, gekleidet in einen weissen Pelz aus Kalbfell und eine graue Mütze . . . , damit das Beutetier meint, der Mann gehöre zu seiner Sippe. Während die Robbe auf dem Eis liegt, stösst sich der Mann mittels eines zu diesem Zweck vorhandenen Stabes mit Eisenspitze allmählich vorwärts, wobei er sich mit dem einen Knie auf der Schiene aufstützt . . . ; der Mann gleicht alle seine Bewegungen den eigentümlichen Verrenkungen der Robbe an und kommt dabei immer näher an sie heran; er muss genau verfolgen, wie das Tier seinen Kopf bewegt und danach seine eigenen Bewegungen richten; die sich sonnende Robbe wundert sich über den Mann und ist hoch erfreut, denn sie glaubt, da nahe sich eine andere Robbe, weshalb sie ihrer Zufriedenheit gleichzeitig Ausdruck gibt mit allerlei komischen Bewegungen und Lauten; der Mann hat eine Klapper *(skräfla)* in der Hand, mit der er der Robbe antwortet, wodurch er sie natürlich in noch grösseres Staunen versetzt."[12]

Unrichtig ist zweifellos die häufig geäusserte Vermutung, die Laufkufe sei erst mit den Feuerwaffen aufgekommen und zum Anschleichen und Vorwärtskommen benutzt worden. Schon der finnische Name *ajopuu* ist ein genuines und dem Typ nach altes Wort, desgleichen das weitverbreitete schwedische *skridstång*. Ferner haben wir im Rechenschaftsbericht des Vogts von Südostbottnien aus d.J. 1561, da die Bauern noch keine Feuerwaffen besassen, eine sehr klare Charakterisierung des Seehundfanges unter Benutzung der Gleitschiene: Wenn sie Seehunde und deren Junge im Winter zur Zeit des zugefrorenen Meeres fangen, benutzen die Bauern von Mustasaari und Vöyri (Vörå) Harpunen und Speere mit Widerhaken, nach dem Marientag (25.3.) aber benutzen sie auf dem Eis Gleitschienen. Desgleichen fangen sie im Herbst mit Netzen . . .[13]

Die Kennzeichnung des Vogtes entspricht in all ihrer Kürze genau dem jährlichen Terminkalender der Seehundjagd, wie wir ihn aus späteren Quellen kennen. Es handelt sich hier offenbar um auf vorhistorische Zeit zurück-gehende Transport- bzw. Fortbewegungsmittel auf hartem Schnee und Eis, von denen die Laufschiene ein sehr weit spezialisiertes, vielwertiges Hilfs-mittel für den Seehundjäger auf dem Meereseis darstellt. Das Aufkommen der Feuerwaffen führte natürlich zu zusätzlichen Besonderheiten.

Unnötig erörtert man, was älter ist, die Skier oder die Gleit- und Lauf-schienen. Die ersten Anwohner des Bottnischen Meerbusens in vorhistorischer Zeit jagten jedenfalls wilde Rentiere in den verschneiten Wäldern und See-hunde weit draussen auf dem Eis des Meeres. In Ostbottnien hat man in Närpiö (Närpes) tief im Lehm das Skelett einer grönländischen Robbe *(Phoca groenlandica)* gefunden, mit einer beinernen Harpunenspitze, desgleichen vom Oulujoki das Skelett einer kleineren Ringelrobbe *(Phoca foetida* oder *hispida)* ebenfalls mit Harpunenspitze. Beide Funde werden in die für die jüngere Steinzeit typische Periode der Kammkeramik datiert. Das erstge-nannte Tier war ca. 20 km von der damaligen Uferlinie entfernt 42 m tief im Wasser versunken, die letztere Robbe lag in einer Tiefe von 62 m 30 km von der Küste entfernt.[14] Für die Entwicklung schneller Gleitskier und -schienen war das nördliche Fennoskandien aufgrund seiner Naturverhältnisse beson-ders prädestiniert: das schneereiche Frühjahr hält lange an, und durch den Einfluss des Golfstroms kommt es oft schon nach der Wintermitte zu Tau-wetter, dem sofort wieder Frost folgt, wodurch die eben noch feuchte Ober-fläche des Schnees gefriert und eine für jegliche Fortbewegung äusserst gün-stige Voraussetzung geschaffen wird, indem der Schnee nun trägt.

Anmerkungen

1. Angaben über Aufbau und Masse der Gleitschiene finden sich bei Sven Ekman (Norr-lands jakt och fiske, Uppsala 1910, S. 229–232) und Albert Hämäläinen (Hylkeenpyynti

keskisen Pohjanlahden suomenpuoleisella rannikolla. Suomen Muinaismuistoyhdistyksen Aikakauskirja 37:2, Helsinki 1930, S. 54–59; Referat: Die Seehundsjagd an der finnländischen Küste längs dem mittleren Teil des Bottnischen Meerbusens, S. 147–148).

2. Th. Schwindt, Atlas ethnographique de Finlande. I. Chasse et pêche (Helsingfors 1905), S. 18, Nr. 158. – T. I. Itkonen, Suomenlahden saarelaisten hylkeenpyynti. Suomen Museo 30 (Helsinki 1924), S. 33. – Anders Allardt, Säljakt i Pellinge. Budkavlen 1923 (Vasa), S. 98. – Herman Vendell, Samlingar af ord ur nyländska allmogemålet (Helsingfors 1884), S. 202: »skríd-stang«, S. 242: »šäla-stang Ett slags skida, med tillhjälp hvaraf skytten krypande närmar sig själen.« – F. J. Wiedemann, Estnisch-deutsches Wörterbuch (1869). Dritter unveränderter Druck (Leipzig 1923), Sp. 1118: tang (aus dem Finnischen) 'kurzes, dickes Holz, vermittelst dessen die Seehundsjäger, mit der linken Seite aufliegend und mit dem rechten Fusse sich fortschiebend, sich an den Seehund heranzuschleichen suchen'.

3. Die Sachkultur Estlands. I. (Tartu 1931), S. 84.

4. Sven Andersson, Fångst- och jaktmetoder vid själfänge i den åländska skärgården. Budkavlen 1931 (Åbo 1931), S. 108–111. – Ernst Klein, Runö (Stockholm 1924), S. 252–253. – Manninen, a. a. O., S. 84. – Kustaa Vilkuna, Varsinaissuomalaisten kansanomaisesta taloudesta ja kulkuneuvoista. Varsinais-Suomen historia III (Porvoo 1935), S. 23–24.

5. K. B. Wiklund, Ur skidans och snöskons historia. På skidor. Föreningens för skidlöpnings främjande i Sverige årsskrift 1928 (Malmö 1927), S. 24.

6. Ernst Klein, Vårt äldsta näringsfång. Några drag ur den svenska säljakten. Svenska kulturbilder (Hrg. S. Erixon u. S. Wallin). III. (Stockholm 1930), S. 148. – Manninen, a. a. O. S. 84.

7. Edvin Brännström, Med säljägare ute på Bottenhavet. Svenska kulturbilder. Ny föld. II. (Stockholm 1934), S. 282.

8. T. I. Itkonen, a. a. O. S. 25–32, bes. S. 30. – Sakari Pälsi, Suomenlahden jäiltä (Helsinki 1924), S. 62–104.

9. Ausführlicher darüber s. G. Berg, The origin and the development of the skis throughout the ages. Im Buch: Finds of skis from prehistoric time in Swedish bogs and marshes (Stockholm 1950), S. 40–51.

10. T. I. Itkonen, Suomen lappalaiset vuoteen 1945. I. (Porvoo 1948), S. 392 mit Literaturhinweisen.

11. Terho Itkonen, Suomen kielen suksisanastoa (Referat: Finnische Skiterminologie). Suomalaisen Kirjallisuuden Seuran toimituksia 254 (Helsinki 1957), vor allem die Seiten 13-23, 53–59, 77–84.

12. (Pehr Kalm =) Chr. Salmenius, Hist. och Oeconom. Beskrifning öfwer Calajoki sockn uti Österbotn. Åbo 1754. S. 38.

13. »Bruka Bönderne wdij mustsåre och wöro Sochner wdi villande haffuett mz staaff och krokar om vintrenn vnder Isenn effter Siell och Kutar, menn effter wårfrwdag i fasta bruka the medtt stänger på Isenn Teslikes om hösten medtt nätt . . .« (Finn. Staatsarchiv 4627, 21 r fogderäkenskap); eine ähnliche Bemerkung liegt vor für die Jahre 1567 und 1568 (K. R. Melander, Metsästyksestä maassamme 1500- ja 1600-luvulla. Historiallinen Aikakauskirja 1928, Helsinki), S. 106.

14. Jorma Leppäaho – Matti Sauramo – V. A. Korvenkontio, Närpiön ja Oulujoen hyljelöydöt. (Ref.: Die steinzeitlichen Seehundskelettfunde in den Kirchspielen Närpiö und Oulujoki). Suomen Museo 43/1936 (Helsinki 1937), S. 1–35.

Lapp Skis and Skiing

Two ancient ski finds from Northern Norway

By ØRNULV VORREN

Skis are among the earliest cultural remains found in Same-ædnam, "the land of the Lapps". It is a very extensive area comprising most of Norway, Sweden, Finland and the northern part of Russia west of the White-Sea. It is assumed that the Lapps or their ancestors were the first to settle in these areas.

In this century, already from its first decade a discussion on ancient ski-finds and the origin and development of skiing was carried on in papers by nordic scholars.

One could even say that it started as early as 1890 when Fridtjof Nansen wrote a chapter on the theme in his book "På ski over Grønland". The Finns Appelgren Kivalo, U. T. Sirelius and T. I. Itkonen, the Dane Gudmund Hatt, the Norwegian Nils Lid and the Swedes K. B. Wiklund, Gösta Berg and Ernst Manker have all played an important part in the discussion.

The finds from northern Norway, seven altogether, are not yet published, only mentioned in various papers. This is partly because some of them have only recently been sent to the proper museum and partly because some of them still remain in other museums. It is hard to believe that many new finds will occur hereafter. Most of the finds were made by road-workers or farmers using simple hand-tools. Nowadays, great machinery has taken their place and the chance of observing and taking care of ancient finds is extremely reduced. Our hopes must therefore stick to the big and complex archaeological projects where settlement sites or graves are excavated.

It is high time that the finds of ancient skis in northern Norway were published so that future discussion may take them into account.

Hence I present in this paper the examination of two ski finds, both of single skis, one from Sør-Varanger in Finnmark and one from Balsfjord in Troms county.

The Neiden-Ski

This ski was found in the village of Neiden in the county of Finnmark about 1930. The ski was found by Hilmar Kårby, one of the road-workers who were

470

making a road down to the Neiden river. The place is situated opposite the old Skolt-Lappish settlement just downstream from the biggest waterfall on the river. The exact location of the find, 8 m from the edge of the river bank is now covered by the road. The finder noticed the ski by piercing the turf and thrusting his turf cutter against the fore part of the ski. The marks of the blade are still discernible just where the ski is broken. The fore part or the "spiss" of the ski was thrown away along with the turf and lost. The rest of the ski was taken care of by Hilmar Kårby despite the reluctance of the overseer of the work. A boat made of planks sewn together was found with the ski. The boat lay with the stern pointing to the river. It was so well conserved that the workers might easily have dug it out of the turf in its entirety but were not allowed to do so by the overseer who did not want them to waste the time. All these remnants too were thrown into the river along with the turf and lost.

The ski was found at a depth of 2–2,5 m in marsh or turf. Ca. 30 cm under the ski the turf rested on a layer of clay. Evidently the marsh must have been built up by a rapid change of the environment, and the depth at which the remnants lay reveals little about their age. It is no longer possible to make a pollen analysis at the site. Radio-carbon dating, however, is being made. (21)

The length of the ski is now 145,5 cm from the rear end to the end of the broken fore part. 64 cm from the rear end there is a foot space pierced with a mortise hole. The middle of the hole is 89,5 cm from the rear end and 55,5 cm from the broken end. The breadth is 14,2 cm 36,5 cm from the rear end and narrows backwards to a lance-shaped rear end. At the rear end of the foot space the total breadth must have been 13,5 cm. The inset list on the left side of the foot space is 2,7 cm. The breadth of the foot space is here 8,1 cm. *The breadth of the ski* at the fore end of the foot space must have been 13,8 cm, the breadth of the list on the left side of the foot space being 3,3 cm and the breadth of the foot space 7,2 cm. 36 and 51 cm ahead of the middle of the mortise hole the total breadth has been 13,6 cm.

According to these measurements the total breadth of the ski has not varied more than 7 mm between the broadest part of the rear end and the broken end. If the fore end starts narrowing 51 cm from the middle of the mortise hole, which the form of the ski indicates, and the narrowing has been the same as that of the rear part, *the total length* of the ski must have been (89,5 + 51 + 36) cm = 176,5 cm. The foot space is 36 cm long. The front part of it is destroyed, the whole upper part of it from the front end and 14 cm to the rear being removed by the blows of an axe.

The foot space is scooped out so that its upper side slopes from the mortise

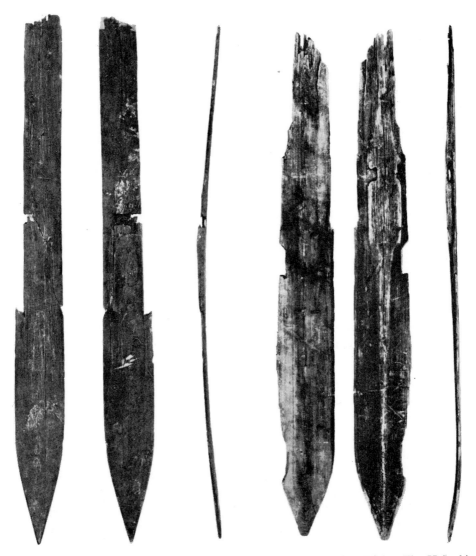

Fig. 1. Left: The Neiden-ski: under side, upper side and right edge. Right: The Heia-ski: under side, upper side and right edge.

hole to the rear end of it and form a thickness of the ski here of 2,2 cm and 1,2 cm respectively. The bottom of the foot space is concave and rises to both sides of it. These are raised 1,2 cm and 0,6 cm above the side list measured at the mortise hole and the rear end respectively.

The upper side of the ski is almost flat, with an almost imperceptible eleva-

472

tion along the mid-line and to both sides. *The under side* is somewhat convex especially towards the edges of the ski.

The thickness is, measured along the mid-line, at the broken end: 0,8 cm, at the fore end of the foot space: 1,2 cm, at the mortise hole: 2,2 cm, at the rear end of the foot space: 1,2 cm, where the rear narrowing starts: 1 cm. The thinnest part at the rear end is 0,9 cm.

The mortise hole has been oblong with a width of 3 to 3,5 cm. The hole curves downwards and was made by a round burning iron piercing the foot space crosswise from either side at the fore and rear part of the hole. The wood between these burned holes could then be cut out to make a proper hole for the binding.

The Neiden-ski is made of pine or red deal and the wood is still so well conserved that we might say that it has the same appearance as it had when it was buried in the marsh. The shape has been altered of course, as the ski is broken, and is no longer flat but bowed.

Originally the ski seems to have been a relatively short one with a length of about 175 cm, the breadth being over 14 cm at the middle part of the rear end and narrowing somewhat to the foot space and the front part.

In Skimuseet in Oslo there is a ski from Elvenes, a place situated only about 40 km from the original location of the Neiden-ski. This ski has a length of 163,3 cm and a breadth of 17 cm. The foot space is elevated, inset and scooped out. The over side is almost flat though with a slight convexity. The ski is also made of pine and resembles the Neiden-ski, although it is somewhat broader.

The Heia-Ski

This fragmentary ancient ski found in Balsfjord parish in Troms county in 1936 was delivered to Tromsø Museum 27 years later, in 1963. It was found by road-workers in the Heia area, near the north-east end of a little mountain lake called Fjellvatnet, ca. 1 km north of the north-east end of lake Takvatnet. The ski lay in a marsh at a depth of ca. 60 cm. The place is now covered by the road E 6. A farmer, Nils Hansgård, took care of the ski and kept it on his farm until it was delivered to Tromsø Museum in 1963.

The ski was unbroken when found, but was broken by the workers and the front part of it with the tip (spiss) was lost. The ski is made of pine which must have grown very slowly according to the annual rings and is so well conserved that one may see how the material has been worn by use. The

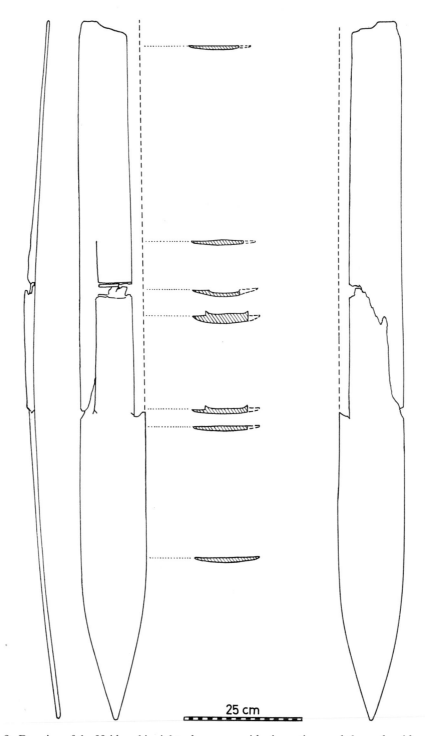

25 cm

Fig. 2. Drawing of the Neiden-ski: right edge, upper side, in sections and the under side.

shape is quite straight except for a slight upturn of the back end which consists of a cross-cut tip.

The length of the fragment is 140 cm, 100 cm from the rear end to the middle of the mortise hole and 40 cm from there to the front end.

The breadth at the broadest conserved part is 16,1 cm. At the rear end of the foot space the breadth is 15,1 cm.

The foot space which is 4,3 cm inset is pierced by a horizontal mortise hole 5 cm broad and 1 cm high. The hole is situated 14,5 cm from the rear end of the foot space. The bottom of the foot space is flat and completely preserved except for a piece over the mortise hole.

The length of the foot space is 23 cm. The breadth of it is 8,6 cm at the back and 9,2 cm at the front.

The under side of the ski is plane except for some places where the knots have been harder to wear down than the wood elsewhere. The erosion of the wood seems mostly to derive from the actual use of the ski because the soft wood is preserved behind the knots and not in front of them.

The over side rises from both edges to a low ridge along the middle part of the ski from the foot space forward and backward. 27 cm back from the foot space the ridge is flat topped and forms a continuation of the foot space.

The thickness of the ski is measured along the low ridge and the middle part of the foot space. At the mortise hole the thickness is 2,5 cm and it thins to 2,1 cm at the rear end of the foot space. Where the ridge is rounded 55 cm from the rear end the thickness is 1,5 cm, and at the thinnest part where the upperside is almost smooth, 28 cm from the rear end, it is 1,2 cm.

The full length of the ski seems to have been over 200 cm. Almost all the ancient skis found in a complete state seem to be a little back-heavy. Taking into consideration the weight of the foot space and a more weighty ridge on the rear part, the fore part seems to have been at least of the same length from the mortise hole to the front end as the rear part.

The inset lists on either side of the foot space have been 4,3 cm broad. The full breadth of the ski must have been 2 × 4,3 = 8,6 cm plus the breadth of the foot space 8,6 cm = 17,2 cm.

The over side is ornamented with hollow moulding lines with fine side lines along the edges of the ski, now most visible at the left side of the rear part.

The characteristic features of the Heia-ski are an elevated, inset and flat foot space which continues in a relative high ridge to both ends. Characteristic also are the ornaments which are found only on a few ancient skis.

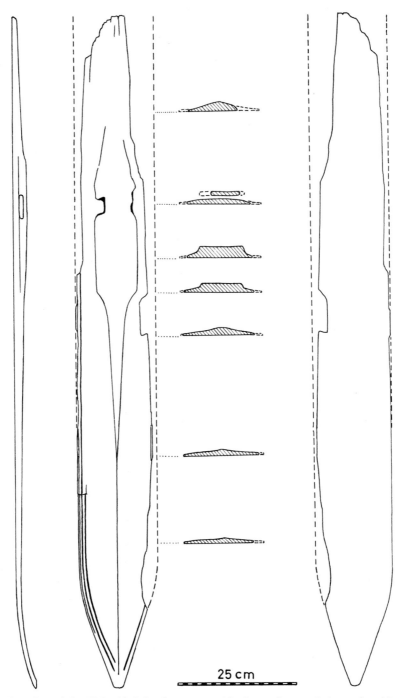

25 cm

Fig. 3. Drawing of the Heia-ski: left edge, upper side, in sections and the under side.

The fore-mentioned discussion on the origin and development of the ski did not result in any definite conclusions about the main problems. But the different analyses which were made brought to light a selection of types or categories. One tried to date the skis according to the types. However, both in Sweden as well as in Finland most of the skis have been dated by pollen analysis. In so far as these are reliable one should be able to identify other finds in a way. Gösta Berg and his co-authors have made the most elaborate and thorough paper on ancient skis, altogether 40 finds, of which 26 are geologically examined. These finds range over a period of 3500 years, stretching from about 2000 B.C. to 1500 A.D. Most of the finds are from areas known to have been occupied by the Lapps. The Swedish skis have been divided into five groups or types, the Southern, the Central Nordic, the Bothnic, the Scanian and the Arctic (3).

A large number of ancient skis have been found in Finland. Dr. T. I. Itkonen suggests that most of the ancient skis found in Finland are of Lapp origin as the Finns came to Finland only between the first and third centuries A.D. Dr. Itkonen divides the ancient Finnish skis into three categories (10):

The first category has a length of between 114 and 165 cm by 11–15 cm broad. The foot space is narrow and scooped out. Both skis of a pair were probably of equal length. They have been in use from the Bronze Age probably through to Historic times.

The second category is 110–115 cm long and 9–12 cm broad. There is a broad groove on the under side, a tip to the "spiss" or point, and ornamentation on the upper side.

The third category of skis is relatively long, 215–235 cm, and 11–14 cm broad. The under side is smooth and has at times been covered with skin. The two skis of a pair were probably not of equal length. Judging from the ornamentation this third category of skis originated during the 11th Century A.D.

This third category of Finnish skis is characterized by one ski of the pair being longer than the other. We have historical records of unequal skis made by the Lapps from the 16th century and later, e.g. Olaus Magnus, in his book written in 1555: "About the Nordic people". Describing their skis he points out that one of the pair was about 30 cm shorter than the other, the shorter one being as long as the skier was tall. The under side of it was covered in soft reindeer calf or seal skin (17).

Dean Tornæus, writing in the mid 17th Century, tells that the Lapps of Finnish Lappland sought the hardest pines—'as black as flint'—to make skis from. The short ski was made from this pine-wood and was convex on the upper side, flat on the under side and between 10 and 12 hand spans

Fig. 4. Lapp ski equipment: 1) Ski stick with spear head and scabbard in the upper end. 2) Skin-covered ski pair and ski stick with scoop in the upper end. 3) Woman's ski of red deal from the southernmost district of northern Norway. 4) Man's ski made of birch from the southernmost district of northern Norway.

long. This short ski the Lapp put on his left foot, the long ski on his right. Then, Tornæus adds: "After doing that, he thrusts and pushes with the spear and the bow as fast as he can, standing steadily with his left foot on the short ski." (23)

The Lapps made many kinds of skis designed to suit different purposes or snow conditions etc. In frozen snow with a hard crust skis of *red deal* (pine) were used, but in loose snow thin, light and much broader *birch* skis were used. Skis for hunting wolves had two grooves on the under side. There were different skis for use in the mountains and for use in the forests. There were skis for the reindeer herders which could be attached to the sledges and towed

478

etc. It is not possible within this paper to describe all the ski types. Here we have room to give only a general description of Lapp skis as they were made in the earlier part of this century.

Lapp skis were normally made out of pine or birch, but in some areas also out of rowan or aspen. The Lapps usually made the skis themselves right up to the last generation, but there have always been special ski makers, particularly among the settled Lapps.

Normally the skis are of an even breadth for most of their length but narrow towards the points at both ends. The "spiss" or front end is usually longer and more pointed than the rear. Along the middle of the ski there is a ridge. The foot space is set in about 1 cm from the borders and its surface may be flat or somewhat convex along and sometimes also across the space in which case there is a small concavity just under the binding. The rear end of the ski may be tipped or rounded and slightly curved up.

The under side of the skis may be quite smooth or may have grooves. Smooth "bottomed" skis may in some districts be covered with reindeer or seal skin. The skin is sewn onto the skis by reindeer sinews, the thread of which runs in a groove along the border on the under side. Every 5 cm or so the thread is taken up in a loop through the wood and through the edge of the skin which is folded up onto the upper side of the ski. At the front and rear of the ski the skin may be fastened by thread crossing the upper side without passing through the wood. Skin covering was chiefly used on skis for steep, hilly terrain and because the foot space was well back on hill skis, the fore part of the ski was heavier.

It was more usual for the skis to have grooves on the under side, and such grooves can be found on ancient skis too. Skis used for wolf hunting had two grooves. The grooves of the different ski pairs are not identical. Some are almost as broad as the ski leaving borders of only 1 or 2 cm, though narrowing to both ends. Some have grooves of only about 3 cm wide and some a very narrow groove like modern skis. A hole was often made in the end of the ski so that it could be attached to the sledges by a leather thong and pulled behind.

The bindings are very simple. As a rule a single broad strap is fastened through a hole abreast of the foot space. The ends of this strap are sewn together so that the strap forms a ring. Sometimes instead of leather straps pieces of willow are used. These are bent over the foot space and fastened into a hole at either side by wooden wedges.

Heel bindings are found only in the southern areas. To attach the heel binding a second strap is passed through the base of the foot space parallel to

Fig. 5. The simple ski binding from the northern area.

the first. The ends of this strap are bent into loops on either side. On each side another strap is fastened around the binding strap and through the loop of the second strap on each side. A little farther back leather thongs are attached to this strap and these tie across the back of the heel. In some areas the foot space is covered with skin or birch bark.

Few sticks have been found along with ancient skis, but one stick and a pair of skis about 4000 years old have been found together in Västerbotten, Sweden. The upper end of this stick was shaped like a shovel or scoop which occupied a quarter of the length of the stick. (3)

Until the introduction of modern ski techniques the Lapps used only one ski stick. This single stick was often, but not always equipped with a wheel of skin or willow at the base.

Dean Tornæus describes the ski sticks used by Finnish Lapps during the 17th century as a combination of light hunting spear and ski stick. The head of the spear was on the upper end of the stick, which might have a wheel near the base. The spear head was mounted in a scabbard often made of reindeer horn, and partly shaped as a shovel. Later the spear seems to have disappeared and the upper end of the ski sticks had only shovel shapes, similar to that of the 4000 year old ski, but smaller. The importance of the shovel was its use by the reindeer herders to dig away snow when searching for food—lichen—for the reindeer.

480

Fig. 6. Binding from the southernmost
district of northern Norway.

In some areas however, two sticks were used, particularly for a special form
of wild reindeer hunting and this is probably the origin of the modern use of
two sticks.

We have now seen glimpses of Lapp skiing and skiing equipment from the
pre-historic period down to modern times. Early historical accounts of skiing
reflect the wonder and admiration of the reporters, but not without scepticism
and disbelief.

Olaus Magnus, arch-bishop of Uppsala, found it necessary to explain that
"even if Pope Paulus III, according to what bishop Saluzzo Philippus Archin-
tus (Governor of the Holy Metropolis) has said, does not trust the records of

the artfulness and ability of the Northerners (Lapps) in skiing, it is however the clear truth". In the Pope's defence we should mention that Olaus Magnus's records are somewhat dramatic, though based on reality. (17)

In the literature dealing with the Lapps and their way of life are constant reminders of their skill at skiing. For instance, Knud Leem, writing in 1767 says: "They may walk or run over rocks and hills. With the stick resting on their shoulders, not even putting it against the ground to support themselves, they run on the ski down precipices and hills at flying speed, so that the wind blows in their ears and their hair lies back in the wind. And if one lays down a cap or something else in their way, they will bend down during the run and pick it up . . .". (12)

One could also cite authors whose descriptions show both how little the writer was acquainted with Lapp skiing, and how clever the Lapps were in using their skis.

Lappland is an extensive area and includes several quite different types of environment: the forests of Finland and Sweden, the barren grounds of Finnmark and the Kola Peninsula, and the wild, steep-sloped, mountains of Troms and Nordland counties in Norway. Each environment must have had an influence on the development of skiing.

In particular the Lapp skiing technique must have been greatly affected by the use of only one ski stick. Consequently, Lapp skiing concentrates more on the use of the weight of the body, and less on the power of the arms, than in modern skiing. The aim of the skiing technique of the Lapps was not speed, but perseverance—the ability to keep skiing all day—and also the use of skis in all possible snow and terrain conditions.

To lubricate the skis, the usual method was to impregnate them with tar in spring time and let them dry out. Then, in the summer, layers of reindeer or fish fat were smeared onto the tar so that the fat could be absorbed by the wood. This layer of fat and tar became "as hard as horn". For sticky or loose snow conditions during the winter the skis might be warmed and greased with more reindeer fat (4–20).

Obviously, in an area where snow lies for more than two thirds of the year, the ski has been vital for the survival of the Lapps. Their hunting and especially their nomadic herding of the reindeer would have been difficult without skis. Skis were also in everyday use about the camps and settlements. For the Lapps their skis were essential to their daily struggle to survive in the harsh Arctic environment. For this reason the use of skis by the Lapps is quite different from the modern, sporting image of skiing.

Thus, it is natural that the Lapps should attach quite different qualities to their skiing equipment and technique than one does to those of modern skiing. These qualities were also to a large extent dictated by the ski maker or skier himself, and were related to the abilities and purposes of the individuals.

Lapps have given much thought and interest to skis and skiing and to the craft of ski-making. This is shown by the very fine differences of details and variations in the craft of the ski makers, and one can also deduce it from the ornamentation of skis which dates from pre-historic time. Indeed some skis were elevated above everyday use. Special "celebration skis" were kept to be used only together with the finest clothes of the owner at special occasions, like weddings (5).

This short and very general examination of Lapp ski forms and functions has shown how diverse the subject is: too diverse to be fully covered in this paper. Also the literature dealing with the subject is rather unbalanced, and in particular, there is a scarcity of material from northernmost Lappland.

Much has been written on the functions of skis; notably by Nils Lid, K. B. Wiklund (26), and Gösta Berg, and much data from the early 19th century was given by Sigrid Drake in her book "Västerbottens-lapparna" (4). However there still remains considerable material which can be gathered from informants, from museum collections, from archives and from the literature. This evidence should be able to throw more light on the problems of Lapp ski form and usage, not only throughout the whole Lapp area, but also through a longer period of time.

This brings us back to the two ski finds in northern Norway, described here. They are from localities which lie some 400 km apart. According to the Swedish classification both skis are of the Bothnic type. It seems better, however, to use T. I. Itkonen's classification. In this the Neiden-ski belongs to the first category and the Heia-ski to the third. Many finds similar to the Neiden-ski have been made in Finland between Lappajärvi in the South and Kolari in the North, and T. I. Itkonen maintains that this type of ski is characteristically Lappish. The Neiden-ski probably belongs to a pair of skis of equal length whereas the Heia-ski seems to be the left gliding-ski of an unequal pair in which the other ski was a short, skin-covered "andor".

Until they have been radio-carbon dated it is not possible to give a definite age to these skis. However, some conclusions about the *function* of the skis can be made from a consideration of their form. (21)

The Neiden kind of ski is convenient for use in loose, dry snow. In wet or heavy snow the snow would collect on the flat upper side. On hard snow surfaces

Fig. 7. How Lapp skiing is illustrated in Knud Leem's book, one of the skiers picking up his cap and the other one keeping the stick on his shoulder during their rapid descent of the hill.

the convex under side would make the gliding, balance and steering difficult, despite the help the concave foot space might give to the steering. Support for the conclusion that the ski has been designed for use in loose, dry snow, comes from the lack of any particular wear on the under side of the ski. Such a ski would be unsuitable for hilly terrain because of the difficulty in steering down hill and the lack of grip for the ascents. In all, this ski type is suited to relatively flat terrain, with low winter temperatures and a relatively small snowfall. The function of this type of ski is similar to that of snowshoes,—that is useful for moving over snow when speed and long distance travel are not required. The function seems to have been for movement during winter hunting in the forests. On the whole the Neiden-ski is well adapted to the ecology, both environmental and cultural.

Irrespective of its actual age the Neiden-ski is connected with the pre-18th century hunting culture of the Skolt Lapps or their ancestors. In this part of Lappland the villages were relatively small and even into the early part of this century the economy of the Skolt Lapps was one of semi-nomadic hunting and not true nomadism. Seasonal transhumance was in winter, generally performed by reindeer transport. Subsistence was gained from hunting animals in the forest and fishing in the rivers and lakes and in the sea. (24–25).

The Heia-ski has a flat under side which has not been covered by skin. The concentration of wear along the right edge, especially by the foot space and at the rear end, indicates that the ski was used on the left foot. At the rear end of the ski the edge and upper part are well worn on the right side, but there is but little wear on the left side, either on the edge or on the upper side.

The under side shows evidence of extensive use on hard surfaces. The front of the knots in the wood have been worn down, but they have protected the softer wood behind. The whole under side of the ski must have been greatly reduced in thickness since the ski was first made.

It is impossible to be certain that the Heia-ski was used with a short "andor"ski and not with another ski of equal length, though this is highly probable. A pair of skis both over 2 m long and about 17 cm broad would be very clumsy and impractical for use even on hard snow surfaces. Another important point is that the traces of wear indicate that the ski has always been pushed and slid forward, implying that it was the other ski that was used for pushing.

This evidence all indicates that the Heia-ski has been used on hard surfaced snow in conjunction with a shorter, skin-covered "andor" steering ski. This kind of ski equipment was used to cover long distances. In his book "Finds of skis from pre-historic time, in Swedish bogs and marshes" (3) Professor Gösta Berg gives a description of the use of this equipment in Jämtland, Sweden. "It was brought out when he wished to cover some long distance, or when the crust on the snow was so hard that the ski could get no grip on it". This does not preclude the use of the ski on loose snow, in fact this may be the reason for the greater breadth of the Heia-ski in comparison with that from Jämtland.

This may be connected with the environmental differences between the two areas. Jämtland has a stable, continental climate with relatively small amounts of snow. Troms on the other hand has an unstable maritime climate with a heavy snowfall. Even during one night it is possible for as much as 50 cm of snow to fall, and the snow is often wet and heavy. Further in Troms the terrain is very varied with high mountain plateaus and long broad valleys. The snow is usually blown into a hard crust on the higher ground, but may remain deep and loose in the valleys. It is obvious that for this kind of environment a more widely adaptable ski is necessary and this requirement seems to be met by the form of the Heia-ski.

It is not so easy to place the cultural context of the Heia-ski as skis of this type, according to Itkonen, were used from about 1000 A.D. Even well before that time there had been Nordic settlements in the Troms area and the ski may be associated with them. However, the ski has so many features characteristic of Lapp skis that it is almost certainly Lappish, in contrast to some other ancient ski finds in North-Norway.

Reindeer herding may, even as early as about 900 A.D. have been of greater importance in the Heia area of Troms than it ever was among the Skolt Lapps of the Neiden area. Migrations with reindeer herds and also seasonal hunting movements would cover greater distances than the movements of the Skolt Lapps. It seems logical therefore that the Heiə-ski should be more suitable for use by reindeer herders than the Neiden-ski.

The identification of the cultural context of the Heia-ski and indeed of most of the ancient ski finds, awaits radio carbon dating (21). This data when it is available may well throw quite a different light on the hypotheses and conclusions made to date.

Nevertheless, to explain the role of skis as cultural elements in Fennoscandia using the present material, it is necessary to stress the assessment of the function of the individual ancient skis, in relation to the ecological circumstances.

Bibliography

1. Berg, Gösta: Förhistoriska skidor i Sverige. "På skidor" 1933. Malmø 1932.
2. – Nya fynd av förhistoriska skidor i Sverige. Skid och Friluftsfrämjandets årsbok 1951. Malmö 1950.
3. – Lundqvist, G., Zettersten, H. and Granlund, E.: Finds of skis from pre-historic time in Swedish bogs and marshes. Stockholm 1950.
4. Drake, Sigrid: Västerbottens-lapparna. Uppsala 1918.
5. Granlund, John: Svensk skidornamentik. "På skidor" 1941. Malmö 1940.
6. Hamberg, Axel: Til skidans femtioårsjubileum vid arktisk forskning. "På skidor" 1933. Malmö 1932.
7. Itkonen, T. I.: Fennoskandia-skienes opprinnelse. Tromsø Museums Skrifter, vol. II.
8. – Finlands fornskidor. "På skidor" 1937. Malmö 1936.
9. – Suomen Museo 1941 – 1946 – 1949.
10. – Suomen Lappalaiset bd. I. Porvoo-Helsinki 1948.
11. Landsmålsarkivets frågelista 24. "På skidor" 1930. Malmö 1929.
12. Leem, Knud: Beskrivelse over Finnmarkens Lapper. København 1767.
13. Lid, Nils: Skifundet frå Øvrebø. Universitetets Oldsaksamlings årbok 1930. Oslo 1932.

14. – Gamle norske skiformer, Syn og Segn. Oslo 1934.
15. – On the history of Norwegian skis. "Ski History 1." Oslo 1937.
16. – Skifundet frå Furnes. Noregs Boklag Oslo 1938.
17. Magnus, Olaus: De Gentibus Septentrionalibus. Antwerpen 1562.
18. Manker, Ernst: Ett förhistorisk skidfynd. Nordiska Museets och Skansens årsbok 1946. "Fataburen" 1946. Stockholm.
19. – En norrbottenslapp som skidmakare. "På skidor" 1948. Malmö 1947.
20. – Den botniska skidtypen i nya myrfynd. Skid och Friluftsfrämjandets årsbok 1957. Malmö 1956.
21. – Fennoskandias fornskidor. Fornvännen. Uppsala 1971.
22. Nansen, Fridtj.: På ski over Grønland. S. 72–127. Kristiania 1890.
23. Tornæus, Joh.: Beskrifning öfwer Tornå och Kemi Lappmarker. Stockholm 1772.
24. Vorren, Ø.: Reindrift og nomadisme i Varangertraktene. Tromsø Museums Skrifter vol. 69 nr. 12. Tromsø 1951.
25. – Om "Nuortalazak" eller skoltesamene. "Ordet" nr. 2. Oslo 1967.
26. Wiklund, K. B.: Ur skidans och snöskons historia. "På skidor" 1928. Malmö.
27. – Mera om skidans historia. "På skidor" 1929. Malmö.
28. – Den södra skidtypens källa. "På skidor" 1933. S. 20 ff.

Bäuerliche Bremsvorrichtungen an Wagen und Schlitten

Von ROBERT WILDHABER

Bremsvorrichtungen sind in der volkskundlichen Literatur bis heute sehr wenig in grösserem Zusammenhang untersucht und behandelt worden.[1] Dabei zeigt eine Sichtung des Materials einen recht beachtlichen Erfindungsreichtum an Behelfsmitteln und einfachen Konstruktionen, bis dann die mechanische Bremse mehr oder weniger allgemein üblich wurde. Die Wagen in ebenen Gebieten besassen üblicherweise keine Bremsvorrichtung; aber im Hügelland und in Berggegenden war es unumgänglich nötig, die Möglichkeit zu besitzen, die Fahrgeschwindigkeit zu verlangsamen oder das Fahrzeug völlig zum Halten zu bringen. Ebenfalls sollte ein Behelfsmittel vorhanden sein, das bei der Aufwärtsfahrt einen Halt gestattete, damit Mensch und Tier für kurze Zeit ausruhen konnten. Die mir aus der Literatur und aus Museumsbestand bekannten europäischen Belege lassen sich folgendermassen einteilen (es handelt sich bei 1 und 2 um Bremsvorrichtungen bei der Abwärtsfahrt):

1. Das Fahrzeug besitzt keine Bremsvorrichtung; die Bremswirkung wird erzielt
   a. durch die Konstruktion des Fahrzeugs oder durch die Art der Beladung,
   b. durch das Zugtier oder durch den vor dem Fahrzeug stehenden Mensch,
   c. durch eine hinter dem Fahrzeug sich befindliche und nicht zu ihm gehörige Massnahme: Bremslast, Tier, Mensch,
   d. durch eine neben dem Fahrzeug (üblicherweise handelt es sich um Schlitten) angebrachte Einrichtung.
2. Am Fahrzeug selbst wird eine Bremsvorrichtung angebracht; ihr Zweck ist die Verringerung der Gleitwirkung durch Unterlagen unter das Rad oder die Schlittenkufe oder durch das Blockieren eines Rades (oder mehrerer Räder, meist zwei, selten vier):
   a. Durchstossen eines Steckens durch die Radspeichen,
   b. Fixieren des Rades mit einer Kette,
   c. Unterlegen einer Kette oder eines Kratzers unter Kufe oder Rad,
   d. Unterlegen eines Radschuhs,
   e. Erschwerung oder Verhinderung der Umdrehung der Nabe,

488

Abb. 1. Schleife aus dem südlichen Tessin. Aus: Freuler (wie Anm. 6).

f. Heben des Rades durch einen Stab,
g. Blockierung der Felgen durch Anpressen eines Steckens an die Hinterräder,
h. die eigentliche "Mechanik" (meist mit Kurbelanzug).
3. Vorrichtungen bei der Aufwährtsfahrt.

1a. Es wird gelegentlich ausdrücklich hervorgehoben, dass die Wagen – auch
in hügeligem Gelände – keinerlei Bremsvorrichtungen besitzen. Dies gilt vor
allem für die französischen Pyrenäen und Gebiete in Spanien. Es wird damit
begründet, dass die Zweiräderkarren mit ihren schwerfälligen Scheibenrädern
ohnehin schon für unebenes Gelände konstruiert seien; auch wirken Steine und
Schlaglöcher auf den schlechten Feldwegen als Bremse.[2] Der primitive
Wagen mit dem niedrigen Rädergestell benötigt auch im hügeligen Gelände
keine Bremsvorrichtung, während der Wagen des Vorlandes mit seinem
hohen Räderpaar eine solche besitzt.[3] Man kann sich auch so behelfen, dass

489

Abb. 2. Wagen mit angehängten Holzstücken. Aus: Egloff (wie Anm. 13).

man den Wagen hinten schwerer beladet als vorne; dadurch wird der Druck, der beim Abwärtsfahren auf dem Ochsengespann lastet, wesentlich vermindert[4]. Auch die schweizerische Enquête I[5] hat eine Antwort (aus Andeer, Graubünden), wonach eine Schleife, die hinten auf dem Boden liegt, durch die Reibung als Hemmvorrichtung wirkt, besonders wenn sie noch belastet ist. Hiezu gehört noch ein interessanter Beleg aus dem Tessin[6]; danach benützten Bauern aus der Gegend Monte Brè-Aldesago um 1900 herum für ihren Eigenbedarf Schleifen ("slitt a carell") zum Transport von Holz vom Berg zum Taldorf. Die Schleife wurde mit Stricken gezogen; die Deichsel diente lediglich als Steuer. Das Fahrzeug wird gebremst, indem man entweder die Deichsel fest gegen den Boden drückt, oder indem man sie in die Höhe hält, wodurch das hinten herausragende Blockholz auf dem Wege reibt (Abb.1).

1b. Mehrfach wird erwähnt, dass keine Bremsen nötig seien, weil die Ochsen im Joch[7] oder auch im schweren Kummet[8] Kraft genug hätten, um den Wagen zurückzuhalten. Dies gilt nur für den Ochsenkarren, nicht aber für den mit Maultieren bespannten Karren, bei dem eine Bremse vorhanden sein muss[9]. Zum Zurückhalten des Wagens bei der Abwärtsfahrt gehört im Tiroler

490

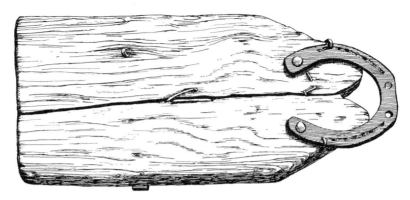

Abb. 3. Kratzeisen, Kt. Bern. Oberseite. Schweiz. Museum für Volkskunde, Basel, Inv.-Nr. VI 21108.

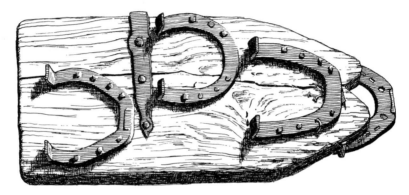

Abb. 4. Wie Abb. 3. Unterseite.

Oetztal ein breiter Lederriemen, welcher den Zugtieren um die Hörner geschlungen und vorn an der Deichsel befestigt wird[10]. Im Schweizerdeutschen versteht man unter "Bruech" einen breiten ledernen Riemen, der den Pferden um den Leib geschlungen wird, um einen Wagen bergab zurückzuhalten[11]. Bei den Hornschlitten für den winterlichen Heuzug stemmt der vorn stehende Fahrer machtvoll seine Füsse gegen den Weg, um das Gefährt abzubremsen[12].

1c. Um eine Bremswirkung zu erzielen, können hinter dem Fahrzeug sich befindliche Massnahmen getroffen werden. Aus dem Kanton Waadt vernehmen wir, dass beim winterlichen Holztransport hinten an den Wagen Holzstücke mit einer Kette angehängt werden, die am Boden nachschleifen (Abb.2)[13]. Die Enquête I enthält weitere derartige Angaben für den Kanton

491

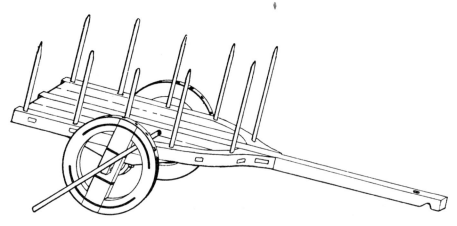

Abb. 5. Stockbremse. Aus: Fernández (wie Anm. 23).

Tessin und für Rickenbach bei Olten; für das Berner Oberland schreibt der Gewährsmann: bei steilen Teilstücken wird eine Last durch Anhängen von Tannästen, beschwert mit Steinen, bergabwärts geschleift; man nennt das "täschen". Durch das "Täsch" wird das Bremsen erleichtert, aber die Wege werden stark hergenommen, deshalb legte 1935 der Gemeinderat von Schwanden bei Brienz einen "Beschluss über das Verbot von jeglichem 'Täschen' auf den Wegen der Gemeinde während des Sommers" der Einwohner-Gemeindeversammlung vor. Aus Spanien[14] haben wir die Angabe, dass man hinter den Karren schwere Steine, häufiger jedoch einen grossen Haufen Ginster, den man zu diesem Zweck abgeschlagen hat, anbindet. Ähnliche Mittel werden auch für das Bremsen des Schlittens im Winter angewendet. Im Zastlertal im Schwarzwald[15] benützt man Pferdestricke und Bremsketten, die mit Ring und Haken Holzbündel zusammenhalten, welche je nach dem Gefälle und den Schneeverhältnissen in grösserer oder geringerer Anzahl nachgeschleift werden. Eigenartig ist die Bremseinrichtung im österreichischen Stubaital, wenn im Winter der Heutransport mit mehreren Schlitten hintereinander ausgeführt wird[16]. Als letzten des Zuges verwendet man einen eigenen Bremsschlitten, bei dem durch einfache Hebelwirkung zwei Eisenzacken an der rechten und linken Kufe zu Boden gedrückt werden. Diese Schlittenart dürfte erst anfangs unseres Jahrhunderts aufgekommen sein. Ihr Vorteil liegt darin, dass man je nach dem Gefälle mehr oder weniger stark bremsen kann, während eine Sperrkette unter den Kufen (siehe 2c) immer gleichmässig bremst. – Im Cervantes sowie in den Ortschaften am Mittellauf des Rio Navia in Spanien spannt der Bauer im gegebenen Fall hinter seinen Karren ein weiteres Ochsenpaar, das als Bremsvorrichtung dient[17]. – Manchmal

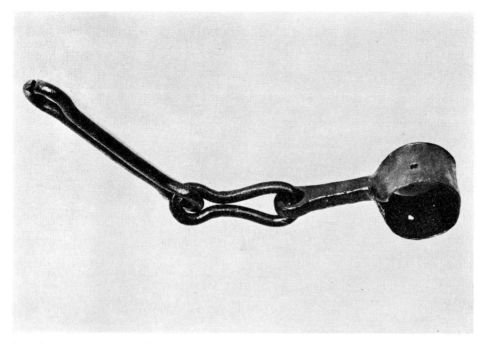

Abb. 6. Schlittenbremse. Guggisberg, Kt. Bern. Schweiz. Museum für Volkskunde, Basel, Inv.-Nr. VI 20293.

genügt auch ein blosses "Hindere haa", wenn Menschen hinten am Wagen mit den Händen die Fahrgeschwindigkeit einzudämmen versuchen; so vernehmen wir es aus dem durch Jeremias Gotthelf bekannten Lützelflüh im Kanton Bern[18].

1d. Eine nicht hinter, sondern neben dem Fahrzeug angebrachte Bremsvorrichtung kommt (in meinen Belegen) nur beim Schlitten vor. Ein besonders schönes Beispiel stammt aus Schwarzenegg bei Thun im Kanton Bern[19]; es heisst "Chratz-Ise" oder "Chritz-Ise"[20]. Es handelt sich um ein starkes Brett, das vorne leicht zugespitzt und etwas eingekerbt ist. Ein altes Hufeisen ist so befestigt, das durch den Hufeisenbogen ein Seil oder eine Kette durchgezogen werden kann (Abb.3). Auf der Unterseite des Brettes sind drei Hufeisen aufgenagelt (manchmal sind es auch nur zwei), die mit ihren vorspringenden Enden die Bremsarbeit zu leisten haben. Um das Spalten des Brettes zu verhindern, wird allenfalls noch ein verstärkendes eisernes Querstück befestigt (Abb.4). Gebraucht wird das "Chritz-Ise" im Winter, wenn mit dem Pferdeschlitten Holz aus dem Wald geholt wird. Es wird mit einer kurzen Kette oder

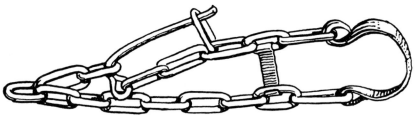

Abb. 7. Radkette. Aus: Dicziunari (wie Anm. 29). a)
Kette am Rad; b) Kette
allein.

mit einem Strick am vordersten Bein des Schlittens angebunden, so dass es
beim Fahren neben dem Schlitten hergleitet. Soll gebremst werden, so stellt
sich der Fuhrmann mit einem Fuss auf die Schlittenkufe, mit dem andern
auf das Bremsbrett. Durch die Belastung werden die Stollen der Hufeisen in
den harten Schnee gepresst und üben auf diese Weise eine bremsende Wirkung aus. Soll stärker gebremst werden, so tritt der Fuhrmann mit beiden
Beinen auf das Kratzeisen. So kann er jederzeit die Schnelligkeit des Schlittens
regulieren, ohne die Fahrt unterbrechen zu müssen. – Man wird hier auch
das Bremsverfahren einreihen dürfen, das Prasch[21] (in nicht ganz klarer
Weise) aus Kärnten erwähnt. Danach wurden Kratzer bei Schlitten so angebracht, dass ihre Schenkel links und rechts der Kufe in den Boden gingen;
der Fuhrmann konnte zum Bremsen einfach auf die über den Kratzhaken
angebrachten Trittbretter stehen.

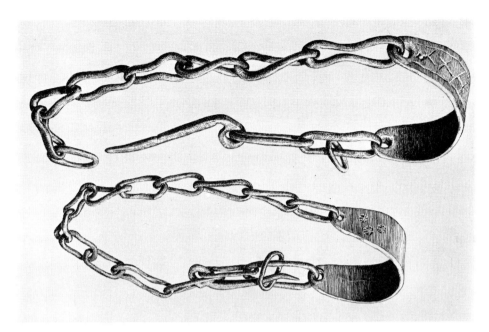

Abb. 8. Radketten. Schweiz. Museum für Volkskunde, Basel, Inv. –Nr. VI 91 und 20286; das bei 91 eingeschlagene Zeichen dürfte Schmiedezeichen sein, bei 20286 ist es vermutlich Ornament.

2a. Bei den Bremsvorrichtungen am Wagen selbst ist wohl die einfachste Art das Durchstossen eines Steckens durch die Radspeichen, um die Drehbewegung zu verhindern. Die schweizerische Enquête I hat mehrere Belege für dieses Vorgehen, so im Kanton Graubünden aus Dalin (mit dem Vermerk "früher") und aus Trimmis, wo man die Stecken als "Spannprügel" bezeichnet; in Gerzensee im Kanton Bern werden sie besonders beim Heutransport an steiler Halde gebraucht. Auch im östlichen Norditalien verzeichnet der AIS[22] verschiedene Punkte, wo ein Stecken zwischen die Räder gesteckt wird, damit diese schleifen. Im spanischen Galizien ist die Vorrichtung ebenfalls bekannt (Abb.5)[23]. Wenn in den Zentralpyrenäen für die mechanische Bremsvorrichtung der Name "garot", Holzknüppel, verwendet wird, so deutet das darauf hin, dass man in früheren Zeiten vermutlich einen Stecken zum Bremsen benutzte[24]. Eine auf den Schlitten übertragene Steckenbremse zeigt die Abb.6; sie stammt aus Guggisberg, Kanton Bern. Es handelt sich um eine Eisenkette; der eine Teil wird hinten unter der Schlittenkufe befestigt; durch den Ring stösst man einen Holzprügel, mit dem man beim winterlichen Holztransport bremsen kann.

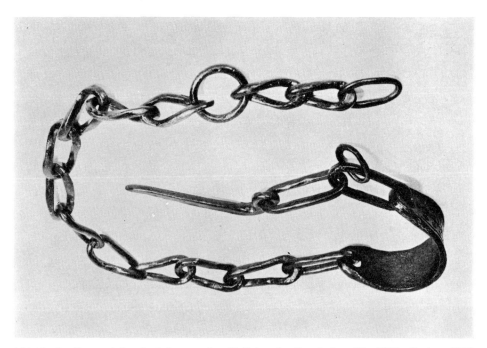

Abb. 9. Radkette. Schweiz. Museum für Volkskunde, Basel, Inv.-Nr. 5270. Datiert 1759, mit Besitzerzeichen ML SCH.

2b. Eine häufige und schon aus frühen Zeiten belegte Bremsvorrichtung besteht im Fixieren eines Hinterrades mit einer Kette. Diese Hemmkette, das "plaustrum", wird schon von Juvenalis (VIII, 148) um 100 n.Chr. erwähnt; es handelt sich um eine Eisenkette, die gewöhnlich an der linken Seite des Wagens eingehängt und dann zwischen zwei Speichen um die Felge gelegt und durch einen Ring und Haken geschlossen wird[25]. Das Schweizerische Idiotikon bringt drei Belege aus dem 16. Jahrhundert: "Die radsperre oder spannstrick, damit man das wagenrad spannet an den halden oder sunst an gehen orten"[26], 1579: "ein par ysin spanstrick"[27], 1574: "ein ysinen sperrstrick ab synem wagen verstollen"[28]. Die Enquête I hat zahlreiche Angaben für die Sperrkette am Hinterrad; Namen dafür werden allerdings nur selten angeführt, so für Metzerlen im Kanton Solothurn "Spannstrick" und "Ruchstrick". Ein schönes Beispiel einer solchen Bremskette, "chadaina", stammt aus Tarasp im Engadin (Abb.7a, b)[29]. Das Schweizerische Museum für Volkskunde in Basel hat Beispiele aus Courroux (Berner Jura) und dem Emmental (Kt. Bern) (Abb.8), ferner aus Buchrain (Kt. Luzern) (Abb.9). Dass diese Ketten mit Schmiede- oder Besitzerzeichen und mit Ornamenten versehen waren

496

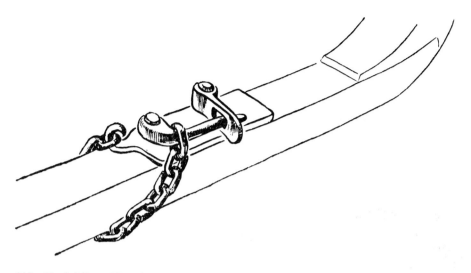

Abb. 10. Schlitten-Unterlegkette. Aus: Schmitter (wie Anm. 49).

beweist, dass man ihnen eine gewisse Wichtigkeit und Wertschätzung beilegte. Zu den bis jetzt erwähnten Namen kommt aus dem bernischen Lützelflüh noch Spannkette ("um eine Radfelge geschlungen") hinzu[30]. Die zahlreichen Namen und die gewisse Unsicherheit in der Beschreibung (es ist gelegentlich nicht eindeutig auszumachen, ob es sich um 2b oder 2c handelt) weisen einerseits darauf hin, dass wir es nicht mit einer allgemein bekannten, unter einem gemeinsamen Namen geläufigen Einrichtung zu tun haben, andrerseits aber zeigt es sich klar, dass wir es mit einem notwendigen Objekt zu tun haben, das vielleicht vom Bauern selbst oder dann vom Dorfschmied hergestellt wurde. Auch im norddeutschen Bereich ist das Anketten eines Rades bekannt; im Niederdeutschen sind Radschuhe kaum im Gebrauch, man hilft sich mit der Radkette[31]; sie heisst "remmkie"[32] oder "spêrkêe"[33]. Besonders zahlreich sind die Belege für die Radketten aus England; besondere Namen dafür sind nicht erwähnt, sondern nur erklärende Bezeichnungen wie "tie chain", "braking chain", "locking chain". In mehreren Gegenden wird die Radkette immer (oder manchmal) mit dem "dogstick" (cf.3) zusammen gebraucht[34], in anderen Gegenden wird sie nur allein verwendet[35]. Als seltene Ausnahme wird erwähnt, dass Radketten für beide Hinterräder gebraucht werden[36].

2c. Das Unterlegen einer Kette unter Rad oder Kufe ist dann belegt, wenn es deutlich als solches bezeichnet ist und nicht mit der Radkette (2b) verwechselt

Abb. 11. Kratzer für Heuzug. Alp Fergen/Klosters (Graubünden). Schweiz. Museum für Volkskunde, Basel, Inv.-Nr. VI 18218.

werden kann. Auch hier zeugen die Namen von einer gewissen Unsicherheit im Schweizerdeutschen; wir haben "Chritzchötti" oder "Underlegchötteli" für Lützelflüh[37], "Heb-Chette" und "Chretz-Kette" für die Kantone Thurgau und Zürich[38], "Verheb-Chette" und "Underleg-Chette" für das Prätigau[39] und "Chretzer" für Glarus, Graubünden, Luzern, Thurgau und Zürich[40]. Auch aus Kärnten kennen wir solche "Kratzer" und "Reissketten"[41]. Wenn das Anketten eines Rades im Niederdeutschen noch nicht genügend zurückhält, windet man eine Kette um den Felgenteil, der auf der Erde schleift[42]. Zahlreich sind die Angaben für das Unterlegen von Schlittenkufen durch Ketten und Kratzer (bei Schlitten kommt ja 2b nicht in Betracht). Bereits 1550 haben wir einen Beleg aus Einsiedeln[43]; "10 guet eisin spannchetten, so man an die schlitten braucht, so man nidsich fahrt". Klosters und Saas im Prätigau haben die Bezeichnung "Schlitten-Chette"[44], Walenstadt-Berg (Kt. St. Gallen) den Einzelbeleg "Strupfkette"[45] für Heu- und Holzschlitten, und das Avers (Kr. Graubünden) ebenfalls den Einzelbeleg "spannig"[46]. Sonst werden im Bündnerdeutschen und Bündnerromanischen recht einheitlich die folgenden Wörter für die Schlittenunterlegkette gebraucht: "fierja", "fierye", "fürje",

498

Abb. 12. Radschuh, 1489. Aus: Feldhaus (wie Anm. 51).

"fiergia", "ferri, pl. ferrene"[47]. Schlittenketten und Kratzer (ohne Namenangabe) sind weiterhin bekannt aus den Bündnerorten Trimmis, Trins, Latsch und Dalin, ferner aus Oberaegeri (Zug) und Fraeschels (Freiburg)[48]. Im Prätigau hat sich seit 1940 eine Neuerung eines Schmiedes in Saas sehr rasch eingebürgert, und sie hat unter dem Namen "Patentkette" die alte "Underlegchötti" ziemlich verdrängt (Abb.10)[49]. Ungebraucht hängt die Patentkette einfach am Haken und schleift nach. Soll sie verwendet werden, zieht man sie unter der Kufe durch, hängt sie in den Arm ein und gibt diesem vorn in der Öffnung der Platte Widerhalt. Soll die Kette ausgeschaltet werden, versetzt man der Platte mit dem Schuh einen Stoss, der sie dreht; der Arm klinkt aus, wird durch den Zug der Kette nach hinten gerissen und muss diese fahren lassen. Vor- und Nachteile des alten und neuen Systems liegen auf der Hand: beim Patentschloss kann man die Ketten nur einlegen, solange der Schlitten stillsteht, kann sie dafür aber mitten in der Fahrt lösen; die alte Kette hingegen kann man je nach Bedürfnis erst mitten im Stich einwerfen, muss sie dafür aber unten mühsam unter den Kufen hervorzerren, was allein manchmal beinahe unmöglich ist. Was Fernández für Spanien feststellt[50], dass viele der dörflichen Bremsen "individuelle Schöpfungen" sind, lässt sich an diesem Prätigauer Beispiel ebenfalls klar zeigen. In Oberschan (Kt. St. Gallen) hat ein Hufschmied Kratzer für Schlitten selber verfertigt und verkauft (Abb.26).

Im Einzelfall, den die Abb.11 zeigt, sind Schleife und "Kratzer" in einem Objekt vereinigt. Es handelt sich um ein ca. 60 cm langes Dreieck aus Holz,

499

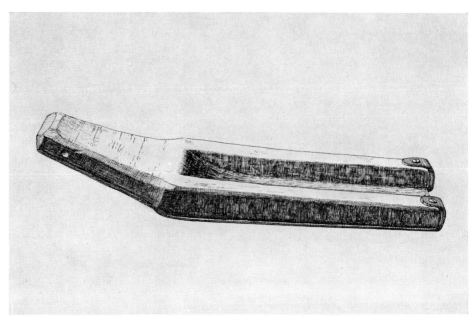

Abb. 13. Radschuh aus Holz mit 2 Eisenschienen. Menzingen, Kt. Zug. Schweiz. Museum für Volkskunde, Basel, Inv.-Nr. VI 5300.

in das acht Holzklötze eingefügt sind, die als starke Bremse wirken. Verwendet wird dieser Kratzer noch gelegentlich (Angabe aus dem Jahr 1947) auf den Alpen in der Umgebung von Klosters (Prätigau) für den Heuzug. Bei steilen Hängen wurde ein solcher Kratzer unter den Heuballen gelegt, und dann zog man das Heu vom Stock hinunter, bis man, auf weniger steilem Gelände, einen Schlitten zum Transport benützen konnte[50a].

2d. Wenn man von Bremsvorrichtungen spricht, mag man wohl zunächst in erster Linie an den Radschuh denken. Er ist eine unter ein Rad geschobene Unterlage, die das Rollen des Rades verhindert und es in eine Schleife umwandelt. Feldhaus[51] hält ihn nicht für sehr alt; er bringt eine Abbildung aus einem Heidelberger Codex von 1489 und fügt hinzu: "Er muss damals neu gewesen sein" (Abb.12). Auch die Bezeichnung "Radschuh" lässt nicht auf ein hohes Alter schliessen. Im norddeutschen Bereich treten ähnliche Wörter auf, so "Hemmschou" oder "Hemschuch"[52], "slepsahl, slepschoh, slöpschoh und sluffschoh"[53] und endlich "remšao"[54]. Arnold[55] verwendet für England nur die Bezeichnung "shoe", während Jenkins[56] neben dem "offiziell" tönenden "drag shoe" auch Formen angibt, die einem regionalen Bereich anzugehören

500

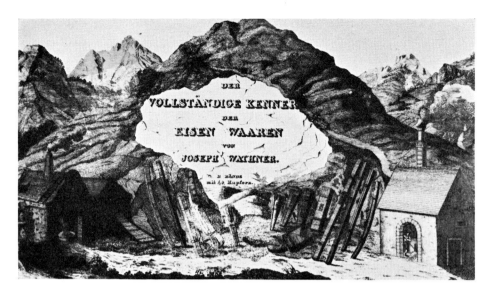

Abb. 14. Titelseite von Wathners Katalog, 1825. Photo: Iván Balassa, Ungarisches Landwirtschaftliches Museum, Budapest.

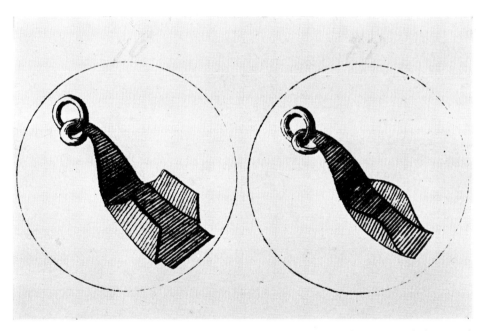

Abb. 15. Radschuhe aus Wathners Katalog, 1825. Photo: Iván Balassa, Ungarisches Landwirtschaftliches Museum, Budapest.

Abb. 16. Eiserner Radschuh aus dem Komitat Nógrád, Ungarn. Länge 37 cm, Breite 7 cm. Photo: Iván Balassa, Ungarisches Landwirtschaftliches Museum, Budapest, Inv.-Nr. 61. 1097. 1–2.

scheinen: "drug shoe, skid pin, skid pan, drug bat, drag bat". Wenn für Sardinien[57] notiert wird, dass der Radschuh – "soweit ein solcher bekannt ist" – "mekkánika" heisst, so bedeutet das, dass er erst aufgekommen ist, nachdem die moderne mechanische Bremse bereits in Gebrauch war. In all den bisher erwähnten Beispielen dürfte der Radschuh aus Eisen bestanden haben und vom Dorfschmied angefertigt worden sein.[57a] Daneben gibt es aber Ausdrücke, die klar darauf hinweisen, dass es auch Radschuhe aus Holz gab (und wohl noch gibt), die dann vom Bauern selbst angefertigt worden sein dürften; sie wurden mit dem Dechsel aus einem Stück Holz ausgehauen. Benützt wurden starke Wurzeln; Buchenholz und Birkenholz werden erwähnt. Manchmal werden unten zum grösseren Schutz vor der Abnützung zwei alte Eisenschienen oder ein Stück von einem alten Radreif aufgeschlagen (Abb. 13)[58]. Die Bezeichnung "Schleipftrog" für einen (ursprünglich) hölzernen Radschuh ist belegt für Lützelflüh[59], und "Schleiftrog" für Gontenschwil, Reinach (beide Kt. Aargau) und Rickenbach (Kt. Luzern)[60]. Dem "ausgehöhlten Trog" entspricht es, wenn der Radschuh französisch mit "sabot" (= Holzschuh, ebenfalls aus einem Stück Holz ausgehöhlt)[61] und rätoromanisch mit "calzer"[62] bezeichnet wird. Angaben über hölzerne Radschuhe, aus dem Jahre

502

Abb. 17. Eiserner Radschuh. Uerzlikon am Albis. Kt. Zürich. Länge 46 cm, Breite 8 cm.
Schweiz. Museum für Volkskunde, Basel, Inv.-Nr. VI 2913.

1838, stammen von den Ungarn im Szeklerland im östlichen Teil von Sieben-
bürgen (heute Rumänien); die Namen dafür sind "talabor" und "talpaló"[63].
In Ungarn haben kleine Hüttenwerke schon in der ersten Hälfte des 19. Jahrhunderts, und auch später noch, Radschuhe aus Eisen hergestellt. 1825 hat
Joseph Wathner einen Katalog von Eisenwaren herausgegeben (Abb.14), in
dem sich Radschuhe abgebildet finden (Abb.15).
  Der Radschuh ist keine ideale Bremsvorrichtung. Er gestattet keine Abstu-
fung der Hemmung und wird daher vom Zugtier stellenweise als lästiges Hin-
dernis empfunden.[64] Die Einsendungen für die Enquête I, 318 erwähnen
immer wieder, dass er die Strassen aufreisse; er wird deshalb "jetzt nicht
mehr erlaubt" (Sent, Kt. Graubünden) oder "nur noch bei ganz schweren
Lasten benützt" (Benken, Kt. Zürich). Schäden zeigten sich vor allem bei den
schmalen Radschuhen, wie sie der Bauer meist benützte (Abb. 16 u. 17). Deshalb wurden gelegentlich ausdrücklich breite Radschuhe vorgeschrieben, so in
einem Patent der Kaiserin Maria Theresia, gegeben 1747 in Klagenfurt[65]:
"...was Massen Wir zu gedeylich – und besserer Erhaltung deren hier
Landes kostbar angelegten Comercial-Strassen eine ohn-umgängliche Noth-

Abb. 18. Eiserner Radschuh. Fallera/Fellers, Kt. Graubünden. Länge 39,5 cm, Breite 15,5 cm. Schweiz. Museum für Volkskunde, Basel, Inv.-Nr. VI 19490.

wendigkeit zu seyn befunden / und dahero allergnädigst resolviret haben: dass erstlich die über 30 Centen führende Fuhrleuth (wann / und so oft sie über die Berge zu Thall fahren) die dabei gesperrte Wägen-Räder mit einem wenigstens sieben Zoll breiten eisen- oder höltzenen Rad-Schuh zu belegen schuldig seyn sollen...". Einen solchen breiten Radschuh zeigt die Abb.18; er stammt von Fallera / Fellers (Kt. Graubünden) und wurde benützt vom alten Pöstler Chistell in Fallera für seine steile und mühsame Fahrt über Laax zur Station Valendas-Sagens hinunter.

2e. Die mir bekannten Belege der Bremswirkung durch eine Erschwerung oder Verhinderung der Umdrehung der Nabe stammen alle aus Spanien. Bei der Abb.19[66] besteht die Bremse aus einer unter der Achse durchlaufenden Kette. Sie wird betätigt, indem die Kette am hinteren Ende angezogen wird, wodurch sich diese strafft und die Achse nach oben drängt und damit die Umdrehung erschwert. Die Kette wird zuweilen durch einen Strick ersetzt, der aber wegen seiner Dehnbarkeit von geringer Wirkung ist; ausserdem besteht die Möglichkeit, dass er durch die Hitze der Reibung verbrennt. Die

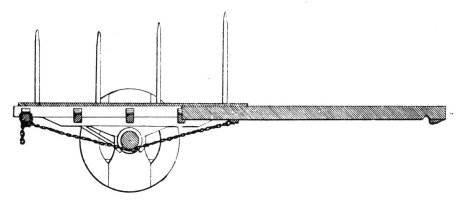

Abb. 19. Spanischer Wagen mit Achsenbremse. Aus: Fernández (wie Anm. 66).

Konstruktion hat den Nachteil, dass die Kette den mittleren Teil der Achse angreift, was schliesslich zu einem Bruch der Achse führen kann. Die Bremse kann nur an einem Wagen wirken, dessen Räder sich mit der Achse drehen. – Bei einer anderen Art (Abb.20)[67] besteht die Bremse aus einem waagrechten Knüttel, der aussen unter der Nabe des Rades entlang läuft und dessen Enden mit Stricken oder Ketten am Wagen befestigt sind. Wird er angepresst, so drückt er auf Nabe und Reifen des Rades. Bei der Bremse in Abb.21[68] ist der Knüttel oberhalb der Nabe angebracht; er wirkt nur auf das Rad, ohne die Nabe zu berühren.

2f. Dass man die Bremswirkung durch das Heben des Rades vermittelst eines Stabes erzielt, ist nur aus einer Abbildung bekannt, die möglicherweise gar nicht in Wirklichkeit umgesetzt wurde, sondern nur als Anregung gedacht war. Um 1595 gab Faustus Verantius (Fausto Veranzio, 1561–1617) in Venedig sein Abbildungswerk "Machinae novae" heraus. Das letzte Blatt zeigt eine Bremsvorrichtung (Abb.22)[69]. Die am Wagenkasten angebundenen Knüppel gehen unter den Hinterradnaben durch, sodass die Räder den Boden nicht berühren. Die ganze Zeichnung erweckt nicht den Eindruck, diese Bremse sei in Wirklichkeit versucht worden.

2g. Bei dieser Bremsart werden die Felgen blockiert durch Anpressen eines Steckens an die Hinterräder. So haben wir etwa aus der Enquête I die Angabe aus den Bündner Orten Davos-Glaris und Lavin: "ein dickes Holzstück, das an einer Kette unten am Wagen vor den Hinterrädern hängt und angezogen werden kann, es heisst Spannbrügel"[70]. Solche Querhölzer als Bremsen sind auch für Italien belegt[71]; ebenfalls bekannt sind sie in Spanien (die Abb.23

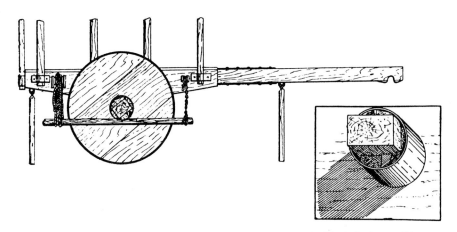

Abb. 20. Spanischer Wagen mit Nabenbremse. Aus: Fernández (wie Anm. 67).

zeigt den Wagen und die Funktionsweise der Bremse von unten)[72], und zwar in Galizien und der Provinz Lugo[73]. In den französischen Zentralpyrenäen besitzen die Enden des Querbalkens je einen Bremsklotz; diese Klötze heissen entweder "esklóts" (wie die Holzblöcke, aus denen die Holzschuhe geschnitzt werden) oder "sabóts"[74].

2h. Das für die moderne Bremse ganz allgemein gebrauchte Wort "Mechanik" (oder Ableitungen davon)[75] zeigt, dass wir es nun nicht mehr mit individuellen und dörflichen Ausformungen, sondern mit einer industriellen Vorrichtung zu tun haben. Eine altertümliche Form dieser Bremse, die noch nicht den Kurbelanzug aufweist, zeigt die Abb.24 aus Corsica[76]. Der Holzklotz wird mit einem Stecken von unten gegen das Rad gedrückt. Dieser Stecken ist schräg gestellt; er wird von oben mit einem Seil heruntergezogen. Das Seil kann an irgendeiner Stelle fixiert und damit die Bremswirkung reguliert werden. Beim Ändern der Bremswirkung muss allerdings das Seil immer wieder verstellt und neu festgebunden werden.

3. Es sollen hier noch kurz einige Vorrichtungen bei der Aufwärtsfahrt angeführt werden, die man verwendet, um Mensch und Tier einen Ausruhehalt zu ermöglichen; das Gefährt muss in diesem Fall zu völligem Stillstand gebracht werden. Das Unterschieben eines Steines oder Holzklotzes oder das völlige Anziehen einer mechanischen Bremse sind selbstverständlich. Etwas gänzlich anderes aber ist eine Einrichtung, für die ich vorläufig nur Belege aus der Schweiz und aus England kenne. Unter der Hinterachse des Wagens schwebt

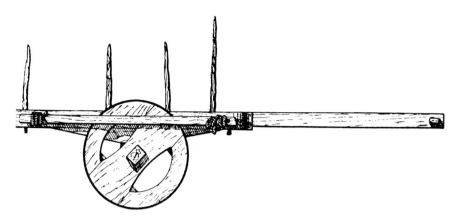

Abb. 21. Spanischer Wagen mit Radbremse. Aus: Fernández (wie Anm. 68).

an zwei Kettchen ein etwa meterlanges Holzstück, um im Augenblick des Anhaltens bergan mit den beiden Eisenspitzen seines zweizinkigen Ausläufers in den Boden einzustechen und den Wagen zum Stillstehen zu bringen. (Abb. 25). Für Lützelflüh, Kt. Bern, ist der Name "Wagenhund" angegeben (man vergleiche damit die englische Bezeichnung!)[77] das Schweiz. Idiotikon[78] gibt "Krätz-Isen, Chretz-Isen" für den Kanton Zürich, und aus dem Lugnez haben wir die rätoromanische Benennung "fuortga de carr" (Wagengabel). Auffällig ist das besonders häufige Auftreten in England, wo die Bezeichnung "dogstick" gebraucht wird[79]. In England kommt daneben noch eine weitere Einrichtung vor (ich habe sonst keine weiteren Belege dafür), die als "roller scotch" (oder nur "scotch") bezeichnet wird[80]. Es ist eine kleine Holzrolle hinten am Hinterrad, damit das Rad sofort blockiert wird, falls der Wagen rückwärts gleitet. Für wirklich steile Stellen dürfte diese Vorrichtung allerdings kaum genügen.

Anmerkungen

1. In: Schweizer Volkskunde, Korrespondenzblatt (Basel) 44:5 (1954) 61–63 erschien ein kleiner Aufsatz von *Rudolf Trüb*, Ein eigenartiger Bremsklotz aus dem Bernbiet. Aus dem Material des Sprachatlasses der deutschen Schweiz. – Anschliessend daran habe ich europäisches Vergleichsmaterial herangezogen: *Robert Wildhaber*, Ueber Bremsvorrichtungen. Idem 63–68, 5 Abb. – Diese Aufsätze bildeten die Grundlage für einen Beitrag in: Die Kärntner Landsmannschaft, Mitteilungsblatt der Heimatverbände Kärntens (Klagenfurt) 1963, Nr. 4, 10–11: *Oskar Moser*, Vom »Reifeisen« zum Radschuh. Ein wenig Kulturgeschichte um kleine vergessene Dinge. – Im gleichen Heft der Kärntner Landsmann-

Abb. 22. Bremse des Faustus Verantius, 1595. Aus: Feldhaus (wie Anm. 69).

schaft, 11–13, erschien ferner: *Helmut Prasch*, »Bin a lustiger Fuhrmann ...«, allerlei Bremszeug. – Endlich ist zu erwähnen *Joaquín Lorenzo Fernández*, Die Bremse am galizischen Wagen. In: Volkstum und Kultur der Romanen (Hamburg) 11 (1938) 282–289. – Das weitere Material findet sich recht zerstreut; in Sprachatlanten und Mundartwörterbüchern stösst man gelegentlich auf willkommene Belege. – Die Schweizerische Gesellschaft für Volkskunde hatte in ihrer Enquête I für den Atlas der schweizerischen Volkskunde die Frage 318 »Welche Hemmvorrichtungen gibt es?« (im folgenden bezeichnet als: Enquête I, 318); die Antworten geben den Stand von etwa 1930 (und »früher«) wieder; ausgewertet wurde diese Frage nicht.

2. *Fernández* (wie Anm. 1) 283. Bremsen sind nur erforderlich auf den besseren Wegen »in der Nähe bedeutenderer Siedlungen«.

3. *Walter Schmolke*, Transport und Transportgeräte in den französischen Zentralpyrenäen (Hamburg 1938) 54.

4. *W. Ebeling*, Die landwirtschaftlichen Geräte im Osten der Provinz Lugo (Spanien). In: Volkstum und Kultur der Romanen 5 (1932) 87.

5. siehe Anm. 1. – Vergleiche auch *Karl Haiding*, Fahrzeuge des steirischen Ennsbereiches und des Ausseer Landes. In: Zeitschrift des historischen Vereines für Steiermark 60 (1969) 185 und 61 (1970) 135.

6. *Bernhard Freuler*, Die Holz- und Kohlentransportmittel im südlichen Tessin. In: Schweizerisches Archiv für Volkskunde 10 (1906) 7 und Abb. 18.

7. *E. Schüle*, La terminologie du joug dans une région du Plateau central. In: Mélanges A. Duraffour = Romanica Helvetica 14 (1939) 190: »comme les chars agricoles ne sont pas encore tous pourvus de freins, il faut les retenir dans la descente par le joug même«;

508

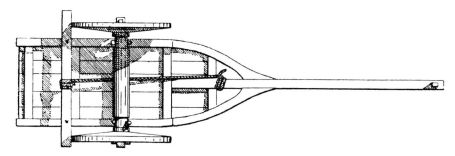

Abb. 23. Prügelbremse. Aus: Fernández (wie Anm. 72).

gilt für die Gegend von Tarn et Garonne, Aveyron, Lozère, Cantal. – Vergleiche dazu: *W. Egloff*, Le joug pour boeufs à Provence (Vaud). In: Folklore suisse 36 (1946) 6.

8. Glossaire des patois de la Suisse romande 2, 514, s.v. bòri; besonders für die Kantone Freiburg und Waadt.

9. Sprach- und Sachatlas Italiens und der Südschweiz 6 (1935), Karte 1245 »frenare il carro«, für die Punkte 739 und 748, beide in Apulien (im folgenden bezeichnet AIS).

10. *Franz Josef Gstrein*, Die Bauernarbeit im Oetztal einst und jetzt (Innsbruck 1933) 24 (mit Abb.).

11. Schweiz. Idiotikon 5, 385.

12. Vgl. etwa *Prasch* (wie Anm. 1) 13.

13. *Egloff* (wie Anm. 7) 7 und Abb. 6.

14. *Ebeling* (wie Anm. 4) 87.

15. *Ernst M. Wallner*, Zastler. Eine Holzhauergemeinde im Schwarzwald (Freiburg i.Br. 1953) 77.

16. *Erika Hubatschek*, Zur bäuerlichen Arbeits- und Gerätekunde des inneren Stubaitales. In: Volk und Heimat, Festschrift für Viktor von Geramb (Graz-Salzburg-Wien 1949) 111. – Vergleiche auch *Haiding* (wie Anm. 5) 61 (1970) 147: »Das Bremsen der Fuhre beim Bergabfahren geschieht auch durch Anhängen einer 'Zig'.«

17. *Ebeling* (wie Anm. 4) 87.

18. *Emanuel Friedli*, Bärndütsch. Band 1: Lützelflüh (Bern 1905) 345.

19. Beschrieben von *Trüb* (wie Anm. 1). Das Objekt ist heute im Schweiz. Museum für Volkskunde, Basel.

20. Das Schweiz. Idiotikon 1, 541 verwendet das Wort für ein anderes Bremsobjekt (s. Anm. 78).

21. *Prasch* (wie Anm. 1) 12.

22. So: 299 Sermide, 356 San Stino die Livenza, 364 Campo San Martino. – Für die Steiermark vergleiche *Haiding* (wie Anm. 5) 61 (1970) 145.

23. *Fernández* (wie Anm. 1) 286 u. Abb. 3 auf S. 284.

24. *Schmolke* (wie Anm. 3) 66. Zum Wort »garot« v. *Meyer-Lübke*, Romanisches etymologisches Wörterbuch, Nr. 3690 »garra«.

25. *Albert Neuburger*, Die Technik des Altertums (Leipzig 1921) 217. *F. M. Feldhaus*, Die Technik der Vorzeit, der geschichtlichen Zeit und der Naturvölker (Leipzig u. Berlin 1914) 524 f.

26. Schweiz. Idiotikon 10, 252; »Radsperre« auch bei 10, 423.

27. 11, 2189 f.

28. 11, 2190.

Abb. 24. Mechanik. Aus: Bottiglioni (wie Anm. 76).

29. Dicziunari rumantsch grischun 3, 145 u. Abb. C 14 a, b.

30. *Friedli* (wie Anm. 18) 346.

31. *Walther Niekerken*, Das Feld und seine Bestellung im Niederdeutschen (Hamburg 1935) 198, § 319; 268, § 390.

32. *Jos. Bröcker*, Die Sprache des Schmiedehandwerkes im Kreise Olpe auf Grund der Mundart von Rhonard (Diss. Münster 1907) 45. Ebenfalls *Woeste*, Wörterbuch der westfälischen Mundart 213. *Bauer*, Waldeckisches Wörterbuch 1, 85 (riemekiede).

33. *Schambach*, Wörterbuch der niederdeutschen Mundart der Fürstenthümer Göttingen und Grubenhagen (Hannover 1858) 204.

34. *J. Geraint Jenkins*, The English farm wagon (Reading 1961) 125 (East Anglia), 129 f. (Hertfordshire), 134 (Rutland), 193 (Wiltshire).

35. *Jenkins* (wie Anm. 34) 139 (West Midland), 150 (Shropshire), 173 (Dorset), 209 (Somerset).

36. *James Arnold*, The farm waggons of England and Wales (London 1969) Taf. 14 (Glamorganshire), Taf. 16 (Staffordshire); weitere Angaben zu »tie chain« 21 u. Taf. 3, 5, 8, 12, 13, 15, 20, 21.

37. *Friedli* (wie Anm. 18) 346.

38. Schweiz. Idiotikon 3, 566.

39. Schweiz. Idiotikon 3, 566.

510

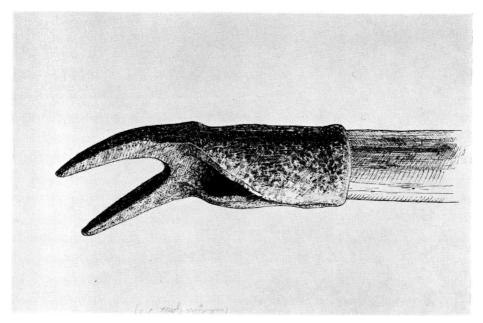

Abb. 25. Haltevorrichtung bei der Aufwärtsfahrt: »fuortga de carr«. Villa, Lugnez (Kt. Graubünden). Schweiz. Museum für Volkskunde, Basel, Inv.-Nr. VI 17196.

40. Schweiz. Idiotikon 3, 933.
41. *Prasch* (wie Anm. 1) 12. – Ob die Angabe aus AIS (wie Anm. 9), Punkt 5 Ems-Domat (Kt. Graubünden) zu 2 b oder 2 c gehört, ist nicht klar.
42. *Niekerken* (wie Anm. 31) 268, § 390.
43. Schweiz. Idiotikon 3, 567.
44. Schweiz. Idiotikon 3, 567.
45. Enquête I, 318.
46. *Martin Tschumpert*, Versuch eines bündnerischen Idiotikon (Chur 1880) 375.
47. *Valentin Bühler*, Davos in seinem Walserdialekt, 1. Teil (Heidelberg 1870) 286. *Tschumpert* (wie Anm. 46) 375. *Pallioppi*, Dizionari dels idioms romauntschs (Samedan 1895) 293. Schweiz. Idiotikon 1, 918 u. 926. Enquête I für Fetan (fiörgia). Das Dicziunari (wie Anm. 29) kennt allerdings auch das blosse »chadaina« für die Schlittenkette.
48. AIS (wie Anm. 9), Punkt 27, und Enquête I, 318.
49. *Werner Schmitter*, Waldarbeit und Waldarbeiter im Prätigau (Schiers 1953) 174 f. u. Abb. 17.
50. *Fernández* (wie Anm. 1) 286.
50 a. Eine entsprechende Abbildung eines solchen »Chretzers« aus Davos-Wolfgang findet sich im »Jahresbericht 1968 des Rätischen Museums in Chur« (im: Jahresbericht 1968 der Historisch-Antiquarischen Gesellschaft von Graubünden, Chur 1970), Abb. 12; dieser Kratzer wird beim Heuzug aber unter ein Brett, ein »Heuschiit«, gelegt.
51. *Feldhaus* (wie Anm. 25) 524 f, u. Abb. 356 (zur Abbildung fügt er aber bei: nach U. Bessnitzer, 1486).

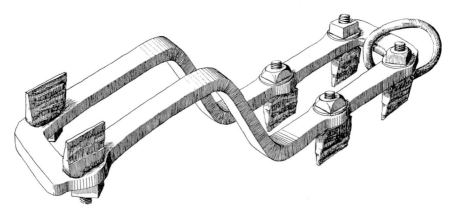

Abb. 26. Kratzer für Schlitten, ca. 55 cm lang. Oberschan (Kt. St. Gallen). Schweiz. Museum für Volkskunde, Basel, Inv.-Nr. VI 35462.

52. *Niekerken* (wie Anm. 31) 198, § 319. *Weigand-Hirt*, Deutsches Wörterbuch 1, 847. Zu »Radschuh«: Schweiz. Idiotikon 8, 482.

53. *Mensing*, Schleswig-Holsteinisches Wörterbuch 4, 542.

54. *Bröcker* (wie Anm. 32) 45.

55. *Arnold* (wie Anm. 36) 20.

56. *Jenkins* (wie Anm. 34) 100 u. 162.

57. *Max Leopold Wagner*, Das ländliche Leben Sardiniens im Spiegel der Sprache. Wörter und Sachen, Beiheft 4 (Heidelberg 1921) 69.

57 a. In Strachilovo (nördlich von Tirnovo, Bulgarien) sah ich beim Wagner einen Radschuh, wie er von ihm für die Bauern des Dorfes angefertigt wird. Ein Radschuh aus der bulgagarischen Dobrudscha ist abgebildet bei *Chr. Vakarelski*, Добруджа (Sofia 1964) 13, Fig. 5.

58. Radreifen unten, belegt aus Gontenschwil (Kt. Aargau): Enquête I, 318. Ferner *Egloff* (wie Anm. 7) 7. Einen schönen Radschuh aus Holz besitzt das Museum Schwarzenberg in Vorarlberg, Österreich.

59. *Friedli* (wie Anm. 18) 345.

60. Angaben aus Enquête I, 318.

61. *Félix Boillot*, Le français régional de La Grand'Combe (Doubs) (Paris 1929) 273.

62. Dicziunari rumantsch grischun 3, 30 (für Disentis).

63. Ich verdanke diese und die folgenden Angaben aus Ungarn der Liebenswürdigkeit von Herrn Direktor Iván Balassa, Budapest. – Ich verdanke ihm auch die Photographie einer Verkehrstafel, die noch heute in der Nähe von Nürnberg zu sehen sein soll und die die Postkutscher daran mahnte, die Radschuhe unter das Rad zu schieben. – Eine Abb. eines hölzernen Radschuhs in A magyarság néprajza, Bd. 2 (Budapest z, s. a.) 218.

64. *Friedli* (wie Anm. 18) 345.

65. Abgedruckt bei *Moser* (wie Anm. 1) 11.

66. *Fernández* (wie Anm. 1) 287 f. u. Abb. 5.

67. *Fernández* (wie Anm. 1) 288 u. Abb. 6. *Ebeling* (wie Anm. 4) 87 f. (für die Provinz Lugo).

68. *Fernández* (wie Anm. 1) 289 u. Abb. 7.

69. Abgebildet bei *Feldhaus* (wie Anm. 25) 524, Abb. 357.

70. Eine ähnliche Angabe aus Gontenschwil, Kt. Aargau. Das Schweiz. Idiotikon verzeichnet das Wort nicht. *Prasch* (wie Anm. 1) nennt diese Art Bremse »Prügelbremse«.

71. AIS (wie Anm. 9) Punkte 356 (San Stino di Livenza), 520 (Camaione: Eisenstange), 541 (Fauglia), 752 (Saracena).
72. *Fernández* (wie Anm. 1) 289 u. Abb. 8.
73. *Ebeling* (wie Anm. 4) 87.
74. *Schmolke* (wie Anm. 3) 66.
75. Schweiz. Idiotikon 4, 59. *Friedli* (wie Anm. 18) 346. *G. A. Seiler*, Die Basler Mundart (Basel 1879) 205. *Fischer*, Schwäbisches Wörterbuch 4, 1658 (Micke, Mickel, Mickeni, Mekeni). *Martin/Lienhart*, Wörterbuch der elsässischen Mundarten 1, 660 (Mick). *Egloff* (wie Anm. 7) 6 (la mécanique). *Gino Bottiglioni*, Atlante linguistico, etnografico italiano della Corsica, vol. 7 (Pisa 1938), Karte 1209: mekkániga. *Günther Fahrholz*, Wohnen und Wirtschaft im Bergland der oberen Ariège. Sach- und Wortkundliches aus den Pyrenäen (Hamburg 1931) 146 (mekaníko). *A. Dornheim*, Die bäuerliche Sachkultur im Gebiet der oberen Ardèche. In: Volkstum und Kultur der Romanen 9 (1936) 388 (mekaníko).
76. *Bottiglioni* (wie Anm. 75), Fig. 1 der Karte 1209.
77. *Friedli* (wie Anm. 18) 346.
78. Schweiz. Idiotikon 1, 541. Es ist sehr wohl denkbar, dass diese Bezeichnung falsch verstanden wurde, da es sich ja nicht um ein »Kratzen«, sondern um ein »Einbohren« handelt.
79. *Jenkins* (wie Anm. 34) 99 f. *Arnold* (wie Anm. 36) 20 f.
80. *Jenkins* (wie Anm. 34) 99 f. *Arnold* (wie Anm. 36) 20 f.